East Tennessee Tax Records Index

Volume I: Washington County 1778–1821

Compiled by
Geoffrey D. Rasmussen

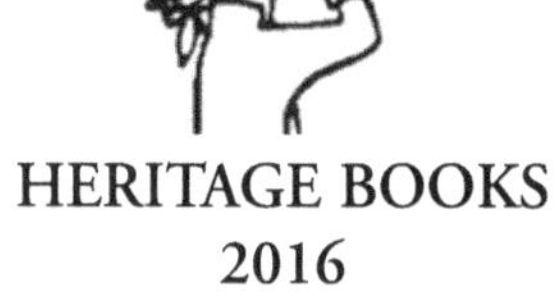

HERITAGE BOOKS
2016

HERITAGE BOOKS
AN IMPRINT OF HERITAGE BOOKS, INC.

Books, CDs, and more—Worldwide

For our listing of thousands of titles see our website
at
www.HeritageBooks.com

Published 2016 by
HERITAGE BOOKS, INC.
Publishing Division
5810 Ruatan Street
Berwyn Heights, Md. 20740

Heritage Books by the author:

East Tennessee Tax Records Index
Volume I: Washington County, 1778–1821

East Tennessee Tax Records Index
Volume II: Washington County, 1822–1839

East Tennessee Tax Records Index
Volume III: Washington County, 1840–1850

International Standard Book Numbers
Paperbound: 978-0-7884-3807-3
Clothbound: 978-0-7884-6393-8

To my Washington County, Tennessee ancestors and their descendants

Contents

Preface

In the search for my Washington County, Tennessee ancestors I quickly learned about the importance of tax records. I had located John McCall and his family of six children in other records, but did not know if they were the only McCall families in the area. Because there was no master index for the tax records, I searched every year and recorded all the McCall entries.

I learned that the first McCall individual to appear in the tax records was John McCall, located in 1792 in Depew's Company. He also appears in 1793, 1797, 1798, 1805, 1807, 1809, 1810, 1811, 1814, 1815, 1816, 1817, 1818, and 1819. With this information, I learned the following:

1. John may have moved to the area about 1792.
2. John may have become of age in 1792.
3. John may have left the area about 1819.
4. John may have died about 1819.
5. Some of the tax records were alphabetically recorded; some lists suggested who his neighbors and associates were.

Though these records do not appear to provide much genealogical information, even their index entries have golden information:

1811 McCray's Company: George Brown, of **Kentucky**
1811 McCray's Company: John Brown, of **North Carolina**
1815 Carcathers' Company: John Blair, **son of Jane**
1824 McCray's Company: Richard Roberts, **deceased**
1826 Kitzmiller's Company: William Crouch, **of Jesse**

Volume one of this index covers 44 years and contains 23,479 individuals. The records prior to 1830 are vitally important because very few Tennessee federal census returns survived before then. In 1935, the Works Progress Administration (WPA) oversaw the transcription of the original tax records. The 1778-1827 portion of this index was compiled using these records. The remaining records were indexed from the originals, which were microfilmed by the Tennessee State Library and Archives.

This index is arranged alphabetically. The names are indexed exactly as they appear in the records. For example, in 1798, John McCall was listed as John *McAll*. Thus, in this index, this entry appears before the rest of the McCalls. Be sure to search for all possible spelling variations of the individual you are researching, including given names. Ezekiel is found throughout the records with the following variants: Esekiel, Ezakel, Ezchail, Ezecal, Ezechel, Ezecial, Ezekeel, Ezihaiel, Ezikiel, Ezkiel, Ezkkel, Zeakel, Zecall, Zekel, and Zekiel.

Once the index entry is located, obtain a copy of the original record.

These films may be viewed at the Family History Library in Salt Lake City, borrowed via your local LDS Family History Center, or they are available at the Tennessee State Library & Archives in Nashville.

Surname, Given names	Year	Comp./Dist.
AAIKENS, James	1809	Roadmas
AALLESON, Robert	1809	Gwin
AALLISON, Robt	1799	Duncan
ABBET, Samuel	1812	McLin
ABBITT, William	1813	Copas
ABBOTT, Elijah	1778	
ABBOTT, James	1778	
ABLE, Abraham	1801	Longmire
ABNER, Elisha	1794	Ford
ABNER, Elisha	1795	Ford
ACARS, Uriah	1781	
ACKEN, James	1798	Hannah
ACTON, James	1793	Hale
ACTON, James	1794	Brown
ACTON, James	1797	Longmire
ACTON, James	1812	Hartsell
ACTON, James	1818	Fine
ACTON, James	1819	Howard
ACTON, James Sr.	1796	Longmire
ACTON, James Sr.	1797	Longmire
ADAER, James	1798	Duncan
ADAIR, James	1798	Duncan
ADAIR, James	1799	Duncan
ADAIR, James	1806	Guin
ADAIR, James	1807	Givins
ADAIR, James	1814	McLin
ADAIR, James	1821	Hunt
ADAIR, James Jr.	1812	McLin
ADAIR, James Jr.	1814	McLin
ADAIR, James Jr.	1815	McLin
ADAIR, James Jr.	1816	Hunt
ADAIR, James Jr.	1818	Hunt
ADAIR, James Sr.	1808	Guin
ADAIR, James Sr.	1812	McLin
ADAIR, James Sr.	1818	Hunt
ADAIR, John	1793	Depew
ADAM, Jame	1779	Wilson
ADAM, James	1801	Taylor
ADAM, James Sr.	1819	Hunt
ADAMS, Alexander	1796	Calvert
ADAMS, Alexander	1797	Calvert
ADAMS, Alexander	1799	Duncan
ADAMS, Alexander	1805	Stephenson
ADAMS, Alexander	1806	Payn
ADAMS, Hugh W.	1806	Guin
ADAMS, James	1817	Hunt
ADAMS, Jesse	1794	Thornton
ADAMS, Jno	1796	Longmire
ADAMS, John	1779	Wilson
ADAMS, John	1781	
ADAMS, John	1794	Scot
ADAMS, John	1796	Jonesboro
ADAMS, John	1797	Calvert
ADAMS, John	1798	Duncan
ADAMS, John	1798	Duncan
ADAMS, John	1799	Duncan
ADAMS, John	1801	Squibb
ADAMS, John	1806	Anderson
ADAMS, John	1807	Anderson
ADAMS, John	1809	Roadmas
ADAMS, John	1811	Rodman
ADAMS, John	1814	McCracken
ADAMS, John	1780-1781 (Undated)	
ADAMS, Josa	1795	Thornton
ADAMS, Sam (heirs of)	1811	McAlister
ADAMS, Saml (Dec'd)	1820	Smith
ADAMS, Saml (decd; estate)	1821	Smith
ADAMS, Samuel (Dec.)	1816	Smith
ADAMS, Samuel (Dec.)	1817	Smith
ADAMS, Samuel (Dec.)	1819	Smith
ADAMS, Samuel A.	1818	Smith
ADAMS, William	1794	Milliken
ADAMS, Wm	1790	Milleken
ADAMS, Wm	1791	Milliken
ADAMS, Wm	1792	Milliken
ADAMS, Wm	1793	Milliken
ADAMS, Wm	1797	Gann
ADARE, James	1811	Davis
ADCOCKS, Leonard	1778	
ADERSON, James	1781	
ADIOR, James	1797	Duncan
ADKIN, Charles	1780-1781 (Undated)	
ADKINSON, Wilton	1817	Smith
ADMONS, John	1781	
AERSTON, Benjamin	1818	Harris
AETON, James	1816	Fine
AETON, James	1817	Fine
AGNES, Barnabas	1798	Morrison
-AHN, William	1793	Hale
AICKEN, Benjamin	1815	Carcathers
AICKENS, James	1811	Rodman
AICKENS, Mathew	1811	Rodman
AIKEN, James	1795	Milliken
AIKEN, James	1805	Stephenson
AIKEN, James	1806	Anderson
AIKEN, James	1807	Anderson
AIKEN, James	1815	Crookshanks
AIKEN, John	1806	Anderson
AIKEN, John	1807	Anderson
AIKEN, John	1816	Smith
AIKEN, John A.	1817	Smith

Surname, Given names	Year	Comp./Dist.
AIKEN, John A.	1819	Smith
AIKEN, John A.	1820	Smith
AIKEN, John A.	1821	Smith
AIKEN, John T.	1814	McCracken
AIKEN, Julian A.	1818	Smith
AIKEN, Martha	1814	McCracken
AIKEN, Mathew	1801	Aiken
AIKEN, Mathew	1806	Anderson
AIKEN, Mathew	1815	Garner
AIKEN, Mathew	1816	Smith
AIKEN, Mathew	1817	Smith
AIKEN, Mathew	1818	Smith
AIKEN, Mathew	1819	Smith
AIKEN, Mathew	1820	Smith
AIKEN, Mathew	1821	Smith
AIKEN, William	1817	Smith
AIKENS, Mathew	1807	Anderson
AIKENS, Mathew	1809	Roadmas
AIKIN, John	1812	Crawford [2]
AIKINS, James	1805	Aikin
AIKINS, John	1805	Aikin
AIKINS, Mosses	1805	Aikin
AKEN, Homer	1812	Crawford [2]
AKEN, James	1812	Crawford
AKEN, John	1812	Crawford
AKER, William	1821	McGee
AKERS, Uria	1780-1781 (Undated)	
ALDRIDGE, Thomas	1781	
ALESON, Frank	1792	Scott
ALEXANDER, Frances	1797	Biddle
ALEXANDER, Frances	1798	Biddle
ALEXANDER, Frances	1807	Shields
ALEXANDER, Frances	1814	Couthers
ALEXANDER, Francis	1790	Biddle
ALEXANDER, Francis	1791	Biddle
ALEXANDER, Francis	1792	Biddle
ALEXANDER, Francis	1793	Biddle
ALEXANDER, Francis	1794	Blair
ALEXANDER, Francis	1798	Biddle
ALEXANDER, Francis	1801	Biddle
ALEXANDER, Francis	1806	Carson
ALEXANDER, Francis	1811	
ALEXANDER, Francis	1815	Carcathers
ALEXANDER, Francis	1816	Hunt
ALEXANDER, James V.	1817	Smith
ALEXANDER, John	1781	
ALEXANDER, John	1790	Biddle
ALEXANDER, John	1791	Biddle
ALEXANDER, John	1792	Biddle
ALEXANDER, John	1793	Biddle
ALEXANDER, John	1794	Blair

Surname, Given names	Year	Comp./Dist.
ALEXANDER, John	1797	Biddle
ALEXANDER, John	1798	Biddle
ALEXANDER, John	1806	Guin
ALEXANDER, John	1808	Guin
ALEXANDER, John	1809	Gwin
ALEXANDER, John	1811	Davis
ALEXANDER, John	1815	McLin
ALEXANDER, John	1816	Hunt
ALEXANDER, John	1817	Hunt
ALEXANDER, John	1818	Hunt
ALEXANDER, John	1819	Hunt
ALEXANDER, John	1821	Hunt
ALEXANDER, John Jr.	1798	Biddle
ALEXANDER, John Jr.	1801	Biddle
ALEXANDER, John Sr.	1801	Biddle
ALEXANDER, Jonathan	1797	Biddle
ALEXANDER, Jonathan	1798	Biddle
ALEXANDER, Jonathan	1798	Biddle
ALEXANDER, Jonathan	1801	Biddle
ALEXANDER, Jonathan	1783 [after]	Blair
ALEXR, Francis	1809	Patterson
ALISON, Charles	1780-1781 (Undated)	
ALISON, Frances	1794	Scot
ALISON, Frank	1808	Parker
ALISON, Franses (Of Maryland returned by James Alison)	1794	Brown
ALISON, James	1794	Brown
ALISON, James	1780-1781 (Undated)	
ALISON, John	1780-1781 (Undated)	
ALISON, Robert	1818	Smith
ALISON, Robert (and the heirs of Rob't Alison D.)	1817	Hunt
ALISON, Robt (dec'd)	1821	Smith
ALISON, Robt (Dec'd)	1820	Smith
ALISTEN, James M.	1814	Crookshanks
ALITON, Robert	1779	Wilson
ALLASON, Robart	1798	Duncan
ALLASON, Robart	1807	Givins
ALLASON, Robart Jr.	1807	Givins
ALLBRIGHT, John	1801	Gann
ALLEN, Isaac	1821	Howard
ALLEN, John	1796	Longmire
ALLEN, John	1799	Stuart
ALLEN, John	1801	Aiken
ALLEN, John Sr.	1797	Calvert
ALLEN, Robert	1792	Depew
ALLEN, Robert	1797	Biddle
ALLEN, Robert	1799	Stuart
ALLEN, Robert	1801	Aiken
ALLEN, Robert	1801	Biddle
ALLEN, Robert	1807	Anderson

Surname, Given names	Year	Comp./Dist.
ALLEN, Robert	1809	Gwin
ALLEN, Zachariah	1779	
ALLESON, Frank	1805	Jas Parker
ALLESON, Robert	1796	Handly
ALLEXANDER, Francis	1810	Dimmons
ALLIEN, Robert	1793	Depew
ALLIEN, Robert	1794	Depew
ALLIEN, Robert	1812	McLin
ALLIN, John (Marchast)	1797	Calvert
ALLIN, Robart	1798	Duncan
ALLIN, Robart	1807	Givins
ALLIN, William	1779	
ALLISON, Ann	1794	Depew
ALLISON, Ann	1797	Duncan
ALLISON, Ann	1798	Duncan
ALLISON, Ann	1799	Duncan
ALLISON, Ann	1783 [after]	Depew
ALLISON, Ann (Widow)	1792	Depew
ALLISON, Charles	1778	
ALLISON, Charles	1781	
ALLISON, Charles	1781	
ALLISON, Charles	1796	Shipley
ALLISON, Charles	1798	Shipley
ALLISON, Charles	1799	Duncan
ALLISON, Charles	1815	Grimsley
ALLISON, Elizabeth	1796	Longmire
ALLISON, Frances	1801	Calvert
ALLISON, Francis	1791	Willey
ALLISON, Francis	1796	Jonesboro
ALLISON, Francis	1797	Calvert
ALLISON, Francis	1797	Calvert
ALLISON, Francis	1797	Gann
ALLISON, Frank	1793	Scott
ALLISON, Frank	1796	Calvert
ALLISON, Frank	1798	Calvert
ALLISON, Frank	1799	Stuart
ALLISON, Frank	1809	Parker
ALLISON, James	1781	
ALLISON, James	1791	North
ALLISON, James	1780-1781 (undated)	
ALLISON, James (and Lura)	1794	Scot
ALLISON, James (Deceased)	1796	Jonesboro
ALLISON, James (Heirs Of)	1809	Roadmas
ALLISON, Jane	1819	Hunt
ALLISON, John	1778	
ALLISON, John	1779	
ALLISON, John	1781	
ALLISON, John	1790	Hanley
ALLISON, John	1791	Hanley
ALLISON, John	1791	Willey
ALLISON, John	1793	Brown
ALLISON, John	1806	Crouch
ALLISON, John	1815	Carcathers
ALLISON, John Sullivan (by Robert Allison Exe)	1806	Brown
ALLISON, R.	1819	Hunt
ALLISON, Robart	1797	Duncan
ALLISON, Robert	1778	
ALLISON, Robert	1781	
ALLISON, Robert	1793	Depew
ALLISON, Robert	1794	Depew
ALLISON, Robert	1797	Calvert
ALLISON, Robert	1797	Gann
ALLISON, Robert	1798	Duncan
ALLISON, Robert	1798	Gann
ALLISON, Robert	1799	Gann
ALLISON, Robert	1799	Moore
ALLISON, Robert	1801	Taylor
ALLISON, Robert	1807	Payne
ALLISON, Robert	1807	
ALLISON, Robert	1808	Guin
ALLISON, Robert	1809	Roadmas
ALLISON, Robert	1811	Davis
ALLISON, Robert	1814	McLin
ALLISON, Robert	1815	McLin
ALLISON, Robert	1816	Hunt
ALLISON, Robert	1819	Hunt
ALLISON, Robert	1780-1781 (Undated)	
ALLISON, Robert (Dec.)	1819	Smith
ALLISON, Robert (deceased)	1818	Hunt
ALLISON, Robert (Exe. of John Sullivan Allison.)	1806	Brown
ALLISON, Robert Sr.	1806	Guin
ALLISON, Robert Sr.	1812	McLin
ALLISON, Samuel	1796	Handly
ALLISON, William	1780-1781 (Undated)	
ALLISON, Wm	1778	
ALLISON, Wm	1781	
ALMON, Thomas	1816	Fine
ALMON, Thomas	1817	Fine
ALSOP, Thomas	1806	Crouch
ALTON, James	1821	Brown
AMBRIE, Faler	1812	Brown
AMBROES, Farler	1815	Hartsell
AMBROSE, David	1819	Brown
AMBROSE, David	1821	Haines
AMBROSE, Forlet	1821	Haines
AMBROSE, Foster	1819	Brown
AMBROSE, Henry	1780-1781	District 7
AMBROSS, Earler	1811	Brown
AMBROUS, Farler	1810	Cove
AMBROUS, Fowler	1814	Brown

Surname, Given names	Year	Comp./Dist.
AMBROUSE, Farler	1808	Odell
AMBROVES, Farler	1809	Viney
AMBRUS, Farler	1807	Odell
ANDERSON, Barnabas	1779	Wilson
ANDERSON, Barnabas	1780-1781 (Undated)	
ANDERSON, Barnaha	1778	
ANDERSON, Barnard	1781	
ANDERSON, Eph	1805	Jas Parker
ANDERSON, Ephraim	1808	Parker
ANDERSON, Ephrian	1809	Parker
ANDERSON, Frederick	1794	North
ANDERSON, Frederick	1797	Young
ANDERSON, Frederick	1806	Parker
ANDERSON, Fredrick	1798	Young
ANDERSON, Isaac	1780-1781 (Undated)	
ANDERSON, James	1805	Aikin
ANDERSON, James	1807	Anderson
ANDERSON, James	1816	Smith
ANDERSON, James	1818	Smith
ANDERSON, James	1819	Smith
ANDERSON, James	1780-1781 (Undated)	
ANDERSON, James C.	1805	Aikin
ANDERSON, James V.	1807	Anderson
ANDERSON, James V.	1809	Roadmas
ANDERSON, James V.	1811	Rodman
ANDERSON, James V.	1814	McCracken
ANDERSON, James V.	1815	Garner
ANDERSON, Jas. D.	1820	Smith
ANDERSON, Jas. V.	1821	Smith
ANDERSON, John	1792	Depew
ANDERSON, John	1793	Depew
ANDERSON, John	1794	Depew
ANDERSON, John	1797	Duncan
ANDERSON, John	1798	Duncan
ANDERSON, John	1799	Duncan
ANDERSON, John	1801	Taylor
ANDERSON, John	1806	Guin
ANDERSON, John	1807	Givins
ANDERSON, John	1808	Guin
ANDERSON, John	1809	Gwin
ANDERSON, John	1780-1781 (Undated)	
ANDERSON, John	1783 [after]	Depew
ANDERSON, Joshua	1795	Ford
ANDERSON, Lewis	1814	McCracken
ANDERSON, Lewis	1815	Garner
ANDERSON, Lewis	1821	Smith
ANDERSON, Thomas	1791	White
ANDERSON, Thomas	1793	Thornton
ANDERSON, Thomas	1794	Ford
ANDERSON, Thomas	1795	Ford
ANDERSON, Thos	1795	Ford
ANDERSON, William	1792	Coye
ANDERSON, William	1793	Hale
ANDERSON, William	1809	Gwin
ANDERSON, William	1811	Davis
ANDERSON, William	1812	McLin
ANDERSON, William	1814	McLin
ANDERSON, William	1815	McLin
ANDERSON, William	1816	Hunt
ANDERSON, William	1817	Hunt
ANDERSON, William	1818	Hunt
ANDERSON, William	1819	Hunt
ANDERSON, Wm	1799	Duncan
ANDERSON, Wm	1821	Hunt
ANDES, Adam	1814	Hartsell
ANDES, Adam	1815	Fines
ANDES, Adam	1821	Howard
ANDES, Frederick	1796	Young
ANDES, Frederick	1801	Taylor
ANDES, Frederick	1810	Hartzel
ANDES, Frederick	1812	Hartsell
ANDES, Frederick	1815	Fines
ANDES, Frederick	1816	Fine
ANDES, Frederick	1817	Fine
ANDES, Frederick	1819	Howard
ANDES, Fredrick	1805	Parker
ANDES, Fredrick	1807	Parker
ANDES, Fredrick	1808	Parker
ANDES, Fredrick	1814	Hartsell
ANDES, Fredrick	1821	Howard
ANDES, John	1821	Howard
ANDES, William	1812	Hartsell
ANDES, William	1814	Hartsell
ANDES, William	1815	Fines
ANDES, William	1816	Fine
ANDES, William	1817	Fine
ANDES, William	1818	Fine
ANDES, William	1819	Howard
ANDES, William	1821	Howard
ANDIS, Frederick	1792	North
ANDIS, Fredrick	1791	North
ANDIS, Fredrick	1793	North
ANDRESS, Fred	1809	Par
ANDREW, Dan	1821	Brown
AND-S, Fredrick	1795	Young
ANDY, Frederick	1818	Fine
ANGLEHAND, Adrew	1778	
ANTHONY, Abraham	1795	Young
ANTHONY, Wm	1778	
ANTONEY, Abam	1794	North

Surname, Given names	Year	Comp./Dist.
ANTONEY, Abraham	1791	North
ANTONY, Abrahm	1793	North
ANYAN, Ransom	1806	Guin
ARC---A, Benjamin	1791	Milliken
ARCHER, __man	1792	Brown
ARCHER, Aaron	1821	Sands
ARCHER, Arron	1819	Sands
ARCHER, Bengemin	1806	Guin
ARCHER, Benj	1801	Glasscock
ARCHER, Benjaman	1797	Shipley
ARCHER, Benjaman	1821	Sands
ARCHER, Benjamin	1798	Shipley
ARCHER, Benjamin	1808	Guin
ARCHER, Benjamin	1814	Couthers
ARCHER, Benjamin	1816	Giles
ARCHER, Benjamin	1817	Gillises
ARCHER, Benjamin	1818	Land
ARCHER, Benjamin	1819	Sands
ARCHER, Benjamin	1783 [after]	Depew
ARCHER, Benjeman	1798	Duncan
ARCHER, Benjeman	1807	Givins
ARCHER, James	1798	Duncan
ARCHER, John	1794	Depew
ARCHER, John	1795	Taylor
ARCHER, John	1783 [after]	Depew
ARCHER, Joseph	1808	Guin
ARCHER, Joseph	1815	McLin
ARCHER, Joseph	1816	Hunt
ARCHER, Joseph	1817	Hunt
ARCHER, Joseph	1818	Hunt
ARCHER, Thomas	1798	Duncan
ARCHER, William	1794	Taylor
ARCHER, William	1795	Taylor
ARCHER, Wm	1793	Depew
Archibald	1780-1781 (Undated)	
--ARD, Robart	1798	Duncan
ARDEN, Joseph	1819	Hunt
ARENDEL, Jno	1790	Greer
ARENDER, William	1811	Barron
ARENTON, Jas	1809	Par
ARINGTON, James	1821	Howard
ARMSTRONG, John	1797	Robertson
ARMSTRONG, John	1798	Roberson
ARMSTRONG, John	1799	Robertson
ARMSTRONG, Lanty	1781	
ARMSTRONG, Lanty	1780-1781 (Undated)	
ARMSTRONG, Lantz	1779	Wilson
ARMSTRONG, Nathenial	1792	Coye
ARMSTRONG, Robert	1780-1781 (undated)	
ARMSTRONG, Samuel	1819	Smith

Surname, Given names	Year	Comp./Dist.
ARNET, Jacob	1781	
ARNET, Jacob	1780-1781 (Undated)	
ARNETT, Jacob (Single)	1779	Wilson
ARNNOLD, Nathannial	1794	Thornton
ARNNOLD, William	1794	Thornton
ARNOLD, John	1778	
ARNOLD, John	1792	Carriger
ARNOLD, John	1792	Greer
ARRENDELL, John	1794	Carriger
ARRINGTON, Thomas	1819	Jones
ARRINGTON, Thomas	1821	Jones
ARTHUR, Matthew	1778	
ARTHUR, Matthew	1779	
ARVIN, Samuel	1801	Longmire
ARVINE, John	1806	Anderson
ARWIN, Benjamin	1797	Young
ARWOOD, Jesse	1816	Fine
ARWOOD, Jessie	1815	Fines
ARWOOD, Jessy	1814	Hartsell
ASBEN, More	1780-1781	District 7
ASBURT, William	1778	
ASH, Thos Lewis	1792	Maxwell
ASH, Thos. Lewis	1793	Maxwell
ASHER, Charles	1778	
ASHER, Charles Sr.	1778	
ASHER, David	1795	Ford
ASHER, John	1778	
ASHER, John	1794	Ford
ASHER, John	1795	Ford
ASHER, Roberson	1795	Ford
ASHER, Thomas	1778	
ASHER, Wm	1778	
ASHLEY, Robart	1798	Duncan
ASHLEY, Robart	1798	Duncan
ASHORE, James	1781	
ASHURST, David	1791	White
ASHURST, David	1793	Thornton
ASHURST, John	1790	White
ASHURST, John	1791	White
ASHURST, John	1792	White
ASHURST, John	1793	Campbell
ASHURST, Robertson	1791	White
ASHURST, Robinson	1793	Campbell
ASHURST, William	1779	
A--SIMAR, Philip	1795	Young
ASTON, James	1796	Longmire
ASTON, James Jr.	1801	Longmire
ASTON, James Sr.	1801	Longmire
ATKEMAN, Milton	1821	Smith
ATKEMAN, William	1821	Smith
ATKINS, Charles	1778	

Surname, Given names	Year	Comp./Dist.
ATKINS, Charles	1780-1781 (undated)	
ATKINSON, Milton	1819	Smith
ATKINSON, Robt	1795	Young
ATKINSON, William	1819	Smith
ATKINSON, Witton	1818	Smith
ATTCESON, William	1820	Smith
ATTCESON, Wilton	1820	Smith
AUSMUS, Henery	1796	Young
AUSMUS, Henery	1797	Young
AUSMUS, Philip	1796	Young
AUSMUS, Phillip	1794	North
AUSMUS, Phillip	1797	Young
AUSTIN, Benjamin	1817	Harris
AUSTIN, Benjamin	1819	Harris
AUSTIN, Benjamin	1821	Hampton
AUSTIN, John	1790	Shipley
AUSTIN, John	1791	Shipley
AUSTIN, John	1794	Murray
AUSTIN, John	1795	Murray
AUSTIN, Samuel	1819	Harris
AYLOT, James	1781	
BABSON, Enoca	1821	Martin
BACOME, James	1810	Barron
BACOME, James	1812	Barnes
BACON, Carls	1821	Martin
BACON, Charles	1798	Shipley
BACON, Charles	1801	Glasscock
BACON, Charles	1805	Rector
BACON, Charles	1809	Cade
BACON, Charles	1809	Right
BACON, Charles	1811	Barron
BACON, Charles	1812	Barnes
BACON, Charles	1815	Grimsley
BACON, Charles	1817	Grimsley
BACON, Charles	1817	Grisham
BACON, Charles	1818	Grimsley
BACON, Charles	1818	Grisham
BACON, Charles	1819	Grimsley
BACON, Charles	1819	Grisham
BACON, Isaac	1793	Melvan
BACON, Isaac	1794	Melvan
BACON, Isaac	1795	Melvan
BACON, Isaac	1796	Melvin
BACON, Isaac	1809	Cade
BACON, Isaac	1809	Right
BACON, Isaac	1812	Ellis
BACON, Isaac	1814	Bean
BACON, Isaac	1816	Hair
BACON, Isaac	1817	Haire
BACON, Isaac	1818	Hair
BACON, Isaac	1819	Hair
BACON, Isaac	1821	Louis
BACON, J.D.	1821	Martin
BACON, James	1798	Shipley
BACON, James	1801	Glasscock
BACON, James	1805	Rector
BACON, James	1809	Cade
BACON, James	1809	Gwin
BACON, James	1811	Barron
BACON, James	1812	Barnes
BACON, James	1815	Grimsley
BACON, James	1816	Grimsley
BACON, James	1817	Grimsley
BACON, James	1818	Grimsley
BACON, James	1818	Grimsley
BACON, James	1819	Grimsley
BACON, James	1819	Grimsley
BACON, James	1821	Martin
BACON, James	1821	Martin
BACON, Jaremiah	1811	Britten
BACON, Jaremiah	1813	Copas
BACON, Jaremiah	1821	Hale
BACON, Jeremiah	1815	Copas
BACON, Jeremiah	1816	Copas
BACON, Jeremiah	1817	Grisham
BACON, Jeremiah	1818	Grisham
BACON, Jesse	1812	Ellis
BACON, Jesse	1814	Bean
BACON, Jesse	1814	Bean
BACON, Jesse	1816	Hair
BACON, Jesse	1817	Haire
BACON, Jesse	1818	Hair
BACON, Jesse	1819	Hair
BACON, John	1794	Melvan
BACON, John	1795	Melvan
BACON, John	1796	Melvin
BACON, John	1805	Rector
BACON, John	1809	Cade
BACON, John	1809	Right
BACON, John	1812	Barnes
BACON, John	1812	Ellis
BACON, John	1814	Barns
BACON, John	1814	Bean
BACON, John	1815	Grimsley
BACON, John	1815	Haire
BACON, John	1816	Hair
BACON, John	1817	Haire
BACON, John	1818	Grimsley
BACON, John	1818	Hair
BACON, John	1819	Grimsley
BACON, John	1819	Hair
BACON, John	1821	Hampton

Surname, Given names	Year	Comp./Dist.
BACON, John	1821	Louis
BACON, John	1821	Martin
BACON, John Jr.	1816	Grimsley
BACON, Jonathan	1795	Murray
BACON, Jonathan	1798	Shipley
BACON, Jonathan	1801	Glasscock
BACON, Jonathan	1805	Rector
BACON, Jonathan	1809	Cade
BACON, Jonathan	1811	Barron
BACON, Jonathan	1812	Barnes
BACON, Jonathan	1815	Grimsley
BACON, Jonathan	1817	Grimsley
BACON, Jonathan	1818	Grimsley
BACON, Jonathan	1818	Grimsley
BACON, Jonathan	1819	Grimsley
BACON, Jonathan	1819	Grimsley
BACON, Jonathan	1821	Hampton
BACON, Jonathan	1821	Martin
BACON, Jonathan Jr.	1812	Barnes
BACON, Jonathan Jr.	1815	Grimsley
BACON, Jonathan Jr.	1817	Grimsley
BACON, Jonnathan	1794	Melvan
BACON, Joseph	1817	Haire
BACON, Joseph	1818	Hair
BACON, Joseph	1819	Hair
BACON, Joseph	1821	Louis
BACON, Michael	1778	
BACON, Michael	1779	Wilson
BACON, Robert	1821	Louis
BACON, Thomas	1809	Right
BACON, Thomas	1812	Ellis
BACON, Thomas	1814	Bean
BACON, Thomas	1816	Hair
BACON, Thomas	1817	Haire
BACON, Thomas	1818	Grimsley
BACON, Thomas	1818	Hair
BACON, Thomas	1819	Grimsley
BACON, Thomas	1819	Hair
BACON, Thos	1821	Louis
BADLEY, Andrew	1793	Morrison
BADLEY, Andrew	1794	Morrison
BAHMER, Nathan	1816	Crookshanks
BAIL, David	1818	Hunt
BAIL, Isaac	1818	Hunt
BAIL, Levey	1818	Hunt
BAIL, Thomas	1798	Biddle
BAILE, Isaac	1811	Davis
BAILES, Abraham	1801	Calvert
BAILES, David	1806	Guin
BAILES, David	1809	Gwin
BAILES, David	1811	Davis
BAILES, Isaac	1794	Depew
BAILES, Isaac	1799	Duncan
BAILES, Isaac	1809	Gwin
BAILES, Isaac	1815	McLin
BAILES, Isaac	1816	Hunt
BAILES, Jacob	1799	Duncan
BAILES, Jacob Sr.	1799	Duncan
BAILES, John	1819	Findley
BAILES, Samel	1799	Duncan
BAILES, Samuel	1793	Scott
BAILES, Solomon	1799	Duncan
BAILEY, Aritha	1809	Hartzell
BAILEY, David	1815	McLin
BAILEY, Levi	1815	McLin
BAILEY, Reuben	1791	Chisom
BAILEY, Reuden	1792	Chisolm
BAILEY, William	1779	
BAILEY, Wm	1778	
BAILS, Abraham	1798	Calvert
BAILS, Danael	1797	Duncan
BAILS, Daniel	1798	Duncan
BAILS, Daniel	1798	Duncan
BAILS, David	1794	Depew
BAILS, David	1797	Duncan
BAILS, David	1807	Givins
BAILS, David	1808	Guin
BAILS, David	1812	McLin
BAILS, David	1814	McLin
BAILS, David	1816	Hunt
BAILS, George	1812	McLin
BAILS, Isaac	1792	Depew
BAILS, Isaac	1797	Duncan
BAILS, Isaac	1798	Duncan
BAILS, Isaac	1798	Duncan
BAILS, Isaac	1806	Guin
BAILS, Isaac	1807	Givins
BAILS, Isaac	1808	Guin
BAILS, Isaac	1812	McLin
BAILS, Isaac	1814	McLin
BAILS, Isaac Sr.	1801	Taylor
BAILS, Jacob	1797	Duncan
BAILS, Jacob	1798	Duncan
BAILS, Jacob	1798	Duncan
BAILS, Jacob	1801	Glasscock
BAILS, Jacob	1801	Taylor
BAILS, Jacob Jr.	1797	Duncan
BAILS, Jacob Sr.	1798	Duncan
BAILS, Joseph	1801	Taylor
BAILS, Joseph	1818	Hunt
BAILS, Levi	1816	Hunt
BAILS, Soloman	1801	Glasscock

Surname, Given names	Year	Comp./Dist.
BAILY, John	1821	McGee
BAILY, Samuel	1796	Calvert
BAILY, William	1796	Calvert
BAIN, Jessee Sr.	1806	Payn
BAIN, Ruban	1798	Gann
BAINS, William	1812	Barnes
BAIRD, Andrew	1793	Handley
BAIRD, Robert	1811	Ellis
BAITS, Henry Jr.	1778	
BAITS, Henry Sr.	1778	
BAKEN, Charels	1807	Cade
BAKEN, Charles	1808	Cade
BAKEN, Charles	1810	Barron
BAKEN, Isaac	1801	Norwood
BAKEN, Isaac	1806	Crouch
BAKEN, Isaac	1807	Cade
BAKEN, Isaac	1808	Cade
BAKEN, Isaac	1811	Ellis
BAKEN, Isaac	1815	Haire
BAKEN, James	1807	Cade
BAKEN, James	1808	Cade
BAKEN, James	1810	Barron
BAKEN, Jenny	1801	Norwood
BAKEN, Jerimiah	1798	Crouch
BAKEN, Jesse	1815	Haire
BAKEN, John	1801	Norwood
BAKEN, John	1806	Crouch
BAKEN, John	1807	Cade
BAKEN, John	1811	Ellis
BAKEN, Jonathan	1807	Cade
BAKEN, Jonathan	1808	Cade
BAKEN, Jonathan	1810	Barron
BAKEN, Joseph	1815	Haire
BAKEN, Thomas	1815	Haire
BAKER, Charles	1797	Shipley
BAKER, Charls	1814	Barns
BAKER, Frances	1791	Willey
BAKER, Frances	1794	Scot
BAKER, Francis	1792	Scott
BAKER, Francis	1793	Scott
BAKER, Francis	1795	Young
BAKER, James	1797	Shipley
BAKER, Jams	1814	Barns
BAKER, Jean	1790	Stone
BAKER, Jean	1791	Stone
BAKER, Jeremiah	1814	Copes
BAKER, Jermiah	1812	Britton
BAKER, John	1794	Thornton
BAKER, John	1795	Thornton
BAKER, Jonathan	1797	Shipley
BAKER, Jonathan	1814	Barns
BAKER, Jonathan Jr.	1814	Barns
BAKER, Mary	1817	Brown
BAKER, Massey	1815	Hartsell
BAKER, William	1790	White
BAKER, William	1791	White
BAKER, William	1792	White
BAKER, William	1793	Campbell
BAKER, William	1817	Brown
BAKER, Wm	1781	
BAKER, Wm	1821	McGee
BAKERS, William	1780-1781 (Undated)	
BAKMAN, Henry	1780-1781	District 7
BALAH, Isaac	1780-1781 (Undated)	
BALDRIDGE, James	1793	Milliken
BALEDEN, Wm.	1792	Milliken
BALELS, Henery	1812	Crawford
BALES, Abner	1807	Cade
BALES, Abner	1808	Cade
BALES, Jacob	1805	Rector
BALES, Jacob	1809	Cade
BALES, John	1791	North
BALES, Reubin	1796	Brown
BALES, Ruben	1792	Brown
BALES, Samuel	1794	Scot
BALES, Solomon	1805	Rector
BALEY, Cateral	1794	Taylor
BALEY, Daniel	1796	Young
BALEY, John	1796	Young
BALIN, Henry	1809	Bayles
BALINGER, James	1819	McClure
BALIS, Danal	1791	North
BALISS, Danel	1794	Scot
BALISS, John	1794	Scot
BALL, Ames	1798	Morrison
BALL, Ames	1806	Carr
BALL, Amos	1790	Williams
BALL, Amos	1791	Williams
BALL, Amos	1792	Tulley
BALL, Amos	1793	Morrison
BALL, Amos	1794	Morrison
BALL, Amos	1795	Morrison
BALL, Amos	1798	Morrison
BALL, Amos	1798	Morrison
BALL, Amos	1799	Morrison
BALL, Amos	1801	Morrison
BALL, Amos	1807	Carr
BALL, Amos	1808	Carr
BALL, Amos	1809	Carr
BALL, Amos	[1796] 1797	Morris
BALL, Andrew	1818	Riley

Surname, Given names	Year	Comp./Dist.
BALL, Andrew	1821	McGee
BALL, Jacob	1794	Murray
BALL, Jacob	1795	Murray
BALL, Jacob	1797	Shipley
BALL, John	1805	Doak
BALL, Joseph	1811	McCray
BALL, Joseph	1812	McCray
BALL, Joseph	1812	McCray
BALL, Joseph	1814	McCray
BALL, Joseph	1816	Harrison
BALL, Joseph	1817	Harris
BALL, Joseph	1819	Harris
BALL, Joseph	1821	Hampton
BALL, Joseph E.	1811	McCray
BALL, Sam	1809	Parker
BALL, Sammuel	1812	McCray
BALL, Samuel	1811	McCray
BALL, Samuel	1812	McCray
BALL, Samuel	1816	Waddell
BALL, Samuel	1817	Riley
BALL, Samuel	1818	Riley
BALL, Samuel	1821	McGee
BALL, Thomas	1794	Milliken
BALL, Thomas	1795	Calvert
BALL, Thomas	1797	Calvert
BALL, Thomas	1797	Calvert
BALL, Thomas	1799	Stuart
BALL, Thomas	1805	Jas Parker
BALL, Thomas	1811	McCray
BALL, Thomas	1812	McCray
BALL, Thomas	1812	McCray
BALL, Thomas	1814	McCray
BALL, Thomas	1816	Harrison
BALL, Thomas	1818	Harris
BALL, Thomas	1819	Harris
BALL, Thomas	1821	Hampton
BALL, Thos	1798	Calvert
BALL, Thos	1801	Calvert
BALL, Thos	1808	Parker
BALL, Thos	1809	Parker
BALLANGER, Jacob	1799	Robertson
BALLANGER, James	1798	Roberson
BALLANGER, Jonnathan	1801	Roberson
BALLENGER, Jacob	1797	Robertson
BALLENGER, James	1797	Robertson
BALLENGER, James	1816	Hampton
BALLER, Samuel	1792	Depew
BALLINGER, James	1806	Brown
BALLINGER, James	1809	Bayles
BALLINGER, James	1821	McClure
BALSTON, John	1801	Taylor

Surname, Given names	Year	Comp./Dist.
BALY, Daniel	1797	Young
BALY, John	1797	Young
BALYS, John	1814	Hartsell
BANDEY, Ebenezer	1814	McLin
BANDEY, John	1814	McLin
BANE, Alexander	1791	Chisom
BANGOR, Wylley	1814	McLin
BANNER, Liener	1780-1781	District 7
BARACROFT, Jonathan	1819	Hunt
BARAGRAFF, Johnathan	1808	Guin
BARAGROFF, Jonathen	1814	McLin
BARBER, Francis	1797	Gann
BARBER, John	1781	
BARCLAY, Daniel	1812	McLin
BARCLAY, Ebenezar	1818	Hunt
BARCRAFT, Johnth	1798	Biddle
BARCRAFT, Jonathan	1809	Gwin
BARCROFF, Jonathan	1818	Hunt
BARCROFT, Johnathen	1806	Guin
BARCROFT, Jonathan	1801	Biddle
BARCROFT, Jonathan	1811	Davis
BARCROFT, Jonathan	1815	McLin
BARCROFT, Jonathan	1816	Hunt
BARDSEN, John	1811	Barron
BARE, Alexr	1792	Chisolm
BARECRAFT, Jonathan	1807	Givins
BARELEY, John	1808	Guin
BAREN, Joshuah	1797	Young
BARGAN, George	1810	Dimmons
BARGAR, Willey	1812	McLin
BARGER, George	1791	Willey
BARGER, George	1811	
BARGER, George	1814	Couthers
BARGER, George	1815	Carcathers
BARGER, George	1817	Gillises
BARGER, Henry	1811	
BARGER, Henry	1815	Carcathers
BARGER, Henry	1816	Giles
BARGER, Henry	1817	Gillises
BARGER, Welond	1818	Land
BARGER, Wilby	1816	Hunt
BARGER, Wiley	1815	McLin
BARGER, Wiley	1818	Hunt
BARGER, Willard	1817	Hunt
BARGER, Willie	1819	Sands
BARGER, Wylend	1821	Sands
BARKELY, Daniel	1819	Hunt
BARKELY, Ebenezer	1819	Hunt
BARKER, Daniel	1817	Little
BARKER, Josiah	1809	Par
BARKER, Thomas	1778	

Surname, Given names	Year	Comp./Dist.
BARKER, Thomas	1821	Jones
BARKLEY, Daniel	1815	McLin
BARKLEY, Daniel	1817	Gillises
BARKLEY, Daniel	1821	Hunt
BARKLEY, Ebenezer	1821	Hunt
BARKLEY, Ebenzer	1815	McLin
BARKLEY, John	1806	Guin
BARKLEY, John	1809	Gwin
BARKLEY, John	1809	Gwin
BARKLEY, William	1809	Bayles
BARKLY, George	1780-1781 (Undated)	
BARKLY, John	1811	Davis
BARKSDELL, Clewis	1779	
BARKSDILL, Cleavers	1779	
BARKSDILL, Clevers	1778	
BARLET, Whisler (Young)	1809	Roadmas
BARNES, Charles	1821	Haines
BARNES, Jacob	1814	Hampton
BARNES, James	1806	Carr
BARNES, James	1813	Hoss
BARNES, James	1814	Hoss
BARNES, James	1815	Hoss
BARNES, James	1816	Hoss
BARNES, James	1817	Little
BARNES, James	1818	Jones
BARNES, James	1819	Jones
BARNES, James	1821	Jones
BARNES, Joseph	1793	Melvan
BARNES, Joseph	1807	Odell
BARNES, Joseph	1809	Viney
BARNES, Joseph	1810	Cove
BARNES, Mary	1812	Brown
BARNES, Mary	1814	Brown
BARNES, Mary	1815	Hartsell
BARNES, Mary	1816	Brown
BARNES, Mary	1817	Brown
BARNES, Mary	1818	Brown
BARNES, Mary	1819	Brown
BARNES, Mary	1821	Haines
BARNES, Nathan	1815	Crookshanks
BARNES, Nathan	1817	McClure
BARNES, Nathan	1818	McClure
BARNES, Nathan	1819	McClure
BARNES, Waker	1821	Martin
BARNES, William	1798	Morrison
BARNET, Wm	1792	Chisolm
BARNEYWELL, Joseph	1797	Calvert
BARNIT, William	1791	Chisom
BARNS, Amon	1812	Barnes
BARNS, James	1807	Carr
BARNS, James	1808	Carr
BARNS, Joseph	1794	Melvan
BARNS, Joseph	1795	Melvan
BARNS, Joseph	1801	Longmire
BARNS, Joseph	1806	Odel
BARNS, Joseph Jr.	1808	Odell
BARNS, Mary (widow)	1811	Brown
BARNS, Nathan	1821	McClure
BARNS, Nathen	1812	Crawford [2]
BARNS, Walker	1812	Barnes
BARNS, William	1810	Dimmons
BARON, Charles	1816	Grimsley
BARON, Wilam	1821	Martin
BARON, William	1818	Grimsley
BARRAN, William	1809	Patterson
BARRCROFT, Jonathon	1821	Hunt
BARREN, Absolem	1793	North
BARREN, John	1801	Glasscock
BARREN, Thomas	1819	Grisham
BARREN, Walker	1809	Cade
BARREN, Walker	1819	Grimsley
BARREN, William	1819	Grimsley
BARREN, Wm	1801	Glasscock
BARRENS, James	1809	Carr
BARRET, James	1798	Roberson
BARRETT, James	1799	Robertson
BARRON, Amon	1807	Cade
BARRON, Amon	1808	Cade
BARRON, Amon	1809	Cade
BARRON, Daniel	1821	Hale
BARRON, Dossey	1793	North
BARRON, Ezkl	1793	North
BARRON, George	1821	Martin
BARRON, James	1793	North
BARRON, John	1795	Murray
BARRON, John	1796	Shipley
BARRON, John	1797	Shipley
BARRON, John	1816	Grimsley
BARRON, Joseph	1793	Murray
BARRON, Joseph	1794	Murray
BARRON, Joseph	1795	Murray
BARRON, Joseph	1796	Shipley
BARRON, Joseph	1797	Shipley
BARRON, Joseph	1798	Shipley
BARRON, Joseph	1801	Glasscock
BARRON, Thomas	1796	Shipley
BARRON, Thomas	1797	Shipley
BARRON, Thomas	1798	Shipley
BARRON, Thomas	1805	Doak
BARRON, Thomas	1807	Britton
BARRON, Thomas	1811	Britten
BARRON, Thomas	1814	Copes

Surname, Given names	Year	Comp./Dist.
BARRON, Thomas	1815	Copas
BARRON, Thomas	1816	Copas
BARRON, Thomas	1817	Grisham
BARRON, Thomas	1818	Grisham
BARRON, Thomas	1821	Hale
BARRON, Thos	1813	Copas
BARRON, Walker	1794	Murray
BARRON, Walker	1795	Murray
BARRON, Walker	1796	Shipley
BARRON, Walker	1797	Shipley
BARRON, Walker	1805	Rector
BARRON, Walker	1807	Cade
BARRON, Walker	1808	Cade
BARRON, Walker	1810	Barron
BARRON, Walker	1811	Barron
BARRON, Walker	1814	Barns
BARRON, Walker	1815	Grimsley
BARRON, Walker	1816	Grimsley
BARRON, Walker	1817	Grimsley
BARRON, Walter	1798	Shipley
BARRON, Wilam	1807	Cade
BARRON, William	1795	Murray
BARRON, William	1796	Shipley
BARRON, William	1797	Shipley
BARRON, William	1798	Shipley
BARRON, William	1805	Rector
BARRON, William	1808	Cade
BARRON, William	1809	Cade
BARRON, William	1810	Barron
BARRON, William	1814	Barns
BARRON, William	1815	Grimsley
BARRON, William	1816	Grimsley
BARRON, William	1817	Grimsley
BARRONS, Thomas	1812	Britton
BARRYMAN, Havum	1780-1781	District 7
BARTELABEN, Arther D.	1797	Robertson
BARTLEY, Robert	1821	Brown
BARTLEY, William	1808	Bayles
BARTLY, Robert	1819	Brown
BASCTER, John	1815	Grimsley
BASKET, Charles	1815	Haire
BASKET, Charles	1816	Hair
BASKET, Charles	1817	Haire
BASKET, Charles	1818	Hair
BASKET, Charles	1819	Hair
BASKET, Charles	1821	Louis
BASKET, John	1815	Copas
BASKET, John	1816	Copas
BASKET, John	1818	Grisham
BASKET, John	1819	Grisham
BASKET, Richard	1815	Haire
BASKET, Richard	1816	Hair
BASKET, Richard	1817	Haire
BASKET, Richard	1818	Hair
BASKET, Richard	1819	Hair
BASKET, Richard	1821	Louis
BASKET, William	1809	Cade
BASKETT, John	1813	Copas
BASKETT, John	1814	Copes
BASKETT, John	1817	Grisham
BASKETT, John	1821	Hale
BASKINS, John	1780-1781 (undated)	
BASON, Charles	1793	Milliken
BASS, Barbara (Widow)	1792	North
BASS, Edward	1799	Moore
BASS, Jeremiah	1790	Greer
BASS, Jeremiah	1792	Greer
BASS, Jeremiah	1794	Carriger
BASS, Jeremiah	1795	Carriger
BASS, Jermiah	1792	Carriger
BASSET, William	1779	
BATTLES, Henery	1795	Calvert
BATTLES, Henry	1797	Hannah
BATTLES, Henry	1819	McClure
BATTLES, Henry	1821	McClure
BATTLES, William	1819	McClure
BATTLES, William	1821	McClure
BATTY, John	1807	Givins
BAXSTER, Frances	1791	Willey
BAXTER, Frances	1795	Calvert
BAXTER, Frances	1798	Gann
BAXTER, Frances	1799	Gann
BAXTER, Frances	1799	Moore
BAXTER, Francis	1792	Milliken
BAXTER, Francis	1793	Scott
BAXTER, Francis	1796	Handly
BAXTER, Francis	1801	Gann
BAXTER, John	1814	Barns
BAXTER, Levi	1816	Grimsley
BAXTOR, Levi	1812	Barnes
BAYES, Edward	1805	Guir
BAYHILL, Richard	1790	Biddle
BAYHILL, Richard	1791	Biddle
BAYHILL, Richard	1792	Biddle
BAYLES, Abner	1819	Brown
BAYLES, Abraham	1819	Smith
BAYLES, Dan	1809	Parker
BAYLES, Daneal	1798	Calvert
BAYLES, Daniel	1793	North
BAYLES, Daniel	1798	Young
BAYLES, Daniel	1801	Taylor
BAYLES, Daniel	1805	Jas Parker

Surname, Given names	Year	Comp./Dist.
BAYLES, Daniel	1806	Brown
BAYLES, Daniel	1806	Parker
BAYLES, Daniel	1807	Parker
BAYLES, Daniel	1808	Parker
BAYLES, Daniel	1809	Par
BAYLES, Daniel	1811	McCray
BAYLES, Daniel	1812	Hartsell
BAYLES, Daniel	1812	McCray
BAYLES, Daniel	1812	McCray
BAYLES, Daniel	1814	McCray
BAYLES, Daniel	1815	Fines
BAYLES, Daniel	1815	Harris
BAYLES, Daniel	1816	Fine
BAYLES, Daniel	1816	Harrison
BAYLES, Daniel	1817	Hampton
BAYLES, Daniel	1817	Harris
BAYLES, Daniel	1818	Brown [2]
BAYLES, Daniel	1818	Fine
BAYLES, Daniel	1819	Harris
BAYLES, Daniel	1819	Howard
BAYLES, Daniel	1821	Brown
BAYLES, Daniel	1821	Hampton
BAYLES, Daniel	1821	Howard
BAYLES, Daniel (Capt.)	1806	Brown
BAYLES, Daniel Jr.	1795	Young
BAYLES, Daniel L.	1809	Bayles
BAYLES, Daniel L.	1816	Hampton
BAYLES, Daniel L.	1819	Brown
BAYLES, Daniel Sr.	1795	Young
BAYLES, Danl Sr.	1801	Taylor
BAYLES, Danniel	1807	Bayles
BAYLES, Danniel	1808	Bayles
BAYLES, Danniel L.	1814	Hampton
BAYLES, David	1818	Harris
BAYLES, George	1801	Roberson
BAYLES, George	1806	Brown
BAYLES, George	1807	Bayles
BAYLES, George	1808	Bayles
BAYLES, George	1818	Harris
BAYLES, George	1819	Howard
BAYLES, George	1821	Howard
BAYLES, Hezekiah	1816	Harrison
BAYLES, Hezekiah	1817	Harris
BAYLES, Hezekiah	1818	Harris
BAYLES, Hezekiah	1819	Harris
BAYLES, Hezekiah	1821	Hampton
BAYLES, Jacob	1819	Brown
BAYLES, Jesse	1816	Fine
BAYLES, Jesse	1818	Fine
BAYLES, Jesse	1819	Howard
BAYLES, Jesse	1821	Brown
BAYLES, Jno	1808	Parker
BAYLES, John	1792	Scott
BAYLES, John	1795	Young
BAYLES, John	1801	Taylor
BAYLES, John	1805	Jas Parker
BAYLES, John	1805	Parker
BAYLES, John	1807	Parker
BAYLES, John	1808	Parker
BAYLES, John	1809	Par
BAYLES, John	1809	Parker
BAYLES, John	1811	McCray
BAYLES, John	1812	Hartsell
BAYLES, John	1812	McCray
BAYLES, John	1812	McCray
BAYLES, John	1815	Fines
BAYLES, John	1816	Fine
BAYLES, John	1816	Harrison
BAYLES, John	1817	Harris
BAYLES, John	1817	Riley
BAYLES, John	1818	Fine
BAYLES, John	1818	Harris
BAYLES, John	1818	Riley
BAYLES, John	1819	Harris
BAYLES, John	1819	Howard
BAYLES, John	1821	Hampton
BAYLES, John	1821	Howard
BAYLES, John Jr.	1814	McCray
BAYLES, John Sr.	1821	Howard
BAYLES, Rease	1821	Howard
BAYLES, Rees	1812	Hartsell
BAYLES, Rees	1815	Fines
BAYLES, Rees (Rev.)	1818	Fine
BAYLES, Reuben	1806	Brown
BAYLES, Reuben	1809	Bayles
BAYLES, Reuben	1809	Parker
BAYLES, Reuben	1811	McCray
BAYLES, Reuben	1814	Hampton
BAYLES, Reuben	1814	Hampton
BAYLES, Reuben	1815	Hoss
BAYLES, Reuben	1816	Hampton
BAYLES, Reuben	1817	Hampton
BAYLES, Reuben	1818	Brown [2]
BAYLES, Reuben	1818	Brown [2]
BAYLES, Reuben	1821	Brown
BAYLES, Reuben Chas B.	1821	Brown
BAYLES, Reuben Jr.	1809	Bayles
BAYLES, Reuben Jr.	1816	Hampton
BAYLES, Reuben Jr.	1819	Brown
BAYLES, Reubin	1801	Roberson
BAYLES, Rien	1819	Howard
BAYLES, Riis	1816	Fine

Surname, Given names	Year	Comp./Dist.
BAYLES, Riis	1817	Fine
BAYLES, Ruben	1793	Brown
BAYLES, Ruben	1807	Bayles
BAYLES, Ruben	1808	Bayles
BAYLES, Ruben L.	1814	Hoss
BAYLES, Sam Jr.	1808	Parker
BAYLES, Sam Jr.	1809	Parker
BAYLES, Sammuel Jr.	1812	McCray
BAYLES, Sammuel Sr.	1812	McCray
BAYLES, Samuel	1797	Calvert
BAYLES, Samuel	1798	Calvert
BAYLES, Samuel	1801	Calvert
BAYLES, Samuel	1808	Parker
BAYLES, Samuel	1810	Hartzel
BAYLES, Samuel	1811	McCray
BAYLES, Samuel	1812	Hartsell
BAYLES, Samuel	1815	Fines
BAYLES, Samuel	1816	Fine
BAYLES, Samuel	1817	Fine
BAYLES, Samuel	1817	Fine
BAYLES, Samuel	1818	Fine
BAYLES, Samuel	1818	Harris
BAYLES, Samuel	1819	Howard
BAYLES, Samuel	1821	Howard
BAYLES, Samuel	1780-1781 (Undated)	
BAYLES, Samuel Jr.	1805	Jas Parker
BAYLES, Samuel Jr.	1811	McCray
BAYLES, Samuel Jr.	1812	McCray
BAYLES, Samuel Jr.	1814	McCray
BAYLES, Samuel Jr.	1816	Harrison
BAYLES, Samuel Jr.	1817	Harris
BAYLES, Samuel Jr.	1819	Harris
BAYLES, Samuel Jr.	1821	Hampton
BAYLES, Samuel Sr.	1805	Jas Parker
BAYLES, Samuel Sr.	1812	McCray
BAYLES, Samuel Sr.	1814	McCray
BAYLES, Samuel Sr.	1815	Harris
BAYLES, Samuel Sr.	1816	Harrison
BAYLES, Samuel Sr.	1817	Harris
BAYLES, Samuel Sr.	1818	Harris
BAYLES, Samuel Sr.	1819	Harris
BAYLES, Samuel Sr.	1821	Hampton
BAYLES, Uriah	1815	Harris
BAYLES, William	1797	Calvert
BAYLES, William	1798	Calvert
BAYLES, William	1811	McCray
BAYLES, William	1812	McCray
BAYLES, William	1812	McCray
BAYLES, William	1817	Harris
BAYLES, William	1818	Harris
BAYLES, William	1819	Harris

Surname, Given names	Year	Comp./Dist.
BAYLES, William	1821	Hampton
BAYLES, Wm	1805	Jas Parker
BAYLES, Wm	1808	Parker
BAYLES, Wm	1809	Parker
BAYLESS, Anet	1821	Haines
BAYLESS, Daniel	1801	Calvert
BAYLESS, John	1810	Hartzel
BAYLESS, Saml	1795	Calvert
BAYLESS, Samuel	1810	Hartzel
BAYLESS, Wm	1801	Calvert
BAYLEY, Cotret	1795	Taylor
BAYLEY, Cottrel	1790	Williams
BAYLEY, Cottrel	1791	Williams
BAYLEY, John	1778	
BAYLEY, Robert	1778	
BAYLIS, Daniel	1797	Calvert
BAYLIS, Daniel	1799	Stuart
BAYLIS, Daniel	1805	Parker
BAYLIS, George	1797	Robertson
BAYLIS, George	1798	Roberson
BAYLIS, Hhenlins S.	1813	Hoss
BAYLIS, John	1793	North
BAYLIS, Rheubin	1798	Roberson
BAYLIS, Rubin	1797	Robertson
BAYLIS, Saml	1797	Calvert
BAYLIS, Samuel	1799	Stuart
BAYLIS, Willm	1797	Calvert
BAYLIS, Wm	1799	Stuart
BAYLS, Abraham	1797	Calvert
BAYLS, Danl	1814	Hartsell
BAYLS, John	1806	Parker
BAYLS, Rees	1814	Hartsell
BAYLS, Samuel	1814	Hartsell
BAYLSE, Sam	1809	Parker
BEACON, Charles	1812	Ellis
BEAGLES, John	1809	Right
BEAGLES, John	1811	Ellis
BEAGLES, John	1812	Ellis
BEAGLES, John	1814	Bean
BEAGLES, Mary	1815	Haire
BEAGLES, Mary	1816	Hair
BEAL, David	1819	Hunt
BEALES, David	1817	Hunt
BEALES, Isaac	1817	Hunt
BEALES, Levi	1817	Hunt
BEALEY, Samuel	1780-1781 (undated)	
BEALIS, John	1809	Hartzell
BEALS, David	1821	Hunt
BEALS, Isaac	1819	Hunt
BEALS, Isaac	1821	Hunt
BEALS, Jacob	1783 [after]	Depew

Surname, Given names	Year	Comp./Dist.
BEALS, Joseph	1819	Hunt
BEALS, Joseph	1821	Hunt
BEALS, Levi	1819	Hunt
BEALS, Levi	1821	Hunt
BEAMS, James	1795	Ford
BEAN, Abraham	1814	Couthers
BEAN, Agnes (Widow)	1791	Tullis
BEAN, Baxter	1814	McCracken
BEAN, Baxter	1815	Garner
BEAN, Charles	1818	Harris
BEAN, Edmon	1793	Melvan
BEAN, Edmon	1795	Melvan
BEAN, Edmon	1796	Melvin
BEAN, Edmon	1798	Crouch
BEAN, Edmon	1801	Norwood
BEAN, Edmond	1790	Stone
BEAN, Edmond	1791	Stone
BEAN, Edmond	1806	Crouch
BEAN, George	1790	Stone
BEAN, George	1791	Stone
BEAN, Jesse	1818	Hair
BEAN, John	1793	Morrison
BEAN, John	1794	Morrison
BEAN, John	1795	Morrison
BEAN, John	1798	Morrison
BEAN, John	1812	Ellis
BEAN, John	1814	Bean
BEAN, John	[1796] 1797	Morris
BEAN, Joseph	1821	Howard
BEAN, Marget	1814	Bean
BEAN, Mark	1811	Britten
BEAN, Mark	1812	Britton
BEAN, Mark	1813	Copas
BEAN, Mark	1814	Copes
BEAN, Mark	1817	Grisham
BEAN, Mark	1819	Grisham
BEAN, Pollark	1818	Grisham
BEAN, Robert	1819	Hair
BEAN, Rusell	1805	Aikin
BEAN, Russel	1801	Aiken
BEAN, Russel	1814	McCracken
BEAN, Russell	1790	Stone
BEAN, Russell	1791	Stone
BEAN, Russell	1806	Anderson
BEAN, Russell	1807	Anderson
BEAN, Russell	1809	Roadmas
BEAN, Russell	1815	Garner
BEAN, William	1798	Morrison
BEANE, Barter	1821	Howard
BEANE, Baxter	1816	Smith
BEANE, Baxter	1817	Smith
BEANE, Margaret	1815	Haire
BEANE, Margaret	1816	Hair
BEANE, Mark	1815	Copas
BEANE, Mark	1816	Copas
BEANE, Robert	1817	Smith
BEANE, Russell	1816	Smith
BEANE, Russell	1817	Smith
BEAR, Mark	1821	Hale
BEARD, Andrew	1794	Handly
BEARD, Andrew	1795	Handly
BEARD, James	1809	Patterson
BEARD, James	1810	Dimmons
BEARD, James	1812	McLin
BEARD, James	1815	Carcathers
BEARD, James	1817	Little
BEARD, James	1818	Jones
BEARD, James	1819	Jones
BEARD, James	1821	Jones
BEARD, John	1797	Calvert
BEARD, John	1798	Calvert
BEARD, Robard	1798	Crouch
BEARD, Robart	1794	Melvan
BEARD, Robart	1795	Melvan
BEARD, Robart	1801	Norwood
BEARD, Robert	1790	Stone
BEARD, Robert	1791	Stone
BEARD, Robert	1793	Melvan
BEARD, Robert	1796	Melvin
BEARD, Robert	1806	Crouch
BEARD, Robert	1809	Right
BEARD, Robert	1812	Ellis
BEARD, Robert	1814	Bean
BEARD, Robert	1815	Haire
BEARD, Robert	1816	Hair
BEARD, Robert	1817	Haire
BEARD, Robert	1818	Hair
BEARD, Robert	1819	Hair
BEARD, Robert	1819	Jones
BEARD, William	1812	Ellis
BEARD, William	1819	Brown
BEARDE, Robert	1821	Louis
BEARDEN, Samuel	1818	Brown [2]
BEAS, Jacob	1797	Biddle
BEATY, Robert	1793	Scott
BEATY, William	1793	Scott
BEAVRORS, Thomas	1780-1781 (Undated)	
BECKMAN, Michael	1791	White
BECKSOME, Jams	1814	Barns
BEDFOURD, Andw	1806	Parker
BEDGLES, John	1806	Crouch
BEEL, John	1793	North

Surname, Given names	Year	Comp./Dist.
BEEL, Joseph	1807	Parker
BEEN, Jesse	1778	
BEEN, John	1778	
BEEN, John	1791	Tullis
BEEN, Robert	1778	
BEEN, Wm (Esq.)	1778	
BEEN, Wm Jr.	1778	
BEETLEBOUGH, Peter	1809	Par
BEFFAUR, Andrew	1820	Smith
BEISL, Thomas	1798	Biddle
B-ELET, William	1798	Shipley
BELEW, Margaret B.	1817	Brown
BELFOR, Andrew	1821	Smith
BELFORD,	1811	Rodman
BELFORD, Andrew	1818	Smith
BELFORE, Andrew	1819	Smith
BELIS, Danel	1794	North
BELIS, Reubin	1794	Brown
BELIS, Samuel	1791	Willey
BELL, Andrew	1819	Findley
BELL, Brooks	1812	Crawford [2]
BELL, Brooks	1821	McGee
BELL, Brooksey	1818	Riley
BELL, Brooksey	1819	Findley
BELL, Elizabeth	1792	Depew
BELL, Elizabeth	1793	Biddle
BELL, Elizabeth	1794	Depew
BELL, George	1792	Depew
BELL, George	1793	Depew
BELL, George	1794	Depew
BELL, George	1797	Duncan
BELL, George	1798	Duncan
BELL, George	1798	Duncan
BELL, George	1799	Duncan
BELL, George	1801	Taylor
BELL, George	1806	Guin
BELL, George	1807	Givins
BELL, George	1808	Guin
BELL, George	1809	Gwin
BELL, George	1811	Davis
BELL, George	1812	McLin
BELL, George	1814	McLin
BELL, George	1815	McLin
BELL, George	1818	Hunt
BELL, George	1819	Hunt
BELL, George	1821	Hunt
BELL, James	1790	Biddle
BELL, James	1791	Biddle
BELL, James	1792	Biddle
BELL, James	1793	Biddle
BELL, James	1794	Blair
BELL, James	1816	Fine
BELL, James	1817	Fine
BELL, James	1818	Fine
BELL, James	1819	Howard
BELL, James	1821	Howard
BELL, John	1791	Tullis
BELL, John	1792	Depew
BELL, John	1792	North
BELL, John	1793	Murray
BELL, John	1794	North
BELL, John	1795	Young
BELL, John	1797	Young
BELL, John	1801	Taylor
BELL, John	1805	Parker
BELL, John	1806	Parker
BELL, John	1807	Parker
BELL, John	1808	Parker
BELL, John	1809	Par
BELL, John	1810	Hartzel
BELL, John	1814	Hartsell
BELL, John	1815	Fines
BELL, John	1816	Fine
BELL, John	1816	Hunt
BELL, John	1817	Fine
BELL, John	1817	Hunt
BELL, John	1818	Fine
BELL, John	1819	Howard
BELL, Joseph	1810	Hartzel
BELL, Joseph	1812	Hartsell
BELL, Joseph	1814	Hampton
BELL, Joseph E.	1812	McCray
BELL, Joseph E.	1812	McCray
BELL, Joseph E.	1815	Waddell
BELL, Samuel	1819	Findley
BELL, Samuel S.	1821	Hunt
BELL, Thomas	1796	Young
BELL, Thomas	1797	Young
BELL, Thomas	1812	Crawford [2]
BELL, William	1792	Depew
BELL, William	1816	Hair
BELLEMY, Elisha	1791	Milliken
BELLS, John	1796	Young
BENCH, Richard	1798	Shipley
BENGER, Kagan W.	1807	Cade
BENMAN, Elias Sr.	1818	Hunt
BENNET, Brook	1821	Hunt
BENNET, John	1781	
BENNIT, John	1780-1781 (Undated)	
BERCKLEY, Ebenzer	1817	Hunt
BERGAMEN, Peter	1818	Riley
BERKLEY, Daniel	1816	Hunt

Surname, Given names	Year	Comp./Dist.
BERKLEY, Ebenzer	1816	Hunt
BERKLEY, Robert	1816	Hampton
BERRICRAFT, John	1798	Biddle
BERRIMAN, Sammuel	1808	Bayles
BERRIMAN, Samuel	1807	Bayles
BERRON, William	1794	Murray
BERRY, John	1797	Duncan
BERRY, John	1798	Duncan
BERRY, John	1819	Hunt
BERRY, John	1821	Hunt
BERRY, Wm	1781	
BERRYMEN, Samuel	1806	Brown
BETTSENLISK, Elisa	1821	Martin
BETTY, William	1780-1781 (Undated)	
BEVACK, Gails	1794	North
BEWLEY, Anthony	1801	Taylor
BEWLEY, Anthony	1806	Parker
BEWLEY, Anthony	1807	
BEYINS, Andrew	1792	Coye
BEYINS, Morgan	1792	Coye
BEYS, Edward	1798	Gann
BIBBER, James	1821	Martin
BICKNELL, James	1821	Jones
BIDDLE, Jame	1808	
BIDDLE, James	1805	Carson
BIDDLE, James	1806	Carson
BIDDLE, James	1807	Shields
BIDDLE, James	1811	
BIDDLE, James	1814	Couthers
BIDDLE, James	1815	Carcathers
BIDDLE, James	1816	Giles
BIDDLE, James	1817	Gillises
BIDDLE, Saml	1814	Couthers
BIDDLE, Samuel	1815	Carcathers
BIDDLE, Samuel	1816	Giles
BIDDLE, Samuel	1817	Gillises
BIDDLE, Samuel	1818	Land
BIDDLE, Samuel	1819	Sands
BIDDLE, Samuel	1821	Sands
BIDDLE, Thomas	1781	
BIDDLE, Thomas	1790	Biddle
BIDDLE, Thomas	1791	Biddle
BIDDLE, Thomas	1792	Biddle
BIDDLE, Thomas	1793	Biddle
BIDDLE, Thomas	1794	Blair
BIDDLE, Thomas	1797	Biddle
BIDDLE, Thomas	1798	Biddle
BIDDLE, Thomas	1798	Biddle
BIDDLE, Thomas	1801	Biddle
BIDDLE, Thomas	1805	Carson
BIDDLE, Thomas	1806	Carson
BIDDLE, Thomas	1807	Shields
BIDDLE, Thomas	1810	Dimmons
BIDDLE, Thomas	1811	
BIDDLE, Thomas	1815	Carcathers
BIDDLE, Thomas	1817	Gillises
BIDDLE, Thomas	1818	Land
BIDDLE, Thomas	1819	Sands
BIDDLE, Thomas	1821	Sands
BIDDLE, Thomas Jr.	1818	Land
BIDDLE, Thomas Jr.	1819	Sands
BIDDLE, Thomas Jr.	1821	Sands
BIDDLE, Thos	1814	Couthers
BIDDLE, Thos	1780-1781 (Undated)	
BIDDLECOM, William	1792	Coye
BIDDLECUM, William	1806	Odel
BIDDLETON, William	1796	Longmire
BIDLE, Thomas	1808	
BIERD, Henry	1795	Melvan
BIGOLEE, Michel	1798	Morrison
BIGSBA, James	1810	Cove
BILLINGELY, Samuel	1796	Shipley
BILLINGESLEY, Samuel	1798	Shipley
BILLINGLEY, James	1814	Copes
BILLINGLEY, Jesse	1814	Copes
BILLINGSBY, Jacob	1815	Copas
BILLINGSBY, Jacob	1816	Copas
BILLINGSBY, Jacob	1818	Grisham
BILLINGSBY, Jacob	1819	Grisham
BILLINGSBY, James	1805	Doak
BILLINGSBY, James	1816	Copas
BILLINGSBY, James	1817	Grisham
BILLINGSBY, James	1818	Grisham
BILLINGSBY, James	1819	Grisham
BILLINGSBY, Jesse	1815	Copas
BILLINGSBY, Jesse	1816	Copas
BILLINGSBY, Jesse	1817	Grisham
BILLINGSBY, Jesse	1818	Grisham
BILLINGSBY, Jesse	1819	Grisham
BILLINGSBY, John	1815	Copas
BILLINGSBY, John	1816	Copas
BILLINGSBY, John	1817	Grisham
BILLINGSBY, John	1818	Grisham
BILLINGSBY, John	1819	Grisham
BILLINGSBY, Joseph	1817	Grisham
BILLINGSBY, Samuel	1797	Shipley
BILLINGSLEY, James	1801	Lane
BILLINGSLEY, James	1806	Doke
BILLINGSLEY, James	1807	Britton
BILLINGSLEY, James	1811	Britten
BILLINGSLEY, James	1812	Britton
BILLINGSLEY, James	1813	Copas

Surname, Given names	Year	Comp./Dist.
BILLINGSLEY, Jas	1821	Hale
BILLINGSLEY, Jesse	1813	Copas
BILLINGSLEY, Jesse	1821	Hale
BILLINGSLEY, Jessee	1811	Britten
BILLINGSLEY, Jessee	1812	Britton
BILLINGSLEY, John	1807	Britton
BILLINGSLEY, John	1811	Britten
BILLINGSLEY, John	1813	Copas
BILLINGSLEY, John	1814	Copes
BILLINGSLEY, John	1821	Hale
BILLINGSLEY, John Sr.	1812	Britton
BILLINGSLEY, Samuel	1801	Lane
BILLINGSLEY, William	1801	Lane
BILLINGSLY, Jacob	1821	Hale
BILLINGSLY, John	1806	Doke
BILLINGSLY, Samuel	1795	Murray
BIMAL, John	1805	Guir
B--IN, Samuel	1817	Hunt
BINKLY, Jacob	1814	McCray
BIRAM, Ebenezer	1780-1781 (undated)	
BIRAM, Ebnezer	1780-1781 (Undated)	
BIRCH, George	1811	Britten
BIRCH, George	1813	Copas
BIRCH, Richard	1806	Doke
BIRCH, Richard	1807	Britton
BIRCHER, John	1816	Waddell
BIRCHER, William	1816	Waddell
BIRD, Amos	1778	
BIRD, Amos	1780-1781 (Undated)	
BIRD, George	1794	Blair
BIRD, James	1795	Carriger
BIRD, James	1811	Barron
BIRD, James	1815	Grimsley
BIRD, Jams	1814	Barns
BIRD, Jonathan	1778	
BIRDWELL, Benjamin	1809	Right
BIRDWELL, Benjamin	1813	Copas
BIRDWELL, Benjamin	1814	Bean
BIRDWELL, George	1812	Ellis
BIRDWELL, William	1805	Rector
BIRDWELL, William	1807	Cade
BIRELY, Michel	1806	Carr
BIRLEY, Mickel	1801	Norwood
BISBEY, John	1779	Wilson
BISHOP, Joseph	1794	Ford
BISHOP, Joseph	1795	Ford
BITNER, John	1790	Hanley
BITNER, John	1791	Hanley
BITNER, John	1793	Handley
BITNER, John	1794	Handly

Surname, Given names	Year	Comp./Dist.
BITNER, John	1794	North
BITNER, John	1795	Handly
BITNER, John	1796	Handly
BITNER, John	1797	Gann
BITNER, John	1798	Gann
BITNER, John	1799	Gann
BITNER, John	1799	Moore
BITNER, John	1801	Gann
BITNER, John	1801	Taylor
BITNER, John	1814	Waddell
BITNER, John	1815	Waddell
BITNER, John	1816	Waddell
BITNER, John	1817	Riley
BITNER, Margaret	1819	Findley
BITNER, Margaret	1821	McGee
BITNER, Samuel	1806	Grur
BITNER, Samuel	1809	Green
BITNER, Samuel	1811	Green
BITNER, Samuel (estate of)	1815	Waddell
BITNER, Samuel (estate)	1816	Waddell
BITNER, Samuel (estate)	1817	Riley
BITNER, Samuel (estate)	1818	Riley
BLACK, Archibald	1814	Waddell
BLACK, Benjamin	1814	Waddell
BLACK, Danial	1805	Carson
BLACK, Jacob	1805	Guir
BLACK, Jacob	1806	Grur
BLACK, James	1811	Rodman
BLACK, James	1812	McCray
BLACK, James	1812	McCray
BLACK, James	1814	McCray
BLACK, James	1816	Harrison
BLACK, John	1780-1781	District 7
BLACK, Thomas	1821	Howard
BLACKBORNE, Archibald	1808	Gwin
BLACKBORNE, Benjamin	1808	Gwin
BLACKBORNE, Samuel	1808	Gwin
BLACKBOURN, Archibald	1805	Guir
BLACKBOURN, Benjamin	1809	Green
BLACKBOURNE, Archebald	1809	Green
BLACKBOURNE, Archibald	1810	Green
BLACKBOURNE, Archibald	1812	Waddill
BLACKBOURNE, Benjamin	1810	Green
BLACKBOURNE, Samuel	1809	Green
BLACKBOURNE, Samuel	1810	Green
BLACKBOURNE, Samuel	1812	Waddill
BLACKBOURNE, William	1812	Waddill
BLACKBURN, Abe	1817	Riley
BLACKBURN, Arch	1818	Riley
BLACKBURN, Arch	1819	Findley
BLACKBURN, Archabald	1807	

Surname, Given names	Year	Comp./Dist.
BLACKBURN, Archabald	1811	Green
BLACKBURN, Archable	1798	Gann
BLACKBURN, Archd	1793	Handley
BLACKBURN, Archd	1794	Handly
BLACKBURN, Archd	1795	Handly
BLACKBURN, Archd	1796	Handly
BLACKBURN, Archd	1799	Moore
BLACKBURN, Archibald	1790	Hanley
BLACKBURN, Archibald	1791	Hanley
BLACKBURN, Archibald	1797	Gann
BLACKBURN, Archibald	1801	Gann
BLACKBURN, Archibald	1806	Grur
BLACKBURN, Archibald	1815	Waddell
BLACKBURN, Archibald	1816	Waddell
BLACKBURN, Archibald	1821	McGee
BLACKBURN, Ben	1806	Grur
BLACKBURN, Benjamin	1811	Green
BLACKBURN, Benjamin	1815	Waddell
BLACKBURN, Benjamin	1816	Waddell
BLACKBURN, Benjamin	1817	Riley
BLACKBURN, Benjamin	1818	Riley
BLACKBURN, Gabrail	1793	Depew
BLACKBURN, Natheenal	1806	Grur
BLACKBURN, Robart	1780-1781 (Undated)	
BLACKBURN, Robert	1778	
BLACKBURN, Robert	1781	
BLACKBURN, Samuel	1806	Grur
BLACKBURN, Samuel	1811	Green
BLACKBURN, Samuel	1818	Riley
BLACKBURN, Samuel	1821	Louis
BLACKBURN, Thomas	1796	Millikin
BLACKBURN, Thomas	1816	Waddell
BLACKBURN, Thomas	1817	Riley
BLACKBURN, Thomas	1818	Riley
BLACKBURN, William	1811	Green
BLACKBURN, William	1815	Waddell
BLACKBURN, William	1816	Waddell
BLACKBURN, William	1817	Riley
BLACKBURN, William	1818	Riley
BLACKBURN, William	1819	Findley
BLACKBURN, Wm	1821	McGee
BLACKELY, Daniel	1816	Giles
BLACKLEY, Daniel	1794	Blair
BLACKLEY, Daniel	1798	Biddle
BLACKLEY, Daniel	1801	Biddle
BLACKLEY, Daniel	1819	Sands
BLACKLEY, John	1798	Biddle
BLACKLEY, John	1801	Biddle
BLACKLEY, Robert	1781	
BLACKLEY, Robert	1792	Depew
BLACKLEY, Robert	1793	Biddle
BLACKLEY, Robert	1801	Biddle
BLACKLEY, Robert	1816	Giles
BLACKLEY, Robert	1819	Sands
BLACKLEY, Thomas	1816	Giles
BLACKLEY, William	1801	Biddle
BLACKLY, Danial	1810	Dimmons
BLACKLY, Daniel	1797	Biddle
BLACKLY, Daniel	1806	Carson
BLACKLY, Daniel	1807	Shields
BLACKLY, Daniel	1811	
BLACKLY, Daniel	1821	Sands
BLACKLY, James	1809	Patterson
BLACKLY, James	1811	
BLACKLY, John	1797	Biddle
BLACKLY, John	1805	Carson
BLACKLY, John	1806	Carson
BLACKLY, John	1807	Shields
BLACKLY, John	1809	Patterson
BLACKLY, John	1810	Dimmons
BLACKLY, John	1811	
BLACKLY, John	1814	Couthers
BLACKLY, Robert	1797	Biddle
BLACKLY, Robert	1805	Carson
BLACKLY, Robert	1810	Dimmons
BLACKLY, Robert	1811	
BLACKLY, Robert	1821	Sands
BLACKLY, Robert	1780-1781 (Undated)	
BLACKLY, Robt	1807	Shields
BLACKLY, Robt	1814	Couthers
BLACKLY, Samel	1814	Couthers
BLACKLY, Thomas	1810	Dimmons
BLACKLY, Thomas	1811	
BLACKLY, Thomas	1814	Couthers
BLACKLY, Thomas Jr.	1814	Couthers
BLACKLY, William	1810	Dimmons
BLACKLY, William Jr.	1821	Sands
BLACKLY, Wm	1806	Carson
BLACKLY, Wm	1807	Shields
BLACKLY, Wm	1811	
BLACKLY, Wm	1814	Couthers
BLACKWELL, David	1781	
BLACKWELL, John	1778	
BLACKWELL, John	1781	
BLACKWELL, John	1780-1781 (Undated)	
BLACKWILL, David	1780-1781 (Undated)	
BLAIN, P.	1818	Smith
BLAIN, Tom	1817	Gillises
BLAIR & PARSONS,	1821	Smith
BLAIR, Brice	1793	Biddle
BLAIR, Brice	1794	Depew

Surname, Given names	Year	Comp./Dist.
BLAIR, Brice	1795	Milliken
BLAIR, Brice	1796	Millikin
BLAIR, Brice	1797	Biddle
BLAIR, Brice	1801	Biddle
BLAIR, Brice	1805	Carson
BLAIR, Bruce	1799	Duncan
BLAIR, Hugh	1778	
BLAIR, Hugh	1781	
BLAIR, Hugh	1793	Biddle
BLAIR, Hugh	1797	Biddle
BLAIR, Hugh	1798	Duncan
BLAIR, Hugh	1783 [after]	Blair
BLAIR, James	1814	Couthers
BLAIR, James	1783 [after]	Depew
BLAIR, Jane	1806	Carson
BLAIR, Jane	1807	Shields
BLAIR, Jean	1805	Carson
BLAIR, Jenny	1810	Dimmons
BLAIR, Jinny	1809	Patterson
BLAIR, Jinny	1811	
BLAIR, Jno	1819	Smith
BLAIR, Jno. F. Parson	1820	Smith
BLAIR, John	1781	
BLAIR, John	1792	Depew
BLAIR, John	1793	Biddle
BLAIR, John	1794	Blair
BLAIR, John	1796	Millikin
BLAIR, John	1797	Biddle
BLAIR, John	1798	Biddle
BLAIR, John	1798	Biddle
BLAIR, John	1805	Stephenson
BLAIR, John	1806	Payn
BLAIR, John	1807	Payne
BLAIR, John	1808	McAllister
BLAIR, John	1810	Dimmons
BLAIR, John	1810	Dimmons
BLAIR, John	1811	McAlister
BLAIR, John	1812	Crawford
BLAIR, John	1812	Crawford [2]
BLAIR, John	1814	Couthers
BLAIR, John	1814	Couthers
BLAIR, John	1814	McCracken
BLAIR, John	1815	Crookshanks
BLAIR, John	1815	Garner
BLAIR, John	1816	Smith
BLAIR, John	1817	Smith
BLAIR, John	1817	Smith
BLAIR, John	1818	McClure
BLAIR, John	1818	Smith
BLAIR, John	1819	Sands
BLAIR, John	1819	Smith
BLAIR, John	1820	Smith
BLAIR, John	1821	Smith
BLAIR, John	1783 [after]	Blair
BLAIR, John	1783 [after]	Depew
BLAIR, John (Big)	1797	Biddle
BLAIR, John (Big)	1798	Biddle
BLAIR, John (Big)	1798	Biddle
BLAIR, John (big)	1801	Biddle
BLAIR, John (Coln.)	1793	Biddle
BLAIR, John (Coln.)	1794	Blair
BLAIR, John (Maj.)	1790	Biddle
BLAIR, John (Maj.)	1791	Biddle
BLAIR, John (Maj.)	1792	Biddle
BLAIR, John (Major)	1780-1781 (Undated)	
BLAIR, John (minor)	1810	Dimmons
BLAIR, John (son of Jane)	1815	Carcathers
BLAIR, John Jr.	1809	Patterson
BLAIR, John Jr.	1811	Davis
BLAIR, John Jr.	1811	
BLAIR, John Jr.	1815	Carcathers
BLAIR, John Miller	1815	Carcathers
BLAIR, John Sr.	1794	Depew
BLAIR, John Sr.	1795	Milliken
BLAIR, John Sr.	1797	Biddle
BLAIR, John Sr.	1797	Hannah
BLAIR, John Sr.	1809	Patterson
BLAIR, John Sr.	1811	Davis
BLAIR, John Sr.	1811	
BLAIR, John Sr.	1815	McLin
BLAIR, John Sr.	1816	Hunt
BLAIR, John Sr.	1817	Hampton
BLAIR, Joseph	1793	Depew
BLAIR, Joseph	1805	Stephenson
BLAIR, Joseph	1806	Payn
BLAIR, Joseph	1807	Payne
BLAIR, Joseph	1809	Patterson
BLAIR, Joseph	1810	Dimmons
BLAIR, Joseph	1811	McAlister
BLAIR, Joseph Jr.	1794	Depew
BLAIR, Lane	1814	Couthers
BLAIR, Parsons P.	1817	Smith
BLAIR, Richard	1790	Biddle
BLAIR, Richard	1791	Biddle
BLAIR, Richard	1792	Biddle
BLAIR, Richard	1793	Biddle
BLAIR, Richard	1793	Milliken
BLAIR, Richard	1794	Depew
BLAIR, Richard	1795	Milliken
BLAIR, Richard	1798	Biddle
BLAIR, Richard	1798	Biddle
BLAIR, Richard	1801	Biddle

Surname, Given names	Year	Comp./Dist.
BLAIR, Richard	1805	Carson
BLAIR, Richard	1806	Carson
BLAIR, Richd	1807	Shields
BLAIR, Richd	1809	Patterson
BLAIR, Richd	1810	Dimmons
BLAIR, Robart	1798	Biddle
BLAIR, Robert	1790	Biddle
BLAIR, Robert	1791	Biddle
BLAIR, Robert	1792	Biddle
BLAIR, Robert	1798	Biddle
BLAIR, Robert	1799	Duncan
BLAIR, Robert	1801	Biddle
BLAIR, Robert (Capt.)	1794	Blair
BLAIR, Samuel	1793	Depew
BLAIR, Samuel	1797	Duncan
BLAIR, Samuel	1807	Shields
BLAIR, Samuel	1809	Patterson
BLAIR, Samuel	1810	Dimmons
BLAIR, Samuel	1811	Davis
BLAIR, Samuel	1812	McLin
BLAIR, Samuel	1815	McLin
BLAIR, Samuel	1816	Hunt
BLAIR, Samuel	1783 [after]	Depew
BLAIR, Tom	1816	Giles
BLAIR, Tom	1819	Sands
BLAIR, William	1797	Biddle
BLAIR, William	1798	Biddle
BLAIR, William	1801	Biddle
BLAIR, William	1805	Carson
BLAIR, William	1806	Carson
BLAIR, William	1810	Dimmons
BLAIR, William	1817	Hampton
BLAIR, William	1818	Brown [2]
BLAIR, Wm	1798	Biddle
BLAIR, Wm	1807	Shields
BLAIR, Wm	1809	Patterson
BLAIR, Wm	1811	
BLAIR, Wm K.	1821	Smith
BLAIRE, Thomes	1806	Guin
BLAKBURN, Archeble	1799	Gann
BLAKELY, Daniel	1815	Carcathers
BLAKELY, Daniel	1817	Gillises
BLAKELY, James	1819	Sands
BLAKELY, John	1815	Carcathers
BLAKELY, John	1816	Giles
BLAKELY, John	1819	Sands
BLAKELY, Robert	1779	Wilson
BLAKELY, Robert	1815	Carcathers
BLAKELY, Thomas	1815	Carcathers
BLAKELY, William	1815	Carcathers
BLAKLEY, John	1817	Gillises
BLAKLEY, Robert	1794	Blair
BLAKLEY, Robert	1817	Gillises
BLAKLEY, William	1817	Gillises
BLANK, Peter	1811	McCray
BLAR, Brice	1798	Hannah
BLAR, Joseph	1798	Hannah
BLAR, Mebery (home man)	1808	McAllister
BLARE, Joseph	1812	McCray
BLASE, John	1780-1781 (Undated)	
BLEAKLEY, Daniel	1818	Land
BLEAKLEY, John	1818	Land
BLEAKLEY, Robert	1818	Land
BLEAKLEY, Thomas	1817	Gillises
BLEAKLEY, Thomas	1818	Land
BLEAKLEY, William	1818	Land
BLEAKLY, William	1805	Carson
BLEAR, John	1821	Sands
BLECKLEY, Robart	1798	Biddle
BLEEKLY, John Jr.	1821	Sands
BLEEKLY, William	1821	Sands
BLEKLEY, Danial	1798	Biddle
BLESLEY, John	1798	Biddle
BLEVINS, David	1806	Crouch
BLEVINS, Phillip	1819	Smith
BLEVINS, William	1792	Coye
BLEYTH, Samuel	1791	Tullis
BLEYTHE, Samuel	1794	North
BLFON, Andrew	1805	Aikin
BLICKLY, John	1821	Sands
BLIGH, Sammuel	1793	Morrison
BLIGH, Sammuel	1794	Morrison
BLITHE, Saml	1801	Taylor
BLITHE, Samuel	1792	Tulley
BLUM, Frederick	1808	Gwin
BLUM, Frederick	1809	Green
BLUSTARD, Claudis	1817	Riley
BLYE, James	1816	Grimsley
BLYETH, Hugh	1807	Britton
BLYTH, Hugh	1806	Parker
BLYTH, Samuel	1806	Parker
BLYTHE, Saml	1795	Young
BLYTHE, Samual	1805	Parker
BLYTHE, Samual	1807	Parker
BOARKS, Nicoli	1791	Milliken
BODENEAL, Wm	1814	Barns
BOG, Abraham	1809	Carr
BOGARD, Abraham	1807	Carr
BOGARD, Abraham	1808	Carr
BOGARD, Samuel	1795	Morrison
BOGART, Abraham	1798	Morrison
BOGART, Abraham	1806	Carr

Surname, Given names	Year	Comp./Dist.
BOGART, Hanerey	1794	Taylor
BOGART, Henery	1791	Tullis
BOGART, Henry	1787	Fains
BOGART, Henry	1792	Tulley
BOGART, Henry	1793	Maxwell
BOGART, Henry	1798	Morrison
BOGART, Henry	[1796] 1797	Morris
BOGART, Samuel	1787	Fains
BOGART, Samuel	1791	Tullis
BOGART, Samuel	1793	Morrison
BOGART, Samuel	1794	Morrison
BOGART, Samuel	[1796] 1797	Morris
BOGERD, Henery	1795	Morrison
BOHANNAN, Ezekiel	1795	Calvert
BOID, George	1793	Biddle
BOID, Joseph	1798	Morrison
BOID, Joseph	1798	Morrison
BOILS, Abraham	1799	Stuart
BOLAND, Wilam	1821	Martin
BOLELS, Henery	1812	Crawford [2]
BOLEN, Phillip	1819	Findley
BOLEN, Thomas	1819	Grimsley
BOLIN, Philip	1818	Riley
BOLIN, Thomas	1817	Grimsley
BOLINGER, Fredrick	1796	Young
BOLISH, John	1795	Ford
BOLLINGER, James	1814	Hampton
BOLTON, James	1816	Fine
BOMAN, Barnel	1809	Par
BOMAN, Elias	1793	Depew
BOMAN, Elias	1797	Duncan
BOMAN, Elias	1806	Guin
BOMAN, Elias	1783 [after]	Depew
BOMAN, George	1806	Guin
BOMAN, Henry	1806	Crouch
BOMAN, Jacob	1795	Morrison
BOMAN, Jacob	1821	Hale
BOMAN, Jacob Jr.	1821	Hale
BOMAN, John	1814	Hartsell
BOMAN, Peter	1798	Young
BOMAN, Peter	1809	Par
BOMAN, Peter	1810	Hartzel
BOMAN, Peter Jr.	1805	Parker
BOMAN, Peter Jr.	1807	Parker
BOMAN, William	1805	Carson
BOMAN, William	1812	Barnes
BOMEN, Barney	1805	Parker
BOND, Charles	1778	
BOND, George	1783 [after]	Blair
BOND, Jesse	1778	
BONESER, George	1821	Martin
BONESER, John	1821	Martin
BONMAN, John	1806	Crouch
BONNETS, Wm	1779	Wilson
BOON, Joseph	1793	Brown
BOONE, David	1821	Brown
BOONE, Sallamon	1795	Thornton
BOOTH, David	1798	Roberson
BOOTH, David	1799	Robertson
BOOTH, David	1801	Taylor
BOOTH, David	1806	Brown
BOOTH, David	1807	Bayles
BOOTH, David	1808	Bayles
BOOTH, David	1814	Hampton
BOOTH, David	1816	Hampton
BOOTH, David	1817	Hampton
BOOTH, David	1818	Brown [2]
BOOTH, John	1814	Hampton
BOOTH, John	1816	Hampton
BOOTH, John	1817	Hampton
BOOTH, John	1818	Brown [2]
BOOTH, John	1819	Brown
BOOTH, Joseph	1798	Roberson
BOOTH, Joseph	1799	Robertson
BOOTH, Joseph	1806	Parker
BOOTH, Joseph	1807	Parker
BOOTH, Joseph	1808	Parker
BOOTH, Joseph	1810	Hartzel
BOOTH, Joseph	1814	Hampton
BOOTH, Joseph	1816	Hampton
BOOTH, Joseph	1817	Hampton
BOOTH, Joseph	1817	Hampton
BOOTH, Joseph	1818	Brown [2]
BOOTH, Joseph	1821	Brown
BOOTH, Sarah	1806	Brown
BOOTH, Sarah	1807	Bayles
BOOTH, Sarah	1808	Bayles
BOOTH, Sarah	1809	Bayles
BOOTHE, David	1809	Bayles
BOOTHE, David	1819	Brown
BOOTHE, Joseph	1791	Milliken
BOOTHE, Joseph	1797	Robertson
BOOTHE, Joseph	1801	Roberson
BOR, Vallentine	1798	Roberson
BORAN, Chanea	1805	Parker
BORAN, Chanea	1807	Parker
BORAN, Chaney	1814	Hartsell
BORAN, Chany	1812	Hartsell
BORAN, Elijah	1805	Parker
BORAN, Elijah	1807	Parker
BORAN, Elijah	1814	Hartsell
BORAN, Ezekiel	1795	Young

Surname, Given names	Year	Comp./Dist.
BORAN, James Jr.	1795	Young
BORAN, James Sr.	1795	Young
BORAN, Tempenes	1810	Hartzel
BORAN, Zeakel	1807	Parker
BORDER, Michael	1778	
BORDERS, Michael	1779	Wilson
BOREEFF, Valtentine	1797	Robertson
BOREING, James	1798	Morrison
BOREING, Joshua	1798	Morrison
BOREING, William	1798	Morrison
BOREING, William	[1796] 1797	Morris
BOREN, Abraham	1817	Smith
BOREN, Absolom	1799	Morrison
BOREN, Absolom	1807	Parker
BOREN, Absolom	1818	Smith
BOREN, Chanea	1808	Parker
BOREN, Chaney	1816	Fine
BOREN, Chaney	1817	Fine
BOREN, Chaney	1818	Fine
BOREN, Chansy	1810	Hartzel
BOREN, Chany	1819	Howard
BOREN, Cheany	1801	
BOREN, Cheney	1793	North
BOREN, Elijah	1816	Fine
BOREN, Elijah	1817	Fine
BOREN, Elijah	1818	Fine
BOREN, Elijah	1819	Howard
BOREN, Greenbury	1816	Hoss
BOREN, Henry	1818	Hair
BOREN, Hezekiah	1815	Haire
BOREN, Hezekiah	1816	Hair
BOREN, Hezekiah	1817	Haire
BOREN, Hezekiah	1819	Hair
BOREN, James	1799	Morrison
BOREN, Jerock	1819	Grisham
BOREN, John	1799	Morrison
BOREN, John	1815	Garner
BOREN, John	1816	Smith
BOREN, John	1817	Haire
BOREN, Joshua	1799	Morrison
BOREN, Joshua	1808	Parker
BOREN, Joshua	1817	Little
BOREN, Temprens	1808	Parker
BOREN, William	1793	Morrison
BOREN, William	1794	Morrison
BOREN, William	1795	Morrison
BOREN, William	1799	Morrison
BOREZE, Vellentine	1799	Robertson
BORGER, Henry	1814	Couthers
BORIFF, Chana	1797	Young
BORIFF, Phebty	1796	Young

Surname, Given names	Year	Comp./Dist.
BORIN, Absolam	1795	Young
BORIN, Absolem	1801	Taylor
BORIN, Absolem	1806	Parker
BORIN, Absolem Sr.	1801	Taylor
BORIN, Absolom	1796	Young
BORIN, Absolom	1797	Young
BORIN, Amon	1813	Hoss
BORIN, Chana	1796	Young
BORIN, Chanay	1806	Parker
BORIN, Chaney	1801	Taylor
BORIN, Chaney	1815	Fines
BORIN, Elijah	1806	Parker
BORIN, Elijah	1815	Fines
BORIN, Ezekiel	1796	Young
BORIN, Ezekiel	1797	Young
BORIN, Ezekiel	1801	Taylor
BORIN, Ezekiel	1806	Parker
BORIN, Joshua	1801	Taylor
BORIN, Joshua	1806	Parker
BORIN, Nicholas	1796	Young
BORIN, Nicholis	1797	Young
BORING, Ablam	1791	North
BORING, Absolam	1809	Par
BORING, Absolem	1798	Young
BORING, Absolem	1814	Hoss
BORING, Absoleon	1792	Tulley
BORING, Absolom	1794	North
BORING, Absolom	1801	Morrison
BORING, Absolom	1806	Carr
BORING, Absolom	1811	Mitchell
BORING, Absolum	1798	Morrison
BORING, Absolum	1807	Carr
BORING, Absolum	1808	Carr
BORING, Absolum	1809	Carr
BORING, Amon	1811	Mitchell
BORING, Asolem	1813	Hoss
BORING, Chane	1798	Young
BORING, Chaney	1809	Par
BORING, Chaney	1821	Howard
BORING, Chenia	1792	North
BORING, China	1821	Jones
BORING, Dansey	1792	North
BORING, Eligah	1821	Howard
BORING, Elijah	1798	Morrison
BORING, Elijah	1812	Hartsell
BORING, Ezekiel	1792	North
BORING, Ezekill	1791	North
BORING, Greenberry	1811	Mitchell
BORING, Greenbery	1809	Carr
BORING, Gremsley	1819	Jones
BORING, Gren Barry	1808	Carr

Surname, Given names	Year	Comp./Dist.
BORING, Gwenberg	1818	Jones
BORING, Hezekiah	1818	Hair
BORING, Hezekiah	1821	Louis
BORING, Isaac	1821	Howard
BORING, James	1791	North
BORING, James	1792	North
BORING, James Jr.	1794	North
BORING, James Sr.	1794	North
BORING, John	1806	Carr
BORING, John	1813	Hoss
BORING, John	1818	Hair
BORING, Joshua	1798	Young
BORING, Joshua	1809	Carr
BORING, Joshua	1811	Mitchell
BORING, Joshua	1818	Jones
BORING, Joshua	1819	Jones
BORING, Joshua	1821	Jones
BORING, Nicholas	1790	Williams
BORING, Nicholas	1791	Williams
BORING, Nickoles	1798	Young
BORING, Sigh	1809	Par
BORING, Templ	1809	Par
BORING, William	1790	Williams
BORING, William	1791	Williams
BORING, William	1792	Tulley
BORING, William	1801	Morrison
BORING, William	1806	Carr
BORING, William	1807	Carr
BORING, William	1811	Mitchell
BORING, William	1814	Hoss
BORING, Wm	1808	Carr
BORING, Wm	1809	Carr
BORING, Zecall	1794	North
BORLING, William	1798	Morrison
BORRENS, James	1811	Mitchell
BORRIAN, Barny	1819	Howard
BORRING, Jacob	1801	Morrison
BOSASTG, Chene	1791	North
BOSERS, Elijah	1814	Hampton
BOSTON, Frances	1794	Scot
BOTELS, Henery	1798	Hannah
BOTELS, Henery	1806	Payn
BOTELS, Henery	1808	McAllister
BOTTLE, Hennry	1791	Milliken
BOTTLES, Henery	1792	Milliken
BOTTLES, Henery	1805	Stephenson
BOTTLES, Henery	1807	Payne
BOTTLES, Henery	1809	McAlister
BOTTLES, Henery	1811	McAlister
BOTTLES, Henery	1814	Crookshanks
BOTTLES, Hennery	1793	Milliken
BOTTLES, Hennery	1794	Milliken
BOTTLES, Henry	1796	Millikin
BOTTLES, Henry	1799	Hannah
BOTTLES, Henry	1815	Crookshanks
BOTTLES, Henry	1816	Crookshanks
BOTTLES, Henry	1817	McClure
BOTTLES, Henry	1818	McClure
BOTTLES, Jacob	1821	Brown
BOUGHRAN, Elijah	1795	Morrison
BOUNDS, Jesse	1791	Chisom
BOUNDS, Jessie	1792	Chisolm
BOUNDS, Obadiah	1792	Chisolm
BOUNDS, Obediah	1791	Chisom
BOUSER, George	1819	Grimsley
BOUSER, John	1807	Cade
BOUSER, John	1819	Grimsley
BOUTH, Joseph	1809	Par
BOUTWELL, Stephen	1792	Scott
BOUZER, John	1812	Barnes
BOWAN, Elias	1812	McLin
BOWEN, Henry	1816	Hair
BOWERS, Henery	1814	Bean
BOWERS, Henry	1809	Right
BOWERS, Henry	1811	Ellis
BOWERS, Henry	1812	Ellis
BOWERS, Henry	1815	Haire
BOWERS, Henry	1817	Haire
BOWERS, Jesse	1792	North
BOWERS, Leonard	1790	Greer
BOWERS, Leonard	1792	Carriger
BOWERS, Leonard	1792	Greer
BOWERS, Leonard	1794	Carriger
BOWERS, Leonard	1795	Carriger
BOWERS, Nancey	1821	Louis
BOWERS, Nancy	1819	Hair
BOWLIN, Philip	1821	McGee
BOWMAN, Anoch	1798	Hannah
BOWMAN, Barneby	1806	Parker
BOWMAN, Cornelius (Over age)	1790	White
BOWMAN, Cornelius (Over age)	1791	White
BOWMAN, Daniel	1806	Crouch
BOWMAN, Daniel	1809	Right
BOWMAN, Daniel	1811	Ellis
BOWMAN, Daniel	1812	Ellis
BOWMAN, Daniel	1814	Bean
BOWMAN, Daniel	1815	Haire
BOWMAN, Daniel	1816	Hair
BOWMAN, Daniel	1817	Haire
BOWMAN, Daniel	1818	Hair
BOWMAN, Daniel	1819	Hair
BOWMAN, Daniel	1821	Louis

Surname, Given names	Year	Comp./Dist.
BOWMAN, Danl	1807	
BOWMAN, David	1817	Hunt
BOWMAN, David	1818	Hunt
BOWMAN, David	1819	Hunt
BOWMAN, David	1821	Hunt
BOWMAN, Elias	1792	Depew
BOWMAN, Elias	1798	Duncan
BOWMAN, Elias	1798	Duncan
BOWMAN, Elias	1799	Duncan
BOWMAN, Elias	1801	Taylor
BOWMAN, Elias	1807	Givins
BOWMAN, Elias	1808	Guin
BOWMAN, Elias	1809	Gwin
BOWMAN, Elias	1809	Gwin
BOWMAN, Elias	1811	Davis
BOWMAN, Elias	1814	McLin
BOWMAN, Elias	1816	Hunt
BOWMAN, Elias Jr.	1818	Hunt
BOWMAN, Elias Jr.	1819	Hunt
BOWMAN, Elias Jr.	1821	Hunt
BOWMAN, Elias Sr.	1815	McLin
BOWMAN, Elias Sr.	1817	Hunt
BOWMAN, Elias Sr.	1819	Hunt
BOWMAN, Elias Sr.	1821	Hunt
BOWMAN, Ellis Jr.	1816	Hunt
BOWMAN, Enoch	1796	Millikin
BOWMAN, Enoch	1797	Hannah
BOWMAN, Enoch	1799	Hannah
BOWMAN, Georg	1808	Guin
BOWMAN, George	1807	Givins
BOWMAN, George	1809	Gwin
BOWMAN, Jacob	1797	Longmire
BOWMAN, Jacob	1817	Haire
BOWMAN, Jacob	1818	Hair
BOWMAN, Jacob	1819	Hair
BOWMAN, Jas.	1819	Jones
BOWMAN, John	1790	Milleken
BOWMAN, John	1797	Duncan
BOWMAN, John	1798	Duncan
BOWMAN, John	1798	Duncan
BOWMAN, John	1799	Duncan
BOWMAN, John	1801	Norwood
BOWMAN, John	1809	Right
BOWMAN, John	1811	Ellis
BOWMAN, John	1812	Ellis
BOWMAN, John	1814	Bean
BOWMAN, John	1814	McCracken
BOWMAN, John	1814	McLin
BOWMAN, John	1815	Fines
BOWMAN, John	1815	Haire
BOWMAN, John	1816	Fine
BOWMAN, John	1816	Hair
BOWMAN, John	1817	Fine
BOWMAN, John	1817	Haire
BOWMAN, John	1818	Fine
BOWMAN, John	1818	Hair
BOWMAN, John	1819	Hair
BOWMAN, John	1819	Howard
BOWMAN, John	1821	Louis
BOWMAN, Joseph	1792	Milliken
BOWMAN, Joseph	1806	Carr
BOWMAN, Joseph	1807	Carr
BOWMAN, Joseph	1808	Carr
BOWMAN, Joseph	1811	Mitchell
BOWMAN, Joseph	1813	Hoss
BOWMAN, Joseph	1814	Hoss
BOWMAN, Joseph	1815	Hoss
BOWMAN, Joseph	1817	Little
BOWMAN, Joseph	1818	Jones
BOWMAN, Joseph	1819	Jones
BOWMAN, Joseph	1821	Jones
BOWMAN, Peter	1801	Taylor
BOWMAN, Peter	1806	Parker
BOWMAN, Peter Jr.	1808	Parker
BOWMAN, William	1816	Giles
BOWMAN, William	1817	Gillises
BOWMAN, William	1818	Land
BOWMAN, William	1819	Sands
BOWSER, John	1805	Rector
BOWSER, John	1808	Cade
BOWSER, John	1810	Barron
BOWSER, John	1814	Barns
BOWSER, John	1815	Grimsley
BOWZER, John	1801	Glasscock
BOWZER, John	1809	Cade
BOWZER, John	1817	Grimsley
BOX, Edward	1778	
BOX, Edward	1779	Wilson
BOX, James	1778	
BOY, Henery	1794	Brown
BOYCE, Henry	1791	Chisom
BOYCE, Henry	1816	Fine
BOYCE, William	1821	Smith
BOYD, Barley	1821	Haines
BOYD, Benj	1801	Calvert
BOYD, David	1812	Hartsell
BOYD, David	1819	McClure
BOYD, Henry	1792	Brown
BOYD, Henry	1793	Brown
BOYD, Henry	1797	Robertson
BOYD, Henry	1798	Roberson
BOYD, Henry	1801	Taylor

Surname, Given names	Year	Comp./Dist.
BOYD, Henry	1807	Parker
BOYD, Henry	1809	Par
BOYD, Henry	1810	Hartzel
BOYD, Henry	1812	Hartsell
BOYD, Henry	1814	Hartsell
BOYD, Henry	1815	Fines
BOYD, Henry	1818	Fine
BOYD, Henry	1819	Howard
BOYD, Jeremiah	1814	McCray
BOYD, Jeremiah	1815	Harris
BOYD, Jeremiah	1818	Harris
BOYD, Jerimiah	1812	McCray
BOYD, John	1781	
BOYD, William	1808	Parker
BOYD, William	1809	Par
BOYD, William	1780-1781 (undated)	
BOYD, Wm	1780-1781	District 7
BOYE, Henry	1792	Chisolm
BOYER, Henry	1817	Fine
BOYL, Edward	1801	Gann
BOYLE, Thomas	1781	
BOYLES, Abraham	1792	Maxwell
BOYLES, Cottrel	1792	Maxwell
BOYLES, Daniel	1792	Scott
BOYLES, Daniell Sr.	1797	Young
BOYLES, George	1799	Robertson
BOYLES, Reuben	1799	Robertson
BOYLES, Richard	1821	Howard
BOYLES, William	1814	McCray
BOYS, John	1801	Gann
BRABSEN, Epheam	1814	McCracken
BRABSON, Ephraim	1805	Jas Parker
BRABSON, Ephraim	1811	McCray
BRABSON, Ephraim	1817	Harris
BRABSON, Ephrain	1808	Parker
BRABSON, Ephrefrem	1798	Hannah
BRABSON, Ephriam	1818	Harris
BRABSON, Thomas	1806	Guin
BRABSON, Thomas	1808	Guin
BRABSON, Thomas	1809	Gwin
BRABSON, Thomas	1809	Gwin
BRABSON, Thomas	1811	
BRABSON, Thomas	1815	Carcathers
BRABSON, Thomas	1816	Giles
BRABSON, Thomas	1817	Gillises
BRABSON, Thomas	1818	Land
BRABSON, Thos	1814	Couthers
BRABSTON, Epheriam	1812	McCray
BRABSTON, Ephraim	1801	Taylor
BRABSTON, Ephrain	1809	Patterson
BRABSTON, Thomas	1799	Stuart

Surname, Given names	Year	Comp./Dist.
BRABSTON, Thomas	1801	Taylor
BRABSTON, Thos	1807	Shields
BRABSTONE, Epheriam	1812	McCray
BRADEN, James	1793	Melvan
BRADEN, James	1794	Melvan
BRADEN, James	1795	Melvan
BRADEN, James	1796	Shipley
BRADEN, James	1798	Crouch
BRADLEY, Andrew	1791	Tullis
BRADLEY, Andrew	1793	Melvan
BRADLEY, James	1778	
BRADLEY, John	1793	Morrison
BRADLEY, John	1794	Morrison
BRADLEY, Jonathan	1791	Tullis
BRADSHA, John	1781	
BRAILS, Nicholas	1809	McAlister
BRANAN, Thos	1814	Couthers
BRANAN, William	1814	Copes
BRANDEN, Thomas	1781	
BRANDON, Joshua	1799	Stuart
BRANDON, Joshua	1801	Aiken
BRANHAM, James	1797	Longmire
BRANHAM, Thomas	1797	Longmire
BRANHAN, Thomas	1796	Longmire
BRANHUM, James	1796	Longmire
BRANNEN, John	1818	Grimsley
BRANNON, James	1812	Crawford [2]
BRANNON, James	1815	McLin
BRANNON, Thomas	1815	Carcathers
BRANNON, william	1807	Britton
BRANNON, William	1801	Lane
BRANNON, William	1805	Doak
BRANNON, William	1806	Doke
BRANNON, William	1811	Britten
BRANNON, William	1812	Britton
BRANNON, William	1812	McLin
BRANNON, William	1813	Copas
BRANON, James	1812	Crawford
BRANON, James	1812	McLin
BRANON, Thomas	1812	McLin
BRANSTTEN, Peter	1795	Thornton
BRANSTUTTER, Peter	1794	Thornton
BRATT, Barned	1809	Roadmas
BRAWS, Alaxndew	1821	Martin
BREADON, John	1779	
BREDDIN, Wm	1791	Milliken
BREDEN, James	1798	Morrison
BREDIN, James	1793	Brown
BREDING, William	1796	Millikin
BREECHER, John	1815	Waddell
BREECHER, William	1815	Waddell

Surname, Given names	Year	Comp./Dist.
BREED, Avery	1780-1781 (Undated)	
BREED, Avrey	1780-1781 (undated)	
BREED, Mery	1780-1781 (Undated)	
BREEDEN, Brian	1795	Handly
BREEDEN, Wm	1790	Milleken
BREEDEN, Wm	1793	Milliken
BREEDEN, Wm	1794	Milliken
BREEDIN, Wm	1795	Milliken
BREEDING, Wm (Soloman Yeager for Wm Breeding)	1797	Hannah
BREEDLOVE, James	1809	McAlister
BREEDLOVE, James	1810	Green
BREEDLOVE, Wm	1810	Green
BREEDLOW, James	1808	Gwin
BREEKERS, Michael (estate)	1816	Waddell
BRELABOGH, Peter	1808	Parker
BRELAR, Joseph	1780-1781 (Undated)	
BREWER, Benjamin	1816	Smith
BREWER, Samuel	1799	Duncan
BRIANS, Ambros	1807	Carr
BRIANT, Ambrus	1801	Roberson
BRIANT, Ambus	1799	Robertson
BRIANT, Josiah	1797	Robertson
BRIANT, M Ambrus	1798	Roberson
BRIBLE, Peter (Docot)	1812	Hartsell
BRICKEN, John	1817	Riley
BRICKEN, John	1818	Riley
BRICKEN, Michael (estate)	1817	Riley
BRICKEN, William	1817	Riley
BRICKEN, William	1818	Riley
BRICKENS, Michael (estate)	1818	Riley
BRICKER, John	1806	Grur
BRICKER, John	1808	Gwin
BRICKER, John	1810	Green
BRICKER, John	1812	Waddill
BRICKER, John	1814	Waddell
BRICKER, John	1819	Findley
BRICKER, John	1821	McGee
BRICKER, Michael	1806	Grur
BRICKER, Michael	1808	Gwin
BRICKER, Michael	1821	McGee
BRICKER, Michael (heirs)	1819	Findley
BRICKER, William	1819	Findley
BRICKER, Wm	1812	Waddill
BRICKER, Wm	1814	Waddell
BRICKER, Wm	1821	McGee
BRIDGES, Edward	1778	
BRIENHART, John	1807	Bayles
BRIENHART, John	1808	Bayles
BRIGHT, Isaac	1798	Morrison

Surname, Given names	Year	Comp./Dist.
BRIKER, John	1805	Guir
BRIKER, John	1809	Green
BRISCON, Samuel	1814	McLin
BRISON, Samuel	1797	Duncan
BRISON, Samuel	1815	McLin
BRISON, Samuel	1816	Hunt
BRIT, John	1815	Copas
BRIT, John	1819	Grisham
BRITAIN, Joseph	1798	Shipley
BRITAIN, William	1798	Shipley
BRITT, John	1806	Doke
BRITT, John	1811	Britten
BRITT, John	1813	Copas
BRITT, John	1814	Copes
BRITT, John	1816	Copas
BRITT, John	1817	Grimsley
BRITT, John	1817	Grisham
BRITT, John	1818	Grisham
BRITTAIN, Abraham	1817	Hunt
BRITTAIN, Abraham	1818	Hunt
BRITTAN, Cornelious	1814	Copes
BRITTAN, Joseph Jr.	1814	Copes
BRITTAN, Joseph Sr.	1814	Copes
BRITTEN, Abraham	1814	McLin
BRITTEN, Abraham	1816	Hunt
BRITTEN, Cornelius	1806	Doke
BRITTEN, Cornelius	1811	Britten
BRITTEN, Jas Jr.	1813	Copas
BRITTEN, Joseph	1790	Shipley
BRITTEN, Joseph	1791	Shipley
BRITTEN, Joseph	1794	Murray
BRITTEN, Joseph	1797	Shipley
BRITTEN, Joseph	1801	Lane
BRITTEN, Joseph	1805	Doak
BRITTEN, Joseph	1806	Doke
BRITTEN, Joseph	1811	Britten
BRITTEN, Joseph	1815	Copas
BRITTEN, Joseph	1817	Grisham
BRITTEN, Joseph (Esq.)	1793	Murray
BRITTEN, Joseph (Esq.)	1807	Britton
BRITTEN, Joseph Jr.	1816	Copas
BRITTEN, Joseph Sr.	1812	Britton
BRITTEN, Joseph Sr.	1813	Copas
BRITTEN, Joseph Sr.	1818	Grisham
BRITTEN, William	1793	Murray
BRITTEN, William (estate of)	1797	Shipley
BRITTEN, William (estate of)	1801	Lane
BRITTEN, William (estate of)	1806	Doke
BRITTEN, William (estate of)	1807	Britton
BRITTEN, William (Estate of)	1796	
BRITTEN, Wm (The estate of)	1794	Murray

Surname, Given names	Year	Comp./Dist.
BRITTON, Abraham	1812	McLin
BRITTON, Abraham	1815	McLin
BRITTON, Cornelius	1812	Britton
BRITTON, Joseph Sr.	1819	Grisham
BROBECK, Philip	1821	Hampton
BROCK, Christian	1796	Young
BROILES, Adam	1793	Handley
BROILES, Adam	1794	Handly
BROILES, Adam	1795	Handly
BROILES, Danial	1794	Handly
BROILES, Danial	1795	Handly
BROILES, Daniel	1793	Handley
BROILES, David	1811	Green
BROILES, James	1795	Handly
BROILES, Mathius Jr.	1811	Green
BROILES, Reuben	1793	Handley
BROILES, Reuben	1794	Handly
BROILES, Reuben	1795	Handly
BROILES, Samuel	1793	Handley
BROILES, Samuel	1794	Handly
BROILES, Samuel	1795	Handly
BROILES, Suries	1795	Handly
BROILES, Syries	1793	Handley
BROILES, Syries	1794	Handly
BROILES, Tabias	1794	Handly
BROILES, Tabias	1795	Handly
BROILES, Tobias	1811	Green
BROILS, Abraham	1791	Milliken
BROILS, Abraham	1795	Milliken
BROILS, Abraham	1805	Stephenson
BROILS, Adam	1798	Gann
BROILS, Adam	1805	Stephenson
BROILS, Adam	1811	McAlister
BROILS, Adam	1814	Crookshanks
BROILS, Cyrus	1805	Stephenson
BROILS, Daniel	1805	Stephenson
BROILS, James	1798	Gann
BROILS, James	1799	Gann
BROILS, Nichlos	1814	Crookshanks
BROILS, Nicholis	1807	Payne
BROILS, Nickloas	1811	McAlister
BROILS, Nicklos	1805	Stephenson
BROILS, Nicoles	1795	Milliken
BROILS, Samuel	1811	McAlister
BROILS, Samuele	1805	Stephenson
BROILS, Samuil	1807	Payne
BROILS, Sires	1798	Gann
BROILS, Thomas	1811	McAlister
BROILS, Thomas	1814	Crookshanks
BROILS, Tobias	1805	Stephenson
BROLLEN, John	1818	Grimsley
BRONEN, John	1821	Martin
BROOKS & FOWLER,	1815	McLin
BROOKS, Giles	1791	North
BROOKS, Giles	1793	North
BROOKS, Giles	1795	Young
BROOKS, Giles	1798	Young
BROOKS, Giles	1810	Hartzel
BROOKS, Jane	1801	Taylor
BROOKS, Jiles	1797	Young
BROOKS, Jiles	1806	Parker
BROOKS, Joiles	1796	Young
BROOKS, Moses	1812	McLin
BROOKS, T.	1815	Fines
BROOKSHIRE, Joseph	1793	Depew
BROTHERS, William (estate of)	1805	Doak
BROW, John Jr.	1807	Odell
BROWN,	1792	Brown
BROWN, Abraham	1791	Willey
BROWN, Abraham	1793	Scott
BROWN, Abraham	1794	Scot
BROWN, Abraham	1795	Calvert
BROWN, Abraham	1796	Longmire
BROWN, Abraham	1797	Calvert
BROWN, Abraham	1797	Calvert
BROWN, Abraham	1798	Calvert
BROWN, Abraham	1799	Stuart
BROWN, Abraham	1801	Calvert
BROWN, Abraham	1811	McCray
BROWN, Abraham	1812	McCray
BROWN, Abraham	1812	McCray
BROWN, Abraham	1816	Harrison
BROWN, Abraham	1818	Harris
BROWN, Abraham	1818	Harris
BROWN, Abraham	1819	Harris
BROWN, Abraham	1821	Hampton
BROWN, Abraham Jr.	1817	Harris
BROWN, Abraham Jr.	1819	Harris
BROWN, Abraham Sr.	1821	Hampton
BROWN, Abram	1805	Jas Parker
BROWN, Abram	1808	Parker
BROWN, Abram	1809	Parker
BROWN, Abram	1814	McCray
BROWN, Abreham	1792	Scott
BROWN, Austin	1795	Ford
BROWN, Ben	1797	Robertson
BROWN, Ben	1798	Roberson
BROWN, Ben	1799	Robertson
BROWN, Bengamen	1794	Brown
BROWN, Benj	1793	Brown
BROWN, Benjamin	1791	Chisom
BROWN, Benjamin	1792	Chisolm

Surname, Given names	Year	Comp./Dist.
BROWN, Benjamin	1796	Brown
BROWN, Benjamin	1801	Roberson
BROWN, Benjamin	1814	Hampton
BROWN, Benjamin	1817	Smith
BROWN, C. John	1815	Hartsell
BROWN, Christian	1817	Haire
BROWN, Christian	1819	Hair
BROWN, Christinah	1815	Haire
BROWN, Christinah	1816	Hair
BROWN, Christinah	1818	Hair
BROWN, Conrad	1798	Calvert
BROWN, Conrad	1811	McCray
BROWN, Conrad	1812	McCray
BROWN, Conrad	1814	McCray
BROWN, Conrad	1816	Harrison
BROWN, Conrad	1818	Harris
BROWN, Conrad	1819	Harris
BROWN, Conred	1799	Stuart
BROWN, Conrod	1805	Jas Parker
BROWN, Coonrad	1808	Parker
BROWN, Coonrad	1809	Parker
BROWN, Coonrad	1812	McCray
BROWN, Coonrad	1821	Hampton
BROWN, Cunrod	1797	Calvert
BROWN, Cunrod	1797	Calvert
BROWN, Daniel	1797	Calvert
BROWN, Daniel	1797	Calvert
BROWN, Daniel	1798	Calvert
BROWN, Daniel	1799	Stuart
BROWN, Daniel	1801	Calvert
BROWN, David	1781	
BROWN, David	1790	Biddle
BROWN, David	1791	Biddle
BROWN, David	1792	Biddle
BROWN, David	1793	Biddle
BROWN, David	1794	Blair
BROWN, David	1797	Biddle
BROWN, David	1797	Calvert
BROWN, David	1797	Calvert
BROWN, David	1798	Biddle
BROWN, David	1798	Calvert
BROWN, David	1799	Stuart
BROWN, David	1801	Biddle
BROWN, David	1801	Calvert
BROWN, David	1805	Carson
BROWN, David	1805	Jas Parker
BROWN, David	1806	Carson
BROWN, David	1807	Shields
BROWN, David	1808	McAllister
BROWN, David	1808	Parker
BROWN, David	1809	Parker

Surname, Given names	Year	Comp./Dist.
BROWN, David	1809	Right
BROWN, David	1810	Dimmons
BROWN, David	1811	McCray
BROWN, David	1812	McCray
BROWN, David	1812	McCray
BROWN, David	1812	Waddill
BROWN, David	1814	Couthers
BROWN, David	1814	McCray
BROWN, David	1814	Waddell
BROWN, David	1815	Carcathers
BROWN, David	1815	Waddell
BROWN, David	1816	Giles
BROWN, David	1816	Harrison
BROWN, David	1816	Hunt
BROWN, David	1816	Waddell
BROWN, David	1817	Gillises
BROWN, David	1817	Harris
BROWN, David	1817	Riley
BROWN, David	1818	Harris
BROWN, David	1818	Land
BROWN, David	1818	Riley
BROWN, David	1819	Findley
BROWN, David	1819	Harris
BROWN, David	1821	Hampton
BROWN, David	1821	McGee
BROWN, David	1780-1781 (Undated)	
BROWN, Ezekel	1778	
BROWN, Frederick	1806	Crouch
BROWN, Gabrile	1821	Brown
BROWN, Geo	1808	Parker
BROWN, Geo (of Ken.)	1809	Parker
BROWN, George	1801	Calvert
BROWN, George	1809	Parker
BROWN, George	1812	McCray
BROWN, George	1814	McCray
BROWN, George (Kentucky)	1812	McCray
BROWN, George (of Kentucky)	1811	McCray
BROWN, George Jr.	1805	Jas Parker
BROWN, George Jr.	1811	McCray
BROWN, George Sr.	1805	Jas Parker
BROWN, Henery	1814	Bean
BROWN, Hiram	1817	Harris
BROWN, Hugh	1814	McCracken
BROWN, Isaac	1812	McCray
BROWN, Isaac	1815	Harris
BROWN, Isaac	1816	Harrison
BROWN, Isaac	1817	Harris
BROWN, Isaac N.	1811	McCray
BROWN, Isaac N.	1812	McCray
BROWN, Isaac N.	1818	Harris
BROWN, Jacob	1778	

Surname, Given names	Year	Comp./Dist.
BROWN, Jacob	1791	Chisom
BROWN, Jacob	1791	Willey
BROWN, Jacob	1792	Brown
BROWN, Jacob	1792	Chisolm
BROWN, Jacob	1792	Scott
BROWN, Jacob	1793	Brown
BROWN, Jacob	1793	Scott
BROWN, Jacob	1794	Scot
BROWN, Jacob	1795	Calvert
BROWN, Jacob	1796	Brown
BROWN, Jacob	1796	Calvert
BROWN, Jacob	1797	Calvert
BROWN, Jacob	1797	Calvert
BROWN, Jacob	1798	Roberson
BROWN, Jacob	1799	Robertson
BROWN, Jacob	1801	Roberson
BROWN, Jacob	1806	Brown
BROWN, Jacob	1806	Crouch
BROWN, Jacob	1807	Bayles
BROWN, Jacob	1808	Bayles
BROWN, Jacob	1808	Parker
BROWN, Jacob	1809	Bayles
BROWN, Jacob	1809	Parker
BROWN, Jacob	1809	Right
BROWN, Jacob	1811	Ellis
BROWN, Jacob	1812	McCray
BROWN, Jacob	1814	McCray
BROWN, Jacob	1815	Garner
BROWN, Jacob	1817	Hampton
BROWN, Jacob	1817	Harris
BROWN, Jacob	1818	Brown [2]
BROWN, Jacob	1818	Brown [2]
BROWN, Jacob	1818	Harris
BROWN, Jacob	1819	Brown
BROWN, Jacob	1819	Harris
BROWN, Jacob	1821	Brown
BROWN, Jacob (Capt.)	1791	
BROWN, Jacob (Capt.)	1794	Brown
BROWN, Jacob (Maj.)	1797	Robertson
BROWN, Jacob (of Abram)	1814	McCray
BROWN, Jacob (of David)	1811	McCray
BROWN, Jacob (of David)	1812	McCray
BROWN, Jacob (of David)	1814	McCray
BROWN, Jacob Jr.	1798	Calvert
BROWN, Jacob Jr.	1799	Stuart
BROWN, Jacob Jr.	1801	Calvert
BROWN, Jacob Jr.	1805	Jas Parker
BROWN, Jacob Jr.	1808	Parker
BROWN, Jacob Jr.	1809	Parker
BROWN, Jacob Jr.	1811	McCray
BROWN, Jacob Jr.	1812	McCray
BROWN, Jacob Jr.	1812	McCray
BROWN, Jacob Jr.	1814	Hampton
BROWN, Jacob Jr.	1814	Hampton
BROWN, Jacob Jr.	1816	Hampton
BROWN, Jacob Jr.	1817	Hampton
BROWN, Jacob Jr.	1817	Harris
BROWN, Jacob Jr.	1819	Harris
BROWN, Jacob Jr.	1821	Brown
BROWN, Jacob Jr.	1821	Hampton
BROWN, Jacob Sr.	1797	Calvert
BROWN, Jacob Sr.	1798	Calvert
BROWN, Jacob Sr.	1799	Stuart
BROWN, Jacob Sr.	1801	Calvert
BROWN, Jacob Sr.	1805	Jas Parker
BROWN, Jacob Sr.	1811	McCray
BROWN, Jacob Sr.	1812	McCray
BROWN, Jacob Sr.	1812	McCray
BROWN, Jacob Sr.	1816	Hampton
BROWN, Jacob Sr.	1816	Harrison
BROWN, Jacob Sr.	1818	Harris
BROWN, Jacob Sr.	1819	Brown
BROWN, Jacob Sr.	1821	Hampton
BROWN, James	1792	Scott
BROWN, James	1796	Handly
BROWN, James	1797	Shipley
BROWN, James	1798	Gann
BROWN, James	1798	Shipley
BROWN, James	1799	Gann
BROWN, James	1799	Moore
BROWN, James	1801	Gann
BROWN, James	1801	Glasscock
BROWN, James	1816	Grimsley
BROWN, James	1817	Harris
BROWN, James	1820	Smith
BROWN, James	1821	Hampton
BROWN, James	1821	Smith
BROWN, Jeremiah	1799	Robertson
BROWN, Jesse	1810	Cove
BROWN, Jesse	1812	Brown
BROWN, Jesse	1816	Brown
BROWN, Jesse	1817	Brown
BROWN, Jesse	1818	Brown
BROWN, Jesse	1819	Brown
BROWN, Jesse	1821	Haines
BROWN, Jessee	1811	Brown
BROWN, Jessee	1814	Brown
BROWN, Jessie	1815	Hartsell
BROWN, Jno	1808	Parker
BROWN, Jno	1809	Parker
BROWN, Jno (M)	1798	Calvert
BROWN, Jno (of N.C.)	1809	Parker

Surname, Given names	Year	Comp./Dist.
BROWN, Joel	1795	Calvert
BROWN, John	1778	
BROWN, John	1778	
BROWN, John	1790	Stone
BROWN, John	1791	Stone
BROWN, John	1792	Brown
BROWN, John	1793	Melvan
BROWN, John	1794	Brown
BROWN, John	1794	Melvan
BROWN, John	1795	Melvan
BROWN, John	1796	Brown
BROWN, John	1796	Melvin
BROWN, John	1797	Calvert
BROWN, John	1797	Calvert
BROWN, John	1797	Calvert
BROWN, John	1797	Longmire
BROWN, John	1797	Robertson
BROWN, John	1798	Longmire
BROWN, John	1798	Roberson
BROWN, John	1799	Robertson
BROWN, John	1799	Stuart
BROWN, John	1799	Stuart
BROWN, John	1801	Aiken
BROWN, John	1801	Biddle
BROWN, John	1801	Calvert
BROWN, John	1801	Longmire
BROWN, John	1805	Aikin
BROWN, John	1805	Carson
BROWN, John	1805	Jas Parker
BROWN, John	1806	Anderson
BROWN, John	1806	Carson
BROWN, John	1806	Odel
BROWN, John	1807	Anderson
BROWN, John	1807	Bayles
BROWN, John	1807	Cade
BROWN, John	1807	Odell
BROWN, John	1807	Shields
BROWN, John	1807	
BROWN, John	1808	Cade
BROWN, John	1808	Odell
BROWN, John	1809	Cade
BROWN, John	1809	Viney
BROWN, John	1810	Barron
BROWN, John	1810	Barron
BROWN, John	1810	Cove
BROWN, John	1810	Cove
BROWN, John	1810	Cove
BROWN, John	1811	Barron
BROWN, John	1811	Ellis
BROWN, John	1811	McCray
BROWN, John	1812	Barnes
BROWN, John	1812	Brown
BROWN, John	1812	McCray
BROWN, John	1812	McCray
BROWN, John	1814	Barns
BROWN, John	1814	Brown
BROWN, John	1814	Waddell
BROWN, John	1815	Grimsley
BROWN, John	1815	Hartsell
BROWN, John	1815	Waddell
BROWN, John	1816	Brown
BROWN, John	1816	Grimsley
BROWN, John	1816	Waddell
BROWN, John	1817	Brown
BROWN, John	1817	Brown
BROWN, John	1817	Grimsley
BROWN, John	1817	Grimsley
BROWN, John	1817	Hunt
BROWN, John	1817	Riley
BROWN, John	1818	Brown
BROWN, John	1818	Brown
BROWN, John	1818	Grimsley
BROWN, John	1818	Hunt
BROWN, John	1818	Riley
BROWN, John	1819	Brown
BROWN, John	1819	Findley
BROWN, John	1819	Grimsley
BROWN, John	1819	Hunt
BROWN, John	1821	Hunt
BROWN, John (of David)	1816	Harrison
BROWN, John (of Jacob)	1816	Harrison
BROWN, John (of N. Carolina)	1811	McCray
BROWN, John C.	1806	Odel
BROWN, John C.	1814	Brown
BROWN, John C.	1821	Haines
BROWN, John C. Jr.	1816	Brown
BROWN, John C. Jr.	1817	Brown
BROWN, John C. Jr.	1819	Brown
BROWN, John C. Sr.	1819	Brown
BROWN, John G.	1792	Chisolm
BROWN, John G.	1801	Roberson
BROWN, John G.	1808	Bayles
BROWN, John G.	1809	Bayles
BROWN, John G.	1814	Hampton
BROWN, John Jr.	1798	Calvert
BROWN, John Jr.	1806	Odel
BROWN, John Jr.	1809	Viney
BROWN, John Jr.	1811	Brown
BROWN, John Jr.	1812	Brown
BROWN, John Jr.	1814	McCray
BROWN, John Jr.	1817	Harris
BROWN, John Jr.	1818	Harris

Surname, Given names	Year	Comp./Dist.
BROWN, John Jr.	1819	Harris
BROWN, John Jr.	1821	Haines
BROWN, John Jr.; (Cove)	1811	Brown
BROWN, John Sr.	1779	
BROWN, John Sr.	1808	Odell
BROWN, John Sr.	1811	Brown
BROWN, John Sr.	1815	Harris
BROWN, John Sr.	1817	Harris
BROWN, John Sr.	1818	Harris
BROWN, John Sr.	1819	Harris
BROWN, John Sr.	1821	Haines
BROWN, John W.	1821	Martin
BROWN, Joseph	1792	Greer
BROWN, Joseph	1796	Calvert
BROWN, Joseph	1796	Jonesboro
BROWN, Joseph	1797	Calvert
BROWN, Joseph	1797	Calvert
BROWN, Joseph	1799	Stuart
BROWN, Joseph	1801	Aiken
BROWN, Joseph	1805	Aikin
BROWN, Joseph	1805	Guir
BROWN, Joseph	1806	Anderson
BROWN, Joseph	1806	Crouch
BROWN, Joseph	1807	Anderson
BROWN, Joseph	1809	Roadmas
BROWN, Joseph	1811	Rodman
BROWN, Joseph	1814	McCracken
BROWN, Joseph	1815	Garner
BROWN, Joseph	1815	Harris
BROWN, Joseph	1816	Harrison
BROWN, Joseph	1816	Smith
BROWN, Joseph	1817	Harris
BROWN, Joseph	1817	Smith
BROWN, Joseph	1818	Smith
BROWN, Joseph	1819	Harris
BROWN, Joseph	1821	Hampton
BROWN, Joseph	1821	McGee
BROWN, Joseph	1780-1781 (Undated)	
BROWN, Joseph (Single)	1779	
BROWN, Koonrod	1801	Calvert
BROWN, Mary	1814	McCracken
BROWN, Mary	1815	Garner
BROWN, Mary	1816	Smith
BROWN, Mary	1817	Smith
BROWN, Mary	1818	Smith
BROWN, Mary	1819	Smith
BROWN, Mary	1820	Smith
BROWN, Mary	1821	Smith
BROWN, Michael	1805	Guir
BROWN, Michael	1806	Grur
BROWN, Michael	1808	Gwin
BROWN, Michael	1810	Green
BROWN, Michael	1811	Green
BROWN, Michael	1812	Waddill
BROWN, Michael	1815	Waddell
BROWN, Michael	1816	Waddell
BROWN, Michael	1817	Riley
BROWN, Michael	1818	Riley
BROWN, Michael	1819	Findley
BROWN, Michael	1821	McGee
BROWN, Micheal	1809	Green
BROWN, Michiel	1814	Waddell
BROWN, Moses	1795	Carriger
BROWN, Peter	1790	Stone
BROWN, Peter	1791	Stone
BROWN, Peter	1793	Melvan
BROWN, Peter	1794	Melvan
BROWN, Peter	1795	Melvan
BROWN, Peter	1796	Melvin
BROWN, Peter	1806	Odel
BROWN, Peter	1807	Odell
BROWN, Peter	1808	Odell
BROWN, Peter	1809	Viney
BROWN, Peter	1810	Cove
BROWN, Peter	1811	Brown
BROWN, Philip	1798	Calvert
BROWN, Philip	1799	Stuart
BROWN, Philip	1809	Parker
BROWN, Philip	1811	McCray
BROWN, Philip	1812	McCray
BROWN, Philip	1812	McCray
BROWN, Philip	1816	Harrison
BROWN, Phillip	1797	Calvert
BROWN, Phillip	1797	Calvert
BROWN, Phillip	1801	Calvert
BROWN, Richard	1818	Land
BROWN, Ruth	1791	Chisom
BROWN, Ruth	1792	Brown
BROWN, Ruth	1792	Chisolm
BROWN, Ruth	1797	Robertson
BROWN, Ruth	1799	Robertson
BROWN, Ruth	1801	Roberson
BROWN, Ruth	1806	Brown
BROWN, Ruth	1807	Bayles
BROWN, Ruth	1808	Bayles
BROWN, Ruth	1809	Bayles
BROWN, Ruthe	1796	Brown
BROWN, Samuel	1798	Morrison
BROWN, Samuel	1819	Smith
BROWN, Sol	1809	Parker
BROWN, Sollomon	1797	Calvert
BROWN, Soloman	1797	Calvert

Surname, Given names	Year	Comp./Dist.
BROWN, Soloman	1812	McCray
BROWN, Soloman	1818	Harris
BROWN, Soloman	1819	Harris
BROWN, Solomon	1798	Calvert
BROWN, Solomon	1799	Stuart
BROWN, Solomon	1801	Roberson
BROWN, Solomon	1808	Parker
BROWN, Solomon	1814	McCray
BROWN, Solomon	1815	Harris
BROWN, Solomon	1816	Harrison
BROWN, Solomon	1817	Harris
BROWN, Solomon	1821	Hampton
BROWN, Stephen	1801	Aiken
BROWN, Stephen	1811	McCray
BROWN, Stephen	1812	McLin
BROWN, Stephen	1814	McLin
BROWN, Stephen	1815	McLin
BROWN, Stephen	1816	Hunt
BROWN, Stephen	1819	Hunt
BROWN, Stephen	1821	Hunt
BROWN, Stephenson	1817	Hunt
BROWN, Thomas	1778	
BROWN, Thomas	1781	
BROWN, Thomas	1791	Chisom
BROWN, Thomas	1792	Brown
BROWN, Thomas	1792	Chisolm
BROWN, Thomas	1793	Brown
BROWN, Thomas	1796	Brown
BROWN, Thomas	1797	Robertson
BROWN, Thomas	1798	Roberson
BROWN, Thomas	1801	Roberson
BROWN, Thomas	1806	Brown
BROWN, Thomas	1807	Bayles
BROWN, Thomas	1808	Bayles
BROWN, Thomas	1809	Bayles
BROWN, Thomas	1812	McCray
BROWN, Thomas	1812	McCray
BROWN, Thomas	1817	Hampton
BROWN, Thomas	1818	Brown [2]
BROWN, Thomas	1818	Brown [2]
BROWN, Thomas	1819	Brown
BROWN, Thomas	1819	Harris
BROWN, Thomas	1821	Brown
BROWN, Thomas (iron worker)	1816	Hampton
BROWN, Thomas J.	1821	Brown
BROWN, Thomas Jr.	1816	Hampton
BROWN, Thomas Jr.	1817	Hampton
BROWN, Thomas Jr.	1819	Brown
BROWN, Thomas Sr.	1816	Hampton
BROWN, Thos	1794	Brown
BROWN, Thos	1799	Robertson

Surname, Given names	Year	Comp./Dist.
BROWN, Thos	1814	Hampton
BROWN, Thos I.	1814	Hampton
BROWN, W. John	1819	Grimsley
BROWN, William	1781	
BROWN, William	1790	Hanley
BROWN, William	1790	Hanley
BROWN, William	1793	Handley
BROWN, William	1794	Blair
BROWN, William	1794	Handly
BROWN, William	1795	Handly
BROWN, William	1796	Handly
BROWN, William	1797	Biddle
BROWN, William	1798	Biddle
BROWN, William	1798	Gann
BROWN, William	1799	Gann
BROWN, William	1805	Carson
BROWN, William	1805	Guir
BROWN, William	1806	Carson
BROWN, William	1809	Viney
BROWN, William	1810	Cove
BROWN, William	1811	Brown
BROWN, William	1812	Brown
BROWN, William	1816	Hampton
BROWN, William	1817	Brown
BROWN, William	1817	Hampton
BROWN, William	1817	Smith
BROWN, William	1818	Brown
BROWN, William	1818	Brown [2]
BROWN, William	1818	Brown [2]
BROWN, William	1818	Harris
BROWN, William	1818	Smith
BROWN, William	1819	Brown
BROWN, William	1819	Brown
BROWN, William	1819	Brown
BROWN, William	1819	Harris
BROWN, William	1821	Brown
BROWN, William	1793	Biddle
BROWN, William (of Thomas)	1816	Hampton
BROWN, William (Single)	1779	
BROWN, William Jr.	1821	Brown
BROWN, Wm	1778	
BROWN, Wm	1779	
BROWN, Wm	1791	Hanley
BROWN, Wm	1791	Hanley
BROWN, Wm	1797	Gann
BROWN, Wm	1798	Biddle
BROWN, Wm	1799	Moore
BROWN, Wm	1801	Gann
BROWN, Wm	1807	Shields
BROWN, Wm	1809	Patterson
BROWN, Wm	1814	Hampton

Surname, Given names	Year	Comp./Dist.
BROWN, Zekel	1778	
BROWNING, Charles	1816	Fine
BROWNING, Charles	1819	Brown
BROWNING, Charles	1821	Brown
BROWNING, Francis	1781	
BROYLE, Abraham	1797	Hannah
BROYLE, Abram	1799	Hannah
BROYLE, Adam	1797	Hannah
BROYLE, Adam	1799	Hannah
BROYLE, Adam	1808	Gwin
BROYLE, Adam Jr.	1806	Grur
BROYLE, Ciras	1814	Waddell
BROYLE, Cyrus	1797	Hannah
BROYLE, Cyrus	1799	Hannah
BROYLE, Daniel	1797	Hannah
BROYLE, Daniel	1799	Hannah
BROYLE, James	1808	Gwin
BROYLE, James	1809	Green
BROYLE, James	1810	Green
BROYLE, James	1814	Waddell
BROYLE, John	1805	Guir
BROYLE, Julias	1816	Waddell
BROYLE, Julious	1814	Waddell
BROYLE, Julius	1808	Gwin
BROYLE, Julius	1809	Green
BROYLE, Mathias	1808	Gwin
BROYLE, Mathias	1814	Waddell
BROYLE, Mathias Sr.	1809	Green
BROYLE, Mathias Sr.	1810	Green
BROYLE, Michiel	1814	Waddell
BROYLE, Nicholas	1797	Hannah
BROYLE, Nicholas	1799	Hannah
BROYLE, Samuel	1797	Hannah
BROYLE, Samuel	1799	Hannah
BROYLE, Samuel	1814	Waddell
BROYLE, Samuel	1816	Waddell
BROYLE, Saras	1808	Gwin
BROYLE, Simeon	1808	Gwin
BROYLE, Simion	1809	Green
BROYLE, Simon	1814	Waddell
BROYLE, Simon	1816	Waddell
BROYLE, Siras	1809	Green
BROYLE, Siras	1810	Green
BROYLE, Tobias	1799	Hannah
BROYLE, Tobias	1808	Gwin
BROYLE, Tobias	1809	Green
BROYLE, Tobias	1810	Green
BROYLES,	1796	Handly
BROYLES, Abraham	1790	Milleken
BROYLES, Abraham	1792	Milliken
BROYLES, Abraham	1793	Milliken
BROYLES, Abraham	1794	Milliken
BROYLES, Abraham	1796	Millikin
BROYLES, Abraham	1801	Squibb
BROYLES, Abraham	1806	Payn
BROYLES, Adam	1790	Hanley
BROYLES, Adam	1791	Hanley
BROYLES, Adam	1791	Hanley
BROYLES, Adam	1796	Handly
BROYLES, Adam	1797	Gann
BROYLES, Adam	1809	McAlister
BROYLES, Adam	1812	Crawford
BROYLES, Adam	1815	Crookshanks
BROYLES, Adam	1816	Crookshanks
BROYLES, Adam	1817	McClure
BROYLES, Adam	1818	McClure
BROYLES, Adam	1819	McClure
BROYLES, Adam	1821	McClure
BROYLES, Addam	1799	Moore
BROYLES, Cyras	1812	Waddill
BROYLES, Cyrus	1790	Hanley
BROYLES, Cyrus	1791	Hanley
BROYLES, Cyrus	1799	Moore
BROYLES, Cyrus	1801	Gann
BROYLES, Cyrus	1815	Waddell
BROYLES, Cyrus	1816	Waddell
BROYLES, Cyrus	1818	Riley
BROYLES, Cyrus	1819	Findley
BROYLES, Cyrus	1821	McGee
BROYLES, Danial	1796	Handly
BROYLES, Daniel	1806	Grur
BROYLES, Daniel	1808	Gwin
BROYLES, Daniel	1809	McAlister
BROYLES, Daniel	1810	
BROYLES, Daniel	1811	Green
BROYLES, David	1808	McAllister
BROYLES, David	1809	McAlister
BROYLES, David	1821	McGee
BROYLES, Ezekial	1819	Findley
BROYLES, Ezekiel	1815	Waddell
BROYLES, Ezekiel	1816	Waddell
BROYLES, Ezekiel	1817	Riley
BROYLES, Ezekiel	1818	Riley
BROYLES, Ezekiel	1821	McGee
BROYLES, Jame	1799	Moore
BROYLES, James	1796	Handly
BROYLES, James	1796	Millikin
BROYLES, James	1797	Gann
BROYLES, James	1801	Squibb
BROYLES, James	1812	Waddill
BROYLES, James	1815	Waddell
BROYLES, James	1816	Waddell

Surname, Given names	Year	Comp./Dist.
BROYLES, James	1817	Riley
BROYLES, James	1818	Riley
BROYLES, James	1819	Findley
BROYLES, James	1821	McGee
BROYLES, Jukas	1815	Waddell
BROYLES, Julias	1810	Green
BROYLES, Julious	1812	Waddill
BROYLES, Julius	1819	Findley
BROYLES, Julus	1821	McGee
BROYLES, Lemon	1818	Riley
BROYLES, Lewis	1817	Riley
BROYLES, Lewis	1818	Riley
BROYLES, Michael	1815	Waddell
BROYLES, Michael	1816	Waddell
BROYLES, Michael	1817	Riley
BROYLES, Michael	1818	Riley
BROYLES, Michael	1819	Findley
BROYLES, Michael	1821	McGee
BROYLES, Nathan	1812	Waddill
BROYLES, Nathan	1818	McClure
BROYLES, Nathan	1819	McClure
BROYLES, Nathan Sr.	1812	Waddill
BROYLES, Nicholas	1801	Squibb
BROYLES, Nicholas	1815	Crookshanks
BROYLES, Nicholas (estate)	1818	McClure
BROYLES, Nicholas (estate)	1819	McClure
BROYLES, Nicholes	1798	Hannah
BROYLES, Nicholes	1812	Crawford
BROYLES, Nicholis (estate)	1816	Crookshanks
BROYLES, Nicholis (estate)	1817	McClure
BROYLES, Nicolas	1794	Milliken
BROYLES, Nicolas	1808	McAllister
BROYLES, Nicoles	1792	Milliken
BROYLES, Nicoles	1793	Milliken
BROYLES, Reuben	1790	Hanley
BROYLES, Reuben	1791	Hanley
BROYLES, Ruben	1796	Handly
BROYLES, Samuel	1790	Hanley
BROYLES, Samuel	1791	Hanley
BROYLES, Samuel	1796	Handly
BROYLES, Samuel	1801	Squibb
BROYLES, Samuel	1808	McAllister
BROYLES, Samuel	1809	McAlister
BROYLES, Samuel	1812	Crawford
BROYLES, Samuel	1812	Crawford [2]
BROYLES, Samuel	1815	Waddell
BROYLES, Samuel	1817	Riley
BROYLES, Simion	1810	Green
BROYLES, Simion	1812	Waddill
BROYLES, Simon	1815	Waddell
BROYLES, Simon	1817	Riley
BROYLES, Simon	1819	Findley
BROYLES, Simon	1821	McGee
BROYLES, Syrus	1811	Green
BROYLES, Syrus	1817	Riley
BROYLES, Tabbias	1812	Waddill
BROYLES, Thomas	1809	McAlister
BROYLES, Thomas	1812	Crawford
BROYLES, Toby	1799	Moore
BROYLES, William	1818	Riley
BROYLES, William Jr.	1817	Hampton
BROYLS, Abraham	1798	Hannah
BROYLS, Adam	1798	Hannah
BROYLS, Adam	1812	Crawford [2]
BROYLS, Aron (South Carolina land)	1801	Gann
BROYLS, Daniel	1798	Hannah
BROYLS, Daniel	1801	Gann
BROYLS, David	1812	Waddill
BROYLS, James	1805	Guir
BROYLS, James	1806	Grur
BROYLS, James	1811	Green
BROYLS, John	1806	Grur
BROYLS, Julius	1811	Green
BROYLS, Mathas	1806	Grur
BROYLS, Michael	1806	Grur
BROYLS, Michael	1812	Waddill
BROYLS, Nicholas	1796	Millikin
BROYLS, Nicolas	1806	Payn
BROYLS, Nicoles	1812	Crawford [2]
BROYLS, Obediah	1801	Gann
BROYLS, Samuel	1798	Hannah
BROYLS, Samuel	1806	Payn
BROYLS, Samuel (heirs of)	1812	Crawford [2]
BROYLS, Sears	1805	Guir
BROYLS, Simeon	1811	Green
BROYLS, Thomas	1812	Crawford [2]
BROYLS, Thomas	1812	Waddill
BROYLS, Tobias	1806	Grur
BROYLS, Toby	1798	Gann
BROYLS, Tyrus	1806	Grur
BRUER, Samuel	1798	Duncan
BRUMBLEY, Thomas	1781	
BRUMET, John	1821	Howard
BRUMET, Macajah	1805	Parker
BRUMET, Mecaga	1821	Howard
BRUMET, Mecagah	1821	Howard
BRUMET, Miciah	1801	Taylor
BRUMET, Samuel	1805	Jas Parker
BRUMET, Samuel	1809	Par
BRUMET, William	1821	Howard
BRUMET, William Jr.	1821	Howard
BRUMIT, James	1807	Parker

Surname, Given names	Year	Comp./Dist.
BRUMIT, James	1808	Parker
BRUMIT, James	1814	Hartsell
BRUMIT, Micager	1807	Parker
BRUMIT, Micager	1808	Parker
BRUMIT, Mileagen	1814	Hartsell
BRUMIT, Samual	1807	Parker
BRUMIT, Samuel	1791	Willey
BRUMIT, Samuel	1792	Scott
BRUMIT, Samuel	1794	Scot
BRUMIT, Samuel	1810	Hartzel
BRUMIT, Samuel	1814	Hartsell
BRUMIT, William	1814	Hartsell
BRUMMER, Samuel	1795	Young
BRUMMER, Samuel	1801	Calvert
BRUMMET, Macjah	1809	Par
BRUMMIT, James	1809	Par
BRUMMIT, James	1815	Fines
BRUMMIT, James	1816	Fine
BRUMMIT, James	1818	Fine
BRUMMIT, James	1819	Howard
BRUMMIT, Jesse	1817	Fine
BRUMMIT, Jesse	1818	Fine
BRUMMIT, Micajah	1806	Parker
BRUMMIT, Micajah	1815	Fines
BRUMMIT, Micajah	1816	Fine
BRUMMIT, Micajah	1817	Fine
BRUMMIT, Micajah	1818	Fine
BRUMMIT, Micasah	1819	Howard
BRUMMIT, Saml	1797	Calvert
BRUMMIT, Samuel	1815	Fines
BRUMMIT, Samuel	1816	Fine
BRUMMIT, Samuel	1817	Fine
BRUMMIT, Samuel	1818	Fine
BRUMMIT, Samuel	1819	Howard
BRUMMIT, William	1815	Fines
BRUMMIT, William	1816	Fine
BRUMMIT, William	1817	Fine
BRUMMITT, Samuel	1799	Stuart
BRUNK,	1780-1781 (Undated)	
BRUNK, Chris (Dunkard)	1781	
BRUNK, Christephils	1780-1781 (Undated)	
BRUNK, Christopher (Dunkard)	1781	
BRUNK, John	1780-1781 (Undated)	
BRUNK, John (Dunkard)	1781	
BRUSTER, Claudious	1814	Waddell
BRYAN, William	1781	
BRYANT, Ambros	1806	Carr
BRYONS, Ambros	1808	Carr
BUCAN, James	1811	Barron
BUCHANAN, James	1778	

Surname, Given names	Year	Comp./Dist.
BUCK, Abijah	1816	Fine
BUCK, Abraham	1795	Thornton
BUCK, Abram	1791	White
BUCK, Elijah	1818	Fine
BUCK, Elijah	1821	Howard
BUCK, Robert	1817	Grisham
BUCKHAMMER, Zecal	1791	Willey
BUCKHANON, Ezekel	1792	Scott
BUCKINGHAM, Thomas	1805	Doak
BUCKINGHAM, Thomas	1806	Crouch
BUCKINGHAM, Thomas	1809	Right
BUCKINGHAM, Thomas	1812	Ellis
BUCKINGHAM, Thomas	1814	Bean
BUCKINGHAM, Thomas	1815	Haire
BUCKINGHAM, Thomas	1817	Grisham
BUCKINGHAM, Thomas	1818	Grisham
BUCKINGHAM, Thomas	1819	Grisham
BUCKINGHAM, Thos	1821	Hale
BUCKINHAM, Thomas	1816	Copas
BUCKMAN, Michel	1795	Ford
BUCKNAL, William	1791	White
BUCKNER, William	1794	Thornton
BUCKNER, William	1795	Thornton
BUHANNAN, Ezekiel	1793	Scott
BUKHAM, James	1807	
BUKMAN, Michael	1790	White
BULENBOGHEN, Peter	1810	Hartzel
BULEY, Anthony	1795	Young
BULEY, Anthony	1796	Young
BULEY, Anthony	1807	Parker
BULEY, Atoney	1794	North
BULL, Elesebeth	1783 [after]	Depew
BULL, Eliash	1816	Copas
BULL, Elisha	1813	Copas
BULL, Elisha	1815	Copas
BULL, Elisha	1817	Grisham
BULL, Elisha	1818	Grisham
BULL, Elisha	1819	Grisham
BULL, George	1816	Hunt
BULL, Jacob	1790	Shipley
BULL, Jacob	1791	Shipley
BULL, Jacob	1793	Murray
BULL, Jacob	1796	Shipley
BULL, Jacob	1801	Lane
BULL, Jacob	1805	Doak
BULL, Jacob	1805	Doak
BULL, Jacob	1806	Doke
BULL, Jacob	1807	Britton
BULL, Jacob	1809	Britten
BULL, Jacob	1809	Right
BULL, Jacob	1811	Britten

Surname, Given names	Year	Comp./Dist.
BULL, Jacob	1812	Britton
BULL, Jacob	1813	Copas
BULL, Jacob	1814	Copes
BULL, Jacob	1815	Copas
BULL, Jacob	1816	Copas
BULL, Jacob	1817	Grisham
BULL, Jacob	1818	Grimsley
BULL, Jacob	1818	Grisham
BULL, Jacob	1819	Grimsley
BULL, Jacob	1819	Grisham
BULL, Jacob	1821	Hale
BULL, Jesse	1815	Copas
BULL, Jesse	1816	Copas
BULL, John	1801	Lane
BULL, John	1806	Doke
BULL, John	1811	Britten
BULL, John	1812	Britton
BULL, William	1815	Haire
BULLARD, John	1778	
BULLARD, Joseph	1778	
BULLARD, Joseph	1781	
BULLEN, Philip	1817	Harris
BULLINGER, Peter	1790	White
BULLINGER, Peter	1791	White
BULLINGER, Peter	1795	Ford
BULLINGTON, Benjamin	1798	Duncan
BULLINGTON, Benjamin	1799	Duncan
BULLINGTON, Benjamin	1801	Taylor
BULLINGTON, William	1790	Shipley
BULLINGTON, William	1791	Shipley
BULLINGTON, William	1794	Murray
BULLINGTON, William	1795	Murray
BULLINGTON, William	1796	Shipley
BULLINGTON, William	1797	Duncan
BULLINGTON, William	1798	Duncan
BULLINGTON, William	1801	Taylor
BULLOCK, Ritchd	1781	
BULOCK, Richard	1780-1781 (Undated)	
BULY, Anthony	1797	Young
BULY, Anthony	1808	Parker
BULY, Anthony Jr.	1805	Parker
BULY, Anthony Sr.	1805	Parker
BULY, Antony	1793	North
BUNDARY, Simon	1779	
BUNKER, John	1805	Jas Parker
BUNN, John G.	1806	Brown
BUNTON, Andrew	1778	
BURAS, Thomas	1780-1781	District 7
BURASS, Elijah	1792	Coye
BURASS, Elijah	1801	Longmire
BURCH, Richard	1790	Shipley

Surname, Given names	Year	Comp./Dist.
BURCH, Richard	1791	Shipley
BURCH, Richard	1793	Murray
BURCH, Richard	1794	Murray
BURCH, Richard	1795	Murray
BURCH, Richard	1797	Shipley
BURCH, Richard	1801	Lane
BURCK, Robert	1805	Doak
BURDEN, Charles	1792	Greer
BURDEN, Jarret	1792	Greer
BURDWELL, Benjamin	1812	Ellis
BURGENER, Peter	1821	McGee
BURGES, Charles	1792	Carriger
BURGES, Jaret	1792	Carriger
BURGET, George	1799	Robertson
BURGISS, Elijah	1798	Longmire
BURGNER, Peter	1806	Grur
BURGNER, Peter	1809	Green
BURGNER, Peter	1810	Green
BURGNER, Petter	1808	Gwin
BURGNES, Peter	1819	Findley
BURIS, John	1818	Fine
BURK, Arthur	1794	Ford
BURK, Arthur	1795	Ford
BURK, John	1779	
BURK, John	1793	Biddle
BURK, John	1794	Blair
BURK, John	1783 [after]	Blair
BURK, Reuben	1812	McLin
BURK, Robert	1811	Britten
BURK, Robert	1812	Britton
BURK, Robert	1813	Copas
BURK, Robert	1815	Copas
BURK, Robert	1816	Copas
BURK, Robert	1818	Grisham
BURK, Robert	1819	Grisham
BURK, Robert	1821	Hale
BURK, Ruben	1808	Guin
BURK, Rubin	1806	Crouch
BURK, William	1794	Depew
BURK, William	1783 [after]	Depew
BURKE, Robert	1814	Copes
BURKER, George	1801	Roberson
BURKET, Andrew	1801	Roberson
BURKET, George	1797	Robertson
BURKET, Simon	1806	Payn
BURKET, Simon	1807	Payne
BURKHART, George	1793	Brown
BURKHART, George	1798	Calvert
BURKS, William	1807	Anderson
BURLESON, Aron	1778	
BURLESON, Thomas	1778	

Surname, Given names	Year	Comp./Dist.
BURLINGTON, Wm	1799	Duncan
BURLISTON, Aaron	1779	Wilson
BURMINGHAM, James	1795	Morrison
BURNER, Daniel	1779	
BURNINGHAM, James	1793	Morrison
BURNINGHAM, James	1794	Morrison
BURNS, Amos	1812	McLin
BURRESS, Jno	1801	Taylor
BURRESS, John	1809	Par
BURRIS, Elijah	1806	Odel
BURRIS, John	1806	Parker
BURRIS, John	1816	Fine
BURRIS, John	1819	Howard
BURRIS, Timothy	1821	Haines
BURRISS, Elijah	1807	Odell
BUSH, William	1796	Handly
BUSTARD, Claudias	1815	Waddell
BUSTARD, Claudius	1816	Waddell
BUTTRON, William	1801	Norwood
BUZARD, Jno	1780-1781 (Undated)	
BYERLY, Mical	1812	Ellis
BYERLY, Mical Jr.	1812	Ellis
BYERLY, Michael	1809	Right
BYERLY, Michael	1818	Land
BYERLY, Nickel	1821	Sands
BYERLY, Samuel	1818	Land
BYERS, Absolom B.	1818	Smith
BYRD, Thomas	1781	
BYRD, William	1781	
BYRLY, Samuel	1821	Sands
BYSONS, James	1810	Barron
CADE, Hews	1801	Glasscock
CADE, Hines	1809	Cade
CADE, Huss	1807	Cade
CADE, Keese	1808	Cade
CADWELL, Robert	1779	
CADWELL, Sarah	1780-1781 (undated)	
CAGE, Elizabeth	1817	Grisham
CAGE, Elizabeth	1818	Grisham
CAGE, Elizabeth	1819	Grisham
CAGE, James	1819	Grisham
CA-IL, Alex	1778	
CAIN, Hugh	1792	Milliken
CAIN, Hugh	1794	Milliken
CAIN, Peter	1794	Thornton
CAIN, Richd	1806	Anderson
CALAT, Isaak	1794	North
CALDHOON, David	1817	Little
CALDHOON, David	1819	Jones
CALDHOON, David	1821	Jones
CALDWELL, John	1815	Grimsley
CALDWELL, John	1816	Grimsley
CALDWELL, John	1817	Grimsley
CALE, Joseph	1812	Brown
CALHOON, David	1809	Carr
CALHOON, David	1815	Hoss
CALHOUN, David	1818	Jones
CALLAM, George	1799	Moore
CALLED, J-al	1796	Brown
CALLER, William	1796	Brown
CALLET, Isaac	1791	Chisom
CALLIHAM, Joel	1778	
CALLIHAM, John	1778	
CALLOM, George	1797	Gann
CALLOM, Jonathan	1814	Waddell
CALLOMS, Junr	1797	Gann
CALRTON, Enouch	1805	Carson
CALS, Jacob	1807	Cade
CALUITS, Fredrick	1779	
CALVAN, J. Pelam (Capt.)	1794	Scot
CALVART, Wm	1791	Willey
CALVERT, Jno	1808	Parker
CALVERT, John	1805	Jas Parker
CALVERT, John	1809	Parker
CALVERT, Leonard	1809	Parker
CALVERT, Leonard	1811	McCray
CALVERT, Leonard	1812	McCray
CALVERT, Leonard	1812	McCray
CALVERT, Leonard	1814	McCray
CALVERT, Leonard	1818	Harris
CALVERT, Leonard	1819	Harris
CALVERT, William	1792	Scott
CALVERT, William	1793	Scott
CALVERT, William	1798	Calvert
CALVERT, William	1811	McCray
CALVERT, William	1812	McCray
CALVERT, William	1812	McCray
CALVERT, William	1814	McCray
CALVERT, William	1818	Harris
CALVERT, William	1819	Harris
CALVERT, William (Capt.)	1796	Calvert
CALVERT, William (Capt.)	1801	Calvert
CALVERT, Willm	1797	Calvert
CALVERT, Wm	1795	Calvert
CALVERT, Wm	1797	Calvert
CALVERT, Wm	1799	Stuart
CALVERT, Wm	1808	Parker
CALVERT, Wm	1809	Parker
CALVERT, Wm Jr.	1805	Jas Parker
CALVERT, Wm Sr.	1805	Jas Parker
CAMBEL, Robert	1779	Wilson

Surname, Given names	Year	Comp./Dist.
CAMBELL, James	1780-1781 (Undated)	
CAMBELL, James Jr.	1780-1781 (Undated)	
CAMBELL, Richard	1796	Brown
CAMBLE, Alexander	1815	McLin
CAMBLE, Hugh	1805	Carson
CAMBLEANCH, Hugh	1810	Dimmons
CAMBREL, Bradley	1778	
CAMEDY, Scott	1812	Crawford [2]
CAMMEL, Joseph	1807	Cade
CAMPBEL, Alexander	1812	McLin
CAMPBEL, Alexander	1780-1781 (Undated)	
CAMPBEL, Hugh	1807	Shields
CAMPBEL, Hugh	1811	
CAMPBEL, Hugh	1814	Couthers
CAMPBEL, John	1793	Depew
CAMPBEL, John	1801	Taylor
CAMPBELL,	1817	Harris
CAMPBELL, Abraham	1792	Depew
CAMPBELL, Abraham	1799	Duncan
CAMPBELL, Abraham	1801	Taylor
CAMPBELL, Abraham	1815	McLin
CAMPBELL, Abraham	1816	Hunt
CAMPBELL, Alex	1778	
CAMPBELL, Alex	1817	Hunt
CAMPBELL, Alex	1819	Harris
CAMPBELL, Alexander	1805	Aikin
CAMPBELL, Alexander	1814	McLin
CAMPBELL, Alexander	1816	Hunt
CAMPBELL, Alexander	1818	Harris
CAMPBELL, Alexander	1821	Hampton
CAMPBELL, Alexdr	1781	
CAMPBELL, Alexdr	1781	
CAMPBELL, Archibald	1819	Grimsley
CAMPBELL, David	1778	
CAMPBELL, George	1797	Biddle
CAMPBELL, Haskiah (Over age)	1790	White
CAMPBELL, Hugh	1794	Blair
CAMPBELL, Hugh	1797	Biddle
CAMPBELL, Hugh	1801	Biddle
CAMPBELL, Hugh	1806	Carson
CAMPBELL, Hugh	1815	Carcathers
CAMPBELL, Hugh	1816	Giles
CAMPBELL, Hugh	1817	Gillises
CAMPBELL, Hugh	1818	Land
CAMPBELL, Hugh	1819	Sands
CAMPBELL, Hugh	1821	Sands
CAMPBELL, Isaac	1791	White
CAMPBELL, Isaac	1793	Thornton
CAMPBELL, Isaac	1794	Ford
CAMPBELL, Isaac	1795	Ford
CAMPBELL, James	1781	
CAMPBELL, James	1781	
CAMPBELL, James	1791	White
CAMPBELL, James	1792	Depew
CAMPBELL, James	1793	Thornton
CAMPBELL, James	1794	Ford
CAMPBELL, James	1795	Ford
CAMPBELL, James	1814	McLin
CAMPBELL, James	1815	McLin
CAMPBELL, James	1816	Hunt
CAMPBELL, James	1817	Hunt
CAMPBELL, James	1818	Harris
CAMPBELL, James	1818	Hunt
CAMPBELL, James	1819	Harris
CAMPBELL, James	1819	Hunt
CAMPBELL, James	1821	Hampton
CAMPBELL, James	1821	Hunt
CAMPBELL, Jeremiah	1791	White
CAMPBELL, Jeremiah	1795	Ford
CAMPBELL, Jerimiah	1794	Ford
CAMPBELL, Jerimiah (Capt.)	1793	Campbell
CAMPBELL, John	1781	
CAMPBELL, John	1790	Biddle
CAMPBELL, John	1790	Milleken
CAMPBELL, John	1791	Biddle
CAMPBELL, John	1792	Biddle
CAMPBELL, John	1792	Depew
CAMPBELL, John	1797	Duncan
CAMPBELL, John	1799	Duncan
CAMPBELL, John	1783 [after]	Depew
CAMPBELL, John (Capt.)	1791	
CAMPBELL, John (Esq.)	1794	Blair
CAMPBELL, John Jr.	1797	Biddle
CAMPBELL, John Sr.	1797	Biddle
CAMPBELL, Leeroy	1821	Hunt
CAMPBELL, Leroy	1821	Smith
CAMPBELL, Robert	1781	
CAMPBELL, Robert	1794	Blair
CAMPBELL, Robert	1797	Biddle
CAMPBELL, Saml (heirs of)	1821	Hale
CAMPBELL, Soloman (Capt.)	1791	
CAMPBELL, Solomon	1779	
CAMPBELL, Solomon	1791	White
CAMPBELL, Solomon	1795	Ford
CAMPBELL, William	1778	
CAMPBELL, William	1781	
CAMPBELL, William	1797	Biddle
CAMPBELL, William	1821	Hunt
CAMPBELL, Wm	1781	
CAMPBELL, Zachariah	1794	Ford
CAMPBELL, Zachariah	1795	Ford

Surname, Given names	Year	Comp./Dist.
CAMPBELL, Zachariah	1795	Ford
CAMPBELL, Zachariah Jr.	1794	Ford
CAMPBELL, Zachriah	1791	White
CAMPBELL, Zackriah	1793	Campbell
CAMPBILL, Abraham	1798	Duncan
CAMPBILL, John	1798	Duncan
CAMPBILL, John	1798	Duncan
CAMPBLE, Abraham	1798	Biddle
CAMPBLE, Alexander	1780-1781 (Undated)	
CAMPBLE, Hugh	1798	Biddle
CAMPBLE, John	1798	Biddle
CAMPBLE, John	1780-1781 (Undated)	
CAMPBLE, Robert	1780-1781 (Undated)	
CAMPBLE, William	1780-1781 (Undated)	
CAMPBLE, William	1780-1781 (Undated)	
CAMSON, John	1821	McClure
CANE, Peter	1795	Thornton
CANEDY, David	1812	Crawford [2]
CANNEDEY, David	1812	Crawford
CANNEDEY, Scott	1812	Crawford
CANNON, James	1821	McClure
CANNON, Wm	1778	
CANON, Robert (Deceased)	1796	Handly
CANTHERS, Jonathan	1819	Jones
CAPBLE, Robert	1798	Biddle
CAPE, Thomas	1796	Shipley
CAPER, Joseph	1791	North
CAPLINGER, Jacob	1806	Brown
CAPLINGER, John	1806	Brown
CAPLINGER, John	1809	Bayles
CAPLINGER, Samuel	1806	Brown
CAPON, Isaac	1814	Couthers
CAPON, John	1814	Couthers
CAPOR, John	1790	Biddle
CAPOR, John	1791	Biddle
CAPOR, John	1792	Biddle
CAPP, Thomas	1798	Shipley
CAPPOCH, Aaron	1798	Duncan
CAR, Thomas	1790	Stone
CAR, Thomas	1791	Stone
CAR, Thomas	1793	Melvan
CAR, Thomas	1794	Melvan
CAR, Thomas	1801	Norwood
CAR, Thomas	1801	Taylor
CAR, Walter	1807	Parker
CARATHERS, Jonathan	1808	Carr
CARATHERS, Jonathan	1809	Carr
CARATHERS, Jonathan	[1796] 1797	Morris
CARATHERS, Jonthen	1801	Morrison
CARATHRES, Jonathan	1811	Mitchell
CARCATHERS, James	1818	Jones
CARCATHERS, Jonathan	1815	Hoss
CARCATHERS, Jonathan	1817	Little
CARCATHERS, Jonathan	1818	Jones
CARCATHERS, Samuel	1815	Carcathers
CARCATHERS, Samuel	1816	Giles
CARCATHERS, Samuel	1818	Land
CARDER, Thomas	1779	
CARE, William	1813	Hoss
CARETHERS, Saml	1806	Carson
CARETHERS, Saml	1811	
CAREY, Joseph	1812	Britton
CAREY, Joseph	1814	Copes
CAREY, Joseph	1815	Copas
CAREY, Joseph	1817	Grisham
CARIK, Jno	1780-1781 (Undated)	
CARITHERS, James	1819	Jones
CARITHERS, Samuel	1817	Gillises
CARITHERS, Samuel	1819	Sands
CARL, John	1821	McGee
CARLEY, Thomas	1779	
CARLHOONE, David	1808	Carr
CARLY, John	[1796] 1797	Morris
CARMACLES, Archl	1814	McLin
CARMEN, Michal	1812	McCray
CARMICAL, Esbal	1805	Carson
CARMICAL, John	1805	Carson
CARMICALL, Esbald	1810	Dimmons
CARMICHAEL, Hannah	1821	Hunt
CARMICHAEL, James	1792	Depew
CARMICHAEL, James	1793	Depew
CARMICHAEL, James	1794	Depew
CARMICHAEL, John	1794	Blair
CARMICHAEL, John	1797	Biddle
CARMICHAL, John	1798	Biddle
CARMICL, William	1821	Sands
CARMICLE,	1814	Couthers
CARMICLE, Abel	1814	Couthers
CARMICLE, Arch	1817	Gillises
CARMICLE, Archable	1810	Dimmons
CARMICLE, Archibald	1811	
CARMICLE, Archibald	1815	Carcathers
CARMICLE, Archibald	1816	Giles
CARMICLE, Archibald	1818	Land
CARMICLE, Isabell	1816	Giles
CARMICLE, Isabella	1817	Gillises
CARMICLE, Isbel	1806	Carson
CARMICLE, Isbel	1811	
CARMICLE, Isbell	1801	Biddle
CARMICLE, William	1815	Carcathers

Surname, Given names	Year	Comp./Dist.
CARMICLE, William	1816	Giles
CARMICLE, William	1817	Gillises
CARMICLE, William	1818	Land
CARMICLE, William	1819	Sands
CARMILLER, Jessey	1780-1781 (Undated)	
CARNEAHIOUS, William	1778	
CARNEATHERS, Jonathan	1793	Morrison
CARNEATHERS, Jonathan	1794	Morrison
CARNEY, John	1793	Melvan
CARNEY, John	1794	Melvan
CARNEY, John	1795	Melvan
CARNEY, John	1796	Melvin
CARNEY, John	1798	Crouch
CARNEY, Thomas	1794	Melvan
CARNEY, Thomas Jr.	1795	Melvan
CARNEY, Thomas Jr.	1796	Melvin
CARNEY, Thomas Sr.	1790	Stone
CARNEY, Thomas Sr.	1791	Stone
CARNEY, Thomas Sr.	1793	Melvan
CARNEY, Thomas Sr.	1794	Melvan
CARNEY, Thomas Sr.	1795	Melvan
CARNEY, Thomas Sr.	1796	Melvin
CARON, Robert	1781	
CARPENDAR, Owla	1780-1781 (Undated)	
CARPENDER, Barton	1781	
CARPENTER, Wm	1781	
CARR, John	1787	Fains
CARR, John	1791	Tullis
CARR, John	1792	Tulley
CARR, John	1795	Morrison
CARR, John	1795	Morrison
CARR, John	1798	Morrison
CARR, John	1798	Morrison
CARR, John	1798	Shipley
CARR, John	1799	Morrison
CARR, John	1801	Lane
CARR, John	1801	Morrison
CARR, John	1805	Doak
CARR, John	1807	Carr
CARR, John	1809	Carr
CARR, John	1811	Mitchell
CARR, John	1813	Hoss
CARR, John	1814	Hoss
CARR, John	1815	Hoss
CARR, John	1816	Hoss
CARR, John	1817	Little
CARR, John	1818	Jones
CARR, John Jr.	1793	Morrison
CARR, John Jr.	1794	Morrison
CARR, John Jr.	1806	Doke
CARR, John Jr.	[1796] 1797	Morris
CARR, John Sr.	1793	Morrison
CARR, John Sr.	1794	Morrison
CARR, John Sr.	1806	Carr
CARR, John Sr.	1808	Carr
CARR, John Sr.	[1796] 1797	Morris
CARR, Richard	1807	Carr
CARR, Richard	1809	Carr
CARR, Richard	1811	Mitchell
CARR, Richard	1813	Hoss
CARR, Richard	1814	Hoss
CARR, Richard	1814	Hoss
CARR, Richard	1815	Hoss
CARR, Richard	1816	Hoss
CARR, Richard	1817	Little
CARR, Richard	1818	Jones
CARR, Richard	1819	Jones
CARR, Richard	1821	Jones
CARR, Ritchard	1806	Carr
CARR, Ritchard	1808	Carr
CARR, Thomas	1792	Depew
CARR, Thomas	1794	Depew
CARR, Thomas	1795	Melvan
CARR, Thomas	1796	Shipley
CARR, Walter	1806	Parker
CARR, William	1807	Carr
CARR, William	1808	Carr
CARR, William	1811	Mitchell
CARR, William	1813	Hoss
CARR, William	1814	Hoss
CARR, William	1815	Hoss
CARR, William	1816	Hoss
CARR, William	1817	Harris
CARR, William	1817	Little
CARR, William	1818	Jones
CARR, William	1819	Jones
CARR, Wm	1809	Carr
CARRACK, John	1778	
CARRATHERS, Jonathan	1799	Morrison
CARREATHERS, Jonathan	1798	Morrison
CARREL, Hickmen	1821	Brown
CARREL, John	1807	Odell
CARREL, John	1808	Odell
CARREL, William	1812	Brown
CARREL, William	1814	Brown
CARREL, William Jr.	1809	Viney
CARRIGER, Godfrey	1794	Carriger
CARRIGER, Godfrey	1795	Carriger
CARRIGER, Godfrey Jr.	1794	Carriger
CARRIGER, Godfrey Jr.	1795	Carriger
CARRIGER, Godfrey Sr.	1790	Greer

Surname, Given names	Year	Comp./Dist.
CARRIGER, Godfrey Sr.	1792	Carriger
CARRIGER, Godfrey Sr.	1792	Greer
CARRIGER, Michael	1790	Greer
CARRIGER, Michael	1792	Carriger
CARRIGER, Michael	1794	Carriger
CARRIGER, Michael	1795	Carriger
CARRIGER, Nicholas	1790	Greer
CARRIGER, Nicholas	1794	Carriger
CARRIGER, Nicholas	1795	Carriger
CARRIGER, Nicolas	1792	Carriger
CARROAL, Delaney	1778	
CARROL, John	1806	Odel
CARROL, Luke	1814	McLin
CARROLD, James	1798	Longmire
CARROLL, Henry	1818	Land
CARROLL, Henry	1819	Hunt
CARROLL, Hickman	1819	Brown
CARROLL, John	1821	Hunt
CARROLL, Luke	1811	Davis
CARROLL, Luke	1815	McLin
CARROLL, Luke	1816	Hunt
CARROLL, Luke	1818	Land
CARROLL, William	1801	Longmire
CARROLL, William Jr.	1811	Brown
CARRUTHERS, James	1821	Jones
CARRUTHERS, John	1821	Jones
CARRUTHERS, Jonathan	1821	Jones
CARRY, Jonathan	1781	
CARSNER, Jacob	1801	Roberson
CARSNER, Jacob	1807	Bayles
CARSON, Absolom	1818	Land
CARSON, Adrone	1798	Biddle
CARSON, Andes	1814	Couthers
CARSON, Andrew	1790	Biddle
CARSON, Andrew	1791	Biddle
CARSON, Andrew	1792	Biddle
CARSON, Andrew	1797	Biddle
CARSON, Andrew	1798	Biddle
CARSON, Andrew	1801	Biddle
CARSON, Andrew	1805	Carson
CARSON, Andrew	1807	Shields
CARSON, Andrew	1809	Patterson
CARSON, Andrew	1810	Dimmons
CARSON, Andrew	1811	
CARSON, Andrew	1815	Carcathers
CARSON, Andrew	1816	Giles
CARSON, Andrew	1818	Land
CARSON, Andrew	1819	Sands
CARSON, Andrew	1821	Sands
CARSON, Archd	1806	Carson
CARSON, David	1792	Depew
CARSON, David	1793	Depew
CARSON, David	1794	Depew
CARSON, David	1794	Depew
CARSON, David	1797	Duncan
CARSON, David	1797	Duncan
CARSON, David	1798	Duncan
CARSON, David	1798	Duncan
CARSON, David	1798	Duncan
CARSON, David	1799	Duncan
CARSON, David	1801	Taylor
CARSON, David	1806	Guin
CARSON, David	1807	Givins
CARSON, David	1808	Guin
CARSON, David	1809	Gwin
CARSON, David	1783 [after]	Depew
CARSON, David (Little)	1792	Depew
CARSON, David Jr.	1792	Depew
CARSON, David Sr.	1792	Depew
CARSON, David Sr.	1793	Depew
CARSON, David Sr.	1794	Depew
CARSON, David Sr.	1798	Duncan
CARSON, John	1792	Tulley
CARSON, John	1798	Duncan
CARSON, John	1812	McLin
CARSON, John	1814	McLin
CARSON, John	1815	McLin
CARSON, John	1816	Hunt
CARSON, John E.	1805	Carson
CARSON, John Jr.	1806	Carson
CARSON, Lemual	1810	Dimmons
CARSON, Lemuel	1806	Carson
CARSON, Lemuel	1807	Shields
CARSON, Lemuel	1809	Patterson
CARSON, Lemuel	1811	
CARSON, Lemuel	1821	Sands
CARSON, Margarett	1819	Sands
CARSON, Mary	1805	Carson
CARSON, Mears W.	1818	Land
CARSON, Mose Jr.	1810	Dimmons
CARSON, Moses	1790	Biddle
CARSON, Moses	1791	Biddle
CARSON, Moses	1792	Biddle
CARSON, Moses	1794	Blair
CARSON, Moses	1797	Biddle
CARSON, Moses	1798	Biddle
CARSON, Moses	1805	Carson
CARSON, Moses	1806	Carson
CARSON, Moses	1807	Shields
CARSON, Moses	1809	Patterson
CARSON, Moses	1809	Patterson
CARSON, Moses	1810	Dimmons

Surname, Given names	Year	Comp./Dist.
CARSON, Moses	1814	Couthers
CARSON, Moses	1815	Carcathers
CARSON, Moses (younger)	1814	Couthers
CARSON, Moses Jr.	1811	
CARSON, Moses Jr.	1815	Carcathers
CARSON, Moses Jr.	1816	Giles
CARSON, Moses Jr.	1817	Gillises
CARSON, Moses Jr.	1818	Land
CARSON, Moses Jr.	1819	Sands
CARSON, Moses Jr.	1821	Sands
CARSON, Moses Sr.	1811	
CARSON, Moses Sr.	1816	Giles
CARSON, Moses Sr.	1817	Gillises
CARSON, Moses Sr.	1819	Sands
CARSON, Mosses	1801	Biddle
CARSON, Nancy	1816	Hunt
CARSON, Nancy	1818	Hunt
CARSON, Nancy	1819	Hunt
CARSON, Nancy	1821	Hunt
CARSON, Newton	1821	Sands
CARSON, Polly	1806	Carson
CARSON, Polly	1807	Shields
CARSON, Polly	1809	Patterson
CARSON, Polly	1811	
CARSON, Polly	1814	Couthers
CARSON, Polly	1815	Carcathers
CARSON, Polly	1816	Giles
CARSON, Polly	1817	Gillises
CARSON, Polly	1818	Land
CARSON, Polly	1819	Sands
CARSON, Polly	1821	Sands
CARSON, Robart	1797	Duncan
CARSON, Robart	1798	Duncan
CARSON, Robart	1807	Givins
CARSON, Robert	1793	Depew
CARSON, Robert	1794	Depew
CARSON, Robert	1798	Duncan
CARSON, Robert	1799	Duncan
CARSON, Robert	1801	Taylor
CARSON, Robert	1806	Guin
CARSON, Robert	1808	Guin
CARSON, Robert	1809	Gwin
CARSON, Robert	1811	Davis
CARSON, Robert	1812	McLin
CARSON, Robert	1814	McLin
CARSON, Robert	1815	McLin
CARSON, Robert	1816	Hunt
CARSON, Robert	1818	Hunt
CARSON, Robert	1819	Hunt
CARSON, Robert	1821	Hunt
CARSON, Robert	1783 [after]	Depew

Surname, Given names	Year	Comp./Dist.
CARSON, Robert Jr.	1792	Depew
CARSON, Robert Sr.	1792	Depew
CARSON, Samuel	1805	Carson
CARSON, Samuel	1814	Couthers
CARSON, Samuel	1815	Carcathers
CARSON, Samuel	1816	Giles
CARSON, Samuel	1817	Gillises
CARSON, Samuel	1818	Land
CARSON, Samuel	1819	Sands
CARSON, W. Moses	1821	Sands
CARSON, William	1793	Depew
CARSON, William	1793	Murray
CARSON, William	1794	Depew
CARSON, William	1806	Guin
CARSON, William	1807	Givins
CARSON, William	1808	Guin
CARSON, William	1809	Gwin
CARSON, William	1811	Davis
CARSON, William	1812	McLin
CARSON, William	1815	McLin
CARSON, William	1821	Hunt
CARSON, William Sr.	1814	McLin
CARSONER, Jacob	1791	Chisom
CARSONS, Jacob	1792	Chisolm
CARTER,	1790	
CARTER, Abm	1781	
CARTER, Agustine	1779	
CARTER, Caleb	1781	
CARTER, Emanuel	1778	
CARTER, Emanuel	1779	
CARTER, James	1819	Harris
CARTER, James Jr.	1819	Harris
CARTER, James P.	1818	Harris
CARTER, John	1781	
CARTER, John	1791	Willey
CARTER, John	1792	Carriger
CARTER, John	1792	Greer
CARTER, John	1793	Morrison
CARTER, John	1794	Carriger
CARTER, John	1794	Morrison
CARTER, John	1795	Carriger
CARTER, John	1798	Morrison
CARTER, John (Esq.)	1778	
CARTER, John (Esqr.)	1779	
CARTER, Joseph	1781	
CARTER, Joseph	1780-1781 (Undated)	
CARTER, Landon	1779	
CARTER, Landon	1792	Greer
CARTER, Landon	1794	Carriger
CARTER, Landon	1795	Carriger
CARTER, Landon (Col.)	1792	Carriger

Surname, Given names	Year	Comp./Dist.
CARTER, Levy	1781	
CARTER, Tom B.	1817	Smith
CARTER, William B.	1818	Smith
CARUTHERS, Jonathan	1795	Morrison
CARUTHERS, Jonathan	1807	
CARUTHERS, Jonathan	1814	Hoss
CARUTHERS, Saml	1807	Shields
CARVER, Michael	1811	McCray
CARVER, Michael	1814	McCray
CARVER, Michael	1816	Harrison
CARVER, Michal	1812	McCray
CARY, Benjamin	1817	Grisham
CARY, Benjamin	1818	Grisham
CARY, Joseph	1811	Britten
CARY, Joseph	1813	Copas
CARY, Joseph	1818	Grisham
CARY, Joseph	1821	Hale
CASADA, James	1810	Hartzel
CASADA, James	1812	Hartsell
CASADA, Robert	1807	Parker
CASADA, Robert	1808	Parker
CASADA, Robin	1812	Hartsell
CASADAY, Jas	1809	Par
CASEADY, James	1806	Carr
CASEDAY, John	1798	Young
CASEDAY, Rob	1809	Par
CASEDAY, Robert	1798	Young
CASEDE, Robert	1806	Carr
CASEDY, John	1778	
CASEDY, Robert	1806	Parker
CASEY, Bey	1819	Grisham
CASEY, Joseph	1819	Grisham
CASH, Benjamin	1808	Parker
CASH, Ingsdasher	1792	Brown
CASH, Jacob	1808	Gwin
CASH, James	1791	Willey
CASH, James	1792	Scott
CASH, James	1794	Scot
CASH, James	1794	Scot
CASH, James	1796	Longmire
CASH, James	1797	Calvert
CASH, James	1798	Calvert
CASH, James	1799	Stuart
CASH, James	1801	Calvert
CASH, James	1805	Jas Parker
CASH, James (estate of)	1811	McCray
CASH, James (Sr.)	1793	Scott
CASH, James Jr.	1793	Scott
CASH, Jas (estate of)	1808	Parker
CASH, Jas Jr.	1795	Calvert
CASH, Jas. Sr.	1795	Calvert
CASH, Jmgs	1791	Willey
CASH, John	1797	Calvert
CASH, John	1797	Calvert
CASH, John	1797	Calvert
CASH, John	1799	Stuart
CASH, John	1801	Calvert
CASH, Lenard	1807	Bayles
CASH, Leonard	1797	Calvert
CASH, Leonard	1806	Brown
CASH, Michael	1808	Gwin
CASH, William	1790	White
CASH, William	1799	Stuart
CASH, William	1801	Calvert
CASH, Willm	1797	Calvert
CASH, Willm	1797	Calvert
CASH, Wm	1805	Jas Parker
CASH, Wm	1808	Parker
CASH, Wm	1809	Parker
CASHADY, John	1779	
CASHADY, Robt	1795	Young
CASHEDY, James	1818	Fine
CASHER, James (Estate Of)	1809	Parker
CASIDA, Robert	1805	Parker
CASIDAY, James	1805	Parker
CASIDAY, John	1821	Howard
CASIDY, Jas	1801	Taylor
CASIDY, Robert	1796	Young
CASIDY, Robert	1797	Young
CASIDY, Robert	1801	Taylor
CASKEDY, Robert	1815	Fines
CASKIDY, James	1815	Fines
CASKIDY, James	1816	Fine
CASKIDY, James	1817	Fine
CASKIDY, Robert	1816	Fine
CASKIDY, Robert	1817	Fine
CASNER, Jacob	1792	Brown
CASNER, Jacob	1797	Robertson
CASNER, Jacob	1799	Robertson
CASNER, Jacob	1806	Brown
CASNER, Jacob	1808	Bayles
CASON, John	1794	Blair
CASON, John (Rev.)	1797	Biddle
CASPN, Charla	1814	Barns
CASSADA, James	1819	Howard
CASSADA, Robert	1819	Howard
CASSADA, Ruben	1810	Hartzel
CASSIDAY, James	1821	Howard
CASSIDAY, Robert	1821	Howard
CASSIMORE, Amos	1781	
CASSIMORE, Mathew	1781	
CASSON, John Sr. (Mr.)	1809	Patterson

Surname, Given names	Year	Comp./Dist.
CASSON, Margret	1814	Couthers
CASWELL, Richard (heirs)	1811	Britten
CATHEY, Archiblad	1816	Brown
CATRIL, John	1790	Shipley
CATRIL, John	1791	Shipley
CAULSON, Enoch	1818	Land
CAUSDSO, John (Rev.)	1798	Biddle
CAUSON, John	1818	Brown [2]
CAUSON, John	1821	Smith
CAVEHAUER, Nickolaus	1799	Morrison
CAWOOD, John (In Virga.)	1778	
CAYLOR, Wilam	1794	Brown
CELSEY, Samuel (estate of)	1806	Payn
CENDAL, James	1808	McAllister
CENLAN, Joseph	1812	Crawford [2]
CERANER, Jacob	1796	Brown
CERLEN, William	1808	McAllister
CERLEN, William	1812	Crawford [2]
CERREL, Luck	1821	Sands
CERSONER, Jacob	1793	Brown
CERTAIN, James	1778	
CERTAIN, Jo	1778	
CHALTON, Thomas	1810	Barron
CHAMBERLAIN,	1818	Grisham
CHAMBERLAIN, James	1790	Shipley
CHAMBERLAIN, James	1791	Shipley
CHAMBERLAIN, James	1793	Murray
CHAMBERLAIN, James	1795	Murray
CHAMBERLAIN, James	1796	Shipley
CHAMBERLAIN, James	1797	Shipley
CHAMBERLAIN, James	1798	Shipley
CHAMBERLAIN, James	1801	Lane
CHAMBERLAIN, James	1805	Doak
CHAMBERLAIN, James	1806	Doke
CHAMBERLAIN, James	1807	Britton
CHAMBERLAIN, James	1815	Copas
CHAMBERLAIN, James	1816	Copas
CHAMBERLAIN, James	1817	Grisham
CHAMBERLAIN, James	1819	Grisham
CHAMBERLIN, -Inian	1781	
CHAMBERLIN, James	1794	Murray
CHAMBERLIN, James	1811	Britten
CHAMBERLIN, Jas	1813	Copas
CHAMBERLIN, Jas	1821	Hale
CHAMBERS,	1780-1781 (undated)	
CHAMBERS, Alexander	1780-1781 (undated)	
CHAMBERS, Alexander	1780-1781 (Undated)	
CHAMBERS, David	1778	
CHAMBERS, David	1780-1781 (undated)	
CHAMBERS, David	1780-1781 (Undated)	
CHAMBERS, John	1778	
CHAMBERS, John	1790	White
CHAMBERS, John	1780-1781 (Undated)	
CHAMBERS, William	1778	
CHAMBLE, Jacob	1778	
CHAMBLE, Jacob	1779	
CHAMPLAIN, James	1814	Copes
CHAMTON, Thomas	1815	Grimsley
CHANCE, Ezekel	1793	Morrison
CHANCE, Ezekel	1794	Morrison
CHANCEY, William	1807	Britton
CHANCY, William	1816	Copas
CHANDLER, Isaac	1814	McCray
CHANDLER, James	1812	McCray
CHANDLER, Simeon	1812	Brown
CHANDLER, Timethy	1812	Brown
CHANDLER, Timothy	1806	Doke
CHANEY, William	1805	Doak
CHANEY, William	1806	Doke
CHANEY, William	1814	Copes
CHANEY, William	1815	Copas
CHANEY, William	1817	Grisham
CHANEY, William	1818	Grisham
CHANNEY, William	1812	Britton
CHANY, William	1819	Grisham
CHANY, Wm	1813	Copas
CHAPMAN, Benja	1801	Lane
CHAPMAN, Benja	1813	Copas
CHAPMAN, Benja	1821	Hale
CHAPMAN, Benjaman	1798	Crouch
CHAPMAN, Benjaman	1806	Doke
CHAPMAN, Benjaman	1814	Copes
CHAPMAN, Benjamin	1805	Doak
CHAPMAN, Benjamin	1811	Britten
CHAPMAN, Benjamin	1812	Britton
CHAPMAN, Benjamin	1815	Copas
CHAPMAN, Benjamin	1816	Copas
CHAPMAN, Benjamin	1817	Grisham
CHAPMAN, Benjamin	1818	Grisham
CHAPMAN, Benjamin	1819	Grisham
CHAPMAN, David	1811	Britten
CHAPMAN, David	1812	Britton
CHAPMAN, John	1790	Shipley
CHAPMAN, John	1791	Shipley
CHAPMAN, John	1793	Murray
CHAPMAN, John	1794	Murray
CHAPMAN, John	1795	Murray
CHAPMAN, John	1796	Shipley
CHAPMAN, John	1801	Lane

Surname, Given names	Year	Comp./Dist.
CHAPMAN, John	1805	Doak
CHAPMAN, John	1806	Doke
CHAPMAN, John	1811	Britten
CHAPMAN, John	1812	Britton
CHAPMAN, John	1813	Copas
CHAPMAN, John Jr.	1814	Copes
CHAPMAN, John Jr.	1815	Copas
CHAPMAN, John Sr.	1814	Copes
CHAPMAN, John Sr.	1815	Copas
CHAPMAN, Robert	1806	Doke
CHAPMAN, Robert	1807	Britton
CHAPMAN, Robert	1811	Britten
CHAPMAN, Robert	1812	Britton
CHAPMAN, Robert	1813	Copas
CHAPMAN, Robert	1814	Copes
CHAPMAN, Robert	1815	Copas
CHAPMAN, Robert	1816	Copas
CHAPMAN, Sam'l	1821	Hale
CHAPMAN, Samuel	1812	Britton
CHAPMAN, Samuel	1814	Copes
CHAPMAN, Samuel	1815	Copas
CHAPMAN, Samuel	1816	Copas
CHAPMAN, Samuel	1817	Grisham
CHAPMAN, Samuel	1818	Grisham
CHAPMAN, Samuel	1819	Grisham
CHAPMAS, Saml	1813	Copas
CHARELTON, Simson	1807	Payne
CHARELTON, Simson	1809	McAlister
Charles	1793	Thornton
CHARLETON, John	1815	Carcathers
CHARLETON, John	1816	Hunt
CHARLETON, Painter	1816	Hunt
CHARLETON, Painter Jr.	1816	Hunt
CHARLETON, Pointen	1807	Shields
CHARLETON, Simpson	1811	McAlister
CHARLETON, Thomas	1816	Grimsley
CHARLETON, Thomas	1817	Grimsley
CHARLINGTON, Jimpsy	1805	Carson
CHARLINTON, Thomas	1812	Barnes
CHARLONS, James	1791	Willey
CHARLTON, Benten	1817	Hunt
CHARLTON, John	1807	Givins
CHARLTON, John	1808	Guin
CHARLTON, John	1809	Gwin
CHARLTON, John	1811	Davis
CHARLTON, John	1812	McLin
CHARLTON, John	1814	Couthers
CHARLTON, John	1815	McLin
CHARLTON, John	1817	Hunt
CHARLTON, John	1819	Hunt
CHARLTON, John	1821	Hunt
CHARLTON, John Jr.	1818	Hunt
CHARLTON, Painter Jr.	1814	McLin
CHARLTON, Painter Sr.	1814	McLin
CHARLTON, Paintor Jr.	1811	Davis
CHARLTON, Paintor Jr.	1821	Hunt
CHARLTON, Paintor Sr.	1821	Hunt
CHARLTON, Pointer	1801	Taylor
CHARLTON, Pointer Jr.	1809	Gwin
CHARLTON, Pointing	1798	Duncan
CHARLTON, Pointing Sr.	1798	Duncan
CHARLTON, Pointon	1799	Duncan
CHARLTON, Pointon	1809	Gwin
CHARLTON, Pointon	1818	Hunt
CHARLTON, Pointon Jr.	1806	Guin
CHARLTON, Pointon Jr.	1808	Guin
CHARLTON, Pointon Jr.	1811	Davis
CHARLTON, Pointon Jr.	1812	McLin
CHARLTON, Pointon Jr.	1815	McLin
CHARLTON, Pointon Jr.	1819	Hunt
CHARLTON, Pointon Sr.	1808	Guin
CHARLTON, Pointon Sr.	1809	Gwin
CHARLTON, Pointon Sr.	1812	McLin
CHARLTON, Pointon Sr.	1815	McLin
CHARLTON, Pointon Sr.	1819	Hunt
CHARLTON, Pointtin	1797	Duncan
CHARLTON, Pounton Sr.	1806	Guin
CHARLTON, Sempson	1812	Crawford
CHARLTON, Simpson	1806	Carson
CHARLTON, Simpson	1812	Crawford [2]
CHARLTON, Simson	1808	McAllister
CHARLTON, Thomas	1806	Guin
CHARLTON, Thomas	1811	Barron
CHARLTON, Thomas	1818	Grimsley
CHARLTON, Thomas	1819	Grimsley
CHARLTON, Thos	1821	Martin
CHARTER, James	1779	
CHARTER, James	1792	Scott
CHARTER, James	1793	Scott
CHARTER, James	1796	Jonesboro
CHASEWOOD, Alex	1778	
CHASONS, Charles	1778	
CHEATE, Austin	1778	
CHENETH, Nicholis	1816	Copas
CHENNETH, Nicholas	1796	Shipley
CHENUTH, Nicholas	1795	Murray
CHESM, John	1792	Chisolm
CHESTER, John	1799	Stuart
CHESTER, John	1801	Aiken
CHESTER, John	1805	Jas Parker
CHESTER, John	1807	Anderson
CHESTER, John	1809	Roadmas

Surname, Given names	Year	Comp./Dist.
CHESTER, John	1811	Rodman
CHESTER, John	1812	Crawford
CHESTER, John	1815	Garner
CHESTER, John	1816	Smith
CHESTER, John	1817	Smith
CHESTER, John	1818	Smith
CHESTER, John	1819	Smith
CHESTER, John	1820	Smith
CHESTER, John	1821	Smith
CHESTER, John D.	1818	Smith
CHESTER, John Jr.	1819	Smith
CHESTER, P. William	1821	McClure
CHESTER, Robert	1815	Garner
CHESTER, Robert	1816	Smith
CHESTER, Saml G.	1821	Smith
CHESTER, Sam'l G.	1820	Smith
CHESTER, Samuel G.	1817	Smith
CHESTER, Samuel G.	1818	Smith
CHESTER, Samuel G.	1819	Smith
CHESTER, William	1796	Calvert
CHESTER, William	1817	Hampton
CHESTER, William	1818	Brown [2]
CHESTER, William H.	1797	Calvert
CHESTER, William P.	1801	Roberson
CHESTER, William P.	1809	Roadmas
CHESTER, William P.	1811	Rodman
CHESTER, William P.	1816	Hampton
CHESTER, William P.	1818	Smith
CHESTER, William P.	1819	Brown
CHESTER, William P. (for Ruffin)	1811	Rodman
CHESTER, Willm P.	1797	Calvert
CHESTER, Wm Jr.	1805	Jas Parker
CHESTER, Wm P.	1799	Stuart
CHESTER, Wm P.	1801	Aiken
CHESTER, Wm P.	1808	Parker
CHESTER, Wm P.	1809	Parker
CHESTER, Wm P.	1814	Hampton
CHESTER, Wm P.	1820	Smith
CHESTER, Wm P.	1821	Smith
CHESTOR, John	1814	McCracken
CHINACITH, Nicholis	1817	Grisham
CHINETH, Nicholas	1819	Grisham
CHINEUTH, Nicholas	1807	Britton
CHINEWTH, Nicholas	1798	Shipley
CHINITH, Nicholas	1815	Copas
CHINITH, Nicholis	1818	Grisham
CHINNETH, Nicholas	1806	Doke
CHINOTH, Archibald	1813	Copas
CHINOTH, Nicholas	1811	Britten
CHINOTH, Nicholas	1813	Copas
CHINOTH, Nicholas	1814	Copes

Surname, Given names	Year	Comp./Dist.
CHINOTH, Nick	1821	Hale
CHINOUTH, Archibald	1814	Copes
CHINOUTH, Nicholas	1801	Lane
CHINUETH, Nicholas	1812	Britton
CHISM, George	1799	Stuart
CHISM, John	1791	Chisom
CHIS'M, John (Esq.)	1778	
CHOAT, Ann (Relict of Tho. Choat)	1779	
CHOAT, Austin	1779	
CHOATE, Edward	1778	
CHOATE, Richard	1778	
CHOATS, Christopher	1778	
CHOATS, Thomas	1778	
CHRESSLIES, John	1817	Hampton
CHRISELLES, John	1798	Young
CHRISTEN, Israil	1795	Murray
CHRISTIAN, Ezeral	1793	Murray
CHRISTIAN, John	1793	Murray
CHRISTIE, Ezzeral	1794	Murray
CHRISTIE, Georg	1798	Biddle
CHRISTY, Israel	1780-1781 (Undated)	
CHRISTY, Isreal	1812	Barnes
CHURCH, Robert	1814	McCracken
CHURCH, Robert	1815	Garner
CHURCH, Robert	1816	Smith
CHURCH, Robert	1817	Smith
CHURCH, Robert	1818	Smith
CHURCH, Robert	1819	Smith
CIBLER, Joab	1821	Martin
CIRBIE, Danel	1798	Crouch
CIRLIM, Joseph	1811	Green
CIRRIL, Henry	1821	Sands
CITTSMILLER, Martin	1801	Morrison
CLACK, Joseph	1821	Hale
CLACKSON, Miller	1814	Couthers
CLACKSON, Widow	1814	Couthers
CLANTON, Edward	1779	
CLANTON, William	1779	
CLANTON, William	1779	
CLARK, David	1821	Hampton
CLARK, George	1816	Waddell
CLARK, Henderson	1806	Grur
CLARK, Henderson	1808	Gwin
CLARK, Henderson	1809	Green
CLARK, Henderson	1810	Green
CLARK, Henderson	1811	Green
CLARK, Henderson	1812	Waddill
CLARK, Henderson	1814	Waddell
CLARK, Henderson	1815	Waddell
CLARK, Henderson	1817	Riley

Surname, Given names	Year	Comp./Dist.
CLARK, Henderson	1818	Riley
CLARK, Henderson	1819	Findley
CLARK, Henderson	1821	McGee
CLARK, Henry	1778	
CLARK, Hiram	1821	McGee
CLARK, James	1807	Shields
CLARK, James	1809	Patterson
CLARK, James	1810	Dimmons
CLARK, James	1811	
CLARK, Jesse	1795	Handly
CLARK, Jesse	1798	Gann
CLARK, Jesse	1799	Gann
CLARK, Jesse	1799	Moore
CLARK, Jessee	1812	Waddill
CLARK, John	1778	
CLARK, John	1790	Hanley
CLARK, John	1791	Hanley
CLARK, John	1797	Gann
CLARK, John	1798	Gann
CLARK, John	1799	Gann
CLARK, John	1799	Moore
CLARK, John	1801	Gann
CLARK, John	1805	Guir
CLARK, John	1806	Grur
CLARK, John	1808	Gwin
CLARK, John	1809	Green
CLARK, John	1810	Green
CLARK, John	1812	Waddill
CLARK, John	1814	Waddell
CLARK, John	1816	Waddell
CLARK, John	1817	Riley
CLARK, John	1818	Riley
CLARK, John	1819	Findley
CLARK, John	1821	McGee
CLARK, Joseah	1794	Taylor
CLARK, Joseph	1816	Copas
CLARK, Joseph	1817	Grisham
CLARK, Joseph	1818	Grisham
CLARK, Joseph	1819	Grisham
CLARK, Josiah	1792	Maxwell
CLARK, Josiah	1793	Maxwell
CLARK, Josiah	1795	Taylor
CLARK, Lewis	1815	Haire
CLARK, Lewis	1816	Hair
CLARK, Malihia	1816	Waddell
CLARK, Nancy	1806	Brown
CLARK, Nancy	1807	Bayles
CLARK, Nancy	1808	Bayles
CLARK, Nancy	1814	Hampton
CLARK, Nancy	1816	Hampton
CLARK, Nancy	1817	Hampton
CLARK, Nancy	1818	Brown [2]
CLARK, Nancy	1819	Brown
CLARK, Nathl	1778	
CLARK, Tenet	1805	Carson
CLARK, Willam	1799	Gann
CLARK, Willam	1799	Gann
CLARK, William	1790	Hanley
CLARK, William	1791	Hanley
CLARK, William	1797	Gann
CLARK, William	1798	Gann
CLARK, William	1805	Guir
CLARK, William	1809	Green
CLARK, William	1811	Green
CLARK, William	1815	Waddell
CLARK, William	1816	Waddell
CLARK, William	1817	Riley
CLARK, William	1818	Riley
CLARK, William	1819	Findley
CLARK, William (Esq.)	1778	
CLARK, William Jr.	1808	Gwin
CLARK, Wm	1799	Moore
CLARK, Wm	1810	Green
CLARK, Wm	1812	Waddill
CLARK, Wm	1814	Waddell
CLARK, Wm	1821	McGee
CLARK, Wm Jr.	1801	Gann
CLARK, Wm Jr.	1806	Grur
CLARKE, Barnes	1809	Bayles
CLARKE, Henderson	1816	Waddell
CLARKE, Isaac	1793	Handley
CLARKE, Jesse	1793	Handley
CLARKE, Jesse	1794	Handly
CLARKE, John	1778	
CLARKE, John	1793	Handley
CLARKE, John	1794	Handly
CLARKE, John	1795	Handly
CLARKE, John	1796	Handly
CLARKE, Nancey	1809	Bayles
CLARKE, Nancey	1821	Brown
CLARKE, William	1793	Handley
CLARKE, William	1794	Handly
CLARKE, William	1795	Handly
CLARKE, William	1796	Handly
CLASON, Charles	1808	Cade
CLAUS, George	1809	Viney
CLAUSE, Aaron	1809	Viney
CLAUSE, Aaron	1814	Brown
CLAUSE, Christopher	1809	Viney
CLAUSE, Elijah	1801	Longmire
CLAUSE, George (estate of)	1812	Brown
CLAUSE, George Jr.	1797	Longmire

Surname, Given names	Year	Comp./Dist.
CLAUSE, George Jr.	1801	Longmire
CLAUSE, George Sr.	1801	Longmire
CLAUSE, John	1801	Longmire
CLAUSE, William	1809	Viney
CLAUSE, William	1814	Brown
CLAUSE, William	1819	Brown
CLAUSON, Jacob	1811	Davis
CLAUSON, Jacob	1818	Hunt
CLAUSON, Samuel	1818	Hunt
CLAUSS, George Sr.	1797	Longmire
CLAUZIN, Jacob	1817	Hunt
CLAWSON, Jacob	1806	Guin
CLAWSON, Jacob	1807	Givins
CLAWSON, Jacob	1808	Guin
CLAWSON, Jacob	1809	Gwin
CLAWSON, Jacob	1812	McLin
CLAWSON, Jacob	1814	McLin
CLAWSON, Jacob	1816	Hunt
CLAWSON, Jacob	1819	Hunt
CLAWSON, Samuel	1819	Hunt
CLAWSON, William	1778	
CLEAK, Marten	1790	Milleken
CLEAK, Peter	1793	Milliken
CLEAK, Petter	1799	Gann
CLEARY, Joseph M.	1814	McCray
CLECK, David	1806	Grur
CLECK, George	1801	Gann
CLECK, George	1806	Grur
CLECK, Henry	1806	Grur
CLECK, Lewis	1792	Milliken
CLECK, Lewis	1793	Milliken
CLECK, Lewis	1796	Millikin
CLECK, Peter	1792	Milliken
CLECK, Peter	1796	Millikin
CLECK, Peter	1801	Gann
CLEEK, George	1815	Waddell
CLEEK, Luis	1798	Gann
CLEEK, Moleher	1815	Waddell
CLEEK, Peter	1798	Gann
CLEEK, Peter	1816	Hampton
CLEEK, Quens	1790	Milleken
CLEM, Michael	1821	Smith
CLEMANS, Joseph	1806	Anderson
CLEMONS, Joseph	1805	Jas Parker
CLENGERY, George	1816	Hampton
CLENGERY, George	1817	Hampton
CLEPPER, Jacob	1821	Louis
CLEVHOWEN, Nicoles	1801	Morrison
CLICK, David	1821	Brown
CLICK, Georg	1805	Guir
CLICK, George	1809	Green
CLICK, George	1810	Green
CLICK, George	1811	Green
CLICK, George	1812	Waddill
CLICK, George	1814	Waddell
CLICK, George	1819	Findley
CLICK, George	1821	McGee
CLICK, George Jr.	1817	Riley
CLICK, George Jr.	1818	Riley
CLICK, George L.	1819	Findley
CLICK, George S.	1821	McGee
CLICK, George Sr.	1817	Riley
CLICK, George Sr.	1818	Riley
CLICK, Henery	1808	McAllister
CLICK, Henery	1811	McAlister
CLICK, Henry	1805	Guir
CLICK, Henry	1812	Waddill
CLICK, Henry	1814	Hampton
CLICK, Henry	1817	Riley
CLICK, Henry	1818	Riley
CLICK, Henry	1819	Findley
CLICK, Henry	1821	McClure
CLICK, Lewis	1791	Milliken
CLICK, Lewis	1794	Milliken
CLICK, Lewis	1797	Hannah
CLICK, Lewis	1799	Hannah
CLICK, Lewis	1799	Moore
CLICK, Lewis	1801	Gann
CLICK, Luis	1799	Gann
CLICK, Malekia	1810	Green
CLICK, Malikia	1812	Waddill
CLICK, Malikia	1814	Waddell
CLICK, Melcher	1811	Green
CLICK, Nicholis	1817	Riley
CLICK, Peter	1790	Milleken
CLICK, Peter	1797	Hannah
CLICK, Peter	1799	Hannah
CLICK, Peter	1799	Moore
CLICK, Peter	1806	Brown
CLICK, Peter	1807	Bayles
CLICK, Peter	1808	Bayles
CLICK, Peter	1809	Bayles
CLICK, Peter	1814	Hampton
CLICK, Peter	1817	Hampton
CLICK, Peter	1818	Brown [2]
CLICK, Peter	1819	Brown
CLICK, Peter	1821	Brown
CLIFTON, Osten	1821	Sands
CLINE, Daniel	1798	Roberson
CLINGAN, Jno B.	1808	Parker
CLINGAN, Jno P.	1809	Parker
CLINGEN, John	1814	Hampton

Surname, Given names	Year	Comp./Dist.
CLIPER, John	1821	Howard
CLIPOR, Jacob	1821	Hunt
CLIPPER, Jacob	1819	Hair
CLIPPER, John	1819	Hair
CLOID, James	1808	Bayles
CLOID, Samuel	1814	Hampton
CLOPOR, Samuel	1821	Hunt
CLOUSE, Aaron	1806	Odel
CLOUSE, Aaron	1810	Cove
CLOUSE, Aaron	1811	Brown
CLOUSE, Aaron	1812	Brown
CLOUSE, Adam	1811	Brown
CLOUSE, Adam	1812	Brown
CLOUSE, Aron	1807	Odell
CLOUSE, Aron	1808	Odell
CLOUSE, Christian	1811	Brown
CLOUSE, Cristian	1810	Cove
CLOUSE, Elijah	1806	Odel
CLOUSE, Elijah	1807	Odell
CLOUSE, Elijah	1808	Odell
CLOUSE, Elizabeth	1812	Brown
CLOUSE, George	1806	Odel
CLOUSE, George	1810	Cove
CLOUSE, George Jr.	1798	Longmire
CLOUSE, George Jr.	1806	Odel
CLOUSE, George Jr.	1807	Odell
CLOUSE, George Jr.	1808	Odell
CLOUSE, George Sr.	1798	Longmire
CLOUSE, George Sr.	1807	Odell
CLOUSE, George Sr.	1808	Odell
CLOUSE, John	1806	Odel
CLOUSE, John	1808	Odell
CLOUSE, John	1811	Brown
CLOUSE, John	1812	Brown
CLOUSE, William	1806	Odel
CLOUSE, William	1808	Odell
CLOUSE, William	1810	Cove
CLOUSE, William	1811	Brown
CLOUSE, William	1812	Brown
CLOUSE, William	1815	Hartsell
CLOUSE, William	1816	Brown
CLOUSE, William	1817	Brown
CLOUSE, William	1818	Brown
CLOUSE, William	1821	Haines
CLOYD, James	1807	Bayles
CLOYD, James	1809	Bayles
CLOYD, James	1814	Hampton
CLOYD, James	1816	Hampton
CLOYD, James	1817	Hampton
CLOYD, James	1818	Brown [2]
CLOYD, James	1819	Brown
CLOYD, James	1821	Brown
CLOYD, Samuel	1816	Hampton
CLOYD, Samuel	1817	Hampton
CLOYD, Samuel	1818	Brown [2]
CLOYD, Samuel	1819	Brown
CLOYD, Samuel	1821	Brown
CLOYD, Wiliam	1795	Calvert
CLOYD, William	1792	Scott
CLOYD, William	1793	Scott
CLOYD, William	1816	Harrison
CLOYD, William	1817	Harris
CLOYD, William	1818	Harris
CLOYD, William	1819	Harris
CLOYD, William Jr.	1812	McCray
CLOYD, William Jr.	1812	McCray
CLOYD, William Jr.	1814	McCray
CLOYD, William Jr.	1815	Harris
CLOYD, William Jr.	1815	Harris
CLOYD, William Sr.	1812	McCray
CLOYD, William Sr.	1814	McCray
CLOYD, William Sr.	1815	Harris
CLOYD, Willm	1797	Calvert
CLOYD, Willm	1797	Calvert
CLOYD, Wm	1798	Calvert
CLOYDE, James B.	1805	Jas Parker
CLOYDE, Samuel	1805	Jas Parker
CLOYDE, William	1801	Calvert
CLOYDE, William	1805	Jas Parker
CLOYDE, William	1808	Parker
CLOYDE, William	1821	Hampton
CLOYDE, William Jr.	1811	McCray
CLOYDE, Wm	1809	Parker
CLOYDE, Wm Jr.	1809	Parker
CLOYER, Richard	1807	Odell
CLUN, William	1801	Taylor
CLUN, Wm	1799	Duncan
COACH, William	1817	Smith
COAL, Solomon	1778	
COARBY, Dannel	1796	Melvin
COBB, Arthur	1778	
COBB, Arthur	1779	
COBB, Been	1791	Tullis
COBB, Benjamin	1778	
COBB, Benjamin	1779	
COBB, Benjamin	1792	Tulley
COBB, Ethel	1795	Taylor
COBB, Pharaoh	1790	
COBB, Pharaoh	1794	Carriger
COBB, Pharo	1792	Greer
COBB, Pharoah	1791	
COBB, Pharoah	1792	Carriger

Surname, Given names	Year	Comp./Dist.
COBB, Pharoah	1795	Carriger
COBB, Pharoh	1778	
COBB, William	1790	
COBB, William	1792	
COBB, William	1793	Morrison
COBB, William	1794	Morrison
COBB, William	1798	Morrison
COBB, William (Capt.)	1792	Tulley
COBB, Wm	1778	
COBENGER, Hagins	1809	Cade
COBENGER, Jogan	1808	Cade
COCHRAN, George	1819	Hunt
COCHRAN, George	1821	Hunt
COCHRON, George	1817	Smith
COCHS, William	1801	Morrison
COCKE, William	1779	
COCKE, Wm	1778	
COCKS, Elijah	1798	Shipley
COCKS, Isaac	1821	McClure
COCKS, William	1806	Carr
COFFEE, Chealey	1790	White
COFFEE, Chesley	1791	White
COFFER, James	1819	Harris
COFMAN, John	1806	Brown
COFMON, John	1807	Bayles
COHEE, John	1797	Robertson
COHEE, John	1798	Roberson
COHOON, David	1814	Hoss
COILE, John	1816	Waddell
COILES, John	1815	Waddell
COILES, John	1817	Riley
COILES, John	1818	Riley
COL, Isral	1808	Odell
COLBOTH, Henry	1779	
COLBRETH, Alexdr	1781	
COLE, Israel	1801	Longmire
COLE, Israel	1806	Odel
COLE, Israel	1807	Odell
COLE, Jno Jr.	1809	Parker
COLE, John	1814	Hampton
COLE, John	1816	Harrison
COLE, John	1817	Harris
COLE, John	1818	Harris
COLE, John	1819	Brown
COLE, John Jr.	1811	McCray
COLE, Joseph	1814	Brown
COLE, Joseph	1815	Hartsell
COLE, Joseph	1816	Brown
COLESEN, James	1778	
COLESEN, Joseph	1778	
COLHOON, David	1813	Hoss
COLLAM, George	1794	Handly
COLLAM, George	1795	Handly
COLLAM, George	1796	Handly
COLLAM, Jonathan	1793	Handley
COLLAM, Jonathan	1796	Handly
COLLAM, Jonathan	1801	Gann
COLLAM, Jonathen	1794	Handly
COLLAM, Jonathen	1795	Handly
COLLENS, Charles	1821	Jones
COLLENS, Jonathan	1798	Gann
COLLENS, Joseph	1795	Morrison
COLLENS, Joseph	1798	Morrison
COLLENS, Joseph	1801	Morrison
COLLENS, Joseph	1812	Ellis
COLLENS, Joshua	1795	Morrison
COLLENS, Uriah	1809	Carr
COLLET,	1792	Brown
COLLET, Isaac	1792	Chisolm
COLLET, Isaac	1793	Brown
COLLETT, John	1821	Hunt
COLLETT, Richard	1778	
COLLIN, Jonathan	1815	Waddell
COLLIN, Joseph Sr.	1816	Hoss
COLLINGS, Joshua	1809	Right
COLLINS, Ambrose	1821	Hunt
COLLINS, Andrew	1819	Hunt
COLLINS, John	1815	McLin
COLLINS, John	1816	Hunt
COLLINS, John	1819	Hunt
COLLINS, John	1821	Brown
COLLINS, Jonathan	1816	Hoss
COLLINS, Jonathan	1817	Little
COLLINS, Joseph	1787	Griggs
COLLINS, Joseph	1792	Tulley
COLLINS, Joseph	1793	Morrison
COLLINS, Joseph	1794	Morrison
COLLINS, Joseph	1798	Morrison
COLLINS, Joseph	1799	Morrison
COLLINS, Joseph	1806	Carr
COLLINS, Joseph	1807	Carr
COLLINS, Joseph	1808	Carr
COLLINS, Joseph	1814	Hoss
COLLINS, Joseph	1815	Hoss
COLLINS, Joseph	[1796] 1797	Morris
COLLINS, Joseph Sr.	1817	Little
COLLINS, Joseph Sr.	1818	Jones
COLLINS, Joseph Sr.	1821	Jones
COLLINS, Joshua	1790	Shipley
COLLINS, Joshua	1791	Shipley
COLLINS, Joshua	1798	Morrison
COLLINS, Joshua	1815	Haire

Surname, Given names	Year	Comp./Dist.
COLLINS, Joshua	1816	Hair
COLLINS, Joshua	1817	Haire
COLLINS, Thomas	1821	Hunt
COLLINS, Uriah	1811	Mitchell
COLLINS, Uriah	1813	Hoss
COLLION, Jonathan	1817	Riley
COLLIT, James	1795	Ford
COLLOM, David	1811	Mitchell
COLLOM, George	1798	Gann
COLLOM, John	1815	Waddell
COLLOM, Jonathan	1791	Hanley
COLLOM, Jonathan	1806	Grur
COLLOM, Jonathan	1810	Green
COLLOM, Jonathan	1819	Findley
COLLOM, Jonathan	1821	McGee
COLLOM, William	1819	Harris
COLLOME, Jonathan	1808	Gwin
COLLOMS, Gorge	1799	Gann
COLLOMS, Jonathan	1799	Gann
COLLOMS, Jonathan	1799	Moore
COLLON, Cullen	1816	Grimsley
COLLON, Jonathan	1812	Waddill
COLLON, Jonathan	1816	Waddell
COLLON, Jonathan	1818	Riley
COLLON, William	1818	Riley
COLLONS, Joseph Sr.	1813	Hoss
COLLONS, Joseph Sr.	1819	Jones
COLLONS, Thomas	1819	Hunt
COLLUM, Johnathen	1809	Green
COLLUM, Jonithan	1805	Guir
COLLUM, Jonnathan	1795	Milliken
COLSON, Enoch	1807	Shields
COLSON, Enoch	1815	Carcathers
COLSON, Enoch	1816	Giles
COLSTAN, Enoch	1821	Sands
COLSTON, Enoc	1814	Couthers
COLSTON, Enoch	1806	Carson
COLSTON, Enoch	1809	Patterson
COLSTON, Enoch	1819	Sands
COLSTON, Enouch	1810	Dimmons
COLTON, Enoc	1811	
COLUM, William	1821	Hampton
COLVERT, Leonard	1816	Harrison
COLVERT, Leonard	1817	Harris
COLVERT, William	1817	Harris
COLYAR, (administrator of)	1821	Brown
COLYAR, Alexander	1814	Hampton
COLYAR, Alexander	1816	Hampton
COLYAR, Alexander	1818	Brown [2]
COLYAR, Alexander	1821	Brown
COLYAR, Leonard	1821	Brown
COLYAR, Steven	1797	Robertson
COLYAR, William	1798	Roberson
COLYAR, William	1801	Roberson
COLYAR, William	1818	Brown [2]
COLYAR, William	1818	Brown [2]
COLYAR, William	1821	Brown
COLYAR, William Jr.	1808	Bayles
COLYAR, William Jr.	1816	Hampton
COLYAR, William Sr.	1807	Bayles
COLYAR, William Sr.	1816	Hampton
COLYAR, Wm	1797	Robertson
COLYAR, Wm Jr.	1814	Hampton
COLYAR, Wm Jr.	1814	Hampton
COLYAR, Wm Sr.	1808	Bayles
COLYAR, Wm Sr.	1809	Bayles
COLYER, Alexander	1817	Hampton
COLYER, Alexander	1819	Brown
COLYER, Charles	1793	Hale
COLYER, Charles	1801	Longmire
COLYER, William	1792	Brown
COLYER, William	1799	Robertson
COLYER, William	1817	Hampton
COLYER, William	1819	Brown
COLYER, William	1819	Brown
COLYER, William Jr.	1806	Brown
COLYER, William Sr.	1806	Brown
COLYER, William Sr.	1817	Hampton
COLYER, Wm	1792	Chisolm
COLYER, Wm	1793	Brown
COLZON, Enoch	1817	Gillises
COMBS, Joseph	1781	
COMENS, Hugh	1798	Biddle
COMINS, Gilbrel	1798	Biddle
COMPTON, Jeremiah	1795	Young
COMPTON, Jerimiah	1797	Young
COMPTON, Jermia	1794	North
COMTON, John	1793	Morrison
COMTON, John	1794	Morrison
CONARD, Zackariah	1781	
CONATHERS, Jonathan	1792	Tulley
CONCH, George	1801	Glasscock
CONDREA, William	1793	Handley
CONDREN, William	1794	Handly
CONDREN, William	1795	Handly
CONDRUM, William	1792	Milliken
CONEHAM, John	1806	Payn
CONELEY, David	1793	Depew
CONINGHAM, John	1808	McAllister
CONINGHAM, Martha	1812	Crawford [2]
CONKEN, George	1805	Rector
CONKEN, John	1805	Rector

Surname, Given names	Year	Comp./Dist.
CONKIN, George	1812	Barnes
CONKIN, Gorge	1807	Cade
CONKIN, John	1801	Glasscock
CONKIN, John	1807	Cade
CONKIN, John	1811	Barron
CONKIN, John	1812	Barnes
CONKIN, Moses	1812	Barnes
CONKLIN, David	1791	Hanley
CONKLIN, David	1792	Brown
CONKLIN, David	1793	Brown
CONKLON, Enoch	1801	Biddle
CONLEY, David	1797	Duncan
CONLY, David	1798	Duncan
CONNANGHAM, Hugh	1798	Hannah
CONNANGHAM, John	1798	Hannah
CONNE, James	1795	Young
CONNEHAM, Martha	1812	Crawford
CONNER, Jacob	1814	Waddell
CONNER, John	1801	Glasscock
CONNER, Julius	1795	Taylor
CONNER, Lewis	1798	Shipley
CONNINGHAM, Samuel	1798	Hannah
CONNINHAM, William	1780-1781 (Undated)	
CONSTABLE, Jacob	1812	Brown
CONSTABLE, Jacob	1814	Brown
CONWAY, Phillip	1778	
COOK, James	1781	
COOK, Wandle	1814	McCray
COOK, William	1792	White
COOK, William	1793	Campbell
COOK, William	1794	Ford
COOK, William	1818	Smith
COOK, Wm	1795	Ford
COON, Catherine	1814	Hoss
COON, Catherine	1815	Hoss
COOPER, Abraham	1791	
COOPER, Abraham	1792	Maxwell
COOPER, Abraham	1793	Maxwell
COOPER, Abraham	1794	Taylor
COOPER, Edward	1793	Maxwell
COOPER, Edward	1794	Taylor
COOPER, James	1778	
COOPER, James	1794	Carriger
COOPER, James	1795	Carriger
COOPER, James	1797	Gann
COOPER, James	1799	Gann
COOPER, James	1801	Gann
COOPER, Job	1790	Williams
COOPER, Job	1791	Williams
COOPER, Job	1792	Maxwell
COOPER, Job	1793	Maxwell
COOPER, Jobe	1794	Taylor
COOPER, Joel	1790	Williams
COOPER, Joel	1791	Williams
COOPER, Joel	1795	Taylor
COOPER, Joel Jr.	1792	Maxwell
COOPER, Joel Jr.	1793	Maxwell
COOPER, Joel Jr.	1794	Taylor
COOPER, Joel Sr.	1790	Williams
COOPER, Joel Sr.	1791	Williams
COOPER, Joel Sr.	1792	Maxwell
COOPER, Joel Sr.	1793	Maxwell
COOPER, Joel Sr.	1794	Taylor
COOPER, John	1793	Maxwell
COOPER, John (Son of Widow Cooper)	1794	Taylor
COOPER, Joseph	1792	North
COOPER, Joseph	1793	North
COOPER, Joseph	1795	Young
COOPER, Joseph	1796	Longmire
COOPER, Joseph	1801	Taylor
COOPER, Joseph	1806	Parker
COOPER, Joseph	1809	Par
COOPER, Nathan	1793	Maxwell
COOPER, Nathan	1794	Taylor
COOPER, Patience	1778	
COOPER, Patience	1779	
COOPER, Patience	1793	Maxwell
COOPER, Patricia (Widow)	1792	Maxwell
COOPER, Robert	1793	Campbell
COOPER, Robert	1801	Gann
COOPER, Thomas	1809	Par
COOPER, Thomas	1815	Fines
COOPER, Thomas	1816	Fine
COOPER, Thomas	1817	Fine
COOPER, Thomas	1818	Fine
COOPER, Thomas	1821	Howard
COOPPER, Phillop	1780-1781 (Undated)	
COOS, Jacob	1819	Findley
COOS, Michael	1819	Findley
COP, Jacob	1811	Green
COP, Jacob	1814	Waddell
COP, Michael	1805	Guir
COP, Michael	1806	Grur
COP, Michael	1812	Waddill
COP, Michal	1811	Green
COP, Micheal	1809	Green
COP, Michial	1814	Waddell
COPAS, John	1816	Copas
COPAS, John	1818	Grisham
COPAS, John	1821	Hale
COPECK, Nicholas	1798	Morrison

Surname, Given names	Year	Comp./Dist.
COPEN, John	1801	Biddle
COPENGER, Smith	1816	Hampton
COPIAS, John	1817	Grisham
COPLE, Nicholas	1798	Morrison
COPP, Jacob	1817	Riley
COPP, Jacob	1818	Riley
COPP, Jacob	1821	McGee
COPP, John	1821	McGee
COPP, Michael	1815	Waddell
COPP, Michael	1818	Riley
COPP, Michael	1821	McGee
COPP, Nicholis	1817	Riley
COPPICK, Arron	1797	Calvert
COPPIK, Aaron	1797	Calvert
CORATHERS, Jonathen	1807	Carr
CORDAIN, James	1817	Hunt
CORETHERS, Jonathan	1798	Morrison
CORETHERS, Samuel	1805	Carson
CORITHER, Samuel	1810	Dimmons
CORNETT, John	1780-1781	District 7
COROTHERS, Saml	1809	Patterson
CORRAN, James	1819	Hunt
CORRAN, John	1819	Hunt
CORREL, William	1815	Hartsell
CORRELIUS, John	1818	Fine
CORSELIUS, John	1819	Brown
CORTHERS, Jonthen	1806	Carr
CORZON, Andrew	1817	Gillises
CORZON, Nancy	1817	Hunt
CORZON, Roland	1817	Hunt
COSC, Benjamin	1816	Hair
COSC, Benjamin	1818	Hair
COSC, George	1815	Grimsley
COSC, George	1816	Grimsley
COSC, James	1815	Copas
COSC, James	1816	Copas
COSC, James	1817	Grisham
COSC, John	1816	Hair
COSC, John	1818	Hair
COSC, William	1816	Giles
COSC, William	1817	Grisham
COSON, John G.	1814	McCracken
COSS, Jacob	1810	Green
COSS, Jacob	1816	Waddell
COSS, John	1818	Riley
COSS, Michael	1810	Green
COSSASS, John	1819	Grisham
COSSON, Isaac	1815	Carcathers
COSSON, Isaac	1817	Gillises
COSSON, Isaac	1818	Land
COSSON, Isaac N.	1816	Giles
COSSON, John	1815	Carcathers
COSSON, John E.	1816	Giles
COSSON, John E.	1818	Land
COSSON, John E. Jr.	1809	Patterson
COSSON, John Jr.	1807	Shields
COSSON, John Jr.	1811	
COSSON, John S.	1817	Gillises
COSSON, John Sr.	1807	Shields
COSSON, John Sr.	1811	
COSSON, Margaret	1815	Carcathers
COSSON, Margaret	1816	Giles
COSSON, Margaret	1817	Gillises
COTTEN, Cullen	1817	Harris
COTTON, Cullen	1815	Crookshanks
COTTON, Cullen	1818	Harris
COTTON, Cullen	1819	Harris
COU, John	1819	Findley
COUFF, Felty	1797	Young
COULEY, David	1798	Duncan
COUP, Jacob	1809	Green
COUTHERS, Saml	1814	Couthers
COVENGER, Hagan	1805	Rector
COVENGER, Hazan	1812	Barnes
COWAN, Elizabeth	1816	Hair
COWAN, Elizabeth	1819	Hair
COWAN, James	1821	Hunt
COWAN, John	1794	Depew
COWAN, John	1806	Crouch
COWAN, John	1809	Gwin
COWAN, John	1812	Ellis
COWAN, John	1814	McLin
COWAN, John	1817	Hunt
COWAN, John	1818	Hunt
COWAN, John	1821	Hunt
COWAN, John	1783 [after]	Depew
COWAN, John Jr.	1812	McLin
COWAN, John Jr.	1814	McLin
COWAN, John Jr.	1816	Hunt
COWAN, John Jr.	1817	Hunt
COWAN, John Sr.	1812	McLin
COWAN, John Sr.	1818	Hunt
COWAN, Nat	1791	Willey
COWAN, Nath L.	1795	Calvert
COWAN, Nathaniel	1796	Jonesboro
COWAN, Natheial	1792	Scott
COWAN, Samuel	1791	Willey
COWAN, Susana	1793	Handley
COWAN, Susanna	1790	Hanley
COWARD, James	1778	
COWARD, John	1778	
COWARD, Zachiah	1780-1781 (Undated)	

Surname, Given names	Year	Comp./Dist.
COWEN, Elizabeth	1817	Haire
COWEN, Elizabeth	1818	Hair
COWEN, Elizabeth	1821	Louis
COWEN, John	1793	Melvan
COWEN, John	1794	Melvan
COWEN, John	1795	Melvan
COWEN, John	1796	Melvin
COWEN, John	1798	Crouch
COWEN, John	1801	Norwood
COWEN, John	1806	Guin
COWEN, John	1809	Right
COWEN, John	1811	Davis
COWEN, John	1811	Ellis
COWEN, John Jr.	1815	McLin
COWEN, John Sr.	1815	McLin
COWEN, Susannah	1791	Hanley
COWER, William	1791	Chisom
COWIN, John	1790	Stone
COWIN, John	1791	Stone
COWIN, John	1797	Duncan
COWIN, John	1798	Duncan
COWIN, John	1798	Duncan
COWIN, John	1799	Duncan
COWLEY, Isaac	1812	Crawford [2]
COWON, John	1810	Dimmons
COWSON, Isaac	1811	Green
COX, Abraham	1778	
COX, Abraham	1790	Greer
COX, Abraham	1792	Tulley
COX, Abraham	1794	Taylor
COX, Abraham	1795	Taylor
COX, Benjamin	1811	Ellis
COX, Benjamin	1815	Haire
COX, Benjamin	1817	Haire
COX, Benjamin	1819	Hair
COX, Benjamin	1821	Louis
COX, Caleb	1819	Smith
COX, Charles	1821	Hale
COX, Elija	1797	Shipley
COX, Elijah	1793	Murray
COX, Elijah	1795	Murray
COX, Elijah	1796	Shipley
COX, Elijah	1801	Aiken
COX, Elijah	1805	Aikin
COX, Eliza	1806	Anderson
COX, Ephraim	1781	
COX, Ezekiel	1809	Right
COX, George	1809	Right
COX, George	1811	Ellis
COX, George	1812	Ellis
COX, Giles	1807	Britton
COX, Giles	1809	Right
COX, Isaac	1817	Little
COX, Isaac	1818	Jones
COX, Isaac	1819	Hair
COX, James	1790	Stone
COX, James	1791	Stone
COX, James	1793	Melvan
COX, James	1794	Melvan
COX, James	1795	Melvan
COX, James	1796	Melvin
COX, James	1798	Crouch
COX, James	1801	Norwood
COX, James	1806	Crouch
COX, James	1809	Right
COX, James	1818	Grisham
COX, James	1821	Hale
COX, James (Esq.)	1811	Ellis
COX, James Jr.	1809	Right
COX, James Jr.	1811	Ellis
COX, Jas (Decd, heirs of)	1812	Ellis
COX, John	1778	
COX, John	1779	
COX, John	1805	Aikin
COX, John	1806	Anderson
COX, John	1809	Green
COX, John	1809	McAlister
COX, John	1811	Ellis
COX, John	1812	Ellis
COX, John	1813	Copas
COX, John	1815	Haire
COX, John	1817	Haire
COX, John	1819	Hair
COX, John	1821	Hale
COX, John	1821	Louis
COX, Jorge	1814	Barns
COX, Maberry	1812	Barnes
COX, Mabry	1812	Ellis
COX, McBerry	1814	Barns
COX, Richard	1792	Carriger
COX, Richard	1792	Greer
COX, Richard	1794	Carriger
COX, Richard	1795	Carriger
COX, Richd	1790	Greer
COX, William	1778	
COX, William	1779	
COX, William	1807	Carr
COX, William	1808	Carr
COX, William	1814	Couthers
COX, William	1814	Hoss
COX, William	1815	Carcathers
COX, William	1815	Hoss

Surname, Given names	Year	Comp./Dist.
COX, William	1817	Gillises
COX, William	1817	Little
COX, William	1818	Grisham
COX, William	1818	Jones
COX, William	1819	Grisham
COX, William	1819	Jones
COX, William	1821	Hale
COX, William	1821	Jones
COX, Wm	1791	Milliken
COX, Wm	1811	Mitchell
COYLER, Charles	1792	Coye
COZIAH, Britton	1818	Harris
COZIAH, Buston	1819	Harris
COZIAH, William	1818	Harris
COZIAH, William	1819	Harris
COZIAH, William	1821	Hampton
CRABTRE, Barnet	1791	Tullis
CRABTREE, Barnat	1794	Melvan
CRABTREE, Barnat	1796	Melvin
CRABTREE, Barnat	1798	Crouch
CRABTREE, Barnet	1792	Tulley
CRABTREE, Barnet	1793	Melvan
CRABTREE, James	1801	Norwood
CRABTREE, James	1806	Crouch
CRABTREE, James	1809	Right
CRABTREE, James	1811	Ellis
CRABTREE, John	1790	Stone
CRABTREE, John	1791	Stone
CRABTREE, John	1793	Melvan
CRABTREE, John	1794	Melvan
CRABTREE, John	1795	Melvan
CRABTREE, John	1796	Melvin
CRABTREE, John	1801	Norwood
CRABTREE, William	1790	Stone
CRABTREE, William	1791	Stone
CRABTREE, William	1795	Melvan
CRABTREE, William	1798	Crouch
CRABTREE, William	1806	Brown
CRABTREE, William	1808	Bayles
CRABTREE, William	1809	Bayles
CRABTREE, Wm	1796	Melvin
CRADDICK, David	1778	
CRADIK, David	1780-1781 (Undated)	
CRAFFORD, Isack	1780-1781 (Undated)	
CRAFFORD, James	1814	Crookshanks
CRAFFORD, Moses	1780-1781 (Undated)	
CRAFFORD, William	1808	Cade
CRAFFORD, William	1818	Grimsley
CRAFFORD, Wm	1810	Dimmons
CRAFFORED, William	1808	Cade

Surname, Given names	Year	Comp./Dist.
CRAFORD, E. William	1821	Sands
CRAFORD, Isaac	1780-1781 (undated)	
CRAFORD, James	1811	McAlister
CRAFORD, James	1812	Crawford
CRAFORD, James	1812	Crawford [2]
CRAFORD, John	1798	Biddle
CRAFORD, M. John	1821	Sands
CRAGUNER, Patrick	1779	
CRAIG, Robert	1779	
CRAIG, Thomas	1794	Depew
CRAIG, Thomas	1783 [after]	Depew
CRASAN, Samuel	1794	Taylor
CRAUTHERS, John	1779	
CRAWFORD,	1814	Couthers
CRAWFORD, Ann	1815	Copas
CRAWFORD, Anne	1816	Copas
CRAWFORD, James	1778	
CRAWFORD, James	1813	Copas
CRAWFORD, James	1815	Crookshanks
CRAWFORD, James	1816	Crookshanks
CRAWFORD, James	1817	McClure
CRAWFORD, James	1818	McClure
CRAWFORD, James	1819	McClure
CRAWFORD, James	1821	McClure
CRAWFORD, John	1778	
CRAWFORD, John	1798	Biddle
CRAWFORD, John	1814	Couthers
CRAWFORD, John	1816	Giles
CRAWFORD, John	1817	Gillises
CRAWFORD, John	1819	Hair
CRAWFORD, John M.	1818	Land
CRAWFORD, John N.	1815	Carcathers
CRAWFORD, John W.	1819	Sands
CRAWFORD, Saml	1778	
CRAWFORD, Sam'l	1820	Smith
CRAWFORD, Sam'l	1821	Smith
CRAWFORD, Samuel	1801	Glasscock
CRAWFORD, Samuel	1816	Smith
CRAWFORD, Samuel	1817	Smith
CRAWFORD, Samuel	1819	Smith
CRAWFORD, Thomas	1795	Murray
CRAWFORD, Tom I.	1818	Smith
CRAWFORD, William	1805	Rector
CRAWFORD, William	1809	Cade
CRAWFORD, William	1812	Barnes
CRAWFORD, William	1816	Giles
CRAWFORD, William	1817	Gillises
CRAWFORD, William	1818	Land
CRAWFORD, William A.	1819	Sands
CRAWFORD, Wm	1811	
CRAWLY, Elijah	1780-1781	District 7

Surname, Given names	Year	Comp./Dist.
CRAWTHERS, John	1779	
CRECELIUS, John	1801	Taylor
CRECILES, John	1807	Parker
CREKLIAS, John	1817	Fine
CREKLIAS, John Jr.	1815	Fines
CREKLIAS, John Jr.	1816	Fine
CREKLIAS, John Sr.	1815	Fines
CREKLIAS, John Sr.	1816	Fine
CRENSLAS, Isac	1794	Scot
CRESELINS, Jacob	1805	Jas Parker
CRESELINS, John	1808	Parker
CRESELOUS, John	1801	Calvert
CRESELOUS, John	1814	Hartsell
CRESELOUS, John	1821	Brown
CRESELUS, Isaac	1797	Calvert
CRESELYS, Isaac	1796	Longmire
CRESILEAS, John	1797	Young
CRESILEAS, John	1806	Brown
CRESILES, John	1805	Parker
CRESILES, John Jr.	1812	Hartsell
CRESILES, John Sr.	1812	Hartsell
CRESILLIS, John	1796	Young
CRESOLIOUS, John Jr.	1814	Hartsell
CRESON, John	1793	Morrison
CRESON, John	1794	Morrison
CRESON, John	1795	Morrison
CRESSELIS, Isaac	1793	Scott
CRESSEN, Thomas	1810	Hartzel
CRESSLINS, Jacob	1808	Parker
CRESSOR, Thomas	1819	Howard
CRETCELUS, John	1807	Bayles
CRETCELUS, John	1814	Hampton
CREZELOUS, Jacob	1809	Bayles
CREZELOUS, John	1809	Bayles
CRISELEAS, Isaac	1795	Calvert
CRISELEAS, John	1795	Calvert
CRISTY, Isreal	1799	Duncan
CRITNILIAS, John	1816	Hampton
CRITULUS, John	1808	Bayles
CRLEN, Joseph	1812	Crawford
CRLEN, William	1812	Crawford
CRO--, George	1821	Hale
CROCH, Joseph	1794	Melvan
CROFFARD, John	1801	Biddle
CROFFORD, James	1814	Copes
CROOKSHANK, George	1819	McClure
CROOKSHANK, William	1819	McClure
CROOKSHANK, William	1821	McClure
CROOKSHANKES, George	1795	Milliken
CROOKSHANKS, George	1790	Milleken
CROOKSHANKS, George	1791	Milliken

Surname, Given names	Year	Comp./Dist.
CROOKSHANKS, George	1792	Milliken
CROOKSHANKS, George	1793	Milliken
CROOKSHANKS, George	1794	Milliken
CROOKSHANKS, George	1797	Hannah
CROOKSHANKS, George	1798	Hannah
CROOKSHANKS, George	1799	Hannah
CROOKSHANKS, George	1801	Squibb
CROOKSHANKS, George	1805	Stephenson
CROOKSHANKS, George	1806	Payn
CROOKSHANKS, George	1807	Payne
CROOKSHANKS, George	1808	McAllister
CROOKSHANKS, George	1809	McAlister
CROOKSHANKS, George	1811	McAlister
CROOKSHANKS, George	1812	Crawford [2]
CROOKSHANKS, George	1814	Crookshanks
CROOKSHANKS, George	1815	Crookshanks
CROOKSHANKS, George	1818	McClure
CROOKSHANKS, Grow	1816	Crookshanks
CROOKSHANKS, Robert	1812	Crawford [2]
CROOKSHANKS, Robt	1814	Crookshanks
CROOKSHANKS, William	1806	Payn
CROOKSHANKS, William	1807	Payne
CROOKSHANKS, William	1808	McAllister
CROOKSHANKS, William	1811	McAlister
CROOKSHANKS, William	1812	Crawford [2]
CROOKSHANKS, William	1815	Crookshanks
CROOKSHANKS, William	1816	Crookshanks
CROOKSHANKS, William	1817	McClure
CROOKSHANKS, William	1818	McClure
CROOKSHANKS, Willm	1809	McAlister
CROOKSHANKS, Wm	1814	Crookshanks
CROSS, Benjamin	1779	
CROSS, Henry	1778	
CROSWHITE, Abraham	1795	Thornton
CROUCE, Michael	1818	Hair
CROUCH, Elijah	1795	Murray
CROUCH, Elijah	1796	Melvin
CROUCH, Elijah	1798	Crouch
CROUCH, Elijah	1801	Lane
CROUCH, Elijah	1812	Ellis
CROUCH, Elijah	1815	Copas
CROUCH, Elijah	1816	Copas
CROUCH, Elijah	1817	Grisham
CROUCH, Elijah	1818	Grisham
CROUCH, Elijah	1819	Grisham
CROUCH, Elijah	1821	Hale
CROUCH, George	1806	Crouch
CROUCH, George	1809	Right
CROUCH, George	1815	Haire
CROUCH, George	1816	Hair
CROUCH, George	1817	Haire

Surname, Given names	Year	Comp./Dist.
CROUCH, George	1818	Hair
CROUCH, George	1819	Grisham
CROUCH, George	1819	Hair
CROUCH, George	1821	Louis
CROUCH, Henry	1807	Shields
CROUCH, James	1793	Morrison
CROUCH, James	1794	Morrison
CROUCH, James	1795	Taylor
CROUCH, James	1799	Morrison
CROUCH, James	1819	Brown
CROUCH, James (Son of David)	1793	Melvan
CROUCH, Jeams	1798	Morrison
CROUCH, Jess	1814	Bean
CROUCH, Jesse	1798	Crouch
CROUCH, Jesse	1801	Norwood
CROUCH, Jesse	1806	Crouch
CROUCH, Jesse	1809	Right
CROUCH, Jesse	1812	Ellis
CROUCH, Jesse	1815	Haire
CROUCH, Jesse	1816	Hair
CROUCH, Jesse	1817	Haire
CROUCH, Jesse	1818	Hair
CROUCH, Jesse	1819	Hair
CROUCH, Jessee	1811	Ellis
CROUCH, Jessie	1821	Louis
CROUCH, John	1794	Taylor
CROUCH, John	1798	Crouch
CROUCH, John	1801	Norwood
CROUCH, John	1809	Right
CROUCH, John	1814	Bean
CROUCH, John	1815	Haire
CROUCH, John	1816	Hair
CROUCH, John	1817	Haire
CROUCH, John	1818	Hair
CROUCH, John	1819	Hair
CROUCH, John	1821	Louis
CROUCH, John Jr.	1795	Murray
CROUCH, John Jr.	1797	Shipley
CROUCH, John Jr.	1806	Crouch
CROUCH, John Jr.	1811	Ellis
CROUCH, John Sr.	1790	Shipley
CROUCH, John Sr.	1791	Shipley
CROUCH, John Sr.	1793	Murray
CROUCH, John Sr.	1794	Murray
CROUCH, John Sr.	1795	Murray
CROUCH, John Sr.	1796	Shipley
CROUCH, John Sr.	1797	Shipley
CROUCH, John Sr.	1806	Crouch
CROUCH, John Sr.	1812	Ellis
CROUCH, Joseph	1790	Stone
CROUCH, Joseph	1791	Stone
CROUCH, Joseph	1793	Melvan
CROUCH, Joseph	1796	Melvin
CROUCH, Joseph	1806	Crouch
CROUCH, Joseph	1809	Right
CROUCH, Joseph	1812	Ellis
CROUCH, Joseph	1814	Bean
CROUCH, Joseph	1814	Hampton
CROUCH, Joseph	1815	Haire
CROUCH, Joseph	1816	Hair
CROUCH, Joseph	1816	Hampton
CROUCH, Joseph	1817	Grisham
CROUCH, Joseph	1817	Haire
CROUCH, Joseph	1817	Hampton
CROUCH, Joseph	1818	Brown [2]
CROUCH, Joseph	1818	Grisham
CROUCH, Joseph	1818	Hair
CROUCH, Joseph	1819	Brown
CROUCH, Joseph	1819	Grisham
CROUCH, Joseph	1819	Hair
CROUCH, Joseph	1821	Brown
CROUCH, Joseph	1821	Hale
CROUCH, Joseph	1821	Louis
CROUCH, Joseph (of Jesse)	1817	Grisham
CROUCH, Joseph (of John)	1819	Grisham
CROUCH, Joseph (of Sr.)	1818	Grisham
CROUCH, Joseph Jr.	1809	Right
CROUCH, Joseph Jr.	1812	Ellis
CROUCH, Joseph Jr.	1812	Ellis
CROUCH, Joseph Jr.	1814	Bean
CROUCH, Joseph Jr.	1815	Copas
CROUCH, Joseph Jr.	1816	Copas
CROUCH, Joseph Sr.	1811	Ellis
CROUCH, Michael	1819	Hair
CROUCH, William	1809	Right
CROUCH, William	1815	Haire
CROUCH, William	1816	Hair
CROUCH, William	1817	Haire
CROUCH, William	1817	Haire
CROUCH, William	1818	Hair
CROUCH, William	1819	Hair
CROUCH, William	1819	Hair
CROUCH, Wm (of Jessie)	1821	Louis
CROUCH, Wm (of Joseph)	1821	Louis
CROUSE, George	1796	Longmire
CROUSE, Michael	1806	Crouch
CROUSE, Michael	1815	Haire
CROUSE, Michael	1816	Hair
CROUSE, Michael	1817	Haire
CROUSE, Michael	1821	Louis
CROUSE, Michel	1807	Britton
CROUSE, Michel	1811	Ellis

Surname, Given names	Year	Comp./Dist.
CROUSE, Michel	1814	Bean
CROUSON, Samuel	1793	Maxwell
CROW, George	1816	Copas
CROW, George	1818	Grisham
CROW, John	1781	
CROW, John	1805	Carson
CROW, John	1780-1781 (Undated)	
CROW, Michael	1809	Right
CROWE, John	1806	Carson
CROWFORD, Wm	1801	Glasscock
CROWN, George	1817	Grisham
CRSUCH, John Jr.	1794	Murray
CRUATHERS, Jonithan	1813	Hoss
CRUMLEY, David	1810	Green
CRUMP, Adam	1780-1781 (undated)	
CRUSEN, Jacob	1792	Tulley
CRUSHON, John	[1796] 1797	Morris
CRUSOE, John	1816	Hampton
CRUSOE, John	1819	Brown
CRUSS, John	1821	Brown
CUBERSAN, Samuel	1793	Hale
CULBERSON, Joseph	1778	
CULBERSON, Joseph	1792	Coye
CULBERSON, Saml.	1792	Coye
CULBERSON, Samuel	1778	
CULBERSON, Samuel	1779	
CULBERTSON, Joseph	1801	Longmire
CULBERTSON, Joseph	1801	Longmire
CULBERTSON, Saml. (Estate Of)	1801	Longmire
CULBERTSON, Samuel	1797	Longmire
CULBUTH, Donnal	1795	Thornton
CULLAM, George	1801	Gann
CULVERSON, Joseph	1798	Longmire
CULVERSON, Saml	1798	Longmire
CUMINGHAM, Hugh	1797	Hannah
CUMINGS, Hugh	1807	Shields
CUMINGS, Hugh	1811	
CUMINGS, Hugh	1814	Couthers
CUMINGS, Hugh Jr.	1806	Carson
CUMINS, Gibriell	1797	Biddle
CUMINS, Hugh Jr.	1801	Biddle
CUMINS, Hugh Sr.	1801	Biddle
CUMMINS, Gabarel	1798	Biddle
CUMMINS, John	1812	McLin
CUMMINS, John	1816	Hampton
CUMMINS, Joseph (Dunkard)	1781	
CUMMONS, Hugh	1805	Carson
CUMMONS, Hugh Sr.	1805	Carson
CUMMONSE, Hugh	1810	Dimmons
CUMPTON, Jerimiah	1796	Young

Surname, Given names	Year	Comp./Dist.
CUMTON, John	1795	Morrison
CUNINGHAM, James	1811	Davis
CUNINGHAM, John	1807	Givins
CUNINGHAM, John	1809	McAlister
CUNINGHAM, John Jr.	1797	Hannah
CUNINGHAM, John Jr.	1805	Stephenson
CUNINGHAM, Martha	1814	Crookshanks
CUNINGHAME, Christopher	1779	
CUNNINGHAM, Chris Jr.	1778	
CUNNINGHAM, Christopher	1778	
CUNNINGHAM, Christopher Sr.	1779	
CUNNINGHAM, E. Jno.	1807	Payne
CUNNINGHAM, Hugh	1792	Milliken
CUNNINGHAM, Hugh	1794	Milliken
CUNNINGHAM, Hugh	1795	Milliken
CUNNINGHAM, Hugh	1796	Millikin
CUNNINGHAM, Hugh	1799	Hannah
CUNNINGHAM, Hugh	1801	Squibb
CUNNINGHAM, Hugh	1815	Carcathers
CUNNINGHAM, James	1798	Duncan
CUNNINGHAM, James	1801	Taylor
CUNNINGHAM, James	1807	Givins
CUNNINGHAM, James	1812	McLin
CUNNINGHAM, James	1816	Hunt
CUNNINGHAM, James	1817	Hunt
CUNNINGHAM, James	1818	Hunt
CUNNINGHAM, James	1819	Hunt
CUNNINGHAM, James	1821	Hunt
CUNNINGHAM, James Jr.	1815	McLin
CUNNINGHAM, James Sr.	1815	McLin
CUNNINGHAM, Jno Jr.	1799	Hannah
CUNNINGHAM, John	1792	Milliken
CUNNINGHAM, John	1794	Milliken
CUNNINGHAM, John	1795	Milliken
CUNNINGHAM, John	1796	Millikin
CUNNINGHAM, John	1801	Squibb
CUNNINGHAM, John	1811	McAlister
CUNNINGHAM, John Sr.	1793	Milliken
CUNNINGHAM, Martha	1815	Crookshanks
CUNNINGHAM, Martha	1816	Crookshanks
CUNNINGHAM, Martha	1817	McClure
CUNNINGHAM, Martha	1818	McClure
CUNNINGHAM, Martha	1819	McClure
CUNNINGHAM, Martha	1821	McClure
CUNNINGHAM, Mary	1790	Williams
CUNNINGHAM, Mary	1791	Williams
CUNNINGHAM, Mary	1793	Maxwell
CUNNINGHAM, Mary	1795	Taylor
CUNNINGHAM, Mary (Widow)	1792	Maxwell
CUNNINGHAM, Samuel	1797	Hannah
CUNNINGHAM, Samuel	1801	Squibb

Surname, Given names	Year	Comp./Dist.
CUNNINGHAM, Wm	1781	
CUNTON, Jeremiah	1793	North
CUP, Jacob	1809	Patterson
CUPER, Joseph	1805	Parker
CUPER, Joseph	1807	Parker
CUPER, Joseph	1808	Parker
CUPER, Thomas	1812	Hartsell
CUPER, Thomas	1814	Hartsell
CUREY, Joseph	1816	Copas
CURSEALES, John	1806	Parker
CURSEALUS, John	1799	Stuart
CURTIS, David	1778	
CURTIS, Joshua	1778	
CURTS, John	1801	Taylor
CUTBARTH, Benjn Sr.	1795	Thornton
CUTBERTH, Daniel	1794	Thornton
CUTBERTSON, Joseph	1796	Longmire
CUTBERTSON, Samuel	1796	Longmire
CUTHBSON, Joseph	1797	Longmire
DALE, James	1780-1781 (Undated)	
DALY, William	1810	Barron
DANBAKER, Thomas	1818	Grimsley
DANEL, Duke	1810	Barron
DANEL, John	1806	Carr
DANEL, Mameduke	1821	Martin
DANEL, Maremaduke	1807	Cade
DANEL, Marmaduke	1808	Cade
DANEL, Richard	1807	Cade
DANEL, Richard	1808	Cade
DANEL, Richard	1814	Barns
DANEL, Richard	1821	Martin
DANELY, Hezekiah	1814	Couthers
DANIALL, Wm	1791	Tullis
Daniel	1821	Howard
DANIEL, Duke	1809	Cade
DANIEL, John	1798	Morrison
DANIEL, John	1799	Morrison
DANIEL, John	1815	Grimsley
DANIEL, John	1818	Grimsley
DANIEL, Marmaduke	1805	Rector
DANIEL, Marmaduke	1819	Grimsley
DANIEL, Marmeduke	1811	Barron
DANIEL, Richard	1801	Glasscock
DANIEL, Richard	1805	Rector
DANIEL, Richard	1809	Cade
DANIEL, Richard	1810	Barron
DANIEL, Richard	1811	Barron
DANIEL, Richard	1815	Grimsley
DANIEL, Richard	1817	Grimsley
DANIEL, Richard	1818	Grimsley
DANIEL, Richard	1819	Grimsley

Surname, Given names	Year	Comp./Dist.
DANIEL, William	1792	Tulley
DANIEL, William	1798	Morrison
DANIEL, William	1799	Morrison
DANIEL, William	[1796] 1797	Morris
DANIEL, Wm	1792	Maxwell
DANIELS, Anne	1801	Morrison
DANIELS, Duke	1812	Barnes
DANIELS, John	1795	Morrison
DANIELS, Richard	1812	Barnes
DANIELS, William	1795	Morrison
DANIL, John	1798	Morrison
DANIL, John	1798	Morrison
DANNEL, John	1793	Morrison
DANNEL, John	1794	Morrison
DANNEL, William	1787	Fains
DANNEL, William	1793	Morrison
DANNEL, William	1794	Morrison
DANNIEL, Marmarde	1818	Grimsley
DANTON, Jonathon	1794	Milliken
DARNEL, Henry	1807	Givins
DARY, Michael	1792	Greer
DAUGETY, George	1779	Wilson
DAVALT, Folde	1809	Carr
DAVALT, Frederick	1811	Mitchell
DAVALT, Valentine	1811	Mitchell
DAVALT, Valintine	1813	Hoss
DAVE, Denton	1819	Grimsley
DAVE, John	1819	Grimsley
DAVENPORT, Harmon	1780-1781	District 7
DAVES, Jacob	1808	Gwin
DAVICE, George	1798	Biddle
DAVICE, Jacob	1810	Green
DAVICE, John	1821	Sands
DAVICE, Nathan	1794	Taylor
DAVICE, Samuel	1798	Biddle
DAVICE, Thomas	1793	Morrison
DAVICE, Thomas	1794	Morrison
DAVICE, William	1794	Taylor
David	1795	Morrison
DAVID, John	1815	Carcathers
DAVIDSON, Egnew	1816	Smith
DAVIES, James	1779	Wilson
DAVIS,	1807	Givins
DAVIS, Charles	1815	Fines
DAVIS, Charles	1816	Fine
DAVIS, Charles	1817	Fine
DAVIS, Charles	1818	Fine
DAVIS, Charles	1819	Howard
DAVIS, Charles Jr.	1814	Hartsell
DAVIS, Charles Jr.	1821	Howard
DAVIS, Charles Sr.	1814	Hartsell

Surname, Given names	Year	Comp./Dist.
DAVIS, Daniel	1817	Fine
DAVIS, Daniel	1818	Fine
DAVIS, Daniel	1821	Brown
DAVIS, George	1790	Biddle
DAVIS, George	1791	Biddle
DAVIS, George	1792	Biddle
DAVIS, George	1794	Blair
DAVIS, George	1797	Biddle
DAVIS, George	1801	Biddle
DAVIS, George	1805	Carson
DAVIS, George	1806	Carson
DAVIS, George	1807	Shields
DAVIS, George	1810	Dimmons
DAVIS, Gorg	1798	Biddle
DAVIS, Gorge	1798	Morrison
DAVIS, Isaac	1781	
DAVIS, Isaac	1780-1781 (Undated)	
DAVIS, Jacob	1806	Brown
DAVIS, Jacob	1811	Green
DAVIS, James	1781	
DAVIS, James	1794	Ford
DAVIS, James	1795	Ford
DAVIS, James	1812	McLin
DAVIS, James	1814	McLin
DAVIS, James	1815	Haire
DAVIS, James	1815	McLin
DAVIS, James	1816	Hunt
DAVIS, James	1817	Hunt
DAVIS, James	1818	Hunt
DAVIS, James	1819	Hunt
DAVIS, John	1778	
DAVIS, John	1796	Jonesboro
DAVIS, John	1797	Calvert
DAVIS, John	1801	Taylor
DAVIS, John	1806	Crouch
DAVIS, John	1809	Gwin
DAVIS, John	1809	Gwin
DAVIS, John	1811	Davis
DAVIS, John	1812	Hartsell
DAVIS, John	1814	Couthers
DAVIS, John	1815	Fines
DAVIS, John	1816	Giles
DAVIS, John	1817	Gillises
DAVIS, John	1818	Land
DAVIS, John	1819	Sands
DAVIS, John (for P. Young)	1816	Fine
DAVIS, John (for Polly Young)	1819	Howard
DAVIS, John (for Polly, Young)	1817	Fine
DAVIS, John (Single)	1779	Wilson
DAVIS, John E.	1808	Guin
DAVIS, John P. Jr.	1818	Fine

Surname, Given names	Year	Comp./Dist.
DAVIS, Joseph	1780-1781 (Undated)	
DAVIS, Micajah	1818	Brown
DAVIS, Micajah	1821	Haines
DAVIS, Micasah	1819	Brown
DAVIS, Mijah	1817	Brown
DAVIS, Nathan	1778	
DAVIS, Nathan	1792	Maxwell
DAVIS, Nathan	1793	Maxwell
DAVIS, Nathan	1795	Taylor
DAVIS, Nathan	1780-1781 (Undated)	
DAVIS, Nathanael	1798	Duncan
DAVIS, Nathanel Sr.	1797	Duncan
DAVIS, Nathaniel	1796	Jonesboro
DAVIS, Nathaniel	1797	Calvert
DAVIS, Nathaniel	1798	Duncan
DAVIS, Nathaniel	1799	Duncan
DAVIS, Nathaniel	1801	Taylor
DAVIS, Nathaniel	1807	Givins
DAVIS, Nathaniel	1808	Guin
DAVIS, Nathaniel	1809	Gwin
DAVIS, Nathaniel	1811	Davis
DAVIS, Nathaniel	1812	McLin
DAVIS, Nathaniel	1814	McLin
DAVIS, Nathaniel	1815	Haire
DAVIS, Nathaniel	1815	McLin
DAVIS, Nathaniel	1816	Hunt
DAVIS, Nathaniel	1817	Hunt
DAVIS, Nathaniel	1818	Hunt
DAVIS, Nathaniel	1819	Hunt
DAVIS, Nathaniel	1780-1781 (Undated)	
DAVIS, Nathaniel	1780-1781 (Undated)	
DAVIS, Nathaniel Jr.	1799	Stuart
DAVIS, Natheniel	1806	Guin
DAVIS, Nathl. Jr.	1798	Calvert
DAVIS, Robert	1781	
DAVIS, Saml	1797	Biddle
DAVIS, Saml	1806	Carson
DAVIS, Saml	1809	Patterson
DAVIS, Samuel	1779	
DAVIS, Samuel	1794	Blair
DAVIS, Samuel	1798	Biddle
DAVIS, Samuel	1801	Biddle
DAVIS, Samuel	1805	Carson
DAVIS, Samuel	1807	Shields
DAVIS, Samuel	1810	Dimmons
DAVIS, Samuel	1811	
DAVIS, Samuel G.	1806	Carson
DAVIS, Samuel G.	1809	Patterson
DAVIS, Thomas	1795	Morrison

Surname, Given names	Year	Comp./Dist.
DAVIS, Thomas	1814	Hartsell
DAVIS, Thomas	1815	Fines
DAVIS, Thomas	1816	Fine
DAVIS, Thomas	1817	Fine
DAVIS, Thomas	1818	Fine
DAVIS, Thomas	1819	Howard
DAVIS, Thomas	1821	Howard
DAVIS, William	1779	
DAVIS, William	1790	Williams
DAVIS, William	1791	Williams
DAVIS, William	1792	Maxwell
DAVIS, William	1793	Maxwell
DAVIS, William	1795	Taylor
DAVISON, Joseph	1778	
DAWALD, Vollintine	1808	Carr
DAWOLD, Falty	1807	Carr
DAWOLD, Fraderick	1808	Carr
DAWOLD, Fradric	1807	Carr
DAWOLD, Fradrick	1806	Carr
DAWOLD, Vallentine	1806	Carr
DEACKIN, Richard	1809	Viney
DEACKINS, John	1809	Viney
DEACKINS, John	1814	Brown
DEACONS, James	1798	Longmire
DEACONS, John	1798	Longmire
DEACONS, Richard	1798	Longmire
DEADERICK, Dav'd A.	1821	Smith
DEADERICK, David	1781	
DEADERICK, David	1792	Scott
DEADERICK, David	1805	Aikin
DEADERICK, David	1815	Garner
DEADERICK, David	1816	Smith
DEADERICK, David	1817	Smith
DEADERICK, David	1818	Smith
DEADERICK, David	1820	Smith
DEADERICK, David	1821	Smith
DEADERICK, David (& Co)	1805	Guir
DEADERICK, David A.	1818	Smith
DEADERICK, David A.	1820	Smith
DEADERICK, David Jr.	1819	Smith
DEADERICK, David Sr.	1819	Smith
DEADERICK, William	1815	Garner
DEADRICK, David	1796	Jonesboro
DEADRICK, David	1797	Calvert
DEADRICK, David	1798	Calvert
DEADRICK, David	1799	Stuart
DEADRICK, David	1801	Aiken
DEADRICK, David	1809	Roadmas
DEADRICK, David	1811	Rodman
DEADRICK, David	1814	McCracken
DEAHEART, Elisha	1796	Young

Surname, Given names	Year	Comp./Dist.
DEAKEN, James	1814	Bean
DEAKENCE, Absolum	1808	Odell
DEAKENS, Absolom	1806	Odel
DEAKENS, James	1811	Ellis
DEAKENS, James	1812	Ellis
DEAKENS, John	1806	Odel
DEAKENS, John	1812	Brown
DEAKENS, Richard	1806	Odel
DEAKENS, Richard	1808	Odell
DEAKIN, John	1819	Brown
DEAKINS, Absolem	1811	Brown
DEAKINS, Absolom	1809	Viney
DEAKINS, Absolom	1810	Cove
DEAKINS, Charles	1821	Hunt
DEAKINS, Daniel	1816	Hair
DEAKINS, Daniel	1817	Haire
DEAKINS, Daniel	1818	Hair
DEAKINS, Daniel	1819	Hair
DEAKINS, Daniel	1821	Louis
DEAKINS, Evan	1791	Chisom
DEAKINS, Henry	1815	Haire
DEAKINS, Henry	1816	Hair
DEAKINS, Henry	1817	Haire
DEAKINS, Henry	1818	Hair
DEAKINS, Henry	1819	Hair
DEAKINS, Henry	1821	Louis
DEAKINS, James	1796	Longmire
DEAKINS, James	1797	Longmire
DEAKINS, James	1801	Longmire
DEAKINS, James	1806	Crouch
DEAKINS, James	1807	
DEAKINS, James	1809	Right
DEAKINS, James	1815	Haire
DEAKINS, James	1817	Hunt
DEAKINS, James	1819	Hunt
DEAKINS, James	1821	Hunt
DEAKINS, John	1796	Longmire
DEAKINS, John	1797	Longmire
DEAKINS, John	1801	Longmire
DEAKINS, John	1808	Odell
DEAKINS, John	1810	Cove
DEAKINS, John	1811	Brown
DEAKINS, John	1815	Hartsell
DEAKINS, John	1816	Brown
DEAKINS, John	1817	Brown
DEAKINS, John	1818	Brown
DEAKINS, John	1821	Haines
DEAKINS, Richard	1797	Longmire
DEAKINS, Richard	1801	Longmire
DEAKINS, Richard	1810	Cove
DEAKINS, Richard	1818	Brown

Surname, Given names	Year	Comp./Dist.
DEAKINS, Richard	1821	Haines
DEAKINS, Rickard	1819	Brown
DEAKINS, Thomas	1817	Haire
DEAL, James	1780-1781 (Undated)	
DEAL, Martha	1781	
DEAL, William	1781	
DEALL, James	1781	
DEAN, John	1817	Gillises
DEARHAM, Phillip	1801	Morrison
DEARICK, William	1811	Rodman
DEBALEM, Arter	1796	Brown
DEBART, Elisha	1805	Stephenson
DEBENPORT, Absolum	1821	Brown
DEDRICK, David	1791	Willey
DEDRICK, David	1795	Calvert
DEDRICK, David	1797	Calvert
DEDRICK, David	1807	Anderson
DEHART,	1809	Right
DEKINS, Jas.	1795	Calvert
DELANEY, France	1780-1781 (undated)	
DELANEY, James	1806	Parker
DELANEY, James	1807	Parker
DELANEY, James	1815	Fines
DELANEY, James	1816	Fine
DELANEY, James	1817	Fine
DELANEY, James	1819	Howard
DELANEY, James	1780-1781 (Undated)	
DELANEY, Jas.	1801	Taylor
DELANEY, William	1819	Howard
DELANY, Francis	1781	
DELANY, James	1812	Hartsell
DELANY, James	1814	Hartsell
DELANY, Jas	1809	Par
DELANY, John	1781	
DELANY, William	1812	Hartsell
DELANY, William	1814	Hartsell
DELASMUS, Moses	1780-1781	District 7
DELASTMENT, John	1815	Hartsell
DELFORD, Andrew	1807	Anderson
DELONEY, James	1821	Howard
DELONEY, William	1821	Howard
DELONG, James	1779	Wilson
DEMOTT, Robert	1790	Shipley
DEMOTT, Robert	1791	Shipley
DEMPSON, Robert	1801	Taylor
DENGINS, Jeremiah	1801	Morrison
DENHAM, Charles	1795	Murray
DENHAM, Charles	1796	Shipley
DENHAM, Charles	1797	Shipley
DENHAM, Charles	1805	Rector
DENHAM, Charles	1816	Grimsley
DENHAM, David	1795	Melvan
DENHAM, David	1796	Shipley
DENHAM, David	1797	Shipley
DENHAM, David	1801	Norwood
DENHAM, David	1806	Crouch
DENHAM, David	1809	Right
DENHAM, John	1806	Doke
DENHAM, William	1809	Right
DENHAM, William	1811	Ellis
DENLEY, Hezekiah	1817	Gillises
DENNY, Samuel	1778	
DENTEN, Jonathan	1795	Milliken
DENTEN, Joseph	1795	Morrison
DENTEN, Samuel	1795	Morrison
DENTIN, Jonathan	1791	Milliken
DENTON, Danel	1821	Martin
DENTON, Daniel	1818	Grimsley
DENTON, Isaac	1790	Williams
DENTON, Isaac	1791	Williams
DENTON, Isaac	1792	Maxwell
DENTON, Isaac	1793	Maxwell
DENTON, Isaac	1794	Taylor
DENTON, Isaac	1795	Morrison
DENTON, Isaac	[1796] 1797	Morris
DENTON, Isaac Jr.	1792	Maxwell
DENTON, Isaac Jr.	1793	Maxwell
DENTON, Isaac Jr.	1793	Morrison
DENTON, Isaac Jr.	1794	Morrison
DENTON, Isaac Sr.	1793	Morrison
DENTON, Isaac Sr.	1794	Morrison
DENTON, Isac	1805	Doak
DENTON, Iseec	1798	Morrison
DENTON, James	1778	
DENTON, James	1779	
DENTON, James	1798	Morrison
DENTON, James	1798	Morrison
DENTON, James	1801	Morrison
DENTON, James	1809	Par
DENTON, James	1810	Hartzel
DENTON, James	1819	Howard
DENTON, James	[1796] 1797	Morris
DENTON, Jas	1792	Maxwell
DENTON, Jeremiah	1795	Morrison
DENTON, Jeremiah	1798	Morrison
DENTON, Jeremiah	[1796] 1797	Morris
DENTON, Jerry	1793	Morrison
DENTON, Jerry	1794	Morrison
DENTON, Johanan	1793	Milliken
DENTON, John	1781	
DENTON, John	1811	Mitchell

Surname, Given names	Year	Comp./Dist.
DENTON, John	1812	Hartsell
DENTON, Jonas	1806	Parker
DENTON, Jonas	1807	Parker
DENTON, Jonas	1815	Fines
DENTON, Jonas	1816	Fine
DENTON, Jonas	1817	Fine
DENTON, Jonas	1818	Fine
DENTON, Jonathan	1778	
DENTON, Jonathan	1779	Wilson
DENTON, Jonathan	1781	
DENTON, Jonathan	1790	Milleken
DENTON, Jonathan	1792	Milliken
DENTON, Jonathan	1797	Hannah
DENTON, Jonathan	1799	Hannah
DENTON, Jonathan	1780-1781 (Undated)	
DENTON, Jonathon	1796	Millikin
DENTON, Jones	1808	Parker
DENTON, Jones	1812	Hartsell
DENTON, Jones	1821	Howard
DENTON, Joseph	1778	
DENTON, Joseph	1779	
DENTON, Joseph	1790	Williams
DENTON, Joseph	1791	Williams
DENTON, Joseph	1793	Morrison
DENTON, Joseph	1794	Morrison
DENTON, Joseph	1798	Morrison
DENTON, Joseph	1798	Morrison
DENTON, Joseph	1799	Morrison
DENTON, Joseph	1801	Morrison
DENTON, Joseph	1806	Carr
DENTON, Joseph	1808	Carr
DENTON, Joseph	[1796] 1797	Morris
DENTON, Martha	1815	Fines
DENTON, Martha	1816	Fine
DENTON, Martha	1817	Fine
DENTON, Martha	1819	Howard
DENTON, Marthy	1818	Fine
DENTON, Saml	1781	
DENTON, Saml	1787	Fains
DENTON, Samuel	1778	
DENTON, Samuel	1791	Tullis
DENTON, Samuel	1791	Tullis
DENTON, Samuel	1793	Morrison
DENTON, Samuel	1794	Morrison
DENTON, Samuel	1798	Morrison
DENTON, Samuel	1798	Morrison
DENTON, Samuel	1801	Morrison
DENTON, Samuel	1806	Carr
DENTON, Samuel	1807	Carr
DENTON, Samuel	1808	Carr
DENTON, Samuel	1809	Carr
DENTON, Samuel	1811	Mitchell
DENTON, Samuel	1813	Hoss
DENTON, Samuel	1814	Hoss
DENTON, Samuel	[1796] 1797	Morris
DENTON, Samuel	1780-1781 (Undated)	
DENTON, Samuel (exec of Tom Martin Deceased)	1813	Hoss
DENTON, Samuel (executor Jas Martin)	1814	Hoss
DENTON, Samuel Jr.; (Single man)	1779	
DENTON, Samuel Sr.	1779	
DENTON, Thomas	1808	Carr
DENTON, Thomas	1810	Hartzel
DENVALD, Gaberel	1799	Morrison
DENWADDEK, James	1792	Milliken
DEPEW, Isaac	1798	Duncan
DEPEW, Isaac	1798	Duncan
DEPEW, Isaac	1806	Guin
DEPEW, Isaac	1807	Givins
DEPEW, Isaac	1809	Gwin
DEPEW, Isaac	1811	Davis
DEPEW, Isaac	1780-1781 (Undated)	
DEPEW, Isaac (Capt.)	1792	Depew
DEPEW, James	1815	Haire
DEPEW, James	1816	Hair
DEPEW, James	1817	Haire
DEPEW, James	1819	Grisham
DEPEW, James	1821	Hale
DEPEW, John	1817	Grisham
DEPEW, John	1818	Grisham
DEPEW, John	1819	Grisham
DEPEW, John	1821	Hale
DEPREAST, Randal	1779	
DEPUE, Isaac	1793	Depew
DEPUE, Isaac	1801	Taylor
DEPUE, Isaac	1808	Guin
DEPUE, Isaac (Capt.)	1794	Depew
DEPUE, Isaac (Esq.)	1799	Duncan
DERHAM, Thomas	1816	Grimsley
DERRICK, William	1809	Roadmas
DERRICK, William E.	1818	Smith
DERRICK, William E.	1819	Smith
DERRICK, Wm E.	1820	Smith
DERRICK, Wm E.	1821	Smith
DESANEY, Thos	1809	Par
DESKINS, Richard	1796	Longmire
DESNEY, Thomas	1792	Brown
DEVALT, Fredrick	1813	Hoss
DEVAULT, Felty	1816	Hoss
DEVAULT, Frederick	1815	Hoss
DEVAULT, Frederick	1819	Jones

Surname, Given names	Year	Comp./Dist.
DEVAULT, Jacob	1818	Hair
DEVAULT, Jacob	1819	Hair
DEVAULT, Jacob	1821	Louis
DEVAULT, Valentine	1815	Hoss
DEVAULT, Valentine	1817	Little
DEVAULT, Valentine	1818	Jones
DEVAULT, Valentine	1819	Jones
DEVAULT, Valentine	1821	Jones
DEVOLT, Frederick	1814	Hoss
DEVOLT, Valentine	1814	Hoss
DEVOULT, Fredrick	1821	Hunt
DEWALD, Gabriel	1801	Morrison
DEWALD, Henry	1801	Morrison
DIARMENT, James	1779	Wilson
DICK, Zedic	1809	Par
DICKENS, James	1793	Hale
DICKENS, James	1818	Hunt
DICKENS, Richard	1793	Hale
DICKERD, George	1797	Calvert
DICKEY, Samual	1805	Parker
DICKINGS, James	1780-1781 (Undated)	
DICKINS, Absalam	1807	Odell
DICKINS, James	1792	Coye
DICKINS, John	1807	Odell
DICKINS, Richard	1792	Coye
DICKINS, Richard	1807	Odell
DICKS, Jacob	1780-1781 (Undated)	
DICKSON, Hugh	1781	
DICKSON, John	1797	Gann
DICKSON, John	1798	Gann
DICKSON, John	1799	Moore
DICKSON, Richard	1814	Brown
DICKSON, Thos	1791	North
DIEL, Patrick	1793	Hale
DIER, John	1794	Melvan
DILFORD, Elisha	1780-1781 (undated)	
DILLARD, Benjamin	1808	Odell
DILLARD, Benjamin	1810	Cove
DILLARD, Benjamin	1811	Brown
DILLARD, Benjamin	1812	Brown
DILLARD, Elizebeth	1807	
DILLARD, John	1806	Odel
DILLARD, John	1807	Odell
DILLARD, John	1808	Odell
DILLARD, John	1809	Viney
DILLARD, John	1810	Cove
DILLARD, Marth	1793	Hale
DILLARD, Martha	1792	Coye
DILLARD, Martha	1796	Longmire
DILLARD, Martha	1797	Longmire
DILLARD, Martha	1801	Longmire
DILLARD, Martha	1806	Odel
DILLARD, Martha	1807	Odell
DILLARD, Martha	1812	Brown
DILLARD, Martha	1814	Brown
DILLARD, Martha	1815	Hartsell
DILLARD, Martha	1816	Brown
DILLARD, Martha	1817	Brown
DILLARD, Martha	1818	Brown
DILLARD, Martha	1819	Brown
DILLARD, Martha (widow)	1811	Brown
DILLARD, Marthien	1809	Viney
DILLARD, Marthierd	1810	Cove
DILLARD, Mathew	1808	Odell
DILLARD, Thomas	1792	Coye
DILLARD, Thomas	1796	Longmire
DILLARD, Thomas	1797	Longmire
DILLENHAM, Vachworth	1778	
DILLIN, Daniel	1780-1781 (Undated)	
DILLIN, Elizabeth	1801	
DINKEN, William	1812	Ellis
DINWIDDIE, Adam (estate of)	1799	Hannah
DISNAY, Thomas	1806	Parker
DISNEY, Thomas	1791	Willey
DISNEY, Thomas	1796	Calvert
DISNEY, Thos	1795	Young
DISNEY, Thos	1801	Taylor
DISNY, Thomas	1807	Parker
DIXON, Clement Sr.	1778	
DIZNEY, Thos	1797	Calvert
DIZNY, Thomas	1805	Parker
DOAK, Alexander	1805	Doak
DOAK, Alexander	1807	Britton
DOAK, John	1815	Crookshanks
DOAK, John	1817	McClure
DOAK, John (Rev.)	1811	McAlister
DOAK, John (Rev.)	1819	McClure
DOAK, John (Rev.)	1821	McClure
DOAK, John (Rev.)	1818	McClure
DOAK, John (Revd.)	1805	Stephenson
DOAK, John (Revd.)	1809	McAlister
DOAK, John W. (Revd)	1814	Crookshanks
DOAK, Robert	1805	Doak
DOAK, Sam (Rev.)	1790	Milleken
DOAK, Saml	1793	Milliken
DOAK, Sam'l (Rev.)	1791	Milliken
DOAK, Saml (Revd.)	1799	Hannah
DOAK, Saml (Revd.)	1807	Payne
DOAK, Samuel	1781	
DOAK, Samuel	1792	Milliken
DOAK, Samuel	1793	Scott

Surname, Given names	Year	Comp./Dist.
DOAK, Samuel	1794	Milliken
DOAK, Samuel	1797	Hannah
DOAK, Samuel	1815	Crookshanks
DOAK, Samuel	1817	McClure
DOAK, Samuel	1818	McClure
DOAK, Samuel (Rev.)	1811	McAlister
DOAK, Samuel (Revd)	1814	Crookshanks
DOAK, Samuel (Revd.)	1795	Milliken
DOAK, Samuel (Revd.)	1805	Stephenson
DOAK, Samuel (Revd.)	1809	McAlister
DOAK, Samuel (Reverent)	1796	Millikin
DOAK, Thomas	1805	Doak
DOAK, W. John	1807	Payne
DOAKE, John (Rev.)	1816	Crookshanks
DOAKE, Sam (Rev.)	1816	Crookshanks
DOAN, John	1815	Carcathers
DOAN, John	1816	Giles
DOAN, John	1818	Land
DOAN, John	1819	Sands
DOBBIN,	1792	Brown
DOBBINS, Evins	1793	Brown
DOBKINS, Evan	1792	Chisolm
DODAN, Charles	1781	
DODD, James	1811	Britten
DODDY, Howell	1778	
DODDY, Powell	1780-1781 (Undated)	
DODSON, Charls	1780-1781 (Undated)	
DODSON, William	1793	Murray
DODSON, William	1794	Murray
DODY, Howel	1781	
DOGAT, Milar	1780-1781 (Undated)	
DOGGETT, Miller	1781	
DOIL, Patrick	1792	Coye
DOK, John	1808	McAllister
DOKE, Allexander	1806	Doke
DOKE, John	1806	Payn
DOKE, Johne	1812	Crawford
DOKE, Robin	1806	Crouch
DOKE, Samuel	1798	Hannah
DOKE, Samuel	1806	Payn
DOKE, Samuel	1812	Crawford
DOKE, Samuel	1812	Crawford [2]
DOLPHIN, Will	1796	Millikin
DONLEY, Hezekiah	1816	Giles
DONNALY, Thos	1797	Calvert
DOODY, Howell	1779	
DOOSE, John	1795	Thornton
DOSSER, William	1821	Howard
DOTSON, Jonathan	1793	North
DOTTY, Eazra	1781	

Surname, Given names	Year	Comp./Dist.
DOTTY, John	1781	
DOUGGLASS, James	1794	Thornton
DOUGLAS, John	1812	Barnes
DOUGLAS, John	1814	Barns
DOUGLAS, Jonathan	1809	Gwin
DOUGLAS, Thos	1814	Barns
DOUGLAS, William	1812	Barnes
DOUGLASS, John	1811	Barron
DOUGLASS, William	1811	Barron
DOVE, John	1814	Couthers
DOWN, John	1821	Sands
DOWNEY, Francis	1807	Carr
DOWOODY, James (Decd)	1807	Payne
DOYEL, Patrick	1796	Longmire
DOYLE, Patrick	1797	Longmire
DOYLE, Patrick	1798	Longmire
DOYLE, Patrick	1801	Longmire
DRAIN, Benjaman	1805	Parker
DRAIN, Benjaman	1807	Parker
DRAIN, Benjamin	1798	Hannah
DRAIN, Benjamin	1806	Parker
DRAIN, Benjamin	1808	Parker
DRAIN, Benjamin	1810	Hartzel
DRAIN, Benjamin	1812	Hartsell
DRAIN, Benjamin	1814	Hartsell
DRAIN, Benjamin	1815	Fines
DRAIN, Benjamin	1816	Fine
DRAIN, Benjamin	1817	Fine
DRAIN, Benjamin	1818	Fine
DRAIN, Benjamin	1819	Howard
DRAINE, Binjm	1801	Taylor
DRAKE, Abraham	1792	Carriger
DRAKE, Abraham	1794	Carriger
DRAKE, Abraham	1795	Carriger
DRAKE, Benjamin	1778	
DRAKE, Ephraim	1819	Howard
DRAKE, Ephrem	1814	Hartsell
DRAKE, Eppram	1821	Howard
DRAKE, John	1778	
DRANE, Benjamin	1797	Hannah
DRANE, Benjn	1809	Par
DRONE, Benjamin	1821	Howard
DUGAN, Jeremiah	1813	Hoss
DUGAN, William	1811	Mitchell
DUGAN, William (Rev.)	1819	Jones
DUGGAR, William	1792	Greer
DUGGAR, Wm	1778	
DUGGARD, Julius	1790	White
DUGGARD, Julius	1791	White
DUGGARD, Julius	1793	Campbell
DUGGARD, Julius	1795	Ford

Surname, Given names	Year	Comp./Dist.
DUGGARD, William	1790	Greer
DUGGARD, William	1793	Campbell
DUGGARD, William (Single man)	1779	
DUGGER, Julias	1794	Ford
DUGGER, William	1794	Ford
DUGGLAS, John	1796	Shipley
DUGLAS, John	1797	Shipley
DUGLAS, John	1805	Rector
DUGLAS, John	1807	Cade
DUGLAS, John	1818	Grimsley
DUGLAS, John	1818	Grimsley
DUGLASS, John	1819	Grimsley
DUGLASS, John Jr.	1819	Grimsley
DUGLES, John	1808	Cade
DUGLES, John	1810	Barron
DUGLES, John	1815	Grimsley
DUGLES, John	1816	Grimsley
DUGLES, John	1817	Grimsley
DUGLES, John	1821	Martin
DUGLES, Samuel	1816	Grimsley
DUGLES, Samuel	1821	Martin
DUGLES, Thomas	1815	Grimsley
DUGLES, William	1810	Barron
DUGLESS, John	1809	Cade
DUHAM, Carles	1821	Martin
DULANEY, James	1781	
DULANEY, James	1818	Fine
DUN, Daniel	1795	Murray
DUN, James	1794	Murray
DUN, Jerimiah	1809	Carr
DUNCAN, Alvice	1821	Jones
DUNCAN, Andrew	1792	Depew
DUNCAN, Andrew	1793	Depew
DUNCAN, Andrew	1794	Depew
DUNCAN, Andrew	1797	Duncan
DUNCAN, Andrew	1798	Duncan
DUNCAN, Andrew	1798	Duncan
DUNCAN, Andrew	1799	Duncan
DUNCAN, Andrew	1801	Taylor
DUNCAN, Andrew	1807	Givins
DUNCAN, Andrew	1811	Davis
DUNCAN, Andrew	1812	McLin
DUNCAN, Andrew	1814	McLin
DUNCAN, Andrew	1815	McLin
DUNCAN, Andrew	1816	Hunt
DUNCAN, Andrew	1818	Hunt
DUNCAN, Andrew	1819	Hunt
DUNCAN, Andrew	1783 [after]	Depew
DUNCAN, Charles	1787	Fains
DUNCAN, Charles	1791	Tullis
DUNCAN, Charles	1793	Morrison
DUNCAN, Charles	1794	Morrison
DUNCAN, Charles	1795	Morrison
DUNCAN, Charles	1798	Morrison
DUNCAN, Charles	1801	Morrison
DUNCAN, Charles	1808	Carr
DUNCAN, Charles	1809	Carr
DUNCAN, Charles	1811	Mitchell
DUNCAN, Charles	1814	Hoss
DUNCAN, Charles	1815	Hoss
DUNCAN, Charles	1816	Hoss
DUNCAN, Charles	1817	Little
DUNCAN, Charles	1818	Jones
DUNCAN, Charles	[1796] 1797	Morris
DUNCAN, Charles (estate)	1819	Jones
DUNCAN, Charles (heirs)	1821	Jones
DUNCAN, Charls	1807	Carr
DUNCAN, Cranen	1780-1781 (Undated)	
DUNCAN, Danl	1781	
DUNCAN, Elizabeth	1795	Murray
DUNCAN, Francis	1819	Hunt
DUNCAN, Gean	1808	Guin
DUNCAN, James	1807	Givins
DUNCAN, James	1808	Guin
DUNCAN, James	1812	McLin
DUNCAN, James	1814	McLin
DUNCAN, James	1815	McLin
DUNCAN, James	1816	Hunt
DUNCAN, James	1817	Hunt
DUNCAN, James	1818	Hunt
DUNCAN, James	1819	Hunt
DUNCAN, James	1821	Hunt
DUNCAN, James	1821	Jones
DUNCAN, Jane	1821	Hunt
DUNCAN, Jesse	1801	Lane
DUNCAN, Jesse	1805	Doak
DUNCAN, Jesse	1806	Doke
DUNCAN, Jesse	1807	Britton
DUNCAN, Jesse	1811	Britten
DUNCAN, Jesse	1812	Britton
DUNCAN, Jesse	1813	Copas
DUNCAN, Jesse	1814	Copes
DUNCAN, Jesse	1816	Copas
DUNCAN, Jesse	1817	Grisham
DUNCAN, Jesse	1818	Grisham
DUNCAN, Jesse	1819	Grisham
DUNCAN, John	1781	
DUNCAN, John	1811	Mitchell
DUNCAN, John	1815	Hoss
DUNCAN, John	1816	Hoss
DUNCAN, John	1817	Little
DUNCAN, John	1818	Jones

Surname, Given names	Year	Comp./Dist.
DUNCAN, John	1819	Jones
DUNCAN, John	1821	Jones
DUNCAN, Joseph	1792	Depew
DUNCAN, Joseph	1793	Depew
DUNCAN, Joseph	1794	Depew
DUNCAN, Joseph	1797	Duncan
DUNCAN, Joseph	1797	Shipley
DUNCAN, Joseph	1798	Duncan
DUNCAN, Joseph	1798	Duncan
DUNCAN, Joseph	1799	Duncan
DUNCAN, Joseph	1801	Lane
DUNCAN, Joseph	1801	Taylor
DUNCAN, Joseph	1805	Doak
DUNCAN, Joseph	1806	Doke
DUNCAN, Joseph	1807	Britton
DUNCAN, Joseph	1807	Givins
DUNCAN, Joseph	1808	Guin
DUNCAN, Joseph	1811	Davis
DUNCAN, Joseph	1812	McLin
DUNCAN, Joseph	1814	McLin
DUNCAN, Joseph	1817	Hunt
DUNCAN, Joseph	1821	Hunt
DUNCAN, Joseph (for Robert Allison & for the heirs of Robert All)	1818	Hunt
DUNCAN, Joseph Jr.	1812	McLin
DUNCAN, Joseph Jr.	1814	McLin
DUNCAN, Joseph Jr.	1815	McLin
DUNCAN, Joseph Jr.	1816	Hunt
DUNCAN, Joseph Jr.	1817	Hunt
DUNCAN, Joseph Jr.	1821	Hunt
DUNCAN, Joseph Jr. (Ex of Jane Allison & Heirs of Robert Allison)	1819	Hunt
DUNCAN, Joseph Jr.; (Ext of the Estate of R. Allison)	1819	Hunt
DUNCAN, Joseph Sr.	1808	Guin
DUNCAN, Joseph Sr.	1815	McLin
DUNCAN, Joseph Sr.	1816	Hunt
DUNCAN, Joseph Sr.	1818	Hunt
DUNCAN, Joseph Sr.	1819	Hunt
DUNCAN, Lawrance	1795	Ford
DUNCAN, Lawrence	1794	Ford
DUNCAN, Marshall	1798	Morrison
DUNCAN, Mary	1818	Jones
DUNCAN, Patrick	1795	Ford
DUNCAN, Patterick	1794	Ford
DUNCAN, Price	1818	Grisham
DUNCAN, Rice	1801	Lane
DUNCAN, Rice	1805	Doak
DUNCAN, Rice	1806	Doke
DUNCAN, Rice	1807	Britton
DUNCAN, Rice	1811	Britten
DUNCAN, Rice	1812	Britton
DUNCAN, Rice	1813	Copas
DUNCAN, Rice	1814	Copes
DUNCAN, Rice	1817	Grisham
DUNCAN, Rice	1819	Grisham
DUNCAN, Rice	1821	Hale
DUNCAN, Richard	1817	Hunt
DUNCAN, Robert	1801	Lane
DUNCAN, Robert	1818	Jones
DUNCAN, Robert	1819	Jones
DUNCAN, Robert	1821	Jones
DUNCAN, Rue	1816	Copas
DUNCAN, Samuel	1819	Sands
DUNCAN, Thomas	1792	Coye
DUNCAN, Thomas	1794	Carriger
DUNCAN, Thomas	1795	Carriger
DUNCAN, Thos	1790	Greer
DUNCAN, Thos	1792	Carriger
DUNCAN, William	1807	Carr
DUNCAN, William	1808	Carr
DUNCAN, William	1811	Mitchell
DUNCAN, William	1814	Hoss
DUNCAN, William	1816	Hoss
DUNCAN, William	1817	Little
DUNCAN, William	1818	Jones
DUNCAN, William	1819	Jones
DUNCAN, William	1821	Jones
DUNCAN, William (Revd.)	1821	Jones
DUNCAN, Wm	1809	Carr
DUNCOM, Jesse	1815	Copas
DUNCOM, Price	1815	Copas
DUNCOME, Elizabeth	1778	
DUNCOME, John	1778	
DUNCOME, Joseph	1778	
DUNCON, Francis	1821	Hunt
DUNCON, Jesse	1821	Hale
DUNCON, Jesse	1821	Hale
DUNDSON, Charles	1790	Shipley
DUNDSON, Charles	1791	Shipley
DUNGAN, Jaremiah	1807	Carr
DUNGAN, Jeremiah	1795	Taylor
DUNGAN, Jeremiah	1795	Taylor
DUNGAN, Jeremiah	1796	Morrison
DUNGAN, Jeremiah	1798	Morrison
DUNGAN, Jerrmiah	1793	Maxwell
DUNGAN, Mary	1814	Hoss
DUNGAN, Mary	1815	Hoss
DUNGAN, Mary	1816	Hoss
DUNGAN, Mary	1817	Little
DUNGAN, Mary	1819	Jones
DUNGANS, Jeremiah	1792	Tulley
DUNGEN, Jariha	1799	Morrison

Surname, Given names	Year	Comp./Dist.
DUNGEN, Jeremiah	1798	Morrison
DUNGENS, Jaremiah	1794	Taylor
DUNGENS, Jeremiah	1806	Carr
DUNGHAN, Jeremiah	1779	
DUNGING, Jaramiah	1778	
DUNGINGE, Jaremiah	1808	Carr
DUNGINGS, Jeremiah	1811	Mitchell
DUNGURTH, Charles	1793	Melvan
DUNGWORK, Charles	1794	Melvan
DUNGWORTH, Charles	1795	Melvan
DUNGWORTH, Charles	1796	Melvin
DUNGWORTH, Charles	1798	Crouch
DUNGWORTH, Charles	1801	Norwood
DUNGWORTH, Charles	1809	Right
DUNGWORTH, Charles	1811	Ellis
DUNGWORTH, Charles	1814	Bean
DUNGWORTH, Thomas	1809	Right
DUNGWORTH, Thomas	1811	Ellis
DUNGWORTH, Thomas	1814	Bean
DUNGWORTH, Thomas	1815	Haire
DUNGWORTH, Thomas	1816	Hair
DUNGWORTH, Thomas	1817	Haire
DUNGWORTH, Thomas	1818	Hair
DUNHAM, Charles	1793	Murray
DUNHAM, Charles	1794	Murray
DUNHAM, Charles	1798	Shipley
DUNHAM, Charles	1808	Cade
DUNHAM, Charles	1809	Cade
DUNHAM, Charles	1810	Barron
DUNHAM, Charles	1812	Barnes
DUNHAM, Charles	1817	Grimsley
DUNHAM, Charles	1819	Grimsley
DUNHAM, Charls	1814	Barns
DUNHAM, Daniel	1778	
DUNHAM, David	1790	Stone
DUNHAM, David	1791	Stone
DUNHAM, David	1793	Melvan
DUNHAM, David	1794	Melvan
DUNHAM, Henry	1778	
DUNHAM, Henry	1779	Wilson
DUNHAM, Henry	1781	
DUNHAM, John	1778	
DUNHAM, John	1778	
DUNHAM, John	1807	Britton
DUNHAM, Joseph	1778	
DUNHAM, Joseph	1779	Wilson
DUNHAM, Joseph	1780-1781 (undated)	
DUNHAM, Joseph	1780-1781 (Undated)	
DUNHAM, Ruben	1781	
DUNHAM, Shanks	1807	Cade
DUNHAM, Thomas	1817	Grimsley
DUNHAM, Thomas	1819	Grimsley
DUNHAND, Reubin	1778	
DUNKAN, Jn	1780-1781 (Undated)	
DUNKEN, Charles	1792	Tulley
DUNKEN, Charles	1799	Morrison
DUNKEN, Charls	1806	Carr
DUNKEN, Joel	1801	Morrison
DUNKEN, Joseph Sr.	1809	Gwin
DUNKEN, Marchel	1799	Morrison
DUNKEN, Marshal	1801	Morrison
DUNKENS, William	1806	Carr
DUNKEON, Thomas	1792	Greer
DUNKIN, Andrew	1806	Guin
DUNKIN, Andrew	1809	Gwin
DUNKIN, Charles	1778	
DUNKIN, Charles	1813	Hoss
DUNKIN, Crauen	1780-1781 (undated)	
DUNKIN, James	1806	Guin
DUNKIN, James	1811	Davis
DUNKIN, John	1778	
DUNKIN, John	1813	Hoss
DUNKIN, Joseph	1806	Guin
DUNKIN, Joseph	1809	Gwin
DUNKIN, Joseph	1811	Barron
DUNKIN, Joseph	1811	Davis
DUNKIN, William	1813	Hoss
DUNKING, Benjamin	1793	Thornton
DUNKING, Patrick	1791	White
DUNKING, Patrick	1793	Thornton
DUNLOP, Ephraim	1779	
DUNN, Thos	1793	Milliken
DUNN, William	1781	
DUNNAM, Thos	1821	Martin
DUNSWORTH, Charles	1806	Crouch
DUNSWORTH, Charles	1812	Ellis
DUNSWORTH, Thomas	1812	Ellis
DUNWADY, James	1806	Payn
DUNWIDAY, Adam (Estate Of)	1801	Squibb
DUNWOODY, Adam	1781	
DUNWORTH, Charles	1790	Stone
DUNWORTH, Charles	1791	Stone
DUNWOYOLE, Adam	1797	Hannah
DURAN, William	1798	Morrison
DURHAM, Charles	1815	Grimsley
DURHAM, Charles	1818	Grimsley
DURHAM, David	1811	Ellis
DURHAM, Thomas	1815	Grimsley
DURICK, William	1814	McCracken
DURRAM, Nath	1778	

Surname, Given names	Year	Comp./Dist.
DUSAN, William (Revd)	1814	Hoss
DUZAN, William	1798	Morrison
DUZAN, William	1807	Carr
DUZAN, William	1808	Carr
DUZAN, William	1813	Hoss
DUZAN, William	1818	Jones
DUZAN, William (Rev.)	1815	Hoss
DUZAN, William (Rev.)	1817	Little
DUZAN, Wm	1809	Carr
DUZANN, William	1801	Morrison
DYER, Alexander	1821	Hale
DYER, David	1790	Stone
DYER, David	1791	Stone
DYER, David	1821	Hale
DYER, Edward	1819	Smith
DYER, John	1790	Stone
DYER, John	1791	Stone
DYER, John	1793	Melvan
DYER, John	1795	Melvan
DYER, John	1821	Hale
EAGAN, Barnbus	1799	Morrison
EAGAN, Barnebe	1796	Morrison
EAGAN, Barnebes	1801	Morrison
EAGAN, James	1796	Morrison
EAGAN, James	1798	Morrison
EAGAN, James	1798	Morrison
EAGAN, James	1799	Morrison
EAGEN, Barnebe	1798	Morrison
EAGEN, Hugh	1799	Morrison
EAGIN, Barney	1790	Williams
EAGIN, Barney	1791	Williams
EARAGROFF, Jonathan	1812	McLin
EARINGTON, Thomas	1816	Hair
EARINGTON, Thomas	1817	Haire
EARLEY, Samuel	1817	Fine
EARLEY, Thomas	1817	Fine
EARLY, Benjaman	1812	McCray
EARLY, Samuel	1816	Fine
EARLY, Samuel	1818	Fine
EARLY, Samuel	1819	Howard
EARLY, Thomas	1816	Fine
EARLY, Thomas	1818	Fine
EARLY, Thomas	1819	Howard
EARNEST, Henry	1778	
EARNEST, Henry	1779	
EASON, Franses	1795	Calvert
EASON, John G.	1815	Garner
EASON, John G.	1816	Smith
EASON, John G.	1817	Smith
EASON, John G.	1818	Smith
EASON, John G.	1819	Smith
EASON, John G.	1820	Smith
EASON, John G.	1821	Smith
EASTES, John B.	1818	Smith
EASTIGS, Moses	1791	White
EASTIL, Sollamen	1809	Gwin
EASTIN, John B.	1820	Smith
EASTRIDGE, Richard	1793	Campbell
EASTRIGE, Richard	1791	White
EATEN, Edward	1779	Wilson
EATON, James Jr.	1792	Coye
EATON, James Sr.	1792	Coye
EAVANS, John	1796	Longmire
EAVANS, Thomas	1796	Longmire
EAVINS, Charlow	1797	Longmire
EAVINS, John	1797	Longmire
EAVINS, Thomas	1797	Longmire
ECEY, Thomas	1814	Copes
ECTON, James	1814	Hartsell
ECTON, James Jr.	1798	Longmire
ECTON, James Sr.	1798	Longmire
ECTON, John	1798	Longmire
EDCOCK, Danial	1780-1781 (Undated)	
EDDLEMAN, Michael	1805	Doak
EDDLEMAN, Michael	1807	Britton
EDDLEMAN, Michel	1806	Doke
EDEN, Austin	1794	Taylor
EDEN, Austin	1795	Taylor
EDEN, James	1794	Taylor
EDMONDS, Dixson	1792	Coye
EDMONDS, John	1779	Wilson
EDMONS, Jno	1780-1781 (Undated)	
EDWARD, Abel Jr.	1808	Odell
EDWARD, Abel Sr.	1808	Odell
EDWARD, Ely	1807	Bayles
EDWARD, Ely	1814	Hampton
EDWARD, Evans	1780-1781 (undated)	
EDWARD, Soloman	1792	Maxwell
EDWARDS, Abal Sr.	1810	Cove
EDWARDS, Abel	1806	Odel
EDWARDS, Abel	1809	Viney
EDWARDS, Abel	1811	Brown
EDWARDS, Abel	1814	Brown
EDWARDS, Abel	1816	Harrison
EDWARDS, Abel	1818	Harris
EDWARDS, Abel	1819	Harris
EDWARDS, Abel	1821	Hampton
EDWARDS, Abel Jr.	1806	Odel
EDWARDS, Abel Jr.	1807	Odell
EDWARDS, Abel Jr.	1809	Viney
EDWARDS, Abel Jr.	1810	Cove

Surname, Given names	Year	Comp./Dist.
EDWARDS, Abel Jr.	1815	Hartsell
EDWARDS, Abel Jr.	1821	Haines
EDWARDS, Abel Sr.	1807	Odell
EDWARDS, Abel Sr.	1815	Hartsell
EDWARDS, Abel Sr.	1816	Brown
EDWARDS, Abell	1817	Harris
EDWARDS, Abell Sr.	1817	Brown
EDWARDS, Abell Sr.	1818	Brown
EDWARDS, Able	1801	Longmire
EDWARDS, Able	1812	Brown
EDWARDS, Able Jr.	1812	Brown
EDWARDS, Alex	1819	Brown
EDWARDS, Arther	1809	Viney
EDWARDS, Arthor	1810	Cove
EDWARDS, Arthur	1811	Brown
EDWARDS, Arthur	1814	Brown
EDWARDS, Arthur	1815	Hartsell
EDWARDS, Arthur	1816	Brown
EDWARDS, Arthur	1817	Brown
EDWARDS, Arthur	1818	Brown
EDWARDS, Arthur	1819	Brown
EDWARDS, Eli	1797	Calvert
EDWARDS, Eli	1801	Roberson
EDWARDS, Eli	1806	Brown
EDWARDS, Eli	1809	Bayles
EDWARDS, Eli	1816	Hampton
EDWARDS, Eli	1817	Hampton
EDWARDS, Ely	1801	Squibb
EDWARDS, Ely	1805	Parker
EDWARDS, Ely	1808	Bayles
EDWARDS, Evan	1779	Wilson
EDWARDS, Evan	1781	
EDWARDS, Evans	1778	
EDWARDS, Henry	1798	Morrison
EDWARDS, James	1795	Ford
EDWARDS, John	1797	Longmire
EDWARDS, John	1798	Longmire
EDWARDS, John	1801	Longmire
EDWARDS, John	1806	Odel
EDWARDS, John	1807	Odell
EDWARDS, John	1808	Odell
EDWARDS, John	1809	Viney
EDWARDS, John	1811	Brown
EDWARDS, John	1812	Brown
EDWARDS, John	1814	Brown
EDWARDS, John	1815	Hartsell
EDWARDS, John	1816	Brown
EDWARDS, John	1817	Brown
EDWARDS, John	1818	Brown
EDWARDS, John	1819	Brown
EDWARDS, John	1821	Haines

Surname, Given names	Year	Comp./Dist.
EDWARDS, Jonathan	1798	Morrison
EDWARDS, Jonathan	1798	Morrison
EDWARDS, Jonathan	1798	Morrison
EDWARDS, Jonathan	1799	Morrison
EDWARDS, Jonathan	1807	Carr
EDWARDS, Jonathan	1808	Carr
EDWARDS, Jonathan	1809	Carr
EDWARDS, Jonathen	1806	Carr
EDWARDS, Joshoua	1806	Odel
EDWARDS, Joshua	1798	Morrison
EDWARDS, Joshua	1807	Odell
EDWARDS, Solomon	1791	
EDWARDS, Solomon	1795	Taylor
EDWARDS, Thomas	1801	Longmire
EDWARDS, Thomas	1806	Odel
EDWARDS, Thomas	1807	Odell
EDWARDS, Thomas	1808	Odell
EDWARDS, Thomas	1809	Viney
EDWARDS, Thomas	1810	Cove
EDWARDS, Thomas	1812	Brown
EDWARDS, Thomas	1815	Hartsell
EDWARDS, Thomas	1817	Brown
EDWARDS, Thomas	1818	Brown
EDWARDS, Thomas	1819	Brown
EDWARDS, Thomas	1821	Haines
EDWARDS, Thommas	1814	Brown
EDWARDS, William (estate)	1819	Harris
ELAXNDER, David	1780-1781 (Undated)	
ELEMAN, John	1798	Duncan
ELENSON, Charles	1811	Barron
ELESON, James	1791	Tullis
ELESON, Robert	1806	Payn
ELIMON, John	1801	Calvert
ELIOT, George	1815	Harris
ELIOT, George	1815	Harris
ELIOT, Patrick	1815	Harris
ELIS, Jacob	1815	Hoss
ELISON, Charles	1807	Cade
ELISON, Charles	1812	Barnes
ELKIN, David	1801	Roberson
ELKINS, David	1797	Longmire
ELKINS, David	1798	Longmire
ELKINS, William	1793	Melvan
ELKINS, William	1801	Longmire
ELKINS, William	1806	Odel
ELKINS, Willm	1798	Longmire
ELKINS, Wm	1797	Longmire
ELLAMAN, John	1798	Duncan
ELLASON, Charles	1810	Barron
ELLEMAN, John	1796	Handly
ELLEMAN, John	1797	Calvert

Surname, Given names	Year	Comp./Dist.
ELLESON, Charles	1801	Glasscock
ELLET, John	1811	McCray
ELLET, Patrick	1811	McCray
ELLICE, Ephraim	1781	
ELLINGNER, John	1811	Green
ELLIOT, George	1816	Smith
ELLIOT, George	1817	Grimsley
ELLIOT, George	1817	Smith
ELLIOT, George	1818	Grimsley
ELLIOT, George	1819	Grimsley
ELLIOT, John	1814	McCracken
ELLIOT, John	1815	Garner
ELLIOT, John	1816	Smith
ELLIOT, John	1817	Smith
ELLIOT, John	1818	Smith
ELLIOT, John	1819	Smith
ELLIOT, Patrick	1814	McCracken
ELLIOT, Patrick	1816	Smith
ELLIOT, Patrick	1817	Smith
ELLIOT, Patrick	1818	Smith
ELLIOT, Patrick	1819	Smith
ELLIOTT, John	1820	Smith
ELLIOTT, John	1821	Smith
ELLIOTT, Patrick	1805	Jas Parker
ELLIOTT, Pattrick	1820	Smith
ELLIOTT, Pattrick	1821	Smith
ELLIS, Clarke	1821	Hunt
ELLIS, Elijah	1814	Bean
ELLIS, Elijah	1816	Hair
ELLIS, Elijah	1817	Haire
ELLIS, Elijah	1818	Hair
ELLIS, Elijah	1819	Hair
ELLIS, Ezekel	1814	Copes
ELLIS, Ezekiel	1812	Britton
ELLIS, Ezekiel	1813	Copas
ELLIS, Ezekiel	1815	Copas
ELLIS, Ezekiel	1817	Grisham
ELLIS, Ezekiel	1818	Grisham
ELLIS, Ezekiel	1819	Grisham
ELLIS, Ezekiel	1821	Hale
ELLIS, Jacob	1812	Ellis
ELLIS, Jacob	1816	Hair
ELLIS, Jacob	1817	Haire
ELLIS, Jacob	1818	Hair
ELLIS, Jacob	1819	Hair
ELLIS, Jacob	1821	Louis
ELLIS, Jacob (Capt.)	1811	Ellis
ELLIS, Jacob (Esqr.)	1812	Ellis
ELLIS, Jacob (Esqr.)	1814	Hoss
ELLIS, James	1798	Crouch
ELLIS, James	1801	Norwood
ELLIS, James	1806	Crouch
ELLIS, James	1809	Right
ELLIS, James	1811	Ellis
ELLIS, James	1812	Ellis
ELLIS, James	1814	Copes
ELLIS, James	1815	Copas
ELLIS, James	1816	Copas
ELLIS, James	1817	Grisham
ELLIS, James	1818	Grisham
ELLIS, James	1819	Grisham
ELLIS, James	1821	Hale
ELLIS, John	1790	Shipley
ELLIS, John	1791	Shipley
ELLIS, John	1793	Murray
ELLIS, John	1794	Murray
ELLIS, John	1795	Murray
ELLIS, John	1796	Shipley
ELLIS, John	1797	Shipley
ELLIS, John	1798	Shipley
ELLIS, John	1801	Lane
ELLIS, John	1805	Doak
ELLIS, John	1805	Stephenson
ELLIS, John	1806	Doke
ELLIS, John	1807	Britton
ELLIS, John	1812	Britton
ELLIS, John	1813	Copas
ELLIS, John	1814	Copes
ELLIS, John	1816	Copas
ELLIS, John	1817	Grisham
ELLIS, John	1818	Grisham
ELLIS, John	1819	Grisham
ELLIS, John	1821	Hale
ELLIS, Martha	1812	Ellis
ELLIS, Shabble	1790	Stone
ELLIS, Shabble	1791	Stone
ELLIS, Tilmon	1798	Shipley
ELLIS, Tilmon	1801	Norwood
ELLIS, William	1790	Stone
ELLIS, William	1791	Stone
ELLIS, William	1793	Melvan
ELLIS, William	1794	Melvan
ELLIS, William	1795	Melvan
ELLIS, William	1798	Crouch
ELLIS, William	1801	Norwood
ELLIS, William	1806	Crouch
ELLIS, William	1809	Right
ELLIS, Wm	1796	Melvin
ELLISON, Charles	1797	Shipley
ELLISON, Charles	1809	Cade
ELLISON, John	1811	
ELLISON, John	1814	Couthers

Surname, Given names	Year	Comp./Dist.
ELLISON, Robert	1821	Louis
ELLISON, Saml	1797	Gann
ELLIT, Patrict	1812	McCray
ELLOTT, John	1805	Jas Parker
ELLOTT, John	1812	McCray
ELLOTTE, Jno	1808	Parker
ELLOTTE, John	1812	McCray
ELLOTTE, Pattrick	1808	Parker
ELLOTTE, Pattrick	1809	Parker
ELLOTTE, Pattrick	1812	McCray
ELSEY, Isaac	1817	Grisham
ELSEY, Isaac	1818	Grisham
ELSEY, Isaac	1819	Grisham
ELSEY, Isaac	1821	Hale
ELSEY, John	1811	Britten
ELSEY, John	1812	Britton
ELSEY, John	1813	Copas
ELSEY, John	1814	Bean
ELSEY, John	1815	Haire
ELSEY, John	1816	Hair
ELSEY, John	1817	Haire
ELSEY, John	1818	Hair
ELSEY, John	1819	Hair
ELSEY, John	1821	Louis
ELSEY, Martin	1816	Hair
ELSEY, Martin	1817	Haire
ELSEY, Nathaniel	1820	Smith
ELSEY, Thomas	1811	Britten
ELSEY, Thomas	1812	Britton
ELSEY, Thomas	1813	Copas
ELSEY, Thomas	1815	Copas
ELSEY, Thomas	1816	Copas
ELSEY, Thomas	1817	Grisham
ELSEY, Thomas	1818	Grisham
ELSEY, Thomas	1819	Grisham
ELSEY, Thomas	1821	Hale
EMBEER,	1821	Brown
EMBENTON, Richard	1794	Murray
EMBERTON, Richard	1795	Murray
EMBILL, Isaac	1791	Chisom
EMBRE, Even	1807	Parker
EMBRE, Jobe	1796	Brown
EMBREE,	1792	Brown
EMBREE, Elihu	1805	Stephenson
EMBREE, Elihu	1807	Payne
EMBREE, Elihu	1808	McAllister
EMBREE, Even	1806	Brown
EMBREE, Isaac	1792	Chisolm
EMBREE, Isaac	1793	Brown
EMBREE, Isaac	1797	Robertson
EMBREE, Isaac	1798	Roberson

Surname, Given names	Year	Comp./Dist.
EMBREE, Isaac	1799	Robertson
EMBREE, Isaac	1801	Roberson
EMBREE, Jacob	1792	Brown
EMBREE, Jacob	1796	Brown
EMBREE, Jacob	1797	Robertson
EMBREE, Jacob	1798	Roberson
EMBREE, Jacob	1799	Robertson
EMBREE, Jacob	1801	Roberson
EMBREE, Jacob	1806	Brown
EMBREE, John	1791	Milliken
EMBREE, John	1792	Milliken
EMBREE, John	1793	Milliken
EMBREE, John	1794	Milliken
EMBREE, John	1796	Millikin
EMBREE, John	1797	Hannah
EMBREE, John	1798	Hannah
EMBREE, John	1799	Hannah
EMBREE, John	1801	Squibb
EMBREE, Margret	1796	Brown
EMBREE, Margret	1799	Robertson
EMBREE, Margrett	1797	Robertson
EMBREE, Moser	1792	Brown
EMBREE, Moses	1791	Chisom
EMBREE, Moses	1792	Chisolm
EMBREE, Moses	1793	Brown
EMBREE, Thomas	1791	Milliken
EMBREE, Thomas	1792	North
EMBREE, Thomas	1793	Milliken
EMBREE, Thomas	1795	Milliken
EMBREE, Thomas	1796	Millikin
EMBREE, Thomas	1797	Hannah
EMBREE, Thomas	1798	Hannah
EMBREE, Thomas	1801	Squibb
EMBREE, Thomas	1805	Stephenson
EMBREE, Thos	1799	Hannah
EMBRERE, Elishu	1809	Viney
EMBRY, Elihu	1806	Payn
EMEBY, John	1795	Calvert
EMMERSON, Thomas	1818	Smith
EMMERT, George	1794	Carriger
EMMET, George	1795	Carriger
EMMONS, Eliza	1808	Gwin
EMUN, William	1821	Howard
ENGIL, John	[1796] 1797	Morris
ENGILL, John	1798	Morrison
ENGILL, Michal	1798	Morrison
ENGLAND, Charles	1778	
ENGLAND, John	1778	
ENGLAND, Joseph	1778	
ENGLE, George	1790	Stone
ENGLE, George	1791	Stone

Surname, Given names	Year	Comp./Dist.
ENGLE, George	1793	Melvan
ENGLE, John	1791	Tullis
ENGLE, John	1792	Tulley
ENGLE, John	1793	Morrison
ENGLE, John	1794	Morrison
ENGLE, John	1798	Morrison
ENGLE, John	1799	Morrison
ENGLE, John	1801	Morrison
ENGLE, John	1806	Carr
ENGLE, John	1807	Carr
ENGLE, John Jr.	1815	Hoss
ENGLE, Michael	1793	Melvan
ENGLE, Michel	1790	Stone
ENGLE, Michel	1791	Stone
ENGLE, Michel	1794	Morrison
ENGLE, Nichel	1793	Morrison
ENGLE, William	1806	Brown
ENGLE, Wm	1814	Bean
ENGLES, D. D. (estate)	1818	Harris
ENGLES, Wm (estate)	1819	Harris
ENGLISH, Alexander	1815	Grimsley
ENGLISH, Alexander	1816	Grimsley
ENGLISH, Andrew	1779	Wilson
ENGLISH, Elizabeth	1816	Grimsley
ENGLISH, Elizabeth	1817	Grimsley
ENGLISH, Elizabeth	1818	Grimsley
ENGLISH, James	1778	
ENGLISH, John	1801	Glasscock
ENGLISH, John	1805	Rector
ENGLISH, John	1809	Cade
ENGLISH, John	1812	Barnes
ENGLISH, John	1814	Barns
ENGLISH, John	1815	Grimsley
ENGLISH, John	1816	Grimsley
ENGLISH, John	1817	Grimsley
ENGLISH, John	1818	Grimsley
ENGLISH, John	1819	Grimsley
ENGLISH, John	1780-1781 (Undated)	
ENGLISH, Joseph	1778	
ENGLISH, Joseph	1778	
ENGLISH, Joseph	1779	Wilson
ENGLISH, Robert	1790	Williams
ENGLISH, Robert	1791	Williams
ENGLISH, Robert	1792	Maxwell
ENGLISH, Robert	1793	Maxwell
ENGLISH, Robert	1794	Taylor
ENGLISH, Stephen	1812	Ellis
ENGLISH, Thomas	1801	Glasscock
ENGLISH, Thomas	1805	Rector
ENGLISH, Thomas	1809	Cade
ENGLISH, Thomas	1812	Barnes
ENGLISH, Thomas	1814	Barns
ENGLISH, Thomas	1815	Grimsley
ENGLISH, Wm	1778	
ENGLISH, Wm	1817	Harris
ENLISH, John	1807	Cade
ENLISH, Tomas	1807	Cade
ENSOR, Mary	1812	Britton
ENSOR, Thomas	1790	Stone
ENSOR, Thomas	1791	Stone
ENSOR, Thomas	1793	Murray
ENSOR, Thomas	1794	Murray
ENSOR, Thomas	1795	Murray
ENSOR, Thomas	1796	Shipley
ENSOR, Thomas	1805	Doak
ENSOR, Thomas	1806	Crouch
ENSOR, Thomas	1806	Doke
ENSOR, Thomas	1807	Britton
ENSOR, Thomas	1812	Ellis
ENSOR, William	1797	Shipley
ENSOR, William	1806	Crouch
ENSOR, William	1809	Right
ENSOR, William T.	1811	Ellis
ENSOR, William T.	1812	Ellis
ENSOR, Wm T.	1814	Bean
EPERSON, Anthony	1801	Glasscock
EPERSON, Anthony	1807	Cade
EPHESON, Anthoney	1790	Shipley
EPHESON, Anthoney	1791	Shipley
EPHESON, Samuel	1790	Shipley
EPHESON, Samuel	1791	Shipley
EPPERSON, Antho	1813	Copas
EPPERSON, Anthony	1794	Murray
EPPERSON, Anthony	1795	Murray
EPPERSON, Anthony	1796	Shipley
EPPERSON, Anthony	1797	Shipley
EPPERSON, Anthony	1798	Shipley
EPPERSON, Anthony	1801	Lane
EPPERSON, Anthony	1805	Doak
EPPERSON, Anthony	1807	Britton
EPPERSON, Anthony	1809	Cade
EPPERSON, Anthony	1813	Copas
EPPERSON, Anthony	1814	Copes
EPPERSON, Anthony	1814	Copes
EPPERSON, Anthony Jr.	1805	Doak
EPPERSON, Anthony Jr.	1812	Britton
EPPERSON, Antony	1808	Cade
EPPERSON, Benjaman	1814	Copes
EPPERSON, Benjamin	1813	Copas
EPPERSON, Benjamin	1815	Copas
EPPERSON, Benjamin	1816	Copas
EPPERSON, Elijah	1805	Rector

Surname, Given names	Year	Comp./Dist.
EPPERSON, Elijah	1809	Cade
EPPERSON, Elijah	1810	Barron
EPPERSON, Jesse	1801	Lane
EPPERSON, Peter	1794	Murray
EPPERSON, Peter	1795	Murray
EPPERSON, Peter	1796	Shipley
EPPERSON, Peter	1797	Shipley
EPPERSON, Peter	1798	Shipley
EPPERSON, Peter	1801	Glasscock
EPPERSON, Samuel	1794	Murray
EPPERSON, Samuel	1795	Murray
EPPERSON, Samuel	1796	Shipley
EPPERSON, Samuel	1797	Duncan
EPPERSON, Samuel	1801	Lane
EPPERSON, Samuel	1805	Doak
EPPERSON, Samuel	1807	Britton
EPPERSON, Samuel	1811	Britten
EPPERSON, Samuel	1812	Britton
EPPERSON, Samuel	1813	Copas
EPPERSON, Samuel	1814	Copes
EPPERSON, Samuel	1815	Copas
EPPERSON, Samuel	1816	Copas
EPPERSON, Thomas	1813	Copas
EPPERSON, Thomas	1814	Copes
EPPERSON, Thomas	1815	Copas
EPPESON, Anthoney	1793	Murray
EPPESON, Anthoney	1806	Doke
EPPESON, Benjamin	1797	Shipley
EPPESON, Peter	1793	Murray
EPPESON, Samuel	1793	Murray
EPPESON, Samuel	1806	Doke
EPPISON, Anthoney Jr.	1812	Britton
ERLE, Samuel	1821	Howard
ERLEY, Thomas	1821	Howard
-ERLING, Joseph	1806	Payn
EROIN, Alex (In Burk.)	1778	
ERVIN,	1793	North
ERVIN, Jas.	1791	North
ERVIN, John	1805	Aikin
ERVIN, Patrik	1805	Aikin
ERVIN, Rob	1791	North
ERVIN, Sam	1791	North
ERVIN, Samuel	1794	Scot
ERVIN, William	1806	Parker
ERVIN, William	1807	Parker
ERVIN, William	1810	Hartzel
ERVIN, William	1814	Brown
ERWENE, Benjamin	1798	Young
ERWIN, Alexander	1815	Grimsley
ERWIN, Alexander	1816	Grimsley
ERWIN, Frances	1812	McCray
ERWIN, George	1809	Cade
ERWIN, George	1815	Grimsley
ERWIN, George	1816	Grimsley
ERWIN, George	1817	Grimsley
ERWIN, George	1818	Grimsley
ERWIN, George	1819	Grimsley
ERWIN, Gorge	1812	Barnes
ERWIN, John	1801	Aiken
ERWIN, Pattrick	1806	Guin
ERWIN, Samuel	1796	Brown
ERWIN, William	1814	Hartsell
ERWIN, William	1815	Fines
ERWIN, William	1815	Hartsell
ERWIN, William	1816	Brown
ERWIN, William	1816	Fine
ERWIN, William	1817	Brown
ERWIN, William	1817	Fine
ERWIN, William	1818	Brown
ERWIN, William	1818	Fine
ERWIN, William	1819	Brown
ERWIN, William	1819	Howard
ERWIN, William	1821	Haines
ERWINE, Robert	1798	Young
ESKERSON, Rob	1791	Willey
ESPAY, Thomas	1781	
ESTER, John B.	1821	Smith
ESTES, John B.	1816	Smith
ESTES, John B.	1819	Smith
ESTILL, Solomon	1809	Right
ESTREGE, Richard	1794	Thornton
ESTRIDGE, Richard	1795	Thornton
ETES, John B.	1817	Smith
EUIT, John	1817	Hampton
EVANS, Archer	1793	Maxwell
EVANS, Archibald	1795	Taylor
EVANS, Farlar	1806	Odel
EVANS, Farlor	1801	Longmire
EVANS, George	1793	Depew
EVANS, George	1795	Calvert
EVANS, George	1797	Hannah
EVANS, George	1799	Hannah
EVANS, John	1778	
EVANS, John	1792	Coye
EVANS, Thomas	1778	
EVANS, Thomas	1792	Coye
EVANS, Thomas	1801	Longmire
EVANS, Thomas	1806	Odel
EVANS, Thos	1793	Scott
EVENS, Archer	1794	Taylor
EVENS, George	1792	Scott
EVENS, George	1798	Hannah

Surname, Given names	Year	Comp./Dist.
EVENS, John	1793	Hale
EVENS, Thomas	1793	Hale
EVERETT, James	1790	Stone
EVERETT, James	1791	Stone
EVINS, Forlen	1798	Longmire
EVINS, George	1794	Scot
EVINS, George	1796	Millikin
EVINS, John	1798	Longmire
EVINS, Samuel	1795	Carriger
EVINS, Thos	1798	Longmire
EWEN, John	1796	Calvert
FAGUSON, Thomas	1808	Guin
FAIN, Abenezor	1814	McCray
FAIN, Agnes (Widow)	1792	Tulley
FAIN, Agness	1795	Morrison
FAIN, David	1805	Jas Parker
FAIN, Ebeneaser	1812	McCray
FAIN, Ebenezer	1819	Harris
FAIN, Ebenzer	1816	Harrison
FAIN, John	1787	Fains
FAIN, John	1799	Stuart
FAIN, John	1801	Aiken
FAIN, John	1805	Guir
FAIN, John	1806	Grur
FAIN, John	1808	Gwin
FAIN, John	1809	Green
FAIN, John	1813	Hoss
FAIN, John	1814	McCray
FAIN, John	1815	Hoss
FAIN, John	1816	Harrison
FAIN, John	1816	Hoss
FAIN, John	1817	Harris
FAIN, John	1821	Jones
FAIN, Nancey	1793	Morrison
FAIN, Nancey	1794	Morrison
FAIN, Nicholas	1807	Anderson
FAIN, Niclos	1781	
FAIN, Saml	1787	Fains
FAIN, Samuel	1778	
FAIN, Samuel	1791	Tullis
FAIN, Samuel	1792	Tulley
FAIN, Samuel	1793	Morrison
FAIN, Samuel	1794	Morrison
FAIN, Samuel	1817	Harris
FAIN, Samuel (deceased)	1811	McCray
FAIN, Samuel (estate of)	1799	Morrison
FAIN, Samuel (heirs of)	1813	Hoss
FAIN, Samuel (heirs)	1815	Hoss
FAIN, Samuel W.	1816	Harrison
FAIN, Thomas	1813	Hoss
FAIN, Thomas	1815	Hoss
FAIN, Thomas	1819	Hair
FAIN, William	1781	
FAIN, William	1796	Longmire
FAIN, William	1798	Calvert
FAIN, William	1801	Calvert
FAIN, William	1805	Aikin
FAIN, William	1805	Jas Parker
FAIN, William	1806	Anderson
FAIN, William	1807	Anderson
FAIN, William	1811	McCray
FAIN, William	1812	McCray
FAIN, William	1814	McCray
FAIN, William D. (estate)	1816	Harrison
FAIN, Wm	1791	Willey
FAIN, Wm	1792	Scott
FAIN, Wm	1795	Calvert
FAIN, Wm	1799	Stuart
FAIN, Wm	1808	Parker
FAIN, Wm	1809	Parker
FAINE, John	1797	Calvert
FAINE, John	1797	Calvert
FAINE, John	1814	Hoss
FAINE, Saml (heirs of)	1814	Hoss
FAINE, Thomas	1814	Hoss
FAINE, William	1809	Roadmas
FAINE, Willm	1797	Calvert
FAINS, Samuel (estate of)	1801	Morrison
FAIR, William	1812	McCray
F-AKER, Michal	1797	Duncan
FALLS, James	1811	McAlister
FALLS, John	1796	Millikin
FALLS, John	1797	Hannah
FANE, Thomas	1808	Carr
FANEELER, Frederick	1821	Hunt
FANN, Mapy	1805	Aikin
FANNAN, Nathan	1812	McCray
FANNCAN, Frederick	1817	Hunt
FANNING, Nathan	1811	McCray
FANSLAR, Frederick	1811	Davis
FARGASON, John	1811	Davis
FARGASON, Samuel	1811	Davis
FARGASON, Thomas	1811	Davis
FARGESON, Henry	1811	Davis
FARGESON, Henry	1815	McLin
FARGESON, John	1811	Davis
FARGESON, John	1815	McLin
FARGESON, Thomas	1814	McLin
FARGESON, Thomas	1815	McLin
FARGISON, John	1781	
FARGISSON, Alexander	1799	Duncan
FARGISSON, John	1799	Duncan

Surname, Given names	Year	Comp./Dist.
FARGISSON, Thomas	1799	Duncan
FARGUSON, Alexander	1794	Depew
FARGUSON, Alexander	1808	Guin
FARGUSON, Alexander	1783 [after]	Depew
FARGUSON, Henry	1812	McLin
FARGUSON, Jean	1812	McLin
FARGUSON, John	1792	Depew
FARGUSON, John	1793	Depew
FARGUSON, John	1794	Depew
FARGUSON, John	1808	Guin
FARGUSON, John	1812	McLin
FARGUSON, John	1812	McLin
FARGUSON, John Taylor	1815	McLin
FARGUSON, Samuel	1808	Guin
FARGUSON, Thomas	1783 [after]	Depew
FARGUSSON, Henry	1799	Duncan
FARIS, Gideon	1816	Hampton
FARIS, Gideon	1818	Brown [2]
FARIS, Gideon	1819	Brown
FARLEN, Ambrous	1817	Brown
FARLER, Ambrose	1818	Brown
FARLER, Ambrous	1816	Brown
FARLER, Obadiah	1793	Depew
FARLER, Obadiah	1794	Depew
FARLEY, Obediah	1790	Shipley
FARLEY, Obediah	1791	Shipley
FARRAN, Nathan	1812	McCray
FARRIS, Jilian	1817	Hampton
FARRIS, Thomas	1781	
FARRIS, William	1793	Thornton
FAUBUSH, David	1798	Crouch
FAUBUSH, Hugh	1798	Crouch
FAUBUSH, Hugh	1806	Guin
FAULING, William (Decd.)	1778	
FAWBUSH, Hugh	1809	Right
FAWBUSH, Hugh	1814	Bean
FAWBUSH, Hugh	1815	Haire
FAWBUSH, Hugh	1816	Hair
FAWBUSH, Thomas	1815	Haire
FAWBUSH, Thomas	1816	Hair
FAWBUSH, Thomas	1817	Haire
FAZEL, Martin	1819	Findley
FAZIE, Martin	1815	Waddell
FEASLE, Martin	1821	McGee
FEASTER, Levi	1815	Carcathers
FEASTON, Abraham	1819	Grimsley
FEAZEL, Mark	1818	Riley
FEAZEL, Martin	1811	Green
FEAZEL, Martin	1814	Waddell
FEAZEL, Martin	1816	Waddell
FEAZEL, Martin	1817	Riley

Surname, Given names	Year	Comp./Dist.
FEIMAH, Peter	1801	Roberson
FELAN, Christelton	1791	Willey
FELKER, Jonathan	1807	Parker
FELKER, Jonathan	1808	Parker
FELKIN, Jonathan	1812	Hartsell
FELKS, Jonathan	1817	Fine
FELLONS, Jacob G.	1819	Findley
FELLOW, Jacob	1815	Waddell
FELLOWS, Jacob	1806	Grur
FELLOWS, Jacob	1808	Gwin
FELLOWS, Jacob	1809	Green
FELLOWS, Jacob	1810	Green
FELLOWS, Jacob	1816	Waddell
FELLOWS, Jacob	1817	Riley
FELLOWS, Jacob	1821	McGee
FELSAWS, Adam	1792	Scott
FELTS, William	1814	McCracken
FELTS, William	1815	Garner
FELTS, William	1817	Smith
FELTS, William	1818	Smith
FENALIN, Frederick	1819	Hunt
FENDLEY, Daniel	1816	Waddell
FENEELES, Fredrick	1814	McLin
FENILL, Smythe (Single)	1779	Wilson
FENSLER, Frederick	1812	McLin
FENULER, Frederick	1816	Hunt
FENULES, Frederick	1815	McLin
FERAL, Smith	1780-1781 (Undated)	
FERGASON, Thomas	1806	Guin
FERGERSON, John	1791	White
FERGERSON, John	1795	Ford
FERGESON & HODGES,	1779	
FERGUSON, Alexander	1797	Duncan
FERGUSON, Alexander	1801	Taylor
FERGUSON, Alexander	1809	Gwin
FERGUSON, Henry	1797	Duncan
FERGUSON, Henry	1801	Taylor
FERGUSON, Henry	1809	Gwin
FERGUSON, Henry	1814	McLin
FERGUSON, Henry	1816	Hunt
FERGUSON, Henry	1817	Hunt
FERGUSON, Henry	1818	Hunt
FERGUSON, Henry	1819	Hunt
FERGUSON, John	1797	Duncan
FERGUSON, John	1801	Taylor
FERGUSON, John	1806	Guin
FERGUSON, John	1809	Gwin
FERGUSON, John	1809	Gwin
FERGUSON, John	1818	Hunt
FERGUSON, John	1819	Hunt
FERGUSON, John	1821	Hunt

Surname, Given names	Year	Comp./Dist.
FERGUSON, John Jr.	1801	Taylor
FERGUSON, John Layton	1817	Hunt
FERGUSON, John Sr.	1806	Guin
FERGUSON, John Taylor	1816	Hunt
FERGUSON, Larkin	1819	Smith
FERGUSON, Nelly	1821	Hunt
FERGUSON, Samuel	1809	Gwin
FERGUSON, Thomas	1797	Duncan
FERGUSON, Thomas	1812	McLin
FERGUSON, Thomas	1816	Hunt
FERGUSON, Thomas	1817	Hunt
FERGUSON, Thomas	1818	Hunt
FERGUSON, Thomas	1819	Hunt
FERGUSON, Thomas	1821	Hunt
FERGUSSON, John	1806	Guin
FERREL, Smith	1781	
FERYLER, Frederick	1818	Hunt
FESTER, Grey	1821	Martin
FEZEL, Martin	1812	Waddill
FICKE, John	1796	Brown
FILLORYM, Jacob	1818	Riley
FINCH, Calvan	1814	McCray
FINCH, Calvin	1792	Scott
FINCH, Calvin	1795	Calvert
FINCH, Calvin	1796	Calvert
FINCH, Calvin	1797	Calvert
FINCH, Calvin	1797	Calvert
FINCH, Calvin	1798	Calvert
FINCH, Calvin	1801	Calvert
FINCH, Calvin	1805	Jas Parker
FINCH, Calvin	1808	Parker
FINCH, Calvin	1809	Parker
FINCH, Calvin	1811	McCray
FINCH, Calvin	1812	McCray
FINCH, Calvin	1812	McCray
FINCH, Calvin	1816	Harrison
FINCH, Calvin	1817	Harris
FINCH, Calvin	1818	Harris
FINCH, Calvin	1819	Harris
FINCH, Calvin	1821	Hampton
FINCH, Colven	1793	Scott
FINCH, Elemezar	1818	Harris
FINCH, John	1818	Harris
FINCH, Thomas	1811	McCray
FINCH, Thomas	1812	McCray
FINCH, Thomas	1812	McCray
FINCH, Thomas	1814	McCray
FINCH, Thomas	1816	Harrison
FINCH, Thomas	1817	Harris
FINCH, Thomas	1818	Harris
FINCH, Thomas	1819	Harris

Surname, Given names	Year	Comp./Dist.
FINCH, Thomas	1821	Hampton
FINCH, Thos	1809	Parker
FINCH, William	1819	Harris
FINDLEY, Daniel	1817	Riley
FINDLEY, Daniel	1818	Riley
FINDLEY, James	1816	Waddell
FINDLEY, James	1817	Riley
FINDLEY, James	1818	Riley
FINDLEY, James	1819	Findley
FINE, Abraham	1812	Hartsell
FINE, Abraham	1814	Hartsell
FINE, Abraham	1815	Fines
FINE, Abraham	1816	Fine
FINE, Abraham	1817	Fine
FINE, Abraham	1818	Fine
FINE, Abraham	1819	Howard
FINE, Abraham	1821	Howard
FINE, Elijah	1805	Parker
FINE, Elijah	1806	Parker
FINE, Elijah	1807	Parker
FINE, Elijah	1808	Parker
FINE, Elijah	1810	Hartzel
FINE, Elijah	1812	Hartsell
FINE, Elijah	1814	Hartsell
FINE, Elijah	1815	Fines
FINE, Elijah	1816	Fine
FINE, Elijah	1817	Fine
FINE, Elijah	1818	Fine
FINE, Elijah	1819	Howard
FINE, Elijah	1821	Howard
FINE, Jno	1809	Par
FINE, John	1791	North
FINE, John	1792	North
FINE, John	1793	North
FINE, John	1794	North
FINE, John	1795	Young
FINE, John	1796	Young
FINE, John	1797	Young
FINE, John	1798	Young
FINE, John	1801	Taylor
FINE, John	1805	Parker
FINE, John	1806	Parker
FINE, John	1807	Parker
FINE, John	1808	Parker
FINE, John	1810	Hartzel
FINE, John	1812	Hartsell
FINE, John	1814	Hartsell
FINE, John	1815	Fines
FINE, John	1816	Fine
FINE, John	1817	Fine
FINE, John	1818	Fine

Surname, Given names	Year	Comp./Dist.
FINE, John	1819	Howard
FINE, John	1821	Howard
FINE, Sigh	1809	Par
FINKES, William	1792	Coye
FINLEY, Christian	1798	Shipley
FINLEY, Daniel	1797	Calvert
FINLEY, Daniel	1799	Stuart
FINLEY, Daniel	1812	Waddill
FINLEY, Daniel	1814	Waddell
FINLEY, Daniel	1815	Waddell
FINLEY, James	1812	Waddill
FINLEY, James	1815	Waddell
FINLEY, Thomas	1790	Shipley
FINLEY, Thomas	1791	Shipley
FINLY, Daniel	1806	Grur
FINLY, Daniel	1811	Green
FINLY, Dannel	1805	Guir
FINN, Jesse	1779	
FINN, Peter	1790	Shipley
FINN, Peter	1791	Shipley
FINTCH, Calvin	1791	Willey
FINTCH, Calvin	1794	Scot
FINTER, Andrew	1805	Guir
FINTER, Andrew	1808	Gwin
FINTER, Andrew	1810	Green
FIRAIN, George	1821	Martin
FIRGUSON, Alaxander	1798	Duncan
FIRGUSON, Alexander	1798	Duncan
FIRGUSON, Alexander	1807	Givins
FIRGUSON, Henry	1798	Duncan
FIRGUSON, John	1798	Duncan
FIRGUSON, John	1798	Duncan
FIRGUSON, John	1807	Givins
FIRGUSON, John	1807	Givins
FIRGUSON, Samuel	1798	Duncan
FIRGUSON, Samuel	1807	Givins
FIRGUSON, Thomas	1798	Duncan
FIRGUSON, Thomas	1798	Duncan
FIRGUSON, Thomas	1807	Givins
FITCHGARREL, Geog	1793	North
FITCHGERALD, George	1794	North
FITCHGERALL, George	1791	North
FITSGARRETT, Aiken	1821	Hale
FITSGARRETT, James	1821	Hale
FITSGERILL, Aiken	1818	Grisham
FITSGERILL, James	1818	Grisham
FITSZARRALD, James	1815	Copas
FITSZARRELL, Aiken	1817	Grisham
FITSZARRELL, James	1817	Grisham
FITZARREL, Aiken	1816	Copas
FITZARREL, James	1816	Copas
FITZGARROLD, George	1801	Taylor
FITZGERALD, George	1798	Young
FITZGERILL, Aiken	1819	Grisham
FITZGERILL, James	1819	Grisham
FLANARY, William	1778	
FLANARY, William	1790	White
FLANARY, William	1791	White
FLANARY, William	1793	Thornton
FLANARY, William	1794	Carriger
FLEMING, Samuel	1809	Gwin
FLETCHER, Richd	1778	
FLETCHER, Thomas	1778	
FLETCHER, William	1819	Hunt
FLID, Isaac	1813	Hoss
FLIN, George	1809	Roadmas
FLINN, George	1815	Garner
FLIPPING, Thomas	1781	
FLOYD, Isaac	1814	Hoss
FLOYD, Isaac	1818	Jones
FLOYD, Isaac	1819	Jones
FLOYDE, Isaac	1817	Little
FOARD, Grant	1815	Copas
FOARD, Grant	1816	Copas
FOARD, Horatio	1806	Carr
FOARD, Horatio Jr.	1815	Hoss
FOARD, Horatio Jr.	1816	Hoss
FOARD, Horatio Sr.	1815	Hoss
FOARD, Horatio Sr.	1816	Hoss
FOARD, James	1815	Copas
FOARD, John	1797	Shipley
FOARD, John	1815	Copas
FOARD, John	1815	Grimsley
FOARD, John	1816	Copas
FOARD, John	1816	Grimsley
FOARD, Loyd	1815	Copas
FOARD, Loyd (of Loyd)	1815	Copas
FOARD, Loyd Jr.	1815	Copas
FOARD, Loyd Jr.	1816	Copas
FOARD, Loyd Sr.	1816	Copas
FOARD, Mary	1815	Hoss
FOARD, Mary	1816	Hoss
FOARD, May	1816	Copas
FOARD, Morduai	1815	Copas
FOARD, Morduai	1816	Copas
FOARD, Stephen	1815	Grimsley
FOARD, Stephen	1816	Grimsley
FOARD, Thomas	1815	Copas
FOARD, Thomas	1815	Hoss
FOARD, Thomas Jr.	1816	Copas
FOARD, Thomas Sr.	1815	Copas
FOARD, Thomas Sr.	1816	Copas

Surname, Given names	Year	Comp./Dist.
FOASE, Nicholas	1791	Chisom
FOLKESIN, John	1808	Carr
FOLLET, George	1814	Waddell
FOLLET, George	1815	Waddell
FOLLET, George	1816	Waddell
FOLLET, George	1819	Findley
FOLLET, Jeremiah	1811	Green
FOLLET, Jeremiah	1815	Waddell
FOLLET, Jeremiah	1816	Waddell
FOORD, Loyd Sr.	1793	Murray
FOORD, Mordiai	1790	Shipley
FOORD, Mordiai	1791	Shipley
FOORD, Mordicai	1793	Murray
FOORD, Thomas	1793	Murray
FOOSE, Nicholas	1792	Chisolm
FORBES, Hugh	1808	
FORBUGH, Hugh	1796	Shipley
FORBUSH, Andrew	1795	Murray
FORBUSH, David	1805	Doak
FORBUSH, David	1806	Doke
FORBUSH, David	1807	Britton
FORBUSH, Hugh	1794	Carriger
FORBUSH, Hugh	1795	Murray
FORBUSH, Hugh	1811	Ellis
FORBUSH, Hugh	1812	Ellis
FORBUSH, Thomas	1812	Ellis
FORBUSH, Thomas	1813	Copas
FORD, Alexander	1821	Hale
FORD, Barney	1807	Carr
FORD, Benjamin	1816	Copas
FORD, Ezekial	1819	Jones
FORD, Ezekiel	1817	Little
FORD, Ezekiel	1818	Jones
FORD, Grand	1818	Grisham
FORD, Grant	1819	Grisham
FORD, Grant	1821	Hale
FORD, Haratio	1801	Morrison
FORD, Horash	1798	Morrison
FORD, Horatia Jr.	1819	Jones
FORD, Horatio	1798	Morrison
FORD, Horatio	1798	Morrison
FORD, Horatio	1799	Morrison
FORD, Horatio	1807	Carr
FORD, Horatio	1808	Carr
FORD, Horatio	1809	Carr
FORD, Horatio	[1796] 1797	Morris
FORD, Horatio Jr.	1811	Mitchell
FORD, Horatio Jr.	1813	Hoss
FORD, Horatio Jr.	1814	Hoss
FORD, Horatio Jr.	1817	Little
FORD, Horatio Jr.	1818	Jones
FORD, Horatio Jr.	1821	Jones
FORD, Horatio Sr.	1811	Mitchell
FORD, Horatio Sr.	1813	Hoss
FORD, Horatio Sr.	1814	Hoss
FORD, Horatio Sr.	1817	Little
FORD, Horatio Sr.	1818	Jones
FORD, Horatio Sr.	1821	Jones
FORD, James	1794	Murray
FORD, James	1795	Murray
FORD, James	1798	Shipley
FORD, James	1801	Lane
FORD, James	1805	Doak
FORD, James	1807	Britton
FORD, James	1807	Britton
FORD, James	1811	Britten
FORD, James	1812	Britton
FORD, James	1813	Copas
FORD, James	1817	Grisham
FORD, James	1818	Grisham
FORD, James	1819	Grisham
FORD, James	1821	Hale
FORD, James (of Loyd Jr.)	1814	Copes
FORD, James (of Loyd Sr.)	1814	Copes
FORD, James (of Loyd)	1812	Britton
FORD, James (the older)	1806	Doke
FORD, James (the younger)	1806	Doke
FORD, James Jr.	1805	Doak
FORD, James Jr.	1811	Britten
FORD, James Jr.	1813	Copas
FORD, John	1793	Murray
FORD, John	1794	Murray
FORD, John	1795	Murray
FORD, John	1798	Shipley
FORD, John	1801	Glasscock
FORD, John	1801	Lane
FORD, John	1805	Doak
FORD, John	1805	Rector
FORD, John	1807	Britton
FORD, John	1807	Cade
FORD, John	1808	Cade
FORD, John	1809	Cade
FORD, John	1811	Barron
FORD, John	1811	Britten
FORD, John	1811	Green
FORD, John	1812	Barnes
FORD, John	1812	Britton
FORD, John	1814	Barns
FORD, John	1817	Grimsley
FORD, John	1817	Grimsley
FORD, John	1817	Grisham
FORD, John	1818	Grimsley

Surname, Given names	Year	Comp./Dist.
FORD, John	1818	Grisham
FORD, John	1819	Grimsley
FORD, John	1819	Grisham
FORD, John	1821	Hale
FORD, John	1821	Martin
FORD, John (of Loyd Sr.)	1806	Doke
FORD, John (of Loyd Sr.)	1814	Copes
FORD, John Jr.	1818	Grimsley
FORD, John Jr.	1819	Grimsley
FORD, Joseph	1790	White
FORD, Joseph	1791	White
FORD, Joseph	1792	White
FORD, Joseph	1793	Campbell
FORD, Joseph	1795	Ford
FORD, Loid	1798	Shipley
FORD, Loid Jr.	1798	Shipley
FORD, Loyd	1796	Shipley
FORD, Loyd	1801	Lane
FORD, Loyd	1812	Britton
FORD, Loyd	1817	Grisham
FORD, Loyd	1818	Grisham
FORD, Loyd	1819	Grisham
FORD, Loyd (the younger)	1807	Britton
FORD, Loyd Jr.	1793	Murray
FORD, Loyd Jr.	1794	Murray
FORD, Loyd Jr.	1795	Murray
FORD, Loyd Jr.	1797	Shipley
FORD, Loyd Jr.	1801	Lane
FORD, Loyd Jr.	1805	Doak
FORD, Loyd Jr.	1806	Doke
FORD, Loyd Jr.	1807	Britton
FORD, Loyd Jr.	1811	Britten
FORD, Loyd Jr.	1813	Copas
FORD, Loyd Jr.	1816	Copas
FORD, Loyd Jr.	1817	Grisham
FORD, Loyd Jr.	1818	Grisham
FORD, Loyd Jr.	1819	Grisham
FORD, Loyd Jr.	1821	Hale
FORD, Loyd Sr.	1794	Murray
FORD, Loyd Sr.	1795	Murray
FORD, Loyd Sr.	1796	Shipley
FORD, Loyd Sr.	1797	Shipley
FORD, Loyd Sr.	1805	Doak
FORD, Loyd Sr.	1806	Doke
FORD, Loyd Sr.	1807	Britton
FORD, Loyd Sr.	1811	Britten
FORD, Loyd Sr.	1813	Copas
FORD, Loyd Sr.	1814	Copes
FORD, Loyd Sr.	1821	Hale
FORD, Mary	1808	Carr
FORD, Mary	1809	Carr
FORD, Mary	1811	Mitchell
FORD, Mary	1813	Hoss
FORD, Mary	1814	Hoss
FORD, Mary	1817	Little
FORD, Mary	1818	Jones
FORD, Mary	1819	Jones
FORD, Mary	1821	Jones
FORD, Medicai	1819	Grisham
FORD, Merdica	1809	Roadmas
FORD, Merdicai	1819	Grisham
FORD, Micasah	1819	Jones
FORD, Mordecai	1798	Shipley
FORD, Mordecia	1814	Copes
FORD, Mordge	1808	Carr
FORD, Mordian	1796	Shipley
FORD, Mordica	1801	Lane
FORD, Mordica	1805	Doak
FORD, Mordica	1811	Britten
FORD, Mordica	1811	Mitchell
FORD, Mordica	1813	Copas
FORD, Mordica	1817	Grisham
FORD, Mordica	1818	Grisham
FORD, Mordica	1818	Grisham
FORD, Mordica Jr.	1817	Grisham
FORD, Mordica Jr.	1821	Hale
FORD, Mordicai	1794	Murray
FORD, Mordicai	1795	Murray
FORD, Mordicai	1797	Shipley
FORD, Mordicai	1806	Doke
FORD, Mordicai	1807	Britton
FORD, Mordicai	1812	Britton
FORD, Mordicia	1821	Hale
FORD, Nimord	1821	Jones
FORD, Nimrod	1818	Jones
FORD, Pruit	1817	Grisham
FORD, Sisley	1821	Hale
FORD, Thomas	1794	Murray
FORD, Thomas	1795	Murray
FORD, Thomas	1796	Shipley
FORD, Thomas	1797	Shipley
FORD, Thomas	1798	Shipley
FORD, Thomas	1801	Lane
FORD, Thomas	1811	Britten
FORD, Thomas	1812	Britton
FORD, Thomas	1813	Hoss
FORD, Thomas	1814	Hoss
FORD, Thomas	1818	Grisham
FORD, Thomas	1821	Hale
FORD, Thomas Jr.	1813	Copas
FORD, Thomas Jr.	1814	Copes
FORD, Thomas Jr.	1817	Grisham

Surname, Given names	Year	Comp./Dist.
FORD, Thomas Sr.	1813	Copas
FORD, Thomas Sr.	1814	Copes
FORD, William	1793	Murray
FORD, William	1794	Murray
FORD, William	1795	Murray
FORD, William	1796	Shipley
FORD, William	1797	Shipley
FORD, William	1798	Shipley
FORD, William	1821	Hale
FORD, Wm	1801	Glasscock
FORGESON, Alexander	1806	Guin
FORGESON, Thomas	1809	Gwin
FORGISON, Cumberland	1801	Biddle
FOSTER, James	1811	McCray
FOSTER, James	1812	McCray
FOSTER, James	1812	McCray
FOSTER, Levi	1807	Anderson
FOSTER, Mark	1780-1781	District 7
FOSTER, Peter R.	1819	Hunt
FOSTER, Robert	1811	McCray
FOSTER, Robert	1812	McCray
FOSTER, Robert	1812	McCray
FOSTER, Thomas	1807	Odell
FOSTER, Thomas	1817	Brown
FOSTER, Thomas	1818	Brown
FOSTER, Thomas	1819	Brown
FOSTER, Thomas	1821	Haines
FOSTER, William	1811	McCray
FOSTER, William	1812	McCray
FOSTER, William	1812	McCray
FOULS, James	1812	Crawford [2]
FOWBUSH, Thos	1821	Louis
FOWER, Samuel	1814	Waddell
FOWLER, Joseph	1778	
FOWLER, Thomas	1781	
FOWLER, Thomas	1780-1781 (Undated)	
FOWLS, James	1812	Crawford
FOX, Adam	1821	Louis
FOX, Daniel	1821	Louis
FOX, Jacob	1810	Green
FOX, Jacob	1811	Green
FOX, Jacob	1812	Waddill
FOX, Jacob	1814	Waddell
FRAKER, John	1801	Lane
FRAKER, Michael	1799	Duncan
FRAKER, Michal	1796	Longmire
FRAKER, Michel	1798	Duncan
FRALEY, Christian	1793	Melvan
FRALEY, Christian	1794	Melvan
FRALEY, Christian	1795	Murray
FRALEY, Christopher	1797	Shipley

Surname, Given names	Year	Comp./Dist.
FRANCE, Archable	1821	Sands
FRANCE, Archibald	1811	
FRANCE, Archibald	1815	Carcathers
FRANCE, Archibald	1816	Giles
FRANCE, Archibald	1818	Land
FRANCE, Archibald	1819	Sands
FRANCE, Daniel	1819	Howard
FRANCE, Daniel	1821	Howard
FRANCE, Ephram	1821	Howard
FRANCE, Jno	1809	Par
FRANCE, John	1801	Taylor
FRANCE, John	1807	Parker
FRANCE, John	1810	Hartzel
FRANCE, John	1814	Hartsell
FRANCE, John	1815	Fines
FRANCE, John	1817	Fine
FRANCE, John	1818	Fine
FRANCE, John	1819	Howard
FRANCE, John	1819	Howard
FRANCE, John Jr.	1821	Howard
FRANCE, John Sr.	1812	Hartsell
FRANCES, John	1797	Young
FRANCIS, Archibald	1817	Gillises
FRANCIS, John	1798	Young
FRANCIS, John	1805	Parker
FRANCIS, John	1816	Fine
FRANCIS, John	[1796] 1797	Morris
FRANCIS, John Sr.	1821	Howard
FRANCISCO, John	1781	
FRANKEN, Michael	1798	Duncan
FRANKLIN, Josiah	1811	McCray
FRANKLIN, Josiah (estate)	1814	McCray
FRANKS, Keith	1795	Taylor
FRANKS, Richard	1794	Taylor
FRAZER, Alexander	1795	Carriger
FRAZOR, Henery	1814	Crookshanks
FREIND, Jacob	1801	Aiken
FREINTEH, Peeter	1794	Brown
FRENCH, Henrey	1792	Scott
FRENCH, L. William	1821	McClure
FRENCH, Peter	1791	Chisom
FRENCH, Peter	1792	Chisolm
FRENCH, Peter	1793	Brown
FRENCH, Petter	1796	Brown
FRENCH, William L.	1819	Smith
FRENCH, Wm L.	1820	Smith
FRENCH, Wm L.	1821	Smith
FRENTCH, Henery	1791	Willey
FRESOR, Henery	1812	Crawford [2]
FRESUR, Henery	1812	Crawford
FRIEND, Jacob	1801	

Surname, Given names	Year	Comp./Dist.
FRIER, Robert	1793	Scott
FRINCH, Peter	1797	Robertson
FRINCH, Peter	1799	Robertson
FRINTCH, George	1791	North
FRY, John	1809	Gwin
FRY, John	1811	Britten
FRY, John	1812	Ellis
FRY, John	1814	Bean
FRY, John	1815	Haire
FRY, John	1816	Hair
FRYER, Robert	1795	Calvert
F-SS, Isiah	1792	Brown
FUKEY, John	1797	Robertson
FULK, George	1819	McClure
FULK, Henry	1818	Harris
FULK, Henry	1819	Harris
FULKASON, Abraham	1814	Barns
FULKASON, Alexander	1814	Barns
FULKASON, John	1807	Cade
FULKASON, John	1808	Cade
FULKASON, John	1810	Barron
FULKASON, John	1814	Barns
FULKER, Jonathan	1806	Parker
FULKERS, John	1821	Martin
FULKERSON, Abraham	1815	Grimsley
FULKERSON, Abraham	1816	Grimsley
FULKERSON, Abraham	1817	Grimsley
FULKERSON, Abraham	1818	Grimsley
FULKERSON, Alexander	1815	Grimsley
FULKERSON, Alexander	1816	Hoss
FULKERSON, Alexander	1817	Little
FULKERSON, Alexander	1818	Jones
FULKERSON, Alexander	1819	Jones
FULKERSON, Alexander	1821	Jones
FULKERSON, James	1819	Grimsley
FULKERSON, James	1821	Jones
FULKERSON, John	1801	Glasscock
FULKERSON, John	1809	Cade
FULKERSON, John	1809	Carr
FULKERSON, John	1811	Barron
FULKERSON, John	1811	Mitchell
FULKERSON, John	1813	Hoss
FULKERSON, John	1814	Hoss
FULKERSON, John	1815	Grimsley
FULKERSON, John	1816	Grimsley
FULKERSON, John	1816	Hoss
FULKERSON, John	1817	Grimsley
FULKERSON, John	1817	Little
FULKERSON, John	1818	Grimsley
FULKERSON, John	1818	Jones
FULKERSON, John	1819	Grimsley
FULKERSON, John	1819	Jones
FULKERSON, John	1821	Jones
FULKES, Jonathan	1818	Fine
FULKES, Thomas	1817	Grimsley
FULKESON, Abraham	1812	Barnes
FULKINSON, John	1805	Rector
FULKISON, John	1812	Barnes
FULKS, David	1801	Roberson
FULKS, David	1805	Parker
FULKS, David	1806	Parker
FULKS, David	1807	Parker
FULKS, David	1809	Par
FULKS, David	1814	Hampton
FULKS, David	1816	Hampton
FULKS, David	1817	Hampton
FULKS, David	1818	Brown [2]
FULKS, David	1819	Brown
FULKS, George	1821	McClure
FULKS, John	1821	McGee
FULKS, Jonathan	[1796] 1797	Morris
FULKSON, Abraham	1821	Martin
FULLEN, Jacob	1811	Barron
FULLEN, James	1821	McClure
FULLEN, Samuel	1806	Crouch
FULLEN, Samuel	1809	Right
FULLER, Francis	1821	Brown
FULLER, Lamar	1821	Brown
FULMER, John	1819	Jones
FULMER, John	1821	Louis
FULTON, John	1801	Taylor
FURGESON, John	1790	White
FURGUSON, John	1814	McLin
FUSTON, John	1798	Duncan
FUSTON, John	1799	Duncan
GADIS, Samuel	1821	Martin
GAFORTH, Absolum	1801	Roberson
GAIN, John	1806	Parker
GAIN, Joshua	1814	Hartsell
GAIN, Joshua	1815	Fines
GAINS, Jno	1809	Par
GAINS, John	1807	Parker
GAINS, John	1813	Hoss
GAINS, John	1819	Hair
GALDSTON, Rubean	1805	Parker
GALEMOOR, Abraham	1801	Glasscock
GALKINS, Francis	1780-1781 (Undated)	
GALLAHER, James	1790	Hanley
GALLAHER, James	1791	Hanley
GALLAHER, John	1793	Handley
GALLAHER, John	1794	Handly
GALLAHER, John	1795	Handly

Surname, Given names	Year	Comp./Dist.
GALLAHER, John	1796	Handly
GALLAWAY, Thomas	1812	Britton
GALLIHAR, William	1796	Millikin
GALLOWAY, Daniel	1821	Hale
GALLOWAY, John	1816	Copas
GALLOWAY, John	1817	Grisham
GALLOWAY, John	1818	Grisham
GALLOWAY, John	1821	Hale
GALLOWAY, Pritchard	1811	Green
GALLOWAY, Thomas	1801	Glasscock
GALLOWAY, Thomas	1811	Britten
GALLOWAY, Thomas	1815	Copas
GALLOWAY, Thomas	1816	Copas
GALLOWAY, Thomas	1817	Grisham
GALLOWAY, Thomas	1818	Grisham
GALLOWAY, Thomas	1821	Hale
GALOGER, John	1779	Wilson
GALOWAY, John	1819	Grisham
GALOWAY, Thomas	1819	Grisham
GALWORTH, John	1815	Carcathers
GAMBEL, Andr	1807	Shields
GAMBELL, Samuel	1805	Doak
GAMBELL, Samuel	1807	Britton
GAMBELL, Samuel	1811	Britten
GAMBELL, Samuel	1812	Britton
GAMBELL, Samuel	1813	Copas
GAMBLE, Andrew	1794	Blair
GAMBLE, Andrew	1805	Carson
GAMBLE, Hugh	1798	Biddle
GAMBLE, Robert	1798	Biddle
GAMBLE, Samuel	1814	Copes
GAMBLE, Samuel	1816	Copas
GAMBLE, Samuel (heirs)	1817	Grisham
GAMBLE, Samuel (heirs)	1818	Grisham
GAMBLE, Samuel (heirs)	1819	Grisham
GAMM, Adam Jr.	1790	Milleken
GAMM, Adam Sr.	1790	Milleken
GAMM, Adam Sr.	1793	Handley
GAMM, Nathan	1790	Milleken
GAMM, Thos	1790	Milleken
GAMMEL, Robert	1781	
GAMS, Adam	1820	Smith
GAN, Adam	1790	Hanley
GAN, Adam	1790	Hanley
GAN, Adam	1791	Hanley
GAN, Adam	1791	Hanley
GAN, Adam	1814	Crookshanks
GAN, Daniel	1801	Gann
GAN, John	1790	Hanley
GAN, John	1791	Hanley
GAN, Thomas	1790	Hanley
GAN, Thomas	1791	Hanley
GAN, Thomas Sr.	1808	Gwin
GANER, John	1790	Milleken
GANN,	1780-1781 (undated)	
GANN, Adam	1781	
GANN, Adam	1796	Handly
GANN, Adam	1798	Gann
GANN, Adam	1799	Gann
GANN, Adam	1799	Moore
GANN, Adam	1805	Guir
GANN, Adam	1806	Grur
GANN, Adam	1808	Gwin
GANN, Adam	1811	Green
GANN, Adam	1811	McAlister
GANN, Adam	1812	Crawford
GANN, Adam	1812	Crawford [2]
GANN, Adam	1815	Crookshanks
GANN, Adam	1817	McClure
GANN, Adam	1818	McClure
GANN, Adam	1819	McClure
GANN, Adam	1821	Smith
GANN, Adam Jr.	1794	Handly
GANN, Adam Jr.	1795	Handly
GANN, Adam Jr.	1796	Handly
GANN, Adam Jr.	1797	Gann
GANN, Adam Jr.	1801	Gann
GANN, Adam Sr.	1793	Handley
GANN, Adam Sr.	1794	Handly
GANN, Adam Sr.	1795	Handly
GANN, Adam Sr.	1797	Gann
GANN, Adam Sr.	1801	Gann
GANN, Clam	1793	Handley
GANN, Clam	1796	Handly
GANN, Clamins	1794	Handly
GANN, Clem	1791	Hanley
GANN, Clem	1799	Moore
GANN, Clem	1801	Gann
GANN, Clemens	1795	Handly
GANN, Clement	1805	Guir
GANN, Clement	1808	Gwin
GANN, Clement	1809	Green
GANN, Clement	1810	Green
GANN, Clement	1812	Waddill
GANN, Clemm	1790	Hanley
GANN, Clemment	1811	Green
GANN, Clemon	1798	Gann
GANN, Daniel	1806	Grur
GANN, Daniel	1808	Gwin
GANN, Daniel	1809	Green
GANN, Daniel	1810	Green
GANN, Daniel	1811	Green

Surname, Given names	Year	Comp./Dist.
GANN, Daniel	1812	Waddill
GANN, Daniel	1814	Waddell
GANN, Daniel	1815	Waddell
GANN, Daniel	1816	Waddell
GANN, Daniel	1817	Riley
GANN, Daniel	1818	Riley
GANN, Daniel	1819	Findley
GANN, Daniel	1821	McGee
GANN, Dannel	1805	Guir
GANN, George	1811	Green
GANN, George	1812	Waddill
GANN, George	1817	Riley
GANN, George	1818	Riley
GANN, George	1819	Findley
GANN, George	1821	McGee
GANN, Isaac	1790	Hanley
GANN, Isaac	1791	Hanley
GANN, Isaac	1793	Handley
GANN, Isaac	1795	Handly
GANN, Isaac	1796	Handly
GANN, Isaac	1798	Gann
GANN, Isaac	1799	Moore
GANN, Isaac	1806	Grur
GANN, Isaac	1808	Gwin
GANN, Isaac	1811	Green
GANN, Isaac	1812	Waddill
GANN, Isaac	1814	Waddell
GANN, Isaac	1815	Waddell
GANN, Isaac	1816	Waddell
GANN, Isaac	1817	Riley
GANN, Isaac	1818	Riley
GANN, Isaac	1819	Findley
GANN, Isaac	1821	McGee
GANN, Isaach	1811	Green
GANN, Isac Jr.	1806	Grur
GANN, Isach Sr.	1810	Green
GANN, Jacob	1799	Gann
GANN, Jacob	1801	Gann
GANN, Jacob	1806	Brown
GANN, Jacob	1817	Riley
GANN, Jacob	1818	McClure
GANN, Jacob	1819	McClure
GANN, Jacob	1821	McClure
GANN, John	1793	Handley
GANN, John	1794	Handly
GANN, John	1795	Handly
GANN, John	1796	Handly
GANN, John	1797	Gann
GANN, John	1798	Gann
GANN, John	1799	Gann
GANN, John	1799	Moore
GANN, John	1806	Grur
GANN, John	1808	Gwin
GANN, John	1810	Green
GANN, John	1811	Green
GANN, John	1812	Crawford [2]
GANN, John	1812	Waddill
GANN, John	1815	Crookshanks
GANN, John	1815	Waddell
GANN, John	1816	Crookshanks
GANN, John	1816	Waddell
GANN, John	1817	McClure
GANN, John	1817	Riley
GANN, John	1818	McClure
GANN, John	1818	Riley
GANN, John	1819	Findley
GANN, John	1821	McGee
GANN, Joshau	1818	McClure
GANN, Joshua	1817	McClure
GANN, Mathan	1805	Guir
GANN, Nance	1791	Hanley
GANN, Nase	1790	Hanley
GANN, Nathan	1797	Gann
GANN, Nathan	1799	Gann
GANN, Nathan	1799	Moore
GANN, Nathan	1801	Gann
GANN, Nathan	1806	Grur
GANN, Nathan	1810	Green
GANN, Nathan	1812	Waddill
GANN, Nathan	1814	Waddell
GANN, Nathan	1815	Waddell
GANN, Nathan	1816	Waddell
GANN, Nathan	1817	Riley
GANN, Nathan	1818	Riley
GANN, Nathan	1819	Findley
GANN, Nathan	1821	McGee
GANN, Nathan Sr.	1809	Green
GANN, Nathan Sr.	1810	Green
GANN, Nathan Sr.	1811	Green
GANN, Nathaniel	1783 [after]	Depew
GANN, Nathen	1793	Handley
GANN, Nathen	1794	Handly
GANN, Nathen	1795	Handly
GANN, Nathen	1796	Handly
GANN, Nathern	1808	Gwin
GANN, Nethen	1798	Gann
GANN, Peggy	1805	Guir
GANN, Reuben	1812	Crawford [2]
GANN, Reuben	1815	Crookshanks
GANN, Reuben	1816	Crookshanks
GANN, Reuben	1817	McClure
GANN, Reuben	1818	McClure

Surname, Given names	Year	Comp./Dist.
GANN, Reuben	1819	McClure
GANN, Thomas	1793	Handley
GANN, Thomas	1794	Handly
GANN, Thomas	1795	Handly
GANN, Thomas	1796	Handly
GANN, Thomas	1797	Gann
GANN, Thomas	1798	Gann
GANN, Thomas	1799	Gann
GANN, Thomas	1799	Moore
GANN, Thomas	1801	Gann
GANN, Thomas	1806	Brown
GANN, Thomas	1810	Green
GANN, Thomas	1812	Waddill
GANN, Thomas Jr.	1811	Green
GANN, William	1805	Guir
GANN, William	1810	Hartzel
GANN, William	1814	McCracken
GANN, William	1815	Garner
GANN, Wm	1801	Gann
GANN, Wm	1806	Grur
GANS, Adam	1780-1781 (Undated)	
GANS, Clement	1780-1781 (Undated)	
GANS, Nathan	1780-1781 (Undated)	
GANT, John	1795	Young
GANT, John	1795	Young
GANTT, John	1793	North
GAR, Thomas	1793	Depew
GARDEN, James	1796	Calvert
GARDENER, Frances	1812	Britton
GARDENER, Francis	1814	Copes
GARDIN, James	1799	Stuart
GARDINI, Francis	1815	Copas
GARDNER, Francis	1811	Britten
GARDNER, Francis	1813	Copas
GARDNER, Francis	1816	Copas
GARDNER, Peter	1815	Haire
GARDNER, Peter	1816	Hair
GARDNER, Peter	1817	Haire
GARLAN, Gutridge	1793	Hale
GARLAND, Daniel	1819	Brown
GARLAND, Daniel	1821	Haines
GARLAND, Gutradge	1792	Greer
GARLAND, Humphrey	1792	Carriger
GARLAND, Humphrey	1792	Greer
GARLAND, Humphrey	1794	Carriger
GARLAND, Humphrey	1806	Odel
GARLAND, Humphrey	1811	Brown
GARLAND, Humphrey	1812	Brown
GARLAND, Humphrey	1814	Brown
GARLAND, Humphrey	1815	Hartsell
GARLAND, Humphrey	1816	Brown
GARLAND, Jesse	1816	Brown
GARLAND, John	1792	Carriger
GARLAND, John	1792	Greer
GARLAND, John	1792	Maxwell
GARLAND, John	1794	Carriger
GARLAND, John	1795	Carriger
GARLAND, John	1817	Brown
GARLAND, Joseph	1792	Maxwell
GARLAND, Joseph	1793	Maxwell
GARLAND, Joseph	1794	Taylor
GARLAND, Josheia	1816	Brown
GARLAND, Joshua	1811	Brown
GARLAND, Joshua	1812	Brown
GARLAND, Joshua	1814	Brown
GARLAND, Joshua	1815	Hartsell
GARLAND, Joshua	1817	Brown
GARLAND, Joshua	1818	Brown
GARLAND, Joshua	1819	Brown
GARLAND, Samuel	1791	White
GARLAND, Samuel	1793	Campbell
GARLAND, Samuel	1794	Thornton
GARLAND, Umphrey	1807	Odell
GARLAND, Umphrey	1809	Viney
GARLAND, Umphrey	1810	Cove
GARLAND, Umprees	1791	Tullis
GARNER, Brice	1798	Crouch
GARNER, Brice	1801	Norwood
GARNER, Brice M.	1806	Crouch
GARNER, Brice M.	1811	Ellis
GARNER, Brise N.	1814	Bean
GARNER, Bruce M.	1815	Haire
GARNER, Griffin G.	1815	Garner
GARNER, Samuel	1816	Hunt
GARNES, Adam	1818	Smith
GARNON, Griffin G.	1814	McCracken
GARNS, Adam	1819	Smith
GARROTT, Amos	1778	
GARVESS, William	1807	Odell
GARVIS, Alexander	1796	Longmire
GARVIS, Alexander	1797	Longmire
GAT, John	1794	North
GATES, Jacob	1790	Stone
GATES, Jacob	1791	Stone
GATES, Jacob	1793	Melvan
GATES, Jacob	1794	Melvan
GATES, Jacob	1795	Melvan
GATES, Jacob	1796	Melvin
GATES, Jacob	1798	Crouch
GATES, Jacob Jr.	1801	Norwood
GATES, Jacob Sr.	1801	Norwood

Surname, Given names	Year	Comp./Dist.
GATES, John	1795	Melvan
GATES, John	1796	Melvin
GATES, John	1798	Crouch
GATES, John	1801	Norwood
GATES, John	1806	Crouch
GATES, John	1809	Right
GATES, John	1811	Ellis
GATES, John	1812	Ellis
GATES, John	1814	Bean
GATES, John	1815	Haire
GATES, John	1816	Hair
GATES, John	1817	Haire
GATES, John	1818	Hair
GATES, John	1821	Louis
GATES, Richard	1790	Stone
GATES, Richard	1791	Stone
GATES, Richard	1793	Melvan
GATES, Richard	1795	Melvan
GATES, Richard	1796	Melvin
GATES, Richard	1798	Crouch
GATES, Richard	1801	Norwood
GATES, Richart	1794	Melvan
GATT, John	1814	Copes
GATT, Joshua	1814	Copes
GATTS, John	1819	Hair
GAUGHT, Dott	1798	Shipley
GAUT, John	1792	North
GAYMON, Abrm	1795	Young
GAYNOR, John	1814	Waddell
GEHAM, Charles	1814	Crookshanks
GELASPEE, Allen	1798	Hannah
GELASPEE, George	1798	Hannah
GELASPEE, George Jr.	1812	Crawford
GELASPEE, James	1798	Hannah
GELASPEE, James	1808	McAllister
GELASPEE, James	1812	Crawford
GELASPEE, Thomas	1798	Hannah
GELASPEE, Thomas	1806	Payn
GELASPEE, Thomas	1808	McAllister
GELASPEE, Thomas	1812	Crawford [2]
GELASSPE, Thomas	1812	Crawford
GENHERT, John	1816	Hair
GENKINS, Adam	1818	Hair
GENKINS, Aron	1815	Haire
GENKINS, Aron	1816	Hair
GENKINS, Aron	1817	Haire
GENKINS, George	1798	Crouch
GENKINS, George	1816	Hair
GENKINS, George	1817	Haire
GENKINS, George	1818	Hair
GENKINS, George Jr.	1795	Melvan
GENKINS, George Sr.	1795	Melvan
GENKINS, Gorge Jr.	1796	Melvin
GENKINS, Gorge Sr.	1796	Melvin
GENKINS, John	1815	Haire
GENKINS, John	1817	Haire
GENKINS, John	1818	Hair
GENN, Adam	1816	Crookshanks
GENTREY, Joseph	1791	White
GENTREY, Joseph	1793	Thornton
GENTREY, Robert	1780-1781 (Undated)	
GENTRY, Charles	1778	
GENTRY, Charles	1780-1781 (undated)	
GENTRY, Charles	1780-1781 (Undated)	
GENTRY, Joseph	1778	
GENTRY, Joseph	1790	White
GENTRY, Joseph	1792	White
GENTRY, Joseph	1794	Thornton
GENTRY, Robert	1778	
George	1807	Parker
GEORGE, Isaac	1821	Smith
GEORGE, Thomas	1821	Smith
GERE, Jacob	1798	Calvert
GESS, Benjamin Sr.	1780-1781 (Undated)	
GEST, Benj	1778	
GEST, Benjamin	1780-1781 (undated)	
GEST, John	1780-1781 (undated)	
GEST, Joseph	1778	
GEST, Joseph	1780-1781 (undated)	
GETTINGS, Clark	1790	Shipley
GETTINGS, Clark	1791	Shipley
GHOLSEN, Anthoney	1795	Melvan
GIAR, Jacob Jr.	1796	Longmire
GIBBINS, James	1799	Moore
GIBBINS, James	1801	Roberson
GIBBONS, Thos	1779	
GIBBS, Thomas	1798	Morrison
GIBBS, Thomas	1798	Morrison
GIBBS, Thomas	1799	Morrison
GIBBS, Thomas	1801	Morrison
GIBBS, Thomas	1806	Carr
GIBBS, Thomas	1807	Carr
GIBBS, Thomas	1808	Carr
GIBBS, Thomas	[1796] 1797	Morris
GIBBSON, James	1781	
GIBINS, James	1798	Hannah
GIBSON, Benj	1778	
GIBSON, Billindy	1809	Cade
GIBSON, Billingly	1810	Barron

Surname, Given names	Year	Comp./Dist.
GILLASPIE, James	1811	McAlister
GILLASPIE, James	1821	McClure
GILLASPIE, Thomas	1811	McAlister
GILLASPIE, Thomas	1821	McClure
GILLASPIE, Thomas Sr.	1779	Wilson
GILLASPIE, Thos	1790	Milleken
GILLASPY, George	1779	Wilson
GILLASPY, George	1780-1781 (Undated)	
GILLASPY, Thomas	1780-1781 (undated)	
GILLASPY, Thomas	1780-1781 (Undated)	
GILLEHAM, John	1781	
GILLEHAND, John	1778	
GILLELAND, William	1816	Waddell
GILLES, George	1816	Giles
GILLES, George	1817	Gillises
GILLESPEE, Thomas	1805	Stephenson
GILLESPIE, Allen	1797	Calvert
GILLESPIE, Allen	1798	Calvert
GILLESPIE, George	1793	Milliken
GILLESPIE, George	1795	Milliken
GILLESPIE, George	1796	Millikin
GILLESPIE, George	1797	Hannah
GILLESPIE, James	1809	McAlister
GILLESPIE, Thomas	1778	
GILLESPIE, Thomas	1779	Wilson
GILLESPIE, Thomas	1791	Milliken
GILLESPIE, Thomas	1793	Milliken
GILLESPIE, Thomas	1794	Milliken
GILLESPIE, Thomas	1795	Milliken
GILLESPIE, Thomas	1796	Millikin
GILLESPIE, Thomas	1797	Hannah
GILLESPIE, Thomas	1809	McAlister
GILLESPIE, Thos	1799	Hannah
GILLESPIE, Thos.	1792	Milliken
GILLESPY, George	1781	
GILLILAND, John	1779	
GILLILAND, William	1818	Riley
GILLILAND, William	1819	Findley
GILLIS, George	1814	Couthers
GILLIS, James	1805	Stephenson
GILLIS, John	1796	Melvin
GILLIS, John	1798	Crouch
GILLISPEE, Thomas	1814	Waddell
GILLISPIE, George	1817	McClure
GILLISPIE, George	1818	McClure
GILLISPIE, George T.	1816	Crookshanks
GILLISPIE, George T.	1819	McClure
GILLISPIE, James	1815	Crookshanks
GILLISPIE, James	1816	Crookshanks
GILLISPIE, James	1817	McClure
GILLISPIE, James	1818	McClure
GILLISPIE, James	1819	McClure
GILLISPIE, Thomas	1816	Crookshanks
GILLISPIE, Thomas	1817	McClure
GILLISPIE, Thomas	1818	McClure
GILLISPIE, Thomas	1819	McClure
GILLONLAND, William	1812	Waddill
GILLUM, John	1792	Greer
GILLUM, John	1795	Carriger
GILLWORTH, John	1797	Biddle
GILLYON, William	1817	Riley
GILS, Richard	1819	Brown
GILWORTH, John	1798	Biddle
GILWORTH, John	1801	Biddle
GILWORTH, John	1805	Carson
GILWORTH, John	1806	Carson
GILWORTH, John	1807	Shields
GILWORTH, John	1810	Dimmons
GILWORTH, John	1811	
GINIS, Robt	1809	Patterson
GINKENS, John	1821	Louis
GINKINS, Aaron	1806	Crouch
GINKINS, Aaron	1811	Ellis
GINKINS, Aaron	1819	Hair
GINKINS, George	1811	Ellis
GINKINS, George Jr.	1806	Crouch
GINKINS, George Jr.	1806	Crouch
GINKINS, George Jr.	1809	Gwin
GINKINS, Gorge	1794	Melvan
GINKINS, John	1806	Crouch
GINKINS, John	1811	Ellis
GINKINS, John	1819	Hair
GIPSON, Belling	1808	Cade
GIPSON, Billingsley	1807	Cade
GIPSON, Thomas	1807	Cade
GIPSON, Thomas	1808	Cade
GIVEN, James	1790	Shipley
GIVEN, James	1791	Shipley
GIVENS, James	1798	Gann
GIVENS, James	1799	Gann
GIVEWS, James	1799	Gann
GIVIN, William	1821	Hunt
GIVINS, Thomas Jr.	1807	Givins
GIVINS, Thomas Sr.	1807	Givins
GIVINS, William	1807	Givins
GLAISE, Lawrance	1801	
GLAIZE, Larance	1805	Guir
GLAS, William Sr.	1801	Taylor
GLASCOCK, Archabald	1795	Murray
GLASCOCK, Archable	1797	Shipley
GLASCOCK, Archable	1798	Shipley

Surname, Given names	Year	Comp./Dist.
GLASCOCK, Archeble	1793	Murray
GLASCOCK, Archeble	1796	Shipley
GLASCOCK, Archibald	1819	Grimsley
GLASCOCK, Gregory	1819	Grimsley
GLASCOCKE, Archibald	1815	Grimsley
GLASCOCKE, Gregory	1815	Grimsley
GLASS, Hiram	1817	Hunt
GLASS, Hiram	1818	Hunt
GLASS, Hiram	1819	Hunt
GLASS, Hiram	1821	Hunt
GLASS, Joseph	1798	Duncan
GLASS, Joseph	1798	Duncan
GLASS, Joseph	1799	Duncan
GLASS, Joseph	1806	Guin
GLASS, Joseph	1807	Givins
GLASS, Joseph	1809	Gwin
GLASS, Joseph	1811	Davis
GLASS, Joseph	1812	McLin
GLASS, Wililam	1783 [after]	Depew
GLASS, William	1781	
GLASS, William	1792	Depew
GLASS, William	1793	Depew
GLASS, William	1794	Depew
GLASS, William	1797	Duncan
GLASS, William	1798	Duncan
GLASS, William	1798	Duncan
GLASS, William	1806	Guin
GLASS, William	1807	Givins
GLASS, William	1808	Guin
GLASS, William	1811	Davis
GLASS, William	1812	McLin
GLASS, William	1815	McLin
GLASS, William	1817	Hunt
GLASS, William	1819	Hunt
GLASS, William	1821	Hunt
GLASS, William	1780-1781 (Undated)	
GLASS, William Jr.	1801	Taylor
GLASS, William Jr.	1809	Gwin
GLASS, William Sr.	1806	Guin
GLASS, Wm	1799	Duncan
GLASS, Wm Sr.	1799	Duncan
GLASSCOCK, Archabald	1805	Rector
GLASSCOCK, Archabald	1808	Cade
GLASSCOCK, Archabald	1810	Barron
GLASSCOCK, Archabald	1811	Barron
GLASSCOCK, Archabald	1812	Barnes
GLASSCOCK, Archabld	1809	Cade
GLASSCOCK, Archd	1801	Glasscock
GLASSCOCK, Archeble	1794	Murray
GLASSCOCK, Archibald	1807	Cade
GLASSCOCK, Archibald	1814	Barns
GLASSCOCK, Gregory	1814	Barns
GLASSCOCK, Gregory	1818	Grimsley
GLASSCOCKE, Archibald	1816	Grimsley
GLASSCOCKE, Archibald	1817	Grimsley
GLASSCOCKE, Archibald	1818	Grimsley
GLASSCOCKE, Gregroy	1817	Grimsley
GLASSCOCKE, Grimsley	1816	Grimsley
GLAYS, Henry	1811	Green
GLAYS, Larence Sr.	1811	Green
GLAYS, Larrence Jr.	1811	Green
GLAZE, Henry	1812	Waddill
GLAZE, Henry	1815	Waddell
GLAZE, Henry	1816	Waddell
GLAZE, Henry	1817	Riley
GLAZE, Henry	1818	Riley
GLAZE, Henry	1819	Findley
GLAZE, Henry	1821	McGee
GLAZE, Larence Jr.	1821	McGee
GLAZE, Larewnce	1818	Riley
GLAZE, Laurence	1809	Green
GLAZE, Lawrence	1810	Green
GLAZE, Lawrence	1814	Waddell
GLAZE, Lawrence	1814	Waddell
GLAZE, Lawrence	1817	Riley
GLAZE, Lawrence	1819	Findley
GLAZE, Lawrence	1819	Findley
GLAZE, Lawrence	1821	McGee
GLAZE, Lawrence Jr.	1810	Green
GLAZE, Lawrence Jr.	1815	Waddell
GLAZE, Lawrence Jr.	1816	Waddell
GLAZE, Lawrence Jr.	1817	Riley
GLAZE, Lawrence Jr.	1818	Riley
GLAZE, Lawrence Sr.	1815	Waddell
GLAZE, Lawrence Sr.	1816	Waddell
GLEN, Henry	1821	Howard
GLEN, Robert	1821	Smith
GLEZER, Samel	1821	Howard
GLISPEE, George T.	1814	Waddell
GLONOCK, Gregory	1821	Martin
GLZE, Lawrence	1812	Waddill
GLZE, Lawrence	1812	Waddill
GMATE, David	1807	Parker
GNAMM, Archbald	1814	Couthers
GOFORTH, Absolum	1799	Robertson
GOFORTH, Zacharia	1807	Anderson
GOFORTH, Zachariah	1814	McCracken
GOID, David	1817	Harris
GOIER, Jacob	1797	Robertson
GOIR, Henry	1797	Robertson
GOIS, Richard	1805	Doak
GOLLIS, James	1778	

Surname, Given names	Year	Comp./Dist.
GOLSTON, Rubent	1806	Parker
GOOD, Christian	1808	Gwin
GOOD, Christian	1809	Green
GOOD, David	1810	Green
GOOD, David	1811	Green
GOOD, David	1812	Hartsell
GOOD, David	1814	McCray
GOOD, David	1816	Harrison
GOOD, Emaniel	1817	Riley
GOOD, Emanuel	1815	Waddell
GOOD, Emanuel	1816	Waddell
GOOD, Emanuel	1818	Riley
GOOD, Emanuel	1819	Findley
GOOD, Emanuel	1821	McGee
GOOD, Jacob	1810	Green
GOOD, Jacob	1810	Green
GOOD, Jacob	1812	Waddill
GOOD, Jacob	1821	Hunt
GOOD, Jacob	1821	Sands
GOOD, Jacob Jr.	1808	Gwin
GOOD, Jacob Jr.	1809	Green
GOOD, Jacob Jr.	1811	Green
GOOD, Jacob Sr.	1808	Gwin
GOOD, Jacob Sr.	1809	Green
GOODEN, Ben Jr.	1781	
GOODEN, Drewry	1779	
GOODEN, James	1781	
GOODEN, Thos	1781	
GOODING, Drury	1778	
GOODMAN, Andrew	1821	Hale
GOODPASTOR, Abraham	1794	North
GOODPASTOR, Abram	1793	North
GOODPASTOR, Isaac	1795	Young
GOODPASTOR, J.	1793	North
GOODPASTOR, Leab	1794	North
GOODPASTOR, Solom	1793	North
GOODPASTOR, Soloman	1794	North
GOODPASTOR, Solomon	1791	North
GOODPASTURE, Abraham	1792	North
GOODPASTURE, Isec	1792	North
GOODPASTURE, John	1792	North
GOODPASTURE, Soloman	1792	North
GOOPASTOR, Isack	1791	North
GOOT, John	1815	Copas
GORDON, James	1797	Calvert
GORDON, Jas	1801	Aiken
GORDON, John	1790	Hanley
GORDON, John	1791	Chisom
GORDON, John	1791	Hanley
GORDON, Lewis	1791	Milliken
GORDON, Lewis	1792	Milliken

Surname, Given names	Year	Comp./Dist.
GORDON, Lewis	1793	Milliken
GOT, Casper	1808	Gwin
GOT, John	1791	North
GOTCHER, Henry	1778	
GOTT, Anthoney	1790	Shipley
GOTT, Anthoney	1791	Shipley
GOTT, Anthoney	1793	Murray
GOTT, Anthoney	1796	Shipley
GOTT, Anthoney	1805	Doak
GOTT, Anthoney	1806	Doke
GOTT, Anthony	1794	Murray
GOTT, Anthony	1795	Murray
GOTT, Anthony	1797	Shipley
GOTT, Anthony	1798	Shipley
GOTT, Anthony	1801	Lane
GOTT, Anthony	1807	Britton
GOTT, Anthony	1811	Britten
GOTT, Anthony	1812	Britton
GOTT, Jesse	1801	Lane
GOTT, John	1790	Shipley
GOTT, John	1791	Shipley
GOTT, John	1793	Murray
GOTT, John	1794	Murray
GOTT, John	1795	Murray
GOTT, John	1796	Shipley
GOTT, John	1797	Shipley
GOTT, John	1798	Shipley
GOTT, John	1801	Lane
GOTT, John	1806	Doke
GOTT, John	1807	Britton
GOTT, John	1811	Britten
GOTT, John	1813	Copas
GOTT, John	1816	Copas
GOTT, John	1817	Grisham
GOTT, John	1818	Grisham
GOTT, John	1819	Grisham
GOTT, John	1821	Hale
GOTT, Lott	1797	Shipley
GOTT, Lott	1801	Lane
GOTT, Sarah	1815	Copas
GOTT, Sarah	1817	Grisham
GOTT, Sarah	1818	Grisham
GOTT, Sarah	1821	Hale
GOTT, William	1815	Copas
GOTT, William	1816	Copas
GOTT, William	1817	Grisham
GOTT, William	1818	Grisham
GOTT, William	1819	Grisham
GOTT, William	1821	Hale
GOURLEY, Loften	1812	Barnes
GOURLEY, Thos (Capt.)	1793	Maxwell

Surname, Given names	Year	Comp./Dist.
GOURLEY, Thos.	1790	Williams
GOURLEY, Thos.	1791	Williams
GOURLEY, Thos.	1792	Maxwell
GOWERS, William	1807	Parker
GOZACH, Sandofar	1778	
GRABAM, Thos	1780-1781 (Undated)	
GRAG, John	1801	Taylor
GRAHAM, Andrew	1806	Guin
GRAHAM, Andrew	1807	Givins
GRAHAM, Andrew	1808	Guin
GRAHAM, Andrew	1811	Davis
GRAHAM, Andrew	1812	McLin
GRAHAM, Andrew	1814	McLin
GRAHAM, Andrew	1815	McLin
GRAHAM, Andrew	1817	Hunt
GRAHAM, Charles	1797	Hannah
GRAHAM, Charles	1799	Hannah
GRAHAM, Charles	1809	McAlister
GRAHAM, Charles	1811	McAlister
GRAHAM, Charles	1818	McClure
GRAHAM, Charles	1819	McClure
GRAHAM, Charles	1821	McClure
GRAHAM, George	1809	McAlister
GRAHAM, James	1797	Hannah
GRAHAM, James	1798	Hannah
GRAHAM, James	1799	Hannah
GRAHAM, James	1806	Payn
GRAHAM, James	1809	McAlister
GRAHAM, James	1811	McAlister
GRAHAM, James	1812	Crawford
GRAHAM, James	1814	Crookshanks
GRAHAM, James Sr.	1809	McAlister
GRAHAM, John	1798	Duncan
GRAHAM, Samuel	1819	McClure
GRAHAM, Thomas	1809	McAlister
GRAHAM, Thomas	1811	McAlister
GRAHAM, William	1818	McClure
GRAHAM, William	1819	McClure
GRAHAM, William	1821	McClure
GRAHAM, Wm	1799	Duncan
GRAHAMS, John	1790	Milleken
GRAHL, Augustus	1817	Smith
GRAM, Hiram	1780-1781 (Undated)	
GRASTEY, Gog	1798	Biddle
GRATE, David	1792	Tulley
GRATE, David	1798	Morrison
GRATE, David	1798	Young
GRATE, David	1806	Parker
GRAUER, James	1792	White
GRAVES, James	1793	Campbell
GRAVES, James	1794	Thornton
GRAVES, James	1795	Thornton
GRAY, Abslom	1794	Melvan
GRAY, Absolom	1793	Melvan
GRAY, Absolom	1795	Melvan
GRAY, Absolom	1798	Crouch
GRAY, Benjamin	1815	Garner
GRAY, Geo	1778	
GRAY, George	1790	Shipley
GRAY, George	1791	Shipley
GRAY, George	1793	Murray
GRAY, George	1794	Murray
GRAY, George	1795	Murray
GRAY, George	1796	Shipley
GRAY, James	1797	Gann
GRAY, James	1798	Gann
GRAY, James	1799	Gann
GRAY, James	1799	Moore
GRAY, James	1805	Guir
GRAY, James	1806	Grur
GRAY, James	1809	McAlister
GRAY, James	1811	Britten
GRAY, James	1811	McAlister
GRAY, James	1812	Britton
GRAY, James	1813	Copas
GRAY, James	1814	Copes
GRAY, James	1814	Crookshanks
GRAY, James	1815	Copas
GRAY, James	1815	Crookshanks
GRAY, James	1816	Copas
GRAY, James	1816	Crookshanks
GRAY, James	1817	Grisham
GRAY, James	1818	Grisham
GRAY, James	1818	McClure
GRAY, James	1819	Grisham
GRAY, James	1821	Hale
GRAY, John	1794	Melvan
GRAY, John	1795	Morrison
GRAY, John	1801	Aiken
GRAY, John	1801	Gann
GRAY, John	1806	Carr
GRAY, John	1807	Carr
GRAY, John	1808	Carr
GRAY, John	1809	Carr
GRAY, John	1811	Green
GRAY, John	1811	Mitchell
GRAY, John	1812	Waddill
GRAY, John	1814	Crookshanks
GRAY, John	1814	Waddell
GRAY, John	1815	Crookshanks
GRAY, John	1815	Waddell

Surname, Given names	Year	Comp./Dist.
GRAY, John	1816	Crookshanks
GRAY, John	1816	Waddell
GRAY, John	1817	McClure
GRAY, John	1817	Riley
GRAY, John	1818	McClure
GRAY, John	1818	Riley
GRAY, John	1821	McGee
GRAY, John	[1796] 1797	Morris
GRAY, Nathan	1813	Copas
GRAY, Nathan	1814	Copes
GRAY, Nathan	1815	Copas
GRAY, Nathan	1816	Copas
GRAY, Nathan	1817	Grisham
GRAY, Nathan	1818	Grisham
GRAY, Nathan	1819	Grisham
GRAY, Nathan	1821	Hale
GRAY, Roben	1797	Shipley
GRAY, Robert	1790	Shipley
GRAY, Robert	1791	Shipley
GRAY, Robert	1793	Murray
GRAY, Robert	1794	Murray
GRAY, Robert	1795	Murray
GRAY, Robert	1796	Shipley
GRAY, Robert	1798	Shipley
GRAY, Robert	1801	Lane
GRAY, Robert	1805	Doak
GRAY, Robert	1806	Doke
GRAY, Robert	1807	Britton
GRAY, Robert	1811	Britten
GRAY, Robert	1812	Britton
GRAY, Robert	1813	Copas
GRAY, Robert	1814	Copes
GRAY, Robert	1814	Crookshanks
GRAY, Robert	1815	Copas
GRAY, Robert	1815	Crookshanks
GRAY, Robert	1816	Copas
GRAY, Robert	1816	Crookshanks
GRAY, Robert	1817	Grisham
GRAY, Robert	1817	McClure
GRAY, Robert	1818	Grisham
GRAY, Robert	1818	Harris
GRAY, Robert	1819	Grisham
GRAY, Robert	1819	Harris
GRAY, Robert	1821	Hale
GRAY, Robert	1821	Hampton
GRAY, Willes	1792	North
GRAY, William	1795	Young
GRAY, William	1797	Duncan
GRAY, William	1798	Young
GRAY, William	1801	Taylor
GRAY, Willis	1793	North
GRAY, Willis	1796	Young
GRAY, Willis	1797	Young
GRAY, Wm	1799	Duncan
GRAYHAM, Andrew	1816	Hunt
GRAYHAM, Charles	1805	Stephenson
GRAYHAM, Charles	1815	Crookshanks
GRAYHAM, Charles	1816	Crookshanks
GRAYHAM, Charles	1817	McClure
GRAYHAM, James Jr.	1805	Stephenson
GRAYHAM, James Sr.	1805	Stephenson
GRAYHAM, Nelly	1815	Crookshanks
GRAYHAM, Thomas	1816	Crookshanks
GRAYHAM, William	1816	Crookshanks
GRAYSON, Thomas	1815	Crookshanks
GREAN, Arnel	1801	Calvert
GREAR, John	1790	Greer
GREAT, David	1787	Fains
GREAT, David	1791	Tullis
GREAT, David	1793	Morrison
GREAT, David	1794	Morrison
GREAT, David	1805	Parker
GREATE, David	[1796] 1797	Morris
GREECE, Sam'l G.	1821	Smith
GREEN, Aleson	1792	Greer
GREEN, Andrew	1797	Gann
GREEN, Arnal	1806	Grur
GREEN, Arnold	1805	Guir
GREEN, Arnold	1809	Green
GREEN, Arnold	1810	Green
GREEN, Arnold	1811	Green
GREEN, Arnold	1812	Waddill
GREEN, Arnold	1814	Waddell
GREEN, Arnold	1815	Waddell
GREEN, Arnold	1817	Riley
GREEN, Arnold	1818	Riley
GREEN, Arnold	1819	Findley
GREEN, Arnold	1821	McGee
GREEN, Artsey	1814	Waddell
GREEN, Frederick	1819	Brown
GREEN, Ira	1801	Gann
GREEN, Ira	1805	Guir
GREEN, Ira	1806	Grur
GREEN, Ira	1808	Gwin
GREEN, Ira	1809	Green
GREEN, Ira	1810	Green
GREEN, Ira	1812	Crawford [2]
GREEN, Ira	1814	Crookshanks
GREEN, Ira	1815	Crookshanks
GREEN, Ira	1817	McClure
GREEN, Ira	1818	McClure
GREEN, Ira	1819	McClure

Surname, Given names	Year	Comp./Dist.
GREEN, Iva	1811	Green
GREEN, James	1819	Smith
GREEN, Jess	1812	Crawford
GREEN, Jesse	1781	
GREEN, Jessey	1799	Gann
GREEN, John	1781	
GREEN, John	1793	Brown
GREEN, Joisua	1812	Waddill
GREEN, Joseph	1821	McClure
GREEN, Joshua	1791	Milliken
GREEN, Joshua	1792	Milliken
GREEN, Joshua	1793	Milliken
GREEN, Joshua	1794	Milliken
GREEN, Joshua	1798	Gann
GREEN, Joshua	1799	Moore
GREEN, Joshua	1801	Gann
GREEN, Joshua	1806	Grur
GREEN, Joshua	1811	Green
GREEN, Joshua	1817	McClure
GREEN, Joshua	1818	McClure
GREEN, Joshua	1819	McClure
GREEN, Joshua	1821	McClure
GREEN, Joshua (estate of)	1810	Green
GREEN, Jossua	1805	Guir
GREEN, Josua	1814	Waddell
GREEN, Peter	1809	Right
GREEN, Richard	1796	Young
GREEN, Richard	1797	Young
GREEN, Samuel	1817	Hunt
GREEN, Samuel	1818	Smith
GREEN, Sosanah	1811	Green
GREEN, Susannah	1810	Green
GREEN, Sussanah	1812	Waddill
GREEN, Thomas	1795	Carriger
GREEN, Wilis	1794	North
GREEN, William	1791	Chisom
GREEN, William	1792	Chisolm
GREEN, William	1792	North
GREEN, William	1793	Brown
GREEN, William	1780-1781 (undated)	
GREENAWAY, William	1794	Handly
GREENAWAY, William	1795	Handly
GREENAWAY, William	1811	Green
GREENE, F. Dick	1821	Brown
GREENE, John	1816	Hunt
GREENE, Richd	1795	Young
GREENEWAY, William	1796	Millikin
GREENWAY, William	1792	Tulley
GREENWAY, William	1793	Melvan
GREENWAY, William	1797	Hannah
GREENWAY, William	1798	Gann
GREENWAY, William	1799	Gann
GREENWAY, William	1808	Gwin
GREENWAY, William	1810	Green
GREENWAY, William	1815	Waddell
GREENWAY, William	1816	Waddell
GREENWAY, William	1817	Riley
GREENWAY, William	1818	Riley
GREENWAY, William	1819	Findley
GREENWAY, William Sr.	1819	Findley
GREENWAY, Wm	1797	Gann
GREENWAY, Wm	1799	Moore
GREENWAY, Wm	1809	Green
GREENWAY, Wm	1812	Waddill
GREENWAY, Wm	1814	Waddell
GREENWAY, Wm	1821	McGee
GREER, Acob	1795	Calvert
GREER, Alex	1795	Carriger
GREER, Alexander	1779	
GREER, Alexd (Capt.)	1790	Greer
GREER, Alexd (Capt.)	1791	
GREER, Alexr	1792	Carriger
GREER, Alexr	1794	Carriger
GREER, Andrew	1794	Carriger
GREER, Andrew (Esq.)	1778	
GREER, Andrew (Esq.)	1795	Carriger
GREER, Andrew (Esqr.)	1779	
GREER, Andrew Jr.	1792	Carriger
GREER, Andrew Jr.	1795	Carriger
GREER, Andrew Sr.	1790	Greer
GREER, Andrew Sr.	1792	Carriger
GREER, Andw Sr.	1792	Greer
GREER, Charles	1792	Scott
GREER, Charles	1793	Morrison
GREER, Charles	1794	Morrison
GREER, David	1792	Carriger
GREER, John	1814	McLin
GREER, John	1815	McLin
GREER, John	1818	Hunt
GREER, John	1819	Hunt
GREER, Joseph	1778	
GREER, Joseph	1790	Greer
GREER, Joseph	1792	Greer
GREER, Josheway	1795	Calvert
GREER, S. Kenedy	1821	Smith
GREER, Sam'l G.	1820	Smith
GREER, Samuel	1814	McLin
GREER, Samuel	1815	Garner
GREER, Samuel	1816	Smith
GREER, Samuel	1817	Smith
GREER, Samuel G.	1818	Hunt
GREER, Samuel Jr.	1819	Smith

Surname, Given names	Year	Comp./Dist.
GREER, Samuel Sr.	1819	Hunt
GREER, Samuel Sr.	1821	Hunt
GREER, Susanah	1814	Waddell
GREER, Tho	1792	Carriger
GREER, Thomas	1794	Carriger
GREER, Thomas	1801	Biddle
GREER, Thomas	1815	Grimsley
GREER, Thomas	1818	Smith
GREER, Thomas	1819	Smith
GREER, Thomas	1820	Smith
GREER, Thomas	1821	Smith
GREER, William	1779	
GREERS, Thomas	1792	Greer
GREHAM, Charles	1807	Payne
GREHAM, Charles	1808	McAllister
GREHAM, Charles	1812	Crawford [2]
GREHAM, Charls	1798	Hannah
GREHAM, Charls	1806	Payn
GREHAM, Charls	1812	Crawford
GREHAM, Chas	1801	Squibb
GREHAM, George	1812	Crawford [2]
GREHAM, James	1798	Hannah
GREHAM, James	1807	Payne
GREHAM, James	1808	McAllister
GREHAM, James	1812	Crawford
GREHAM, James	1812	Crawford [2]
GREHAM, Thomas	1812	Crawford
GREHAM, Thomas	1812	Crawford [2]
GREHAM, William	1812	Crawford
GRENAWAY, Wm	1806	Grur
GRENEY, Wm	1791	Tullis
GRENSWAY, Wm	1801	Gann
GRENWAY, William	1805	Guir
GRESHAM, George	1815	Copas
GRESHAM, George	1816	Copas
GRESHAM, George	1818	Grisham
GRESHAM, John	1816	Copas
GRESHAM, John	1818	Grisham
GRESHAM, Price	1816	Copas
GRESHAM, Thomas	1815	Copas
GRESHAM, Thomas	1816	Copas
GRESHAM, Thomas	1821	Hale
GRESHAM, Thomas Jr.	1821	Hale
GRESHAM, William	1817	McClure
GREST, Robert	1817	Smith
GREY, Andrew	1798	Hannah
GREY, James	1812	Crawford
GREY, James	1817	McClure
GREY, Robert	1812	Crawford [2]
GRIEMS, James	1781	
GRIER, Samuel	1812	Waddill

Surname, Given names	Year	Comp./Dist.
GRIFFEN, William	1794	Thornton
GRIFFIN, Stansberry	1819	Harris
GRIFFIN, William	1778	
GRIFFIN, William	1790	White
GRIFFIN, William	1791	White
GRIFIN, William	1795	Thornton
GRILLS, Richard	1795	Murray
GRILLS, Richard	1796	Shipley
GRIMELEY, William	1796	Shipley
GRIMES, Andrew	1809	Gwin
GRIMES, Henry	1778	
GRIMES, James	1794	Milliken
GRIMES, James	1797	Calvert
GRIMES, John	1778	
GRIMES, John	1791	White
GRIMES, John	1793	Campbell
GRIMES, John	1794	Ford
GRIMES, Thomas	1781	
GRIMESLEY, John	1821	Martin
GRIMESLY, John	1809	Cade
GRIMESLY, Loften	1809	Cade
GRIMLY, Loftin	1808	Cade
GRIMSLEY, Cage	1811	Ellis
GRIMSLEY, Cage	1812	Ellis
GRIMSLEY, Caston	1818	Grimsley
GRIMSLEY, John	1807	Cade
GRIMSLEY, John	1811	Barron
GRIMSLEY, John	1812	Barnes
GRIMSLEY, John	1812	Ellis
GRIMSLEY, John	1815	Grimsley
GRIMSLEY, John	1816	Grimsley
GRIMSLEY, John	1817	Grimsley
GRIMSLEY, John	1818	Grimsley
GRIMSLEY, John	1819	Grimsley
GRIMSLEY, Lafton	1810	Barron
GRIMSLEY, Loffton	1801	Glasscock
GRIMSLEY, Loften	1815	Grimsley
GRIMSLEY, Loften	1816	Grimsley
GRIMSLEY, Loften	1817	Grimsley
GRIMSLEY, Loften	1819	Grimsley
GRIMSLEY, Loftin	1798	Shipley
GRIMSLEY, Loftin	1807	Cade
GRIMSLEY, Loftin	1811	Barron
GRIMSLEY, Loftin	1814	Barns
GRIMSLEY, William	1797	Shipley
GRIMSLEY, William	1798	Shipley
GRIMSLEY, William	1811	Ellis
GRIMSLEY, William	1812	Barnes
GRIMSLEY, William	1812	Ellis
GRIMSLEY, William	1814	Barns
GRIMSLEY, William	1815	Grimsley

Surname, Given names	Year	Comp./Dist.
GRIMSLEY, William	1816	Grimsley
GRIMSLEY, William	1817	Grimsley
GRIMSLEY, William	1818	Grimsley
GRIMSLEY, William	1819	Grimsley
GRIMSLEY, Wm	1801	Glasscock
GRIMSLY, John	1805	Rector
GRIMSLY, John	1808	Cade
GRIMSLY, John	1810	Barron
GRIMSLY, John	1814	Barns
GRIMSLY, Lofton	1805	Rector
GRIMSLY, William	1809	Right
GRINDS, William	1821	Martin
GRINDSTAFF, Catharinah	1794	Ford
GRINDSTAFF, Catharine	1790	White
GRINDSTAFF, Catherine	1791	White
GRINDSTAFF, John	1794	Thornton
GRINDSTAFF, Wm	1780-1781	District 7
GRINSTAF, John	1795	Thornton
GRINSTAFF, Catherin	1795	Ford
GRINTHAM, Thomas	1794	Murray
GRISHAM, Darcas	1806	Doke
GRISHAM, Dorcas	1805	Doak
GRISHAM, Fuller	1801	Lane
GRISHAM, George	1817	Grisham
GRISHAM, George	1819	Grisham
GRISHAM, George	1819	Grisham
GRISHAM, George	1821	Hale
GRISHAM, Jno	1813	Copas
GRISHAM, John	1801	Lane
GRISHAM, John	1805	Doak
GRISHAM, John	1806	Doke
GRISHAM, John	1807	Britton
GRISHAM, John	1811	Britten
GRISHAM, John	1817	Grisham
GRISHAM, Price	1819	Grisham
GRISHAM, Pryer	1817	Grisham
GRISHAM, Pryer	1818	Grisham
GRISHAM, Thomas	1801	Lane
GRISHAM, Thomas	1811	Britten
GRISHAM, Thomas	1813	Copas
GRISHAM, Thomas	1814	Copes
GRISHAM, Thomas	1817	Grisham
GRISHAM, Thomas	1818	Grisham
GRISHAM, Thomas	1818	Grisham
GRISHAM, Thomas	1819	Grisham
GRISHAM, Thomas	1819	Grisham
GRISHAM, Tryor	1821	Hale
GRISHOLM, John	1814	Copes
GRISM, James	1778	
GRISMBY, Lofton	1821	Martin
GRISOM, Wm	1778	
GRISS, Robert	1818	Smith
GRISSOM, James	1779	
GRISSOM, William	1787	Griggs
GRISSUM, William	1779	
GRIST, Robert	1812	McCray
GRIST, Robert	1815	McLin
GRIST, Robert	1819	Smith
GRIST, Robert	1820	Smith
GRIST, Robert	1821	Smith
GRIST, Robt	1809	Parker
GRISTHAM, Thomas	1790	Shipley
GRISTHAM, Thomas	1791	Shipley
GRISTHAM, Thomas	1793	Murray
GRISTHAM, Thomas	1795	Murray
GRISTHAM, Thomas	1796	Shipley
GRISTHAM, Thomas	1797	Shipley
GRO-ARD, Phillip Sr.	1790	Stone
GRO-ARD, Phillip Sr.	1791	Stone
GRRENTON, Charles	1780-1781 (Undated)	
GRUBBS, Weslley	1812	Ellis
GRUM, John	1819	Hunt
GRYER, Jacob	1797	Calvert
GRYMES, James	1778	
GRYSHAM, Fullor	1798	Crouch
GUILLING, Thomas	1812	Brown
GUIME, Champ	1790	White
GUIME, James Sr.; (Over age)	1791	White
GUIN, Arnold	1808	Gwin
GUIN, Champ	1795	Ford
GUIN, Hugh	1791	Milliken
GUIN, James Jr.	1795	Ford
GUIN, James Sr.	1795	Ford
GUIN, John	1808	Parker
GUIN, John	1810	Hartzel
GUIN, Thomas	1801	Taylor
GUIN, Thomas	1810	Barron
GUIN, Thomas	1811	Barron
GUIN, Thomas Jr.	1808	Guin
GUIN, William	1801	Taylor
GUIN, William	1808	Guin
GUIN, William	1809	Gwin
GUIN, William	1818	Hunt
GUIN, William	1819	Hunt
GUINN AND HARRIS,	1818	Smith
GUINN, Arnold	1816	Waddell
GUINN, Champ	1793	Campbell
GUINN, Champness	1791	White
GUINN, Champness	1792	White
GUINN, George	1816	Waddell
GUINN, Ira	1816	Crookshanks
GUINN, Jaims	1814	McCracken

Surname, Given names	Year	Comp./Dist.
GUINN, James	1793	Campbell
GUINN, James	1815	Garner
GUINN, James	1816	Smith
GUINN, James	1817	Smith
GUINN, James	1818	Smith
GUINN, James (Over age)	1792	White
GUINN, James Jr.	1791	White
GUINN, James Jr.	1793	Campbell
GUINN, John	1817	Hunt
GUINN, Joshua	1816	Crookshanks
GUINN, Samuel	1815	McLin
GUINN, Thomas	1818	Grimsley
GUINN, Thomas	1819	Grimsley
GUINN, William	1817	Hunt
GULLISHER, Thomas	1815	Crookshanks
GURLEY, Ben	1809	Par
GUST, Robert	1816	Smith
GUWYN, Thomas	1809	Cade
GWIN, Champ	1794	Ford
GWIN, James	1820	Smith
GWIN, James	1821	Smith
GWIN, Thomas	1799	Duncan
GWIN, Thomas	1812	Barnes
GWIN, Thomas	1816	Grimsley
GWIN, Thomas Sr.	1806	Guin
GWIN, William	1806	Guin
GWIN, William	1815	Carcathers
GWINE, James Sr.	1794	Thornton
GWYER, Henry	1809	Hartzell
GYER, Christan	1807	Bayles
GYER, Christian	1809	Green
GYER, Cristian	1808	Bayles
GYER, Henry	1801	Roberson
GYER, Henry	1808	Bayles
GYER, Henry	1812	Hartsell
GYER, Henry	1814	Hartsell
GYER, Henry	1821	Howard
GYER, Henry (Adminstrator Jacob Hyer decd)	1807	Bayles
GYER, Jacob	1807	Bayles
GYER, Jacob	1809	Bayles
GYER, Jacob	1814	Hampton
GYER, Jacob	1816	Hampton
GYER, Jacob	1821	Brown
GYER, Jacob (Administrators of Jacob Gyer Dec'd)	1808	Bayles
GYERS, Henry	1810	Hartzel
GYNE, Christian	1806	Brown
GYNE, Henry	1806	Brown
GYNE, Henry	1815	Fines
GYNE, Henry	1817	Fine
GYNE, Henry	1818	Fine

Surname, Given names	Year	Comp./Dist.
GYNE, Jacob	1806	Brown
GYNE, Jacob	1817	Hampton
GYNE, Jacob	1818	Brown [2]
GYNE, Jacob (Decd estate)	1806	Brown
GYRE, Christain	1801	Roberson
GYRE, Henry	1798	Roberson
GYRE, Henry	1819	Howard
GYRE, Henry (Administrator of Jacob Gyre)	1801	Roberson
GYRE, Jacob	1799	Robertson
GYRE, Jacob	1801	Roberson
GYRE, Jacob	1801	Roberson
GYRE, Jacob	1819	Brown
GYRE, Jacob (administrator of Jacob Gyre)	1801	Roberson
H, Ann	1807	Britton
HA, Arther	1801	Norwood
HADAN, Elisah	1780-1781 (Undated)	
HADDEN, Elisha	1781	
HADLE, Abednega	1791	Shipley
HADLE, Abedneza	1790	Shipley
HADLER, Lebaston	1795	Calvert
HADLER, Sibbaston	1799	Gann
HAG, Ruben	1798	Morrison
HAGAN, Arther	1796	Melvin
HAGAN, Arther	1798	Crouch
HAGAN, Barnabas	1792	Maxwell
HAGEN, Barney	1794	Taylor
HAGEN, James	1794	Taylor
HAGER, Solomon	1799	Hannah
HAGGARD, John	1818	Grimsley
HAGGARD, William	1795	Young
HAGIN, Arter	1795	Melvan
HAGIN, Barney	1793	Maxwell
HAGINS, Arthor	1793	Melvan
HAGWORTH, Absolom	1780-1781 (undated)	
HAIL, Abedengo (The older)	1795	Murray
HAIL, Abednego	1798	Shipley
HAIL, Abednego	1801	Glasscock
HAIL, Abednego	1811	Barron
HAIL, Abednego	1780-1781 (Undated)	
HAIL, Abednego Jr.	1794	Melvan
HAIL, Abednego Jr.	1805	Rector
HAIL, Abednego Sr.	1805	Rector
HAIL, Abednego Sr.	1811	Barron
HAIL, Abego	1821	Martin
HAIL, Abenego Sr.	1798	Shipley
HAIL, Aledinga	1819	Grimsley
HAIL, Amon	1798	Shipley
HAIL, Amon	1811	Barron
HAIL, Amon	1818	Grimsley

Surname, Given names	Year	Comp./Dist.
HAIL, Amon	1818	Grisham
HAIL, Amon	1819	Grimsley
HAIL, Amon	1819	Grisham
HAIL, Archibald	1815	Haire
HAIL, Bird	1811	Barron
HAIL, Bird	1818	Grimsley
HAIL, Bird	1819	Grimsley
HAIL, Chase	1819	Grimsley
HAIL, George	1798	Shipley
HAIL, George	1818	Grisham
HAIL, George	1819	Grimsley
HAIL, George Jr.	1798	Shipley
HAIL, Henry	1818	Grisham
HAIL, Henry (son of John)	1798	Shipley
HAIL, Hezekiah	1818	Grimsley
HAIL, Hezekiah	1819	Grimsley
HAIL, James	1818	Grisham
HAIL, James	1819	Grisham
HAIL, John	1793	Maxwell
HAIL, John	1798	Shipley
HAIL, John	1818	Grisham
HAIL, Joseph	1798	Shipley
HAIL, Joseph	1811	Barron
HAIL, Joseph	1818	Grimsley
HAIL, Joseph	1819	Grimsley
HAIL, Joseph (Elder)	1798	Shipley
HAIL, Joshua	1798	Shipley
HAIL, Joshua	1819	Grisham
HAIL, Mark	1815	Haire
HAIL, Mashack	1818	Grisham
HAIL, Meashack	1798	Shipley
HAIL, Mesach	1779	
HAIL, Meshech (son of Shadrach Hail)	1798	Shipley
HAIL, Micajah	1818	Grisham
HAIL, Micasah R.	1819	Grisham
HAIL, Naman	1811	Barron
HAIL, Nathan	1798	Shipley
HAIL, Nathan	1818	Grisham
HAIL, Nicholas Sr.	1798	Shipley
HAIL, Richard	1805	Rector
HAIL, Richard	1818	Grisham
HAIL, Samuel	1798	Shipley
HAIL, Samuel	1806	Crouch
HAIL, Shaderick	1818	Grimsley
HAIL, Shadrach	1798	Shipley
HAIL, Shadrack	1801	Glasscock
HAIL, Shadrack	1805	Rector
HAIL, Shadrick	1811	Barron
HAIL, Shadrick	1819	Grimsley
HAIL, Sharach	1798	Shipley
HAIL, Thomas	1818	Grisham

Surname, Given names	Year	Comp./Dist.
HAIL, Walter	1814	McCracken
HAIL, Walter	1815	Garner
HAIL, Walter	1818	Smith
HAIL, William	1798	Shipley
HAIL, William	1780-1781 (undated)	
HAIL, Zachariah	1818	Grisham
HAILE, Abednego	1793	Murray
HAILE, Abednego	1795	Melvan
HAILE, Abednego	1796	Melvin
HAILE, Abednego	1797	Shipley
HAILE, Abednego	1801	Norwood
HAILE, Abednigo	1797	Biddle
HAILE, Abendnego	1794	Murray
HAILE, Alexander	1794	Murray
HAILE, Alexander	1805	Doak
HAILE, Alexander	1807	Britton
HAILE, Allexander	1806	Doke
HAILE, Amon	1806	Doke
HAILE, Amon	1814	Copes
HAILE, Ann	1805	Doak
HAILE, Archabald	1811	Ellis
HAILE, Archibald	1809	Right
HAILE, Archibald	1812	Ellis
HAILE, George	1801	Lane
HAILE, George	1801	Lane
HAILE, George	1805	Doak
HAILE, George	1812	Britton
HAILE, George	1814	Copes
HAILE, George (of George)	1806	Doke
HAILE, George (of John)	1805	Doak
HAILE, George Jr.	1793	Murray
HAILE, George Jr.	1794	Murray
HAILE, George Jr.	1795	Murray
HAILE, George Jr.	1796	Shipley
HAILE, George Jr.	1797	Shipley
HAILE, George Jr.	1801	Lane
HAILE, George Sr.	1793	Murray
HAILE, George Sr.	1794	Murray
HAILE, George Sr.	1795	Murray
HAILE, George Sr.	1796	Shipley
HAILE, George Sr.	1797	Shipley
HAILE, Hannah	1805	Doak
HAILE, Hannah	1807	Britton
HAILE, Henry	1796	Shipley
HAILE, Jemima	1795	Murray
HAILE, John	1793	Murray
HAILE, John	1794	Murray
HAILE, John	1795	Murray
HAILE, John	1797	Shipley
HAILE, Joseph	1807	Britton
HAILE, Joseph	1821	Martin

Surname, Given names	Year	Comp./Dist.
HAILE, Joseph (elder)	1801	Lane
HAILE, Joseph (elder)	1805	Doak
HAILE, Joseph (of George)	1797	Shipley
HAILE, Joseph (the older)	1796	Shipley
HAILE, Joseph (the older)	1797	Shipley
HAILE, Joseph (the older)	1806	Doke
HAILE, Joseph (the older)	1812	Britton
HAILE, Joseph (the older)	1814	Copes
HAILE, Joseph (The older)	1795	Murray
HAILE, Joseph (The Older)	1794	Murray
HAILE, Joseph (The Younger)	1794	Murray
HAILE, Joseph Jr.	1801	Lane
HAILE, Joshua	1790	Shipley
HAILE, Joshua	1791	Shipley
HAILE, Joshua	1793	Murray
HAILE, Joshua	1794	Murray
HAILE, Joshua	1795	Murray
HAILE, Joshua	1796	Shipley
HAILE, Joshua	1797	Shipley
HAILE, Joshua	1801	Lane
HAILE, Joshua	1806	Doke
HAILE, Machach	1806	Doke
HAILE, Machash	1797	Shipley
HAILE, Mark	1811	Ellis
HAILE, Mark	1812	Ellis
HAILE, Marshall	1794	Murray
HAILE, Mashech	1805	Doak
HAILE, Mashuch	1807	Britton
HAILE, Mechach	1814	Copes
HAILE, Meshach	1795	Murray
HAILE, Meshack	1796	Shipley
HAILE, Michael (Little)	1795	Murray
HAILE, Mosah	1797	Shipley
HAILE, Mozhack (Son of George)	1793	Murray
HAILE, Nathan	1793	Murray
HAILE, Nathan	1794	Murray
HAILE, Nathan	1795	Murray
HAILE, Nathan	1796	Shipley
HAILE, Nathan	1797	Shipley
HAILE, Nathan	1801	Lane
HAILE, Nathan	1805	Doak
HAILE, Nathan	1806	Doke
HAILE, Nathan	1807	Britton
HAILE, Nathan	1812	Britton
HAILE, Nathan	1814	Copes
HAILE, Ncholas (Estate)	1795	Murray
HAILE, Nicholas	1801	Lane
HAILE, Nicholas	1805	Doak
HAILE, Nicholas	1805	Doak
HAILE, Nicholas	1806	Doke
HAILE, Nicholas	1807	Britton

Surname, Given names	Year	Comp./Dist.
HAILE, Nicholas	1812	Britton
HAILE, Nicholas	1814	Copes
HAILE, Nicholas (The estate of)	1794	Murray
HAILE, Nicholas Jr.	1793	Murray
HAILE, Nicholas Sr.	1793	Murray
HAILE, Nicholas Sr.	1794	Murray
HAILE, Nicholas Sr.	1795	Murray
HAILE, Nicholas Sr.	1796	Shipley
HAILE, Nicholas Sr.	1797	Shipley
HAILE, Richard	1793	Murray
HAILE, Richard	1794	Murray
HAILE, Richard	1795	Murray
HAILE, Richard	1801	Lane
HAILE, Richard	1805	Doak
HAILE, Richard	1806	Doke
HAILE, Richard	1812	Britton
HAILE, Richard (of John)	1814	Copes
HAILE, Richard Jr.	1796	Shipley
HAILE, Richard Sr.	1796	Shipley
HAILE, Richard Sr.	1814	Copes
HAILE, Ruth	1806	Crouch
HAILE, Ruth	1809	Right
HAILE, Ruth	1811	Ellis
HAILE, Ruth (widow)	1812	Ellis
HAILE, Samuel	1793	Murray
HAILE, Samuel	1794	Murray
HAILE, Samuel	1795	Murray
HAILE, Samuel	1796	Shipley
HAILE, Samuel	1797	Shipley
HAILE, Samuel	1801	Lane
HAILE, Samuel	1809	Right
HAILE, Shadrack	1795	Murray
HAILE, Shadrack	1797	Shipley
HAILE, Shadrock	1794	Murray
HAILE, Thomas	1796	Shipley
HAILE, Thomas	1797	Shipley
HAILE, Thomas	1801	Lane
HAILE, Thomas	1805	Doak
HAILE, Thomas	1807	Britton
HAILE, Thomas	1812	Britton
HAILE, Thomas	1814	Copes
HAILE, William	1793	Murray
HAILE, William	1794	Murray
HAILE, William	1795	Murray
HAILE, William	1801	Lane
HAILE, William (of Nicholas)	1796	Shipley
HAILE, William (of Nicholas)	1797	Shipley
HAILE, William (of Richard Sr.)	1796	Shipley
HAILE, William (of Richard)	1797	Shipley
HAILE, Zachariah	1812	Britton
HAILE, Zachariah	1814	Copes

Surname, Given names	Year	Comp./Dist.
HAILES, Abedneg	1783 [after]	Blair
HAILL, Abednego	1798	Crouch
HAINE, Isaac	1797	Calvert
HAINE, John C.	1820	Smith
HAINES, George	1790	Williams
HAINES, George	1791	Williams
HAINES, George M.	1821	Haines
HAINEY, Barney	1779	
HAINEY, John	1779	
HAINEY, Thomas	1779	
HAINS, James M.	1780-1781	District 7
HAINS, William	1812	Crawford
HAIR, Danl	1778	
HAIR, Henery	1814	Bean
HAIR, Henry	1799	Duncan
HAIR, Henry	1801	Taylor
HAIR, Henry	1816	Hair
HAIR, Henry	1817	Haire
HAIR, Henry	1818	Hair
HAIR, Henry	1821	Louis
HAIR, Isaac	1793	Scott
HAIR, Isaac	1798	Calvert
HAIR, Isaac	1799	Stuart
HAIR, Isaac	1801	Calvert
HAIR, Isaac	1814	McCray
HAIR, Isaac	1816	Hair
HAIR, Isaac	1816	Harrison
HAIR, Isaac	1817	Hunt
HAIR, Isaac	1818	Hunt
HAIR, Isaac	1819	Hunt
HAIR, Isaac	1821	Hunt
HAIR, Jacob	1814	Bean
HAIR, Jacob	1816	Hair
HAIR, Jacob	1817	Haire
HAIR, Jacob	1818	Hair
HAIR, Jacob	1819	Hair
HAIR, Jacob	1821	Louis
HAIR, John	1821	Hunt
HAIR, Joseph	1814	McCray
HAIRE, Handsil	1808	Bayles
HAIRE, Hen	1809	Parker
HAIRE, Henry	1798	Duncan
HAIRE, Henry	1808	Parker
HAIRE, Henry Jr.	1812	Ellis
HAIRE, Isaac	1797	Calvert
HAIRE, Isaac	1808	Parker
HAIRE, Isaac	1809	Parker
HAIRE, Isaac	1811	McCray
HAIRE, Isaac	1812	McCray
HAIRE, Isaac	1812	McCray
HAIRE, Jacob	1808	Parker
HAIRE, Jacob	1809	Parker
HAIRE, Jacob	1812	Ellis
HAIRS, Clem	1779	
HAIS, Henry	1819	Hair
HAISLIP, Robert (Single man)	1779	
HAITE, George Jr.	1790	Shipley
HAITE, George Jr.	1791	Shipley
HAITE, Joseph (the Elder)	1793	Murray
HAL, Elisha W.	1814	Barns
HALE, (Capt.)	1793	Hale
HALE, Abedenego Jr.	1809	Cade
HALE, Abednago	1807	Cade
HALE, Abednago	1807	Cade
HALE, Abednego	1814	Barns
HALE, Abednego	1814	Barns
HALE, Abednego	1815	Grimsley
HALE, Abednego	1815	Grimsley
HALE, Abednego	1816	Grimsley
HALE, Abednego	1817	Grimsley
HALE, Abednego	1818	Grimsley
HALE, Abednego (J.)	1808	Cade
HALE, Abednego Sr.	1809	Cade
HALE, Abednego Sr.	1816	Grimsley
HALE, Abenago Jr.	1810	Barron
HALE, Abenago Sr.	1810	Barron
HALE, Alexander	1811	Britten
HALE, Alexander	1813	Copas
HALE, Amon	1807	Cade
HALE, Amon	1808	Cade
HALE, Amon	1809	Cade
HALE, Amon	1810	Barron
HALE, Amon	1811	Britten
HALE, Amon	1812	Barnes
HALE, Amon	1813	Copas
HALE, Amon	1814	Barns
HALE, Amon	1815	Copas
HALE, Amon	1815	Grimsley
HALE, Amon	1816	Copas
HALE, Amon	1816	Grimsley
HALE, Amon	1817	Grimsley
HALE, Amon	1817	Grisham
HALE, Amon Sr.	1807	Britton
HALE, Amond	1821	Martin
HALE, Archabald	1821	Louis
HALE, Archbald	1814	Bean
HALE, Archibald	1816	Hair
HALE, Archibald	1817	Haire
HALE, Archibald	1818	Hair
HALE, Archibald	1819	Hair
HALE, Baldwin	1797	Calvert
HALE, Bednigo	1812	Barnes

Surname, Given names	Year	Comp./Dist.
HALE, Bednigo Sr.	1812	Barnes
HALE, Bird	1809	Cade
HALE, Bird	1810	Barron
HALE, Bird	1812	Barnes
HALE, Bird	1815	Grimsley
HALE, Bird	1816	Grimsley
HALE, Bird	1817	Grimsley
HALE, Birel	1814	Barns
HALE, Butler	1807	Cade
HALE, Butler	1808	Cade
HALE, Caleb	1814	McCray
HALE, Chase	1815	Copas
HALE, Chase	1816	Copas
HALE, Chase	1821	Martin
HALE, David	1821	Martin
HALE, Elisha W.	1814	Barns
HALE, Esakial	1814	Barns
HALE, Ezekiel	1815	Grimsley
HALE, Fredrick	1801	Gann
HALE, Geo	1813	Copas
HALE, George	1811	Britten
HALE, George	1815	Copas
HALE, George	1816	Copas
HALE, George	1817	Grisham
HALE, George	1819	Grisham
HALE, George	1821	Hale
HALE, George	1821	Martin
HALE, Gess	1814	Barns
HALE, Guy	1812	Barnes
HALE, Gy	1815	Grimsley
HALE, Gye	1816	Grimsley
HALE, Henry	1814	McCray
HALE, Henry	1815	Copas
HALE, Henry	1816	Copas
HALE, Henry	1817	Grisham
HALE, Henry	1819	Grisham
HALE, Henry	1819	Hair
HALE, Henry	1821	Hale
HALE, Henry	1821	Louis
HALE, Hezekiah	1816	Grimsley
HALE, Hezekiel	1812	Barnes
HALE, Hisaciah	1821	Martin
HALE, James	1809	Right
HALE, James	1815	Grimsley
HALE, James	1817	Grisham
HALE, Jesse	1815	Copas
HALE, Jesse	1816	Copas
HALE, Jesse	1816	Grimsley
HALE, Jesse	1817	Grisham
HALE, John	1792	Coye
HALE, John	1792	Maxwell

Surname, Given names	Year	Comp./Dist.
HALE, John	1794	Taylor
HALE, Joseph	1807	Cade
HALE, Joseph	1809	Cade
HALE, Joseph	1810	Barron
HALE, Joseph	1811	Britten
HALE, Joseph	1812	Barnes
HALE, Joseph	1813	Copas
HALE, Joseph	1816	Grimsley
HALE, Joseph	1817	Grimsley
HALE, Joseph (Son of George)	1795	Murray
HALE, Joshiah	1821	Hale
HALE, Joshua	1817	Grimsley
HALE, Joshua S.	1817	Grisham
HALE, Leroy	1807	Cade
HALE, Leroy	1808	Cade
HALE, Leroy	1812	Barnes
HALE, Mack	1818	Hair
HALE, Mark	1814	Bean
HALE, Mark	1816	Grimsley
HALE, Mark	1816	Hair
HALE, Mark	1817	Haire
HALE, Mark	1819	Hair
HALE, Mark	1821	Louis
HALE, Mashack	1817	Grisham
HALE, Mashech	1813	Copas
HALE, Masheek	1816	Copas
HALE, Mesbach	1819	Grisham
HALE, Mesheck	1811	Britten
HALE, Mesheck	1821	Hale
HALE, Micajah	1815	Copas
HALE, Micajah	1816	Copas
HALE, Micajah	1817	Grisham
HALE, Michal	1821	Hale
HALE, Nathan	1811	Britten
HALE, Nathan	1813	Copas
HALE, Nathan	1815	Copas
HALE, Nathan	1816	Copas
HALE, Nathan	1817	Grisham
HALE, Nathan	1819	Grisham
HALE, Nathan	1821	Hale
HALE, Nathanael	1809	Right
HALE, Nicholas	1811	Britten
HALE, Nicholas Sr.	1813	Copas
HALE, Nicholis	1815	Copas
HALE, Nicholis	1816	Copas
HALE, Nicholis	1817	Grisham
HALE, Rd Sr.	1813	Copas
HALE, Richard	1807	Cade
HALE, Richard	1809	Cade
HALE, Richard	1821	Hale
HALE, Richard (of John)	1815	Copas

Surname, Given names	Year	Comp./Dist.
HALE, Richard Jr.	1811	Britten
HALE, Richard Jr.	1815	Copas
HALE, Richard Jr.	1817	Grisham
HALE, Richard Sr.	1811	Britten
HALE, Richard Sr.	1816	Copas
HALE, Richard Sr.	1817	Grisham
HALE, Richd Jr.	1813	Copas
HALE, Robert	1819	Grisham
HALE, Rytha	1814	Bean
HALE, Shade	1812	Barnes
HALE, Shaderick	1815	Grimsley
HALE, Shaderick	1816	Grimsley
HALE, Shaderick	1817	Grimsley
HALE, Shadrac	1807	Cade
HALE, Shadrac	1810	Barron
HALE, Shadrac	1814	Barns
HALE, Shadral	1808	Cade
HALE, Shadrick	1809	Cade
HALE, Thadrick	1821	Martin
HALE, Thomas	1813	Copas
HALE, Thomas	1815	Copas
HALE, Thomas	1816	Copas
HALE, Thomas	1817	Grisham
HALE, Thomas	1819	Grisham
HALE, Thomas	1821	Hale
HALE, Walter	1819	Smith
HALE, Walter	1820	Smith
HALE, Walter	1821	Smith
HALE, William	1809	Right
HALE, William	1814	Barns
HALE, Zachariah	1813	Copas
HALE, Zachariah	1815	Copas
HALE, Zachariah	1816	Copas
HALE, Zachariah	1817	Grisham
HALE, Zachariah	1819	Grisham
HALE, Zachariah	1821	Hale
HALES, Abednago	1808	Cade
HALES, Jacob	1808	Cade
HALL, Alex	1793	Milliken
HALL, Alex	1794	Milliken
HALL, Alexander	1792	Milliken
HALL, George	1807	Britton
HALL, Henrey	1795	Handly
HALL, Henry	1821	Hale
HALL, James	1792	Milliken
HALL, James	1793	Milliken
HALL, James	1793	Scott
HALL, James	1794	Milliken
HALL, James	1794	Scot
HALL, James	1798	Crouch
HALL, James	1801	Norwood
HALL, James	1806	Crouch
HALL, James	1811	Ellis
HALL, James	1812	Ellis
HALL, James	1814	Bean
HALL, James	1815	Haire
HALL, James	1816	Hair
HALL, James	1817	Haire
HALL, James	1818	Hair
HALL, James	1819	Hair
HALL, James	1821	Louis
HALL, John	1792	Milliken
HALL, John	1793	Milliken
HALL, John	1821	Louis
HALL, Joshua	1814	Hampton
HALL, Joshua	1819	Brown
HALL, Nath	1801	Norwood
HALL, Nathanael	1793	Melvan
HALL, Nathanael	1794	Melvan
HALL, Nathanail	1795	Murray
HALL, Nathanel	1796	Melvin
HALL, Nathaniel	1790	Shipley
HALL, Nathaniel	1791	Shipley
HALL, Nathaniel	1806	Crouch
HALL, Nathaniel	1812	Ellis
HALL, Nathl	1807	
HALL, Sammuel	1795	Melvan
HALL, Samuel	1790	Stone
HALL, Samuel	1791	Stone
HALL, Samuel	1793	Melvan
HALL, Samuel	1794	Melvan
HALL, Samuel	1798	Crouch
HALL, Samuel	1805	Doak
HALL, Samuel	1806	Doke
HALL, Thomas	1793	Melvan
HALL, Thomas	1794	Melvan
HALL, Thomas	1795	Melvan
HALL, Thomas	1796	Melvin
HALL, Thomas	1811	Britten
HALL, William	1794	Melvan
HALL, William	1795	Murray
HALL, William	1798	Crouch
HALL, William	1801	Norwood
HALL, William	1806	Crouch
HALL, William	1811	Ellis
HALL, Wm	1790	Milleken
HALL, Wm	1796	Melvin
HALL, Wm Jr.	1791	Milliken
HALL, Wm Jr.	1792	Milliken
HALL, Wm Jr.	1793	Milliken
HALL, Wm Sr.	1791	Milliken
HALL, Wm Sr.	1793	Milliken

Surname, Given names	Year	Comp./Dist.
HALLAND, Benjamin	1798	Shipley
HALLES, David	1811	McAlister
HALLEY, James (The Heirs Of)	1799	Robertson
HALTSINGER, John	1809	McAlister
HAM, Henry	1815	Haire
HAM, Jacob	1815	Haire
HAMAR, Jacob	1791	Tullis
HAMAR, John	1791	Tullis
HAMBELTON, John	1780-1781 (Undated)	
HAMBERGER, Jacob	1810	Hartzel
HAMBLE, Peter	1809	Par
HAMEL, Peter	1808	Parker
HAMEL, Peter	1810	Hartzel
HAMELL, Peter	1801	Taylor
HAMELL, Peter	1807	Parker
HAMILTON, Frances	1781	
HAMILTON, Frances Sr.	1780-1781 (Undated)	
HAMILTON, Francis	1778	
HAMILTON, Francis	1778	
HAMILTON, Isiah	1778	
HAMILTON, Jacob	1778	
HAMILTON, John	1779	Wilson
HAMILTON, John	1781	
HAMILTON, Saml (of Coaller free)	1809	McAlister
HAMILTON, Samuel	1805	Jas Parker
HAMILTON, Samuel	1816	Crookshanks
HAMILTON, Samuel	1817	McClure
HAMILTON, Samuel	1818	McClure
HAMILTON, Samuel (a man of Colour)	1819	Hunt
HAMLETON, Isaac	1781	
HAMLETON, John	1781	
HAMMAR, Baltes	1796	Melvin
HAMMAR, Boltis	1798	Crouch
HAMMELL, George	1799	Stuart
HAMMELL, Peter	1799	Stuart
HAMMER, Bathes Jr.	1790	Stone
HAMMER, Bathes Jr.	1791	Stone
HAMMER, Bathes Sr.	1790	Stone
HAMMER, Bathes Sr.	1791	Stone
HAMMER, Battes Sr.	1793	Melvan
HAMMER, Boltis	1794	Melvan
HAMMER, Boltis	1801	Norwood
HAMMER, Christian	1817	Smith
HAMMER, Isaac	1795	Morrison
HAMMER, Isaac	1798	Morrison
HAMMER, Isaac	1798	Morrison
HAMMER, Isaac	1798	Morrison
HAMMER, Isaac	1799	Morrison
HAMMER, Isaac	1806	Carr

Surname, Given names	Year	Comp./Dist.
HAMMER, Isaac	1807	Carr
HAMMER, Isaac	1808	Carr
HAMMER, Isaac	1809	Carr
HAMMER, Isaac	1811	Mitchell
HAMMER, Isaac	1813	Hoss
HAMMER, Isaac	1814	Hoss
HAMMER, Isaac	1815	Hoss
HAMMER, Isaac	1816	Hoss
HAMMER, Isaac	1817	Little
HAMMER, Isaac	1818	Jones
HAMMER, Isaac	1819	Jones
HAMMER, Isaac	1821	Jones
HAMMER, Isacc	1801	Morrison
HAMMER, Jacob	1787	Fains
HAMMER, Jacob	1792	Tulley
HAMMER, Jacob	1793	Morrison
HAMMER, Jacob	1794	Morrison
HAMMER, Jacob	1795	Morrison
HAMMER, Jacob	1798	Morrison
HAMMER, Jacob	1798	Morrison
HAMMER, Jacob	1798	Morrison
HAMMER, Jacob	1801	Morrison
HAMMER, Jacob	1806	Carr
HAMMER, Jacob	1807	Carr
HAMMER, Jacob	1808	Carr
HAMMER, Jacob	1809	Carr
HAMMER, Jacob	1811	Mitchell
HAMMER, Jacob	1813	Hoss
HAMMER, Jacob	1814	Hoss
HAMMER, Jacob	1815	Hoss
HAMMER, Jacob	1816	Hoss
HAMMER, Jacob	1817	Little
HAMMER, Jacob	1819	Jones
HAMMER, Jacob	1821	Jones
HAMMER, Jacob	[1796] 1797	Morris
HAMMER, John	1787	Fains
HAMMER, John	1792	Tulley
HAMMER, John	1793	Morrison
HAMMER, John	1794	Morrison
HAMMER, John	1795	Morrison
HAMMER, John	1811	McCray
HAMMER, John	1818	Jones
HAMMER, John	1819	Jones
HAMMER, John	1821	Jones
HAMMER, John Jr.	1798	Morrison
HAMMER, John Jr.	1798	Morrison
HAMMER, John Jr.	1798	Morrison
HAMMER, John Jr.	1799	Morrison
HAMMER, John Jr.	1801	Morrison
HAMMER, John Jr.	1806	Carr
HAMMER, John Jr.	1807	Carr

Surname, Given names	Year	Comp./Dist.
HAMMER, John Jr.	1808	Carr
HAMMER, John Jr.	1809	Carr
HAMMER, John Jr.	1813	Hoss
HAMMER, John Jr.	1814	Hoss
HAMMER, John Jr.	1815	Hoss
HAMMER, John Jr.	1816	Hoss
HAMMER, John Jr.	1817	Little
HAMMER, John Jr.	1821	Jones
HAMMER, John Jr.	[1796] 1797	Morris
HAMMER, John Jr.; (and Taylor)	1811	Mitchell
HAMMER, John Sr.	1798	Morrison
HAMMER, John Sr.	1798	Morrison
HAMMER, John Sr.	1799	Morrison
HAMMER, John Sr.	1801	Morrison
HAMMER, John Sr.	1806	Carr
HAMMER, John Sr.	1807	Carr
HAMMER, John Sr.	1808	Carr
HAMMER, John Sr.	1809	Carr
HAMMER, John Sr.	1811	Mitchell
HAMMER, John Sr.	1813	Hoss
HAMMER, John Sr.	1814	Hoss
HAMMER, John Sr.	1815	Hoss
HAMMER, John Sr.	1817	Little
HAMMER, John Sr.	[1796] 1797	Morris
HAMMER, Johnathan	1799	Morrison
HAMMER, Jonathan	1798	Morrison
HAMMER, Jonathan	1801	Morrison
HAMMER, Jonathan	1807	Carr
HAMMER, Jonathan	1808	Carr
HAMMER, Jonathan	1809	Carr
HAMMER, Jonathan	1811	Mitchell
HAMMER, Jonathan	1814	Hoss
HAMMER, Jonathan	1815	Hoss
HAMMER, Jonathan	1816	Hoss
HAMMER, Jonathan	1817	Little
HAMMER, Jonathan	1818	Jones
HAMMER, Jonathan	1819	Jones
HAMMER, Jonathen	1806	Carr
HAMMER, Jonathon	1821	Jones
HAMMER, Jonithan	1813	Hoss
HAMMER, Joseph	1798	Morrison
HAMMER, Joseph	1799	Morrison
HAMMER, Joseph	1801	Morrison
HAMMER, Peter	1806	Crouch
HAMMER, Peter	1809	Right
HAMMER, Peter	1811	Britten
HAMMER, Richard	1793	Melvan
HAMMER, Richard	1801	Norwood
HAMMER, Richard	1806	Crouch
HAMMER, Richard	1809	Right
HAMMER, Richard	1811	Ellis
HAMMER, Richard	1812	Ellis
HAMMER, Richard	1814	Bean
HAMMER, Richard	1815	Haire
HAMMER, Richard	1816	Hair
HAMMER, Richard	1817	Haire
HAMMOCK, John	1798	Morrison
HAMMON, Adam	1817	Riley
HAMMON, Bolles	1795	Melvan
HAMMON, Christopher	1792	Chisolm
HAMMON, Christopher	1793	Brown
HAMMON, John	1781	
HAMMON, Thomas	1811	McCray
HAMMON, Thomas	1812	McCray
HAMMON, Thomas	1816	Harrison
HAMMOND, Christefor	1796	Brown
HAMMOND, Christopher	1797	Robertson
HAMMOND, Christopher	1798	Roberson
HAMMOND, Christopher	1799	Robertson
HAMMOND, Christopher	1801	Roberson
HAMMONS, Christopher	1791	Chisom
HAMMONS, Thomas	1821	Hampton
HAMMOR, Richart	1794	Melvan
HAMOCK, John	1798	Morrison
HAMOND, Christefar	1794	Brown
HAMOND, Thomas	1814	McCray
HAMPSON, James	1790	Williams
HAMPSON, James	1791	Williams
HAMPSON, James	1792	Maxwell
HAMPSON, James	1793	Maxwell
HAMPSON, William	1792	Maxwell
HAMPTON, Henrey	1805	Guir
HAMPTON, Isaac	1814	McLin
HAMPTON, Jesse	1816	Harrison
HAMPTON, Jesse	1817	Harris
HAMPTON, Jesse	1818	Harris
HAMPTON, Jesse	1819	Harris
HAMPTON, Jesse	1821	Hampton
HAMPTON, Jessee	1814	Hampton
HAMPTON, John	1807	Bayles
HAMPTON, John	1808	Bayles
HAMPTON, John	1809	Bayles
HAMPTON, John	1814	Hampton
HAMPTON, John	1816	Hampton
HAMPTON, John	1817	Hampton
HAMPTON, John	1818	Brown [2]
HAMPTON, John	1819	Brown
HAMPTON, John	1821	Brown
HAMPTON, Mary	1806	Brown
HAMPTON, Mary	1807	Bayles
HAMPTON, Mary	1808	Bayles
HAMPTON, Robert	1791	Chisom

Surname, Given names	Year	Comp./Dist.
HAMPTON, Robert	1792	Brown
HAMPTON, Robert	1792	Chisolm
HAMPTON, Robert	1807	Bayles
HAMPTON, Robert	1816	Fine
HAMPTON, Robert	1817	Fine
HAMPTON, Robert	1818	Harris
HAMPTON, Robert	1819	Harris
HAMPTON, Robert	1819	Howard
HAMPTON, Robert	1821	Hampton
HAMPTON, Robt	1793	Brown
HAMPTON, Rolins	1818	Fine
HAMPTON, Thomas	1819	Brown
HAMPTON, Thos	1821	Brown
HAMTON, John	1797	Robertson
HAMTON, John	1798	Roberson
HAMTON, John	1799	Robertson
HAMTON, John	1801	Roberson
HAMTON, Mary	1797	Robertson
HAMTON, Mary	1799	Robertson
HAMTON, Mary	1801	Roberson
HAMTON, Robert	1794	Brown
HAMTON, Robert	1807	Carr
HAMTON, Robert	1808	Carr
HANAH, Andrew	1792	Milliken
HANAH, John	1793	Handley
HANAH, Joseph	1793	Handley
HANAH, Samuel	1793	Handley
HANCE, John	1791	North
HANDLEY, George	1814	Hampton
HANDLEY, George Sr.	1792	Chisolm
HANDLEY, Isaac	1814	Hampton
HANDLEY, Isaac	1821	Brown
HANDLEY, Isaach	1808	Bayles
HANDLEY, James	1821	Brown
HANDLEY, John	1808	Bayles
HANDLEY, Joshua	1814	Hampton
HANDLEY, Joshua	1821	Brown
HANDLEY, Saml (Capt.)	1791	
HANDLEY, Samuel	1778	
HANDLY, Lerngdon	1814	McCracken
HANDLY, Samuel	1781	
HANDLY, Samuel	1793	Handley
HANE, Richard	1809	Roadmas
HANELLEY, George	1791	Chisom
HANER, Lewis	1797	Calvert
HANERY, Abreham	1794	Taylor
HANES, David	1812	Brown
HANES, George	1794	Taylor
HANES, James	1819	Grimsley
HANES, Lewis	1801	Calvert
HANGER, John	1799	Stuart
HANLEY, George	1794	Brown
HANLEY, Gorge	1796	Brown
HANLEY, Isaac	1809	Bayles
HANLEY, James	1796	Brown
HANLEY, James	1797	Robertson
HANLEY, James	1798	Roberson
HANLEY, John	1796	Brown
HANLEY, John	1798	Roberson
HANLEY, John	1801	Roberson
HANLEY, John	1809	Bayles
HANLEY, Samuel	1790	Hanley
HANLEY, Samuel	1791	Hanley
HANLEY, Samuel	1796	Brown
HANNA, Andrew	1793	Milliken
HANNA, John	1790	Hanley
HANNA, John	1791	Hanley
HANNAD, Andrew	1790	Milleken
HANNAH, Andr	1794	Milliken
HANNAH, Andrew	1791	Milliken
HANNAH, Andrew	1795	Milliken
HANNAH, Andrew	1796	Millikin
HANNAH, Andrew	1797	Hannah
HANNAH, Andrew	1798	Hannah
HANNAH, Andrew	1799	Hannah
HANNAH, Andrew	1801	Squibb
HANNAH, Andrew	1805	Rector
HANNAH, Andrew	1805	Stephenson
HANNAH, Andrew	1806	Payn
HANNAH, Andrew	1807	Payne
HANNAH, Andrew	1809	McAlister
HANNAH, Andrew	1809	McAlister
HANNAH, Andrew	1811	Green
HANNAH, Andrew	1812	Crawford [2]
HANNAH, Andrew	1815	Crookshanks
HANNAH, Andrew	1816	Crookshanks
HANNAH, Andrew	1817	McClure
HANNAH, Andrew	1818	McClure
HANNAH, Andrew	1819	McClure
HANNAH, Andrew	1821	McClure
HANNAH, Hartsell	1815	Fines
HANNAH, John	1795	Milliken
HANNEH, Andrew	1812	Crawford
HANNEL, John	1791	Willey
HANNET, Andrew	1808	McAllister
HANS, Conra-	1818	Grimsley
HANS, James	1818	Grimsley
HANS, James	1821	Martin
HANS, John	1818	Grimsley
HANS, John	1819	Grimsley
HANS, John	1821	Martin
HAN'S, John	1811	Barron

Surname, Given names	Year	Comp./Dist.
HANS, Thomas	1819	Sands
HAN'S, Thomas	1811	Barron
HANSON, John	1795	Thornton
HAPTON, Mary	1809	Bayles
HARBINSON, William	1791	Hanley
HARBISON, Saml	1795	Handly
HARBISON, Saml	1799	Moore
HARBISON, Samuel	1798	Gann
HARBISON, William	1793	Handley
HARBISON, William	1794	Handly
HARBISON, William	1795	Handly
HARBISON, William	1796	Handly
HARBISON, William	1798	Gann
HARBISON, Wm	1790	Hanley
HARBISON, Wm	1797	Gann
HARBISON, Wm	1799	Moore
HARBISON, Wm	1801	Gann
HARDEN, Ben	1781	
HARDEN, Francis	1819	Brown
HARDEN, Joseph	1781	
HARDEN, William	1794	Carriger
HARDEN, William	1795	Carriger
HARDING, William	1780-1781 (Undated)	
HARE, Isaac	1805	Jas Parker
HARE, Jacob	1801	Roberson
HARE, Jacob	1805	Jas Parker
HARE, William	1819	Hair
HARELIP, Kenher	1812	Barnes
HARES, Benjamen C.	1809	Par
HARESS, Benjamin	1808	Parker
HARESS, George C.	1808	Parker
HARESS, Joshua	1798	Morrison
HARIE, Isaac	1792	Scott
HARIS, Nathaniel	1811	
HARIS, Nathaniel	1812	McLin
HARISON, Thomas	1821	Howard
HARLEN, Joseph	1807	Payne
HARLES, Baldwin	1795	Calvert
HARLIE, Baldwin	1796	Jonesboro
HARMAN, Abraham	1806	Grur
HARMAN, Abram	1805	Jas Parker
HARMAN, Adam	1814	Waddell
HARMAN, Joseph	1809	Parker
HARMAN, Michall	1796	Calvert
HARMEN, Adam	1799	Moore
HARMON, Abraham	1792	Scott
HARMON, Abraham	1793	Scott
HARMON, Abraham	1794	Scot
HARMON, Abraham	1795	Calvert
HARMON, Abraham	1796	Calvert
HARMON, Abraham	1801	Gann
HARMON, Abraham	1808	Gwin
HARMON, Abram	1799	Gann
HARMON, Adam	1791	Willey
HARMON, Adam	1792	Scott
HARMON, Adam	1793	Scott
HARMON, Adam	1795	Calvert
HARMON, Adam	1796	Longmire
HARMON, Adam	1797	Gann
HARMON, Adam	1799	Gann
HARMON, Adam	1801	Gann
HARMON, Adam	1806	Grur
HARMON, Adam	1808	Gwin
HARMON, Adam	1809	Green
HARMON, Adam	1810	Green
HARMON, Adam	1811	Green
HARMON, Adam	1812	Waddill
HARMON, Adam	1816	Waddell
HARMON, Adam	1818	Riley
HARMON, Adam	1819	Findley
HARMON, Adam	1821	McGee
HARMON, Andrew	1814	Crookshanks
HARMON, Jos	1799	Moore
HARMON, Joseph	1791	Willey
HARMON, Joseph	1792	Scott
HARMON, Joseph	1806	Grur
HARMON, Joseph	1808	Parker
HARMON, Joseph	1811	McCray
HARMON, Joseph	1812	McCray
HARMON, Joseph	1812	McCray
HARMON, Joseph	1814	McCray
HARMON, Mikel	1798	Crouch
HARMON, Sha	1799	Moore
HAROLD, Elisha	1799	Duncan
HAROLD, Johnathan	1799	Duncan
HARPER, Josiah	1792	Tulley
HARPER, Josiah	1793	Maxwell
HARPMAN, John	1812	Barnes
HARPMAN, Levi	1812	Barnes
HARRADEN, Susan	1821	Smith
HARRALD, John	1798	Longmire
HARREAH, James	1798	Duncan
HARREL, Amasa	1805	Rector
HARREL, James	1798	Duncan
HARREL, John	1806	Crouch
HARRESS, Benjamin	1805	Jas Parker
HARRESS, Benjamin	1809	Parker
HARRESS, Geo C.	1809	Parker
HARRESS, George C.	1805	Jas Parker
HARRIDEN, Susan	1820	Smith
HARRIE, John	1805	Parker
HARRIL, Benjamin	1817	Harris

Surname, Given names	Year	Comp./Dist.
HARRIL, Jonathan	1798	Shipley
HARRILA, John	1801	Longmire
HARRIMAN, Thomas	1818	Harris
HARRINGTON, Charles	1778	
HARRINGTON, Peter	1819	Jones
HARRINGTON, Peter	1821	Jones
HARRIS & GREEN,	1817	Smith
HARRIS, Benj.	1798	Calvert
HARRIS, Benjaman	1812	McCray
HARRIS, Benjamin	1801	Calvert
HARRIS, Benjamin	1811	McCray
HARRIS, Benjamin	1812	McCray
HARRIS, Benjamin	1814	McCray
HARRIS, Benjamin	1816	Harrison
HARRIS, Benjamin	1818	Harris
HARRIS, Benjamin	1819	Harris
HARRIS, Benjamin (estate)	1821	Hampton
HARRIS, George	1817	Harris
HARRIS, George	1819	Brown
HARRIS, George C.	1811	McCray
HARRIS, George C.	1812	McCray
HARRIS, George C.	1812	McCray
HARRIS, George C.	1814	McCray
HARRIS, George C.	1816	Harrison
HARRIS, George C.	1818	Harris
HARRIS, George C.	1819	Harris
HARRIS, George C.	1821	Hampton
HARRIS, J.C.	1814	McCracken
HARRIS, James	1819	Brown
HARRIS, Jno C.	1806	Parker
HARRIS, John C.	1797	Hannah
HARRIS, John C.	1799	Hannah
HARRIS, John C.	1811	Rodman
HARRIS, John C.	1815	Garner
HARRIS, John C.	1816	Smith
HARRIS, John C.	1817	Smith
HARRIS, John C.	1818	Smith
HARRIS, John C.	1819	Smith
HARRIS, John C.	1821	Smith
HARRIS, Joshua	1798	Morrison
HARRIS, Joshua	1798	Morrison
HARRIS, Joshua	1799	Morrison
HARRISON, Benjamin	1799	Stuart
HARRISON, Daniel	1781	
HARRISON, Daniel	1819	Hunt
HARRISON, Edmund	1796	Longmire
HARRISON, Michael	1790	Biddle
HARRISON, Michael	1791	Biddle
HARRISON, Michael	1792	Biddle
HARRISON, Michael	1793	Scott
HARRISON, Michael	1796	Jonesboro
HARRISON, Michael	1799	
HARRISON, Michael	1800	
HARRISON, Michael	1801	
HARRISON, Michal	1797	Calvert
HARRISON, Michal	1797	Calvert
HARRISON, Michl	1798	Calvert
HARRISON, Michl	1801	Aiken
HARRISON, Samuel	1797	Calvert
HARRISON, Samuel	1819	Findley
HARRISON, Samuel	1821	McGee
HARRISON, Willam	1799	Gann
HARRISON, William	1819	Hunt
HARRISS, Gideon	1779	
HARRISS, Jno C.	1798	Calvert
HARRISS, John	1797	Calvert
HARRISSON, Michael	1807	Bayles
HARROLD, John	1792	Coye
HARSHA, John	1781	
HART, Aaron	1811	McCray
HART, Aaron	1817	Haire
HART, Joseph	1818	Grisham
HART, Piten	1818	Grisham
HART, Thomas	1799	Duncan
HART, Thomas	1801	Biddle
HARTMAN, Adam	1815	Waddell
HARTMAN, Henery	1809	Cade
HARTMAN, Henry	1807	Givins
HARTMAN, Henry	1808	Cade
HARTMAN, Henry	1810	Barron
HARTMAN, Henry	1811	Barron
HARTMAN, Henry	1812	Barnes
HARTMAN, Henry	1814	Barns
HARTMAN, Henry	1815	Grimsley
HARTMAN, Henry	1818	Grimsley
HARTMAN, Henry	1819	Grimsley
HARTMAN, Henry	1821	Martin
HARTMAN, John	1811	Barron
HARTMAN, John	1814	Barns
HARTMAN, John	1815	Grimsley
HARTMAN, John	1816	Grimsley
HARTMAN, John	1817	Grimsley
HARTMAN, John	1818	Grimsley
HARTMAN, John	1819	Grimsley
HARTMAN, Joseph	1812	McLin
HARTMAN, Joseph	1813	Copas
HARTMAN, Joseph	1815	Copas
HARTMAN, Joseph	1815	McLin
HARTMAN, Joseph	1816	Copas
HARTMAN, Joseph	1816	Hunt
HARTMAN, Joseph	1817	Grisham
HARTMAN, Joseph	1817	Hunt

Surname, Given names	Year	Comp./Dist.
HARTMAN, Joseph	1818	Grisham
HARTMAN, Joseph	1818	Hunt
HARTMAN, Joseph	1819	Grisham
HARTMAN, Joseph	1819	Hunt
HARTMAN, Joseph	1821	Hale
HARTMAN, Joseph Jr.	1808	Guin
HARTMAN, Joseph Jr.	1809	Gwin
HARTMAN, Joseph Jr.	1811	Davis
HARTMAN, Joseph Jr.	1812	McLin
HARTMAN, Joseph Sr.	1807	Givins
HARTMAN, Joseph Sr.	1808	Guin
HARTMAN, Joseph Sr.	1809	Gwin
HARTMAN, Joseph Sr.	1811	Davis
HARTMAN, Joseph Sr.	1814	McLin
HARTMAN, Larey	1814	Barns
HARTMAN, Leroy	1808	Cade
HARTMAN, Levi	1801	Taylor
HARTMAN, Levi	1805	Rector
HARTMAN, Levi	1815	Grimsley
HARTMAN, Levi	1816	Grimsley
HARTMAN, Levi	1817	Grimsley
HARTMAN, Levi	1818	Grimsley
HARTMAN, Levi	1819	Grimsley
HARTMAN, Levy	1809	Cade
HARTMAN, Levy	1810	Barron
HARTMAN, Levy	1811	Barron
HARTMAN, Marshall	1815	Carcathers
HARTMAN, Marshel	1814	McLin
HARTMEN, Joseph	1806	Guin
HARTMEN, Levi	1806	Guin
HARTMON, John	1821	Martin
HARTMON, Joseph	1821	Hunt
HARTSEL, Abraham	1801	Taylor
HARTSEL, Hanah	1821	Howard
HARTSEL, Hannah	1801	Taylor
HARTSEL, Isaac	1811	Brown
HARTSEL, Jacob	1817	Fine
HARTSELL, Abraham	1798	Young
HARTSELL, Abraham	1809	Par
HARTSELL, Abraham	1815	Fines
HARTSELL, Abraham	1816	Fine
HARTSELL, Abraham	1817	Fine
HARTSELL, Abraham	1818	Fine
HARTSELL, Abram	1814	Hartsell
HARTSELL, Hannah	1795	Young
HARTSELL, Hannah	1809	Par
HARTSELL, Hannah	1812	Hartsell
HARTSELL, Hannah	1817	Fine
HARTSELL, Hannah	1818	Fine
HARTSELL, Hannah	1819	Howard
HARTSELL, Isaac	1815	Hartsell
HARTSELL, Isaac	1816	Brown
HARTSELL, Isaac	1817	Hampton
HARTSELL, Isaac	1818	Brown [2]
HARTSELL, Isaac	1819	Brown
HARTSELL, Jacob	1809	Par
HARTSELL, Jacob	1812	Hartsell
HARTSELL, Jacob	1815	Fines
HARTSELL, Jacob	1816	Fine
HARTSELL, Jacob	1818	Fine
HARTSELL, Jacob	1819	Howard
HARTSELL, Jacob	1821	Howard
HARTSIL, Hana	1797	Young
HARTSIL, Isaac	1814	Brown
HARTSOOK, Hannah	1816	Fine
HARTZELL, Hanna	1791	North
HARTZELL, Jacob	1806	Brown
HARTZLE, Hanah	1806	Parker
HARVEY, James	1797	Hannah
HARVEY, James	1806	Parker
HARVEY, James	1815	Fines
HARVEY, James	1815	Garner
HARVEY, James	1816	Fine
HARVEY, James	1816	Smith
HARVEY, James	1817	Fine
HARVEY, James	1818	Fine
HARVEY, James	1818	Smith
HARVEY, James	1819	Howard
HARVEY, James	1819	Smith
HARVEY, James	1821	Howard
HARVEY, James	1821	Smith
HARVEY, Jas	1801	Taylor
HARVEY, John	1815	Fines
HARVEY, John	1816	Fine
HARVEY, John	1817	Fine
HARVEY, John	1821	Howard
HARVS, John C.	1801	Taylor
HARVY, Francis	1805	Parker
HARVY, James	1796	Millikin
HARVY, James	1809	Par
HARWOOD, John	1796	Shipley
HARY, Chares	1791	Willey
HAS, Isaac	1814	Hartsell
HASE, William	1818	Hair
HASELET, Kinler	1809	Gwin
HASELET, Kinley	1811	Barron
HASELOT, Hinley	1810	Barron
HASLET, Kindler	1808	Guin
HASLET, Kinler	1806	Guin
HASS, Jacob	1814	Bean
HASS, Sarah	1814	Bean
HATCHER, Henry	1797	Hannah

Surname, Given names	Year	Comp./Dist.
HATCHER, Jameston	1781	
HATCHER, John	1791	Milliken
HATCHER, John	1793	Milliken
HATCHER, Samson	1791	Milliken
HATCHER, William	1781	
HATESPELLER, Jacob	1807	Shields
HATH, Epaham	1797	Longmire
HATH, Jacob	1797	Longmire
HATHAWAY, Abraham	1811	
HATHERLY, Evans	1795	Thornton
HATHERLY, George	1778	
HATHERLY, Hueins	1778	
HATHERLY, Samuel	1778	
HATHEWAY, Elijah	1806	Crouch
HATHHORN, Noah	1793	Scott
HATHORN, Noah	1794	Scot
HATMEN, Leroy	1807	Cade
HATSIPILLAR, Jacob	1814	Waddell
HAUN, Adam	1790	Williams
HAUN, Adam	1791	Williams
HAUN, Adam	1792	Maxwell
HAUN, Adam	1793	Maxwell
HAUN, Adam	1796	Longmire
HAUN, Adam	1797	Longmire
HAUN, Adam	1798	Longmire
HAUN, Adam	1801	Longmire
HAUN, Austin	1795	Taylor
HAUN, Bauston	1790	Williams
HAUN, Bauston	1791	Williams
HAUN, Sebastian	1792	Maxwell
HAUN, Sebastian	1793	Maxwell
HAUN, Sebaustin	1795	Taylor
HAUNBARGER, Jacob	1821	Howard
HAUSE, John	1812	Barnes
HAUSER, John	1821	McGee
HAUTON, Daniel	1812	Barnes
HAUTON, William	1812	Barnes
HAVENRIDGE, John Sr.	1799	Duncan
HAWARD, John	1809	Par
HAWES, Conrad	1816	Grimsley
HAWES, James	1816	Grimsley
HAWES, John	1816	Grimsley
HAWES, Thomas	1816	Grimsley
HAWS, Conrad	1815	Grimsley
HAWS, Conrad	1817	Grimsley
HAWS, Elizabeth	1812	Barnes
HAWS, James	1815	Grimsley
HAWS, James	1817	Grimsley
HAWS, John	1797	Shipley
HAWS, John	1798	Shipley
HAWS, John	1801	Glasscock
HAWS, John	1809	Cade
HAWS, John	1815	Grimsley
HAWS, John	1817	Grimsley
HAWS, John Jr.	1801	Glasscock
HAWS, John Jr.	1805	Rector
HAWS, John Jr.	1809	Cade
HAWS, John Sr.	1805	Rector
HAWS, Thomas	1805	Rector
HAWS, Thomas	1815	Grimsley
HAWS, Thomas	1821	Sands
HAWTHORN, Noah	1792	Scott
HAYNES, George	1792	Coye
HAYNON, Lewis	1799	Stuart
HAYS, Agnes	1795	Taylor
HAYS, Charles	1779	Wilson
HAYS, Charles	1792	Scott
HAYS, Charles	1780-1781 (undated)	
HAYS, Charls	1780-1781 (Undated)	
HAYS, Chas	1781	
HAYS, Chas (James Scott is the executor)	1793	Scott
HAYS, David	1795	Taylor
HAYS, Elijah	1819	Harris
HAYS, Elizah	1818	Harris
HAYS, Ezekiel	1819	Hunt
HAYS, James	1781	
HAYS, James	1797	Shipley
HAYS, John	1817	Hunt
HAYS, John	1818	Hunt
HAYS, John	1819	Hunt
HAYS, Nathaniel	1779	Wilson
HAYS, Wilam	1794	Scot
HEADDRECK, Daniel	1809	Par
HEADERICK, Charles	1815	Fines
HEADERICK, Charles	1816	Fine
HEADERICK, Charles	1817	Fine
HEADERICK, Daniel	1817	Fine
HEADERICK, Jacob	1815	Fines
HEADERICK, Jacob	1816	Fine
HEADERICK, Jacob	1817	Fine
HEADLER, Sebastian	1796	Calvert
HEADRECK, Charles	1809	Par
HEADRECK, Charles	1809	Par
HEADRICK, Charles	1796	Young
HEADRICK, Charles	1797	Young
HEADRICK, Charles	1798	Young
HEADRICK, Charles	1806	Parker
HEADRICK, Charls	1801	Taylor
HEADRICK, Chas	1795	Young
HEADRICK, Joseph	1806	Parker
HEAIR, Henry	1798	Duncan

Surname, Given names	Year	Comp./Dist.
HEAN, Richard	1807	Anderson
HEAR, Isac	1794	Scot
HEARSYL, Hanah	1807	Parker
HEARTSEL, Isaac	1809	Bayles
HEARTSEL, Isaac	1812	Brown
HEARTSEL, Isaac	1821	Brown
HEARTSELL, Hana	1796	Young
HEARVY, James	1807	Parker
HEATH, Jonston	1796	Handly
HEATH, Richard	1796	Handly
HEATHERICK, Jacob	1790	Greer
HEATHERICK, Jacob Jr.	1794	Carriger
HEATHERICK, Jacob Sr.	1790	Greer
HEATHERICK, Joseph	1790	Greer
HEATHERLY, Euins (Over age)	1790	White
HEATHERLY, Euins (Over age)	1792	White
HEATHERLY, Evan	1791	White
HEATHERLY, Ewings	1794	Thornton
HEATHERLY, Ewins	1793	Campbell
HEATHERLY, John	1793	Campbell
HEATHERLY, John	1794	Thornton
HEATON, John	1794	Thornton
HEAVENRIG, John	1798	Duncan
HECKS, Joseph	1817	Smith
HECKS, Joseph	1818	Smith
HECTER, Bengmin	1821	Martin
HEDERICK, Jacob	1821	Hampton
HEDRICK, Abraham	1814	Hartsell
HEDRICK, Charles	1791	North
HEDRICK, Charles	1792	North
HEDRICK, Charles	1793	North
HEDRICK, Charles	1794	North
HEDRICK, Charles	1807	Parker
HEDRICK, Charles	1814	Hartsell
HEDRICK, Charles	1818	Fine
HEDRICK, Charles Jr.	1805	Parker
HEDRICK, Charles Jr.	1810	Hartzel
HEDRICK, Charles Jr.	1812	Hartsell
HEDRICK, Charles Sr.	1805	Parker
HEDRICK, Charles Sr.	1812	Hartsell
HEDRICK, Daniel	1807	Parker
HEDRICK, Daniel	1810	Hartzel
HEDRICK, Daniel	1812	Hartsell
HEDRICK, Jacob	1812	McCray
HEDRICK, Jacob	1814	Hartsell
HEDRICK, Jacob	1818	Fine
HEDRICK, Jacob	1819	Howard
HEDRICK, Jacob Jr.	1792	Carriger
HEDRICK, Jacob Jr.	1792	Greer
HEDRICK, Jacob Sr.	1792	Carriger
HEDRICK, John	1801	Glasscock
HEDRICK, Joseph	1805	Parker
HEDRICK, Joseph	1807	Parker
HEDRICK, Peter	1792	Carriger
HEDRICK, Samel	1821	Howard
HEDRICK, Samual	1805	Parker
HEDRICK, Samuel	1812	Hartsell
HEDRICK, Samuel	1819	Howard
HEINES, George	1818	Brown
HEINS, Andrew	1790	Hanley
HEINS, Andrew	1791	Hanley
HEIR, Isaac	1795	Calvert
HELEM, John	1806	Payn
HELM, Henery	1809	McAlister
HELM, Henery	1812	Waddill
HELM, Henery	1814	Crookshanks
HELM, Henry	1811	Green
HELM, Henry	1819	McClure
HELM, John	1799	Hannah
HELM, John	1805	Stephenson
HELM, John	1807	Payne
HELM, John	1809	McAlister
HELM, John	1811	McAlister
HELM, John	1812	Crawford
HELM, John	1812	Crawford [2]
HELM, John (heirs of)	1819	McClure
HELMIS, John	1779	Wilson
HELMS, Henry	1816	Crookshanks
HELMS, Henry	1817	McClure
HELMS, Henry	1818	McClure
HELMS, Henry	1819	Smith
HELMS, John	1797	Hannah
HELMS, John	1798	Hannah
HELMS, John	1808	McAllister
HELMS, John	1816	Crookshanks
HELMS, John (estate of)	1818	McClure
HELMS, John (estate)	1817	McClure
HELMS, John (heirs of)	1821	McClure
HELMS, William	1821	McClure
HELTON, Abraham	1792	Greer
HELTON, Abraham	1794	Carriger
HELTON, Arnold	1792	Carriger
HELTON, Arnold	1792	Greer
HELTON, John	1792	Carriger
HELTON, John	1794	Carriger
HELTON, Peter	1794	Carriger
HEMP, Casper	1808	Gwin
HEMPHILL, Andw	1781	
HEMPTON, John	1806	Brown
HENAH, Amasa	1797	Duncan
HENAH, Elisha	1797	Duncan
HENAH, Jonathan	1797	Duncan

Surname, Given names	Year	Comp./Dist.
HENARD, Robart	1797	Duncan
HENARD, Robart	1798	Duncan
HENDERSON, Daniel	1781	
HENDERSON, George	1812	Crawford
HENDERSON, George	1812	Crawford [2]
HENDERSON, James	1779	Wilson
HENDERSON, John	1794	North
HENDERSON, John	1795	Young
HENDERSON, John	1796	Young
HENDERSON, John	1797	Young
HENDERSON, John	1810	Dimmons
HENDERSON, John	1811	
HENDERSON, Jos.	1795	Young
HENDERSON, Joseph	1781	
HENDERSON, Joseph	1793	Depew
HENDERSON, Joseph	1794	Depew
HENDERSON, Joseph	1796	Young
HENDERSON, Joseph	1797	Young
HENDERSON, Joseph	1798	Duncan
HENDERSON, Joseph	1798	Duncan
HENDERSON, Joseph	1780-1781 (Undated)	
HENDERSON, Richard	1808	Odell
HENDERSON, William	1812	Barnes
HENDERSON, Wm	1781	
HENDLEY, George	1816	Hampton
HENDLEY, George	1817	Hampton
HENDLEY, George	1818	Brown [2]
HENDLEY, George	1819	Brown
HENDLEY, Isaac	1816	Hampton
HENDLEY, Isaac	1817	Hampton
HENDLEY, Isaac	1818	Brown [2]
HENDLEY, Isaac	1819	Brown
HENDLEY, Isaack	1807	Bayles
HENDLEY, James	1817	Hampton
HENDLEY, James	1818	Brown [2]
HENDLEY, James	1819	Brown
HENDLEY, John	1807	Bayles
HENDLEY, Joshua	1817	Hampton
HENDLEY, Joshua	1818	Brown [2]
HENDLEY, Joshua	1819	Brown
HENDLEY, Samuel	1793	Brown
HENDLEY, Samuel	1780-1781 (Undated)	
HENDLY, George	1792	Brown
HENDRICK, Jacob	1792	Greer
HENDRICK, John	1792	Carriger
HENDRICK, Solomon	1794	Taylor
HENDRICKS, John	1790	
HENDRICKS, John	1791	
HENDRICKS, Jonathan	1795	Thornton
HENDRIX, John	1792	Tulley
HENDRIX, Solomon	1790	Williams
HENDRIX, Solomon	1791	Williams
HENDRIX, Solomon	1792	Maxwell
HENDRIX, Solomon	1793	Maxwell
HENDRY, Eli	1815	Haire
HENDRY, Eli	1817	Haire
HENDRY, Ely	1806	Crouch
HENDRY, Samuel (Single)	1779	Wilson
HENDRY, Thompson	1811	Ellis
HENDRY, Tompson	1814	Bean
HENDRY, Wileson	1806	Crouch
HENDRY, William	1801	Norwood
HENERY, James	1779	
HENERY, William	1779	
HENKLE, George	1811	McCray
HENLEY, George	1793	Brown
HENLEY, John	1799	Robertson
HENLY, John	1797	Robertson
HENNARD, Robert	1801	Lane
HENNER, Jacob	1805	Stephenson
HENNERY, Spencer	1812	McCray
HENNERY, Spencer	1812	McCray
HENON, Luis	1805	Stephenson
HENREY, James	1820	Smith
HENRICK, Charles	1810	Hartzel
HENRICKS, Solomon	1795	Taylor
HENRY, Abraham	1790	Williams
HENRY, Abraham	1791	Williams
HENRY, Abraham	1792	Maxwell
HENRY, Eli	1809	Right
HENRY, Eli	1816	Hair
HENRY, Eli	1818	Hair
HENRY, Eli	1819	Hair
HENRY, Ely	1821	Louis
HENRY, Hugh	1779	
HENRY, James	1778	
HENRY, James	1808	Parker
HENRY, James	1810	Hartzel
HENRY, James	1812	Hartsell
HENRY, James	1814	Hartsell
HENRY, John	1814	Hartsell
HENRY, John	1780-1781 (Undated)	
HENRY, Rachel	1801	Norwood
HENRY, Samuel	1779	
HENRY, Samuel Sr.	1778	
HENRY, Spencer	1814	McCray
HENRY, Spencer	1819	Smith
HENRY, Thompson	1809	Right
HENRY, William	1794	Carriger
HENS, William	1812	Crawford
HENSELL, Jacob	1814	Hartsell

Surname, Given names	Year	Comp./Dist.
HENSELY, John	1819	Brown
HENSLEY, John	1806	Brown
HENSLY, John	1780-1781	District 7
HENTON, Robert	1796	Brown
HENTSELL, Hanah	1810	Hartzel
HENTSELL, Hanah	1814	Hartsell
HENTSELLE, Jacob	1810	Hartzel
HERALD, Amasy	1812	Barnes
HERALD, John	1819	Hair
HERBY, Molicas	1798	Young
HERESON, Danial	1780-1781 (Undated)	
HERIS, Juashey	1791	Willey
HERLD, Jonathan	1805	Carson
HERLIN, Joseph	1805	Stephenson
HERLY, Samuel	1793	Hale
HERMON, Abram	1798	Gann
HERMON, Adam	1798	Gann
HERMON, Joseph	1798	Gann
HERON, Edmon	1811	
HERRAH, Elsha	1798	Duncan
HERREN, Henry	1821	Smith
HERRIS, Josua	1793	Scott
HERTSELL, Abraham	1808	Parker
HERTSELL, Hanah	1805	Parker
HERTSELL, Isaac	1805	Parker
HERTSZLE, Jacob	1807	Parker
HERVY, James	1805	Parker
HESLAN, Abram	1793	North
HESLIN, Abraham	1791	North
HESS, Philip	1799	Duncan
HESSTON, Mathew	1780-1781 (undated)	
HESTARIN, Abraham Sr.	1791	North
HESTARIN, Samuel	1791	North
HETH, Richard	1797	Gann
HETHERIE, Jacob	1795	Carriger
HETLER, Sebastan	1798	Gann
HETTER, Sebastian	1793	Handley
HETTON, Silas	1811	Mitchell
Hezakiah	1814	Bean
HICE, Jacob	1812	Crawford
HICKEY, David	1778	
HICKEY, David	1779	
HICKEY, David	1790	Stone
HICKEY, David	1791	Stone
HICKEY, David	1795	Murray
HICKEY, John	1801	Roberson
HICKKY, Henry	1778	
HICKMAN, Elisha	1798	Duncan
HICKMAN, Henry	1797	Duncan
HICKMAN, Henry	1798	Duncan
HICKMAN, Henry	1798	Duncan
HICKMAN, Henry	1799	Duncan
HICKMAN, Samuel	1808	
HICKMAN, Slisha	1801	Taylor
HICKS, Arilse	1806	Anderson
HICKS, David	1778	
HICKS, David	1778	
HICKS, Jeter	1821	McClure
HICKS, John H.	1821	Howard
HICKS, Joseph	1819	Smith
HICKS, Joseph	1820	Smith
HIDER, Elizabeth (Widow)	1790	Williams
HIDER, Elizabeth (Widow)	1791	Williams
HIDER, Elizabeth (Widow)	1792	Maxwell
HIDER, Elizabeth (Widow)	1793	Maxwell
HIDER, John	1790	Williams
HIDER, John	1791	Williams
HIDER, John	1792	Maxwell
HIDER, John	1793	Maxwell
HIDER, Michael	1778	
HIDER, Michael	1790	Williams
HIDER, Michael	1791	Williams
HIDER, Michael	1792	Maxwell
HIDER, Michael	1793	Maxwell
HIDLER, Sebastan	1799	Moore
HIDLOR, Sabastin	1801	Gann
HIGENS, William	1821	Howard
HIGGANS, John	1778	
HIGGINS, Thomas	1819	Hunt
HIGHIT, Joseph	1798	Duncan
HIGHIT, Joseph	1798	Duncan
HIGHTOWER, Oldum	1778	
HILL, John	1778	
HILL, John	1811	Barron
HILL, Saml	1780-1781 (Undated)	
HILL, Samuel	1781	
HILL, Shedrick	1780-1781 (Undated)	
HILL, Will	1797	Calvert
HILLARD, William	1805	Aikin
HILTEN, Jacob	1814	Barns
HILTON, Abraham	1792	Carriger
HILTON, John	1792	Coye
HINDS, Samuel	1795	Morrison
HINDS, Samuel	1799	Stuart
HINES, Samuel	1794	Melvan
HINES, Samul	1797	Calvert
HINGLE, George	1809	Bayles
HINKLE, Geo	1808	Parker
HINKLE, Geo	1809	Parker
HINKLE, George	1805	Jas Parker

Surname, Given names	Year	Comp./Dist.
HINKLE, George	1812	McCray
HINKLE, George	1812	McCray
HINKLE, George Jr.	1819	Harris
HINKLE, George Jr.	1821	Hampton
HINKLE, Margaret	1807	Britton
HINKLE, Samuel	1812	McCray
HINKS, George	1795	Carriger
HINNAMON, John	1805	Rector
HINTON, William Robert	1779	
HIRLIN, William	1809	McAlister
HITE, Jacob	1812	Barnes
HITE, Jacob	1814	Barns
HITE, Jacob	1815	Grimsley
HITE, Jacob	1816	Grimsley
HITE, Jacob	1817	Grimsley
HITE, Jacob	1818	Grimsley
HITE, Jacob	1819	Grimsley
HITE, Jacob	1821	Martin
HITE, James	1815	Grimsley
HITE, John	1809	Cade
HITE, John	1810	Barron
HITE, John	1812	Barnes
HITE, John	1814	Barns
HITE, John	1815	Grimsley
HITE, John	1816	Grimsley
HITE, John	1817	Grimsley
HITE, John	1818	Grimsley
HITE, John	1819	Grimsley
HITE, John	1821	Martin
HITTLER, Sebastan	1797	Gann
HIX, Abraham	1807	Parker
HIX, Abraham	1810	Hartzel
HIX, Abraham	1815	Fines
HIX, Abraham	1816	Fine
HIX, Abraham	1817	Fine
HIX, Abraham	1818	Fine
HIX, Abraham	1819	Howard
HIX, Abram	1814	Hartsell
HIX, Burrel	1807	Bayles
HIX, Dempsey	1807	Bayles
HIX, Dempy	1806	Brown
HIX, Hankle	1806	Brown
HIX, Hardsil	1807	Bayles
HIX, John	1819	Brown
HIX, Joseph	1816	Smith
HIXON, John	1821	McGee
HMPHIES, Moses	1793	Melvan
HMPLICE, John	1793	Melvan
HOAFMAN, Jesse	1797	Hannah
HOAS, Jacob	1806	Crouch
HOAS, John	1780-1781 (Undated)	
HOAS, Peter	1801	Norwood
HOASE, Jacob	1796	Melvin
HOASE, John Sr.	1798	Shipley
HOASE, Peter	1796	Melvin
HOASS, Jacob	1795	Melvan
HOASS, Jacob	1798	Crouch
HOASS, Jacob	1801	Norwood
HOASS, Peter	1798	Crouch
HOBSON, Edward	1778	
HOBSON, John	1821	Martin
HOCKTON, William	1781	
HODGCASE, Jerred	1798	Calvert
HODGE, Ambrose	1778	
HODGE, Edmond	1818	Grisham
HODGE, Edmond	1819	Grisham
HODGE, Frances	1787	Griggs
HODGE, Hovel	1819	Grisham
HODGE, Howel	1818	Grisham
HODGE, John	1818	Grisham
HODGE, John	1819	Grisham
HODGEASE, Jarred	1799	Stuart
HODGES, Edmond	1815	Copas
HODGES, Edmond	1816	Copas
HODGES, Edmond	1821	Louis
HODGES, Edward	1817	Grisham
HODGES, Edward	1819	Hair
HODGES, Howel	1811	Britten
HODGES, Howel	1812	Britton
HODGES, Howel	1813	Copas
HODGES, Howel	1814	Copes
HODGES, Howel	1815	Copas
HODGES, Howel	1816	Copas
HODGES, Howel	1817	Grisham
HODGES, Howel	1821	Hale
HODGES, John	1798	Crouch
HODGES, John	1801	Norwood
HODGES, John	1812	Ellis
HODGES, John	1817	Grisham
HODGES, John	1821	Hale
HODGES, John Jr.	1795	Melvan
HODGES, John Jr.	1796	Melvin
HODGES, John Jr.	1806	Crouch
HODGES, John Sr.	1790	Stone
HODGES, John Sr.	1791	Stone
HODGES, John Sr.	1793	Melvan
HODGES, John Sr.	1795	Melvan
HODGES, John Sr.	1796	Melvin
HODGES, Robin	1819	Hair
HODGES, Roland	1798	Crouch
HODGES, Roland	1801	Norwood
HODGES, Roland	1815	Haire

Surname, Given names	Year	Comp./Dist.
HODGES, Roland	1817	Haire
HODGES, Rolen	1811	Ellis
HODGES, Rolen	1814	Bean
HODGES, Rolen	1818	Hair
HODGES, Rolen	1821	Louis
HODGES, Rolin	1812	Ellis
HODGES, Rolin	1816	Hair
HODGES, Rolland	1806	Crouch
HODGES, Rowland	1809	Right
HODGKISS, Jeremiah	1797	Calvert
HOFMAN, David	1792	North
HOG, Archable	1798	Morrison
HOG, Obediah	1794	Ford
HOG, Ruben	1798	Morrison
HOGARD, James	1819	Grimsley
HOGART, James	1821	Martin
HOGEN, Arthor	1790	Stone
HOGEN, Arthor	1791	Stone
HOGES, John Sr.	1794	Melvan
HOGG, Obadiah	1795	Ford
HOLBETT, Solomon	1792	Greer
HOLDSINGER, John	1821	Brown
HOLDWAY, Timothy	1778	
HOLEY, John	1780-1781 (Undated)	
HOLINGER, John	1816	Hampton
HOLLAND, Benj	1801	Glasscock
HOLLAND, Benjamin	1790	Shipley
HOLLAND, Benjamin	1791	Shipley
HOLLAND, Benjamin	1793	Murray
HOLLAND, Benjamin	1794	Murray
HOLLAND, Benjamin	1795	Murray
HOLLAND, Benjamin	1796	Shipley
HOLLAND, Benjamon	1797	Shipley
HOLLAND, Peter	1795	Murray
HOLLAND, Peter	1796	Shipley
HOLLAND, Peter	1797	Shipley
HOLLAWAY, John	1792	Coye
HOLLAWAY, William	1792	Coye
HOLLEY, Francis	1778	
HOLLEY, Jacob	1778	
HOLLEY, John	1778	
HOLLEY, John	1781	
HOLLEY, John	1797	Hannah
HOLLEY, John	1798	Hannah
HOLLEY, John	1801	Squibb
HOLLEY, John Jr.	1778	
HOLLEY, Jonathan	1778	
HOLLIT, Solomon	1790	Greer
HOLLY, John	1779	Wilson
HOLLY, John	1796	Millikin
HOLLY, John	1799	Hannah

Surname, Given names	Year	Comp./Dist.
HOLLY, Johnathan	1779	Wilson
HOLMS, James	1819	Sands
HOLMS, James	1821	Sands
HOLMS, John	1815	Crookshanks
HOLSAPULER, Jacob	1806	Parker
HOLSENGER, John	1817	Hampton
HOLSEPIL, Jacob	1821	McGee
HOLSINGER, John	1799	Stuart
HOLSINGER, John	1818	Brown [2]
HOLT, Alex	1790	Milleken
HOLT, Ephraim	1798	Longmire
HOLT, Ephraim	1801	Longmire
HOLT, Jacob	1798	Longmire
HOLT, Jacob	1801	Longmire
HOLT, Jacob	1806	Odel
HOLT, Jacob	1807	Odell
HOLT, Jacob	1808	Odell
HOLT, Jacob	1809	Viney
HOLT, Jacob	1810	Cove
HOLT, Jacob	1811	Brown
HOLT, Jacob	1812	Brown
HOLT, Jacob	1814	Brown
HOLT, Jacob	1815	Hartsell
HOLT, Jacob	1816	Brown
HOLT, Jacob	1817	Brown
HOLT, Jacob	1819	Brown
HOLT, Jacob	1821	Haines
HOLT, Jas	1790	Milleken
HOLT, John	1819	Brown
HOLT, Norman	1819	Brown
HOLT, Peter	1798	Longmire
HOLTSINGER, John	1819	Brown
HOLYBEE, John	1821	Hampton
HOMANEL, Peter	1811	Mitchell
HOMBARGER, Jacob	1806	Parker
HOMBLE, Peter	1806	Parker
HOMEL, Peter	1805	Parker
HOMIL, Peter	1813	Hoss
HONE, Abraham	1794	Taylor
HONE, Adam	1794	Taylor
HONE, Christopher	1794	Taylor
HONE, Mathies	1794	Taylor
HONE, Sabaustian	1794	Taylor
HONEYCUTT, Austin	1778	
HONEYCUTT, John	1778	
HONICUT, Uriah	1806	Parker
HONLEY, John S.	1811	McCray
HONLEY, John S.	1819	Hunt
HONLEY, Lankston	1811	McCray
HOOKER, John	1819	Brown
HOOKER, Robert	1792	Greer

Surname, Given names	Year	Comp./Dist.
HOOKER, William	1795	Carriger
HOOKSHANKS, George	1812	Crawford
HOOKSHANKS, William	1812	Crawford
HOOPER, John	1821	Brown
HOOVER, Jacob	1799	Moore
HOOVER, Mathas	1799	Moore
HOOVER, Mathias	1797	Hannah
HOOVER, Matthias	1799	Hannah
HOPTON, John	1779	Wilson
HORETON, Daniel	1807	Cade
HORLET, Nancy	1817	Grimsley
HORNBARGER, Jacob	1809	Par
HORNBERGER, Jacob	1807	Parker
HORNBERGER, Jacob	1812	Hartsell
HORNBERGER, Jacob	1814	Hartsell
HORNBERGER, Jacob	1817	Fine
HORNBERGER, Jacob	1818	Fine
HORNBERGER, Jacob	1818	Fine
HORNBERGER, Jacob Jr.	1814	Hartsell
HORNBERGER, Jacob Jr.	1815	Fines
HORNBERGER, Jacob Jr.	1816	Fine
HORNBERGER, Jacob Jr.	1817	Fine
HORNBERGER, Jacob Sr.	1815	Fines
HORNBERGER, Jacob Sr.	1816	Fine
HORNCOMPTON, Jeremia	1791	North
HORNCUMTON, Jeremiah	1792	North
HORTEN, Daniel	1798	Shipley
HORTEN, Daniel	1805	Rector
HORTEN, Daniel	1811	Barron
HORTEN, Daniel	1817	Grimsley
HORTEN, Daniel	1818	Grimsley
HORTEN, Isaac	1817	Grimsley
HORTON, Danel	1821	Martin
HORTON, Daniel	1801	Glasscock
HORTON, Daniel	1808	Cade
HORTON, Daniel	1809	Cade
HORTON, Daniel	1814	Barns
HORTON, Daniel	1815	Grimsley
HORTON, Daniel	1816	Grimsley
HORTON, Daniel	1819	Grimsley
HORTON, Isaac	1808	Cade
HORTON, Isaac	1809	Cade
HORTON, Isaac	1810	Barron
HORTON, Isaac	1814	Couthers
HORTON, Isaac	1815	Carcathers
HORTON, Isaac	1816	Grimsley
HORTON, Isaac	1818	Grimsley
HORTON, Isaac	1819	Grimsley
HOSE, William	1798	Morrison
HOSKINS, C._S.	1778	
HOSKINS, Jesse	1778	

Surname, Given names	Year	Comp./Dist.
HOSKINS, John	1778	
HOSKINS, Josiah	1778	
HOSKINS, Neman	1791	White
HOSKINS, Nenian	1790	White
HOSKINS, Nineon	1795	Ford
HOSKINS, Ning	1778	
HOSKINS, Thomas	1791	White
HOSKINS, Thomas	1793	Campbell
HOSKINS, Thomas	1794	Ford
HOSONBERGER, Jacob	1819	Howard
HOSS, Abraham	1806	Carr
HOSS, Abraham	1807	Carr
HOSS, Abraham	1808	Carr
HOSS, Abraham	1809	Carr
HOSS, Abraham	1811	Mitchell
HOSS, Abraham	1814	Hoss
HOSS, Abraham	1815	Hoss
HOSS, Abraham	1816	Hoss
HOSS, Abraham	1817	Little
HOSS, Abraham	1818	Jones
HOSS, Abraham	1819	Jones
HOSS, Abraham	1821	Jones
HOSS, Abriaham	1813	Hoss
HOSS, George	1807	Carr
HOSS, George	1808	Carr
HOSS, George	1809	Carr
HOSS, George	1811	Mitchell
HOSS, George	1814	Hampton
HOSS, Gray	1816	Grimsley
HOSS, Henry	1814	McCracken
HOSS, Henry	1816	Hair
HOSS, Henry	1817	Haire
HOSS, Henry	1818	Hair
HOSS, Henry	1819	Hair
HOSS, Henry	1821	Louis
HOSS, Isaac	1809	Parker
HOSS, Isaac	1809	Right
HOSS, Isaac	1810	Hartzel
HOSS, Isaac	1815	Fines
HOSS, Isaac	1816	Fine
HOSS, Isaac	1817	Fine
HOSS, Isaac	1818	Fine
HOSS, Isaac	1819	Howard
HOSS, Isaac	1821	Howard
HOSS, Jacob	1790	Stone
HOSS, Jacob	1791	Stone
HOSS, Jacob	1793	Melvan
HOSS, Jacob	1794	Melvan
HOSS, Jacob	1808	Carr
HOSS, Jacob	1809	Right
HOSS, Jacob	1813	Hoss

Surname, Given names	Year	Comp./Dist.
HOSS, Jacob	1815	Haire
HOSS, Jacob	1816	Hair
HOSS, Jacob (Esq.)	1811	Mitchell
HOSS, Jacob (Esqr.)	1809	Carr
HOSS, Jacob Jr.	1806	Carr
HOSS, Jacob Jr.	1807	Carr
HOSS, Jacob Sr.	1811	Ellis
HOSS, Jacob Sr.	1812	Ellis
HOSS, John	1806	Carr
HOSS, John	1807	Carr
HOSS, John	1808	Carr
HOSS, John	1809	Carr
HOSS, John	1811	Mitchell
HOSS, John	1813	Hoss
HOSS, John	1814	Hoss
HOSS, John	1815	Hoss
HOSS, John	1816	Hoss
HOSS, John	1817	Haire
HOSS, John	1817	Little
HOSS, John	1818	Hair
HOSS, John	1818	Jones
HOSS, John	1819	Hair
HOSS, John	1819	Jones
HOSS, John	1821	Jones
HOSS, John	1821	Louis
HOSS, Joseph	1779	
HOSS, Joseph	1821	Howard
HOSS, Margaret	1818	Hair
HOSS, Margaret	1819	Hair
HOSS, Margret	1821	Louis
HOSS, Peter	1806	Crouch
HOSS, Peter	1809	Right
HOSS, Peter	1811	Ellis
HOSS, Peter	1812	Ellis
HOSS, Sarah	1815	Haire
HOSS, Sarah	1816	Hair
HOSS, Sarah	1817	Haire
HOSS, Sarah	1818	Hair
HOSS, Sarah	1819	Hair
HOSS, Sarah	1821	Louis
HOTKPILLER, Jacob	1815	Waddell
HOTKSELLER, Jacob	1816	Waddell
HOTSHOTLER, Jacob	1810	Green
HOTSIPILLER, Jacob	1819	Findley
HOTSPELLER, Jacob	1812	Waddill
HOTSPILLER, Jacob	1817	Riley
HOTSPILLER, Jacob	1818	Riley
HOTT, Jacob	1818	Brown
HOTT, John	1818	Brown
HOUC, John	1780-1781 (Undated)	
HOUGHTON, Joshua	1778	
HOUGHTON, Joshua Jr.	1779	
HOUGHTON, Joshua Sr.	1779	
HOUGHTON, Tho (J.P.)	1779	
HOUGHTON, Thomas	1779	
HOUGHTON, Thomas	1779	
HOUGHTON, Thomas (Esq.)	1778	
HOUS, Thomas	1810	Barron
HOUSE, George	1793	Scott
HOUSE, George	1795	Calvert
HOUSE, George	1796	Calvert
HOUSE, George	1796	Jonesboro
HOUSE, George	1797	Calvert
HOUSE, George	1797	Calvert
HOUSE, George	1798	Calvert
HOUSE, George	1799	Stuart
HOUSE, George	1805	Aikin
HOUSE, Go	1801	
HOUSE, Jacob Sr.	1801	Morrison
HOUSE, John	1807	Cade
HOUSE, John	1810	Barron
HOUSE, John Jr.	1808	Cade
HOUSE, John Sr.	1808	Cade
HOUSE, Thomas	1793	Scott
HOUSE, Thomas	1796	Calvert
HOUSE, Thomas	1808	Cade
HOUSE, Thomas	1812	Barnes
HOUSER, John	1819	Findley
HOUSES, John	1807	Cade
HOUSTON, Dungan	1821	Jones
HOUSTON, John	1801	Morrison
HOUSTON, John	1813	Hoss
HOUSTON, John	1815	Hoss
HOUSTON, John	1816	Hoss
HOUSTON, John	1817	Little
HOUSTON, John	1818	Jones
HOUSTON, John	1819	Jones
HOUSTON, John	1821	Howard
HOUSTON, John	1821	Jones
HOUSTON, John (for Dugans estate)	1817	Little
HOUSTON, John (for Dungans' estate)	1816	Hoss
HOUSTON, John (for Dungans' estate)	1818	Jones
HOUSTON, William	1790	Biddle
HOUSTON, William	1791	Biddle
HOUSTON, William	1792	Biddle
HOUSTON, William	1815	Hoss
HOUSTON, William	1816	Hoss
HOUSTON, William	1817	Little
HOUSTON, William	1818	Jones
HOUSTON, William	1819	Jones
HOUSTON, William	1821	Jones

Surname, Given names	Year	Comp./Dist.
HOUTON, Daniel	1810	Barron
HOVEMIDGE, John	1799	Duncan
HOVER, Jacob	1798	Gann
HOVER, Methier	1798	Gann
HOWARD, Daniel	1780-1781	District 7
HOWARD, George	1781	
HOWARD, Jacob	1819	Smith
HOWARD, Jacob	1820	Smith
HOWARD, Jacob	1821	Smith
HOWARD, James	1778	
HOWARD, John	1778	
HOWARD, John	1779	Wilson
HOWARD, John	1781	
HOWARD, John	1794	Thornton
HOWARD, John	1801	Taylor
HOWARD, John	1806	Parker
HOWARD, John	1812	Hartsell
HOWARD, John	1816	Fine
HOWARD, John	1817	Fine
HOWARD, John	1818	Fine
HOWARD, John	1819	Howard
HOWARD, John	1821	Howard
HOWARD, John	1780-1781 (Undated)	
HOWARD, John Jr.	1781	
HOWARD, William	1809	Hartzell
HOWE, Charles	1819	Hunt
HOWEL, Berry	1805	Stephenson
HOWEL, Charles	1807	Anderson
HOWEL, Charles	1809	Gwin
HOWEL, Thomas (estate of)	1808	Odell
HOWEL, Thos (Robert Love Admin)	1807	Odell
HOWEL, Thos Jr.	1798	Longmire
HOWELL, Charles	1821	Hunt
HOWELL, John	1796	Longmire
HOWELL, John	1797	Longmire
HOWELL, Thomas	1797	Longmire
HOWELL, Thomas	1806	Odel
HOWELL, Thomas Jr.	1801	Longmire
HOWELL, Thomas Sr.	1797	Longmire
HOWEND, John	1810	Hartzel
HOWEND, John	1815	Fines
HOWERD, Absolom	1780-1781 (undated)	
HOWERD, John	1807	Parker
HOWERD, John	1780-1781 (Undated)	
HOWLAND, John	1780-1781 (Undated)	
HOYT, Peter	1801	Longmire
HU-, Moses	1809	Carr
HUBARD, James	1780-1781 (Undated)	
HUBBARD, James	1781	
HUCHINS, Thomas	1807	Odell
HUCHINS, William	1807	Odell
HUDEBURK, Thomas	1794	Taylor
HUDIBURG, Thomas	1791	
HUDIBURG, Thos	1792	Maxwell
HUDIBURG, Thos	1793	Maxwell
HUDSON, Geo	1778	
HUFFINE, Phillip	1810	Hartzel
HUFFMAN, Adam	1816	Harrison
HUFFMAN, Adam	1818	Fine
HUFFMAN, Daniel	1792	Maxwell
HUFFMAN, Daniel	1793	Maxwell
HUFFMAN, David	1797	Young
HUFFMAN, David	1798	Young
HUFFMAN, David	1819	Howard
HUFFMAN, Henry	1818	Brown [2]
HUFFMAN, Jacob	1817	Hampton
HUFFMAN, Jacob	1818	Brown [2]
HUFFMAN, Jesse	1796	Handly
HUFFMINE, Phillip	1806	Parker
HUFFMON, Anthoney	1796	Handly
HUFHINE, Jacob	1815	Fines
HUFHINE, Jacob	1816	Fine
HUFHINE, Jacob	1817	Fine
HUFHINE, Jacob	1818	Fine
HUFHINE, Philip	1815	Fines
HUFHINE, Philip	1816	Fine
HUFHINE, Philip	1818	Fine
HUFHINE, Phillip	1807	Parker
HUFHINE, Phillip	1819	Howard
HUFHINE, Phillips	1805	Parker
HUFHINES, Jacob	1821	Howard
HUFHINES, Philip	1821	Howard
HUFHINES, William	1821	Howard
HUFHINS, Philip	1809	Par
HUFINE, Phillip	1814	Hartsell
HUFMAN, Adam	1807	Parker
HUFMAN, Adam	1809	Par
HUFMAN, Adam	1810	Hartzel
HUFMAN, Adam	1812	McCray
HUFMAN, Adam	1812	McCray
HUFMAN, Adam	1814	McCray
HUFMAN, Adam	1817	Fine
HUFMAN, David	1791	North
HUFMAN, David	1793	Brown
HUFMAN, David	1794	Taylor
HUFMAN, David	1795	Young
HUFMAN, David	1796	Young
HUFMAN, David	1801	Taylor
HUFMAN, David	1806	Parker

Surname, Given names	Year	Comp./Dist.
HUFMAN, David	1807	Parker
HUFMAN, David	1809	Par
HUFMAN, David	1810	Hartzel
HUFMAN, David	1814	Hartsell
HUFMAN, David	1815	Fines
HUFMAN, David	1816	Fine
HUFMAN, David	1817	Fine
HUFMAN, David	1818	Fine
HUFMAN, David	1821	Howard
HUFMAN, Henry	1812	Hartsell
HUFMAN, Henry	1816	Fine
HUFMAN, Henry	1816	Hampton
HUFMAN, Henry	1817	Hampton
HUFMAN, Henry	1819	Howard
HUFMAN, Jacob	1778	
HUFMAN, Jacob	1816	Fine
HUFMAN, Jacob	1816	Hampton
HUFMAN, Jesse	1819	Howard
HUFMAN, Peter	1778	
HUFMAN, Philip	1817	Fine
HUGATT, Soleman	1796	Brown
HUGEANS, William	1810	Cove
HUGHES, David	1778	
HUGHES, David	1779	
HUGHES, Francis	1778	
HUGHES, John	1778	
HUGHES, John	1779	Wilson
HUGHES, John	1779	
HUGHES, John	1781	
HUGHES, John (L Creak)	1779	Wilson
HUGHS, David	1780-1781 (Undated)	
HUGHS, Francis	1779	Wilson
HULSE, John	1821	Hale
HUM, Chresten	1812	Crawford
HUM, Christian	1812	Crawford [2]
HUMBARD, John	1791	Willey
HUMBERD, John	1793	Scott
HUMBERD, John	1794	Scot
HUMBERT, John	1792	Scott
HUMBERT, John	1795	Calvert
HUMMINS, Thomas	1815	Harris
HUMMONS, Thomas	1817	Harris
HUMMONS, Thomas	1819	Harris
HUMPHARY, George	1799	Morrison
HUMPHERS, Moses	1806	Carr
HUMPHES, Wm	1798	Biddle
HUMPHR, Richard	1808	Gwin
HUMPHRAY, William	1805	Carson
HUMPHRES, Jeehee	1798	Gann
HUMPHRES, Jehue	1801	Norwood
HUMPHRES, John	1798	Morrison
HUMPHRES, John	1806	Crouch
HUMPHRES, Moses	1801	Morrison
HUMPHRES, Moses	1807	Carr
HUMPHRES, Moses	1808	Carr
HUMPHRES, Moses	1813	Hoss
HUMPHRES, Richard	1809	Green
HUMPHRES, William	1808	
HUMPHREY, David	1816	Giles
HUMPHREY, Elisha	1792	Carriger
HUMPHREY, Elisha	1792	Greer
HUMPHREY, George	1791	Tullis
HUMPHREY, James	1816	Giles
HUMPHREY, Leslie	1816	Giles
HUMPHREY, Lisby	1810	Dimmons
HUMPHREY, Richard	1790	Hanley
HUMPHREY, Richard	1797	Gann
HUMPHREY, Richd	1799	Moore
HUMPHREY, Sisby	1815	Carcathers
HUMPHREY, William	1807	Shields
HUMPHREY, William	1816	Giles
HUMPHREY, Wm	1811	
HUMPHREY, Wm	1814	Couthers
HUMPHREYS, David	1811	
HUMPHREYS, David	1814	Couthers
HUMPHREYS, David	1815	Carcathers
HUMPHREYS, David	1817	Gillises
HUMPHREYS, David	1818	Land
HUMPHREYS, Elisha	1790	Greer
HUMPHREYS, Elisha	1794	Carriger
HUMPHREYS, Elisha	1795	Carriger
HUMPHREYS, George	1795	Morrison
HUMPHREYS, George	1809	Right
HUMPHREYS, George	1811	Ellis
HUMPHREYS, George	1812	Ellis
HUMPHREYS, George	1815	Haire
HUMPHREYS, George	1816	Hair
HUMPHREYS, George	1817	Haire
HUMPHREYS, George	1818	Hair
HUMPHREYS, George	1819	Hair
HUMPHREYS, George	1821	Louis
HUMPHREYS, James	1809	Patterson
HUMPHREYS, James	1809	Patterson
HUMPHREYS, James	1815	Carcathers
HUMPHREYS, James	1817	Gillises
HUMPHREYS, Jesse	1790	Williams
HUMPHREYS, Jesse	1791	Williams
HUMPHREYS, Jesse	1795	Taylor
HUMPHREYS, John	1787	Fains
HUMPHREYS, John	1794	Carriger
HUMPHREYS, John	1795	Morrison
HUMPHREYS, John	1799	Moore

Surname, Given names	Year	Comp./Dist.
HUMPHREYS, John	1805	Carson
HUMPHREYS, John	1816	Hair
HUMPHREYS, John	1817	Haire
HUMPHREYS, John	1818	Hair
HUMPHREYS, John	1819	Hair
HUMPHREYS, John	1821	Louis
HUMPHREYS, Lesley	1817	Gillises
HUMPHREYS, Lesley	1819	Sands
HUMPHREYS, Leslie	1818	Land
HUMPHREYS, Lesly	1814	Couthers
HUMPHREYS, Lisby	1811	
HUMPHREYS, Moses	1811	Mitchell
HUMPHREYS, Moses	1813	Hoss
HUMPHREYS, Moses	1813	Hoss
HUMPHREYS, Moses	1814	Hoss
HUMPHREYS, Moses	1814	Hoss
HUMPHREYS, Moses	1815	Hoss
HUMPHREYS, Moses	1816	Hoss
HUMPHREYS, Moses	1817	Little
HUMPHREYS, Moses	1818	Jones
HUMPHREYS, Moses	1819	Jones
HUMPHREYS, Moses	1821	Jones
HUMPHREYS, Richard	1791	Hanley
HUMPHREYS, Richard	1793	Handley
HUMPHREYS, Richard	1798	Gann
HUMPHREYS, Richard	1806	Grur
HUMPHREYS, Widdow	1810	Green
HUMPHREYS, William	1793	Biddle
HUMPHREYS, William	1797	Biddle
HUMPHREYS, William	1798	Biddle
HUMPHREYS, William	1809	Patterson
HUMPHREYS, William	1810	Dimmons
HUMPHREYS, William	1815	Carcathers
HUMPHREYS, William	1817	Gillises
HUMPHREYS, William	1818	Land
HUMPHREYS, William	1821	Sands
HUMPHREYS, William (of Capt Carsons Co)	1806	Anderson
HUMPHREYS, Wm	1806	Carson
HUMPHRIES, George	1798	Morrison
HUMPHRIES, George	1814	Bean
HUMPHRIES, George	[1796] 1797	Morris
HUMPHRIES, Jehue	1796	Handly
HUMPHRIES, Jese	1794	Taylor
HUMPHRIES, Jesse	1792	Maxwell
HUMPHRIES, Richard	1794	Handly
HUMPHRIES, Richard	1795	Handly
HUMPHRIES, Richard	1805	Guir
HUMPHRIES, Richd	1796	Handly
HUMPHRIS, George	1792	Tulley
HUMPHRYS, Moses	1794	Melvan
HUMPHRYS, Richard	1799	Gann
HUMPHRYS, Richard	1801	Gann
HUMPHYES, Moses	1799	Gann
HUMPRIS, George	1798	Morrison
HUN, Luis	1821	Martin
HUNDLEY, John L.	1815	Garner
HUNDLEY, John S.	1816	Smith
HUNDLEY, John S.	1817	Smith
HUNDLEY, John S.	1821	Hampton
HUNDLEY, Langsdon	1816	Smith
HUNDLEY, Langson	1807	Anderson
HUNDLEY, Lansdon	1815	Garner
HUNDLY, Langston	1805	Aikin
HUNECUT, Ries	1807	Parker
HUNICUT, E.	1808	Parker
HUNLEY, Sangsdon	1806	Anderson
HUNLY, Joshua	1809	Bayles
HUNNEYCUT, Moses	1801	Taylor
HUNNICUT, Uriah	1809	Hartzell
HUNT, Abraham	1798	Young
HUNT, Elizabeth	1816	Hair
HUNT, Elizabeth	1817	Haire
HUNT, Elizabeth	1818	Hair
HUNT, Elizabeth	1819	Hair
HUNT, Henson	1806	Crouch
HUNT, Jean	1794	Murray
HUNT, Jeese	1790	Shipley
HUNT, Jeese	1791	Shipley
HUNT, Jesse	1793	Murray
HUNT, Jesse	1795	Murray
HUNT, Jesse	1796	Shipley
HUNT, Jesse	1797	Shipley
HUNT, Jesse	1798	Shipley
HUNT, Jesse	1801	Lane
HUNT, Jesse	1807	Britton
HUNT, Jesse	1811	Britten
HUNT, Jesse	1817	Grisham
HUNT, Jesse	1821	Hale
HUNT, Jesse	1821	Hunt
HUNT, Jesse Jr.	1805	Doak
HUNT, Jesse Jr.	1809	Right
HUNT, Jesse Jr.	1812	Britton
HUNT, Jesse Jr.	1813	Copas
HUNT, Jesse Jr.	1814	Copes
HUNT, Jesse Sr.	1805	Doak
HUNT, Jesse Sr.	1806	Doke
HUNT, Jesse Sr.	1807	Britton
HUNT, Jesse Sr.	1812	Britton
HUNT, Jesse Sr.	1813	Copas
HUNT, Jesse Sr.	1814	Copes
HUNT, Jessee Jr.	1811	Britten
HUNT, John	1806	Crouch

Surname, Given names	Year	Comp./Dist.
HUNT, John	1807	Cade
HUNT, John	1809	Right
HUNT, John	1811	Ellis
HUNT, John	1812	Ellis
HUNT, John	1814	Bean
HUNT, John	1815	Haire
HUNT, Joseph	1819	Grisham
HUNT, Joshua	1809	Bayles
HUNT, Joshua	1813	Hoss
HUNT, Joshua	1814	Bean
HUNT, Joshua	1815	Haire
HUNT, Joshua	1816	Hair
HUNT, Joshua	1817	Haire
HUNT, Joshua	1818	Hair
HUNT, Joshua	1819	Hair
HUNT, Limon	1806	Brown
HUNT, Peter	1805	Doak
HUNT, Peter	1806	Doke
HUNT, Peter	1807	Britton
HUNT, Peter	1811	Britten
HUNT, Peter	1817	Grisham
HUNT, Peter	1819	Grisham
HUNT, Peter	1821	Hale
HUNT, Saml	1801	Norwood
HUNT, Samuel	1797	Shipley
HUNT, Samuel	1798	Crouch
HUNT, Samuel	1806	Crouch
HUNT, Samuel	1809	Right
HUNT, Samuel	1811	Mitchell
HUNT, Samuel	1813	Hoss
HUNT, Samuel	1814	Hoss
HUNT, Samuel	1815	Hoss
HUNT, Samuel	1817	Little
HUNT, Samuel	1818	Jones
HUNT, Samuel	1819	Jones
HUNT, Samuel	1821	Jones
HUNT, Simmon	1799	Gann
HUNT, Simon	1793	Melvan
HUNT, Simon	1794	Melvan
HUNT, Simon	1796	Handly
HUNT, Simon	1797	Gann
HUNT, Simon	1798	Gann
HUNT, Simon	1799	Moore
HUNT, Simon	1807	Bayles
HUNT, Simon	1808	Bayles
HUNT, Simon	1809	Bayles
HUNT, Simon	1814	Hampton
HUNT, Simon (Joining Wm McGee)	1801	Gann
HUNT, Smith	1814	McLin
HUNT, Smith	1818	Hunt
HUNT, Smith	1819	Hunt
HUNT, Smith	1821	Hunt
HUNT, Thomas	1790	Stone
HUNT, Thomas	1791	Stone
HUNT, Thomas	1793	Melvan
HUNT, Thomas	1794	Melvan
HUNT, Thomas	1795	Melvan
HUNT, Thomas	1796	Melvin
HUNT, Thomas	1798	Crouch
HUNT, Thomas	1801	Norwood
HUNT, Thomas	1806	Crouch
HUNT, Thomas	1807	
HUNT, Thomas	1809	Right
HUNT, Thomas	1811	Davis
HUNT, Thomas	1811	Ellis
HUNT, Thomas	1812	Ellis
HUNT, Thomas	1814	Bean
HUNT, Thomas	1815	Haire
HUNT, Thomas	1816	Hair
HUNT, Thomas	1817	Haire
HUNT, Thomas	1818	Hair
HUNT, Thomas	1819	Hair
HUNT, Uria	1811	Davis
HUNT, Uriad	1790	Shipley
HUNT, Uriad	1791	Shipley
HUNT, Uriah	1778	
HUNT, Uriah	1793	Depew
HUNT, Uriah	1794	Depew
HUNT, Uriah	1797	Duncan
HUNT, Uriah	1798	Duncan
HUNT, Uriah	1798	Duncan
HUNT, Uriah	1799	Duncan
HUNT, Uriah	1801	Taylor
HUNT, Uriah	1806	Guin
HUNT, Uriah	1807	Britton
HUNT, Uriah	1808	Guin
HUNT, Uriah	1809	Gwin
HUNT, Uriah	1810	Barron
HUNT, Uriah	1811	Barron
HUNT, Uriah	1812	Barnes
HUNT, Uriah	1814	Barns
HUNT, Uriah	1814	McLin
HUNT, Uriah	1821	Hunt
HUNT, Uriah	1821	Sands
HUNT, Uriah Sr.	1812	McLin
HUNT, Uriah Sr.	1818	Hunt
HUNT, Uriah Sr.	1819	Hunt
HUNT, Uriak	1815	McLin
HUNT, Urick	1815	Grimsley
HUNT, Urick	1816	Grimsley
HUNT, Urick	1816	Hunt
HUNT, Urick	1817	Grimsley

Surname, Given names	Year	Comp./Dist.
HUNT, Urick	1818	Grimsley
HUNT, Urick L.	1817	Hunt
HUNT, Wesley	1816	Hampton
HUNT, Wesley	1817	Hampton
HUNT, Wesley	1818	Brown [2]
HUNT, Wesley	1819	Brown
HUNT, Westley	1814	Hampton
HUNT, Westly	1821	Brown
HUNT, William	1806	Doke
HUNT, William	1811	Britten
HUNT, William	1812	Britton
HUNTE, Joshua	1821	Louis
HUNTE, Thos	1821	Louis
HUNTER, Abraham	1793	Scott
HUNTER, Abraham	1794	Scot
HUNTER, Abraham	1795	Young
HUNTER, Abraham	1796	Young
HUNTER, Abraham	1797	Young
HUNTER, David	1819	Smith
HUNTER, David	1820	Smith
HUNTER, David C.	1818	Fine
HUNTER, Henery	1794	North
HUNTER, Henery	1796	Young
HUNTER, Henery	1797	Young
HUNTER, Hennery	1795	Young
HUNTER, Isaac	1805	Parker
HUNTER, Isaac	1806	Parker
HUNTER, Isaac	1807	Parker
HUNTER, Jacob	1791	North
HUNTER, Jacob	1796	Young
HUNTER, Jacob	1797	Young
HUNTER, Jacob	1798	Young
HUNTER, Jacob	1801	Taylor
HUNTER, Jacob	1805	Parker
HUNTER, Jacob	1806	Parker
HUNTER, Jacob	1807	Parker
HUNTER, Jacob	1808	Parker
HUNTER, Jacob	1809	Par
HUNTER, Jacob	1812	Hartsell
HUNTER, Jacob	1814	Hartsell
HUNTER, Jacob	1815	Fines
HUNTER, Jacob	1816	Fine
HUNTER, Jacob	1817	Fine
HUNTER, Jacob	1818	Fine
HUNTER, Jacob	1819	Howard
HUNTER, Jacob	1821	Howard
HUNTER, Jacob Sr.	1821	Howard
HUNTER, James	1794	Depew
HUNTER, James	1797	Duncan
HUNTER, James	1798	Duncan
HUNTER, James	1799	Duncan

Surname, Given names	Year	Comp./Dist.
HUNTER, James	1783 [after]	Depew
HUNTER, Jeremiah D.	1819	Jones
HUNTER, Jno	1809	Par
HUNTER, John	1791	North
HUNTER, John	1792	North
HUNTER, John	1793	North
HUNTER, John	1794	North
HUNTER, John	1796	Young
HUNTER, John	1801	Taylor
HUNTER, John	1805	Parker
HUNTER, John	1806	Parker
HUNTER, John	1807	Parker
HUNTER, John	1808	Parker
HUNTER, John	1810	Hartzel
HUNTER, John	1814	Hartsell
HUNTER, John	1814	Hartsell
HUNTER, John	1815	Fines
HUNTER, John	1815	Fines
HUNTER, John	1816	Fine
HUNTER, John	1817	Fine
HUNTER, John	1818	Fine
HUNTER, John	1819	Howard
HUNTER, John	1821	Howard
HUNTER, John (for Brooks heirs)	1817	Fine
HUNTER, John (for Brookshire)	1816	Fine
HUNTER, John Brook	1819	Howard
HUNTER, John Crooks	1818	Fine
HUNTER, John Sr.	1795	Young
HUNTER, John Sr.	1812	Hartsell
HUNTER, John Sr.	1814	Hartsell
HUNTER, Joseph	1801	Taylor
HUNTER, Joseph	1805	Parker
HUNTER, Joseph	1806	Parker
HUNTER, Joseph	1807	Parker
HUNTER, Joseph	1808	Parker
HUNTER, Joseph	1809	Par
HUNTER, Joseph	1810	Hartzel
HUNTER, Joseph	1812	Hartsell
HUNTER, Joseph	1814	Hartsell
HUNTER, Joseph	1815	Fines
HUNTER, Joseph	1816	Fine
HUNTER, Joseph	1817	Fine
HUNTER, Joseph	1818	Fine
HUNTER, Joseph	1819	Howard
HUNTER, Joseph	1821	Howard
HUNTTER, James	1798	Duncan
HUR, Cristopher	1780-1781 (Undated)	
HURD, John	1779	
HURD, John	1779	
HURRING, Shadrick	1814	Copes

Surname, Given names	Year	Comp./Dist.
HURRISON, Michael	1806	Brown
HUS, John	1798	Hannah
HUSELAND, Franses	1780-1781 (Undated)	
HUSTON, Absolam	1790	Hanley
HUSTON, Absolem	1791	Hanley
HUSTON, James L.	1808	McAllister
HUSTON, John	1791	Tullis
HUSTON, John	1792	Tulley
HUSTON, John	1793	Morrison
HUSTON, John	1794	Morrison
HUSTON, John	1795	Morrison
HUSTON, John	1798	Morrison
HUSTON, John	1798	Morrison
HUSTON, John	1799	Morrison
HUSTON, John	1806	Carr
HUSTON, John	1807	Carr
HUSTON, John	1808	Carr
HUSTON, John	1813	Hoss
HUSTON, John	1814	Hoss
HUSTON, John	[1796] 1797	Morris
HUSTON, Preston	1819	Hair
HUSTON, William	[1796] 1797	Morris
HUTCHEN, Charles	1798	Longmire
HUTCHING, Thomas	1808	Odell
HUTCHINGS, Charles	1797	Longmire
HUTCHINGS, William	1808	Odell
HUTCHINS, Charles	1801	Longmire
HUTCHINS, Moses	1811	Brown
HUTCHINS, Thomas	1806	Odel
HUTCHINS, William	1806	Odel
HUTCHINS, William	1811	Brown
HUTER, John Sr.	1821	Howard
HUTTON, John	1811	Mitchell
HUTTON, Samuel	1778	
HUTTON, Samuel	1779	
HUTTON, William	1778	
HUTTON, William	1781	
HUTTON, William	1780-1781 (Undated)	
HYBARGER, David	1808	Gwin
HYDER, John	1794	Taylor
HYDER, Michel	1794	Taylor
HYDER, Michl	1779	
-IBB, Jacob	1821	Martin
ILE, William	1808	McAllister
ILES, William	1801	Biddle
ILES, William	1809	McAlister
ILES, William	1814	McCray
ILES, William	1817	McClure
ILES, William	1821	McGee
ILES, William Sr.	1817	McClure
ILES, Willis	1799	Hannah
INGELL, Mical	1794	Scot
INGELL, Willam	1794	Brown
INGLE, Adam	1798	Roberson
INGLE, Adam	1799	Robertson
INGLE, Adam	1801	Calvert
INGLE, Adam	1805	Guir
INGLE, Adam	1809	Green
INGLE, Adam	1811	Davis
INGLE, Adam	1812	Waddill
INGLE, Adam	1814	Waddell
INGLE, Adam	1815	Waddell
INGLE, Adam	1816	Waddell
INGLE, Adam	1817	Riley
INGLE, Adam	1818	Riley
INGLE, Adam	1819	Findley
INGLE, Adam Jr.	1819	Findley
INGLE, Adam Jr.	1821	McGee
INGLE, Adam Sr.	1818	Riley
INGLE, Adam Sr.	1821	McGee
INGLE, George	1795	Ford
INGLE, John	1795	Morrison
INGLE, John	1816	Hair
INGLE, John	1817	Haire
INGLE, John	1818	Hair
INGLE, John	1819	Hair
INGLE, Mary	1809	Green
INGLE, Mary	1815	Waddell
INGLE, Mary	1816	Waddell
INGLE, Mary	1817	Riley
INGLE, Mary	1818	Riley
INGLE, Mary	1819	Findley
INGLE, Mary	1821	McGee
INGLE, Michael	1799	Stuart
INGLE, Michael	1808	Gwin
INGLE, Michal	1796	Longmire
INGLE, Michal	1797	Calvert
INGLE, Michal	1797	Calvert
INGLE, Michel	1801	Calvert
INGLE, Michel (Agent for Robert Moore)	1798	Calvert
INGLE, Michol	1795	Calvert
INGLE, Willam	1796	Brown
INGLE, William	1793	Brown
INGLE, William	1801	Roberson
INGLE, William	1808	Bayles
INGLE, William	1809	Bayles
INGLE, William	1811	Ellis
INGLE, William	1812	Ellis
INGLE, William	1815	Haire
INGLE, William	1816	Hair
INGLE, William	1817	Haire

Surname, Given names	Year	Comp./Dist.
INGLE, William	1819	Hair
INGLE, William	1821	Louis
INGLE, William (executor of)	1815	Harris
INGLE, Wm	1797	Robertson
INGLE, Wm	1799	Robertson
INGLE, Wm	1807	Bayles
INGLE, Wm (estate of)	1821	Hampton
INGLISH, Andw	1781	
INGLISH, James	1781	
INGLISH, John	1781	
INGLISH, John	1811	Barron
INGLISH, Thomas	1811	Barron
INGRAM, Z.	1798	Duncan
INGRUM, Zedicaiah	1798	Biddle
INKEL, Mary	1812	Crawford
INKEL, Mery	1812	Crawford [2]
INKS, George	1796	Young
INKS, Gorge	1797	Young
INLAND, Thomas	1815	Fines
INLISH, John	1808	Cade
INLISH, Thomas	1808	Cade
INLISH, Thomas	1810	Barron
INMAN, Abdednego	1780-1781 (Undated)	
INMAN, Abednago	1779	Wilson
INMAN, Ebedo	1781	
IREBY, Isam	1778	
IRELAND, Robert	1817	Fine
IRELAND, Thomas	1806	Brown
IRELAND, Thomas	1807	Bayles
IRELAND, Thomas	1812	Hartsell
IRELAND, Thomas	1814	Hartsell
IRELAND, Thomas	1816	Fine
IRELAND, Thomas	1818	Fine
IRELAND, Thomas	1819	Howard
IRELAND, Thos	1801	Roberson
IRELAND, Thos	1808	Bayles
IRLAND, Thos	1809	Par
IRUFIN, William	1805	Parker
IRVAN, Gorge	1807	Cade
IRVIN, Francis	1812	McCray
IRVIN, George	1805	Rector
IRVIN, John	1807	Anderson
IRVIN, Patrick	1818	Hunt
IRVIN, Patrick	1819	Hunt
IRVIN, Saml	1795	Calvert
IRVINE, John	1793	Depew
IRVINE, Robert	1781	
IRVINE, Robert	1781	
IRWIN, Alexnder	1809	Cade
IRWIN, Bengamin	1796	Young
IRWIN, Frances	1801	Taylor
IRWIN, Frances	1805	Jas Parker
IRWIN, Frances	1808	Parker
IRWIN, Francis	1809	Parker
IRWIN, Francis	1811	McCray
IRWIN, James	1795	Young
IRWIN, James (Disputed)	1792	North
IRWIN, John	1801	Taylor
IRWIN, Jorge	1814	Barns
IRWIN, Patrick	1807	Anderson
IRWIN, Patrick	1808	
IRWIN, Patrick	1809	Gwin
IRWIN, Patrick	1815	McLin
IRWIN, Patrick	1816	Hunt
IRWIN, Patrick	1817	Hunt
IRWIN, Patrick	1821	Hunt
IRWIN, Robert	1792	North
IRWIN, Saml	1793	North
IRWIN, Samuel	1797	Robertson
IRWIN, William	1809	Par
IRWIN, Wm	1801	Taylor
ISAACS, Jacob	1809	Green
ISANBARGER, Nicholas	1819	Hair
ISBEL, James R.	1811	Rodman
ISBELL, Godfrey	1778	
ISBELL, James R.	1809	Roadmas
ISBELL, James R.	1814	McCracken
ISBELL, Zach	1778	
ISBELL, Zachariah (Esq.)	1778	
ISENBARGER, Nicholas	1806	Crouch
ISENBARGER, Nicholis	1818	Hair
ISENBERG, Nicholas	1809	Right
ISENBERG, Nicholas	1811	Ellis
ISENBERG, Nicholas	1812	Ellis
ISENBERG, Nicholis	1817	Haire
ISENBERG, Sarah	1811	Ellis
ISENBERG, Sarah (widow)	1812	Ellis
ISENBERGER, Nicholas	1815	Haire
ISENBERGER, Nicholis	1816	Hair
ISEY, William	1819	Hair
ISLES, William	1805	Stephenson
ISLES, William	1814	Crookshanks
ISLES, William	1818	McClure
ISLES, William	1819	Findley
ISLES, William	1819	McClure
ISLES, William Jr.	1818	Harris
ISLES, Willm	1811	McAlister
ISOMBARGE, Nicholas	1814	Bean
ISONBERGER, Daniel	1821	Louis
ISONBERGER, Nicholas	1821	Louis
IVEY, Howel	1792	Maxwell
IVEY, Howel	1793	Morrison

Surname, Given names	Year	Comp./Dist.
IVEY, Howel	1794	Morrison
IVEY, Howell	1790	Williams
IVEY, Howell	1791	Williams
IVEY, Howell	1793	Maxwell
IVEY, James	1794	Carriger
IVY, James	1792	Greer
IVY, James	1795	Carriger
IVY, Jas	1790	Greer
JABB, David	1801	Morrison
Jack (man of colour)	1821	Hale
JACK, Jaremy	1780-1781 (Undated)	
JACK, Jeremiah	1779	Wilson
JACK, Jeremiah	1781	
JACKSON,	1795	Thornton
JACKSON, Bengamin	1809	Gwin
JACKSON, Benjamin	1807	Anderson
JACKSON, Benjamin	1811	Davis
JACKSON, Benjamin	1812	McLin
JACKSON, Benjamin	1814	McLin
JACKSON, Benjamin	1815	McLin
JACKSON, Benjamin	1817	Smith
JACKSON, Benjamin	1818	Smith
JACKSON, George	1794	Murray
JACKSON, George	1796	Shipley
JACKSON, George	1797	Shipley
JACKSON, George	1798	Shipley
JACKSON, George	1805	Rector
JACKSON, George	1806	Doke
JACKSON, George	1806	Odel
JACKSON, George	1807	Britton
JACKSON, George	1808	Odell
JACKSON, George	1811	Barron
JACKSON, George	1811	Britten
JACKSON, George	1812	Barnes
JACKSON, George	1813	Copas
JACKSON, George	1814	Copes
JACKSON, George	1815	Copas
JACKSON, George	1815	Grimsley
JACKSON, George	1815	Grimsley
JACKSON, George	1816	Copas
JACKSON, George	1816	Grimsley
JACKSON, George	1817	Grisham
JACKSON, George	1818	Grimsley
JACKSON, George	1818	Grisham
JACKSON, George	1819	Grimsley
JACKSON, George	1819	Grisham
JACKSON, George	1821	Hale
JACKSON, George Jr.	1817	Grimsley
JACKSON, Gorge	1801	Glasscock
JACKSON, Gorge	1809	Cade
JACKSON, Henry	1806	Brown

Surname, Given names	Year	Comp./Dist.
JACKSON, Henry	1808	Bayles
JACKSON, Jacob	1811	Barron
JACKSON, Jacob	1812	Barnes
JACKSON, Jacob	1815	Grimsley
JACKSON, Jacob	1816	Grimsley
JACKSON, Jacob	1817	Grimsley
JACKSON, Jacob	1818	Grimsley
JACKSON, Jacob	1819	Grimsley
JACKSON, Jarge	1814	Barns
JACKSON, Jeremiah	1805	Rector
JACKSON, Jonathan	1807	Britton
JACKSON, Jonathan	1811	Britten
JACKSON, Jonathan	1812	Britton
JACKSON, Jonathan	1813	Copas
JACKSON, Jonathan	1814	Copes
JACKSON, Jonathan	1815	Copas
JACKSON, Peter	1801	Glasscock
JACKSON, Peter	1818	Grimsley
JACKSON, Peter	1819	Grimsley
JACKSON, Peter	1821	Martin
JACKSON, Sam'l	1821	Smith
JACKSON, Samuel	1811	Rodman
JACKSON, Samuel	1814	Hampton
JACKSON, Samuel	1815	Garner
JACKSON, Samuel	1816	Smith
JACKSON, Samuel	1817	Smith
JACKSON, Samuel	1818	Grimsley
JACKSON, Samuel	1818	Smith
JACKSON, Samuel	1819	Grimsley
JACKSON, Samuel	1819	Smith
JACKSON, Samuel	1820	Smith
JACKSON, Wilam	1821	Martin
JACKSON, William	1794	Murray
JACKSON, William	1794	Thornton
JACKSON, William	1796	Shipley
JACKSON, William	1797	Shipley
JACKSON, William	1798	Shipley
JACKSON, William	1805	Rector
JACKSON, William	1811	Barron
JACKSON, William	1812	Barnes
JACKSON, William	1814	Copes
JACKSON, William	1815	Copas
JACKSON, William	1815	Grimsley
JACKSON, William	1816	Copas
JACKSON, William	1816	Grimsley
JACKSON, William	1817	Grimsley
JACKSON, William	1817	Grisham
JACKSON, William	1818	Grimsley
JACKSON, William	1818	Grisham
JACKSON, William	1819	Grimsley
JACKSON, William	1819	Grisham

Surname, Given names	Year	Comp./Dist.
JACKSON, William	1821	Hale
JACKSON, Wm	1801	Glasscock
JACOBS, Dufty	1796	Calvert
JACOBS, Dufty	1796	Jonesboro
JACOBS, Dufty	1797	Calvert
JACOBS, Dufty	1797	Calvert
JACOBS, Dufty	1798	Calvert
JACOBS, Dufty	1799	Stuart
JACOBS, Dufty	1801	Aiken
JACOBS, Dufty	1805	Aikin
JACOBS, Dufty	1806	Anderson
JACOBS, John	1801	Aiken
JACOON, George	1821	Martin
JACSON, George	1795	Murray
JACSON, George	1807	Odell
JACSON, Gorge	1814	Barns
JACSON, Jacob	1810	Barron
JACSON, Jacob	1814	Barns
JACSON, Jacob	1821	Martin
JACSON, Jorge	1810	Barron
JACSON, Nathan	1814	Barns
JACSON, William	1795	Murray
JACSON, William	1807	Cade
JACSON, William	1810	Barron
JACSON, William	1814	Barns
JAISON, William	1808	Cade
JAMES, (a man of colored living of J. Whites')	1818	Jones
JAMES, (a man of Colour living at Jas. Bowman's)	1819	Jones
JAMES, (a man of colour living at Joseph Bowman's)	1821	Jones
JAMES, Andrew	1780-1781	District 7
JAMES, Isaac	1781	
JAMES, Roland	1795	Thornton
JAMES, Thomas	1797	Calvert
JAMES, Tomisen J.	1808	Parker
JAMES, Tomson I.	1807	Parker
JANTREY, Joseph	1795	Thornton
JARDEN, John	1811	McAlister
JARDEN, Luis	1809	McAlister
JARDEN, Luis	1811	McAlister
JARVIS, Alexander	1801	Longmire
JARVIS, Alexd	1792	Coye
JARVIS, Alexr	1798	Longmire
JARVIS, William	1806	Odel
JARVIS, William	1808	Odell
JASLLY, John	1780-1781 (undated)	
JASON, Robert	1816	Brown
JEKINS, Willam	1799	Gann
JENBRY, William	1817	Fine
JENKINS, George	1807	Givins
JENKINS, George	1808	Guin
JENKINS, George	1809	Right
JENKINS, George	1815	McLin
JENKINS, George	1816	Hunt
JENKINS, George	1817	Hunt
JENKINS, George	1818	Hunt
JENKINS, George	1821	Hunt
JENKINS, George Sr.	1801	Norwood
JENKINS, Hugh	1793	Thornton
JENKINS, Joseph	1795	Thornton
JENKINS, Roland	1794	Thornton
JENKINS, Roland	1795	Thornton
JENKINS, Rowland	1790	White
JENKINS, Rowland	1791	White
JENKINS, Rowland	1793	Thornton
JENKINS, William	1797	Young
JENKINS, Wm	1799	Moore
JENTERY, Robert	1781	
JERDEN, John	1798	Gann
JERRY,	1792	Brown
JESS, Joseph	1780-1781 (Undated)	
Jesse	1795	Taylor
JESTER, Isaac	1798	Morrison
JESTER, Thos	1799	Hannah
JIFFIN, Henry	1783 [after]	Blair
JILES, William	1815	Crookshanks
JILES, William	1816	Crookshanks
JILES, William Jr.	1816	Crookshanks
JINKIN, Isaac	1813	Hoss
JINKINS, Aaron	1812	Ellis
JINKINS, Aaron	1814	Bean
JINKINS, George	1790	Stone
JINKINS, George	1791	Stone
JINKINS, George	1793	Melvan
JINKINS, George	1812	Ellis
JINKINS, George	1812	McLin
JINKINS, George	1814	Bean
JINKINS, George	1814	McLin
JINKINS, George	1819	Hunt
JINKINS, Henry	1801	Roberson
JINKINS, Henry	1806	Brown
JINKINS, John	1812	Ellis
JINKINS, John	1814	Bean
JINKINS, Wilam	1798	Gann
JOANES, Robert	1794	Scot
JOANS, Isac	1794	Scot
JOANS, John	1781	
JOB, Abraham	1798	Morrison
JOB, Abraham	1806	Carr
JOB, Abraham	1807	Carr
JOB, Abraham	1808	Carr

Surname, Given names	Year	Comp./Dist.
JOB, Abraham	1814	Hoss
JOB, Abraham	1815	Hoss
JOB, David	1790	Williams
JOB, David	1791	Williams
JOB, David	1792	Tulley
JOB, David	1793	Morrison
JOB, David	1794	Morrison
JOB, David	1795	Morrison
JOB, David	1798	Morrison
JOB, David	1798	Morrison
JOB, David	[1796] 1797	Morris
JOB, Enoc	1809	Viney
JOB, Enoch	1808	Odell
JOB, Enoch	1810	Cove
JOB, Enoch	1811	Barron
JOB, Enoch	1811	Brown
JOB, Enoch	1814	Brown
JOB, Enoch	1815	Hartsell
JOB, Enoch	1816	Brown
JOB, Enoch	1816	Copas
JOB, Enoch	1817	Brown
JOB, Enoch	1817	Grisham
JOB, Enoch	1818	Brown
JOB, Enoch	1818	Grisham
JOB, Enoch	1819	Brown
JOB, Enoch	1821	Haines
JOB, John	1816	Hoss
JOB, Moses	1816	Brown
JOB, Moses	1817	Brown
JOB, Moses	1818	Brown
JOB, Moses	1819	Brown
JOB, Moses	1821	Haines
JOB, Nathan	1811	Barron
JOB, Nathan	1815	Grimsley
JOB, Nathan	1816	Grimsley
JOB, Nathan	1818	Grimsley
JOB, Nathan	1819	Grimsley
JOB, Nathan	1821	Martin
JOBB, David	1779	
JOBB, David	1799	Morrison
JOBB, Enoch	1812	Brown
JOBE, Abariham	1813	Hoss
JOBE, Abigail	1811	Mitchell
JOBE, Abraham	1816	Hoss
JOBE, Abraham	1817	Little
JOBE, Abraham	1818	Jones
JOBE, Abraham	1819	Jones
JOBE, Abraham	1821	Jones
JOBE, Abraham	1821	Jones
JOBE, Enoch	1807	Cade
JOBE, Enoch	1807	Odell

Surname, Given names	Year	Comp./Dist.
JOBE, Enoch	1808	Cade
JOBE, Enoch	1812	Barnes
JOBE, Enoch	1819	Grisham
JOBE, Enoch	1821	Hale
JOBE, Enuch	1801	Glasscock
JOBE, Enuch	1809	Cade
JOBE, John	1817	Little
JOBE, John	1818	Jones
JOBE, John	1819	Jones
JOBE, Jonathan	1809	Cade
JOBE, Jonathan	1810	Barron
JOBE, Laban	1819	Jones
JOBE, Moses	1793	Maxwell
JOBE, Nathan	1801	Glasscock
JOBE, Nathan	1807	Cade
JOBE, Nathan	1808	Cade
JOBE, Nathan	1809	Cade
JOBE, Nathan	1810	Barron
JOBE, Nathan	1812	Barnes
JOBE, Nathan	1814	Barns
JOBE, Nathan	1817	Grimsley
JODAN, Lewis	1795	Milliken
JOE, Aqulis	1780-1781 (Undated)	
Joh-	1809	Carr
John	1795	Taylor
John	1795	Thornton
John	1806	Parker
John	1810	Green
JOHNSON, David	1779	
JOHNSON, Francis	1798	Duncan
JOHNSON, Isaac	1778	
JOHNSON, Jacob	1781	
JOHNSON, James	1814	Hampton
JOHNSON, James	1821	Smith
JOHNSON, Jas. S.	1820	Smith
JOHNSON, Robert	1814	Brown
JOHNSON, Robert	1817	Brown
JOHNSON, Samuel	1793	Depew
JOHNSON, Suseana	1806	Guin
JOHNSON, William	1779	
JOHNSTON, Benja	1778	
JOHNSTON, Jacob	1780-1781 (Undated)	
JOHNSTON, James	1814	Hoss
JOHNSTON, James	1818	Brown [2]
JOHNSTON, James S.	1816	Hampton
JOHNSTON, James S.	1819	Smith
JOHNSTON, Jonithan F.	1821	Louis
JOHNSTON, Robert	1792	Carriger
JOHNSTON, Robert	1812	Brown
JOHNSTON, Robert	1815	Hartsell

Surname, Given names	Year	Comp./Dist.
JOHNSTON, Robt	1792	Greer
JOHNSTON, Robt	1794	Carriger
JOHNSTON, Samuel	1794	Depew
JOHNSTON, Samuel	1798	Duncan
JOHNSTON, Samuel	1798	Duncan
JOHNSTON, Samuel	1799	Duncan
JOHNSTON, Samuel	1817	Hampton
JOHNSTON, Stephen	1806	Grur
JOHNSTON, William	1819	Smith
JOHNSTON, Wm	1778	
JOHNSTONS, Thos	1780-1781 (Undated)	
JOLLEY, Dudley	1811	Barron
JOLLEY, Dudley	1817	Grimsley
JOLLEY, Dudly	1805	Rector
JOLLEY, Henry	1805	Rector
JOLLEY, Henry	1811	Barron
JOLLEY, Henry	1816	Grimsley
JOLLEY, Henry	1817	Grimsley
JOLLY, Aury	1819	Grimsley
JOLLY, Dudley	1814	Barns
JOLLY, Dudley	1815	Grimsley
JOLLY, Dudley	1816	Grimsley
JOLLY, Dudly	1807	Cade
JOLLY, Dudly	1808	Cade
JOLLY, Dudly	1809	Cade
JOLLY, Dudly	1810	Barron
JOLLY, Hennery	1809	Cade
JOLLY, Henry	1807	Cade
JOLLY, Henry	1808	Cade
JOLLY, Henry	1810	Barron
JOLLY, Henry	1814	Barns
JOLLY, Henry	1815	Grimsley
JOLLY, Henry	1818	Grimsley
JONACKIN, Thomas	1778	
JONAS, William D.	1817	Little
Jonathan	1798	Roberson
JONER, Christian Shoults	1792	Greer
JONES, Allis	1779	
JONES, Christopher	1809	Green
JONES, Culton	1779	
JONES, Darlen	1806	Carr
JONES, Darlin	1808	Carr
JONES, Darling	1791	Tullis
JONES, Darling	1795	Morrison
JONES, Darling	1798	Morrison
JONES, Darling	1798	Morrison
JONES, Darling	1798	Morrison
JONES, Darling	1799	Morrison
JONES, Darling	1801	Morrison
JONES, Darling	1807	Carr
JONES, Darling	1809	Carr

Surname, Given names	Year	Comp./Dist.
JONES, Darling	1811	Mitchell
JONES, Darling	1814	Hoss
JONES, Darling	1815	Hoss
JONES, Darling	1817	Little
JONES, Darling	1818	Jones
JONES, Darling	[1796] 1797	Morris
JONES, Darlins	1813	Hoss
JONES, Henry	1778	
JONES, James	1778	
JONES, James	1790	White
JONES, James	1791	White
JONES, James	1794	Ford
JONES, James	1795	Ford
JONES, James	1806	Payn
JONES, James	1808	McAllister
JONES, James	1815	Crookshanks
JONES, James	1815	Hoss
JONES, James	1817	Little
JONES, Jesse	1817	Brown
JONES, Jesse	1818	Brown
JONES, Jesse	1821	Brown
JONES, John	1812	Britton
JONES, John B.	1821	Hunt
JONES, Jurdan	1809	Viney
JONES, Laben	1817	Little
JONES, Lewis	1778	
JONES, Lewis	1779	
JONES, Lewis	1795	Ford
JONES, Lewis	1817	Fine
JONES, Lewis Jr.	1794	Ford
JONES, Lewis Jr.	1795	Ford
JONES, Lewis Sr.	1793	Campbell
JONES, Lewis Sr.	1794	Ford
JONES, Lewis Sr.; (Over age)	1791	White
JONES, Lewis Sr.; (Over age)	1792	White
JONES, Nancy	1807	Carr
JONES, Nancy	1817	Little
JONES, Nathaneal	1798	Duncan
JONES, Nathanel	1797	Duncan
JONES, Nathanel	1821	Hunt
JONES, Nathaniel	1792	Depew
JONES, Nathaniel	1793	Depew
JONES, Nathaniel	1794	Depew
JONES, Nathaniel	1798	Duncan
JONES, Nathaniel	1799	Duncan
JONES, Nathaniel	1801	Taylor
JONES, Nathaniel	1807	Givins
JONES, Nathaniel	1808	Guin
JONES, Nathaniel	1811	Davis
JONES, Nathaniel	1812	McLin
JONES, Nathaniel	1814	McLin

Surname, Given names	Year	Comp./Dist.
JONES, Nathaniel	1815	McLin
JONES, Nathaniel	1816	Hunt
JONES, Nathaniel	1817	Hampton
JONES, Nathaniel	1817	Hunt
JONES, Nathaniel	1818	Grimsley
JONES, Nathaniel	1818	Hunt
JONES, Nathaniel	1819	Grimsley
JONES, Nathaniel	1819	Hunt
JONES, Nathenial	1809	Gwin
JONES, Natheniel	1806	Guin
JONES, Phillip	1778	
JONES, Richard	1792	Brown
JONES, Richard	1793	Brown
JONES, Richard	1794	Brown
JONES, Richard	1797	Robertson
JONES, Richard	1798	Roberson
JONES, Richard	1799	Robertson
JONES, Richard	1801	Roberson
JONES, Richard	1806	Brown
JONES, Richard	1807	Bayles
JONES, Richard	1808	Bayles
JONES, Richard	1809	Bayles
JONES, Samuel	1819	Grimsley
JONES, Samuel	1821	Martin
JONES, Sevier Jr.	1790	White
JONES, Sevier Sr.; (Over age)	1790	White
JONES, Thomas	1819	Brown
JONES, Thommas	1809	Viney
JONES, William	1779	
JONES, William	1779	
JONES, William	1795	Ford
JONES, William	1812	Brown
JONES, William	1815	Hoss
JONES, William D.	1816	Hoss
JONES, William D.	1818	Jones
JONES, William D.	1819	Jones
JONES, William D.	1821	Jones
JONES, Wm	1779	
JONES, Wm	1779	
JONES, Wm	1814	Hampton
JONS, Evan	1780-1781 (Undated)	
JONS, Richard	1796	Brown
JONSON, Francis	1781	
JONSTEN, James	1799	Gann
JONSTON, James	1821	Louis
JONSTON, James	1780-1781 (undated)	
JONSTON, Moses	1780-1781 (undated)	
JONSTON, Thomas	1781	
JONSTON, Thomas	1812	McCray
JONSTON, Thomas	1812	McCray

Surname, Given names	Year	Comp./Dist.
JORDAN, John	1799	Moore
JORDAN, Lewis	1797	Hannah
JORDAN, Lewis	1799	Hannah
JORDAN, Quena	1790	Milleken
JORDEN, John	1793	Handley
JORDEN, John	1796	Handly
JORDEN, John	1814	Crookshanks
JORDEN, Lewes	1798	Hannah
JORDEN, Lewis	1796	Millikin
JORDEN, Lewis	1814	Crookshanks
JORDEN, Luis	1805	Stephenson
JORDEN, Luis	1807	Payne
JORDON, John	1815	Crookshanks
JORDON, John	1816	Crookshanks
JORDON, John	1817	McClure
JORDON, John	1818	McClure
JORDON, Lewis	1815	Crookshanks
JORDON, Lewis	1816	Crookshanks
JORDON, Lewis	1817	McClure
JORDON, Lewis	1818	McClure
JORDON, Lewis	1819	McClure
JORDON, Lewis	1821	McClure
JUNDON, Lewis	1794	Milliken
JUNEIN, Gorge	1821	Martin
JURDAN, John	1797	Gann
JURDEN, John	1795	Handly
JURDEN, John	1812	Crawford [2]
JURDEN, Lewis	1808	McAllister
JURDEN, Lewis	1812	Crawford
JURDEN, Lewis	1812	Crawford [2]
JURDEN, Wm	1809	Carr
JURDON, Lewis	1801	Squibb
JURVIS, James	1808	Odell
JUSTICE, John	1817	Gillises
JUSTIN, John	1816	Giles
KAMMON, Scott	1817	McClure
KANE, John	1790	White
KANE, John	1791	White
KANE, John	1793	Thornton
KANE, Peter	1790	White
KANE, Peter	1791	White
KANE, Peter	1792	White
KANEDAY, David	1808	McAllister
KAPLINGER, Jacob	1809	Bayles
KAPLINGER, Samuel	1809	Bayles
KARD, Jane	1811	Mitchell
KARLAN, William	1817	McClure
KARR, George	1778	
KARR, Robert Jr.	1781	
KARTY, John	1815	McLin
KARTZ, John	1811	Davis

Surname, Given names	Year	Comp./Dist.
KASEY, Moses	1781	
KEAN, Jona	1810	Barron
KEAN, Jonah	1814	Barns
KEAN, Jonah	1815	Grimsley
KEASE, John	1814	Barns
KEBLER, Jacob	1815	Grimsley
KEBLER, Jacob	1816	Grimsley
KEBLER, Jacob	1817	Grimsley
KEBLER, Jacob Jr.	1815	Grimsley
KEBLER, Jacob Jr.	1816	Grimsley
KEBLER, Jacob Jr.	1817	Grimsley
KEBLER, James	1811	Barron
KEBLER, James	1815	Grimsley
KEBLER, James	1816	Grimsley
KEBLER, James	1817	Grimsley
KEBLER, James	1818	Grimsley
KEBLER, John	1811	Barron
KEBLER, John	1815	Grimsley
KEBLER, John	1816	Grimsley
KEBLER, John	1817	Grimsley
KECHARES, Nicholis	1817	Grisham
KEDRICK, Charles Jr.	1808	Parker
KEDRICK, Charles Sr.	1808	Parker
KEEBLER, Jacob	1801	Glasscock
KEEBLER, Jacob	1805	Rector
KEEBLER, Jacob	1809	Cade
KEEBLER, Jacob	1812	Barnes
KEEBLER, Jacob Jr.	1818	Grimsley
KEEBLER, Jacob Jr.	1819	Grimsley
KEEBLER, Jacob Sr.	1812	Barnes
KEEBLER, Jacob Sr.	1818	Grimsley
KEEBLER, Jacob Sr.	1819	Grimsley
KEEBLER, James	1812	Barnes
KEEBLER, James	1819	Grimsley
KEEBLER, John	1812	Barnes
KEEBLER, John	1818	Grimsley
KEEBLER, John	1819	Grimsley
KEEFAUER, Nicholas	1808	Guin
KEEFHAVER, Nicholas	1811	Britten
KEEFHAVER, Nicholas	1813	Copas
KEEL, James	1781	
KEEL, John	1791	Chisom
KEEL, John	1792	Chisolm
KEEL, John	1793	Brown
KEELE, James	1793	Brown
KEELE, John	1796	Brown
KEEN, Elijah	1818	Grimsley
KEEN, George	1809	Viney
KEEN, Iona	1817	Grimsley
KEEN, Iona	1818	Grimsley
KEEN, Jonah	1811	Barron
KEEN, Jonas	1809	Cade
KEEN, Joney	1821	Martin
KEEN, Lewis	1817	Grimsley
KEENAN, Joseph	1809	Viney
KEENAR, Jonathan	1810	Cove
KEENAR, Joseph	1810	Cove
KEENAR, Joseph	1814	Brown
KEENAR, Peeter	1814	Brown
KEENAR, Peter	1810	Cove
KEENAR, Ulrich	1810	Cove
KEENAR, Ulrich	1814	Brown
KEENE, Jonah	1812	Barnes
KEENE, Jonah	1819	Grimsley
KEENER,	1807	Odell
KEENER, Francis	1779	
KEENER, George	1806	Odel
KEENER, George	1808	Odell
KEENER, George	1811	Brown
KEENER, John	1806	Odel
KEENER, Joseph	1808	Odell
KEENER, Joseph	1811	Brown
KEENER, Joseph	1812	Brown
KEENER, Joseph	1815	Hartsell
KEENER, Joseph	1819	Brown
KEENER, Joseph	1821	Haines
KEENER, Peter	1811	Brown
KEENER, Peter	1812	Brown
KEENER, Peter	1815	Hartsell
KEENER, Peter	1818	Brown
KEENER, Peter	1819	Brown
KEENER, Ulrich	1806	Odel
KEENER, Ulrich	1811	Brown
KEENER, Ulrich	1819	Brown
KEENER, Ulrich	1821	Haines
KEENER, Ulrick	1812	Brown
KEENER, Ulrick	1815	Hartsell
KEENER, Ulrick	1818	Brown
KEENER, Werick	1808	Odell
KEENER, William	1819	Brown
KEENER, William	1821	Haines
KEENEY, John	1779	Wilson
KEENEY, Joseph	1780-1781 (undated)	
KEEPHAVER, Nicholas	1821	Hale
KEER, John	1794	Carriger
KEER, Philip	1815	McLin
KEES, Isaac	1816	Hair
KEES, Isaac	1818	Hair
KEES, Isaac	1819	Hair
KEES, Isaac	1821	Louis
KEES, John	1812	McLin
KEES, John	1816	Hair

Surname, Given names	Year	Comp./Dist.
KEES, John	1818	Hair
KEES, John	1819	Hair
KEES, John	1821	Louis
KEES, Philip	1808	Guin
KEES, Philip	1816	Hunt
KEES, Phillip	1801	Taylor
KEESE, Philip	1809	Gwin
KEETH, Danual	1780-1781 (Undated)	
KEEVER, Jacob	1808	Parker
KEEYS, Philip	1821	Hunt
KEEYS, Phillip	1812	McLin
KEFAUVER, Nicholas	1812	Britton
KEFAUVER, Nicholas	1814	Copes
KEFAVER, Nicholas	1819	Grisham
KEGLEY, John	1818	Land
KEICHER, Coonrad Jr.	1809	Bayles
KEICHER, John	1801	Calvert
KEICHER, John	1809	Bayles
KEICHER, Joseph	1801	Roberson
KEICHER, Joseph	1809	Bayles
KEILL, James	1794	Brown
KEILL, Jse	1794	Brown
KEITH, Daniel	1778	
KELEE, John	1798	Biddle
KELEY, Kinchen	1791	Tullis
KELEY, Kinchen	1798	Morrison
KELEY, Moses	1780-1781 (Undated)	
KELL, John	1794	Brown
KELLER, Hezekiah	1819	Grimsley
KELLER, William	1819	Grimsley
KELLEY, Chinchen	1795	Morrison
KELLEY, Elijah	1821	Brown
KELLEY, James	1778	
KELLEY, Kenchen	1807	Carr
KELLEY, Kimburly	1813	Hoss
KELLEY, Kinchen	1799	Morrison
KELLEY, Kinchen	1801	Morrison
KELLEY, Kinchen	1806	Carr
KELLEY, William	1813	Hoss
KELLO, Hezekiah	1818	Grimsley
KELLOW, Hezekiah	1821	Hale
KELLSAY, Saml (estate of)	1799	Hannah
KELLY, Eli John	1818	Jones
KELLY, Elijah	1816	Hoss
KELLY, Elijah	1817	Little
KELLY, George	1818	Smith
KELLY, George	1819	Smith
KELLY, James	1780-1781 (Undated)	
KELLY, John	1815	Hoss
KELLY, John	1816	Hoss
KELLY, John	1817	Little
KELLY, Joshua	1812	Barnes
KELLY, Joshua	1814	Barns
KELLY, Joshua	1816	Grimsley
KELLY, Joshua	1819	Jones
KELLY, Kenchen	1817	Little
KELLY, Kinchen	1787	Fains
KELLY, Kinchen	1815	Hoss
KELLY, Kincher	1792	Tulley
KELLY, Kincher	1819	Jones
KELLY, Kirchen	1798	Morrison
KELLY, Richard	1780-1781 (Undated)	
KELLY, William	1815	Hoss
KELLY, William	1817	Little
KELSAY, John	1801	Biddle
KELSAY, John	1805	Carson
KELSAY, Samuel	1801	Squibb
KELSAY, William	1797	Biddle
KELSAY, William	1801	Biddle
KELSAY, William	1805	Carson
KELSEY, John	1798	Biddle
KELSEY, John	1806	Carson
KELSEY, John	1807	Shields
KELSEY, John	1811	
KELSEY, John	1814	Couthers
KELSEY, John	1819	Sands
KELSEY, John	1821	Sands
KELSEY, Nath'l	1821	Smith
KELSEY, Sol	1809	McAlister
KELSEY, William	1794	Blair
KELSEY, William	1783 [after]	Depew
KELSEY, Wm	1798	Biddle
KELSO, William	1780-1781 (Undated)	
KELSY, John	1810	Dimmons
KELSY, Saml (estate of)	1807	Payne
KENADEY, David	1805	Guir
KENADY, David	1806	Grur
KENADY, Samuel	1821	Sands
KENE, Iona	1816	Grimsley
KENEADY, David	1797	Gann
KENEDAY, David	1790	Hanley
KENEDY, Daniel	1778	
KENEDY, Daniel	1780-1781 (Undated)	
KENEDY, David	1807	Payne
KENEDY, David	1811	McAlister
KENEDY, David Sr.	1797	Gann
KENEDY, Isaac	1812	McLin
KENEDY, Isaac	1814	McLin
KENEDY, John	1807	Anderson
KENEDY, John	1814	McCracken

Surname, Given names	Year	Comp./Dist.
KENEDY, John	1820	Smith
KENEDY, John	1821	Smith
KENEDY, Scott	1818	McClure
KENIDY, David	1793	Handley
KENIDY, David Jr.	1796	Handly
KENIDY, David Sr.	1796	Handly
KENNADY, David	1801	Gann
KENNADY, John	1799	Stuart
KENNADY, John	1805	Aikin
KENNADY, John	1809	Roadmas
KENNADY, John	1811	Rodman
KENNADY, Moses	1781	
KENNARD, John	1796	Jonesboro
KENNEDA, Samuel	1818	Grimsley
KENNEDAY, David	1798	Gann
KENNEDAY, David	1798	Gann
KENNEDY, Dan	1781	
KENNEDY, Daniel	1779	Wilson
KENNEDY, Daniel	1781	
KENNEDY, David	1791	Hanley
KENNEDY, David	1799	Gann
KENNEDY, David	1799	Moore
KENNEDY, David Sr.	1799	Moore
KENNEDY, Hugh	1819	Sands
KENNEDY, James	1805	Carson
KENNEDY, Jno	1806	Anderson
KENNEDY, John	1801	Aiken
KENNEDY, John	1815	Garner
KENNEDY, John	1816	Smith
KENNEDY, John	1817	Smith
KENNEDY, John	1818	Smith
KENNEDY, John	1819	Smith
KENNEDY, John (Decd.; Enumerated with Matthew Pate)	1779	Wilson
KENNEDY, Samuel	1815	Grimsley
KENNEDY, Samuel	1816	Grimsley
KENNEDY, Samuel	1817	Grimsley
KENNEDY, Samuel	1819	Sands
KENNEDY, Scott	1815	Crookshanks
KENNEDY, William	1815	Carcathers
KENNEDY, William	1816	Giles
KENNEDY, William	1817	Gillises
KENNEDY, William	1818	Land
KENNEDY, William	1819	Sands
KENNEDY, Wm	1814	Couthers
KENNER, George	1807	Odell
KENNER, John	1778	
KENNER, John	1807	Odell
KENNER, Joseph	1816	Brown
KENNER, Joseph	1817	Brown
KENNER, Peter	1816	Brown
KENNER, Peter	1817	Brown
KENNER, Ulrick	1816	Brown
KENNER, Ulrick	1817	Brown
KENNOR, Joseph	1818	Brown
KENTFELL, Hanah	1808	Parker
KEPLENGER, Jacob	1816	Hampton
KEPLENGER, John	1816	Hampton
KEPLENGER, Samuel	1816	Hampton
KEPLINGER, Jacob	1807	Bayles
KEPLINGER, Jacob	1808	Bayles
KEPLINGER, Jacob	1814	Hampton
KEPLINGER, Jacob	1817	Hampton
KEPLINGER, Jacob	1818	Brown [2]
KEPLINGER, Jacob	1819	Brown
KEPLINGER, Jacob	1821	Brown
KEPLINGER, John	1807	Bayles
KEPLINGER, John	1808	Bayles
KEPLINGER, John	1814	Hampton
KEPLINGER, John	1817	Hampton
KEPLINGER, John	1818	Brown [2]
KEPLINGER, John	1819	Brown
KEPLINGER, John	1821	Brown
KEPLINGER, Sammuel	1808	Bayles
KEPLINGER, Samuel	1807	Bayles
KEPLINGER, Samuel	1814	Hampton
KEPLINGER, Samuel	1817	Hampton
KEPLINGER, Samuel	1818	Brown [2]
KEPLINGER, Samuel	1819	Brown
KEPLINGER, Samuel	1821	Brown
KERBY, Christopher	1796	Shipley
KERBY, Malachi	1801	Taylor
KERBY, Malbea	1797	Young
KERBY, Mallaby	1796	Young
KERCHEVALL, John	1781	
KERLAND, Joseph	1819	Brown
KERLEN, Joseph	1816	Hampton
KERLIN, Joseph	1808	Gwin
KERLIN, Joseph	1810	Green
KERLIN, Peter	1807	Anderson
KERLIN, William	1807	Payne
KERLIN, William	1819	McClure
KERLIN, William	1821	McClure
KERLON, William	1818	McClure
KERNAN, John	1795	Milliken
KERR, John	1790	Greer
KERR, John	1792	Greer
KERR, Philip	1795	Melvan
KERR, Robert	1781	
KESLIN, Joseph	1814	Crookshanks
KESLIN, Willm	1814	Crookshanks
KESSON, Nicholis	1818	Grisham
KEY, Phillip	1798	Duncan

Surname, Given names	Year	Comp./Dist.
KEYFAUVER, Necholes	1806	Guin
KEYFAUVER, Nicholas	1807	Givins
KEYFAUVER, Nicholes	1809	Gwin
KEYS, Isaac	1819	Hunt
KEYS, Philip	1806	Guin
KEYS, Philip	1811	Davis
KEYS, Philip	1814	McLin
KEYS, Phillips	1818	Hunt
KEYS, Pillip	1819	Hunt
KEYTH, Daniel	1781	
KIBLER, Jacob	1807	Cade
KIBLER, Jacob	1810	Barron
KIBLER, Jacob	1814	Barns
KIBLER, Jacob Jr.	1814	Barns
KIBLER, James	1810	Barron
KIBLER, Jams	1814	Barns
KIBLER, John	1810	Barron
KIBLER, John	1814	Barns
KICHEN, Conrod	1805	Jas Parker
KICHEN, John	1805	Jas Parker
KICHEN, Joseph	1805	Jas Parker
KICHER, Coonrad	1809	Parker
KICK, George	1811	Davis
KICKEN, Coonard	1808	Parker
KIDLY, Elijah	1819	Brown
KIEFHAVEN, Nicholis	1816	Copas
KIGER, Conrad	1799	Stuart
KIGER, John	1806	Brown
KIIS, Isaac	1817	Haire
KIIS, John	1815	Haire
KIIS, John	1817	Haire
KIIS, Philip	1817	Hunt
KIKER, Conrad	1816	Hampton
KIKER, Conrad	1817	Hampton
KIKER, Conrad	1817	Harris
KIKER, Conrad	1819	Harris
KIKER, John	1816	Hampton
KIKER, Joseph	1808	Parker
KIKER, Joseph	1810	Hartzel
KIKER, Joseph	1816	Hampton
KIKER, Joseph	1817	Hampton
KILBY, John	1815	Carcathers
KILE, John	1808	McAllister
KILLEN, Jacob	1808	Cade
KILLEY, Joshua	1811	Mitchell
KILLEY, Kinchen	1808	Carr
KILLEY, Kinchen	1811	Mitchell
KILLEY, Kinchen	1821	Jones
KILLEY, Kinchen	[1796] 1797	Morris
KILLEY, Kintchen	1793	Morrison
KILLEY, Kintchen	1794	Morrison
KILLEY, William	1811	Mitchell
KILLY, Kinchen	1809	Carr
KILLY, Kinchen	1814	Hoss
KILNY, John	1816	Giles
KILSEY, John	1809	Patterson
KILSEY, John	1817	Gillises
KIMALL, John	1801	Gann
KIMMAN, Robert	1806	Brown
KIMMENS, Robert	1814	Hampton
KIMMINGS, Joseph	1793	Handley
KIMMINS, Robert	1808	Bayles
KIMMISS, Robert	1807	Bayles
KIMMONS, Robert	1809	Bayles
KINARD, John	1796	Calvert
KINCHALO, John	1818	Grimsley
KINCHALOW, George	1819	Grimsley
KINCHALOW, James	1819	Grimsley
KINCHALOW, William	1819	Grimsley
KINCHELOE, Charles	1794	Murray
KINCHELOE, Charles	1795	Murray
KINCHELOE, Charles	1797	Shipley
KINCHELOE, Charles	1805	Rector
KINCHELOE, Charles	1807	Cade
KINCHELOE, Charles	1808	Cade
KINCHELOE, Charles	1810	Barron
KINCHELOE, Charles	1812	Barnes
KINCHELOE, Elijah	1801	Glasscock
KINCHELOE, Elijah	1810	Barron
KINCHELOE, Elijah	1811	Barron
KINCHELOE, Elijah	1812	Barnes
KINCHELOE, Enoch	1797	Shipley
KINCHELOE, Enoch	1798	Shipley
KINCHELOE, Enoch	1805	Rector
KINCHELOE, Enoch	1807	Cade
KINCHELOE, Enoch	1808	Cade
KINCHELOE, Enoch	1812	Barnes
KINCHELOE, Enock	1810	Barron
KINCHELOE, George	1793	Murray
KINCHELOE, George	1794	Murray
KINCHELOE, George	1795	Murray
KINCHELOE, George	1797	Shipley
KINCHELOE, George	1798	Shipley
KINCHELOE, George	1801	Glasscock
KINCHELOE, George	1805	Rector
KINCHELOE, George	1807	Cade
KINCHELOE, George	1808	Cade
KINCHELOE, George	1810	Barron
KINCHELOE, George	1811	Barron
KINCHELOE, George	1812	Barnes
KINCHELOE, George	1815	Haire
KINCHELOE, George	1817	Grimsley

Surname, Given names	Year	Comp./Dist.
KINCHELOE, George	1821	Martin
KINCHELOE, Gorge	1809	Cade
KINCHELOE, Gorge	1814	Barns
KINCHELOE, John	1793	Murray
KINCHELOE, John	1794	Murray
KINCHELOE, John	1795	Murray
KINCHELOE, John	1797	Shipley
KINCHELOE, John	1798	Shipley
KINCHELOE, John	1801	Glasscock
KINCHELOE, John	1805	Rector
KINCHELOE, John	1807	Cade
KINCHELOE, John	1808	Cade
KINCHELOE, John	1809	Cade
KINCHELOE, John	1810	Barron
KINCHELOE, John	1811	Barron
KINCHELOE, John	1811	Barron
KINCHELOE, John	1812	Barnes
KINCHELOE, Lijah	1798	Shipley
KINCHELOE, Wilam	1821	Martin
KINCHELOE, William	1815	Grimsley
KINCHELOR, Enoch	1817	Grimsley
KINCHELOR, George	1816	Hair
KINCHELOR, John	1817	Grimsley
KINCHELOR, William	1817	Grimsley
KINCHER, Killy	1818	Jones
KINCHER, Koonrad Jr.	1806	Brown
KINCHLOE, Charles	1792	Depew
KINCHLOE, Enoch	1816	Grimsley
KINCHLOE, Enoch	1818	Grimsley
KINCHLOE, George	1816	Grimsley
KINCHLOE, George	1818	Grimsley
KINCHLOE, James	1818	Grimsley
KINCHLOE, John	1814	Barns
KINCHLOE, John	1815	Grimsley
KINCHLOE, John	1816	Grimsley
KINCHLOE, William	1816	Grimsley
KINCHLOE, William	1818	Grimsley
KINCHLOW, Enoch	1801	Glasscock
KINCHLOW, Enoch	1819	Grimsley
KINCHLOW, John	1819	Grimsley
KINDAL, Barbary	1797	Calvert
KINDAL, William	1812	McCray
KINDALE, William	1812	McCray
KINDALL, George	1791	Willey
KINDELL, George	1794	Scot
KINDEN, Joseph	1817	Hampton
KINDLE, Barbara	1801	Calvert
KINDLE, Barbary	1796	Calvert
KINDLE, Barbary	1805	Jas Parker
KINDLE, Barbery	1798	Calvert
KINDLE, Barbery	1799	Stuart
KINDLE, Geo	1795	Calvert
KINDLE, James	1809	McAlister
KINDLE, William	1814	McCray
KINEDY, David	1809	McAlister
KINEDY, David	1809	McAlister
KING, Billy (heirs)	1821	Jones
KING, Billy F. (estate of)	1818	Jones
KING, Billy F. (estate)	1817	Little
KING, Billy F. (estate)	1819	Jones
KING, Francis (heirs)	1816	Hoss
KING, Henneary	1813	Hoss
KING, Henry	1790	Biddle
KING, Henry	1791	Biddle
KING, Henry	1792	Biddle
KING, Henry	1793	Biddle
KING, Henry	1793	Hale
KING, Henry	1794	Blair
KING, Henry	1798	Morrison
KING, Henry	1798	Morrison
KING, Henry	1798	Morrison
KING, Henry	1799	Morrison
KING, Henry	1801	Morrison
KING, Henry	1806	Carr
KING, Henry	1807	Carr
KING, Henry	1808	Carr
KING, Henry	1809	Carr
KING, Henry	1811	Mitchell
KING, Henry	1814	Hoss
KING, Henry	1815	Hoss
KING, Henry	1816	Hoss
KING, Henry	1817	Little
KING, Henry	1818	Jones
KING, Henry	1819	Jones
KING, Henry	1821	Jones
KING, Henry Jr.	1821	Jones
KING, Isaac	1806	Crouch
KING, James	1791	Willey
KING, James	1801	Morrison
KING, James	1806	Carr
KING, James	1808	Carr
KING, James	1811	Mitchell
KING, James	1814	Hoss
KING, James	1815	Hoss
KING, James	1816	Hoss
KING, James	1817	Little
KING, James	1821	Jones
KING, James (Rev.)	1818	Jones
KING, James (Rev.)	1819	Jones
KING, John	1815	Hoss
KING, Jonathan	1819	Hair
KING, Kirbe	1794	Murray

Surname, Given names	Year	Comp./Dist.
KING, Martha	1809	Right
KING, Martha	1811	Ellis
KING, -ruth	1796	Shipley
KING, Thomas	1798	Morrison
KING, Thomas	1799	Morrison
KING, Thomas	1801	Morrison
KING, Thomas	1805	Carson
KING, Thomas	1806	Carson
KING, Thomas	1807	Carr
KING, Thomas	1807	Shields
KING, Thomas	1808	Carr
KING, Thomas	1809	Carr
KING, Thomas	1809	Patterson
KING, Thomas	1810	Dimmons
KING, Thomas	1811	Mitchell
KING, Thomas	1811	
KING, Thomas	1815	Carcathers
KING, Thomas	1816	Copas
KING, Thomas	1816	Giles
KING, Thomas	1817	Gillises
KING, Thomas	1817	Grisham
KING, Thomas	1818	Grisham
KING, Thomas	1818	Land
KING, Thomas	1819	Sands
KING, Thomas	1821	Jones
KING, Thomas	1821	Sands
KING, Thomas	[1796] 1797	Morris
KING, Thomes	1806	Carr
KING, Thos	1814	Couthers
KING, Walter	1796	Brown
KING, Walter	1816	Hampton
KING, Walter	1817	Hampton
KING, Walter	1818	Brown [2]
KING, Walter	1819	Brown
KING, Walter	1821	Brown
KING, William	1791	
KING, William	1792	Maxwell
KING, William	1793	Maxwell
KING, William	1798	Morrison
KING, William	1798	Morrison
KING, William	1798	Morrison
KING, William	1799	Morrison
KING, William	1801	Morrison
KING, William	1806	Carr
KING, William	1807	Carr
KING, William	1808	Carr
KING, William	1811	Mitchell
KING, William	1813	Hoss
KING, William	1814	Hoss
KING, William	1816	Hoss
KING, William	1817	Little
KING, William	1818	Jones
KING, William	1819	Jones
KING, William	1821	Jones
KING, William F.	1815	Hoss
KING, William Sr.	1815	Hoss
KING, Wm	1809	Carr
KINNARD, John	1818	Smith
KINNARD, John	1819	Smith
KINNARD, John	1821	Smith
KINNARD, Mary	1820	Smith
KINNARD, Mary	1821	Smith
KINNARD, Thomas	1819	Smith
KINNARD, Thomas	1820	Smith
KINTCHELOE, Charles	1796	Shipley
KIPPEE, Jacob	1811	
KIRDENDAL, Jas	1780-1781 (Undated)	
KIRK, George	1812	McLin
KIRK, George	1814	McLin
KIRK, George	1815	McLin
KIRK, George	1816	Hunt
KIRK, George	1817	Hunt
KIRK, George	1818	Hunt
KIRK, George	1819	Hunt
KIRK, George	1821	Hunt
KIRKENDAL, Adam	1780-1781 (Undated)	
KIRKINDALL, Jno	1780-1781 (Undated)	
KIRLEN, Joseph	1818	Brown [2]
KIRLIN, Joseph	1801	Roberson
KIRLIN, Joseph	1815	Crookshanks
KIRLIN, William	1815	Crookshanks
KIRTZ, John	1806	Guin
KITCLLILAR, Martin	1818	Hair
KITE, Isaac	1792	Greer
KITE, Isaac	1794	Carriger
KITE, Richard	1792	Carriger
KITE, Richard	1794	Carriger
KITE, Richard	1795	Carriger
KITE, Richd	1790	Greer
KITSMILLER, Martain	1806	Crouch
KITSMILLER, Martin	1814	Bean
KITSMILLER, Martin	1815	Haire
KITSMILLER, Martin	1819	Hair
KITSMILLER, Martin	1821	Louis
KITZMILLER, Martin	1809	Right
KITZMILLER, Martin	1811	Ellis
KITZMILLER, Martin	1812	Ellis
KITZMILLER, Martin	1816	Hair
KITZMILLER, Martin	1817	Haire
KNODY, William Jr.	1792	Scott
KNOWLAN, John	1779	

Surname, Given names	Year	Comp./Dist.
KOBENGER, Hogan	1811	Barron
KONIN, John	1808	Cade
KONKEN, John	1815	Grimsley
KONKIN, Gorge	1808	Cade
KONKIN, Moses	1814	Barns
KONKING, John	1814	Barns
KONTZ, John	1814	McLin
KOON, Catherine	1816	Hoss
KOON, Catherine	1817	Little
KOON, Catherine	1818	Jones
KOON, Peter	1817	Little
KOON, Peter	1818	Jones
KOONCE, Catherine	1819	Jones
KOONCE, Peter	1819	Jones
KOONE, Cathrin (widow)	1813	Hoss
KORLEN, William	1811	McAlister
KORTS, John	1819	Hunt
KORTZ, John	1808	Guin
KORTZ, John	1812	McLin
KORTZ, John	1816	Hunt
KORTZ, John	1817	Hunt
KORTZ, John	1818	Hunt
KORTZ, John	1821	Hunt
KREDIL, Willm	1798	Longmire
KROUZ, Michail	1812	Ellis
KUFHAVER, Nicholas	1815	Copas
KUHN, Catharine	1821	Jones
KUHN, Peter	1821	Jones
KUNES, John	1801	Longmire
KUYHENDOL, Abm	1781	
KUYHENDOL, Adam	1781	
KUYHENDOL, James	1781	
KUYHENDOL, Jon	1781	
KUYKENDAL, Petter	1780-1781 (Undated)	
KUYKENDALL, Benjamin	1780-1781 (undated)	
KUYKENDOL, Peter	1781	
KYCKER, Coonrad	1812	McCray
KYCKER, Joseph	1812	McCray
KYE, Phillip	1797	Duncan
KYGLER, Conrad	1798	Calvert
KYKER, Conrad	1811	McCray
KYKER, Conrad	1812	McCray
KYKER, Conrad	1818	Brown [2]
KYKER, Conrad	1818	Harris
KYKER, Conrad	1819	Brown
KYKER, Conrad	1821	Brown
KYKER, Conrod	1807	Bayles
KYKER, Conrod	1808	Bayles
KYKER, Conrod	1814	Hampton
KYKER, Conrod	1814	McCray

Surname, Given names	Year	Comp./Dist.
KYKER, Coonrad	1821	Hampton
KYKER, John	1807	Bayles
KYKER, John	1808	Bayles
KYKER, John	1814	Hampton
KYKER, John	1819	Brown
KYKER, John	1821	Brown
KYKER, Joseph	1811	McCray
KYKER, Joseph	1812	McCray
KYKER, Joseph	1814	McCray
KYKER, Joseph	1818	Brown [2]
KYKER, Joseph	1819	Brown
KYKER, Joseph	1821	Brown
KYKER, Peter	1819	Brown
KYKER, Peter	1821	Brown
LACEY, James	1794	Carriger
LACEY, John	1795	Carriger
LACEY, Philemon	1794	Carriger
LACEY, Philimon	1792	Maxwell
LACHINS, Robert	1798	Biddle
LACHUS, Robert	1801	Biddle
LACKEY, John	1808	Bayles
LACKEY, Thomas	1819	Smith
LACKEY, Thomas	1820	Smith
LACKEY, Thomas	1821	Smith
LACKEY, Thos	1792	Maxwell
LACKEY, Thos	1793	Maxwell
LACKEY, Thos	1805	Aikin
LACKEY, William Jr.	1808	Bayles
LACKEY, Wm W.	1809	Bayles
LACKINS, Wm	1799	Duncan
LACKY, John	1815	Garner
LACKY, John	1816	Smith
LACKY, John	1817	Smith
LACKY, John Jr.	1805	Aikin
LACKY, Joseph	1817	Smith
LACKY, Thomas	1806	Anderson
LACKY, Thomas	1809	Roadmas
LACKY, Thomas	1814	McCracken
LACKY, Thomas	1815	Garner
LACKY, Thomas	1816	Smith
LACKY, Thomas	1817	Smith
LACKY, Thomas	1818	Smith
LACY, Fileman	1792	Carriger
LACY, John	1790	Greer
LACY, John	1792	Carriger
LACY, John	1792	Greer
LACY, Philemon	1795	Carriger
LACY, Thomas	1815	Waddell
LACY, Thomas	1816	Waddell
LACY, Thomas	1818	Riley
LACY, Thomas	1819	Findley

Surname, Given names	Year	Comp./Dist.
LAIN, Corbin	1781	
LAIN, Corbin	1780-1781 (Undated)	
LAIN, Elias	1778	
LAIN, Lewis	1778	
LAIN, Saml	1814	Couthers
LAIN, Samuel	1798	Shipley
LAIN, Samuel	1806	Doke
LAIN, Tidance	1798	Shipley
LAIN, Tidance	1806	Doke
LAINE, Tidance	1795	Murray
LAIRD, Moses	1778	
LAMAN, John	1790	Milleken
LAMEN, Christofer	1805	Parker
LAMEN, John	1805	Parker
LAMMAN, Chrytian	1811	McAlister
LAMMAN, Joseph	1811	McAlister
LAMMEN, Joseph	1817	McClure
LAMMON, Abraham	1779	
LAMMON, Chrisley	1817	McClure
LAMMON, John	1779	
LAMON, Abraham	1809	Bayles
LAMON, Abraham	1812	Hartsell
LAMON, Abraham	1815	Crookshanks
LAMON, Alexn	1793	North
LAMON, Brisley	1806	Brown
LAMON, Chisely	1815	Crookshanks
LAMON, David	1797	Robertson
LAMON, David	1799	Robertson
LAMON, David	1801	Roberson
LAMON, David	1809	Bayles
LAMON, David	1816	Hampton
LAMON, David	1821	Brown
LAMON, David Sr.	1806	Brown
LAMON, Emanuel	1816	Hampton
LAMON, Jacob	1797	Gann
LAMON, Jacob	1821	Brown
LAMON, John	1793	North
LAMON, John	1797	Gann
LAMON, John	1806	Brown
LAMON, John	1809	Bayles
LAMON, John	1816	Hampton
LAMON, Joseph	1806	Brown
LAMON, Joseph	1815	Crookshanks
LAMONS, John	1793	North
LANCY, Joseph	1818	Brown
LAND, Bond (Heirs)	1797	Robertson
LAND, Thomas	1817	Riley
LANDS, Benjamons	1814	Couthers
LANE, Abraham	1815	Carcathers
LANE, Abraham	1816	Giles
LANE, Abraham	1821	Sands
LANE, Adron	1801	Lane
LANE, Dutton	1781	
LANE, Elizabeth	1790	Shipley
LANE, Elizabeth	1791	Shipley
LANE, Robert	1814	Brown
LANE, Samuel	1797	Shipley
LANE, Samuel	1801	Lane
LANE, Samuel	1809	Cade
LANE, Samuel	1810	Barron
LANE, Samuel	1811	Barron
LANE, Samuel	1812	Barnes
LANE, Samuel	1814	Barns
LANE, Samuel	1815	Carcathers
LANE, Samuel	1816	Giles
LANE, Samul	1805	Doak
LANE, Tedance	1811	Britten
LANE, Tidance	1794	Murray
LANE, Tidance	1797	Shipley
LANE, Tidance	1812	Britton
LANE, Tidance	1814	Copes
LANE, Tidenc	1805	Doak
LANE, Tidence	1797	Shipley
LANE, Tidence	1801	Lane
LANE, Tidence	1813	Copas
LANGFORD,	1821	Smith
LANIER, John	1781	
LANIER, Moses Carson	1814	Couthers
LANNER, Massy	1806	Anderson
LARD, Levie	1791	Tullis
LARGE, Joseph	1792	Greer
LARGE, Joseph	1794	Carriger
LARGE, Joseph	1795	Carriger
LARGE, Robert	1793	Maxwell
LARGE, Robert	1794	Carriger
LARKBROOKS, John	1807	Bayles
LARKBROOKS, John	1808	Bayles
LARKBROOKS, Wm	1807	Bayles
LARKIN, John	1810	Barron
LARKINS, James	1793	Scott
LARKINS, Jesse	1792	Milliken
LARMER, Masey	1807	Anderson
LARNS, Abram	1780-1781	District 7
LARRENCE, Jno	1780-1781 (Undated)	
LASCON, Abram	1796	Brown
LASHBROAKS, Wm	1796	Longmire
LASHBROOKS, John	1809	Bayles
LASHBROOKS, William	1806	Brown
LASHBROOKS, William	1809	Bayles
LASHLEY, Charles	1818	Hair
LASHLEY, Jesse	1814	Copes
LASHLEY, Jesse	1815	Haire

Surname, Given names	Year	Comp./Dist.
LASHLEY, Jesse	1816	Hair
LASHLEY, Jesse	1817	Haire
LASHLEY, Jesse	1818	Hair
LASHLEY, Jesse	1819	Hair
LASLEY, Jesse	1813	Copas
LATHAM, John	[1796] 1797	Morris
LAUDEMILK, John	1821	Jones
LAW, Abraham	1817	Gillises
LAW, Abraham	1818	Land
LAW, Andrew	1798	Crouch
LAW, Archibald	1819	Sands
LAW, James	1805	Stephenson
LAW, Rebins	1818	Brown
LAW, Samuel	1818	Brown
LAW, Thomas	1818	Brown
LAY, Jessee	1795	Ford
LAYFOLLET, George	1817	Riley
LAYFOLLET, George	1818	Riley
LAYFOLLET, Jeremiah	1817	Riley
LAYMAN, Chris	1798	Longmire
LAYMAN, Christian	1808	Bayles
LAYMAN, Christopher	1795	Young
LAYMAN, Christopher	1801	Longmire
LAYMAN, David	1808	Bayles
LAYMAN, Jacob	1801	Gann
LAYMAN, John	1793	Handley
LAYMAN, John	1794	Handly
LAYMAN, John	1801	Gann
LAYMAN, John	1808	Bayles
LAYMAN, John Jr.	1795	Young
LAYMAN, Thomas	1805	Stephenson
LAYMON, Christian	1807	Bayles
LAYMON, David	1807	Bayles
LAYMON, David	1814	Hampton
LAYMON, Jacob	1796	Handly
LAYMON, John	1795	Handly
LAYMON, John	1807	Bayles
LAYMON, Nanny	1814	Hampton
LAYMONS, John	1814	Hampton
LAYSAY, Thomas	1821	McGee
LEACH, James	1805	Parker
LEACH, James	1806	Parker
LEACH, James	1810	Hartzel
LEACH, James	1812	Hartsell
LEACH, James	1814	Hartsell
LEACH, James	1815	Fines
LEACH, James	1816	Fine
LEACH, James	1817	Fine
LEACH, James	1819	Howard
LEACH, James	1821	Howard
LEACH, John	1808	Parker
LEACH, Wiliam Sr.	1805	Parker
LEACH, William	1796	Young
LEACH, William	1797	Young
LEACH, William	1806	Brown
LEACH, William	1806	Parker
LEACH, William	1814	Hartsell
LEACH, William	1815	Fines
LEACH, William	1816	Fine
LEACH, William	1817	Fine
LEACH, William	1819	Howard
LEACH, William	1821	Howard
LEACH, William Jr.	1807	Parker
LEACH, William Jr.	1808	Parker
LEACH, William Jr.	1810	Hartzel
LEACH, William Sr.	1806	Parker
LEACH, William Sr.	1807	Parker
LEACH, William Sr.	1808	Parker
LEACH, William Sr.	1810	Hartzel
LEACH, Wm	1792	Scott
LEACH, Wm	1795	Young
LEACH, Wm	1797	Robertson
LEACH, Wm	1801	Taylor
LEAMON, David	1817	Hampton
LEAMON, Jacob	1817	Hampton
LEAMON, John	1791	Hanley
LEAMON, John	1817	Hampton
LEAT, Thos	1790	Milleken
LEATEH, William	1791	North
LEATHERN, John	1795	Morrison
LEAVY, Hartman	1821	Sands
LEAZERWOOD, Natt	1814	Waddell
LECH, John	1792	Milliken
LECH, William	1809	Par
LEE, Clemment	1795	Morrison
LEE, Nicolas	1781	
LEE, Thomas	1781	
LEECH, James	1818	Fine
LEECH, Jas	1809	Par
LEECH, Joseph	1778	
LEECH, William	1793	North
LEECH, William	1809	Par
LEECK, William	1818	Fine
LEEMAN, John	1790	Hanley
LELA, William	1812	Crawford [2]
LELBURN, Andrew	1817	Fine
LELBURN, Andrew Jr.	1815	Fines
LELBURN, Andrew Jr.	1816	Fine
LELBURN, Andrew Jr.	1817	Fine
LELBURN, Andrew Sr.	1815	Fines
LELBURN, Andrew Sr.	1816	Fine
LEMAN, __rid	1792	Brown

Surname, Given names	Year	Comp./Dist.
LEMAN, Abraham	1792	North
LEMAN, John Jr.	1791	North
LEMAN, John Jr.	1792	North
LEMAN, John Sr.	1791	North
LEMAN, John Sr.	1792	North
LEMANS, Chitefor	1794	Brown
LEMANS, David	1794	Brown
LEMANS, Jacob	1794	Brown
LEMANS, Joseph	1814	Crookshanks
LEMENS, William	1780-1781 (Undated)	
LEMMENS, Crestly	1809	McAlister
LEMMON, John	1799	Moore
LEMMON, William	1779	
LEMMONS, David	1796	Brown
LEMMONS, Jacob	1799	Moore
LEMMONS, Joseph	1809	McAlister
LEMON, Chrisley	1819	McClure
LEMON, Christopher	1808	McAllister
LEMON, Cristopher	1812	Crawford [2]
LEMON, David	1818	Brown [2]
LEMON, David	1819	Brown
LEMON, Emanuel	1817	Hampton
LEMON, Emanuel	1818	Brown [2]
LEMON, Emanuel	1819	Brown
LEMON, Jacob	1798	Gann
LEMON, Jacob	1818	Brown [2]
LEMON, Jacob	1819	Brown
LEMON, John	1798	Gann
LEMON, John	1818	Brown [2]
LEMON, John	1819	Brown
LEMON, Joseph	1808	McAllister
LEMON, Joseph	1812	Crawford [2]
LEMONS, Abraham	1814	Crookshanks
LEMONS, Chrisley	1818	McClure
LEMONS, Christy	1814	Crookshanks
LEMONS, Cristopher	1812	Crawford
LEMONS, Jacob	1793	Brown
LEMONS, Joseph	1812	Crawford
LEMONS, Joseph	1818	McClure
LEMONS, William	1781	
LENBERGER, Nicholas	1817	Hampton
-LENO, Nathanal	1780-1781 (Undated)	
LERN, Samuel	1812	Crawford [2]
LESENBY, Charles	1821	Louis
LESLIE, John	1819	Smith
LESSLIE, Jonathan	1820	Smith
LESSLIE, Jonathan	1821	Smith
LETHERMAN, Nicholas	1819	Howard
LETSINGER, Philip	1807	Shields
LETSINGER, Phillip	1806	Carson

Surname, Given names	Year	Comp./Dist.
LETSINGER, Phillip	1809	Patterson
LETSINGOR, Phillip	1805	Carson
LETTERMAN, Nicholis	1816	Fine
LETTERMAN, Nicholis	1817	Fine
LETTERMAN, William	1794	North
LEVER, Joseph	1792	Carriger
LEWES, Joel	1809	Carr
LEWIS, Aaron	1779	
LEWIS, Aaron	1781	
LEWIS, James	1799	Moore
LEWIS, James	1799	Moore
LEWIS, James	1815	Fines
LEWIS, John Sr.	1799	Moore
LEWIS, Jonas	1816	Fine
LEWIS, Obediah	1799	Gann
LEWIS, Obediah	1801	Gann
LEWIS, Samuel	1819	Hunt
LEWIS, Samuel	1821	Smith
LEWIS, Sollomon	1807	Odell
LEWIS, Solomon	1806	Odel
LEWIS, Surrel	1778	
LEWIS, Thos	1790	Williams
LEWIS, Thos	1791	Williams
LEWIS, William	1792	Coye
LEWIS, William	1793	Hale
LEWIS, William	1796	Longmire
LEWIS, William	1797	Longmire
LEWIS, William	1801	Longmire
LEWIS, William	1806	Odel
LEWIS, William	1807	Odell
LEWIS, William	1808	Odell
LEWIS, William	1810	Cove
LEWIS, Wm	1798	Longmire
LIALER, Wymor	1781	
LIDENER, Martin	1801	Calvert
LIGHT, John	1814	Hoss
LIGHTEN, Christian	1819	Sands
LIGHTNEN, Christen	1812	McCray
LIGHTNER, Christain	1812	McCray
LIGHTNER, Christian	1811	McCray
LIGHTNER, Christian	1821	Hampton
LIKEINGS, William	1798	Duncan
LIKUNGS, William	1797	Duncan
LILBIN, Andrew	1805	Parker
LILBORN, Andrew	1796	Young
LILBURN, Andrew	1792	Scott
LILBURN, Andrew	1793	Scott
LILBURN, Andrew	1797	Robertson
LILBURN, Andrew	1801	Taylor
LILBURN, Andrew	1806	Parker
LILBURN, Andrew	1807	Parker

Surname, Given names	Year	Comp./Dist.
LILBURN, Andrew	1808	Parker
LILBURN, Andrew	1809	Par
LILBURN, Andrew	1812	Hartsell
LILBURN, Andrew	1814	Hartsell
LILBURN, Andrew	1818	Fine
LILBURN, Andrew	1818	Fine
LILBURN, Andrew	1821	Howard
LILE, Henry	1779	
LILE, John (Captain)	1780-1781 (Undated)	
LILFORD, Thomas	1808	McAllister
LILLERSEN, Andrew	1819	Howard
LILLERSEN, Andrew Sr.	1819	Howard
LILLOM, Andrew	1795	Calvert
LILLUM, Andrew	1810	Hartzel
LINCKHORN, Isaac	1779	
LINCOLN, Isaac	1790	Greer
LINCOLN, Isaac	1792	Carriger
LINCOLN, Isaac	1792	Greer
LINCOLN, Isaac	1794	Carriger
LINCOLN, Isaac	1795	Carriger
LINCOLN, Isaac	1814	Hoss
LINCOLN, Isaac	1815	Hoss
LINDSAY, Mathew (Over age)	1792	White
LINDSAY, Matthew (Over age)	1791	White
LINDSEY, Matthew	1793	Campbell
LINDSEY, Matthew	1794	Thornton
LINEBARGER, Nicholous	1809	Bayles
LINEBERGER, Nicholas	1806	Brown
LINEBERGER, Nicholas	1807	Bayles
LINEBERGER, Nicholas	1819	Brown
LINEBERGER, Nicolas	1808	Bayles
LINEBERGER, Nicolas	1814	Hampton
LINEBURGER, Charles	1821	Brown
LINEBURGER, Nicholas	1821	Brown
LINEBURGER, Nicholus	1801	Roberson
LINEBURGER, Nicoles	1818	Brown [2]
LINIRT, Moses	1779	Wilson
LINK, John	1819	McClure
LINK, John	1821	McClure
LINKHORN, Isaac	1811	Mitchell
LINKLEY, Charles	1817	Little
LINKLEY, William	1817	Little
LINSALE, Moses	1821	Martin
LINVEL, Thomas	1812	Hartsell
LINVILL, Thomas	1814	McCray
LINVILLE, Thomas	1818	Harris
LION, Asher	1816	Hunt
LION, Ezekel	1807	Givins
LION, Ezekel Jr.	1807	Givins
LION, Ezekiel	1806	Crouch
LION, Ezekiel	1816	Hunt
LION, Ezekiel	1780-1781 (Undated)	
LION, Ezekiel Jr.	1816	Hunt
LION, William	1816	Hunt
LION, Zekel Sr.	1806	Guin
LIONS, Ezekel Jr.	1809	Gwin
LIONS, Ezekel Sr.	1809	Gwin
LIONS, Ezekiel	1809	Viney
LIONS, Ezekiel Jr.	1815	McLin
LIONS, Ezekiel Sr.	1815	McLin
LIONS, John	1807	Odell
LIONS, William	1809	Gwin
LIONS, William	1812	McLin
LIONS, William	1815	McLin
LIONS, Zekiel Jr.	1812	McLin
LISEMBAY, Abraham	1809	Gwin
LISENBY, Abraham	1811	Davis
LISENBY, Abraham	1812	Britton
LISENLY, Charles	1819	Hair
LISENLY, William	1815	McLin
LISENLY, William	1819	Hair
LISSENBAY, Abraham	1808	Guin
LITHERMAN, Nicholis	1818	Fine
LITTELL, Jonas	1791	Tullis
LITTLE, Andrew	1778	
LITTLE, Andrew	1779	
LITTLE, George	1792	Tulley
LITTLE, Isaac	1816	Hoss
LITTLE, Isaac	1817	Little
LITTLE, Isaac	1818	Jones
LITTLE, Isaac	1818	Jones
LITTLE, Isaac	1819	Jones
LITTLE, Isaac (Cap.)	1817	Little
LITTLE, John	1792	Coye
LITTLE, John	1793	Morrison
LITTLE, John	1794	Morrison
LITTLE, John	1795	Morrison
LITTLE, John	1798	Morrison
LITTLE, John	1801	Morrison
LITTLE, John	1806	Carr
LITTLE, John	1807	Carr
LITTLE, John	1808	Carr
LITTLE, John	1809	Carr
LITTLE, John	1811	Mitchell
LITTLE, John	[1796] 1797	Morris
LITTLE, John (estate of)	1815	Hoss
LITTLE, John (estate)	1817	Little
LITTLE, John (estate)	1819	Jones
LITTLE, John (heirs)	1821	Jones
LITTLE, John Eason	1818	Jones
LITTLE, Jonah	1798	Morrison
LITTLE, Jonah	1807	Carr

Surname, Given names	Year	Comp./Dist.
LITTLE, Jonah	1808	Carr
LITTLE, Jonah	[1796] 1797	Morris
LITTLE, Jonas	1778	
LITTLE, Jonas	1779	
LITTLE, Jonas	1779	
LITTLE, Jonas	1779	
LITTLE, Jonas	1792	Tulley
LITTLE, Jonas	1793	Morrison
LITTLE, Jonas	1794	Morrison
LITTLE, Jonas	1809	Carr
LITTLE, Jonas	1811	Mitchell
LITTLE, Jonas	1814	Hoss
LITTLE, Jonas	1815	Hoss
LITTLE, Jonas	1816	Hoss
LITTLE, Jonas	1818	Jones
LITTLE, Jonas (estate)	1819	Jones
LITTLE, Jonas (heirs)	1821	Jones
LITTLE, Jones	1795	Morrison
LITTLE, Jones	1801	Morrison
LITTLE, Jonh	1806	Carr
LITTLE, Jonis	1813	Hoss
LITTLE, Mathias	1778	
LITTLE, Mathias	1779	
LITTLE, Thomas	1794	Carriger
LITTLE, Thomas (Single)	1779	
LITTLE, Valentine	1778	
LITTLE, Valentine	1779	
LOADERMILK, Henry	1817	Little
LOCKERD, John	1807	Parker
LOCKERD, Robert	1794	Taylor
LOCKERD, William	1794	Taylor
LOCKEY, Thomas	1794	Taylor
LODERWICK, John	1819	Jones
LOGAN, Charles	1790	Hanley
LOGAN, Charles	1791	Hanley
LOGAN, Charles	1795	Milliken
LOGAN, George	1795	Ford
LOGGAN, Charles	1793	Handley
LONAIRINAH, Henry	1818	Jones
LONG, Christian	1817	Riley
LONG, Christian	1818	Riley
LONG, Christian	1819	Harris
LONG, Christian	1821	Hampton
LONG, Henry	1790	Stone
LONG, Henry	1791	Stone
LONG, Henry	1817	Riley
LONG, Henry	1818	Riley
LONG, Henry	1819	Findley
LONG, James	1805	Aikin
LONG, James	1806	Anderson
LONG, James	1807	Anderson
LONG, James	1809	Roadmas
LONG, James	1811	Rodman
LONG, James	1814	Hartsell
LONG, James	1815	Fines
LONG, James	1816	Harrison
LONG, James Guinn Sr.	1793	Campbell
LONG, Joseph	1821	Haines
LONG, Nicholas	1799	Hannah
LONG, Patrick	1806	Anderson
LONG, Patrick	1807	Anderson
LONG, Patrick	1809	Right
LONG, Patrik	1805	Aikin
LONGMARIS, Sarah	1816	Brown
LONGMIERS, George	1809	Viney
LONGMIERS, Joseph	1809	Viney
LONGMIERS, Joseph	1810	Cove
LONGMIERS, Joseph	1814	Brown
LONGMIERS, Sary	1814	Brown
LONGMIR, John	1796	Longmire
LONGMIRE, Charles	1792	Coye
LONGMIRE, Charles	1793	Hale
LONGMIRE, Charles	1796	Longmire
LONGMIRE, Charles	1797	Longmire
LONGMIRE, Chas	1798	Longmire
LONGMIRE, George	1806	Odel
LONGMIRE, George	1808	Odell
LONGMIRE, George	1811	Brown
LONGMIRE, George	1812	Brown
LONGMIRE, George	1818	Brown
LONGMIRE, John	1797	Longmire
LONGMIRE, John	1798	Longmire
LONGMIRE, John	1801	Longmire
LONGMIRE, John Everton (for Charles Longmire estate)	1801	Longmire
LONGMIRE, Joseph	1801	Longmire
LONGMIRE, Joseph	1806	Odel
LONGMIRE, Joseph	1808	Odell
LONGMIRE, Joseph	1811	Brown
LONGMIRE, Joseph	1815	Hartsell
LONGMIRE, Joseph	1816	Brown
LONGMIRE, Joseph	1817	Brown
LONGMIRE, Joseph	1818	Brown
LONGMIRE, Joseph	1819	Brown
LONGMIRE, Joseph	1821	Haines
LONGMIRE, Sarah	1815	Hartsell
LONGMIRE, Sarah	1817	Brown
LONGMIRES, George	1807	Odell
LONGMIRES, Joseph	1807	Odell
LONGMIRES, Joseph	1812	Brown
LOPEWASSER, Conrad	1821	Brown
LOPEWASSER, George	1821	Brown
LOPEWASSER, Joseph	1821	Brown

Surname, Given names	Year	Comp./Dist.
LORD, Abel	1794	Blair
LORD, Joseph	1794	Ford
LOSSOSSER, Conrad	1819	Brown
LOT, Casher	1812	Waddill
LOT, Casher	1816	Waddell
LOT, Casper	1805	Guir
LOT, Casper	1811	Green
LOT, Casper	1814	Waddell
LOT, Casper	1819	Findley
LOT, Gasper	1798	Hannah
LOT, John	1819	Findley
LOTT, Casper	1815	Waddell
LOTT, Casper	1817	Riley
LOTT, Casper	1818	Riley
LOTT, Gasper	1790	Milleken
LOTT, Gasper	1792	Milliken
LOTT, Gasper	1796	Millikin
LOTT, Gasper	1797	Hannah
LOTT, Jasper	1793	Milliken
LOTT, Jasper	1799	Hannah
LOTT, Jasper	1806	Grur
LOTT, John	1817	Riley
LOTT, John	1818	Riley
LOTT, John	1821	McGee
LOTT, Roda	1821	McGee
LOTTS, Jesse	1780-1781	District 7
LOUDERWICK, Henry	1819	Jones
LOUIS, Samuel	1821	Louis
LOULY, Wm L.	1792	Scott
LOVE, James (Capt.)	1791	
LOVE, Jesse	1817	Little
LOVE, R.	1801	Longmire
LOVE, R.	1806	Odel
LOVE, R. (Adminr of Thomas Howells Estate)	1806	Odel
LOVE, Robert	1797	Longmire
LOVE, Robert	1798	Longmire
LOVE, Robert	1807	Odell
LOVE, Robert	1808	Odell
LOVE, Robert	1812	Hartsell
LOVE, Robert	1815	Hartsell
LOVE, Robert	1816	Brown
LOVE, Robert	1817	Brown
LOVE, Robert	1821	Haines
LOVE, Robert (for the estate of Thomas Howel)	1808	Odell
LOVE, Robert P.	1810	Cove
LOVE, Samuel	1817	Brown
LOVE, Samuel	1821	Haines
LOVE, Samuel B.	1812	Hartsell
LOVE, Samuel B.	1816	Fine
LOVE, Samuel B.	1821	Howard

Surname, Given names	Year	Comp./Dist.
LOVE, Thomas	1792	Coye
LOVE, Thomas	1817	Brown
LOVE, Thomas	1821	Haines
LOVELADY, John	1780-1781 (Undated)	
LOVELADY, Marshall	1780-1781 (Undated)	
LOVELATY, John	1781	
LOW, Andrew	1801	Norwood
LOW, Aquilla	1780-1781 (undated)	
LOW, Robert	1819	Brown
LOW, Sam C.	1819	Brown
LOW, Thomas	1819	Brown
LOWE, Andrew	1801	Norwood
LOWELL, Lewis	1779	
LOWERY, Adam	1809	Green
LOWERY, Adam	1810	Green
LOWERY, Adam	1811	Green
LOWERY, Samuel	1811	Green
LOWLY, Adam	1805	Stephenson
LOWREY, Adam	1807	Payne
LOWRREY, Robert	1780-1781 (Undated)	
LOWRY, Adam	1795	Milliken
LOWRY, Adam	1796	Millikin
LOWRY, Adam	1797	Hannah
LOWRY, Adam	1798	Hannah
LOWRY, Adam	1799	Hannah
LOWRY, Adam	1801	Squibb
LOWRY, Adam	1808	Gwin
LOWRY, Adam	1815	Waddell
LOWRY, Adam	1816	Waddell
LOWRY, Adam	1817	Riley
LOWRY, Adam	1818	Riley
LOWRY, Adam	1819	Findley
LOWRY, Adam	1821	McGee
LOWRY, John	1780-1781 (Undated)	
LOWRY, Joseph	1819	Brown
LOWRY, Rebeckah	1781	
LOWRY, Samuel	1815	Waddell
LOWRY, Samuel	1816	Waddell
LOWRY, Samuel	1817	Riley
LOWRY, Samuel	1818	Riley
LOYD, James	1795	Ford
LOYD, John	1795	Ford
LOYD, Levy	1795	Ford
LOYD, Wm	1814	Hampton
LUCAS, George	1794	Taylor
LUCAS, George	1796	Morrison
LUCAS, George	1798	Morrison
LUCAS, Robert	1798	Biddle
LUCAS, Robert (Esq.)	1778	

Surname, Given names	Year	Comp./Dist.
LUCES, George	1798	Morrison
LUCIAS, Robert	1779	
LUCKES, George	1799	Morrison
LUCKEY, Andrew	1805	Guir
LUCKEY, Thomas	1807	Anderson
LUIS, James	1798	Gann
LUIS, James	1798	Gann
LUK, George	1806	Payn
Luke	1812	McLin
LUMNERS, Isaac	1814	Brown
LUNAFORD, Jesse	1818	Harris
LUNCEFORD, Jesse	1817	Harris
LUNCEFORD, Samuel	1817	Harris
LUN--ORD, Jesse	1819	Harris
LUNSFORD, Jesse	1821	Hampton
LUSK, Robert	1779	
LUSK, Robert	1790	Williams
LUSK, Robert	1791	Williams
LUSK, Robert	1792	Maxwell
LUSK, Robert	1793	Maxwell
LUSK, Robert	1794	Taylor
LYLE,	1780-1781 (undated)	
LYLE, David	1779	
LYLE, David	1780-1781 (undated)	
LYLE, Henry	1778	
LYLE, John	1790	Milleken
LYLE, John	1791	Milliken
LYLE, John	1792	Milliken
LYLE, Saml	1779	
LYLE, Samuel	1778	
LYLE, Samuel	1781	
LYNCH, Jesse	1792	Coye
LYNCH, John	1795	Ford
LYON, Asher	1817	Hunt
LYON, Asher	1821	Hunt
LYON, David	1808	Odell
LYON, Ezekel	1801	Norwood
LYON, Ezekel	1808	Odell
LYON, Ezekial Jr.	1821	Hunt
LYON, Ezekial Sr.	1821	Hunt
LYON, Ezekiel	1806	Odel
LYON, Ezekiel	1817	Hunt
LYON, Ezekiel Jr.	1817	Hunt
LYON, Ezekiel Jr.	1819	Hunt
LYON, Ezekiel Sr.	1819	Hunt
LYON, John	1796	Melvin
LYON, John	1798	Crouch
LYON, John	1801	Norwood
LYON, John	1806	Crouch
LYON, John	1806	Odel
LYON, John	1808	Odell
LYON, John	1810	Cove
LYON, William	1817	Hunt
LYON, William	1819	Hunt
LYON, William	1821	Hunt
LYON, Zeakel	1796	Melvin
LYONS, Ashur	1814	McLin
LYONS, Ezakel	1811	Davis
LYONS, Ezakel Jr.	1811	Davis
LYONS, Ezekial	1818	Hunt
LYONS, Ezekial Sr.	1818	Hunt
LYONS, Ezekiel Jr.	1808	Guin
LYONS, Ezekiel Sr.	1808	Guin
LYONS, John	1811	Brown
LYONS, William	1811	Davis
LYONS, William	1814	McLin
LYONS, William	1818	Hunt
LYONS, Zekiel	1814	McLin
LYONS, Zekiel Jr.	1814	McLin
LYONS, Zekriel	1812	McLin
MA-, Marke	1809	Carr
MABURY, Gorge Sr.	1796	Melvin
MACALISTER, John	1794	Milliken
MACCOY, William	1808	Bayles
MACCRAY, Charles	1807	Bayles
MACEY, Edward	1799	Stuart
MACEY, Thos	1799	Hannah
MACHIN, Alexander	1783 [after]	Blair
MACHLIN, Robert	1794	Depew
MACINTURFF, Christopher	1790	Williams
MACINTURFF, Christopher	1791	Williams
MACINTURFF, Gasper	1790	Williams
MACINTURFF, Gasper	1791	Williams
MACINTURFF, John	1790	Williams
MACINTURFF, John	1791	Williams
MACINTURFF, John Jr.	1790	Williams
MACINTURFF, John Jr.	1791	Williams
MACK, John	1801	Gann
MACK, Samuel	1817	Riley
MACKEN, Barnabas	1819	Smith
MACKEN, Boring	1818	Smith
MACKEN, Edward	1811	Rodman
MACKEN, Edward	1818	Smith
MACKEN, Edward	1819	Smith
MACKENS, Edward	1807	Anderson
MACKENTURF, Christopher	1794	Taylor
MACKENTURF, John Sr.	1794	Taylor
MACKIN, Edward	1796	Calvert
MACKIN, Edward	1797	Calvert
MACKIN, Edward	1809	Roadmas
MACKIN, John	1796	Calvert

Surname, Given names	Year	Comp./Dist.
MACKIS, Edward	1801	Aiken
MACKLIN, Alexander	1797	Hannah
MACKLIN, Robert	1792	Depew
MACLEN, Robert	1806	Guin
MACLEN, William	1806	Guin
MACLIN, Robert (heirs of)	1821	Hunt
MACON, Ewd	1821	Smith
MACY, Clement	1801	Squibb
MACY, Thomas	1801	Squibb
MADCAP, William (Single)	1779	
MADEN, Andrew	1790	Shipley
MADEN, Andrew	1791	Shipley
MADEN, Andrew	1793	Murray
MADEN, Andrew	1794	Murray
MADEN, Andrew	1795	Murray
MADEN, Andrew	1795	Murray
MADEN, Andrew	1796	Shipley
MADEN, Andrew	1797	Shipley
MADEN, Andrew	1814	Bean
MADEN, Andrew	1815	Copas
MADEN, Andrew	1817	Grisham
MADEN, Andrew	1818	Grisham
MADEN, Andrew	1819	Grisham
MADEN, Andrew Jr.	1811	Britten
MADEN, Andrew Sr.	1813	Copas
MADEN, George	1815	Copas
MADEN, George	1816	Copas
MADEN, George	1817	Grisham
MADEN, George	1818	Grisham
MADEN, George	1821	Hale
MADEWELL,	1821	Smith
MAE, Abraham	1791	Tullis
MAENTAIN, James	1819	Howard
MAFEE, John	1821	Louis
MAGAHAH, Farill	1778	
MAGANESS, John	1801	Calvert
MAGENESS, John Jr.	1801	Calvert
MAGHON, James	1781	
MAGLAUGHLIN, Epperson	1815	Grimsley
MAHES, Anes	1812	Crawford
MAHONEY, James	1819	Hunt
MAHONEY, John	1817	Little
MAHONEY, William	1816	Hunt
MAHONEY, William	1819	Hunt
MAIDEN, Andrew	1798	Shipley
MAINE, David	1811	Ellis
MAINER, David	1821	Louis
MAINES, David	1819	Hair
MAINS, David	1814	Bean
MAINS, David	1818	Hair
MAINS, Isaac	1801	Norwood
MAISEA, Wm	1792	Carriger
MA-K, John	1808	Gwin
MAKERY, William	1817	Hunt
MAKIN, Eward	1799	Stuart
MAKOLS, John	1795	Melvan
MALISTER, John	1817	Smith
MALLENCE, John	1809	Roadmas
MALLOCK, James	1778	
MALLOCK, John	1779	
MALLONEE, John	1811	Rodman
MALLONNE, John	1808	Carr
MALONE, John	1778	
MALONE, John	1814	Hoss
MALONE, John	1815	Hoss
MALONEE, John	1821	Jones
MALSON, William	1809	Viney
MALVEN, James	1807	Carr
MALVEN, Joseph	1807	Carr
MALVEN, William	1806	Carr
MALVIN, James	1808	Carr
MALVIN, Joseph	1806	Carr
MALVIN, Joseph	1808	Carr
MANCY, Martin (Single)	1779	Wilson
MANES, David	1807	Britton
MANES, Joseph	1805	Doak
MANFIELD, Thomas	1795	Carriger
MANFIELD, William	1819	Findley
MANFIELD, William	1819	McClure
MANIFOLD, William	1816	Crookshanks
MANIFOLD, William	1817	McClure
MANIFOLD, Wm	1821	McGee
MANS, William	1816	Hoss
MANS, William	1819	Jones
MAPEL, James	1798	Morrison
MAPELS, James	[1796] 1797	Morris
MAPELS, John	[1796] 1797	Morris
MAPELS, William	[1796] 1797	Morris
MAPER, Joseph	1806	Grur
MAPLES, John	1798	Morrison
MAPLES, John	1798	Morrison
MAPLES, John	1798	Morrison
MAPLES, William	1798	Morrison
MARACFOL, Fredrick	1792	Maxwell
MARCER, Edward	1801	Glasscock
MARCH, Henry Sr.	1819	Hunt
MARCH, Jonas	1818	Hunt
MARCH, Samuel	1816	Waddell
MARES, John	1817	Little
MARES, Mack	1817	Little
MARES, Mark	1811	Mitchell
MARES, Moses	1817	Hunt

Surname, Given names	Year	Comp./Dist.
MARGE, Isaac	1790	Stone
MARGE, Isaac	1791	Stone
MARGINES, David	1815	McLin
MARH, William	1798	Duncan
MARIS, Mark	1815	Hoss
MARK, Mans	1816	Hoss
MARKIN, Edward	1815	Garner
MARKONY, William	1818	Hunt
MARR, Gideon	1819	McClure
MARR, Gideon	1821	McClure
MARR, Melton	1821	McClure
MARR, Milton	1819	McClure
MARR, Widon	1819	McClure
MARR, Widow	1821	McClure
MARS, Mark	1813	Hoss
MARSH, Grannian	1817	Hunt
MARSH, Gravocer	1816	Hunt
MARSH, Grevenes	1815	McLin
MARSH, Henry	1801	Taylor
MARSH, Henry	1808	Guin
MARSH, Henry	1812	McLin
MARSH, Henry	1814	McLin
MARSH, Henry	1815	McLin
MARSH, Henry	1816	Hunt
MARSH, Henry	1817	Hunt
MARSH, Henry	1818	Hunt
MARSH, Henry Jr.	1819	Hunt
MARSH, Henry Sr.	1821	Hunt
MARSH, Jonas	1819	Hunt
MARSH, Jones	1817	Hunt
MARSHAL, Joseph	1819	McClure
MARSHAL, Joseph	1821	McClure
MARTAIN, Andrew	1781	
MARTAIN, James	1781	
MARTAIN, James	1780-1781 (Undated)	
MARTAIN, John	[1796] 1797	Morris
MARTAIN, Joseph	1781	
MARTAIN, Joseph	1805	Carson
MARTAIN, Joseph	1780-1781 (Undated)	
MARTAIN, Richard	1780-1781 (Undated)	
MARTAIN, Ritchd	1781	
MARTEIN, Joseph	1798	Biddle
MARTIAN, Hugh	1798	Morrison
MARTIAN, James	1798	Morrison
MARTIN, (estate of)	1808	Carr
MARTIN, Andrew	1778	
MARTIN, Andrew	1780-1781 (Undated)	
MARTIN, Azarias	1815	Grimsley
MARTIN, Azarias	1816	Grimsley
MARTIN, Azerial	1814	Copes
MARTIN, Caleb	1817	Harris
MARTIN, Edward	1805	Aikin
MARTIN, Edward	1818	Smith
MARTIN, Edward	1819	Smith
MARTIN, Edward L.	1821	Hunt
MARTIN, George	1778	
MARTIN, Henry	1809	Gwin
MARTIN, Henry	1814	Hoss
MARTIN, Henry	1816	Hunt
MARTIN, Henry	1817	Hunt
MARTIN, Henry	1818	Hunt
MARTIN, Henry	1819	Hunt
MARTIN, Henry (heirs of)	1821	Hunt
MARTIN, Hugh	1806	Crouch
MARTIN, Hugh	1818	Grimsley
MARTIN, Hugh	1819	Grimsley
MARTIN, James	1790	Shipley
MARTIN, James	1791	Shipley
MARTIN, James	1793	Murray
MARTIN, James	1794	Murray
MARTIN, James	1795	Murray
MARTIN, James	1796	Shipley
MARTIN, James	1797	Shipley
MARTIN, James	1798	Shipley
MARTIN, James	1813	Hoss
MARTIN, James	1814	Hoss
MARTIN, James	1815	Hoss
MARTIN, James	1816	Fine
MARTIN, James	1818	Fine
MARTIN, Jas	1814	Hoss
MARTIN, Job	1815	Grimsley
MARTIN, Job	1816	Grimsley
MARTIN, John	1821	Hunt
MARTIN, Joseph	1778	
MARTIN, Joseph	1779	Wilson
MARTIN, Joseph	1790	Biddle
MARTIN, Joseph	1791	Biddle
MARTIN, Joseph	1792	Biddle
MARTIN, Joseph	1794	Blair
MARTIN, Joseph	1797	Biddle
MARTIN, Joseph	1798	Biddle
MARTIN, Joseph	1801	Biddle
MARTIN, Joseph	1806	Carson
MARTIN, Joseph	1811	
MARTIN, Joseph	1814	Couthers
MARTIN, Joseph	1815	Carcathers
MARTIN, Joseph	1816	Giles
MARTIN, Joseph	1817	Gillises
MARTIN, Joseph	1818	Land
MARTIN, Joseph	1783 [after]	Blair

Surname, Given names	Year	Comp./Dist.
MARTIN, Josia	1780-1781 (Undated)	
MARTIN, Josiah	1778	
MARTIN, Josiah	1779	Wilson
MARTIN, Micael	1814	Couthers
MARTIN, Michael	1815	McLin
MARTIN, Michael	1817	Gillises
MARTIN, Richard	1821	Hunt
MARTIN, Richard (Single)	1779	Wilson
MARTIN, Stephen	1811	Davis
MARTIN, Tom (deceased)	1813	Hoss
MARVIN, Thomas	1817	McClure
Mary	1801	
MASASENGAIL, Henery	1791	Tullis
MASENGAEL, Henry	1808	Carr
MASENGILL, Blick	1812	Crawford [2]
MASENGILL, Hennery	1795	Morrison
MASENGILL, Henry	1793	Morrison
MASENGILL, Henry	1794	Morrison
MASENGILL, Henry	1798	Morrison
MASENGILL, Henry Jr.	1779	
MASENGILL, Henry Sr.	1801	Morrison
MASENGILL, John	1812	Crawford
MASENGILL, John	1812	Crawford [2]
MASENGILL, Solomon	1793	Morrison
MASENGILL, Solomon	1794	Morrison
MASENGILL, William	1821	Jones
MASH, Henry	1799	Duncan
MASH, Henry	1806	Guin
MASH, Henry	1807	Givins
MASH, Henry	1809	Gwin
MASH, Henry	1811	Davis
MASH, Henry	1821	McClure
MASHBERRE, Wm	1780-1781	District 7
MASINGAILL, William	1807	Carr
MASINGELL, John	1814	Waddell
MASINGIL, John	1812	Waddill
MASINGILL, Blare	1812	Waddill
MASINGILL, Henry	1806	Carr
MASINGILL, John	1809	Green
MASINGILL, William	1806	Carr
MASON, Edward	1807	Cade
MASON, Ewd	1820	Smith
MASSENGEL, Henry	1801	Morrison
MASSENGEL, Wm	1811	Mitchell
MASSENGELL, William	1813	Hoss
MASSENGER, Henry	[1796] 1797	Morris
MASSENGIL, Blake	1811	Green
MASSENGIL, John	1811	Green
MASSENGILL, Blake	1815	Waddell
MASSENGILL, Blake	1816	Crookshanks
MASSENGILL, Blake	1816	Waddell
MASSENGILL, Blake	1817	McClure
MASSENGILL, Blake	1818	McClure
MASSENGILL, George	1818	Riley
MASSENGILL, Henry	1778	
MASSENGILL, Henry	1798	Morrison
MASSENGILL, Henry Sr.	1778	
MASSENGILL, James	1814	Waddell
MASSENGILL, James	1817	Haire
MASSENGILL, James	1818	Hair
MASSENGILL, James	1819	Hair
MASSENGILL, John	1815	Crookshanks
MASSENGILL, John	1816	Crookshanks
MASSENGILL, John	1817	McClure
MASSENGILL, John	1818	McClure
MASSENGILL, William	1814	Hoss
MASSENGILL, William	1815	Hoss
MASSENGILL, William	1816	Crookshanks
MASSENGILL, William	1817	Little
MASSENGILL, William	1817	McClure
MASSENGILL, William	1818	Jones
MASSENGILL, William	1818	McClure
MASSENGILL, William	1819	Jones
MASSER, Joseph	1811	McAlister
MASSEY, John	1818	Smith
MASSINGAEL, William	1808	Carr
MASSINGAIL, Henry	1807	Carr
MASSINGAL, Soloman	1792	Tulley
MASSINGALL, John	1819	McClure
MASSINGALL, William	1819	McClure
MASSINGELL, Michael	1778	
MASSON, Saml	1780-1781 (Undated)	
MATAIN, Joshua	1781	
MATHAS, William (Mr.)	1798	Duncan
MATHERLY,	1814	Couthers
MATHES, Abeham	1812	Crawford [2]
MATHES, Abraham	1817	McClure
MATHES, Abreham	1812	Crawford
MATHES, Alaxander	1798	Hannah
MATHES, Alex	1791	Milliken
MATHES, Alexander	1797	Hannah
MATHES, Alexander	1806	Payn
MATHES, Alexander	1808	McAllister
MATHES, Alexander	1811	McAlister
MATHES, Alexander	1812	Crawford
MATHES, Alexander	1819	McClure
MATHES, Alexander Sr.	1806	Payn
MATHES, Alexd	1814	Crookshanks
MATHES, Alexr	1799	Hannah
MATHES, Allen	1798	Hannah
MATHES, Aney	1812	Crawford [2]
MATHES, Cornelious	1819	Brown

Surname, Given names	Year	Comp./Dist.
MATHES, Cornelious	1821	Brown
MATHES, Ebenezar	1814	Crookshanks
MATHES, Ebenzer	1816	Crookshanks
MATHES, Ebenzer	1817	McClure
MATHES, Ebonezar	1811	McAlister
MATHES, George	1806	Payn
MATHES, George	1808	McAllister
MATHES, George	1811	McAlister
MATHES, George	1812	Crawford [2]
MATHES, George	1816	Crookshanks
MATHES, George	1817	McClure
MATHES, George	1819	McClure
MATHES, George	1821	Hunt
MATHES, George L.	1814	Crookshanks
MATHES, James	1799	Duncan
MATHES, John	1808	McAllister
MATHES, John	1811	McAlister
MATHES, John	1812	Crawford
MATHES, John	1812	Crawford [2]
MATHES, John	1814	Crookshanks
MATHES, John	1816	Crookshanks
MATHES, John	1817	McClure
MATHES, John	1819	McClure
MATHES, John	1821	Hunt
MATHES, Samuel	1780-1781 (Undated)	
MATHES, William	1801	Taylor
MATHESS, William	1781	
MATHEW, Alexander	1818	McClure
MATHEW, Alexd	1795	Milliken
MATHEW, Ebenzer	1818	McClure
MATHEW, George	1818	McClure
MATHEW, John	1818	McClure
MATHEWS, Alex	1792	Milliken
MATHEWS, Alexander	1793	Milliken
MATHEWS, Alexander	1794	Milliken
MATHEWS, Alexander	1801	Squibb
MATHEWS, Alexander	1801	Squibb
MATHEWS, Alexander	1815	Crookshanks
MATHEWS, Cornelius	1818	Harris
MATHEWS, Ebenezer	1819	McClure
MATHEWS, Ebenzer	1815	Crookshanks
MATHEWS, George	1815	Crookshanks
MATHEWS, James	1806	Guin
MATHEWS, John	1815	Crookshanks
MATHEWS, Wm	1799	Duncan
MATHIAS, George L.	1809	McAlister
MATHIES, Ebenzar	1809	McAlister
MATHIES, John	1809	McAlister
MATHIS, Alexander	1796	Millikin
MATHIS, Alexander	1812	Crawford [2]
MATHIS, Alexander Jr.	1805	Stephenson
MATHIS, Alexander Sr.	1805	Stephenson
MATHIS, George	1805	Stephenson
MATHIS, James	1807	Givins
MATHS, George	1812	Crawford
MATLACK, George	1795	Carriger
MATLACK, Giddeon	1795	Carriger
MATLACK, William	1795	Carriger
MATLOCK, Bird	1806	Crouch
MATLOCK, Gideon	1794	Carriger
MATLOCK, Isaac	1818	Grisham
MATLOCK, Isham	1811	Britten
MATLOCK, Isham	1815	Copas
MATLOCK, Ishom	1821	Hale
MATLOCK, Isom	1812	Britton
MATLOCK, John	1778	
MATLOCK, Moore	1797	Shipley
MATLOCK, Ranson	1821	Hale
MATLOCK, William	1794	Carriger
MATLOCK, Wm	1792	Carriger
MATLOCK, Zachariah	1793	Melvan
MATLOCK, Zachariah	1795	Melvan
MATLOCK, Zachariah	1796	Melvin
MATLOCK, Zachariah	1811	Ellis
MATLOCK, Zachariah	1815	Haire
MATLOCK, Zaciarah	1814	Bean
MATLOCK, Zakariah	1790	Stone
MATLOCK, Zakariah	1791	Stone
MATTHES, Alexander	1809	McAlister
MATTHES, Alexr (estate of)	1807	Payne
MATTHES, George	1807	Payne
MATTHEWS, Alexander	1821	McClure
MATTHEWS, Ebenezer	1821	McClure
MATTHEWS, George	1821	McClure
MATTHEWS, John	1821	McClure
MATTHIS, William	1798	Duncan
MATTHS, Alexr	1807	Payne
MATTOCK, George	1816	Hair
MATTOCK, George	1817	Haire
MATTOCK, George	1818	Hair
MATTOCK, George	1819	Hair
MATTOCK, Isham	1816	Copas
MATTOCK, Isham	1817	Grisham
MATTOCK, Isom	1819	Grisham
MATTOCK, John	1814	Copes
MATTOCK, Ransom	1812	Ellis
MATTOCK, Ransom	1816	Hair
MATTOCK, Ransom	1817	Grisham
MATTOCK, Ransom	1817	Haire
MATTOCK, Ransom	1818	Hair
MATTOCK, Zacha	1821	Louis
MATTOCK, Zachariah	1812	Ellis

Surname, Given names	Year	Comp./Dist.
MATTOCK, Zachariah	1816	Hair
MATTOCK, Zachariah	1817	Haire
MATTOCK, Zachariah	1818	Hair
MATTOCK, Zachariah	1819	Hair
MAUGRIN, John	1795	Taylor
MAUK,	1810	Green
MAUK, Daniel	1818	Riley
MAUK, John	1805	Guir
MAUK, John	1809	Green
MAUK, John	1810	Green
MAUK, Joseph	1812	Waddill
MAUK, Samuel	1819	Findley
MAUK, Samuel	1821	McGee
MAUK, Sarah	1821	McGee
MAULDEN,	1778	
MAULDEN, James	1778	
MAURAY, Henry	1807	Bayles
MAXEY, Jesse	1779	
MAXFIELD, Thomas (Captain)	1790	
MAXFIELD, Thomas (Captain)	1791	
MAXFIELD, Thos (Capt.)	1791	
MAXSEY, Jesse	1778	
MAXVIL, Samuel	1806	Anderson
MAXWELL, Saml	1814	McCracken
MAXWELL, Saml	1820	Smith
MAXWELL, Sam'l	1821	Smith
MAXWELL, Samuel	1809	Roadmas
MAXWELL, Samuel	1811	Rodman
MAXWELL, Samuel	1815	Garner
MAXWELL, Samuel	1816	Smith
MAXWELL, Samuel	1817	Smith
MAXWELL, Samuel	1818	Smith
MAXWELL, Samuel	1819	Smith
MAXWELL, Tho.	1792	Carriger
MAXWELL, Thomas (Capt.)	1794	Taylor
MAXWELL, Thos (Capt.)	1792	Maxwell
MAY, Adam	1814	Hampton
MAY, Adam	1816	Hampton
MAY, Adam	1819	Brown
MAY, Adam	1821	Brown
MAY, Casamer	1806	Brown
MAY, Casimore	1801	Roberson
MAY, Casiner	1794	Milliken
MAY, Cassemor	1795	Milliken
MAY, Cassemore	1809	Bayles
MAY, Cassiman	1817	Hampton
MAY, Cassimer	1816	Hampton
MAY, Cassimer	1819	Brown
MAY, Cassimon	1818	Brown [2]
MAY, Cassimore	1797	Robertson
MAY, Cassimore	1798	Roberson
MAY, Cassimore	1799	Robertson
MAY, Cassimore	1807	Bayles
MAY, Cassimore	1808	Bayles
MAY, Cassimore	1821	Brown
MAY, John	1793	Campbell
MAY, John	1795	Ford
MAY, John	1807	Bayles
MAY, John	1808	Bayles
MAY, John	1809	Par
MAY, John	1810	Hartzel
MAY, John	1812	Hartsell
MAY, John	1814	Hampton
MAY, John	1816	Hampton
MAY, John	1817	Hampton
MAY, John	1818	Brown [2]
MAY, John	1819	Brown
MAY, John	1821	Brown
MAY, Peter	1817	Hampton
MAY, Peter	1818	Brown [2]
MAY, Peter	1819	Brown
MAY, Saml	1797	Calvert
MAY, Samuel	1819	Brown
MAY, Samuel	1821	Brown
MAY, Samuel Jr.	1797	Calvert
MAY, Thomas	1817	Riley
MAYFIELD, Charles	1812	Ellis
MAYFIELD, Charles	1821	Howard
MAYO, Peter	1815	Garner
MAYOR, Richard	1818	Smith
MBRIDE, Alexandria A.	1812	Hartsell
McAALLISTER, John	1812	Crawford
McADAM, Jno	1780-1781 (Undated)	
McADAM, John Jr.	1780-1781 (Undated)	
McADAM, Robert	1815	Carcathers
McADAMS, Hugh	1797	Duncan
McADAMS, Hugh	1798	Duncan
McADAMS, Hugh	1798	Duncan
McADAMS, Hugh	1799	Duncan
McADAMS, Hugh	1801	Taylor
McADAMS, Hugh	1807	Givins
McADAMS, Hugh	1808	Guin
McADAMS, Hugh	1809	Gwin
McADAMS, Hugh	1811	Davis
McADAMS, Hugh	1812	McLin
McADAMS, Hugh	1814	McLin
McADAMS, Isabela	1815	McLin
McADAMS, Isbella	1816	Hunt
McADAMS, James	1778	
McADAMS, James	1819	Sands
McADAMS, Robert	1801	Taylor

Surname, Given names	Year	Comp./Dist.
McADAMS, Robert	1806	Guin
McADAMS, Robert	1807	Givins
McADAMS, Robert	1808	Guin
McADAMS, Robert	1809	Gwin
McADAMS, Robert	1811	Davis
McADAMS, Robert	1816	Giles
McADAMS, Robert	1817	Hampton
McADAMS, Robert	1818	Brown [2]
McADAMS, Robert	1819	Brown
McADAMS, Robt	1814	Couthers
McADAMS, Robt	1821	Smith
McADOO, David	1781	
McADOO, John	1781	
McADOO, William	1781	
McADOW, William	1780-1781 (Undated)	
McAFEE, James	1781	
McAFEE, Robert	1781	
McAFFEE, James	1801	Longmire
McAFLE, John	1806	Crouch
McAIMUS, Hannon	1795	Thornton
McAKEN, Edward	1817	Smith
McALERSTER, John Jr.	1811	Rodman
McALISTER, James	1815	Crookshanks
McALISTER, James	1816	Crookshanks
McALISTER, James	1817	McClure
McALISTER, James	1818	McClure
McALISTER, James	1819	McClure
McALISTER, James	1821	McClure
McALISTER, John	1791	Milliken
McALISTER, John	1792	Milliken
McALISTER, John	1796	Millikin
McALISTER, John	1799	Stuart
McALISTER, John	1801	Aiken
McALISTER, John	1807	Anderson
McALISTER, John	1807	Payne
McALISTER, John	1809	McAlister
McALISTER, John	1809	McAlister
McALISTER, John	1809	McAlister
McALISTER, John	1809	Roadmas
McALISTER, John	1811	McAlister
McALISTER, John	1814	McCracken
McALISTER, John	1815	Garner
McALISTER, John	1816	Smith
McALISTER, John	1818	Smith
McALISTER, John	1819	Smith
McALISTER, John	1820	Smith
McALISTER, John	1821	Smith
McALL, John	1798	Biddle
McALLISON, (a foriner)	1801	Gann
McALLISTER, James	1808	McAllister
McALLISTER, James	1812	Crawford [2]
McALLISTER, Jno Jr.	1798	Calvert
McALLISTER, John	1793	Milliken
McALLISTER, John	1798	Hannah
McALLISTER, John	1799	Hannah
McALLISTER, John	1801	Squibb
McALLISTER, John	1806	Payn
McALLISTER, John	1812	Crawford [2]
McALLISTER, John Sr.	1797	Hannah
McANEAR, Robert	1781	
McARDEL, Philip	1821	Hampton
McBAKEN, John	1806	Payn
McBASH, William	1797	Hannah
McBATH, Andrew	1791	Milliken
McBATH, Andrew	1798	Hannah
McBATH, Robart	1796	Millikin
McBATH, Willam	1798	Hannah
McBATH, William	1796	Millikin
McBEATH, Andrew	1793	Milliken
McBEATH, Andrew	1794	Milliken
McBEATH, Andrew	1795	Milliken
McBEATH, Robert	1793	Milliken
McBEE, William	1779	Wilson
McBEE, William	1787	Fains
McBRIDE, Alexander	1806	Parker
McBRIDE, Elexander	1807	Parker
McBRIDE, Elexander	1808	Parker
McBRIDE, Elick	1805	Parker
McBRIDE, Francis	1779	Wilson
McBRIDE, Wm	1779	Wilson
McBRIDGE, Alx	1809	Par
McCALEP, Ann	1806	Guin
McCALISTER, John Jr.	1805	Aikin
McCALL, James	1821	Sands
McCALL, John	1792	Depew
McCALL, John	1793	Biddle
McCALL, John	1797	Biddle
McCALL, John	1798	Biddle
McCALL, John	1805	Carson
McCALL, John	1806	Carson
McCALL, John	1807	Shields
McCALL, John	1809	Patterson
McCALL, John	1810	Dimmons
McCALL, John	1811	
McCALL, John	1815	Carcathers
McCALL, John	1816	Giles
McCALL, John	1816	Giles
McCALL, John	1818	Land
McCALL, John Jr.	1814	Couthers
McCALL, John Jr.	1815	Carcathers
McCALL, John Jr.	1817	Gillises
McCALL, John Jr.	1818	Land

Surname, Given names	Year	Comp./Dist.
McCALL, John Sr.	1814	Couthers
McCALL, John Sr.	1817	Gillises
McCALL, Robert	1817	Gillises
McCALL, Robert	1818	Land
McCALL, Robert	1819	Sands
McCALL, William	1809	Patterson
McCALL, William	1810	Dimmons
McCALL, William	1815	Carcathers
McCALL, William	1816	Giles
McCALL, William	1817	Gillises
McCALL, William	1818	Land
McCALL, William	1819	Sands
McCALL, William	1821	Sands
McCALL, William Sr.	1819	Sands
McCALL, Wm	1811	
McCALL, Wm	1814	Couthers
McCALLISTER, John	1795	Milliken
McCANN, John	1818	Smith
McCANN, William	1818	Smith
McCANNEL, John	1794	Blair
McCARCKLE, Joseph	1794	Depew
McCARD, David	1778	
McCARD, David	1794	Depew
McCARD, James	1794	Depew
McCARD, James	1799	Duncan
McCARDAL, Isaac	1812	McLin
McCARDAL, John	1812	McLin
McCARDALL, Jacob	1812	McCray
McCARDALL, Jacob	1812	McCray
McCARDALL, Philip	1812	McCray
McCARDALL, Philip	1812	McCray
McCARDALL, Phillip	1814	McCray
McCARDEL, Philip	1799	Hannah
McCARDELL, Philip	1808	Parker
McCARDELL, Philip	1809	Parker
McCARDELL, Philip	1811	McCray
McCARDELL, Philip	1819	Harris
McCARDELLY, Philip	1817	Harris
McCARDILL, Philip	1805	Jas Parker
McCARKLE, John	1821	Smith
McCARROLL, James	1812	Barnes
McCARROLL, Philip	1816	Harrison
McCARTHEY, Chas	1781	
McCARTHEY, James	1779	Wilson
McCARTNEY, Charles	1778	
McCARTNEY, James	1778	
McCARTNEY, James	1781	
McCARTNEY, James	1780-1781 (Undated)	
McCARTNY, Charles	1779	Wilson
McCARTY, John	1806	Guin
McCARY, Charles	1796	Longmire

Surname, Given names	Year	Comp./Dist.
McCASDELL, Phillip	1818	Harris
McCASH, Robert	1797	Hannah
McCAY, John	1813	Hoss
McCLAIN, Alexander	1817	McClure
McCLANY, Joseph	1812	McCray
McCLARY, Joseph	1811	McCray
McCLARY, Joseph	1816	Harrison
McCLARY, Joseph	1817	Harris
McCLEARY, Joseph	1806	Guin
McCLEARY, Joseph	1812	Ellis
McCLEARY, Joseph	1818	Smith
McCLEARY, Joseph	1819	Smith
McCLEARY, Joseph	1821	Hunt
McCLELAND, Isaac	1816	Smith
McCLELLAM, Isaac	1815	Garner
McCLELLAN, Isaac	1818	Smith
McCLELLAN, Isaac B.	1819	Smith
McCLELLON, David	1805	Stephenson
McCLELON, Isaac B.	1821	Smith
McCLOUD, Abner	1818	Smith
McCLOUD, Andrew	1798	Crouch
McCLOUD, James	1790	Stone
McCLOUD, James	1791	Stone
McCLOUD, James	1793	Melvan
McCLOUD, James	1795	Melvan
McCLOUD, James	1798	Crouch
McCLOUD, John	1793	Melvan
McCLOUD, John	1794	Melvan
McCLOUD, John	1795	Melvan
McCLOUD, John	1798	Gann
McCLOUD, John	1799	Moore
McCLOUD, Robart	1795	Melvan
McCLOUD, Robert	1798	Crouch
McCLOUD, Thomas	1793	Melvan
McCLOUD, Thomas	1795	Melvan
McCLOUD, William	1794	Melvan
McCLOUD, William	1798	Crouch
McCLOUD, William	1798	Duncan
McCLOUD, William	1801	Morrison
McCLOUD, William	1805	Doak
McCLOUD, William	1806	Crouch
McCLOUD, William	1815	Waddell
McCLOUD, William	1816	Waddell
McCLOUD, William	1817	Riley
McCLOUD, William	1819	Findley
McCLOUD, William Jr.	1790	Stone
McCLOUD, William Jr.	1791	Stone
McCLOUD, William Jr.	1793	Melvan
McCLOUD, William Jr.	1795	Melvan
McCLOUD, William Sr.	1793	Melvan
McCLOUD, William Sr.	1794	Melvan

Surname, Given names	Year	Comp./Dist.
McCLOUD, William Sr.	1795	Melvan
McCLOUD, Wm	1814	Waddell
McCLOUD, Wm	1821	McGee
McCLOWD, Anthony	1796	Melvin
McCLOWD, James	1796	Melvin
McCLOWD, Robert	1796	Melvin
McCLOWD, Wm Jr.	1796	Melvin
McCLOWD, Wm Sr.	1796	Melvin
McCLUAR, John	1797	Duncan
McCLUER, James	1806	Guin
McCLUES, Robert	1821	Sands
McCLURE, Andw	1781	
McCLURE, Edwin	1817	McClure
McCLURE, Edwin	1818	McClure
McCLURE, Ervin	1821	McClure
McCLURE, Erwin	1816	Crookshanks
McCLURE, Erwin	1819	McClure
McCLURE, Ewing	1809	McAlister
McCLURE, James	1801	Taylor
McCLURE, John	1806	Payn
McCLURE, John	1807	Payne
McCLURE, Robert	1805	Jas Parker
McCLURE, Robert	1811	McCray
McCLURE, Robert	1812	McCray
McCLURE, Robert	1812	McCray
McCLURE, Robert	1815	Grimsley
McCLURE, Robt	1808	Parker
McCLURE, Robt	1809	Parker
McCLURE, Thos	1781	
McCLURE, Yewen	1812	Crawford
McCLURE, Yewen	1812	Crawford [2]
McCNAME, Peeter	1791	Willey
McCOAL, Gaberal	1780-1781 (Undated)	
McCOLAM, Thomas	1780-1781 (Undated)	
McCOLLISTER, John	1797	Calvert
McCOLLOM, Jacob	1798	Hannah
McCOLLOM, Jas	1811	Green
McCOLLUM, Thos	1781	
McCONNAL, John	1798	Biddle
McCONNAL, John	1812	McCray
McCONNEL, John	1798	Biddle
McCOOD, William Sr.	1790	Stone
McCOOD, William Sr.	1791	Stone
McCORD, David	1779	Wilson
McCORD, David	1781	
McCORD, David	1792	Depew
McCORD, David	1793	Depew
McCORD, David	1780-1781 (Undated)	
McCORD, James	1778	
McCORD, James	1781	
McCORD, James	1793	Depew
McCORD, James	1797	Duncan
McCORD, James	1780-1781 (Undated)	
McCORD, John	1798	Duncan
McCORKLE, John	1815	Garner
McCORKLE, John	1817	Smith
McCORKLE, John	1818	Smith
McCORKLE, John	1819	Smith
McCORKLE, John	1820	Smith
McCORKLE, Joseph	1792	Depew
McCORKLE, Joseph	1793	Depew
McCORKLE, Joseph	1815	Haire
McCORKLE, Joseph	1816	Hair
McCORKLE, Joseph	1817	Haire
McCORKLES, John	1816	Smith
McCORMACK, Robert	1794	Taylor
McCORMACK, Robert	1795	Taylor
McCORMACK, Wm	1798	Calvert
McCORMICK, Robert	1792	Tulley
McCOY, Enoch	1792	Coye
McCOY, Jacob	1806	Grur
McCOY, Jacob	1808	Gwin
McCOY, Jacob	1810	Green
McCOY, John	1793	Maxwell
McCOY, John	1794	Taylor
McCOY, John	1808	Carr
McCOY, John	1809	Carr
McCOY, John	1811	Mitchell
McCOY, John	1814	Hoss
McCOY, John	1815	Hoss
McCOY, John	1816	Hoss
McCOY, John	1817	Little
McCOY, John	1818	Jones
McCOY, John	1819	Jones
McCOY, John	1821	Jones
McCOY, William	1811	Green
McCOY, William	1815	Waddell
McCOY, William	1816	Waddell
McCOY, William	1817	Riley
McCOY, William	1819	Findley
McCOY, William	1819	Jones
McCOY, Wm	1810	Green
McCOY, Wm	1812	Waddill
McCOY, Wm	1814	Waddell
McCOY, Wm	1821	McGee
McCRACKEN, Henery	1812	Crawford [2]
McCRACKEN, Henry	1815	Garner
McCRACKEN, Henry	1816	Smith
McCRACKEN, Henry	1817	Smith
McCRACKEN, Henry	1818	Smith
McCRACKEN, Henry	1819	Smith

Surname, Given names	Year	Comp./Dist.
McCRACKEN, John	1809	McAlister
McCRACKEN, John	1809	McAlister
McCRACKEN, John	1812	Crawford [2]
McCRACKEN, John	1814	Crookshanks
McCRACKEN, John	1814	McCracken
McCRACKEN, John	1817	McClure
McCRACKEN, John	1817	Smith
McCRACKEN, John	1818	McClure
McCRACKEN, John	1819	McClure
McCRACKEN, John	1819	Smith
McCRACKEN, John	1821	McClure
McCRACKEN, John Jr.	1799	Stuart
McCRACKEN, John Jr.	1807	Payne
McCRACKEN, John Jr.	1815	Crookshanks
McCRACKEN, John Jr.	1816	Crookshanks
McCRACKEN, John Sr.	1801	Squibb
McCRACKEN, John Sr.	1807	Payne
McCRACKEN, Robert	1807	Payne
McCRACKEN, Robert	1809	McAlister
McCRACKEN, Robert	1816	Crookshanks
McCRACKEN, Robert	1817	McClure
McCRACKEN, Robert	1817	Riley
McCRACKEN, Robert	1818	Riley
McCRACKEN, Saml	1807	Payne
McCRACKEN, Samuel	1812	Ellis
McCRACKEN, Samuel	1814	Bean
McCRACKEN, Samuel	1814	McCracken
McCRACKEN, Samuel	1815	Haire
McCRACKEN, Samuel	1816	Hunt
McCRACKEN, Samuel	1817	Haire
McCRACKEN, Samuel	1817	Harris
McCRACKEN, Samuel	1818	McClure
McCRACKEN, Samuel	1819	McClure
McCRACKEN, Samuel	1821	McClure
McCRACKIN, Henery	1814	Crookshanks
McCRACKIN, John Jr.	1805	Stephenson
McCRACKIN, John Sr.	1805	Stephenson
McCRACKIN, Samuel	1816	Hair
McCRACKIN, Wm Sr.	1801	Squibb
McCRAKEN, Henry	1812	Crawford
McCRAKEN, Henry	1820	Smith
McCRAKEN, Henry	1821	Smith
McCRAKEN, Jas (dec'd)	1821	Smith
McCRAKEN, John	1799	Duncan
McCRAKEN, John	1799	Hannah
McCRAKEN, John	1806	Payn
McCRAKEN, John	1808	McAllister
McCRAKEN, John	1808	McAllister
McCRAKEN, John	1812	Crawford
McCRAKEN, John	1820	Smith
McCRAKEN, John Jr.	1811	McAlister

Surname, Given names	Year	Comp./Dist.
McCRAKEN, Robert	1806	Payn
McCRAKEN, Robert	1808	McAllister
McCRAKEN, Robert	1819	Findley
McCRAKEN, Robert	1821	McGee
McCRAKEN, Saml	1809	McAlister
McCRAKEN, Samuel	1808	McAllister
McCRAKEN, Samuel	1809	Roadmas
McCRAKEN, Samuel	1811	McAlister
McCRAKEN, Samuel	1821	Smith
McCRARY, Joseph	1801	Taylor
McCRATH, Ande	1792	Milliken
McCRAY, Charles	1792	Scott
McCRAY, Charles	1797	Longmire
McCRAY, Charles	1806	Brown
McCRAY, Charles	1808	Odell
McCRAY, Dan	1809	Parker
McCRAY, Daniel	1792	North
McCRAY, Daniel	1796	Longmire
McCRAY, Daniel	1801	Calvert
McCRAY, Daniel	1805	Jas Parker
McCRAY, Daniel	1808	Parker
McCRAY, Daniel	1780-1781 (Undated)	
McCRAY, Elijah	1819	Brown
McCRAY, Elisha	1811	Brown
McCRAY, Elisha	1812	Brown
McCRAY, Elisha	1815	Hartsell
McCRAY, Elisha	1816	Brown
McCRAY, Elisha	1817	Hampton
McCRAY, Elisha	1818	Brown [2]
McCRAY, Georg	1801	Norwood
McCRAY, George	1806	Odel
McCRAY, George	1808	Odell
McCRAY, George	1816	Harrison
McCRAY, George	1819	Harris
McCRAY, Hennery	1812	McCray
McCRAY, Hennery	1812	McCray
McCRAY, Henry	1806	Brown
McCRAY, Henry	1808	Carr
McCRAY, Henry	1809	Carr
McCRAY, Henry	1811	McCray
McCRAY, Henry	1814	McCray
McCRAY, Henry	1815	Harris
McCRAY, Henry	1816	Harrison
McCRAY, Henry	1817	Harris
McCRAY, Henry	1818	Harris
McCRAY, Philip	1819	Brown
McCRAY, Phillup	1821	Brown
McCRAY, Thomas	1811	Davis
McCRAY, Thomas	1812	Ellis
McCRAY, Thomas	1814	Bean
McCRAY, Thomas	1815	Haire

Surname, Given names	Year	Comp./Dist.
McCRAY, Thomas	1816	Hair
McCRAY, Thomas	1817	Haire
McCRAY, Thomas	1818	Hair
McCRAY, Thomas	1819	Hair
McCRAY, William	1812	McCray
McCRAY, William	1812	McCray
McCRAY, William	1816	Hair
McCRAY, William	1817	Haire
McCRAY, William	1818	Hair
McCRAY, William	1819	Harris
McCREE, Charles	1791	Willey
McCREE, Danel	1791	North
McCREE, Danell	1791	North
McCUBBIN, John	1801	Lane
McCUBBIN, John	1805	Doak
McCUBBIN, John	1806	Doke
McCUBBIN, John	1807	Britton
McCUBBIN, Zachariah	1790	Shipley
McCUBBIN, Zachariah	1791	Shipley
McCUBBIN, Zachariah	1793	Murray
McCUBBIN, Zachariah	1795	Murray
McCUBBIN, Zachariah	1796	Shipley
McCUBBIN, Zachariah	1797	Shipley
McCUBBIN, Zachariah	1798	Shipley
McCUBBIN, Zachariah	1801	Lane
McCUBBIN, Zachariah	1805	Doak
McCUBBIN, Zachariah	1806	Doke
McCUBBIN, Zachariah	1807	Britton
McCUEN, Alex	1794	Milliken
McCUFFIN, Zachariah	1794	Murray
McCULLAM, David	1801	Gann
McCULLICK, James	1796	Millikin
McCUNE, Alexander	1821	McClure
McCUTCHEN, Willam	1798	Hannah
McCUTCHINS, Wm	1799	Gann
McDAM, Shular	1809	Carr
McDANEL, James	1806	Carr
McDIN, David	1814	McLin
McDONALD, George	1809	Right
McDONALD, George	1814	Bean
McDONALD, George	1817	Gillises
McDONALD, James	1819	Smith
McDONALD, John	1790	Shipley
McDONALD, John	1791	Shipley
McDONALD, John	1806	Crouch
McDONNAL, George	1812	Ellis
McDONNAL, George	1815	Haire
McDONNAL, John	1801	Norwood
McDONNAL, John	1801	Norwood
McDONNALD, Shular	1811	Mitchell
McDONNEL, George	1816	Giles

Surname, Given names	Year	Comp./Dist.
McDONNEL, James	1798	Crouch
McDONNEL, James	1801	Norwood
McDONOLD, George	1811	Ellis
McEFEE, John	1809	Right
McEFEE, John	1812	Ellis
McEFEE, John	1814	Bean
McEFEE, John	1815	Haire
McEFEE, John	1816	Hair
McEFEE, John	1817	Haire
McEFEE, John	1818	Hair
McEFEE, John	1819	Hair
McELROY, John F.	1807	Payne
McERVIN, Ebeneser	1806	Payn
McESEN, Ebenezar	1809	McAlister
McEWEN, Abenesar	1808	McAllister
McEWEN, Alexander	1792	Milliken
McEWEN, Alexander	1793	Milliken
McEWEN, Alexd (heirs of)	1811	McAlister
McEWEN, Alexde	1791	Milliken
McEWEN, Ebenezer	1807	Payne
McEWEN, Margaret	1796	Millikin
McEWEN, Margaret	1797	Hannah
McEWEN, Margret	1799	Hannah
McEWEN, Margret	1801	Squibb
McFALL, Frances	1794	Taylor
McFALL, Frances	1795	Taylor
McFALL, Francis	1790	Williams
McFALL, Francis	1791	Williams
McFALL, Francis	1792	Tulley
McFALL, Francis	1793	Maxwell
McFALLS, John	1811	McAlister
McFARLAND, Alexd	1781	
McFARLAND, Robert	1793	Handley
McFARLIN, Elaxander	1780-1781 (Undated)	
McFARLIN, Robert	1794	Handly
McFARLIN, Robert	1795	Handly
McFARLING, John	1778	
McFARRAN, Andrew	1795	Milliken
McFARRAN, Andrew	1797	Hannah
McFARRON, Andw	1798	Calvert
McFERRIN, Andrew	1796	Millikin
McFERRIN, Andw (heirs)	1806	Brown
McFERSON, Barten	1793	Murray
McFERSON, Bartin	1792	Depew
McFERSON, Charles	1805	Jas Parker
McFERSON, Daniel	1793	Murray
McFERSON, Daniel	1795	Murray
McFERSON, Daniel	1796	Shipley
McFERSON, Henry	1792	Depew
McFERSON, Henry	1792	Depew
McFERSON, Henry	1795	Murray

Surname, Given names	Year	Comp./Dist.
McFITT, Antony	1792	Depew
McGAMSEY, William	1817	Brown
McGANN, John	1819	Smith
McGANN, William	1819	Smith
McGANSEY, William	1821	Haines
McGARNER, Brice	1809	Right
McGARY, Henry	1819	Harris
McGEE, George	1796	Handly
McGEE, George	1799	Moore
McGEE, George	1814	Waddell
McGEE, George	1815	Waddell
McGEE, George	1816	Crookshanks
McGEE, George	1816	Waddell
McGEE, George	1821	McGee
McGEE, John	1793	Handley
McGEE, John	1794	Handly
McGEE, John	1795	Handly
McGEE, John	1796	Handly
McGEE, John	1798	Gann
McGEE, John	1799	Gann
McGEE, John	1799	Moore
McGEE, John	1801	Gann
McGEE, John	1805	Guir
McGEE, John	1806	Grur
McGEE, John	1808	Gwin
McGEE, John	1809	Green
McGEE, John	1810	Green
McGEE, John	1811	Ellis
McGEE, John	1811	Green
McGEE, John	1812	Waddill
McGEE, John	1814	Waddell
McGEE, John	1815	Waddell
McGEE, John	1816	Waddell
McGEE, John	1817	Riley
McGEE, John	1818	Riley
McGEE, John	1819	Findley
McGEE, John	1821	McGee
McGEE, Robert	1816	Waddell
McGEE, Solomen	1799	Gann
McGEE, Thomas	1791	White
McGEE, Thomas	1794	Ford
McGEE, Willam	1799	Gann
McGEE, William	1794	Handly
McGEE, William	1795	Handly
McGEE, William	1796	Handly
McGEE, William	1805	Guir
McGEE, William	1808	Gwin
McGEE, William	1809	Green
McGEE, William	1810	Green
McGEE, William	1811	Green
McGEE, William	1815	Waddell
McGEE, William	1816	Waddell
McGEE, William	1818	Riley
McGEE, William	1819	Findley
McGEE, Wm	1799	Moore
McGEE, Wm	1801	Gann
McGEE, Wm	1806	Grur
McGEE, Wm	1812	Waddill
McGEE, Wm	1814	Waddell
McGEE, Wm	1821	McGee
McGHE, Feral	1780-1781 (Undated)	
McGIMPSAY, Wm	1819	Brown
McGIN, Alexander	1796	Millikin
McGINAS, John	1791	Willey
McGINES, John	1795	Calvert
McGINES, John Sr.	1814	McCray
McGINESS, David	1814	McCray
McGINESS, James	1814	McCray
McGINESS, Jno Jr.	1809	Parker
McGINESS, Jno Sr.	1809	Parker
McGINESS, John Jr.	1805	Jas Parker
McGINESS, John Jr.	1814	McCray
McGINESS, John Sr.	1805	Jas Parker
McGINESS, Wm	1809	Parker
McGINIS, James	1821	McGee
McGINISS, John	1792	Scott
McGINISS, John	1799	Stuart
McGINNES, David	1811	McCray
McGINNES, David	1812	McCray
McGINNES, James	1811	McCray
McGINNES, John Jr.	1811	McCray
McGINNES, John Jr.	1812	McCray
McGINNES, John Sr.	1811	McCray
McGINNESS, David	1812	McCray
McGINNESS, James	1812	McCray
McGINNESS, James	1812	McCray
McGINNESS, Jas	1808	Parker
McGINNESS, Jno	1798	Calvert
McGINNESS, Jno Jr.	1808	Parker
McGINNESS, John	1808	Parker
McGINNESS, John	1812	McCray
McGINNESS, John Jr.	1812	McCray
McGINNIS, David	1816	Hunt
McGINNIS, David	1817	Hunt
McGINNIS, David	1819	Harris
McGINNIS, James	1816	Crookshanks
McGINNIS, James	1819	Findley
McGINNIS, John	1797	Calvert
McGINNIS, John	1797	Calvert
McGINNIS, John	1819	Harris
McGINNIS, John Jr.	1815	Harris
McGINNIS, John Jr.	1816	Harrison

Surname, Given names	Year	Comp./Dist.
McGINNIS, John Jr.	1817	Harris
McGINNIS, John Jr.	1818	Harris
McGINNIS, John Sr.	1815	Harris
McGINNIS, John Sr.	1816	Harrison
McGINNIS, John Sr.	1817	Harris
McGINNIS, John Sr.	1818	Harris
McGINNIS, Joseph	1815	Harris
McGINNIS, Joseph	1817	Harris
McGINNIS, Joseph	1818	Harris
McGINNISS, John Sr.	1812	McCray
McGINNS, John	1796	Calvert
McGINNSAY, William	1818	Brown
McGINTEY, Alexander	1819	Hair
McGINTY, Alexander	1821	Louis
McGLANGHLIN, Henrey	1812	McLin
McGLAUGHLEN, Alexdr	1781	
McGLAUGHLIN, Alexander	1780-1781 (Undated)	
McGLAUGHLIN, Alexd	1781	
McGLAUGHLIN, Willis	1818	Grimsley
McGLOTHIN, Wiles	1821	Martin
McGLOUGHLIN, John	1780-1781 (Undated)	
McINTOUFF, Peter	1791	Tullis
McINTURF, Gaspar	1806	Odel
McINTURF, Gasper	1793	Maxwell
McINTURF, Gasper	1797	Longmire
McINTURF, Gasper	1798	Longmire
McINTURF, Israel	1798	Longmire
McINTURF, Jasper	1796	Longmire
McINTURF, John	1793	Maxwell
McINTURF, John Jr.	1793	Maxwell
McINTURFF, Casper	1792	Maxwell
McINTURFF, Casper	1793	Hale
McINTURFF, Christopher	1792	Maxwell
McINTURFF, Gasper	1801	Longmire
McINTURFF, Gasper	1807	Odell
McINTURFF, John	1792	Maxwell
McINTURFF, John Jr.	1792	Maxwell
McINTURFF, John Jr.	1794	Taylor
McINTURY, Christopher	1793	Maxwell
McJUNE, Ebeneser	1812	Crawford
McKAN, William	1820	Smith
McKAY, William	1818	Riley
McKEE, Adam	1809	Roadmas
McKEE, Adam	1811	Rodman
McKEE, Adam	1814	McCracken
McKEE, Adam	1815	Garner
McKEE, Adam	1816	Smith
McKEE, Adam	1817	Smith
McKEE, Adam	1818	Smith
McKEE, Adam	1819	Smith
McKEE, Adam	1820	Smith
McKEE, Adam	1821	Smith
McKEE, Alaxander	1799	Gann
McKEE, Alex	1790	Hanley
McKEE, Alex	1791	Hanley
McKEE, Alex	1793	Handley
McKEE, Alexander	1798	Gann
McKEE, Alexander	1801	Gann
McKEE, Alexander	1808	Gwin
McKEE, Alexander	1809	Green
McKEE, Alexander	1812	Waddill
McKEE, Alexr	1806	Grur
McKEE, Allen	1796	Handly
McKEE, Allen	1797	Gann
McKEE, Allexr	1799	Moore
McKEE, John	1790	Hanley
McKEE, John	1791	Hanley
McKEE, John	1793	Handley
McKEE, John	1794	Handly
McKEE, John	1795	Handly
McKEE, John	1818	Riley
McKEE, Robert	1806	Grur
McKEE, Robert	1812	Waddill
McKEE, Robert	1814	Waddell
McKEE, Robert	1815	Waddell
McKEE, Robert	1817	Riley
McKEE, Robert	1818	Riley
McKEE, Robert	1819	Findley
McKEE, Robert	1821	McGee
McKEE, William	1817	Riley
McKEEHAM, George	1821	Jones
McKEN, James	1813	Hoss
McKEY, Wm	1809	Bayles
McKICKAN, James	1814	Hoss
McKIN, Edward	1797	Calvert
McKIN, John	1805	Aikin
McKINNEY, John A.	1807	Anderson
McKINNEY, John A.	1809	Roadmas
McKINY, Henrey	1793	Handley
McKIRE, John	1815	Garner
McKIT, Anthony	1815	McLin
McLAIN, John	1798	Duncan
McLAIN, Robert	1781	
McLAND, Alexr	1794	Depew
McLAUGHLIN, John	1819	Grimsley
McLAUGLIN, William	1819	Grimsley
McLEN, Alexander	1816	Crookshanks
McLEN, Robert	1817	Hampton
McLIN, Alaxander	1798	Hannah
McLIN, Alex	1801	Biddle
McLIN, Alexander	1808	McAllister

Surname, Given names	Year	Comp./Dist.
McLIN, Alexander	1812	Crawford
McLIN, Alexander	1812	Crawford [2]
McLIN, Alexander	1815	Crookshanks
McLIN, Alexander	1819	McClure
McLIN, Alexd	1809	McAlister
McLIN, Alexd	1814	Crookshanks
McLIN, Alexr	1807	Payne
McLIN, Alexr	1811	McAlister
McLIN, David	1812	McLin
McLIN, David	1815	McLin
McLIN, John	1799	Duncan
McLIN, John	1808	Guin
McLIN, John B.	1806	Guin
McLIN, John Blair	1807	Givins
McLIN, Joseph	1819	Hunt
McLIN, Joseph	1821	Hunt
McLIN, Robart	1798	Duncan
McLIN, Robart	1807	Givins
McLIN, Robert	1798	Duncan
McLIN, Robert	1799	Duncan
McLIN, Robert	1801	Taylor
McLIN, Robert	1809	Gwin
McLIN, Robert	1811	Davis
McLIN, Robert	1812	McLin
McLIN, Robert	1814	McLin
McLIN, Robert	1815	McLin
McLIN, Robert	1816	Hunt
McLIN, Robert	1817	Hunt
McLIN, Robert	1818	Brown [2]
McLIN, Robert	1818	Hunt
McLIN, Robert	1819	Hunt
McLIN, Robert	1819	Smith
McLIN, Robert	1821	Smith
McLIN, William	1801	Biddle
McLIN, William	1801	Taylor
McLIN, William	1807	Givins
McLIN, William	1808	Guin
McLIN, William	1809	Gwin
McLIN, William	1811	Davis
McLIN, William	1812	McLin
McLIN, William	1814	McLin
McLIN, William	1815	McLin
McLIN, William	1816	Hunt
McLINE, Alexr	1801	Squibb
McLINN, Alexr	1799	Hannah
McLINN, Robt	1820	Smith
McLINS, Edward	1814	McCracken
McLOUD, John	1797	Gann
McLUEN, Alex	1790	Milleken
McMACKIN, John Blair	1793	Morrison
McMACKIN, John Blair	1794	Morrison
McMACKIN, John Blair	1797	Biddle
McMACKIN, John Blair	[1796] 1797	Morris
McMAHAN, John Blair	1787	Fains
McMAHAN, John Blear	1791	Tullis
McMAHEN, John Brs	1798	Morrison
McMAHON, John B.	1778	
McMAHON, John B.	1778	
McMAHON, John Blair	1792	Tulley
McMAKAN, John B.	1795	Morrison
McMAMEE, Peter	1778	
McMAMEE, Peter	1779	Wilson
McMEEN, Robert	1780-1781 (undated)	
McMIN, Robert	1781	
McMITT, Anthoney	1794	Depew
McMITT, John	1794	Depew
McNABB, Baptist	1778	
McNABB, Baptist	1779	
McNABB, Baptist	1794	Taylor
McNABB, Baptist	1795	Taylor
McNABB, David	1778	
McNABB, David	1779	
McNABB, David	1790	Williams
McNABB, David	1791	Williams
McNABB, David	1792	Maxwell
McNABB, David	1793	Maxwell
McNABB, David	1794	Taylor
McNABB, David	1795	Taylor
McNABB, John	1778	
McNABB, John (Esqr.)	1779	
McNABB, William	1790	Williams
McNABB, William	1791	Williams
McNABB, William	1792	Maxwell
McNABB, William	1793	Maxwell
McNABB, William	1794	Taylor
McNABB, William (Esqr.)	1779	
McNABB, Wm	1778	
McNAME, Peter	1781	
McNEACE, Jacob	1815	Waddell
McNEAL, John	1808	Gwin
McNEAL, John	1809	Green
McNEAL, John	1810	Green
McNEAL, John	1812	Waddill
McNEAS, Jacob	1819	Findley
McNEAS, Robert	1779	Wilson
McNEASE, Jacob	1817	Riley
McNEASE, Joab	1821	McGee
McNEASE, Joeb	1816	Waddell
McNEECE, Joal	1818	Riley
McNEEL, Anny	1821	McGee
McNEEL, John	1812	Crawford [2]
McNEES, Joseph	1812	Crawford

Surname, Given names	Year	Comp./Dist.
MEDLOCK, Ranson	1815	Haire
MEDLOCK, Zachariah	1794	Melvan
MEDLOCK, Zachariah	1809	Right
MEENS, William	1812	Crawford [2]
MEER, Abner	1812	Crawford
MEER, Abner	1812	Crawford [2]
MEER, Joseph	1812	Crawford
MEER, Joseph	1812	Crawford
MEER, Thomas	1812	Crawford
MEFFORD, John	1807	Anderson
MEGDAR, Robert	1780-1781 (Undated)	
MEGEE, Gorge	1798	Gann
MEGEE, William	1798	Gann
MEGER, Thomas	1795	Ford
MEGINNIS, John	1793	Depew
MEGINNIS, William	1810	Cove
MEGINS, S. John	1794	Scot
MEHONEY, Philip	1821	Hunt
MEHONEY, William	1821	Hunt
MEINS, David	1798	Crouch
MEINS, Isaa	1796	Melvin
MEINS, Isaac	1795	Melvan
MEINS, Thomas	1795	Melvan
MEINS, Thomas	1796	Melvin
MEL, Alexander	1806	Payn
MELAND, John	1819	Jones
MELEKEN, John	1806	Payn
MELEKEN, John	1808	McAllister
MELIGAN, John	1797	Hannah
M-ELKORE, Andrew (of North Carolina)	1799	Stuart
MELLAN, Tiler	1797	Gann
MELLEN, Edward	1816	Smith
MELLENER, John	1818	Jones
MELON, John	1812	Crawford
MELONE, Williamson	1801	Norwood
MELOUGLAR, John	1779	Wilson
MELSAPS, Thomas	1794	Taylor
MELSKEN, John	1798	Hannah
MELSON, William	1806	Odel
MELSON, William	1807	Odell
MELVAIN, John	1794	Melvan
MELVAIN, Joseph (A son of Thomas)	1794	Melvan
MELVAIN, Samuel	1794	Melvan
MELVAN, Beakly Joseph	1811	Ellis
MELVAN, John	1790	Stone
MELVAN, John	1791	Stone
MELVAN, John	1793	Melvan
MELVAN, John	1795	Melvan
MELVAN, Josep (Son of Thomas)	1793	Melvan
MELVAN, Joseph	1815	Haire
MELVAN, Joseph (Son of Jno)	1794	Murray
MELVAN, Joseph (Son of John)	1793	Melvan
MELVAN, Joseph (Son of John)	1795	Murray
MELVAN, Joseph (The Elder)	1794	Morrison
MELVAN, Joseph (The older)	1793	Morrison
MELVAN, Joseph (The younger)	1795	Melvan
MELVAN, Sammuel	1795	Melvan
MELVAN, Samuel	1790	Stone
MELVAN, Samuel	1791	Stone
MELVAN, Samuel	1793	Melvan
MELVAN, Samuel	1812	Britton
MELVAN, Thomas	1790	Stone
MELVAN, Thomas	1791	Stone
MELVAN, Thomas	1793	Melvan
MELVAN, Thomas	1795	Melvan
MELVEN, James	1809	Carr
MELVEN, John	1798	Crouch
MELVEN, Joseph	1798	Crouch
MELVEN, Joseph	1798	Crouch
MELVEN, Joseph	1799	Morrison
MELVEN, Joseph	1801	Norwood
MELVEN, Joseph	1801	Norwood
MELVEN, Saml	1801	Norwood
MELVEN, Slem Joseph	1811	Ellis
MELVEN, Thomas	1794	Melvan
MELVIN, James	1811	Mitchell
MELVIN, James	1814	Hoss
MELVIN, James	1815	Hoss
MELVIN, James	1816	Hoss
MELVIN, James	1817	Little
MELVIN, James	1818	Jones
MELVIN, James	1821	Jones
MELVIN, John	1796	Melvin
MELVIN, John	1806	Crouch
MELVIN, John	1815	Hoss
MELVIN, John	1817	Little
MELVIN, John	1819	Jones
MELVIN, John	1821	Jones
MELVIN, Jonathan	1818	Jones
MELVIN, Joseph	1791	Tullis
MELVIN, Joseph	1792	Tulley
MELVIN, Joseph	1795	Morrison
MELVIN, Joseph	1798	Morrison
MELVIN, Joseph	1801	Morrison
MELVIN, Joseph	1806	Crouch
MELVIN, Joseph	1806	Crouch
MELVIN, Joseph	1809	Carr
MELVIN, Joseph	1811	Mitchell
MELVIN, Joseph	1812	Ellis
MELVIN, Joseph	1814	Bean

Surname, Given names	Year	Comp./Dist.
MELVIN, Joseph	1815	Hoss
MELVIN, Joseph	1816	Hair
MELVIN, Joseph	1816	Hoss
MELVIN, Joseph	1817	Haire
MELVIN, Joseph	1817	Little
MELVIN, Joseph	1818	Hair
MELVIN, Joseph	1818	Jones
MELVIN, Joseph	1819	Hair
MELVIN, Joseph	1819	Jones
MELVIN, Joseph	1821	Jones
MELVIN, Joseph	1821	Louis
MELVIN, Joseph	[1796] 1797	Morris
MELVIN, Joseph (Berkley)	1809	Right
MELVIN, Joseph (estate)	1817	Little
MELVIN, Joseph Jr.	1796	Melvin
MELVIN, Joseph Jr.	1809	Right
MELVIN, Joseph Jr.	1813	Hoss
MELVIN, Joseph Sr.	1796	Melvin
MELVIN, Joseph Sr.	1813	Hoss
MELVIN, Joseph Sr.	1814	Hoss
MELVIN, Saml	1813	Copas
MELVIN, Samuel	1806	Crouch
MELVIN, Samuel	1809	Right
MELVIN, Samuel	1811	Britten
MELVIN, Samuel	1814	Copes
MELVIN, Samuel	1815	Copas
MELVIN, Samuel	1816	Copas
MELVIN, Thomas	1796	Melvin
MELVIN, Thomas	1806	Crouch
MENNEFOLD, William	1809	Bayles
MENNIFOLD, William	1808	Bayles
MEPECK, William	1807	Anderson
MERAY, Elisha	1810	Cove
MERAY, Elisha	1814	Brown
MERAY, George	1809	Viney
MERCER, Edward	1805	Rector
MERCER, John	1805	Guir
MERCER, John	1815	Crookshanks
MERCER, Joseph	1797	Hannah
MERCER, Joseph	1799	Hannah
MERCER, Joseph	1816	Crookshanks
MERCER, Joseph Jr.	1815	Crookshanks
MERCER, Joseph Sr.	1815	Crookshanks
MERCER, Joseph Sr.	1816	Crookshanks
MERCER, Thomas	1812	Crawford [2]
MERCER, Thomas	1816	Crookshanks
MERCY, Thomas	1806	Payn
MERES, Philip	1817	Fine
MERRY, Wm	1780-1781 (Undated)	
MERSER, Sary	1808	Cade
MERTAIN, James	1821	Sands
MERTAIN, Joseph	1821	Sands
MESER, Joseph	1792	Milliken
MESER, Joseph	1795	Calvert
MESER, Joseph	1798	Hannah
MESER, Joseph	1806	Payn
MESINGILL, Soloman	1791	Tullis
MESSAR, Joseph	1791	Chisom
MESSAR, Joseph	1796	Millikin
MESSAR, Joseph	1801	Squibb
MESSEMORE, Peter	1821	McGee
MESSEN, Abner	1809	McAlister
MESSER, John	1808	McAllister
MESSER, John	1811	McAlister
MESSER, Joseph	1794	Milliken
MESSER, Joseph	1807	Payne
MESSER, Joseph	1808	McAllister
MESSER, Joseph	1809	McAlister
MESSER, Joseph	1811	McAlister
MESSER, Joseph	1814	Crookshanks
MESSER, Joseph	1814	Crookshanks
MESSER, Joseph	1817	McClure
MESSER, Joseph Jr.	1821	McClure
MESSER, Joseph Sr.	1817	McClure
MESSER, Joseph Sr.	1821	McClure
MESSER, Thomas	1818	McClure
MESSOR, Joseph	1819	McClure
MESSOR, Joseph Sr.	1819	McClure
METLOCK, George	1815	Haire
METS, Thomas	1795	Taylor
MGEE, George	1797	Gann
MGEE, John	1797	Gann
MGEE, Wm	1797	Gann
MGINNES, David	1821	Hampton
MGINNIS, John	1821	Hampton
MICHAEL, James	1778	
MICHAEL, Martin H.	1816	Giles
MICHAEL, Thos	1779	Wilson
MICHAEL, William	1810	Dimmons
MICHAL, Robert	1807	Anderson
MICHEL, Adam	1799	Morrison
MICHEL, Adam	1809	Carr
MICHEL, James	1814	McCray
MICHEL, Thomas	1814	McCray
MICHEL, W. M.	1811	
MICKEL, Robart	1801	Norwood
MICY, Thomas	1807	Payne
MIERS, Fredrick	1798	Young
MIERS, Fredrick	1805	Parker
MIERS, Fredrick	1807	Parker
MILBORN, Samuel	1790	Stone
MILBORN, Samuel	1791	Stone

Surname, Given names	Year	Comp./Dist.
MILBORN, Samuel	1801	Norwood
MILBUNN, Samuel	1793	Melvan
MILBURN, Samuel	1794	Melvan
MILBURN, Samuel	1795	Melvan
MILBURN, Samuel	1796	Melvin
MILBURN, Samuel	1798	Crouch
MILEGON, John	1801	Squibb
MILER, Henry	1791	Willey
MILIKEN, John (Capt.)	1791	
MILION, Edward	1794	Scot
MILLANGS, James	1794	Ford
MILLAR, Jacob	1809	Green
MILLAR, Jacob	1814	Waddell
MILLAR, Jacob	1821	McGee
MILLAR, James	1799	Moore
MILLAR, James	1809	Green
MILLAR, James	1814	Waddell
MILLAR, John	1798	Morrison
MILLAR, John	1821	Sands
MILLAR, John	[1796] 1797	Morris
MILLAR, John Blair	1805	Carson
MILLAR, Peter	1798	Morrison
MILLAR, Peter	1798	Morrison
MILLAR, Peter	1799	Moore
MILLAR, Petter	1821	Sands
MILLAR, Theoph	1799	Moore
MILLAR, Wm	1809	Green
MILLARD, Tho	1792	Carriger
MILLARD, Thomas	1794	Carriger
MILLE, Jacob	1815	Waddell
MILLEKEN, John	1790	Milleken
MILLEKEN, John	1792	Milliken
MILLEN, Simion	1810	Hartzel
MILLER, Abraham	1811	Green
MILLER, Adam	1793	Murray
MILLER, Adam	1794	Murray
MILLER, Andrew	1787	Fains
MILLER, Christly	1795	Ford
MILLER, Daniel	1790	White
MILLER, Daniel	1793	Thornton
MILLER, Daniel	1795	Ford
MILLER, Daniel Jr.	1793	Thornton
MILLER, David	1781	
MILLER, David	1780-1781 (Undated)	
MILLER, George	1790	White
MILLER, George	1795	Ford
MILLER, Henery	1794	Scot
MILLER, Henery	1795	Calvert
MILLER, Henry	1792	Scott
MILLER, Henry	1793	Scott
MILLER, Henry	1793	Thornton
MILLER, Henry	1801	Aiken
MILLER, Henry	1805	Jas Parker
MILLER, Henry	1808	Parker
MILLER, Henry Jr.	1795	Ford
MILLER, Henry Sr.	1795	Ford
MILLER, Isaac	1805	Jas Parker
MILLER, Isaac	1808	Parker
MILLER, Isaac	1809	Parker
MILLER, Isaac	1811	McCray
MILLER, Isaac	1812	McCray
MILLER, Isaac	1814	McCray
MILLER, Isaac	1815	Harris
MILLER, Isaac	1817	Harris
MILLER, Isaac	1817	Riley
MILLER, Isaac	1818	Harris
MILLER, Isaac	1818	Riley
MILLER, Isaac	1819	Findley
MILLER, Isaac	1819	Harris
MILLER, Isaac	1821	Hampton
MILLER, Isaac	1821	McGee
MILLER, Jacob	1806	Crouch
MILLER, Jacob	1809	Parker
MILLER, Jacob	1809	Right
MILLER, Jacob	1811	Ellis
MILLER, Jacob	1811	Green
MILLER, Jacob	1812	Ellis
MILLER, Jacob	1812	Waddill
MILLER, Jacob	1813	Hoss
MILLER, Jacob	1814	Bean
MILLER, Jacob	1814	Hoss
MILLER, Jacob	1815	Haire
MILLER, Jacob	1815	Hoss
MILLER, Jacob	1816	Hair
MILLER, Jacob	1816	Hoss
MILLER, Jacob	1816	Waddell
MILLER, Jacob	1817	Haire
MILLER, Jacob	1817	Little
MILLER, Jacob	1817	Riley
MILLER, Jacob	1818	Hair
MILLER, Jacob	1818	Jones
MILLER, Jacob	1818	Riley
MILLER, Jacob	1819	Findley
MILLER, Jacob	1819	Hair
MILLER, Jacob	1819	Jones
MILLER, Jacob	1821	Jones
MILLER, Jacob	1821	Louis
MILLER, Jacobe	1811	McCray
MILLER, James	1778	
MILLER, James	1781	
MILLER, James	1793	Handley
MILLER, James	1794	Handly

Surname, Given names	Year	Comp./Dist.
MILLER, James	1795	Handly
MILLER, James	1796	Handly
MILLER, James	1797	Gann
MILLER, James	1798	Gann
MILLER, James	1799	Gann
MILLER, James	1801	Gann
MILLER, James	1805	Guir
MILLER, James	1806	Grur
MILLER, James	1812	Waddill
MILLER, James	1819	Jones
MILLER, James	1780-1781 (Undated)	
MILLER, James (executor)	1811	Green
MILLER, John	1790	White
MILLER, John	1791	Tullis
MILLER, John	1793	Morrison
MILLER, John	1793	Thornton
MILLER, John	1793	Thornton
MILLER, John	1794	Morrison
MILLER, John	1795	Morrison
MILLER, John	1798	Morrison
MILLER, John	1799	Morrison
MILLER, John	1801	Morrison
MILLER, John	1806	Carr
MILLER, John	1807	Bayles
MILLER, John	1807	Carr
MILLER, John	1808	Bayles
MILLER, John	1808	Carr
MILLER, John	1809	Carr
MILLER, John	1811	Mitchell
MILLER, John	1812	Crawford [2]
MILLER, John	1813	Hoss
MILLER, John	1814	Hartsell
MILLER, John	1814	Hoss
MILLER, John	1815	Fines
MILLER, John	1815	Hoss
MILLER, John	1816	Fine
MILLER, John	1816	Hoss
MILLER, John	1817	Fine
MILLER, John	1817	Little
MILLER, John	1818	Fine
MILLER, John	1818	Jones
MILLER, John	1819	Howard
MILLER, John	1819	Jones
MILLER, John	1821	Jones
MILLER, John Blair	1794	Blair
MILLER, John Blair	1801	Taylor
MILLER, John Blair	1808	Guin
MILLER, John Blair	1814	Couthers
MILLER, John Jr.	1795	Ford
MILLER, John Sr.	1795	Ford
MILLER, Joseph (estate of)	1818	Jones

Surname, Given names	Year	Comp./Dist.
MILLER, Lemon	1816	Harrison
MILLER, Old	1792	Greer
MILLER, Peter	1790	Stone
MILLER, Peter	1791	Stone
MILLER, Peter	1793	Handley
MILLER, Peter	1793	Melvan
MILLER, Peter	1794	Melvan
MILLER, Peter	1795	Handly
MILLER, Peter	1795	Melvan
MILLER, Peter	1798	Gann
MILLER, Peter	1799	Morrison
MILLER, Peter	1801	Gann
MILLER, Peter	1801	Morrison
MILLER, Peter	1806	Carr
MILLER, Peter	1807	Carr
MILLER, Peter	1808	Carr
MILLER, Peter	1809	Carr
MILLER, Peter	1811	Mitchell
MILLER, Peter	1813	Hoss
MILLER, Peter	1814	Hoss
MILLER, Peter	1815	Hoss
MILLER, Peter	1816	Giles
MILLER, Peter	1817	Gillises
MILLER, Peter	1818	Land
MILLER, Peter	1819	Sands
MILLER, Peter	1821	Jones
MILLER, Peter	1821	McGee
MILLER, Peter Jr.	1816	Hoss
MILLER, Peter Jr.	1817	Little
MILLER, Peter Jr.	1818	Jones
MILLER, Peter Jr.	1819	Jones
MILLER, Peter Sr.	1817	Little
MILLER, Peter Sr.	1818	Jones
MILLER, Petter	1796	Handly
MILLER, Samuel	1814	Hartsell
MILLER, Samuel	1814	Hoss
MILLER, Samuel	1815	Fines
MILLER, Samuel	1815	Hoss
MILLER, Samuel	1817	Little
MILLER, Samuel	1818	Fine
MILLER, Samuel	1818	Jones
MILLER, Samuel	1819	Howard
MILLER, Samuel	1821	Jones
MILLER, Simon	1806	Parker
MILLER, Simon	1808	Parker
MILLER, Simon	1809	Par
MILLER, Simon	1814	McCray
MILLER, Simon	1818	Hunt
MILLER, Simon	1819	Hunt
MILLER, Simon	1821	Hunt
MILLER, Soloman	1819	Jones

Surname, Given names	Year	Comp./Dist.
MILLER, Soloman	1821	Jones
MILLER, Solomon	1814	Hoss
MILLER, Solomon	1815	Hoss
MILLER, Solomon	1816	Hoss
MILLER, Solomon	1816	Hoss
MILLER, Solomon	1817	Little
MILLER, Solomon	1818	Jones
MILLER, Theoflis	1801	Gann
MILLER, Theophilas	1806	Brown
MILLER, Theophiles	1798	Gann
MILLER, Theophilus	1797	Gann
MILLER, Theophilus	1808	Bayles
MILLER, Theophilus	1811	Green
MILLER, Thomas	1811	Britten
MILLER, Thomas	1812	Britton
MILLER, Thomas	1813	Copas
MILLER, Thomas	1813	Copas
MILLER, Thomas	1814	Copes
MILLER, Thomas	1815	Copas
MILLER, Thomas	1816	Copas
MILLER, Thomas	1817	Grisham
MILLER, Thomas	1818	Grisham
MILLER, Thomas	1819	Grisham
MILLER, Thomas	1821	Hale
MILLER, Thos	1790	Greer
MILLER, Widow	1818	Hunt
MILLER, William	1805	Guir
MILLER, William	1806	Guin
MILLER, William	1806	Guin
MILLER, William	1807	Givins
MILLER, William	1808	Guin
MILLER, William	1809	Gwin
MILLER, William	1810	Green
MILLER, William	1811	Green
MILLER, William	1812	McLin
MILLER, William	1815	McLin
MILLER, William	1816	Hampton
MILLER, William	1816	Hunt
MILLER, William	1817	Hampton
MILLER, William	1818	Brown [2]
MILLER, William	1819	Brown
MILLER, William	1821	Brown
MILLER, William (Esq.)	1814	McLin
MILLER, William (heirs of)	1821	Hunt
MILLER, Wm	1799	Stuart
MILLER, Wm	1801	Calvert
MILLER, Wm	1806	Grur
MILLER, Wm	1808	Gwin
MILLER, Wm	1814	Hampton
MILLER, Wm (Dec.; heirs of)	1819	Hunt
MILLER, Wm Hezekiah	1817	Hunt

Surname, Given names	Year	Comp./Dist.
MILLERPOLE, Thomas	1780-1781 (Undated)	
MILLES, Christey	1793	Thornton
MILLES, Hurr	1809	Gwin
MILLES, John Blair	1798	Biddle
MILLES, Samuel	1821	Howard
MILLGAN, Edward	1807	Givins
MILLIAN, Edw	1808	Parker
MILLIAN, Edw Jr.	1808	Parker
MILLIAN, Edward	1796	Calvert
MILLIAN, Edward	1814	McCray
MILLIAN, Edward	1819	Harris
MILLIAN, Jacob	1808	Parker
MILLIAN, Jacob	1814	McCray
MILLIAN, Jacob	1815	Harris
MILLIAN, Robert	1808	Parker
MILLIAN, Robert	1817	Harris
MILLIAN, Robert	1819	Harris
MILLICAN, James	1778	
MILLIKEN, Jesse (Capt.)	1791	
MILLIKEN, John	1793	Milliken
MILLIKEN, John	1794	Milliken
MILLIKEN, John	1795	Calvert
MILLIKIN, John	1796	Millikin
MILLIN, Edward	1791	Willey
MILLION, Edw	1809	Parker
MILLION, Edw Jr.	1809	Parker
MILLION, Edward	1792	Scott
MILLION, Edward	1793	Scott
MILLION, Edward	1795	Calvert
MILLION, Edward	1797	Calvert
MILLION, Edward	1797	Calvert
MILLION, Edward	1798	Calvert
MILLION, Edward	1799	Stuart
MILLION, Edward	1801	Calvert
MILLION, Edward	1811	McCray
MILLION, Edward	1812	McCray
MILLION, Edward	1812	McCray
MILLION, Edward	1812	McLin
MILLION, Edward	1815	Harris
MILLION, Edward	1821	Hampton
MILLION, Edward D.	1818	Harris
MILLION, Edward D.	1818	Harris
MILLION, Edward Jr.	1805	Jas Parker
MILLION, Edward Jr.	1816	Harrison
MILLION, Edward Sr.	1805	Jas Parker
MILLION, Edward Sr.	1816	Harrison
MILLION, Edwerd Jr.	1806	Guin
MILLION, Jacob	1805	Jas Parker
MILLION, Jacob	1809	Parker
MILLION, Jacob	1811	McCray
MILLION, Jacob	1812	McCray

Surname, Given names	Year	Comp./Dist.
MILLION, Jacob	1812	McCray
MILLION, John	1797	Calvert
MILLION, John	1801	Calvert
MILLION, John	1806	Guin
MILLION, John	1807	Bayles
MILLION, John	1808	Bayles
MILLION, John	1809	Bayles
MILLION, John	1814	Hampton
MILLION, John	1816	Hampton
MILLION, John	1817	Hampton
MILLION, John	1818	Brown [2]
MILLION, John	1819	Brown
MILLION, John	1821	Brown
MILLION, Robert	1805	Jas Parker
MILLION, Robert	1811	McCray
MILLION, Robert	1812	McCray
MILLION, Robert	1812	McCray
MILLION, Robert	1815	Harris
MILLION, Robert	1816	Harrison
MILLION, Robert	1818	Harris
MILLION, Robert	1821	Hampton
MILLION, Robert	1780-1781 (Undated)	
MILLION, Robt	1809	Parker
MILLON, Jacob	1801	Norwood
MILLON, John	1794	Milliken
MILLOV, Peter	1794	Handly
MILLS, Harr	1811	Davis
MILLS, Henr	1798	Biddle
MILLS, Hir	1798	Biddle
MILLS, Hur	1805	Carson
MILLS, Hurr	1799	Hannah
MILLS, Hurr	1808	Guin
MILLS, John Blen	1798	Biddle
MILLS, Keer	1812	McLin
MILLS, Wier	1806	Carson
MILLSAP, James	1794	Ford
MILLSAPS, Thos	1793	Maxwell
MILLUKEN, James (Single)	1779	
MILROY, George	1815	Harris
MILROY, John T.	1809	McAlister
MILSAPS, James	1792	Greer
MILSAPS, James	1792	White
MILSAPS, James	1795	Ford
MILSAPS, Thomas	1796	Handly
MILSAPS, Thos	1792	Carriger
MILTON, James	1808	Gwin
MIPEY, Wm	1805	Aikin
MIRES, Jacob	1779	Wilson
MIRES, John	1806	Grur
MIRLES, Adam	1779	Wilson
MIRSE, Jacob	1807	Cade

Surname, Given names	Year	Comp./Dist.
MITCHAL, David	1811	Barron
MITCHAL, James	1780-1781 (Undated)	
MITCHEL, Adam	1787	Fains
MITCHEL, Adam	1792	Tulley
MITCHEL, Adam	1793	Morrison
MITCHEL, Adam	1794	Morrison
MITCHEL, Adam	1795	Morrison
MITCHEL, Adam	1806	Carr
MITCHEL, Adam	1813	Hoss
MITCHEL, Adam	1814	Hoss
MITCHEL, Adam	[1796] 1797	Morris
MITCHEL, Adam (Samuel Fain's estate)	1794	Morrison
MITCHEL, Adam (Samuel Fain's Estate)	1793	Morrison
MITCHEL, David	1809	Patterson
MITCHEL, David	1812	Crawford [2]
MITCHEL, David	1812	Crawford [2]
MITCHEL, David	1821	Brown
MITCHEL, David Jr.	1812	Crawford
MITCHEL, Elizabeth	1808	Carr
MITCHEL, Elizabeth	1809	Roadmas
MITCHEL, Elizibath	1812	McCray
MITCHEL, James	1790	Stone
MITCHEL, James	1791	Stone
MITCHEL, James	1808	Parker
MITCHEL, James	1812	McCray
MITCHEL, James	1812	McCray
MITCHEL, James	1821	Hampton
MITCHEL, James A.	1821	Hampton
MITCHEL, John	1798	Morrison
MITCHEL, John	1799	Morrison
MITCHEL, John	1812	Crawford
MITCHEL, John	1812	Crawford [2]
MITCHEL, John	1814	McLin
MITCHEL, John Cove	1821	Brown
MITCHEL, Robart	[1796] 1797	Morris
MITCHEL, Robert	1795	Morrison
MITCHEL, Robert	1797	Calvert
MITCHEL, Robert	1805	Jas Parker
MITCHEL, Robert (estate)	1814	McCray
MITCHEL, Robt	1808	Parker
MITCHEL, Thomas	1805	Jas Parker
MITCHEL, Thomas	1812	McCray
MITCHEL, Thomas	1812	McCray
MITCHEL, Thomas	1821	Brown
MITCHEL, Thos	1808	Parker
MITCHEL, Thos	1780-1781 (Undated)	
MITCHEL, William	1812	McLin
MITCHEL, William	1821	Brown
MITCHEL, William Jr.	1821	Brown

Surname, Given names	Year	Comp./Dist.
MITCHEL, Wm	1807	Shields
MITCHEL, Wm	1809	Patterson
MITCHELL, Adam	1791	Tullis
MITCHELL, Adam	1798	Morrison
MITCHELL, Adam	1801	Morrison
MITCHELL, Adam	1808	Carr
MITCHELL, Adam	1815	Hoss
MITCHELL, Adam	1819	Jones
MITCHELL, Adam	1821	Jones
MITCHELL, Adam Jr.	1798	Morrison
MITCHELL, Adom	1807	Carr
MITCHELL, Andrew	1796	Young
MITCHELL, David	1801	Biddle
MITCHELL, David	1812	Barnes
MITCHELL, David	1812	Waddill
MITCHELL, David	1815	Grimsley
MITCHELL, David	1815	Waddell
MITCHELL, David	1816	Hunt
MITCHELL, David	1816	Waddell
MITCHELL, David	1817	Hampton
MITCHELL, David	1817	Hunt
MITCHELL, David	1817	Riley
MITCHELL, David	1818	Brown [2]
MITCHELL, David	1818	Hunt
MITCHELL, David	1818	Riley
MITCHELL, David	1819	Brown
MITCHELL, David	1819	Findley
MITCHELL, David	1819	Hunt
MITCHELL, David	1821	Hunt
MITCHELL, Elizabeth	1806	Carr
MITCHELL, Elizabeth	1811	McCray
MITCHELL, Elizabeth	1816	Harrison
MITCHELL, Elizabeth	1817	Harris
MITCHELL, Elizabeth	1818	Harris
MITCHELL, Hezekiah	1815	Waddell
MITCHELL, Hezekiah	1817	Riley
MITCHELL, Hezekiah	1819	Findley
MITCHELL, Hezekiah B.	1816	Waddell
MITCHELL, Hezekiah B.	1818	Riley
MITCHELL, James	1779	Wilson
MITCHELL, James	1781	
MITCHELL, James	1815	Hartsell
MITCHELL, James	1816	Brown
MITCHELL, James	1816	Hampton
MITCHELL, James	1817	Brown
MITCHELL, James	1817	Hampton
MITCHELL, James	1817	Smith
MITCHELL, James	1818	Brown [2]
MITCHELL, James	1818	Smith
MITCHELL, James	1819	Harris
MITCHELL, James	1819	Harris
MITCHELL, James	1819	Smith
MITCHELL, James	1819	Smith
MITCHELL, James	1820	Smith
MITCHELL, James	1820	Smith
MITCHELL, James	1821	Smith
MITCHELL, Joab	1778	
MITCHELL, John	1798	Morrison
MITCHELL, John	1801	Morrison
MITCHELL, John	1811	Green
MITCHELL, John	1812	Waddill
MITCHELL, John	1816	Harrison
MITCHELL, John	1819	Brown
MITCHELL, John	1819	Harris
MITCHELL, Nelson	1818	Harris
MITCHELL, Nelson	1819	Harris
MITCHELL, Robert	1797	Calvert
MITCHELL, Robert	1799	Stuart
MITCHELL, Robert	1801	Calvert
MITCHELL, Robert	1805	Aikin
MITCHELL, Robert (heirs of)	1818	Smith
MITCHELL, Robert (heirs)	1819	Smith
MITCHELL, Robt (heirs)	1820	Smith
MITCHELL, Thomas	1816	Harrison
MITCHELL, Thomas	1819	McClure
MITCHELL, Thomas	1780-1781 (Undated)	
MITCHELL, Thos	1781	
MITCHELL, Thos Jr.	1781	
MITCHELL, William	1805	Guir
MITCHELL, William	1808	Gwin
MITCHELL, William	1811	Green
MITCHELL, William	1812	Waddill
MITCHELL, William	1815	Waddell
MITCHELL, William	1816	Hampton
MITCHELL, William	1816	Waddell
MITCHELL, William	1817	Hampton
MITCHELL, William	1817	Riley
MITCHELL, William	1818	Brown [2]
MITCHELL, William	1818	Riley
MITCHELL, William	1819	Brown
MITCHELL, William	1819	Findley
MITCHELL, Wm	1801	Gann
MITCHELL, Wm	1810	Green
MITCHELL, Wm	1821	McGee
MITCHELL, Wm (Capt.)	1806	Grur
MITCHELL, Zebekiah	1821	Jones
MITCHILL, Wm	1809	Green
MITCHL, Robt (Estate Of)	1809	Parker
MITTEN, Simon	1812	Hartsell
MOBSON, Jacob	1821	Martin
MOCK, John (estate of)	1811	Green
MOCK, Joseph	1811	Green

Surname, Given names	Year	Comp./Dist.
MOFFATT, Alex	1793	Maxwell
MOFFET, William	1812	Brown
MOFFETT, William	1807	Odell
MOFFITT, William	1806	Odel
MOFFITT, William	1808	Odell
MOFFITT, William	1809	Viney
MOFFITT, William	1810	Cove
MOHLER, Henery	1814	Bean
MOHLER, Henry	1815	Haire
MO-K, John	1806	Grur
MOLENU, John	1816	Hoss
MOLER,	1817	Grisham
MOLER, Henry	1821	Hale
MOLER, John	1819	Grisham
MOLIN,	1818	Grisham
MONEY, James	1814	McCracken
MONEY, James	1816	Smith
MONTAIN, James	1817	Fine
MONTGOMERY, Alex	1790	Milleken
MONTGOMERY, Alex	1792	Milliken
MONTGOMERY, Alexander	1793	Milliken
MONTGOMERY, Alexdr	1794	Milliken
MONTGOMERY, Hugh	1790	Milleken
MONTGOMERY, James	1791	Milliken
MONTGOMERY, James	1793	Milliken
MONTGOMERY, James	1794	Milliken
MONTGOMERY, James	1795	Milliken
MONTGOMERY, Jas	1790	Milleken
MONTGOMERY, Jas	1792	Milliken
MONTGOMERY, Joe	1781	
MONTGOMERY, John	1797	Duncan
MONTGOMERY, Thomas	1791	Milliken
MONTGOMERY, Thomas	1794	Milliken
MONTGOMERY, Thos	1792	Milliken
MONTGOMERY, Thos	1793	Milliken
MONTGOMERY, William	1792	Depew
MONTGOMERY, William	1794	Depew
MONTGOMERY, Wm	1790	Milleken
MOON, Daniel	1819	Findley
MOON, John	1805	Jas Parker
MOON, Robert	1818	Harris
MOONEY, James	1815	Garner
MOOR, Abselom	1794	Taylor
MOOR, Alex	1791	Hanley
MOOR, Daniel	1794	Taylor
MOOR, Daniel	1811	Green
MOOR, Daniel	1817	Riley
MOOR, Daniel	1818	Riley
MOOR, Jame	1796	Young
MOOR, James	1791	North
MOOR, James	1792	North
MOOR, James	1794	North
MOOR, James	1798	Young
MOOR, James	1809	Patterson
MOOR, James	1817	Riley
MOOR, James	1818	Riley
MOOR, John	1779	
MOOR, John	1779	
MOOR, John	1801	Calvert
MOOR, Moses	1779	Wilson
MOOR, Moses	1812	McLin
MOOR, Moses	1815	McLin
MOOR, Moses Jr.	1781	
MOOR, Robert	1801	Calvert
MOOR, Robert	1816	Harrison
MOOR, Robert	1818	Harris
MOOR, Robert	1821	Hampton
MOOR, Robt	1809	Parker
MOOR, Samuel	1779	Wilson
MOOR, Samuel	1781	
MOOR, William	1781	
MOORE, Abraham	1792	Tulley
MOORE, Abraham	1793	Morrison
MOORE, Abraham	1794	Morrison
MOORE, Absolem	1792	Maxwell
MOORE, Alaxander	1799	Gann
MOORE, Alex	1790	Hanley
MOORE, Alexander	1794	Handly
MOORE, Alexander	1795	Handly
MOORE, Alexr	1793	Handley
MOORE, Allen	1797	Gann
MOORE, Allen	1799	Moore
MOORE, Anthony	1781	
MOORE, Anthony	1781	
MOORE, Anthony	1780-1781 (undated)	
MOORE, Babel	1812	McCray
MOORE, Babel	1812	McCray
MOORE, Daniel	1801	Gann
MOORE, Daniel	1806	Grur
MOORE, Daniel	1808	Gwin
MOORE, Daniel	1815	Waddell
MOORE, Daniel	1816	Waddell
MOORE, Dannel	1805	Guir
MOORE, James	1781	
MOORE, James	1781	
MOORE, James	1793	North
MOORE, James	1795	Young
MOORE, James	1810	Barron
MOORE, James	1821	McGee
MOORE, James	1780-1781 (Undated)	
MOORE, Jeptha	1798	Calvert

Surname, Given names	Year	Comp./Dist.
MOORE, Jepthah	1799	Hannah
MOORE, Jno Parker	1794	Carriger
MOORE, John	1778	
MOORE, John	1812	McCray
MOORE, John	1819	Harris
MOORE, John Parker	1790	Greer
MOORE, John Parker	1792	Greer
MOORE, John Parker	1795	Carriger
MOORE, Moses	1778	
MOORE, Moses	1781	
MOORE, Moses	1811	Davis
MOORE, Moses	1816	Hunt
MOORE, Moses Jr.	1779	Wilson
MOORE, Mosses	1808	Parker
MOORE, Mosses	1809	Parker
MOORE, Peter	1795	Murray
MOORE, Peter	1801	Roberson
MOORE, Rebecca	1821	McGee
MOORE, Robert	1798	Calvert
MOORE, Robert	1811	McCray
MOORE, Robert	1812	McCray
MOORE, Robert	1812	McCray
MOORE, Robert	1815	Harris
MOORE, Robert	1819	Harris
MOORE, Robert (Single)	1779	
MOORE, Robet	1811	McCray
MOORE, Robt	1808	Parker
MOORE, Samuel	1790	Shipley
MOORE, Samuel	1791	Shipley
MOORE, Samuel	1793	Murray
MOORE, Samuel	1794	Murray
MOORE, Samuel	1795	Murray
MOORE, Samuel	1796	Shipley
MOORE, Samuel	1797	Shipley
MOORE, Samuel Jr.	1780-1781 (undated)	
MOORE, William	1793	Handley
MOORE, William	1794	Handly
MOORE, William	1795	Handly
MOORE, William	1797	Gann
MOORE, William	1812	McCray
MOORE, William	1780-1781 (Undated)	
MOORE, Wm	1790	Hanley
MOORE, Wm	1791	Hanley
MOORE, Wm	1799	Moore
MORAY, Morgan	1778	
MORE, Alexander	1798	Gann
MORE, Danial	1799	Gann
MORE, Daniel	1795	Taylor
MORE, James	1797	Young
MORE, James	1798	Morrison

Surname, Given names	Year	Comp./Dist.
MORE, James	1780-1781 (Undated)	
MORE, Moses	1778	
MORE, Moses	1780-1781 (Undated)	
MORE, Peter	1798	Shipley
MORE, Reuben	1795	Morrison
MORE, Robert	1814	McCray
MORE, Robert	1817	Harris
MORE, Ruben	1798	Morrison
MORE, Ruben	1798	Morrison
MORE, Ruben	1799	Morrison
MORE, Ruben	[1796] 1797	Morris
MORE, Samuel	1798	Shipley
MORE, William	1798	Gann
MORELAND, William	1794	Ford
MORELAND, Wm	1795	Ford
MORGAN, Charles	1801	Glasscock
MORGAN, Cornelous	1801	Glasscock
MORGAN, Leonard	1778	
MORGAN, Lewis	1779	Wilson
MORISON, William	1811	Mitchell
MORISON, Wm	1809	Carr
MORLAND, William	1791	White
MORRELL, Glenmore	1821	Smith
MORRELL, John	1779	
MORRELL, Jonathan	1779	
MORRES, Hardy	1821	Martin
MORRESS, Gideon	1778	
MORRESS, Shadrick	1778	
MORRIS, Drury	1781	
MORRIS, Drury	1780-1781 (Undated)	
MORRIS, Gideon	1781	
MORRIS, Hardin	1816	Grimsley
MORRIS, Hardy	1817	Grimsley
MORRIS, Hardy	1819	Grimsley
MORRIS, John	1807	Bayles
MORRIS, John	1816	Smith
MORRIS, John	1817	Smith
MORRIS, John	1819	Smith
MORRIS, John	1820	Smith
MORRIS, John	1821	Smith
MORRIS, Lidsay	1818	Grimsley
MORRIS, Michael	1819	Grimsley
MORRIS, Shedrk	1781	
MORRISON, James	1798	Morrison
MORRISON, James	1798	Morrison
MORRISON, James	1799	Morrison
MORRISON, James	1801	Morrison
MORRISON, James	[1796] 1797	Morris
MORRISON, John	1778	
MORRISON, John	1791	Willey

Surname, Given names	Year	Comp./Dist.
MORRISON, Joseph	1787	Fains
MORRISON, Joseph	1791	Tullis
MORRISON, Joseph	1793	Morrison
MORRISON, Joseph	1794	Morrison
MORRISON, Joseph	1795	Morrison
MORRISON, Joseph	1798	Morrison
MORRISON, Joseph	1798	Morrison
MORRISON, Joseph	1799	Morrison
MORRISON, Joseph	1801	Morrison
MORRISON, Joseph	1806	Carr
MORRISON, Joseph	1808	Carr
MORRISON, Joseph	1814	Hoss
MORRISON, Joseph	1815	Hoss
MORRISON, Joseph	1816	Hoss
MORRISON, Joseph	1817	Little
MORRISON, Joseph	1818	Jones
MORRISON, Joseph	1819	Jones
MORRISON, Joseph	1821	Jones
MORRISON, Joseph	1821	Jones
MORRISON, Joseph	[1796] 1797	Morris
MORRISON, Joseph (Capt.)	1792	Tulley
MORRISON, Robert	1812	Ellis
MORRISON, Robert	1816	Giles
MORRISON, Robert	1817	Gillises
MORRISON, Robert	1821	Sands
MORRISON, Thomas	1793	Thornton
MORRISON, William	1808	Carr
MORRISON, William	1811	Britten
MORRISON, William	1815	Haire
MORRISON, William	1816	Hair
MORRISON, William	1817	Haire
MORRISON, William	1818	Hair
MORRISON, William	1819	Hair
MORRISS, Gidion	1779	
MORRISS, Shaderick	1779	
MORRISSON, Joseph	1807	Carr
MORRISSON, Robert	1809	Right
MORRISSON, William	1807	Carr
MORRON, Alexander	1781	
MORROW, Alexander	1779	Wilson
MORROW, Alexander	1780-1781 (Undated)	
MORROW, James	1781	
MORROW, James	1780-1781 (Undated)	
MORRSON, Joseph	1809	Carr
MORTEN, Caleb	1819	Hunt
MORTEN, John	1819	Hunt
MORTON, Enoch	1811	Green
MORY, William	1781	
MOSECK, William	1806	Anderson
MOSELEY, John	1790	Shipley
MOSELEY, John	1791	Shipley
MOSER, Anthoney	1793	Melvan
MOSES, Anthoney	1790	Stone
MOSES, Anthoney	1791	Stone
MOSES, James	1793	Milliken
MOSES, Mark	1814	Hoss
MOSES, Thomas	1821	Brown
MOTUPILLAR, Jacob	1808	Gwin
MOUNTCASTLE, Wm	1821	Smith
MOUNTGOMERY, Alexde	1791	Milliken
MOYARS, Fredderick	1808	Bayles
MOYER, John	1808	Gwin
MOYERS, Frederick	1806	Parker
MTICHELL, Wm	1814	Waddell
MUCKELROY, John	1805	Guir
MULANS, John	1795	Thornton
MULCHY, Phillip	1778	
MULKER, Jonathan (Rev.)	1805	Doak
MULKEY, James	1779	
MULKEY, James	1795	Ford
MULKEY, Jonathan	1790	Shipley
MULKEY, Jonathan	1791	Shipley
MULKEY, Jonathan	1793	Murray
MULKEY, Jonathan	1794	Murray
MULKEY, Jonathan	1797	Shipley
MULKEY, Jonathan	1798	Duncan
MULKEY, Jonathan (Reverant)	1795	Murray
MULKEY, Philip	1795	Ford
MULLEN, Jessa	1814	Barns
MULLEN, Jesse	1815	Grimsley
MULLEN, Jesse	1818	Grimsley
MULLENS, Jesa	1808	Cade
MULLENS, Jessa	1807	Cade
MULLENS, Jesse	1817	Grimsley
MULLENS, John	1794	Thornton
MULLENS, William	1794	Ford
MULLENS, William Jr.	1794	Ford
MULLENS, Wm	1795	Ford
MULLIN, Jess	1801	Glasscock
MULLIN, Wm Jr.	1795	Ford
MULLING, John	1793	Thornton
MULLINGS, William Jr.	1793	Campbell
MULLINS, Jess	1805	Rector
MULLINS, Jessa	1810	Barron
MULLINS, Jesse	1809	Cade
MULLINS, Jesse	1811	Barron
MULLINS, Jesse	1816	Grimsley
MULLINS, Jesse	1819	Grimsley
MULLINS, Jesse	1821	Martin
MULLINS, Jessee	1812	Barnes
MUNSON, John	1795	Calvert

Surname, Given names	Year	Comp./Dist.
MUR, John	1814	McCray
MUR, John	1815	Harris
MURAY, Charles	1809	Viney
MUREY, Jeriamiah	1795	Morrison
MURPHEY, Dennis	1791	Chisom
MURPHEY, Elijah	1814	McLin
MURPHEY, Joseph	1814	McLin
MURPHY, Dennis	1792	Chisolm
MURPHY, Dinnes	1792	Brown
MURPHY, George	1815	McLin
MURPHY, Jesse	1818	Hunt
MURPHY, Patrick	1778	
MURPHY, Patrick	1792	Coye
MURR, George	1821	Hampton
MURR, John	1799	Stuart
MURR, John	1816	Harrison
MURR, John	1817	Harris
MURR, John	1819	Harris
MURR, John	1821	Hampton
MURRAH, Joshua	1797	Hannah
MURRAY, Christopher	1798	Shipley
MURRAY, Christopher	1819	Grisham
MURRAY, Ephd	1793	North
MURRAY, Ephraim	1806	Parker
MURRAY, Ephraim	1819	Howard
MURRAY, Ephriam	1810	Hartzel
MURRAY, Ephrm	1795	Young
MURRAY, John	1811	Britten
MURRAY, John	1813	Copas
MURRAY, John	1814	Copes
MURRAY, John	1819	Grisham
MURRAY, John	1821	Hale
MURRAY, Morgan	1798	Shipley
MURRAY, Morgan	1801	Lane
MURRAY, Morgan	1805	Doak
MURRAY, Morgan	1814	Barns
MURRAY, Morgan (Capt.)	1791	
MURRAY, Shaderick	1801	Lane
MURRAY, Shadrach	1794	Murray
MURRAY, Shadrach	1798	Shipley
MURRAY, Shadrck	1813	Copas
MURRAY, Shadrick	1805	Doak
MURRAY, Shadrick	1807	Britton
MURRAY, Shadrick	1811	Britten
MURRAY, Shadrick	1819	Grisham
MURRAY, Thomas	1798	Shipley
MURRAY, Thomas	1801	Lane
MURRAY, Thomas	1811	Britten
MURRAY, Thomas	1812	Barnes
MURRAY, Thomas	1813	Copas
MURRAY, Thomas	1814	Copes
MURRAY, Thomas Jr.	1797	Shipley
MURRAY, Thomas Jr.	1798	Shipley
MURRAY, Thos Jr.	1801	Lane
MURRAY, William	1790	Greer
MURREY, Christopher	1795	Murray
MURREY, Ephraim	1801	Taylor
MURREY, Headrick	1812	Britton
MURREY, James	1778	
MURREY, John	1812	Britton
MURREY, Morgan	1794	Murray
MURREY, Morgan	1795	Murray
MURREY, Morgan	1796	Shipley
MURREY, Morgan	1797	Shipley
MURREY, Shadrack	1797	Shipley
MURREY, Shadrick	1806	Doke
MURREY, Thomas Jr.	1795	Murray
MURREYS, Thomas Sr.	1795	Murray
MURROW, Alex	1778	
MURRY, Christopher	1796	Shipley
MURRY, Christopher	1797	Shipley
MURRY, Christopher	1816	Copas
MURRY, Christopher	1817	Grisham
MURRY, Christopher	1818	Grisham
MURRY, Christopher	1821	Hale
MURRY, Ephraim	1797	Young
MURRY, Ephraim	1798	Young
MURRY, Ephraim	1815	Fines
MURRY, Ephraim	1816	Fine
MURRY, Ephraim	1817	Fine
MURRY, Ephraim	1818	Fine
MURRY, Ephrain	1809	Par
MURRY, Ephrem	1796	Young
MURRY, Ephrem	1807	Parker
MURRY, Ephrem	1814	Hartsell
MURRY, Ephrom	1821	Howard
MURRY, Epraim	1792	Greer
MURRY, Hogan	1814	Barns
MURRY, Jeremiah	[1796] 1797	Morris
MURRY, John	1815	Copas
MURRY, John	1816	Copas
MURRY, John	1817	Grisham
MURRY, John	1818	Grisham
MURRY, Joseph	1809	Cade
MURRY, Joseph	1815	Grimsley
MURRY, Joseph	1816	Grimsley
MURRY, Morgan	1793	Murray
MURRY, Morgan	1815	Grimsley
MURRY, Morzan	1816	Grimsley
MURRY, Shaderick	1815	Copas
MURRY, Shaderick	1816	Copas
MURRY, Shaderick	1817	Grisham

Surname, Given names	Year	Comp./Dist.
MURRY, Shaderick	1818	Grisham
MURRY, Shadrach	1795	Murray
MURRY, Shadrack	1793	Murray
MURRY, Shadrack	1796	Shipley
MURRY, Shadrock	1821	Hale
MURRY, Shamal Sr.	1796	Shipley
MURRY, Thomas Jr.	1796	Shipley
MURRY, Thomas Sr.	1793	Murray
MURRY, Thomas Sr.	1794	Murray
MURRY, Thomas Sr.	1797	Shipley
MURRY, William	1812	Hartsell
MURRY, William	1814	Hartsell
MURRY, William	1815	Fines
MURS, Philip	1816	Fine
MURY, Ephriam	1812	Hartsell
MURY, Thomas	1812	Britton
MUSGROVE, John	1792	Greer
MUSGROVE, John	1795	Carriger
MUSGROVE, Robert	1794	Carriger
MUSGROVE, Robert	1795	Carriger
MUSGROVE, Samuel	1795	Carriger
MUSGROVES, John	1792	Carriger
MUSGROVES, John	1794	Carriger
MYERS, Adam	1781	
MYERS, Fredk	1793	North
MYERS, Jacob	1809	Cade
MYERS, Samuel	1807	Anderson
MYRS, Christephor	1781	
NACE, Jesse	1799	Stuart
NA-E, Henry	1778	
NA-E, John	1778	
NA-E, Teter	1779	
NAIL, George	1792	Depew
NAIL, George	1806	Brown
NAIL, Hennery	1812	McCray
NAIL, Jessee	1812	McCray
NAIL, Wm	1793	Brown
NAILE, Jesse	1797	Calvert
NALE, Caleb	1811	McCray
NALE, Henry	1811	McCray
NALE, Jesse	1811	McCray
NALSON, George	1807	Carr
NALSON, James	1807	Carr
NANE, John	1795	Carriger
NARWOOD, John	1793	Murray
NATHERLAND, Isac	1783 [after]	Depew
NAUE, Teter	1778	
NAVE, Abraham	1792	Greer
NAVE, Abraham	1794	Carriger
NAVE, John	1792	Carriger
NAVE, Teter	1790	Greer
NAVE, Teter	1792	Carriger
NAVE, Teter	1792	Greer
NAVE, Teter	1794	Carriger
NAVE, Teter	1795	Carriger
NAY, John	1791	White
NEAL, George	1797	Robertson
NEAL, George	1798	Roberson
NEAL, George	1799	Robertson
NEAL, George	1801	Roberson
NEAL, Gorge	1796	Brown
NEAL, Henery	1796	Brown
NEAL, Henry	1797	Robertson
NEAL, Henry	1798	Roberson
NEAL, Henry	1799	Robertson
NEAL, Henry	1808	Parker
NEAL, Henry	1809	Parker
NEAL, Honey	1801	Roberson
NEAL, Jess	1801	Calvert
NEAL, Jesse	1805	Jas Parker
NEAL, Jesse	1808	Parker
NEAL, Jesse	1809	Parker
NEAL, Jesse	1812	McCray
NEAL, Johneal	1814	Barns
NEAL, Neelass	1780-1781 (undated)	
NEAL, William	1792	Depew
NEAL, William	1795	Calvert
NEAL, William	1796	Brown
NEAL, William	1798	Roberson
NEAL, William	1809	Bayles
NEAL, William Jr.	1801	Roberson
NEAL, William Sr.	1801	Roberson
NEAL, Wm	1797	Robertson
NEAL, Wm	1799	Robertson
NEALL, Samuel	1794	Depew
NEDE, Andrew	1808	Cade
NEDYHALE, Joshua	1821	Martin
NEEL, James	1792	Brown
NEEL, Samuel	1793	Depew
NELLON, Berryman	1798	Longmire
NELSON, Alec M.	1815	Garner
NELSON, Alexander	1812	Crawford [2]
NELSON, Alexander M.	1816	Smith
NELSON, Alexander M.	1817	Smith
NELSON, Benjamin	1817	Hampton
NELSON, Benjamin	1818	Brown [2]
NELSON, Benjamin	1819	Brown
NELSON, Benjman	1801	Longmire
NELSON, Benjmon	1796	Longmire
NELSON, Berriman	1816	Hampton
NELSON, Berrimore	1821	Brown
NELSON, Berry	1797	Longmire

Surname, Given names	Year	Comp./Dist.
NELSON, Berryman	1806	Odel
NELSON, Dan	1819	Findley
NELSON, David	1816	Smith
NELSON, David	1817	Riley
NELSON, David	1817	Smith
NELSON, David	1818	Riley
NELSON, David	1818	Smith
NELSON, David	1819	Smith
NELSON, David	1820	Smith
NELSON, David	1821	McGee
NELSON, David	1821	Smith
NELSON, Elenery	1812	Crawford [2]
NELSON, Elisha	1778	
NELSON, Georg	1806	Carr
NELSON, George	1793	Morrison
NELSON, George	1794	Morrison
NELSON, George	1798	Morrison
NELSON, George	1798	Morrison
NELSON, George	1801	Morrison
NELSON, George	1808	Carr
NELSON, George	1809	Carr
NELSON, George	1811	Mitchell
NELSON, George	[1796] 1797	Morris
NELSON, Henery	1798	Hannah
NELSON, Henery	1806	Payn
NELSON, Henery	1807	Payne
NELSON, Henery	1808	McAllister
NELSON, Henery	1809	McAlister
NELSON, Henery	1809	McAlister
NELSON, Henery	1811	McAlister
NELSON, Henery	1812	Crawford
NELSON, Henery	1814	Crookshanks
NELSON, Hennery	1792	Milliken
NELSON, Hennery	1793	Milliken
NELSON, Hennery	1795	Milliken
NELSON, Henry	1790	Williams
NELSON, Henry	1791	Williams
NELSON, Henry	1794	Milliken
NELSON, Henry	1796	Millikin
NELSON, Henry	1797	Hannah
NELSON, Henry	1799	Hannah
NELSON, Henry	1801	Squibb
NELSON, Henry	1806	Grur
NELSON, Henry	1807	Payne
NELSON, Henry	1809	Green
NELSON, Henry	1811	Green
NELSON, Henry	1812	Waddill
NELSON, Henry	1815	Crookshanks
NELSON, Henry	1815	Waddell
NELSON, Henry	1816	Crookshanks
NELSON, Henry	1816	Waddell
NELSON, Henry	1817	McClure
NELSON, Henry	1817	Riley
NELSON, Henry	1818	McClure
NELSON, Henry	1819	Findley
NELSON, Henry	1819	McClure
NELSON, Henry	1821	McClure
NELSON, Henry	1821	McGee
NELSON, James	1798	Morrison
NELSON, James	1801	Morrison
NELSON, James	1806	Carr
NELSON, James	1806	Carson
NELSON, James	1807	Shields
NELSON, James	1807	
NELSON, James	1808	Carr
NELSON, James	1809	Carr
NELSON, James	1809	Patterson
NELSON, James	1810	Dimmons
NELSON, James	1811	Mitchell
NELSON, James	1811	
NELSON, James	1813	Hoss
NELSON, James	1813	Hoss
NELSON, James	1814	Hoss
NELSON, James	1815	Carcathers
NELSON, James	1815	Hoss
NELSON, James	1816	Giles
NELSON, James	1816	Hoss
NELSON, James	1817	Little
NELSON, James	1818	Jones
NELSON, James N.	1817	Gillises
NELSON, Jane	1793	Morrison
NELSON, Jane	1794	Morrison
NELSON, Jane	1798	Morrison
NELSON, Jane	1798	Morrison
NELSON, Jane	1799	Morrison
NELSON, Jane	[1796] 1797	Morris
NELSON, Jean	1795	Morrison
NELSON, Jean (Widow)	1792	Tulley
NELSON, John	1790	Milleken
NELSON, John	1790	Stone
NELSON, John	1790	Williams
NELSON, John	1791	Milliken
NELSON, John	1791	Stone
NELSON, John	1791	Williams
NELSON, John	1792	Milliken
NELSON, John	1793	Milliken
NELSON, John	1794	Melvan
NELSON, John	1795	Melvan
NELSON, John	1796	Millikin
NELSON, John	1797	Hannah
NELSON, John	1798	Hannah
NELSON, John	1799	Hannah

Surname, Given names	Year	Comp./Dist.
NELSON, John	1801	Squibb
NELSON, John	1806	Payn
NELSON, John	1807	Payne
NELSON, John	1808	McAllister
NELSON, John	1809	McAlister
NELSON, John	1811	McAlister
NELSON, John	1812	Barnes
NELSON, John	1812	Crawford [2]
NELSON, John	1812	Crawford [2]
NELSON, John	1814	Crookshanks
NELSON, John	1814	Crookshanks
NELSON, John	1815	Crookshanks
NELSON, John	1816	Crookshanks
NELSON, John	1818	McClure
NELSON, John	1821	Hunt
NELSON, John A.	1795	Milliken
NELSON, John Jr.	1817	McClure
NELSON, John Jr.	1819	McClure
NELSON, John Sr.	1812	Crawford
NELSON, John Sr.	1812	Crawford [2]
NELSON, John Sr.	1817	McClure
NELSON, John Sr.	1818	McClure
NELSON, John Sr.	1819	McClure
NELSON, John Sr.	1821	McClure
NELSON, Joseph	1798	Biddle
NELSON, Joseph	1808	McAllister
NELSON, Joseph (Esqr.)	1780-1781 (Undated)	
NELSON, Luthey	1793	Handley
NELSON, Mack W.	1817	Little
NELSON, Mark M.	1819	Jones
NELSON, Mark W.	1818	Jones
NELSON, Mark W.	1821	Jones
NELSON, Moses	1817	Riley
NELSON, Moses	1818	Riley
NELSON, Nancy	1813	Hoss
NELSON, Nancy	1814	Hoss
NELSON, Nancy	1815	Hoss
NELSON, Nathan	1797	Duncan
NELSON, Nathan	1798	Duncan
NELSON, Nathan	1799	Duncan
NELSON, Nathan	1801	Taylor
NELSON, Nathan	1807	Givins
NELSON, Nathan	1808	Guin
NELSON, Nathan	1809	Gwin
NELSON, Nathan	1812	McLin
NELSON, Nathan	1814	McLin
NELSON, Nathan	1815	McLin
NELSON, Nathan	1816	Hunt
NELSON, Nathan	1817	Hunt
NELSON, Nathan	1818	Hunt
NELSON, Nathan	1819	Hunt

Surname, Given names	Year	Comp./Dist.
NELSON, Nathan	1821	Hunt
NELSON, Nathen	1811	Davis
NELSON, Natheniel	1806	Guin
NELSON, Sathey	1806	Grur
NELSON, Souther Jr.	1817	Riley
NELSON, Souther Sr.	1817	Riley
NELSON, Southerway	1814	Waddell
NELSON, Southey	1801	Gann
NELSON, Southey	1815	Waddell
NELSON, Southey	1816	Waddell
NELSON, Southmay	1821	McGee
NELSON, Southuay	1819	Findley
NELSON, Southwell	1818	Riley
NELSON, Southy	1778	
NELSON, Southy	1790	Hanley
NELSON, Southy	1791	Hanley
NELSON, Southy	1798	Gann
NELSON, Southy	1799	Moore
NELSON, Suthey	1796	Handly
NELSON, Suthey	1780-1781 (Undated)	
NELSON, Suthy	1812	Waddill
NELSON, Thirssey	1811	Green
NELSON, Thomas	1801	Taylor
NELSON, Thomas	1805	Carson
NELSON, Thomas	1808	Guin
NELSON, Thomas	1809	Gwin
NELSON, Thomas	1811	Davis
NELSON, Thomas	1812	McLin
NELSON, Thomas	1814	McCracken
NELSON, Thomas	1814	McLin
NELSON, Thomas	1815	Crookshanks
NELSON, Thomas	1815	McLin
NELSON, Thomas	1816	Crookshanks
NELSON, Thomas	1816	Hunt
NELSON, Thomas	1817	Hunt
NELSON, Thomas	1817	Smith
NELSON, Thomas	1818	Hunt
NELSON, Thomas	1819	Hunt
NELSON, Thomas	1821	Hunt
NELSON, Thomes	1806	Guin
NELSON, William	1778	
NELSON, William	1779	Wilson
NELSON, William	1787	Fains
NELSON, William	1792	Tulley
NELSON, William	1793	Morrison
NELSON, William	1794	Morrison
NELSON, William	1795	Morrison
NELSON, William	1797	Longmire
NELSON, William	1798	Morrison
NELSON, William	1799	Morrison
NELSON, William	1799	Morrison

Surname, Given names	Year	Comp./Dist.
NELSON, William	1801	Longmire
NELSON, William	1801	Morrison
NELSON, William	1801	Morrison
NELSON, William	1806	Odel
NELSON, William	1807	Carr
NELSON, William	1807	Carr
NELSON, William	1807	Odell
NELSON, William	1808	Carr
NELSON, William	1808	Odell
NELSON, William	1808	Odell
NELSON, William	1809	Green
NELSON, William	1809	Viney
NELSON, William	1810	Cove
NELSON, William	1810	Cove
NELSON, William	1811	Brown
NELSON, William	1811	Green
NELSON, William	1812	Brown
NELSON, William	1814	Brown
NELSON, William	1815	Hartsell
NELSON, William	1816	Brown
NELSON, William	1816	Hampton
NELSON, William	1817	Brown
NELSON, William	1817	Hampton
NELSON, William	1817	Riley
NELSON, William	1817	Riley
NELSON, William	1818	Brown [2]
NELSON, William	1818	Riley
NELSON, William	1819	Brown
NELSON, William	1819	Brown
NELSON, William	1819	Jones
NELSON, William	1821	Brown
NELSON, William	1821	Haines
NELSON, William	1821	Jones
NELSON, William	[1796] 1797	Morris
NELSON, William Jr.	1798	Morrison
NELSON, William Jr.	1798	Morrison
NELSON, William Jr.	1806	Carr
NELSON, William Jr.	1808	Carr
NELSON, William Sr.	1798	Morrison
NELSON, William Sr.	1806	Carr
NELSON, William Sr.	1811	Mitchell
NELSON, William Sr.	1813	Hoss
NELSON, William Sr.	1814	Hoss
NELSON, William Sr.	1815	Hoss
NELSON, William Sr.	1817	Little
NELSON, William Sr.	1818	Jones
NELSON, Wm	1790	Hanley
NELSON, Wm	1791	Hanley
NELSON, Wm	1791	Tullis
NELSON, Wm	1809	Carr
NELSON, Wm	1812	Waddill

Surname, Given names	Year	Comp./Dist.
NELSON, Wm	1814	Hampton
NERSON, William Sr.	1813	Hoss
NEWBURY, Joseph	1812	Waddill
NEWEL, Joseph	1793	Depew
NEWEL, Joseph	1794	Depew
NEWEL, Joseph	1783 [after]	Depew
NEWHOUSE, Sevier	1792	Coye
NEWMAN, Hugh	1797	Calvert
NEWMAN, John	1781	
NEWMAN, John	1781	
NEWMAN, Paul	1797	Calvert
NEWMAN, Peter	1811	Britten
NEWMAN, Peter	1812	Britton
NEWMAN, Peter	1813	Copas
NEWMAN, Peter	1814	Bean
NEWMAN, Peter	1815	Haire
NEWMAN, Peter	1816	Hair
NEWMAN, Peter	1817	Haire
NEWMAN, Peter	1818	Hair
NICHOLAS, Daniel	1792	Maxwell
NICHOLAS, Daniel	1794	Taylor
NICHOLS, Daniel	1793	Maxwell
NICKELS, James	1797	Longmire
NILSON, Joseph	1805	Guir
NILSON, Thomas	1807	Givins
NOBAN, George	1790	Shipley
NOBAN, George	1791	Shipley
NODDING, William	1792	Scott
NODDING, William	1795	Calvert
NODDING, William	1796	Calvert
NODDING, William	1798	Calvert
NODING, Wilam	1794	Scot
NODING, Willim	1797	Calvert
NODING, Wm	1799	Stuart
NODING, Wm	1812	McCray
NODING, Wm Jr.	1791	Willey
NODING, Wm. Sr.	1791	Willey
NODY, Wiliam	1793	Scott
NOLAN, George	1793	Murray
NOLAN, George	1794	Murray
NOLAN, George	1795	Murray
NOLAN, George	1797	Shipley
NOLAN, James	1793	Murray
NOLAN, James	1794	Murray
NOLAN, James	1795	Murray
NOLAN, James	1797	Shipley
NOLAND, James	1796	Shipley
NOLAND, James	1798	Shipley
NOLANG, George	1798	Shipley
NOLEN, George	1801	Lane
NOLEN, George (heirs of)	1813	Copas

Surname, Given names	Year	Comp./Dist.
NOLEN, James	1801	Glasscock
NORRIS, James	1821	Haines
NORRIS, John	1815	Haire
NORRIS, Phillip	1819	Smith
NORRIS, Thomas	1821	Haines
NORTEN, David	1780-1781 (Undated)	
NORTH, Geo	1796	Young
NORTH, Geo (Capt.)	1791	
NORTH, Geore	1795	Young
NORTH, George	1791	North
NORTH, George	1797	Young
NORTH, George	1798	Young
NORTH, George	1801	Taylor
NORTH, George	1805	Parker
NORTH, George	1806	Parker
NORTH, George	1810	Hartzel
NORTH, George	1812	Hartsell
NORTH, George	1814	Brown
NORTH, George	1815	Fines
NORTH, George	1815	Hartsell
NORTH, George	1816	Brown
NORTH, George	1817	Brown
NORTH, George	1818	Brown
NORTH, George	1819	Brown
NORTH, George (Capt.)	1792	North
NORTH, George (Capt.)	1793	North
NORTH, George (Capt.)	1794	North
NORTH, John	1791	North
NORTH, John	1792	North
NORTH, John	1793	North
NORTON, Enoch	1796	Longmire
NORTON, Enoch	1812	McLin
NORWOOD, John	1794	Murray
NORWOOD, John	1795	Murray
NORWOOD, John	1797	Shipley
NORWOOD, John	1798	Crouch
NORWOOD, John	1801	Norwood
NORWOOD, John	1808	Carr
NORWOOD, John Jr.	1806	Carr
NORWOOD, John Jr.	1807	Carr
NORWOOD, John Jr.	1808	Carr
NORWOOD, John Jr.	1809	Carr
NORWOOD, John Sr.	1806	Carr
NORWOOD, John Sr.	1807	Carr
NORWOOD, John Sr.	1809	Carr
NOWLAN, Georg	1796	Shipley
NOWLAN, John	1792	Carriger
NOWLAN, John	1794	Carriger
NOWLAND, John	1792	Greer
NOWLEN, John	1795	Carriger
NULY, Benjamin	1819	Smith

Surname, Given names	Year	Comp./Dist.
NUMON, Peter	1819	Hair
NUMON, Peter	1821	Louis
NUNN, Thorton	1796	Handly
NUNN, Warten	1795	Handly
NUNN, Wharton	1797	Gann
NURMAN, Hugh	1799	Stuart
NUTT, John M.	1811	McAlister
OADEL, Caleb Jr.	1779	
OADLE, Isaac	1779	
OADLE, John	1779	
OADLE, Tompkins	1779	
OADLE, William	1779	
OAR, Robert	1806	Guin
OAR, Robert	1812	McLin
OAR, Thomas	1796	Young
OARE, Robert	1808	Guin
OB?ES, Thos	1795	Young
OBENGER, Daniel	1816	Grimsley
OD---, Calib	1778	
ODARE, James	1809	Gwin
ODDENEAL, Bartholomew	1783 [after]	Depew
ODEL, Abraham	1811	Brown
O'DEL, Abraham	1814	Brown
ODELL, Abraham	1808	Odell
ODELL, Abraham	1809	Viney
ODELL, Abraham	1816	Brown
ODELL, Abraham	1817	Brown
ODELL, Abraham	1818	Brown
ODELL, Abraham	1819	Brown
ODELL, Abraham	1821	Haines
O'DELL, Abraham	1810	Cove
ODELL, Abram	1807	Odell
ODELL, Baillet	1817	Brown
ODELL, Bartholomew	1816	Brown
O'DELL, Bartlett	1814	Brown
ODELL, Benkin	1810	Cove
ODELL, James	1816	Hair
ODELL, James	1818	Brown
ODELL, Job	1791	Tullis
ODELL, John	1816	Brown
ODELL, Reuben	1809	Viney
ODELL, Reuben Jr.	1816	Brown
O'DELL, William	1814	Brown
ODENALE, William	1816	Giles
ODENALE, William B.	1815	Carcathers
ODENEAL, Bartholomew	1808	Cade
ODENEAL, Bartholomy	1797	Shipley
ODENEAL, Bartley	1807	Cade
ODENEAL, William	1807	Cade
ODENEAL, William	1810	Barron
ODENEEL, Bartholomew	1801	Glasscock

Surname, Given names	Year	Comp./Dist.
ODENEEL, Bartholomew	1805	Rector
ODENEEL, William	1805	Rector
ODENEEL, Wm	1801	Glasscock
ODENEIL, William	1809	Cade
ODENELL, William	1821	Sands
ODENIAL, William	1818	Land
ODENUL, Wililam	1817	Gillises
ODINEAL, Bartholom	1798	Shipley
ODINEAL, Bartholomew	1812	Barnes
ODINEAL, William	1819	Grimsley
ODIRHOLSTER, Samuel	1816	Crookshanks
ODLE,	1793	Morrison
ODLE,	1794	Morrison
ODLE, Abraham	1806	Odel
ODLE, Abraham	1812	Brown
ODLE, Abraham	1815	Hartsell
ODLE, Bartlet	1815	Hartsell
ODLE, Caleb	1790	Williams
ODLE, Caleb	1791	Williams
ODLE, Caleb	1792	Tulley
ODLE, James	1815	Hartsell
ODLE, Job	1792	Tulley
ODLE, Job	1793	Morrison
ODLE, Job	1794	Morrison
ODLE, Reuben	1801	Longmire
ODNEAL, Bartholemew	1811	Barron
ODNEAL, Barthomew	1809	Cade
ODNEAL, William	1811	Barron
ODWAL, John	1778	
OEN, James	1796	Melvin
OLDHAM, Henry	1787	Griggs
OLDHAM, Henry	1790	Stone
OLDHAM, Henry	1791	Stone
OLDHAM, Henry	1793	Melvan
OLDHAM, Henry	1794	Melvan
OLDHAM, Henry	1795	Melvan
OLDINGER, Daniel	1814	Barns
OLINGER, Daniel	1815	Grimsley
OLIVER, Henry	1812	Ellis
OLIVER, John	1809	Right
OLIVER, John	1811	Ellis
OLIVER, John	1812	Ellis
OLIVER, John	1812	Ellis
OLIVER, John	1814	McCray
OLIVER, John	1814	McLin
OLIVER, John	1815	Haire
OLIVER, John	1819	Hunt
OLIVER, John (of Wm.)	1811	Ellis
OLIVER, John (wild)	1812	Ellis
OLIVER, Joseph	1809	Right
OLIVER, Joseph	1812	Ellis
OLIVER, Samuel	1812	Ellis
OLIVER, William	1812	Ellis
OLLIVER, Samuel	1809	Right
O'NEAL, Bartholomew	1810	Barron
ONEAL, John	1778	
ONEAL, William	1808	Cade
ORE, Thos	1780-1781 (Undated)	
ORI, Sample	1817	Harris
ORR, Robart	1807	Givins
ORR, Robert	1809	Gwin
ORR, Robert	1811	Davis
ORR, Sample	1821	Brown
ORR, Samuel	1819	Harris
ORR, Thomas	1797	Young
ORR, Thomas	1798	Duncan
ORR, William	1817	Hampton
OSEMUS, Henry	1801	Taylor
OSIMAS, Henery	1798	Young
OSMUS, Philip	1793	North
OUR, Thomas	1799	Duncan
OURHOTSON, Samuel	1819	McClure
OUTLAW, Alexr	1798	Calvert
OUTZ, Adam	1812	Waddill
OVERALL, William	1778	
OVERBOLT, Samuel	1812	Crawford
OVERHOLT, Jacob	1809	Parker
OVERHOLT, Jacob	1811	McAlister
OVERHOLT, Jacob	1812	Crawford [2]
OVERHOLT, Jacob	1815	Crookshanks
OVERHOLT, Jacob	1817	McClure
OVERHOLT, Saml	1814	Crookshanks
OVERHOLT, Samuel	1811	McAlister
OVERHOLT, Samuel	1812	Crawford [2]
OVERHOLT, Samuel	1815	Crookshanks
OVERHOLT, Samuel	1817	McClure
OVERHOLT, Samuel	1818	McClure
OVERHOLT, Samuel	1821	McClure
OVERHOLTS, Jacob	1808	Parker
OVERHOLTSSER, Jacob	1805	Jas Parker
OVERSLACK, Benjamin	1806	Grur
OWEINGA, James	1778	
OWEN, James	1793	Murray
OWEN, James	1794	Murray
OWEN, James	1795	Murray
OWEN, James	1801	Norwood
OWEN, James	1812	Britton
OWEN, James	1813	Copas
OWEN, James	1814	Copes
OWEN, Rachel	1821	Brown
OWENS, Ben	1780-1781 (Undated)	

Surname, Given names	Year	Comp./Dist.
OWENS, Elias	1816	Hunt
OWENS, Elias	1819	Hunt
OWENS, Elias	1821	Hunt
OWENS, James	1810	Barron
OWENS, James	1811	Britten
OWENS, James	1815	Copas
OWENS, Orvin	1781	
OWENS, Owen	1779	Wilson
OWENS, Rachal	1809	Bayles
OWENS, Rachel	1814	Hampton
OWENS, Rachel	1816	Hampton
OWENS, Rachel	1817	Hampton
OWENS, Rachel	1818	Brown [2]
OWENS, Rachel	1819	Brown
OWENS, Robert	1810	Barron
OWENS, Robert	1812	Barnes
OZEMIUS, Philip	1791	North
OZMUS, Petter	1792	North
PADFIELD, Wm	1791	Milliken
PADFIELD, Wm	1792	Milliken
PADFIELD, Wm	1793	Milliken
PAGE, Nathan	1809	Cade
PAGE, Nathan	1810	Barron
PAGE, Nathan	1815	Grimsley
PAGE, Nathan	1816	Grimsley
PAGE, Robert	1808	Cade
PAGE, Robert	1809	Cade
PAGE, Robert	1810	Barron
PAIN, Jese	1794	Scot
PAIN, Jesse	1819	McClure
PAIN, Jesse Jr.	1819	McClure
PAIN, Jesse Jr.	1821	McClure
PAIN, Jesse Sr.	1821	McClure
PAIN, John	1798	Shipley
PAIN, Joseph	1821	McClure
PAIN, Reuben	1799	Moore
PAIN, Reubin	1793	Murray
PAIN, Reubin	1796	Handly
PAIN, Robert	1819	McClure
PAIN, Robert	1821	McClure
PAIN, Ruben	1790	Shipley
PAIN, Ruben	1791	Shipley
PAIN, William	1819	McClure
PAIN, William	1821	McClure
PAINE, Reuben	1796	Handly
PAINTER, Adam	1790	Hanley
PAINTER, Adam	1801	Gann
PAINTER, Adam	1812	Waddill
PAINTER, Adam	1814	Waddell
PAINTER, Adam	1815	Waddell
PAINTER, Adam	1817	Riley
PAINTER, Adam	1819	Findley
PAINTER, Adam	1819	Findley
PAINTER, Adam	1821	McGee
PAINTER, Adam Jr.	1816	Waddell
PAINTER, Adam Jr.	1818	Riley
PAINTER, Adam Sr.	1815	Waddell
PAINTER, Adam Sr.	1816	Waddell
PAINTER, Adam Sr.	1818	Riley
PAINTER, Adam Sr.	1821	McGee
PAINTER, David	1812	Waddill
PAINTER, David	1815	Waddell
PAINTER, David	1816	Waddell
PAINTER, David	1817	Riley
PAINTER, David	1818	Riley
PAINTER, David	1819	Findley
PAINTER, David	1821	McGee
PAINTER, Ezekiel	1801	Gann
PAINTER, Ezekiel	1821	McGee
PAINTER, Jacob	1815	Carcathers
PAINTER, Jese	1821	McGee
PAINTER, Philip	1821	McGee
PAINTER, Phillip	1819	Findley
PAINTER, William	1816	Waddell
PAINTER, William	1817	Riley
PAINTER, William	1818	Riley
PAINTER, William	1819	Findley
PAINTER, William	1821	McGee
PAINTER, Wm	1814	Waddell
PALESTINE, Jonas	1778	
PALLEN, Jacob	1814	Bean
PALMER, John	1816	Hoss
PALMER, Joshua	1809	Bayles
PANE, Daniel	1810	Barron
PANE, John	1799	Robertson
PANTER, Adam	1799	Moore
PANTHER, Adam	1794	Handly
PANTHER, Adam	1795	Handly
PANTHER, Ezekiel	1799	Moore
PANYMORE, Wm	1781	
PAR, Robert	1801	Taylor
PARCE, Ezra	1819	Hunt
PARCE, William	1819	Hunt
PAREMON, Mathew	1780-1781 (Undated)	
PAREMOR, William	1780-1781 (Undated)	
PARKER, Adam	1797	Gann
PARKER, Charles	1778	
PARKER, James	1797	Calvert
PARKER, James	1797	Calvert
PARKER, James	1799	Stuart
PARKER, James	1801	Calvert

Surname, Given names	Year	Comp./Dist.
PARKER, James	1805	Jas Parker
PARKER, James	1805	Parker
PARKER, James	1808	Parker
PARKER, James	1809	Parker
PARKER, James	1811	McCray
PARKER, James	1812	McCray
PARKER, James	1814	McCray
PARKER, James	1815	Harris
PARKER, James	1816	Harrison
PARKER, James	1818	Harris
PARKER, James	1819	Harris
PARKER, James	1821	Hampton
PARKER, John	1794	North
PARKER, John	1795	Young
PARKER, John	1796	Young
PARKER, John	1797	Young
PARKER, John	1798	Young
PARKER, John	1801	Taylor
PARKER, John	1805	Parker
PARKER, John	1806	Parker
PARKER, John	1807	Parker
PARKER, John	1809	Par
PARKER, John	1810	Hartzel
PARKER, John	1812	Britton
PARKER, John	1814	Hartsell
PARKER, John	1815	Fines
PARKER, John	1816	Fine
PARKER, John	1817	Fine
PARKER, John	1818	Fine
PARKER, John	1819	Howard
PARKER, John H.	1821	Howard
PARKER, John Sr.	1821	Howard
PARKER, Joseph	1812	Crawford
PARKER, Joseph	1818	Fine
PARKER, Joshiah	1812	Hartsell
PARKER, Joshiah	1814	Hartsell
PARKER, Josiah	1801	Taylor
PARKER, Josiah	1806	Parker
PARKER, Josiah	1807	Parker
PARKER, Josiah	1810	Hartzel
PARKER, Josiah	1815	Fines
PARKER, Josiah	1816	Fine
PARKER, Josiah	1817	Fine
PARKER, Josiah	1819	Howard
PARKER, Josiah	1821	Howard
PARKER, Philup	1821	Brown
PARKER, Samuel	1817	Harris
PARKER, William	1779	
PARKER, William	1781	
PARKER, Wm	1778	
PARKERSON, George	1779	
PARKERSON, John	1807	Parker
PARKERSON, Mary	1791	White
PARKES, John	1812	Hartsell
PARKESON, John	1805	Parker
PARKS, Alfred	1819	Smith
PARKS, Mathan	1801	Taylor
PARKS, Nathan	1806	Carr
PARKS, Nathen	1807	Carr
PARKS, P. Alfred	1821	Smith
PARKS, Philip	1801	Taylor
PARKS, Philip	1816	Hampton
PARKS, Philip	1817	Hampton
PARKS, Philip	1818	Brown [2]
PARKS, Philip	1819	Brown
PARKS, Phillip	1814	Hampton
PARKS, Phillip Jr.	1808	Bayles
PARKS, Phillip Jr.	1809	Bayles
PARKS, Phillip Sr.	1806	Brown
PARKS, Phillip Sr.	1808	Bayles
PARKS, Phillip Sr.	1809	Bayles
PARKS, Phillup	1806	Brown
PARKS, William	1805	Parker
PARKS, William	1811	Rodman
PARMER, Joshua	1806	Guin
PARMER, Joshuaway	1808	Bayles
PARRIMORE, Ezecial	1781	
PARRIS, Robert	1781	
PARRY, David	1781	
PARSON, P.	1818	Smith
PARSONS,	1819	Smith
PARSONS, James	1819	Findley
PARSONS, Jesse	1795	Ford
PARSONS, Peter	1814	McCracken
PARSONS, Peter	1815	Garner
PARTERS, Henery	1801	Glasscock
PATE, Mathew	1781	
PATE, Matthew (Estate of John Kennedy decd.)	1779	Wilson
PATE, Nathen	1780-1781 (Undated)	
PATEET, Thomas	1814	Barns
PATEN, Alex	1798	Morrison
PATERSON, John	1779	Wilson
PATERSON, William	1797	Longmire
PATON, John	1795	Thornton
PATRICK, James	1794	Carriger
PATRICK, Jesse	1795	Carriger
PATRICK, Jessey	[1796] 1797	Morris
PATRON, John	1817	Smith
PATTEN, Anthoney	1798	Biddle
PATTEN, John	1805	Aikin
PATTEN, Thomas C.	1805	Jas Parker

Surname, Given names	Year	Comp./Dist.
PATTERSO, James	1798	Biddle
PATTERSON, James	1794	Blair
PATTERSON, James	1797	Biddle
PATTERSON, James	1798	Biddle
PATTERSON, James	1801	Biddle
PATTERSON, James	1807	Shields
PATTERSON, James	1809	Patterson
PATTERSON, James	1810	Dimmons
PATTERSON, James	1811	
PATTERSON, James	1814	Couthers
PATTERSON, John	1778	
PATTERSON, John	1781	
PATTERSON, William	1801	Longmire
PATTERSON, Willm	1798	Longmire
PATTERSON, Willm	1814	Crookshanks
PATTERSON, Wm	1796	Longmire
PATTERSON, Wm	1809	Patterson
PATTISON, John	1812	McCray
PATTON, Anthony	1797	Biddle
PATTON, Anthony	1798	Biddle
PATTON, Anthony	1806	Anderson
PATTON, Jacob	1812	Ellis
PATTON, John	1797	Duncan
PATTON, John	1798	Duncan
PATTON, John	1798	Duncan
PATTON, John	1799	Duncan
PATTON, John	1801	Biddle
PATTON, John	1801	Taylor
PATTON, John	1806	Anderson
PATTON, John	1807	Anderson
PATTON, John	1809	Roadmas
PATTON, John	1811	Rodman
PATTON, John	1815	Garner
PATTON, John	1816	Smith
PATTON, John	1818	Smith
PATTON, John	1819	McClure
PATTON, John	1819	Smith
PATTON, John	1820	Smith
PATTON, John	1821	Smith
PATTON, Joseph	1821	McGee
PATTON, Robert	1799	Duncan
PATTON, Robert	1821	Smith
PATTON, Thomas	1807	Bayles
PATTON, Thomas	1808	Bayles
PATTON, Thomas C.	1811	McCray
PATTON, Thomas C.	1812	McCray
PATTON, Thomas C.	1812	McCray
PATTON, Thomas C.	1814	McCray
PATTON, Thomas C.	1818	Harris
PATTON, Thomas C.	1819	Harris
PATTON, Thomas C.	1821	Hampton
PATTON, Thos C.	1809	Parker
PATTON, William	1801	Squibb
PATTON, William	1805	Guir
PATTON, William	1808	Gwin
PATTON, William	1811	Green
PATTON, William	1812	Waddill
PATTON, William	1815	Waddell
PATTON, William	1816	Waddell
PATTON, William	1817	Riley
PATTON, William	1818	Riley
PATTON, William	1819	Findley
PATTON, William	1821	McGee
PATTON, Wm	1806	Grur
PATTON, Wm	1809	Green
PATTON, Wm	1810	Green
PATTON, Wm	1814	Waddell
PAULEY, Edward	1795	Ford
PAYN, Jesse	1796	Millikin
PAYN, John	1801	Roberson
PAYNE, Daniel	1809	Cade
PAYNE, Henery	1808	McAllister
PAYNE, Henery	1809	McAlister
PAYNE, Henery	1812	Crawford
PAYNE, Henery	1812	Crawford [2]
PAYNE, Henery	1814	Crookshanks
PAYNE, Henry	1806	Payn
PAYNE, Henry	1811	McAlister
PAYNE, James	1805	Rector
PAYNE, Jesse	1798	Hannah
PAYNE, Jesse	1806	Payn
PAYNE, Jesse	1808	McAllister
PAYNE, Jesse	1812	Crawford [2]
PAYNE, Jesse	1818	McClure
PAYNE, Jesse (Esq.)	1799	Hannah
PAYNE, Jesse Jr.	1812	Crawford
PAYNE, Jesse Jr.	1814	Crookshanks
PAYNE, Jesse Jr.	1816	Crookshanks
PAYNE, Jesse Jr.	1817	McClure
PAYNE, Jesse Jr.	1818	McClure
PAYNE, Jesse Sr.	1808	McAllister
PAYNE, Jesse Sr.	1814	Crookshanks
PAYNE, Jesse Sr.	1817	McClure
PAYNE, Jessee	1795	Calvert
PAYNE, Jessee	1809	McAlister
PAYNE, Jessee	1809	McAlister
PAYNE, Jessee (Esq.)	1811	McAlister
PAYNE, Jessee Jr.	1811	McAlister
PAYNE, Jessie Jr.	1815	Crookshanks
PAYNE, Jessie Sr.	1801	Squibb
PAYNE, Jessie Sr.	1815	Crookshanks
PAYNE, Jessie Sr.	1816	Crookshanks

Surname, Given names	Year	Comp./Dist.
PAYNE, John	1793	Thornton
PAYNE, Robert	1806	Payn
PAYNE, Robert	1808	McAllister
PAYNE, Robert	1811	McAlister
PAYNE, Robert	1812	Crawford
PAYNE, Robert	1812	Crawford [2]
PAYNE, Robert	1814	Crookshanks
PAYNE, Robert	1815	Crookshanks
PAYNE, Robert	1816	Crookshanks
PAYNE, Robert	1817	McClure
PAYNE, Robert	1818	McClure
PAYNE, Robt	1809	McAlister
PAYNE, Rubin	1799	Stuart
PAYNE, Wilam	1812	Crawford [2]
PAYNE, William	1808	McAllister
PAYNE, William	1811	McAlister
PAYNE, William	1812	Crawford
PAYNE, William	1815	Crookshanks
PAYNE, William	1816	Crookshanks
PAYNE, William	1817	McClure
PAYNE, William	1818	McClure
PAYNE, Willm	1809	McAlister
PAYNE, Wm	1814	Crookshanks
PAYNEE, Jess	1797	Hannah
PEACHEASE, John	1795	Thornton
PEAN, Jessee	1793	Scott
PEARCE, Ezra	1817	Hunt
PEARCE, James	1778	
PEARCE, James	1816	Hoss
PEARCE, James	1817	Little
PEARCE, Joshua	1795	Murray
PEARCE, Joshua	1797	Shipley
PEARCE, Philip Graford	1794	Murray
PEARCE, Philip Groford	1793	Melvan
PEARCEFIELD, Samuel	1795	Morrison
PEARMAN, James	1805	Jas Parker
PEARMAN, Jas	1809	Parker
PEARMON, James	1801	Roberson
PEBELS, Robert	1779	
PEBELS, Robert	1779	
PEBLET, John	1781	
PECTEROW, Alexander	1815	Waddell
PEEKINS, John	1779	Wilson
PEINEL, John	1818	Land
PEIRCE, James	1814	Hoss
PEIRCE, James	1780-1781 (undated)	
PEKINS, John	1780-1781 (Undated)	
PELLOT, John	1779	Wilson
PENNEY, James	1801	Gann
PENNEY, John	1796	Handly
PENNILTON, Reubin	1806	Brown
PENNY, James	1808	Gwin
PENNY, James	1809	Green
PENNY, James	1810	Green
PENNY, James	1811	Green
PENNY, James	1812	Waddill
PENNY, James	1814	Waddell
PENTER, Adam	1791	Hanley
PENTER, Adam	1793	Handley
PENTER, Adam	1799	Gann
PENTER, Esakel	1798	Gann
PENTHER, Adam	1796	Handly
PEOPLES, John	1790	Williams
PEOPLES, John	1791	Williams
PEOPLES, John	1793	Maxwell
PEOPLES, John	1794	Taylor
PEOPLES, John	1795	Taylor
PEOPLES, Nathan	1814	Brown
PEOPLES, Nathan	1815	Hoss
PEOPLES, Nathan	1816	Brown
PEOPLES, Nathan	1821	Howard
PEOPLES, Nathaniel	1815	Hartsell
PEOPLES, William	1791	
PEOPLES, William	1792	Maxwell
PEOPLES, William	1794	Taylor
PEOPLES, William	1795	Taylor
PEOPLES, Wm	1793	Maxwell
PERCE, James	1780-1781 (Undated)	
PERCEFIELD, Samuel	[1796] 1797	Morris
PERCETULL, Sammuel	1793	Morrison
PERCETULL, Sammuel	1794	Morrison
PEREY, David	1780-1781 (Undated)	
PERIGEN, Henry	1805	Jas Parker
PERKESON, Mary	1794	Ford
PERKINS, George	1790	White
PERKINS, George	1791	White
PERKINS, George	1792	White
PERKINS, George	1793	Campbell
PERKINS, George	1795	Carriger
PERKINS, Jacob	1791	White
PERKINS, Jacob	1794	Thornton
PERKINS, James	1793	Campbell
PERKINS, Joshua	1790	White
PERKINS, Joshua	1791	White
PERMAN, James	1808	Bayles
PERREYMORE, Ezekiel	1780-1781 (Undated)	
PERRY, David	1815	Haire
PERRY, David	1816	Hair
PERRY, David	1817	Haire
PERRY, David	1818	Hair

Surname, Given names	Year	Comp./Dist.
PERRYMORE, Ezihaiel	1779	Wilson
PERSELL, John	1821	Sands
PERSON, Aron	1778	
PERSON, Joseph	1780-1781 (Undated)	
Peter	1798	Biddle
PETERS, Christian	1794	Carriger
PETERS, Christian	1795	Carriger
PETERS, Christopher	1792	Greer
PETERS, Daniel	1793	Thornton
PETERS, J. Michael Smith	1792	Greer
PETERS, John Michael Smith	1794	Carriger
PETERS, Michael S.	1795	Carriger
PETERS, Michael Smith	1779	
PETNER, John	1798	Young
PETRE, Adam	1795	Ford
PETRE, Daniel	1795	Ford
PETTERSON, James	1805	Carson
PETTERSON, James	1806	Carson
PEW, Jacob	1805	Rector
PEWET, Joel	1797	Young
PEWET, Joel	1798	Young
PEYBURN, Benjamin	1778	
PHAIN, Nicolus	1780-1781 (Undated)	
PHAIN, William	1780-1781 (Undated)	
PHILIPINT, Thomas	1780-1781 (Undated)	
PHILIPS, John	1811	McCray
PHILLIP, Dyer	1801	Biddle
PHILLIPS,	1795	Ford
PHILLIPS, Baty	1821	McGee
PHILLIPS, Charles	1778	
PHILLIPS, Charles	1779	
PHILLIPS, Charles	1811	Brown
PHILLIPS, David	1797	Duncan
PHILLIPS, David	1798	Duncan
PHILLIPS, David	1798	Duncan
PHILLIPS, Gabl	1793	North
PHILLIPS, Gabrell	1794	North
PHILLIPS, Gabriel	1795	Young
PHILLIPS, Wm	1796	Longmire
PICHARD, Singleton	1815	Haire
PICKENS, James	1781	
PICKERING, Samuel	1806	Payn
PIERCE, Ezrah	1821	Hunt
PIERCE, William	1821	Hunt
PINKLY, Jacob	1812	Hartsell
PINSON, Aron	1778	
PINSON, John	1778	
PINSON, Thomas	1778	
PINTER, Adam	1798	Gann
PIPKIN, John	1797	Calvert
PIRKINDAL, Abram	1780-1781 (Undated)	
PITCKLE, Thomas	1806	Crouch
PITCOCK, John	1794	Melvan
PITCOCK, John	1797	Shipley
PITCOCK, John	1798	Shipley
PITCOCK, John	1801	Norwood
PITCOCK, John	1809	Right
PITCOCK, John	1812	Britton
PITCOCK, John	1821	Louis
PITCOCK, Thomas	1809	Right
PITCOCK, Thomas	1811	Ellis
PITCOCK, Thomas	1816	Hair
PITCOCK, Thomas	1818	Hair
PITCOCK, Thomas	1819	Hair
PITCOCK, Thomas	1821	Louis
PITCOCKE, John	1806	Crouch
PITCOCKE, John	1811	Britten
PITCOCKE, Stephen	1815	Haire
PITCOCKE, Stephen	1816	Hair
PITCOCKE, Stephen	1817	Haire
PITCOCKE, Thomas	1815	Haire
PITCOCKE, Thomas	1817	Haire
PITMAN, Elijah	1818	Riley
PITMAN, William	1818	Riley
PITNER, John	1793	North
PITNER, John	1795	Young
PITNER, John	1796	Young
PITNER, John	1797	Young
PITNER, John	1805	Parker
PITNER, John	1806	Parker
PITNER, John	1807	Parker
PITNER, John	1808	Parker
PITNER, Michael	1798	Young
PLOWMAN, Mary	1801	
PLUM, Fredrick	1801	Gann
PLUM, Fredrick	1806	Grur
PLUME, Frederick	1810	Green
PLUME, Fredrick	1805	Guir
PLUMLY, Daniel	1808	Carr
PLUMLY, Daniel	1809	Carr
PLUMLY, Solomon	1808	Carr
PLUMLY, Solomon	1809	Carr
PLUMLY, Thomas	1808	Carr
PLUMLY, Thomas	1809	Carr
POBLEY, John	1778	
POLAND, Jacob	1815	Haire
POLAND, Jacob	1816	Hair
POLAND, Jacob	1817	Haire
POLAND, John	1792	Maxwell
POLAND, John	1793	Maxwell

Surname, Given names	Year	Comp./Dist.
POLAND, John	1794	Taylor
POLES, Thomas	1818	Grimsley
POLIN, Jacob	1819	Hair
POLKS, David	1810	Hartzel
POLLET, Thomas	1819	Grimsley
POLLEY, James	1796	Longmire
POLLEY, James	1797	Longmire
POLLEY, Jas	1798	Longmire
POLLEY, John	1796	Longmire
POLLEY, John	1797	Longmire
POLLY, Edward	1794	Ford
POLLY, John	1801	Longmire
POLLY, Young	1815	Fines
POLLY, Young	1817	Fine
POLSON, Isarel	1812	Ellis
POOR, Moses	1780-1781 (Undated)	
POORE, Moses	1781	
POPE, John	1781	
PORE, Benjamin	[1796] 1797	Morris
PORTER, Anne	1801	Glasscock
PORTER, Charles	1795	Murray
PORTER, Charles	1796	Shipley
PORTER, Charles	1797	Shipley
PORTER, Charles	1801	Norwood
PORTER, Charles	1806	Crouch
PORTER, Charles	1809	Right
PORTER, Charles	1811	Ellis
PORTER, Charles	1812	Ellis
PORTER, Joseph	1812	Crawford [2]
POSEY, David	1778	
POTEET, Thomas	1815	Grimsley
POTER, Charles	1798	Crouch
POTERSON, Robert	1812	McLin
POTITE, Thomas	1812	Barnes
POTTER, Hannah	1790	White
POTTER, Hannah	1791	White
POTTER, Hannah	1794	Ford
POTTER, Hannah	1795	Ford
POTTS, David	1796	Young
POWEL, Henry	1806	Guin
POWEL, Henry	1808	Guin
POWEL, Henry	1809	Gwin
POWEL, Henry	1811	Davis
POWEL, Henry	1812	McLin
POWELL, Elizabeth	1815	McLin
POWELL, George	1817	Hunt
POWELL, John	1817	Hunt
POWELL, John	1817	Hunt
POWELL, John	1818	Hunt
POWELL, John	1819	Hunt
POWELL, John	1821	Hunt

Surname, Given names	Year	Comp./Dist.
POWERS, John	1781	
PRASEY, Hosea	1796	Young
PRAT, Gilles	1821	Martin
PRAT, John	1808	Cade
PRATER, Isaac	1808	Odell
PRATER, John	1778	
PRATHERSON, Allen	1799	Moore
PRATT, Alexander	1814	Waddell
PRATT, Jno	1798	Shipley
PRATT, John	1801	Glasscock
PRATT, John	1805	Rector
PRATT, Joseph	1796	Brown
PRECHARD, Charles	1793	Melvan
PRECHARD, Charls	1794	Melvan
PRECHARD, Hungleton	1811	Ellis
PREMMER, Mary	1795	Ford
PRESSLEY, William Jr.	1781	
PRESTON, Francis	1807	Anderson
PRETHERO, Alexr	1795	Handly
PRETHEROW, Alex	1821	McGee
PRIBALL, John	1794	North
PRICE, Arthur	1791	White
PRICE, Christopher	1816	Fine
PRICE, Christopher	1817	Fine
PRICE, Christopher	1818	Fine
PRICE, Christopher	1819	Howard
PRICE, Dossey	1821	Howard
PRICE, Ezra	1818	Hunt
PRICE, Harden	1793	North
PRICE, James	1792	Carriger
PRICE, James	1792	Greer
PRICE, James	1794	Carriger
PRICE, James	1795	Carriger
PRICE, James	1807	Parker
PRICE, James	1815	Fines
PRICE, James	1816	Fine
PRICE, James	1817	Fine
PRICE, James	1818	Fine
PRICE, James	1818	Jones
PRICE, James	1819	Howard
PRICE, James	1821	Howard
PRICE, John	1781	
PRICE, John	1792	Carriger
PRICE, John	1792	Greer
PRICE, John	1780-1781 (Undated)	
PRICE, Kit	1814	Hartsell
PRICE, Kit	1815	Fines
PRICE, M.	1790	Williams
PRICE, M.	1791	Williams
PRICE, Madica	1796	Young
PRICE, Mordekie	1792	North

Surname, Given names	Year	Comp./Dist.
PRICE, Mordica	1794	North
PRICE, Mordica	1797	Young
PRICE, Mordicai	1798	Young
PRICE, Mordicka	1795	Young
PRICE, Mordicoy	1821	Howard
PRICE, Noddria	1799	
PRICE, Noddria	1801	
PRICE, Rachel	1801	Taylor
PRICE, Rachel	1806	Parker
PRICE, Rachel	1807	Parker
PRICE, Rachel	1809	Par
PRICE, Rachel	1810	Hartzel
PRICE, Rachel	1814	Hartsell
PRICE, Rachel	1815	Fines
PRICE, Rachel	1816	Fine
PRICE, Rachel	1817	Fine
PRICE, Rachel	1818	Fine
PRICE, Rachel	1819	Howard
PRICE, Sion	1821	Hampton
PRICE, Solomon	1794	Taylor
PRICE, Thomas	1778	
PRICE, Thomas	1793	Maxwell
PRICE, Thomas	1794	Taylor
PRICE, Thomas	1814	Hartsell
PRICE, Thomas	1815	Fines
PRICE, Thomas	1816	Fine
PRICE, Thomas	1817	Fine
PRICE, Thomas	1818	Fine
PRICE, Thomas	1819	Howard
PRICE, Thomas	1821	Howard
PRICE, William	1794	Taylor
PRICHARD, Charles	1790	Stone
PRICHARD, Charles	1791	Stone
PRICHARD, Charles	1811	Ellis
PRICHET, Charles	1796	Melvin
PRICHET, Charles	1812	Ellis
PRICHET, Charles	1814	Bean
PRICHET, Singleton	1812	Ellis
PRICHET, Singleton	1814	Bean
PRICHET, Singleton	1821	Louis
PRICHETT, Charles	1795	Melvan
PRIMAL, Phillip	1810	Green
PRIMER, Mary	1793	Campbell
PRIMER, Mary	1794	Ford
PRIMER, R. James	1821	Smith
PRING, James	1818	Harris
PRING, James	1819	Harris
PRING, Nicholas	1808	Parker
PRING, Nicholas	1809	Parker
PRING, Nicholas	1811	McCray
PRING, Nicholas	1812	McCray

Surname, Given names	Year	Comp./Dist.
PRING, Nicholas	1812	McCray
PRING, Nicholas	1814	McCray
PRING, Nicholas	1821	Hampton
PRING, Nicholis	1816	Harrison
PRING, Nicklas	1791	Willey
PRISE, Abraham	1812	Hartsell
PRISE, Benjamin	1812	Hartsell
PRITCHET, Charles	1798	Crouch
PRITCHET, Charles	1801	Norwood
PRITCHET, Charles	1809	Right
PRITCHET, Singleton	1806	Crouch
PRITCHET, Singleton	1809	Right
PRITCHET, Singleton	1816	Hair
PRITCHET, Singleton	1817	Haire
PRITCHET, Singleton	1818	Hair
PRITCHET, Singleton	1819	Hair
PRITCHET, Thomas	1798	Crouch
PRITCHET, Thomas	1801	Norwood
PRITCHIT, Widdow	1806	Crouch
PRITHAROW, Alexander	1798	Gann
PRITHER, Alexander	1817	Riley
PRITHEROW, Alexander	1818	Riley
PRITHERSON, Alexander	1816	Waddell
PRITHESON, Alexander	1819	Findley
PRIVIS, James	1799	Robertson
PROCTER, Thomas	1812	McCray
PROFFIT, Thomas	1816	Grimsley
PROPHET, John	1794	Thornton
PROTHERO, Alaxander	1799	Gann
PRUET, Martain	1781	
PRUET, William	1781	
PRUET, Wm	1781	
PRUIT, Martin	1780-1781 (Undated)	
PRUIT, William	1780-1781 (Undated)	
PRUITS, William	1779	Wilson
PRUITT, William	1780-1781 (Undated)	
PRUTHORS, Alexander	1801	Gann
PUGH, Susanna (Widow)	1790	Williams
PUGH, Susanna (Widow)	1791	Williams
PUGH, Susanna (Widow)	1792	Maxwell
PURCELL, George	1816	Hunt
PURCELL, George	1818	Hunt
PURCELL, George	1821	Hunt
PURCELL, George (of Greene)	1816	Hunt
PURCELL, John	1818	Hunt
PURCLEY, Wm	1799	Duncan
PURKINS, George	1794	Thornton
PURSALL, Georg	1807	Givins
PURSEL, George	1808	Guin
PURSELL, George	1801	Taylor

Surname, Given names	Year	Comp./Dist.
PURSELL, George	1806	Guin
PURSELL, George	1809	Gwin
PURSELL, George	1811	Davis
PURSELL, George	1812	McLin
PURSELL, George	1815	McLin
PURSELL, John	1809	Gwin
PURSELL, William	1801	Taylor
PURSELLEY, William	1808	Guin
PURSELLY, William	1797	Duncan
PURSELLY, William	1812	McLin
PURSLEY, William	1781	
PURSLEY, William	1793	Depew
PURSLEY, William	1798	Duncan
PURSLEY, William	1798	Duncan
PURSLEY, William	1806	Guin
PURSLEY, William	1807	Givins
PURTON, Francis	1805	Aikin
PURVIS, Calvan	1807	Bayles
PURVIS, Calvin	1806	Brown
PURVIS, James	1801	Roberson
PURVIS, James	1806	Brown
PUSIFELD, Samuel	1791	Willey
PUSLEY, William	1794	Depew
PUSLEY, William	1811	Davis
PUTHRS, Alexander	1796	Handly
PYBURN, Benjamin	1779	Wilson
QUALLS, James	1806	Grur
QUALS, Abraham	1805	Guir
QUALS, Abraham	1806	Grur
QUILLEN, Thomas	1814	Brown
QUILLEN, Thomas	1815	Hartsell
QUILLEN, Thomas	1816	Brown
QUILLEN, Thomas	1817	Brown
QUINN, James	1779	
QUINN, John	1779	
RADER, Abraham	1819	Jones
RADER, Abraham	1821	Jones
RADER, Adam	1791	Tullis
RADER, Adam	1792	North
RADER, Adam	1795	Young
RADER, Adam	1796	Young
RADER, Adam	1797	Young
RADER, Adam	1798	Young
RADER, Adam	1801	Taylor
RADER, Adam	1805	Parker
RADER, Adam	1807	Parker
RADER, Adam	1808	Parker
RADER, Adam	1812	Hartsell
RADER, Avey	1821	Howard
RADER, Henry	1801	Morrison
RADER, Nancy	1815	Fines

Surname, Given names	Year	Comp./Dist.
RADER, Nancy	1817	Fine
RADERM, Nancy	1816	Fine
RAGAN, Benjamin	1799	Robertson
RAGAN, Daniel	1798	Roberson
RAGAN, Jeremiah	1801	Taylor
RAGEN, Jeremiah	1812	Hartsell
RAGIN, Benjamin	1807	Bayles
RAGIN, Benjamin	1808	Bayles
RAGIN, Jeremiah Jr.	1805	Parker
RAGIN, Jeremiah Jr.	1807	Parker
RAGIN, Jeremiah Sr.	1805	Parker
RAGIN, Jeremiah Sr.	1807	Parker
RAGIN, Jeremiah Sr.	1810	Hartzel
RAGIN, Jerimeah Jr.	1821	Howard
RAGON, Jeremiah Jr.	1821	Howard
RAINBOLD, (Widow)	1794	Ford
RAINBOLT, Adam	1790	White
RAINBOLT, Adam	1791	White
RAINBOLT, Adam	1793	Campbell
RAINBOLT, Adam	1794	Ford
RAINBOLT, Adam	1795	Ford
RAINBOLT, Elisha	1795	Ford
RAINBOLT, John	1794	Ford
RAINBOLT, Susannah	1795	Ford
RAINBOLT, Sussanah	1793	Campbell
RAINS, Henry	1778	
RALSTON, John	1819	Hunt
RAMOR, John	1794	Scot
RAMSEY, F.A.	1792	Milliken
RAMSEY, Francis A.	1793	Milliken
RAMSEY, Randolph	1797	Gann
RAMSEY, Robert	1794	Blair
RAMSEY, Thomas	1806	Grur
RAMSEY, Thomas	1808	Gwin
RAMSEY, Thomas	1811	Green
RAMSY, Morgan	1780-1781	District 7
RANALS, William	1781	
RANDAL, James	1778	
RANDEL, Samuel	1821	Brown
RANDLE, Samuel	1819	Brown
RANDOLL, Samuel	1797	Longmire
RANDOLPH, Isom	1780-1781 (undated)	
RANDOLPH, James	1779	Wilson
RANDOLPH, James	1781	
RANDOLPH, James	1780-1781 (Undated)	
RANDOLPH, Jun	1801	Longmire
RANDOLPH, Saml	1798	Longmire
RANDOLPH, Saml Jr.	1798	Longmire
RANDOLPH, Thomas	1779	Wilson
RANDOLPH, Thomas	1781	

Surname, Given names	Year	Comp./Dist.
RANG, John	1813	Hoss
RANGE, Isaac	1818	Jones
RANGE, Isaac	1819	Hair
RANGE, Isaac	1821	Louis
RANGE, Jacob	1814	Hoss
RANGE, Jacob	1815	Hoss
RANGE, Jacob	1816	Hoss
RANGE, Jacob	1817	Little
RANGE, Jacob	1818	Jones
RANGE, Jacob	1819	Jones
RANGE, Jacob	1821	Jones
RANGE, James	1792	Maxwell
RANGE, James	1794	Taylor
RANGE, John	1806	Carr
RANGE, John	1807	Carr
RANGE, John	1808	Carr
RANGE, John	1809	Carr
RANGE, John	1811	Mitchell
RANGE, John	1814	Hoss
RANGE, John	1815	Hoss
RANGE, John	1816	Hoss
RANGE, John	1817	Little
RANGE, John	1818	Jones
RANGE, John	1819	Jones
RANGE, John	1821	Jones
RANGE, Peter	1787	Fains
RANGE, Peter	1791	Tullis
RANGE, Peter	1792	Tulley
RANGE, Peter	1793	Morrison
RANGE, Peter	1794	Morrison
RANGE, Peter	1795	Morrison
RANGE, Peter	1798	Morrison
RANGE, Peter	1799	Morrison
RANGE, Peter	1801	Morrison
RANGE, Peter	1806	Carr
RANGE, Peter	1807	Carr
RANGE, Peter	1808	Carr
RANGE, Peter	1809	Carr
RANGE, Peter	1811	Mitchell
RANGE, Peter	1813	Hoss
RANGE, Peter	1814	Hoss
RANGE, Peter	1816	Hoss
RANGE, Peter	1817	Little
RANGE, Peter	1818	Jones
RANGE, Peter	1819	Jones
RANGE, Peter	1821	Jones
RANGE, Peter	[1796] 1797	Morris
RANGE, Peter Jr.	1815	Hoss
RANGE, Peter Jr.	1817	Little
RANGE, Peter Sr.	1815	Hoss
RANKIN, David	1780-1781 (Undated)	
RANKIN, Gorge	1809	Cade
RANKIN, John	1809	Cade
RANKIN, John	1816	Waddell
RANKINS, John	1817	Riley
RANNALDS, Moses	1791	White
RANSOM, James	1779	
RANSOM, Jas	1779	
RASON, Haze	1794	North
RAULSTON, John	1816	Hunt
RAVEN, Adam	1810	Hartzel
RAWLINGS, Asael	1778	
RAY, Joseph	1779	Wilson
RAY, Joseph	1781	
RAY, Joseph	1780-1781 (Undated)	
RAY, Thomas	1781	
RAY, William	1793	Thornton
RAY, Wm	1795	Ford
READ, Andrew	1790	Hanley
READ, Andrew	1791	Hanley
READ, Andrew	1811	Barron
READ, John	1781	
READER, Adam	1793	North
READER, Adam	1794	North
READER, Adam	1809	Par
READER, Nancy	1819	Howard
READMAN, William C.	1815	McLin
READOR, William	1797	Longmire
REAGON, Jer	1809	Hartzell
REAGON, Jeremiah Jr.	1806	Parker
REASONER, Garnet	1790	Williams
REASONER, Garnet	1791	Williams
REASONER, Garret	1792	Tulley
REASONER, Garret	1795	Taylor
REASONER, Garrett	1793	Maxwell
REAVES, George	1779	
REAVES, Jordan (Dunkard)	1779	
REAVES, William (Single)	1779	
RECKLOW, John	1821	Martin
RECORD, George	1821	Louis
RECORD, Lewis	1806	Crouch
RECORD, Louis	1821	Louis
RECTOR, Bengemin	1809	Gwin
RECTOR, Benjaman	1814	Barns
RECTOR, Benjamin	1810	Barron
RECTOR, Benjamin	1811	Barron
RECTOR, Benjamin	1812	Barnes
RECTOR, Benjamin	1815	Grimsley
RECTOR, Benjamin	1816	Grimsley
RECTOR, Benjamin	1817	Grimsley
RECTOR, Benjamin	1818	Grimsley
RECTOR, Benjamin	1819	Grimsley

Surname, Given names	Year	Comp./Dist.
RECTOR, Daniel	1819	Grimsley
RECTOR, George	1795	Murray
RECTOR, John	1793	Murray
RECTOR, John	1795	Murray
RECTOR, John	1805	Rector
RECTOR, John	1807	Cade
RECTOR, John	1808	Cade
RECTOR, John	1809	Cade
RECTOR, Samuel	1818	Grimsley
RECTOR, Uriah	1795	Murray
RECTTER, Benjeman	1807	Givins
REDE, Andrew	1807	Cade
REDING, John	1778	
REDMAN, Stephen	1794	Carriger
REDMAN, Stephen	1795	Carriger
REDMON, Steven	1792	Greer
REDRION, She	1810	Barron
REED, Andre	1819	Grimsley
REED, Andrew	1801	Glasscock
REED, Andrew	1805	Rector
REED, Andrew	1809	Cade
REED, Andrew	1815	Grimsley
REED, Andrew	1816	Grimsley
REED, Andrew	1817	Grimsley
REED, Andrew	1818	Grimsley
REED, George	1778	
REED, George	1780-1781 (Undated)	
REED, Jacob	1780-1781 (undated)	
REED, James	1792	Depew
REED, James	1792	Depew
REED, James	1793	Scott
REED, James	1796	Calvert
REED, James	1796	Calvert
REED, James	1797	Calvert
REED, James	1797	Calvert
REED, James	1805	Carson
REED, James	1809	Patterson
REED, James	1811	
REED, James	1814	Couthers
REED, James	1815	Carcathers
REED, James	1816	Giles
REED, James	1817	Gillises
REED, James	1818	Land
REED, James	1821	Sands
REED, Jas	1780-1781 (Undated)	
REED, Molest	1817	Hunt
REED, Robert	1815	McLin
REED, Robert	1818	Harris
REED, Robert	1818	Hunt
REED, Robert	1821	Hampton

Surname, Given names	Year	Comp./Dist.
REED, Solomon	1781	
REED, William	1780-1781 (undated)	
REEDER, George	1817	Brown
REEDER, George	1818	Brown
REEDER, George	1819	Brown
REEMS, William	1778	
REES, Jas	1801	Taylor
REESE, William	1806	Payn
REEVES, Edward	1799	Morrison
REEVES, Edward	1801	Morrison
REEVES, Edward	1806	Parker
REEVES, George	1778	
REEVES, John	1808	Parker
REEVES, Jorden	1778	
REEVES, Nancy	1818	Fine
REEVES, Wm	1801	Longmire
REGAR, Jeremiah	1819	Howard
REGISTER, John	1817	Hunt
REID, Andrew	1812	Barnes
REID, Robert	1816	Hunt
REID, Robert	1819	Harris
REID, Thomas	1799	Stuart
REIDER, Adam	1806	Parker
REIVES, Edward	1798	Morrison
RENA, Charles	1792	Maxwell
RENA, John	1792	Maxwell
RENEHURT, Andrew	1808	Odell
RENFRO, Peter	1778	
RENHEN, David	1781	
RENKIN, Samuel	1821	McClure
RENNO, Benjamin	1809	Carr
RENNS, Charles	1793	Maxwell
RENO, Charles	1795	Morrison
RENO, Charles	[1796] 1797	Morris
RENO, John	1793	Morrison
RENO, John	1794	Morrison
RENO, John	1795	Morrison
RENOLDS, Wm	1778	
RENS, Charles	1790	Williams
RENS, Charles	1791	Williams
RENS, Charles	1793	Morrison
RENS, Charles	1794	Morrison
RENS, John Sr.	1793	Maxwell
RERE, John	1818	Brown
RESONER, Garet	1794	Taylor
RESTON, John	1794	Murray
RESTOR, George	1794	Murray
REUBEL, John G.	1808	Parker
REUBEL, John G.	1812	McCray
REUBLE, Jno G.	1809	Parker
REUBLE, John G.	1812	McCray

Surname, Given names	Year	Comp./Dist.
REVES, Edward	1805	Parker
REWFULLY, William	1792	Depew
REYNOLDS, Henry	1795	Ford
RHEA, David	1819	Brown
RHEA, John	1796	Jonesboro
RHEA, John	1799	Stuart
RHEA, John	1801	Aiken
RHEA, John	1805	Aikin
RHEA, John	1806	Anderson
RHEA, John	1807	Anderson
RHEA, John	1808	
RHEA, John	1814	McCracken
RHEA, John	1815	Garner
RHEA, John (by James Reed)	1805	Carson
RHEA, John (Esq.)	1801	Biddle
RHINEHART, John	1811	Brown
RHODS, Elisha	1796	Young
RIANHEART, John	1812	McLin
RICARD, George	1815	Haire
RICARD, George	1815	Waddell
RICARD, George	1816	Hair
RICARD, George	1817	Haire
RICARD, Henry	1815	Waddell
RICARD, Lewis	1815	Haire
RICARD, Lewis	1816	Hair
RICARD, Lewis	1817	Haire
RICE, Charles	1793	Morrison
RICE, Charles	1794	Morrison
RICE, David	1798	Duncan
RICE, David	1799	Duncan
RICE, Edward	1778	
RICE, John	1778	
RICE, Leonard	1778	
RICE, Thomas	1796	Calvert
RICE, Thomas	1797	Calvert
RICH, Daniel	1781	
RICHA, Robart	1798	Duncan
RICHARD, George	1814	Waddell
RICHARD, George	1818	Hair
RICHARD, Henry	1816	Waddell
RICHARD, Henry	1817	Riley
RICHARD, Henry	1818	Riley
RICHARD, Henry	1821	McClure
RICHARD, Isaac	1821	McGee
RICHARD, John	1796	Brown
RICHARD, Lenen	1798	Biddle
RICHARD, Lewis	1801	Taylor
RICHARD, Lewis	1808	Guin
RICHARD, Lewis	1812	McLin
RICHARD, Lewis	1818	Hair
RICHARD, Louis	1814	Bean
RICHARD, Luis	1799	Duncan
RICHARD, Robert	1817	Hampton
RICHARDS, David	1792	Depew
RICHARDS, David	1793	Biddle
RICHARDS, David	1794	Blair
RICHARDS, David	1798	Biddle
RICHARDS, David	1798	Biddle
RICHARDS, Henry	1819	Findley
RICHARDS, Henry	1819	McClure
RICHARDS, Henry	1821	McGee
RICHARDS, Lewis	1797	Biddle
RICHARDS, Luis	1798	Biddle
RICHARDSON, Amos	1793	Campbell
RICHARDSON, Daniel	1794	Ford
RICHARDSON, Geo	1778	
RICHARDSON, Henry	1778	
RICHARDSON, John	1794	Ford
RICHARDSON, John	1795	Ford
RICHARDSON, John	1795	Thornton
RICHARDSON, Mary	1778	
RICHEL, David	1817	Hunt
RICHELL, Anthony	1817	Hampton
RICHERSON, John	1781	
RICHEY, Eli	1814	McLin
RICHEY, James	1794	Depew
RICHEY, William	1779	Wilson
RICHEY, William	1780-1781 (Undated)	
RICHMAN, John	1808	Bayles
RICHMAN, John	1810	Hartzel
RICHY, Eli	1817	Hunt
RICKERD, Luis	1809	Gwin
RICKETS, John	1809	Cade
RICKEY, Eli	1818	Hunt
RICORD, George	1819	Hair
RICORD, Louis	1819	Hair
RIDDLE, Mary	1781	
RIDDLE, Saml	1810	Dimmons
RIDLEGARIN, Randolph	1781	
RIGBY, Thomas	1807	Odell
RIGG, Iseah	1799	Duncan
RIGGS, Edwards	1780-1781 (Undated)	
RIGGS, Edwd	1781	
RIGGS, Isaiah	1819	Grimsley
RIGGS, Jesse	1817	Grimsley
RIGGS, Reuben	1780-1781 (Undated)	
RIGGS, Ruben	1781	
RIGHT, James	1794	Carriger
RIGHT, James	1795	Carriger
RIGHT, James	1801	Norwood
RIGHT, James	1806	Crouch

Surname, Given names	Year	Comp./Dist.
RIGHT, John	1821	Louis
RIGHT, Mathew	1821	Louis
RIGHT, Robert	1795	Carriger
RIGO, Elias	1797	Duncan
RIGO, Isaiah	1797	Duncan
RIGS, Elias	1799	Duncan
RIGS, Elias	1801	Lane
RIGS, Isaiah	1801	Lane
RIGS, Isaiah	1805	Doak
RIGS, Isiah	1798	Duncan
RIGS, Jesse	1818	Grimsley
RIGS, Josiah	1798	Duncan
RIGS, Zain	1818	Grimsley
RIGSBAY, Asa	1806	Odel
RIGSBAY, James	1806	Odel
RIGSBAY, Thomas	1806	Odel
RIGSBAY, Thomas (in trust for Thomas Gibson)	1806	Odel
RIGSBLY, Kennedy	1811	Brown
RIGSBY, James	1808	Odell
RIGSBY, James	1811	Brown
RIGSBY, James	1812	Brown
RIGSBY, James	1815	Hartsell
RIGSBY, James	1816	Brown
RIGSBY, James	1817	Brown
RIGSBY, James	1818	Brown
RIGSBY, James	1819	Brown
RIGSBY, Kenedy	1812	Brown
RIGSBY, Thomas	1796	Longmire
RIGSBY, Thomas	1808	Odell
RIGSHA, James	1809	Viney
RIGSLY, James	1814	Brown
RIKARD, Luis	1811	Davis
RILAND, John	1816	Giles
RILEY, William	1816	Hoss
RILEY, William	1817	Riley
RILEY, William	1818	Riley
RIMAL, John	1791	Willey
RIMAL, Philip	1809	Green
RIMALL, Jacob	1801	Gann
RIMALL, Phillip	1806	Grur
RIMDL, Philip	1808	Gwin
RIMEL, Jacob	1799	Gann
RIMEL, John	1799	Gann
RINDHART, John	1816	Brown
RINDHART, John	1817	Brown
RINEHART, John	1801	Longmire
RINEHART, John	1806	Odel
RINEHART, John	1807	Odell
RINEHART, John	1810	Cove
RINEHART, John	1812	Brown
RINEHART, John	1814	Brown
RINEHART, John	1815	McLin
RINEHART, John	1818	Brown
RINEHART, John	1821	Haines
RINEHEART, John	1798	Longmire
RINEHEART, John	1808	Odell
RINEHURST, John	1819	Brown
RION, James	1792	Depew
RIPLEY, Peasent	1796	Longmire
RIPLY, John	1796	Longmire
RITCHEY, Eli	1815	McLin
RITCHEY, Eli	1816	Hunt
RITCHEY, John	1781	
RITCHEY, William	1778	
RITCHEY, William	1781	
RITCHIE, John	1778	
RIVER, Edward	1807	Parker
ROACH, Jordan	1779	
ROACH, Jorden	1778	
ROACH, Pleasant	1821	Smith
ROADMAN, William C.	1816	Hunt
ROADMAN, William C.	1817	Hunt
ROADMAN, Wm C.	1814	McLin
ROADS, Elisha	1798	Young
ROADS, Elisha	1801	Taylor
ROASE, Hosea	1778	
ROBENS, John	1780-1781 (undated)	
ROBENSON, Jacob	1807	Cade
ROBERSON, Charles	1793	Brown
ROBERSON, Charles	1796	Brown
ROBERSON, Charles	1796	Calvert
ROBERSON, Charles	1799	Robertson
ROBERSON, Charles	1801	Roberson
ROBERSON, Charles	1808	Bayles
ROBERSON, Charles	1809	Bayles
ROBERSON, Charles (Capt.)	1798	Roberson
ROBERSON, Charles (Dec.)	1799	Robertson
ROBERSON, Charles (Executor)	1799	Robertson
ROBERSON, Chas (Capt.)	1797	Robertson
ROBERSON, Chas (executor of, deceased)	1801	Aiken
ROBERSON, Chas Sr.; (Died 1798)	1795	Young
ROBERSON, Daniel	1799	Duncan
ROBERSON, David	1808	Bayles
ROBERSON, David	1809	Bayles
ROBERSON, David	1821	Brown
ROBERSON, George	1801	Roberson
ROBERSON, Jacob	1808	Cade
ROBERSON, Jacob	1810	Barron
ROBERSON, Jacob	1814	Barns
ROBERSON, James	1798	Duncan
ROBERSON, James	1807	Anderson

Surname, Given names	Year	Comp./Dist.
ROBERSON, John	1790	
ROBERSON, John	1791	
ROBERSON, John	1794	Carriger
ROBERSON, Jules	1796	Brown
ROBERSON, Julis	1779	
ROBERSON, Samuel (of Virg.)	1814	Copes
ROBERSON, Susana	1801	Aiken
Robert	1795	Taylor
Robert	1814	McCray
ROBERT, Charles (Executors Of)	1799	Stuart
ROBERT, Jacob	1809	Cade
ROBERT, S. Owen	1821	Smith
ROBERTS, Aaron	1794	Thornton
ROBERTS, Admon	1780-1781 (Undated)	
ROBERTS, Edmd	1781	
ROBERTS, Edmund	1778	
ROBERTS, James	1807	Shields
ROBERTS, James	1810	Dimmons
ROBERTS, James	1811	
ROBERTS, Jesse	1792	Coye
ROBERTS, Jessee	1793	Hale
ROBERTS, John	1790	Milleken
ROBERTS, John	1792	Milliken
ROBERTS, John	1793	Milliken
ROBERTS, John	1794	Milliken
ROBERTS, John	1805	Guir
ROBERTS, John	1815	Fines
ROBERTS, Moses	1794	Thornton
ROBERTS, Moses	1795	Ford
ROBERTS, Reuben	1794	Thornton
ROBERTS, Reuben	1795	Ford
ROBERTS, Rewbin	1791	White
ROBERTS, Richard	1805	Jas Parker
ROBERTS, Richard	1806	Brown
ROBERTS, Richard	1807	Bayles
ROBERTS, Richard	1808	Bayles
ROBERTS, Richard	1809	Bayles
ROBERTS, Richard	1814	Hampton
ROBERTS, Richard	1816	Hampton
ROBERTS, Richard	1818	Brown [2]
ROBERTS, Richard (Dec'd)	1819	Brown
ROBERTS, Richard (Doct.)	1821	Brown
ROBERTS, Thomas O.	1821	Hampton
ROBERTS, William	1794	Thornton
ROBERTS, William	1809	Bayles
ROBERTS, William	1812	Hartsell
ROBERTS, William	1814	Hartsell
ROBERTS, William	1815	Fines
ROBERTS, William	1816	Fine
ROBERTS, William	1817	Fine

Surname, Given names	Year	Comp./Dist.
ROBERTS, William	1818	Fine
ROBERTS, William	1819	Howard
ROBERTS, William	1821	Howard
ROBERTSON,	1778	
ROBERTSON, Charles	1791	Chisom
ROBERTSON, Charles	1806	Brown
ROBERTSON, Charles	1807	Bayles
ROBERTSON, Charles	1814	Hampton
ROBERTSON, Charles	1816	Hampton
ROBERTSON, Charles (Bflo.)	1779	
ROBERTSON, Charles (Esq.)	1778	
ROBERTSON, Charles Jr.	1778	
ROBERTSON, Charles Sr.	1798	Calvert
ROBERTSON, Chas Jr.	1791	Chisom
ROBERTSON, Chas Jr.	1792	Chisolm
ROBERTSON, Col	1780-1781 (undated)	
ROBERTSON, Daniel	1798	Duncan
ROBERTSON, David	1778	
ROBERTSON, David	1792	Depew
ROBERTSON, David	1814	Hampton
ROBERTSON, David	1816	Hampton
ROBERTSON, David	1817	Hampton
ROBERTSON, David	1818	Brown [2]
ROBERTSON, David	1780-1781 (Undated)	
ROBERTSON, David	1780-1781 (Undated)	
ROBERTSON, David	1783 [after]	Depew
ROBERTSON, Enoch	1817	Grimsley
ROBERTSON, George	1790	Hanley
ROBERTSON, George	1791	Hanley
ROBERTSON, George	1797	Calvert
ROBERTSON, George	1797	Calvert
ROBERTSON, Jacob	1801	Glasscock
ROBERTSON, Jacob	1811	Barron
ROBERTSON, Jacob	1815	Grimsley
ROBERTSON, Jacob	1816	Grimsley
ROBERTSON, Jacob	1817	Grimsley
ROBERTSON, James	1779	Wilson
ROBERTSON, James	1794	Blair
ROBERTSON, James	1801	Taylor
ROBERTSON, James	1806	Carson
ROBERTSON, James	1810	Dimmons
ROBERTSON, James	1815	Carcathers
ROBERTSON, James	1815	Fines
ROBERTSON, James	1816	Fine
ROBERTSON, James	1816	Giles
ROBERTSON, James	1817	Fine
ROBERTSON, James	1818	Fine
ROBERTSON, James	1783 [after]	Blair
ROBERTSON, James	1783 [after]	Depew
ROBERTSON, James (Esqr.)	1779	

Surname, Given names	Year	Comp./Dist.
ROBERTSON, John	1778	
ROBERTSON, John	1779	
ROBERTSON, John	1791	Milliken
ROBERTSON, John	1794	Thornton
ROBERTSON, John	1812	McLin
ROBERTSON, Julis	1778	
ROBERTSON, Mark	1812	McCray
ROBERTSON, Marke	1812	McCray
ROBERTSON, William	1812	McCray
ROBERTSON, William	1812	McLin
ROBESO, Charles	1780-1781 (undated)	
ROBESON, James	1780-1781 (Undated)	
ROBINSON, Allen	1819	Smith
ROBINSON, Charles	1793	
ROBINSON, Chas (Col.)	1792	Chisolm
ROBINSON, David	1781	
ROBINSON, David	1821	Hunt
ROBINSON, Enoch	1819	Grimsley
ROBINSON, Ezekiel	1806	Brown
ROBINSON, Jacob	1805	Rector
ROBINSON, Jacob	1812	Barnes
ROBINSON, Jacob	1819	Grimsley
ROBINSON, James	1808	Parker
ROBINSON, James	1810	Hartzel
ROBINSON, James	1812	Hartsell
ROBINSON, James	1814	Couthers
ROBINSON, James	1819	Howard
ROBINSON, John	1779	Wilson
ROBINSON, John	1781	
ROBINSON, John	1792	Carriger
ROBINSON, Luke	1780-1781 (undated)	
ROBINSON, Oliver B.	1819	Smith
ROBINSON, William B.	1819	Smith
ROBISON, Alexander	1806	Parker
ROBISON, David	1779	Wilson
ROBISON, David	1781	
ROBISON, James	1781	
ROBISON, James	1781	
ROBISON, James	1805	Carson
ROBISON, James	1811	
ROBISON, James	1821	Howard
ROBISON, James	1821	Hunt
ROBISON, John	1792	Greer
ROBISON, Mathew	1781	
ROBISON, Samuel	1813	Copas
ROBSON, Carter (executor of Saml. Culbertsons Estate)	1801	Longmire
ROBSON, Charles (Capt.)	1794	Scot
ROBYESON, James	1806	Anderson
ROCKETT, Frances M.	1819	Jones

Surname, Given names	Year	Comp./Dist.
ROCKHOLT, Francis W.	1821	Jones
ROCKWELL, Dorson	1793	Maxwell
ROCKWELL, Dowson	1792	Maxwell
ROCKWELL, Jasen	1794	Taylor
RODEKIN, Andrew	1810	Barron
RODGER, Moses	1790	Biddle
RODGER, Moses	1791	Biddle
RODGER, Moses	1792	Biddle
RODGERS, Andes	1807	Shields
RODGERS, Andr	1806	Carson
RODGERS, Andrew	1801	Biddle
RODGERS, Andrew	1805	Carson
RODGERS, David	1817	Little
RODGERS, Elijah	1816	Hampton
RODGERS, Elijah	1817	Hampton
RODGERS, Elijah	1818	Brown [2]
RODGERS, James	1793	Biddle
RODGERS, James	1801	Biddle
RODGERS, James	1805	Carson
RODGERS, James	1806	Carson
RODGERS, James	1807	Shields
RODGERS, James	1780-1781 (Undated)	
RODGERS, James	1783 [after]	Blair
RODGERS, Jeremiah	1816	Hampton
RODGERS, Jeremiah	1817	Hampton
RODGERS, Jeremiah	1818	Brown [2]
RODGERS, John	1791	North
RODGERS, John	1792	Brown
RODGERS, John	1794	Brown
RODGERS, Joseph	1791	Chisom
RODGERS, Joseph	1792	Chisolm
RODGERS, Joseph	1794	Brown
RODGERS, Joseph	1816	Hampton
RODGERS, Joseph	1817	Hampton
RODGERS, Joseph	1818	Brown [2]
RODGERS, Moses	1793	Biddle
RODGERS, Reuben	1816	Hampton
RODGERS, Reuben	1817	Hampton
RODGERS, Reuben	1818	Brown [2]
RODGERS, Robert	1791	North
RODGERS, Robert	1792	North
RODGERS, Saml	1806	Carson
RODGERS, Samuel	1806	Brown
RODGERS, Samuel	1807	Shields
RODGERS, Thomas	1779	Wilson
RODGERS, Thomas	1790	Biddle
RODGERS, Thomas	1791	Biddle
RODGERS, Thomas	1791	North
RODGERS, Thomas	1792	Biddle
RODGERS, Thomas	1792	North
RODGERS, Thomas	1793	Biddle

Surname, Given names	Year	Comp./Dist.
RODGERS, Thomas	1801	Biddle
RODGERS, Thomas	1805	Carson
RODGERS, Thomas	1783 [after]	Blair
RODGERS, Thomas (estate of)	1801	Biddle
RODGERS, Thos	1781	
RODGERS, Thos	1794	North
RODGERS, William	1808	Guin
RODGERS, William	1812	McLin
RODGERS, William	1814	McLin
RODGERS, William	1816	Hunt
RODGERS, William	1817	Hunt
RODGERS, William	1818	Hunt
RODGERS, Ze-eif	1807	Payne
RODMAN, William C.	1809	Roadmas
RODMAN, William C.	1811	Rodman
ROEARK, William	1812	Ellis
ROGAN, Benjamin	1806	Brown
ROGAN, Samuel	1810	Dimmons
ROGARS, Andrew	1798	Biddle
ROGERS, Andrew	1798	Biddle
ROGERS, David	1821	Jones
ROGERS, Elijah	1819	Brown
ROGERS, Elijah	1821	Brown
ROGERS, Ezechel	1814	Hampton
ROGERS, Ezekel	1797	Robertson
ROGERS, Ezekel	1812	McCray
ROGERS, Ezekiel	1809	Parker
ROGERS, Ezkiel	1808	Parker
ROGERS, James	1781	
ROGERS, James	1811	
ROGERS, John	1793	Brown
ROGERS, John	1796	Brown
ROGERS, John	1797	Robertson
ROGERS, John	1798	Roberson
ROGERS, John	1799	Robertson
ROGERS, Joseph	1792	Brown
ROGERS, Joseph	1793	Brown
ROGERS, Joseph	1796	Brown
ROGERS, Joseph	1797	Robertson
ROGERS, Joseph	1798	Roberson
ROGERS, Joseph	1799	Robertson
ROGERS, Joseph	1801	Roberson
ROGERS, Joseph	1806	Brown
ROGERS, Joseph	1807	Bayles
ROGERS, Joseph	1808	Bayles
ROGERS, Joseph	1809	Bayles
ROGERS, Joseph	1814	Hampton
ROGERS, Joseph	1819	Brown
ROGERS, Joseph	1821	Brown
ROGERS, Moses	1797	Biddle
ROGERS, Moses	1798	Biddle
ROGERS, Reuben	1809	Bayles
ROGERS, Reuben	1814	Hampton
ROGERS, Reuben	1819	Brown
ROGERS, Reuben	1821	Brown
ROGERS, Robert	1795	Taylor
ROGERS, Sammuel	1808	Bayles
ROGERS, Samuel	1809	Bayles
ROGERS, Samuel	1811	
ROGERS, Thomas	1797	Biddle
ROGERS, Thomas Jr.	1797	Biddle
ROGERS, Thomas Sr.	1798	Biddle
ROGERS, Thos	1793	North
ROGERS, Thos	1795	Young
ROGERS, William	1806	Guin
ROGERS, William	1807	Givins
ROGERS, William	1809	Gwin
ROGERS, William	1811	Davis
ROGERS, William	1815	McLin
ROGERS, William	1819	Hunt
ROGERS, William	1821	Hunt
ROGERS, Williams	1799	Robertson
ROGERS, Zekiel	1805	Stephenson
ROGGEN, Thomas	1780-1781 (Undated)	
ROLAND, John	1781	
ROLAND, Selvester	1807	Givins
ROLANS, John C.	1780-1781	District 7
ROLESTON, James	1817	Gillises
ROLINGS, Ashel	1781	
ROLINSON, David	1819	Brown
ROLISON, Enoch	1818	Grimsley
ROLISON, Jacob	1818	Grimsley
ROLLING, Ashel	1780-1781 (Undated)	
ROLLINS, John	1806	Crouch
ROLSTON, John	1797	Duncan
ROLSTON, John	1798	Duncan
ROLSTON, John	1806	Guin
ROLSTON, John	1808	Guin
ROLSTON, John	1809	Gwin
ROLSTON, John	1815	McLin
ROLSTON, John	1821	Hunt
ROLSTON, John	1780-1781	District 7
ROLSTONE, John	1812	McLin
ROLSTONE, John	1814	McLin
ROODS, Elisha	1797	Young
ROOS, Hose	1791	North
ROSE, Hasea	1792	North
ROSE, Hassea	1801	Taylor
ROSE, Hine	1807	Parker
ROSE, Hose	1807	Parker
ROSE, Hosea	1795	Young

Surname, Given names	Year	Comp./Dist.
ROSE, Hosea	1797	Young
ROSE, Hosea	1805	Parker
ROSE, Hosea	1806	Parker
ROSE, Hoseah	1793	North
ROSE, John	1806	Crouch
ROSE, John	1809	Right
ROSE, John	1809	Viney
ROSE, John	1811	Ellis
ROSE, John	1811	Ellis
ROSE, John	1815	Hartsell
ROSE, John	1816	Brown
ROSE, John	1817	Brown
ROSE, John	1821	Haines
ROSE, Kins	1808	Parker
ROSE, Kinsey	1806	Parker
ROSE, Reuben	1805	Doak
ROSE, Reuben	1806	Doke
ROSON, William	1795	Milliken
ROSS, O.B.	1821	Smith
ROSS, Oliver B.	1820	Smith
ROTSTEN, John	1807	Britton
ROULSTON, John	1799	Duncan
ROVEHOUSE, John	1794	Thornton
ROW, John	1819	Brown
ROWLING, Moses	1801	Aiken
ROWLINGS, Asah	1779	
ROYLEY, John	1779	
ROYLSTON, John	1818	Hunt
RUBB, John	1798	Young
RUBEL, Henry	1821	Howard
RUBEL, John	1792	North
RUBEL, John	1807	Bayles
RUBEL, John	1821	Howard
RUBEL, Joseph	1821	Howard
RUBEL, Peter (Doctor)	1821	Howard
RUBELL, Moses	1791	Tullis
RUBIL, John	1795	Young
RUBIL, Peter	1795	Young
RUBLE, Henry	1801	Taylor
RUBLE, Henry	1806	Parker
RUBLE, Henry	1807	Parker
RUBLE, Henry	1808	Parker
RUBLE, Henry	1809	Par
RUBLE, Henry	1810	Hartzel
RUBLE, Henry	1812	Hartsell
RUBLE, Henry	1814	Hartsell
RUBLE, Henry	1815	Fines
RUBLE, Henry	1816	Fine
RUBLE, Henry	1817	Fine
RUBLE, Henry	1818	Fine
RUBLE, Henry	1819	Howard
RUBLE, Jacob	1797	Young
RUBLE, Jacob	1798	Young
RUBLE, Jacob	1806	Parker
RUBLE, Jacob	1807	Parker
RUBLE, Jacob	1808	Parker
RUBLE, Jacob	1809	Par
RUBLE, James Banis	1819	Howard
RUBLE, Jno	1809	Par
RUBLE, John	1793	North
RUBLE, John	1796	Young
RUBLE, John	1797	Young
RUBLE, John	1801	Taylor
RUBLE, John	1806	Brown
RUBLE, John	1806	Parker
RUBLE, John	1807	Parker
RUBLE, John	1810	Hartzel
RUBLE, John	1812	Hartsell
RUBLE, John	1814	Hartsell
RUBLE, John	1814	Hartsell
RUBLE, John	1815	Fines
RUBLE, John	1816	Fine
RUBLE, John	1816	Fine
RUBLE, John	1816	Fine
RUBLE, John	1817	Fine
RUBLE, John	1817	Fine
RUBLE, John	1817	Fine
RUBLE, John	1818	Fine
RUBLE, John	1818	Fine
RUBLE, John	1818	Fine
RUBLE, John	1819	Howard
RUBLE, John G.	1811	McCray
RUBLE, John G.	1821	Howard
RUBLE, John Jr.	1821	Howard
RUBLE, John Waggr	1819	Howard
RUBLE, Peter	1796	Young
RUBLE, Peter	1797	Young
RUBLE, Peter	1801	Taylor
RUBLE, Peter	1806	Parker
RUBLE, Peter	1807	Parker
RUBLE, Peter	1809	Par
RUBLE, Peter	1810	Hartzel
RUBLE, Peter	1814	Hartsell
RUBLE, Peter	1815	Fines
RUBLE, Peter	1816	Fine
RUBLE, Peter	1817	Fine
RUBLE, Peter	1818	Fine
RUBLE, Peter	1819	Howard
RUBLE, Peter Sr.	1812	Hartsell
RUBLE, Peter Sr.	1821	Howard
RUESTON, John	1798	Biddle
RUISHART, John	1815	Hartsell

Surname, Given names	Year	Comp./Dist.
RULANS, Gabword	1780-1781	District 7
RUMBOLT, Joseph	1791	White
RUNNALDA, Henry	1790	White
RUNNALDA, Moses	1790	White
RUNNALS, Moses	1795	Ford
RUNNO, Benjamin	1811	Mitchell
RUPELL, David Jr.	1821	Hunt
RUPELL, David Sr.	1821	Hunt
RUPELL, James	1793	Thornton
RUPELL, William	1821	Hunt
RUSEL, David	1801	Taylor
RUSEL, David Jr.	1814	McLin
RUSH, William	1797	Hannah
RUSH, William	1799	Hannah
RUSH, William	1806	Payn
RUSH, Wm	1801	Squibb
RUSHTON, Robert	1821	Brown
RUSLAND, Wililam	1780-1781 (Undated)	
RUSLE, David	1799	Duncan
RUSSEL, Anthony	1812	McCray
RUSSEL, Anthony	1812	McCray
RUSSEL, Anthony	1821	Brown
RUSSEL, David	1792	Depew
RUSSEL, David	1793	Depew
RUSSEL, David	1794	Depew
RUSSEL, David	1797	Duncan
RUSSEL, David	1798	Duncan
RUSSEL, David	1798	Duncan
RUSSEL, David	1806	Guin
RUSSEL, David	1808	Guin
RUSSEL, David	1812	McLin
RUSSEL, David Sr.	1814	McLin
RUSSEL, Thomas	1811	McCray
RUSSEL, Thomas	1812	McCray
RUSSEL, Thomas	1821	Hampton
RUSSELL, Anthony	1816	Hampton
RUSSELL, Anthony	1818	Brown [2]
RUSSELL, Anthony	1819	Brown
RUSSELL, David	1807	Givins
RUSSELL, David	1809	Gwin
RUSSELL, David	1811	Davis
RUSSELL, David	1818	Hunt
RUSSELL, David Jr.	1815	McLin
RUSSELL, David Jr.	1816	Hunt
RUSSELL, David Jr.	1817	Hunt
RUSSELL, David Jr.	1818	Hunt
RUSSELL, David Jr.	1819	Hunt
RUSSELL, David Sr.	1815	McLin
RUSSELL, David Sr.	1816	Hunt
RUSSELL, David Sr.	1819	Hunt
RUSSELL, George	1778	

Surname, Given names	Year	Comp./Dist.
RUSSELL, George	1814	McLin
RUSSELL, George (Esq.)	1778	
RUSSELL, John	1778	
RUSSELL, John	1778	
RUSSELL, John	1819	Sands
RUSSELL, Samuel	1791	White
RUSSELL, Thomas	1812	McCray
RUSSELL, Thomas	1819	Harris
RUSSELL, William	1819	Hunt
RUSSELLE, Anthony	1814	McCray
RUSSELLE, Thomas	1814	McCray
RUST, David	1812	Ellis
RUST, Jeremiah	1812	Ellis
RUST, Micage	1812	Ellis
RUSTEN, Jesse	1796	Shipley
RUSTEN, John	1817	Hampton
RUSTER, John	1819	Brown
RUSTIN, Jesse	1798	Shipley
RUSTIN, Jesse	1801	Glasscock
RUSTIN, John	1816	Hampton
RUSTIN, John	1818	Brown [2]
RUSTON, Jesse	1797	Shipley
RUTER, Benjamin	1808	Guin
RUTHERFORD, Benjamine	1780-1781 (undated)	
RYAN, James	1795	Morrison
RYANS, John	1812	Barnes
RYBURN, Benjamine	1780-1781 (undated)	
RYBURN, Benjman	1780-1781 (Undated)	
RYBURN, Elias	1780-1781 (Undated)	
RYE, Phillip	1807	Givins
RYEMEAL, Jno	1796	Longmire
RYEN, James	[1796] 1797	Morris
RYENS, James	1798	Morrison
RYLAND, John	1818	Hunt
RYLAND, John	1819	Hunt
RYLAND, John	1821	Hunt
RYLAND, Silvester	1811	Davis
RYLAND, Silvester	1814	Couthers
RYLAND, Sylvester	1818	Hunt
RYLAND, Sylvester	1819	Hunt
RYLEY, John	1778	
RYLEY, William	1815	Waddell
RYLEY, William	1816	Waddell
RYMAL, John	1792	Scott
RYMAL, John	1793	Scott
RYMAL, John	1799	Moore
RYMAL, Philip	1805	Guir
RYMAL, Philip	1811	Green
RYMEL, John	1798	Gann

Surname, Given names	Year	Comp./Dist.
RYNAL, John	1795	Calvert
S. PETERS, John Michael	1792	Carriger
SAILER, John	1814	Hoss
SAILER, John S.	1809	Carr
SAILOR, John	1807	Carr
SAILOR, John	1813	Hoss
SAILOR, John	1818	Jones
SAILOR, John	1819	Jones
SAILORS, John	1817	Little
SAKEN, Nancy	1817	Gillises
SALAS, George	1806	Crouch
SALER, John	1808	Carr
SALT, Henery	1797	Calvert
SALT, Henery	1797	Calvert
SALT, Henry	1798	Calvert
SALTE, John	1812	McCray
SALTER, Robert	1819	Smith
SALTS, Andrew	1819	Harris
SALTS, Daniel	1819	Harris
SALTS, Hen	1809	Parker
SALTS, Hennery	1812	McCray
SALTS, Henry	1799	Stuart
SALTS, Henry	1805	Jas Parker
SALTS, Henry	1808	Parker
SALTS, Jno	1809	Parker
SALTS, John	1805	Jas Parker
SALTS, John	1812	McCray
SALTS, John	1814	McCray
SALTS, John	1817	Harris
SALTS, John	1818	Harris
SALTS, John	1819	Harris
SAMMS, James	1792	Coye
SAMMS, John	1792	Coye
SAMMS, John (In trust for James Samms)	1792	Coye
SAMPLE, Moses	1781	
SAMPLE, Saml	1779	Wilson
SAMPLE, Wm	1781	
SAMPLES, William	1819	Smith
SAMPSON, John	1810	Dimmons
SAMS, James	1793	Hale
SAMS, John	1793	Hale
SAMS, John	1797	Longmire
SAMS, Thos	1780-1781	District 7
SAND, Benjamin	1815	Carcathers
SAND, Benjamin	1816	Giles
SAND, Benjimon	1805	Carson
SAND, Isaac	1815	Carcathers
SAND, Jacob	1815	Carcathers
SAND, Joseph	1781	
SAND, Thomas	1815	Carcathers
SANDER, Freder (estate of)	1805	Doak
SANDER, Frederick	1797	Shipley
SANDER, Fredrick (estate of)	1806	Doke
SANDERS, Frederick	1798	Shipley
SANDERS, Frederick	1801	Lane
SANDERS, Frederick (estate of)	1807	Britton
SANDERS, John	1781	
SANDERS, John	1813	Copas
SANDERS, John	1814	Copes
SANDERS, John	1815	Copas
SANDS, Benjaman	1810	Dimmons
SANDS, Benjamen	1801	Biddle
SANDS, Benjamin	1790	Biddle
SANDS, Benjamin	1791	Biddle
SANDS, Benjamin	1792	Biddle
SANDS, Benjamin	1794	Blair
SANDS, Benjamin	1806	Carson
SANDS, Benjamin	1807	Shields
SANDS, Benjamin	1811	
SANDS, Benjamin	1817	Gillises
SANDS, Benjamin	1818	Land
SANDS, Benjamin	1819	Sands
SANDS, Benjamin	1821	Sands
SANDS, Benjamin	1783 [after]	Blair
SANDS, Isaa	1821	Sands
SANDS, Isaac	1814	Couthers
SANDS, Isaac	1817	Gillises
SANDS, Isaac	1818	Land
SANDS, Jacob	1805	Carson
SANDS, Jacob	1806	Carson
SANDS, Jacob	1807	Shields
SANDS, Jacob	1809	Patterson
SANDS, James	1817	Gillises
SANDS, Joseph	1793	Thornton
SANDS, Joseph	1794	Thornton
SANDS, Joseph	1795	Thornton
SANDS, Joseph	1805	Carson
SANDS, Joseph	1806	Carson
SANDS, Joseph	1807	Shields
SANDS, Joseph	1816	Giles
SANDS, Joseph	1817	Gillises
SANDS, Joseph	1818	Land
SANDS, Joseph	1819	Sands
SANDS, Joseph	1821	Sands
SANDS, Micael	1811	
SANDS, Michall W.	1801	Biddle
SANDS, Michel	1798	Biddle
SANDS, Mikal	1798	Biddle
SANDS, Othanel	1806	Carson
SANDS, Othaniel	1807	Shields
SANDS, Othaniel	1809	Patterson
SANDS, Othaniel	1819	Sands

Surname, Given names	Year	Comp./Dist.
SANDS, Otheniel	1821	Sands
SANDS, Otherical	1805	Carson
SANDS, Thomas	1818	Land
SANS, Benjamin	1797	Biddle
SANS, John	1796	Longmire
SASHBROOKS, John	1806	Brown
SATNFEALE, Samuel	1798	Duncan
SAULTS, Henry	1801	Calvert
SAVENGER, John	1815	Hoss
SAW, James	1801	Squibb
SAWYER, Wm	1778	
SAYLER, John	1821	Jones
SAYLOR, John	1815	Hoss
SCHOT, Absolam	1805	Parker
SCOOT, Absolem	1793	North
SCOT, Absolem	1821	Howard
SCOT, Absolom	1807	Parker
SCOT, Casper	1809	Green
SCOT, Thomas	1792	Milliken
SCOT, Thomas	1801	Squibb
SCOT, Thos	1793	Milliken
SCOTT, Absolem	1806	Parker
SCOTT, James	1791	Willey
SCOTT, James	1792	Scott
SCOTT, James	1793	Scott
SCOTT, James	1796	Jonesboro
SCOTT, James (Executor of Chas Hays)	1793	Scott
SCOTT, John	1816	Smith
SCOTT, John	1817	Smith
SCOTT, Robert	1796	Millikin
SCOTT, Robert	1797	Hannah
SCOTT, Robert	1798	Hannah
SCOTT, Thomas	1778	
SCOTT, Thomas	1791	Milliken
SCOTT, Thomas	1794	Milliken
SCOTT, Thomas	1795	Milliken
SCOTT, Thomas	1796	Millikin
SCOTT, Thomas	1798	Hannah
SCOTT, Thomas	1806	Payn
SCOTT, Thomas	1780-1781 (Undated)	
SCOTT, Thos	1781	
SCOTT, Thos	1797	Hannah
SCOTT, Thos	1799	Hannah
SCOTT, Wilson	1780-1781	District 7
SCOTT, Zachariah	1815	Haire
SCOTT, Zachariah	1816	Hair
SCROGGINS, Benjamin	1819	Harris
SCROGGS, Ebanezer	1790	Milleken
SCROGS, Andrew	1821	Hampton
SCROGS, Ebenezer	1795	Calvert
SCROOGS, Ebanezer	1791	Milliken
SCROUGS, Ebneson	1794	Scot
SEAHORN, Nansey	1807	Shields
SEAHORN, Nansey	1811	
SEAMAN, Jacob	1797	Calvert
SEAMAN, John	1794	North
SEAMONS, Joseph	1796	Longmire
SEAMONS, Joseph	1797	Longmire
SEAVER, John	1790	Hanley
SEAVER, John	1791	Hanley
SEDUXAS, Emanuel	1778	
SEEHORN, Agness	1810	Dimmons
SEEHORN, James	1797	Biddle
SEEHORN, James	1798	Biddle
SEEHORN, James	1798	Biddle
SEEHORN, James	1801	Biddle
SEEHORN, Nancy	1815	Carcathers
SEEHORN, William	1821	Sands
SEEMAN, Jacob	1807	Givins
SEETHONN, Nancy	1818	Land
SEFENCAY, Abraham	1812	McLin
SEFENCAY, William	1812	McLin
SEHORN, Nansey	1806	Carson
SEHORN, Nansey	1814	Couthers
SELLARS, John	1780-1781	District 7
SEMAN, Abraham	1794	North
SEMERLIN, John	1795	Ford
SEMPLE, Saml	1781	
SEPHESON, Mathew	1806	Payn
SEPSON, James	1821	Howard
SERANCY, William	1819	Smith
SERHAM, Agnes	1819	Sands
SERIN, James	1819	Brown
S-ET, John	1798	Biddle
SETSLEER, William	1816	Copas
SETSLEER, William Jr.	1816	Copas
SEVEIR, John Jr.	1793	Scott
SEVERE, John Jr.	1797	Calvert
SEVIER, (Genl.)	1795	Carriger
SEVIER, Abraham	1790	Greer
SEVIER, Abraham	1792	Carriger
SEVIER, Abraham	1792	Greer
SEVIER, Abraham	1794	Carriger
SEVIER, Charles	1798	Roberson
SEVIER, Charles	1799	Robertson
SEVIER, Gavinor	1799	Stuart
SEVIER, Jack	1792	Scott
SEVIER, Jack	1793	Scott
SEVIER, James	1792	Scott
SEVIER, James	1794	Scot
SEVIER, James	1796	Brown

Surname, Given names	Year	Comp./Dist.
SEVIER, James	1797	Gann
SEVIER, James	1797	Robertson
SEVIER, James	1798	Roberson
SEVIER, James	1801	Roberson
SEVIER, James	1806	Brown
SEVIER, James	1807	Bayles
SEVIER, James	1809	Roadmas
SEVIER, James	1814	Hampton
SEVIER, James	1816	Hampton
SEVIER, James	1817	Hampton
SEVIER, James	1818	Brown [2]
SEVIER, James	1821	Brown
SEVIER, James (Esq.)	1791	
SEVIER, James Jr.	1799	Robertson
SEVIER, Jas	1795	Calvert
SEVIER, John	1778	
SEVIER, John	1779	
SEVIER, John	1791	Willey
SEVIER, John	1796	Longmire
SEVIER, John	1797	Robertson
SEVIER, John	1805	Aikin
SEVIER, John	1806	Anderson
SEVIER, John	1813	Hoss
SEVIER, John (Genl.)	1793	Handley
SEVIER, John (Gov.)	1796	Brown
SEVIER, John (Govener)	1798	Gann
SEVIER, John (Governor)	1801	Roberson
SEVIER, John (Govr.)	1797	Robertson
SEVIER, John Jr.	1794	Scot
SEVIER, John Jr.	1796	Jonesboro
SEVIER, John Jr.	1797	Robertson
SEVIER, John Jr.	1798	Roberson
SEVIER, John Jr.	1801	Roberson
SEVIER, Joseph	1790	Greer
SEVIER, Joseph	1792	Greer
SEVIER, Robert	1778	
SEVIER, Valentine	1778	
SEVIER, Valentine Jr.	1779	
SEVIER, Valentine Jr.	1792	Greer
SEVIER, Valentine Sr.	1778	
SEVIER, Valentine Sr.	1790	Greer
SEVIER, Valentine Sr.	1792	Carriger
SEVIER, Valentine Sr.	1792	Greer
SEVIER, Valentine Sr.	1794	Carriger
SEVIER, Valintine Sr.	1779	
SEVIERS, Valentine Sr.	1795	Carriger
SHACELFORD, James	1805	Rector
SHACELFORD, John	1805	Rector
SHACKELFORD, William	1805	Rector
SHACKKELFORD, James	1806	Doke
SHACKLEFORD, James	1807	Britton
SHACKLEFORD, William	1811	Barron
SHACKLEFORD, William	1812	Barnes
SHAFFEY, John	1815	Copas
SHAKLEFORD, James	1808	Cade
SHAKLEFORD, John	1808	Cade
SHAKLEFORD, William	1808	Cade
SHAKLEFORD, William	1809	Cade
SHAKLEFORD, William	1810	Barron
SHAKLESFORD, John	1807	Cade
SHAKLESFORD, William	1807	Cade
SHANAN, John	1791	Willey
SHANAN, John	1794	Brown
SHANAN, Wm	1791	Willey
SHANE, Lonard	1795	Thornton
SHANKS,	1779	Wilson
SHANKS, George Crook	1796	Millikin
SHANKS, Holden	1794	Depew
SHANKS, Holdin	1793	Depew
SHANKS, James	1781	
SHANKS, James	1790	Biddle
SHANKS, James	1791	Biddle
SHANKS, James	1792	Biddle
SHANKS, James	1793	Depew
SHANKS, James	1794	Blair
SHANKS, Joseph	1811	
SHANKS, Joseph	1814	Couthers
SHANKS, Moses	1814	Couthers
SHANKS, Moses	1815	McLin
SHANKS, Moses	1816	Hunt
SHANKS, Nicholas	1805	Carson
SHANKS, Nicolis	1798	Duncan
SHANKS, William	1790	Biddle
SHANKS, William	1791	Biddle
SHANKS, William	1792	Biddle
SHANKS, William	1793	Depew
SHANKS, William	1794	Blair
SHANKS, William	1797	Biddle
SHANKS, William	1798	Biddle
SHANKS, William	1798	Duncan
SHANKS, William	1801	Biddle
SHANKS, William	1805	Carson
SHANKS, William	1806	Carson
SHANKS, William	1810	Dimmons
SHANKS, William	1814	Couthers
SHANKS, William	1815	McLin
SHANKS, William	1816	Hunt
SHANKS, Wm	1798	Biddle
SHANKS, Wm	1809	Patterson
SHANKS, Wm	1811	
SHANNEN, John	1796	Brown
SHANNON, Elijah	1798	Roberson

Surname, Given names	Year	Comp./Dist.
SHANNON, Elijah	1799	Robertson
SHANNON, Elijah	1801	Roberson
SHANNON, Elijah	1806	Brown
SHANNON, Elijah	1807	Bayles
SHANNON, Elijah	1821	Brown
SHANNON, George	1818	Fine
SHANNON, John	1793	Brown
SHANNON, John	1797	Robertson
SHANNON, John	1798	Roberson
SHANNON, John	1799	Robertson
SHANNON, John	1801	Roberson
SHANNON, John	1806	Brown
SHANNON, John	1807	Bayles
SHANNON, John	1808	Bayles
SHANNON, John	1809	Bayles
SHANNON, John	1814	Hampton
SHANNON, John	1816	Hampton
SHANNON, John	1817	Hampton
SHANNON, John	1818	Brown [2]
SHANNON, John	1819	Brown
SHANNON, John	1821	Brown
SHANNON, Joseph	1797	Robertson
SHANNON, Joseph	1798	Roberson
SHANNON, Joseph	1799	Robertson
SHANNON, Joseph	1801	Roberson
SHANNON, Joseph	1806	Brown
SHANNON, Joseph	1807	Bayles
SHANNON, Willm	1797	Calvert
SHANNON, Willm	1797	Calvert
SHANNON, Wm	1796	Longmire
SHANNON, Wm	1799	Stuart
SHANON, Wilam	1794	Scot
SHARP, Joseph	1793	Handley
SHARP, William	1795	Carriger
SHARPE, William	1795	Taylor
SHARREL, Samuel Sr.	1780-1781 (undated)	
SHARRELL, Samuel	1779	Wilson
SHAW, Benjaman	1794	Melvan
SHAW, Benjamin	1790	Shipley
SHAW, Benjamin	1791	Shipley
SHAW, Benjamin	1793	Melvan
SHAW, Benjamin	1795	Murray
SHAW, Francis	1792	Depew
SHAW, Francis	1797	Duncan
SHAW, Francis	1798	Duncan
SHAW, Francis	1798	Duncan
SHAW, Francis	1799	Duncan
SHAW, Francis	1801	Taylor
SHAW, Samuel	1790	Shipley
SHAW, Samuel	1791	Shipley
SHAW, Samuel	1792	Depew

Surname, Given names	Year	Comp./Dist.
SHAW, Samuel	1793	Depew
SHAW, Samuel	1794	Depew
SHAW, Samuel	1797	Duncan
SHAW, Samuel	1798	Duncan
SHAW, Samuel	1798	Duncan
SHAW, Samuel	1799	Duncan
SHEA, Marson	1820	Smith
SHEA, Morgan	1819	Smith
SHEALS, Joseph	1798	Duncan
SHEALS, Joseph	1814	Barns
SHEALS, William	1807	Givins
SHEATS, Daniel	1807	Cade
SHEATS, Daniel	1808	Cade
SHEATS, Daniel	1810	Barron
SHEATS, Daniel	1811	Barron
SHEEP, Joseph	1795	Handly
SHEETS, Daniel	1809	Cade
SHEFFEILD, Gorge	1799	Gann
SHEFFIELD, George	1794	Thornton
SHEFFIELD, George	1801	Roberson
SHEHIG, John	1815	Haire
SHEILDS, John	1806	Guin
SHEILDS, Patrick	1792	Milliken
SHEILDS, Patrick	1795	Milliken
SHEILDS, Patrick	1799	Hannah
SHEILDS, William	1806	Guin
SHEILS, Joseph	1810	Barron
SHELBY, Jno (Esq.)	1778	
SHELBY, John (Esqr.)	1779	
SHELDS, Gog	1798	Biddle
SHELDS, Joseph	1798	Biddle
SHELDS, Joseph	1809	Cade
SHELDS, Patrick	1798	Hannah
SHELL, Andrew	1821	Smith
SHELLS, Arnol	1778	
SHELLS, Arnold	1779	
SHELLY, Phillip	1778	
SHELSER, Jacob	1780-1781 (undated)	
SHELTON, Armstead	1819	Brown
SHELTON, Arnstred	1821	Haines
SHENEN, William	1792	Scott
SHENEN, William	1793	Scott
SHERAL, Jno	1780-1781 (Undated)	
SHERAL, Saml Jr.	1780-1781 (Undated)	
SHERAL, Saml Sr.	1780-1781 (Undated)	
SHEREY, John	1805	Parker
SHERFEY, Benjamin	1821	Jones
SHERFEY, John	1814	Bean
SHERFEY, Samuel	1814	Bean

Surname, Given names	Year	Comp./Dist.
SHERFFEY, John	1821	Hale
SHERFY, John	1807	Parker
SHERFY, John	1808	Parker
SHERILL, Philip	1779	Wilson
SHERILL, William	1798	Roberson
SHERP, Joseph	1794	Handly
SHERRAL, George	1808	Bayles
SHERRAL, John	1808	Bayles
SHERREL, George	1801	Roberson
SHERREL, George	1809	Bayles
SHERREL, Samuel	1799	Robertson
SHERREL, Thomas	1808	Odell
SHERREL, Thomas	1812	Brown
SHERREL, Thomas	1814	Brown
SHERREL, Thommas	1809	Viney
SHERRELL, Samuel	1797	Robertson
SHERRELL, Thomas	1806	Odel
SHERRELL, William	1821	Brown
SHERRIL, Thomas	1810	Cove
SHERRIL, Thomas	1811	Brown
SHERRILL, Adam	1778	
SHERRILL, Phillip	1778	
SHERRILL, Samuel	1778	
SHERRILL, Samuel Jr.	1778	
SHERRILL, Thomas	1807	Odell
SHERRILL, Thomas	1815	Hartsell
SHERRILL, Thomas	1817	Brown
SHERRILL, Thomas	1819	Brown
SHERRILL, Thomas	1821	Haines
SHIBLE, William	1793	Thornton
SHIELD, David	1808	Gwin
SHIELD, David	1814	Waddell
SHIELD, David	1816	Waddell
SHIELD, Georg	1798	Biddle
SHIELD, Patrick	1793	Milliken
SHIELDS, David	1790	Biddle
SHIELDS, David	1791	Biddle
SHIELDS, David	1792	Biddle
SHIELDS, David	1793	Biddle
SHIELDS, David	1797	Biddle
SHIELDS, David	1798	Biddle
SHIELDS, David	1801	Biddle
SHIELDS, David	1809	Green
SHIELDS, David	1810	Green
SHIELDS, David	1811	Green
SHIELDS, David	1812	Waddill
SHIELDS, David	1815	Waddell
SHIELDS, David	1818	Riley
SHIELDS, David	1819	Findley
SHIELDS, David	1821	McGee
SHIELDS, George	1790	Biddle

Surname, Given names	Year	Comp./Dist.
SHIELDS, George	1791	Biddle
SHIELDS, George	1792	Biddle
SHIELDS, George	1794	Blair
SHIELDS, George	1797	Biddle
SHIELDS, George	1809	Patterson
SHIELDS, George	1810	Dimmons
SHIELDS, George	1783 [after]	Blair
SHIELDS, Harvey	1810	Dimmons
SHIELDS, Hennry	1814	McLin
SHIELDS, Henrey	1793	Handley
SHIELDS, Henry	1790	Hanley
SHIELDS, Henry	1797	Biddle
SHIELDS, Henry	1798	Biddle
SHIELDS, Henry	1801	Biddle
SHIELDS, Henry	1805	Carson
SHIELDS, Henry	1806	Carson
SHIELDS, Henry	1807	Shields
SHIELDS, Henry	1809	Patterson
SHIELDS, Henry	1811	
SHIELDS, Henry	1815	Carcathers
SHIELDS, Henry	1815	McLin
SHIELDS, Henry	1816	Giles
SHIELDS, Henry	1816	Hunt
SHIELDS, Henry	1817	Hunt
SHIELDS, Henry	1818	Hunt
SHIELDS, Henry	1819	Hunt
SHIELDS, Joseph	1790	Biddle
SHIELDS, Joseph	1791	Biddle
SHIELDS, Joseph	1792	Biddle
SHIELDS, Joseph	1793	Biddle
SHIELDS, Joseph	1794	Blair
SHIELDS, Joseph	1797	Biddle
SHIELDS, Joseph	1798	Biddle
SHIELDS, Joseph	1799	Duncan
SHIELDS, Joseph	1801	Biddle
SHIELDS, Joseph	1805	Carson
SHIELDS, Joseph	1805	Carson
SHIELDS, Joseph	1806	Carson
SHIELDS, Joseph	1807	Shields
SHIELDS, Joseph	1809	Patterson
SHIELDS, Joseph	1810	Dimmons
SHIELDS, Joseph	1811	Barron
SHIELDS, Joseph	1811	
SHIELDS, Joseph	1812	Barnes
SHIELDS, Joseph	1814	Couthers
SHIELDS, Joseph	1815	Carcathers
SHIELDS, Joseph	1815	Grimsley
SHIELDS, Joseph	1816	Grimsley
SHIELDS, Joseph	1817	Grimsley
SHIELDS, Joseph	1818	Grimsley
SHIELDS, Joseph	1818	Hunt

Surname, Given names	Year	Comp./Dist.
SHIELDS, Joseph	1819	Grimsley
SHIELDS, Joseph	1819	Hunt
SHIELDS, Joseph	1821	Hunt
SHIELDS, Joseph	1783 [after]	Blair
SHIELDS, Joseph Jr.	1808	Guin
SHIELDS, Joshua	1817	Hunt
SHIELDS, Kennery	1798	Biddle
SHIELDS, Patrick	1797	Hannah
SHIELDS, Patrik	1796	Millikin
SHIELDS, Thomas	1811	
SHIELDS, Thomas	1819	Smith
SHIELDS, William	1808	Guin
SHIELDS, William	1809	Gwin
SHIELDS, William	1811	Davis
SHIELDS, William	1812	McLin
SHIELDS, William	1814	McLin
SHIELDS, William	1815	McLin
SHIELDS, William	1816	Hunt
SHIELDS, William	1817	Hunt
SHIELDS, William	1818	Hunt
SHIELDS, William	1819	Hunt
SHIELDS, William	1821	Hunt
SHILDS, David	1799	Stuart
SHIPLEY, Adam	1793	Murray
SHIPLEY, Adam	1812	Ellis
SHIPLEY, Adam	1819	Smith
SHIPLEY, Adam	1820	Smith
SHIPLEY, Adam	1821	Hale
SHIPLEY, Benja	1813	Copas
SHIPLEY, Benja (of Saml)	1813	Copas
SHIPLEY, Benjaman	1814	Copes
SHIPLEY, Benjamin	1790	Shipley
SHIPLEY, Benjamin	1791	Shipley
SHIPLEY, Benjamin	1793	Murray
SHIPLEY, Benjamin	1794	Murray
SHIPLEY, Benjamin	1795	Murray
SHIPLEY, Benjamin	1796	Shipley
SHIPLEY, Benjamin	1797	Shipley
SHIPLEY, Benjamin	1815	Copas
SHIPLEY, Benjamin	1815	Copas
SHIPLEY, Benjamin	1816	Copas
SHIPLEY, Benjamin	1816	Copas
SHIPLEY, Benjamin	1817	Grisham
SHIPLEY, Benjamin	1818	Grisham
SHIPLEY, Benjamin	1818	Hair
SHIPLEY, Benjamin	1819	Grisham
SHIPLEY, Benjamin	1819	Hair
SHIPLEY, Benjamin	1819	Jones
SHIPLEY, Benjamin	1821	Hale
SHIPLEY, Benjamin	1821	Louis
SHIPLEY, Edward	1790	Shipley
SHIPLEY, Edward	1791	Shipley
SHIPLEY, Edward	1793	Murray
SHIPLEY, Edward	1794	Murray
SHIPLEY, Edward	1795	Murray
SHIPLEY, Edward (Capt.)	1791	
SHIPLEY, Enoch	1816	Copas
SHIPLEY, Enoch	1821	Hale
SHIPLEY, James	1793	Murray
SHIPLEY, James	1795	Murray
SHIPLEY, James	1796	Shipley
SHIPLEY, James	1798	Shipley
SHIPLEY, James	1801	Lane
SHIPLEY, James	1805	Doak
SHIPLEY, James	1807	Britton
SHIPLEY, James	1811	Britten
SHIPLEY, James	1812	Britton
SHIPLEY, James	1813	Copas
SHIPLEY, James	1814	Copes
SHIPLEY, James	1815	Copas
SHIPLEY, James	1816	Copas
SHIPLEY, James	1818	Grisham
SHIPLEY, James	1819	Grisham
SHIPLEY, James	1821	Hale
SHIPLEY, Jesse	1815	Copas
SHIPLEY, Jesse	1816	Copas
SHIPLEY, Jesse	1817	Grisham
SHIPLEY, Jesse	1818	Grisham
SHIPLEY, Jesse	1819	Grisham
SHIPLEY, John	1816	Copas
SHIPLEY, John	1817	Grisham
SHIPLEY, John	1818	Grisham
SHIPLEY, John	1819	Grisham
SHIPLEY, Nathan	1793	Murray
SHIPLEY, Nathan	1795	Murray
SHIPLEY, Nathan	1796	Shipley
SHIPLEY, Nathan	1797	Shipley
SHIPLEY, Nathan	1798	Shipley
SHIPLEY, Nathan	1801	Lane
SHIPLEY, Nathan	1805	Doak
SHIPLEY, Nathan	1807	Britton
SHIPLEY, Nathan	1811	Britten
SHIPLEY, Nathan	1812	Britton
SHIPLEY, Nathan	1813	Copas
SHIPLEY, Nathan	1814	Copes
SHIPLEY, Nathan	1815	Copas
SHIPLEY, Nathan	1816	Copas
SHIPLEY, Nathan	1817	Grisham
SHIPLEY, Nathan	1818	Grisham
SHIPLEY, Nathan	1819	Grisham
SHIPLEY, Nathan	1821	Hale
SHIPLEY, Nathan Sr.	1806	Doke

Surname, Given names	Year	Comp./Dist.
SHIPLEY, Pete	1820	Smith
SHIPLEY, Peter	1790	Shipley
SHIPLEY, Peter	1791	Shipley
SHIPLEY, Peter	1793	Murray
SHIPLEY, Peter	1794	Murray
SHIPLEY, Peter	1795	Murray
SHIPLEY, Peter	1797	Shipley
SHIPLEY, Peter	1798	Shipley
SHIPLEY, Peter	1801	Lane
SHIPLEY, Peter	1805	Doak
SHIPLEY, Peter	1806	Doke
SHIPLEY, Peter	1807	Britton
SHIPLEY, Peter	1811	Britten
SHIPLEY, Peter	1812	Britton
SHIPLEY, Peter	1813	Copas
SHIPLEY, Peter	1814	Copes
SHIPLEY, Peter	1815	Copas
SHIPLEY, Peter	1816	Copas
SHIPLEY, Peter	1817	Grisham
SHIPLEY, Peter	1819	Brown
SHIPLEY, Peter	1819	Smith
SHIPLEY, Thomas	1790	Shipley
SHIPLEY, Thomas	1791	Shipley
SHIPLEY, Thomas	1793	Depew
SHIPLEY, Thomas	1794	Depew
SHIPLEY, Thomas	1796	Shipley
SHIPLEY, Thomas	1797	Shipley
SHIPLEY, Thomas	1798	Shipley
SHIPLEY, Thomas	1801	Glasscock
SHIPPEN, William	1819	Smith
SHIRAL, George	1807	Bayles
SHIRER, William	1812	Waddill
SHIRREL, Samuel	1796	Brown
SHIR-Y, John	1806	Parker
SHOFF, Hugh	1819	Smith
SHOFFEN, Omega	1805	Aikin
SHOLEY, Luke	1781	
SHON, Jacob	1809	Green
SHOOTHS, Christian Sr.	1792	Greer
SHORE, Henry	1810	Green
SHORE, Jacob	1808	Gwin
SHORE, Jacob	1810	Green
SHORT, Drury	1819	Hunt
SHOULTS, Christian Jr.	1792	Carriger
SHOULTS, Christian Sr.	1792	Carriger
SHOULTZ, Christian	1794	Carriger
SHOULTZ, Christian Jr.	1794	Carriger
SHOWN, Leonard	1794	Thornton
SHUFFIELD, George	1797	Gann
SHULES, Christian (D.P.)	1779	
SHULES, Martin (Dr.)	1779	
SHULL, Thomas	1816	Brown
SHULL, Thomas	1818	Brown
SHULTZ, Christian	1795	Carriger
SHURLEY, Edward	1778	
SHURLEY, John	1778	
SHURLEY, Robert	1778	
SHURLEY, Thomas	1778	
SICKEL, Van	1797	Shipley
SIDENER, Martin	1797	Calvert
SIDNARR, Martain	1796	Calvert
SIDNER, Martin	1794	Scot
SIDNER, Martin	1795	Calvert
SIDNER, Martin	1797	Calvert
SIDNER, Martin	1798	Calvert
SIDNER, Martin	1799	Stuart
SIGHTERS,	1814	Couthers
SIHORN, Nancy	1816	Giles
SILTY, Christain	1808	Guin
SIMERLY, Adam	1792	Maxwell
SIMERLY, John	1792	White
SIMERLY, John	1793	Campbell
SIMERMAN, Daniel	1806	Crouch
SIMMERLY, Adam	1793	Maxwell
SIMMERLY, John	1794	Ford
SIMMERMAN, Daniel	1812	Ellis
SIMMERMAN, John	1821	Jones
SIMMERMON, Daniel	1814	Bean
SIMMONS, Isaac	1817	Hampton
SIMMONS, Isaac	1818	Brown
SIMMONS, Joseph	1792	Coye
SIMMONS, Joseph	1798	Longmire
SIMMONS, Micajah	1817	Hampton
SIMMONS, Micajah	1818	Brown [2]
SIMMONS, William	1817	Hampton
SIMMONS, William	1818	Hair
SIMMONS, Zachariah	1816	Hampton
SIMMONS, Zachariah	1817	Hampton
SIMMONS, Zachariah	1818	Brown [2]
SIMMONS, Zachariah	1819	Brown
SIMPLE, Samuel	1780-1781 (Undated)	
SIMPSON, James	1799	Duncan
SIMPSON, James	1801	Taylor
SIMPSON, John	1799	Duncan
SIMPSON, John	1801	Taylor
SIMPSON, John	1809	Patterson
SIMPSON, John	1811	Davis
SIMPSON, John	1811	
SIMPSON, John	1814	McLin
SIMPSON, Nathaniel	1801	Glasscock
SIMPSON, Samuel	1780-1781 (Undated)	

Surname, Given names	Year	Comp./Dist.
SIMS, Jacob	1780-1781 (Undated)	
SIMS, Job	1781	
SIMS, John	1798	Longmire
SIMSON, James	1806	Payn
SIMSON, James	1807	Payne
SIMSON, Samuel	1781	
SINCLEAR, Alexander	1794	Brown
SISENBAY, William	1814	McLin
SITSELLER, William	1821	Hale
SITSLLER, William	1817	Grisham
SIZCORN, Abram	1806	Crouch
SKILES, William	1811	Green
SKYLER, Joseph	1795	Ford
SLAGAL, Henry	1821	Howard
SLAGEL, Henry	1805	Parker
SLAGEL, Henry	1807	Parker
SLAGEL, Henry	1808	Parker
SLAGEL, Henry	1809	Par
SLAGEL, Henry	1814	Hartsell
SLAGER, John	1791	Willey
SLAGLE, Christopher	1819	Howard
SLAGLE, Henry	1815	Fines
SLAGLE, Henry	1816	Fine
SLAGLE, Henry	1817	Fine
SLAGLE, Henry	1818	Fine
SLAGLE, Henry	1819	Howard
SLAGLE, John	1814	McCray
SLAGLE, John	1816	Harrison
SLAGLE, John	1817	Harris
SLAGLE, John	1818	Harris
SLAGLE, John	1819	Harris
SLAGLE, John	1821	Hampton
SLAIGER, John Jr.	1792	Scott
SLAIGER, John Sr.	1792	Scott
SLARGER, John Jr.	1793	Scott
SLARNO, Peter	1807	Bayles
SLAUGHTER, Allexander	1806	Crouch
SLAUGHTER, Willam	1798	Hannah
SLAUGHTER, William	1797	Hannah
SLAUGHTER, William	1807	Givins
SLAUGHTER, William	1817	Hunt
SLAUGHTER, William	1818	Hunt
SLAUGHTER, William	1819	Hunt
SLAUGHTER, William Jr.	1807	Givins
SLAUGHTER, William Jr.	1809	Gwin
SLAUGHTER, William Jr.	1811	Davis
SLAUGHTER, William Jr.	1812	McLin
SLAUGHTER, William Jr.	1814	McLin
SLAUGHTER, William Jr.	1815	McLin
SLAUGHTER, William Jr.	1816	Hunt
SLAUGHTER, William Sr.	1809	Gwin

Surname, Given names	Year	Comp./Dist.
SLAUGHTER, William Sr.	1811	Davis
SLAUGHTER, William Sr.	1812	McLin
SLAUGHTER, William Sr.	1814	McLin
SLAUGHTER, William Sr.	1815	McLin
SLAUGHTER, William Sr.	1816	Hunt
SLAUGHTER, Wm	1799	Duncan
SLAWTER, William	1796	Millikin
SLEGAR, Adam	1799	Stuart
SLEGAR, John Jr.	1799	Stuart
SLEGAR, John Sr.	1799	Stuart
SLEGER, John Jr.	1814	McCray
SLEIGAL, Henry	1806	Parker
SLEMMINS, Peter	1780-1781 (Undated)	
SLEMMONS, William	1816	Hampton
SLEMMONS, Wm	1814	Hampton
SLEMONS, William	1807	
SLEMONS, William	1809	Right
SLEMONS, William	1819	Brown
SLIGAR, Adam	1811	McCray
SLIGAR, Christopher	1806	Parker
SLIGAR, Gasper	1796	Longmire
SLIGAR, Henry	1796	Longmire
SLIGAR, Jno	1796	Calvert
SLIGAR, John	1796	Calvert
SLIGAR, John Jr.	1811	McCray
SLIGAR, John Sr.	1811	McCray
SLIGER, Adam	1797	Calvert
SLIGER, Adam	1798	Calvert
SLIGER, Adam	1801	Calvert
SLIGER, Adam	1805	Jas Parker
SLIGER, Adam	1808	Parker
SLIGER, Adam	1809	Parker
SLIGER, Adam	1812	McCray
SLIGER, Adam	1812	McCray
SLIGER, Adam	1814	McCray
SLIGER, Adam	1816	Harrison
SLIGER, Adam	1817	Harris
SLIGER, Adam	1818	Harris
SLIGER, Adam	1819	Harris
SLIGER, Adam	1821	Hampton
SLIGER, Adam (adm. of Wm Loyd)	1814	Hampton
SLIGER, Adam (for Wm. Taylor estate)	1816	Harrison
SLIGER, Adam Jr.	1821	Hampton
SLIGER, Casper	1801	Roberson
SLIGER, Christian	1817	Fine
SLIGER, Christian	1818	Fine
SLIGER, Christo	1809	Par
SLIGER, Christofor	1805	Parker
SLIGER, Christopher	1810	Hartzel
SLIGER, Christopher	1812	Hartsell

Surname, Given names	Year	Comp./Dist.
SLIGER, Christopher	1814	Hartsell
SLIGER, Gasner	1793	Scott
SLIGER, Gasper	1797	Calvert
SLIGER, Henry	1797	Calvert
SLIGER, Henry	1808	Bayles
SLIGER, Henry	1814	Hampton
SLIGER, Henry	1818	Brown [2]
SLIGER, James	1819	Brown
SLIGER, Jasper	1794	Scot
SLIGER, Jasper	1798	Calvert
SLIGER, Jno	1809	Parker
SLIGER, Jno Jr.	1809	Parker
SLIGER, Jno Sr.	1798	Calvert
SLIGER, John	1797	Calvert
SLIGER, John	1808	Parker
SLIGER, John	1819	Harris
SLIGER, John	1821	Hampton
SLIGER, John (Dec'd)	1821	Hampton
SLIGER, John (estate of)	1821	Hampton
SLIGER, John (estate)	1819	Harris
SLIGER, John Jr.	1794	Scot
SLIGER, John Jr.	1794	Scot
SLIGER, John Jr.	1797	Calvert
SLIGER, John Jr.	1798	Calvert
SLIGER, John Jr.	1801	Calvert
SLIGER, John Jr.	1805	Jas Parker
SLIGER, John Jr.	1808	Parker
SLIGER, John Jr.	1812	McCray
SLIGER, John Jr.	1812	McCray
SLIGER, John Jr.	1816	Harrison
SLIGER, John Jr.	1817	Harris
SLIGER, John Jr.	1818	Harris
SLIGER, John Sr.	1793	Scott
SLIGER, John Sr.	1797	Calvert
SLIGER, John Sr.	1801	Calvert
SLIGER, John Sr.	1805	Jas Parker
SLIGER, John Sr.	1812	McCray
SLIGER, John Sr.	1812	McCray
SLIGER, John Sr.	1814	McCray
SLIGER, John Sr.	1816	Harrison
SLIGER, John Sr.	1817	Harris
SLIGER, John Sr.	1818	Harris
SLIGLE, Henry	1810	Hartzel
SLIMMONS, William	1818	Brown [2]
SLIMMONS, William	1821	Brown
SLIMP, Michal	1794	Thornton
SLINGLE, George	1806	Brown
SLOAN, Archibd	1781	
SLOANS, Archl	1779	Wilson
SLOGAL, John	1821	Howard
SLONE, George	1797	Calvert
SLOOM, George	1798	Calvert
SLOT, Absolem	1810	Hartzel
SLOUGHTER, William	1821	Hunt
SLUGGER, Henry	1799	Robertson
SLUMP, Michal	1795	Thornton
SLURA, Charles	1798	Biddle
SLURD, Charles	1798	Biddle
SLYER, Christopher	1821	Howard
SLYGER, Casper	1795	Calvert
SLYGER, Christan	1807	Parker
SLYGER, Christopher	1816	Fine
SLYGER, Harry	1821	Brown
SLYGER, Henery	1795	Calvert
SLYGER, Henry	1801	Roberson
SLYGER, Henry	1806	Brown
SLYGER, Henry	1807	Bayles
SLYGER, Henry	1809	Bayles
SLYGER, Henry	1817	Hampton
SLYGER, John	1795	Calvert
SLYGER, John Jr.	1795	Calvert
SLYSSER, Christopher	1815	Fines
SMALLING, Saml	1792	Maxwell
SMALSER, Jacob	1781	
SMASER, Jacob	1779	Wilson
SMATEIR, Peter	1797	Biddle
SMEETAN, Edward	1778	
SMETSER, Peter	1801	Biddle
SMETZE, Peter	1812	McLin
SMILEY, Thomas	1795	Calvert
SMITH, (Sen.)	1817	Hunt
SMITH, Abraham	1792	Depew
SMITH, Abraham	1793	Depew
SMITH, Abraham	1794	Depew
SMITH, Abraham	1797	Duncan
SMITH, Abraham	1798	Duncan
SMITH, Abraham	1798	Duncan
SMITH, Abraham	1799	Duncan
SMITH, Abraham	1806	Guin
SMITH, Abraham	1807	Givins
SMITH, Abraham	1808	Guin
SMITH, Abraham	1809	Gwin
SMITH, Abraham	1783 [after]	Depew
SMITH, Adam	1806	Odel
SMITH, Adam	1811	
SMITH, Adam Brailes B.	1794	Handly
SMITH, Adam Broiles	1793	Handley
SMITH, Adam Broiles	1795	Handly
SMITH, Adam Broyles B.	1796	Handly
SMITH, Alexander	1817	Smith
SMITH, Alexander	1818	Smith
SMITH, Alexander	1819	Smith

Surname, Given names	Year	Comp./Dist.
SMITH, Alexander	1820	Smith
SMITH, Anderson	1792	Depew
SMITH, Anderson	1793	Murray
SMITH, Anderson	1794	Murray
SMITH, Anderson	1795	Murray
SMITH, Anderson	1797	Shipley
SMITH, Anderson	1798	Shipley
SMITH, Bank	1816	Hunt
SMITH, Banks	1815	McLin
SMITH, Brooks	1792	Maxwell
SMITH, Brooks	1793	Maxwell
SMITH, Brooks	1794	Taylor
SMITH, Charles	1812	McCray
SMITH, Charles	1814	McCracken
SMITH, Charls	1812	McCray
SMITH, Danial	1796	Handly
SMITH, Daniel	1797	Gann
SMITH, Edward	1778	
SMITH, Edward	1790	White
SMITH, Edward	1791	North
SMITH, Edward	1791	White
SMITH, Edward	1792	North
SMITH, Edward	1794	Ford
SMITH, Edward	1795	Young
SMITH, Edward	1796	Young
SMITH, Edward	1797	Young
SMITH, Edward	1798	Shipley
SMITH, Edward	1798	Young
SMITH, Edward	1801	Taylor
SMITH, Edward	1805	Parker
SMITH, Edward (Esq.)	1795	Ford
SMITH, Edward (Over age)	1792	White
SMITH, Edwd	1793	North
SMITH, Eurd	1794	North
SMITH, Ezekiel	1778	
SMITH, Ezekiel	1814	Couthers
SMITH, Ezekiel	1816	Giles
SMITH, Ezekiel	1817	Gillises
SMITH, Ezekiel	1818	Land
SMITH, Ezekiel	1821	Sands
SMITH, Geo	1799	Stuart
SMITH, George	1797	Calvert
SMITH, George	1811	Davis
SMITH, George	1812	McLin
SMITH, George	1815	McLin
SMITH, George	1816	Hunt
SMITH, Henry	1793	Hale
SMITH, Isaac	1817	Hunt
SMITH, Isaac	1818	Hunt
SMITH, Isaac	1819	Hunt
SMITH, Isaac	1821	Hunt
SMITH, Jacob	1790	White
SMITH, Jacob	1791	White
SMITH, Jacob	1793	Campbell
SMITH, Jacob	1794	Ford
SMITH, Jacob	1795	Ford
SMITH, James	1791	Willey
SMITH, James	1794	Scot
SMITH, James	1814	McCracken
SMITH, James	1815	Garner
SMITH, James	1818	Smith
SMITH, James C.	1820	Smith
SMITH, Jeremia M.	1821	Smith
SMITH, Jeremiah	1811	Mitchell
SMITH, Jeremiah	1813	Hoss
SMITH, Jeremiah	1814	Bean
SMITH, Jeremiah	1815	Hoss
SMITH, Jeremiah	1816	Hoss
SMITH, Jeremiah	1817	Little
SMITH, Jeremiah	1818	Smith
SMITH, Jeremiah	1819	Smith
SMITH, Jeremiah	1820	Smith
SMITH, Jeremiah D.	1814	Hoss
SMITH, Jeremiah D.	1816	Hoss
SMITH, Jeremiah D.	1817	Little
SMITH, Jeremiah D.	1818	Jones
SMITH, Jeremiah D.	1819	Jones
SMITH, Jerimiah	1811	Rodman
SMITH, Jermiah D.	1821	Jones
SMITH, Jno	1809	Parker
SMITH, Jno (Mason)	1809	Parker
SMITH, Jno Mason	1821	Smith
SMITH, John	1778	
SMITH, John	1790	White
SMITH, John	1791	Milliken
SMITH, John	1791	White
SMITH, John	1792	Milliken
SMITH, John	1792	Scott
SMITH, John	1793	Scott
SMITH, John	1793	Thornton
SMITH, John	1794	Ford
SMITH, John	1794	Milliken
SMITH, John	1794	Scot
SMITH, John	1795	Ford
SMITH, John	1795	Milliken
SMITH, John	1796	Handly
SMITH, John	1796	Longmire
SMITH, John	1797	Calvert
SMITH, John	1798	Calvert
SMITH, John	1801	Taylor
SMITH, John	1805	Aikin
SMITH, John	1805	Parker

Surname, Given names	Year	Comp./Dist.
SMITH, John	1806	Parker
SMITH, John	1807	Anderson
SMITH, John	1814	McCracken
SMITH, John	1816	Smith
SMITH, John	1817	Smith
SMITH, John	1818	Smith
SMITH, John	1819	Smith
SMITH, John	1820	Smith
SMITH, John	1821	Hunt
SMITH, John	1821	Smith
SMITH, John	1780-1781 (Undated)	
SMITH, John (mason)	1807	Parker
SMITH, John (mason)	1808	Parker
SMITH, John (mason)	1812	McCray
SMITH, John (mason)	1812	McCray
SMITH, John (mason)	1815	Garner
SMITH, John (Mason)	1809	Roadmas
SMITH, John (Mason)	1814	McCracken
SMITH, John Jr.	1797	Calvert
SMITH, John Jr.	1799	Stuart
SMITH, John Jr.	1801	Calvert
SMITH, John Jr.	1805	Jas Parker
SMITH, John Jr.	1808	Parker
SMITH, John Jr.	1812	McCray
SMITH, John Jr.	1812	McCray
SMITH, John Jr.	1814	McCracken
SMITH, John Jr.	1815	Garner
SMITH, John M.	1809	Roadmas
SMITH, John M.	1811	Rodman
SMITH, John Mason	1816	Smith
SMITH, John Mason	1817	Smith
SMITH, John Mason	1819	Smith
SMITH, John Mason	1820	Smith
SMITH, John Michael	1790	Greer
SMITH, John Sr.	1799	Stuart
SMITH, John Sr.	1812	McCray
SMITH, Joseph	1815	McLin
SMITH, Joseph	1816	Hunt
SMITH, Joseph	1818	Harris
SMITH, Joseph	1819	Harris
SMITH, Joseph	1821	Hampton
SMITH, Lurned	1818	Smith
SMITH, Martha	1811	Davis
SMITH, Martha	1812	McLin
SMITH, Martha	1815	McLin
SMITH, Martha	1816	Hunt
SMITH, Martha	1818	Hunt
SMITH, Martha	1819	Hunt
SMITH, Martha	1821	Hunt
SMITH, Mathew	1817	Hunt
SMITH, Nathanel	1814	Couthers

Surname, Given names	Year	Comp./Dist.
SMITH, Nathaniel	1811	
SMITH, Nathaniel	1815	Carcathers
SMITH, Nathaniel	1816	Giles
SMITH, Nathaniel	1817	Gillises
SMITH, Nathaniel	1818	Land
SMITH, Nathaniel	1819	Sands
SMITH, Nathaniel	1821	Sands
SMITH, Nicholas	1794	Ford
SMITH, Nicholas	1795	Ford
SMITH, Phillip	1796	Handly
SMITH, Phillip	1797	Gann
SMITH, Richard	1790	Biddle
SMITH, Richard	1791	Biddle
SMITH, Richard	1792	Biddle
SMITH, Richard	1794	Blair
SMITH, Richard	1797	Biddle
SMITH, Richard	1798	Biddle
SMITH, Richard	1798	Biddle
SMITH, Richard	1801	Biddle
SMITH, Richard	1814	McCracken
SMITH, Richard	1815	Garner
SMITH, Richard	1816	Smith
SMITH, Richard	1817	Smith
SMITH, Richard	1818	Smith
SMITH, Richard	1819	Smith
SMITH, Richard	1820	Smith
SMITH, Richard	1780-1781 (Undated)	
SMITH, Rich'd	1821	Smith
SMITH, Robert	1793	Scott
SMITH, Robert	1795	Calvert
SMITH, Samuel	1778	
SMITH, Samuel	1779	
SMITH, Samuel	1791	White
SMITH, Samuel	1793	Thornton
SMITH, Samuel	1794	Ford
SMITH, Samuel	1795	Ford
SMITH, Seath	1799	Duncan
SMITH, Seth	1797	Duncan
SMITH, Seth	1798	Duncan
SMITH, Seth	1798	Duncan
SMITH, Soloman	1819	Sands
SMITH, Soloman	1821	Sands
SMITH, Solomon	1778	
SMITH, Solomon	1779	
SMITH, Solomon	1818	Land
SMITH, Thomas	1781	
SMITH, Thommas	1780-1781 (Undated)	
SMITH, Turner	1805	Jas Parker
SMITH, Turner	1808	Parker
SMITH, Turner	1809	Parker

Surname, Given names	Year	Comp./Dist.
SMITH, Turner	1811	McCray
SMITH, Turner	1812	McCray
SMITH, Turner	1812	McCray
SMITH, Turner	1814	McCracken
SMITH, Turner	1815	Garner
SMITH, Turner	1816	Smith
SMITH, Turner	1817	Smith
SMITH, Turner	1819	Smith
SMITH, Turner	1820	Smith
SMITH, Turner	1821	Smith
SMITH, William	1779	
SMITH, William	1791	White
SMITH, William	1793	Thornton
SMITH, William	1794	Ford
SMITH, William	1797	Duncan
SMITH, William	1798	Duncan
SMITH, William	1798	Duncan
SMITH, William	1801	Taylor
SMITH, William	1806	Guin
SMITH, William	1809	Gwin
SMITH, William	1811	Davis
SMITH, William	1812	McLin
SMITH, William	1816	Smith
SMITH, William	1817	Smith
SMITH, William	1818	Smith
SMITH, William B.	1812	McLin
SMITH, William B.	1817	Hunt
SMITH, William B.	1818	Hunt
SMITH, William B.	1819	Hunt
SMITH, William B.	1821	Hampton
SMITH, William Bailey	1779	
SMITH, Wm	1779	
SMITH, Wm	1795	Ford
SMITH, Wm	1799	Duncan
SMITH, Zebelum	1794	Taylor
SMITH, Zebsolom	1796	Morrison
SMITH, Zebulen	1798	Morrison
SMITH, Zebulen	1801	Morrison
SMITH, Zebulen	1806	Carr
SMITH, Zebulen	1819	Jones
SMITH, Zebulon	1792	Tulley
SMITH, Zebulon	1793	Maxwell
SMITH, Zebulon	1798	Morrison
SMITH, Zebulon	1798	Morrison
SMITH, Zebulon	1799	Morrison
SMITH, Zebulon	1808	Carr
SMITH, Zebulon	1809	Carr
SMITH, Zebulon	1814	Hoss
SMITH, Zebulon	1815	Hoss
SMITH, Zebulon	1816	Hoss
SMITH, Zebulon	1817	Little
SMITH, Zebulon	1818	Jones
SMITH, Zebulon	1821	Jones
SMITH, Zibulon	1807	Carr
SMITHE, John Jr.	1811	McCray
SNAP, Abraham	1805	Guir
SNAP, Abraham	1806	Grur
SNAP, Abraham	1808	Gwin
SNAP, Abraham	1809	Green
SNAP, Abraham	1810	Green
SNAP, Abraham	1811	Green
SNAP, Abraham	1812	Waddill
SNAP, Abraham	1814	Waddell
SNAP, George	1814	Waddell
SNAP, Larance	1805	Guir
SNAP, Larance	1806	Grur
SNAP, Larence	1811	Green
SNAP, Lawrence	1809	Green
SNAP, Lawrence	1810	Green
SNAP, Lawrence	1812	Waddill
SNAP, Peter	1809	Green
SNAP, Peter	1812	Waddill
SNAP, Peter	1814	Waddell
SNAPP, Abraham	1815	Waddell
SNAPP, Abraham	1816	Waddell
SNAPP, Abraham	1817	Riley
SNAPP, Abraham	1818	Riley
SNAPP, Abraham	1819	Findley
SNAPP, Abraham	1821	McGee
SNAPP, Abraham Sr.	1819	Findley
SNAPP, George	1815	Waddell
SNAPP, George	1816	Waddell
SNAPP, George	1817	Riley
SNAPP, George	1818	Riley
SNAPP, George	1819	Findley
SNAPP, George	1821	McGee
SNAPP, Jacob	1801	Gann
SNAPP, John	1815	Crookshanks
SNAPP, John	1817	McClure
SNAPP, John	1818	McClure
SNAPP, John	1819	McClure
SNAPP, John	1821	McClure
SNAPP, John Sr.	1816	Crookshanks
SNAPP, Joseph	1817	Riley
SNAPP, Joseph	1818	Riley
SNAPP, Lawrence	1814	Crookshanks
SNAPP, Lawrence	1815	Crookshanks
SNAPP, Lawrence	1816	Crookshanks
SNAPP, Lawrence	1817	McClure
SNAPP, Lawrence	1818	McClure
SNAPP, Lawrence	1819	McClure
SNAPP, Lawrence	1821	McClure

Surname, Given names	Year	Comp./Dist.
SNAPP, Peter	1815	Waddell
SNAPP, Peter	1816	Waddell
SNAPP, Peter	1817	Riley
SNAPP, Peter	1818	Riley
SNAPP, Peter	1819	Findley
SNAPP, Peter	1821	McGee
SNIDER, Adam	1790	White
SNIDER, Adam	1791	White
SNIDER, Adam	1792	White
SNIDER, Casper	1811	Davis
SNIDER, Daniel	1806	Carson
SNIDER, Daniel	1807	Shields
SNIDER, Daniel	1816	Hair
SNIDER, Daniel	1817	Haire
SNIDER, Daniel	1819	Hair
SNIDER, Daniel	1821	Louis
SNIDER, David	1818	Hair
SNIDER, Elizabeth	1794	Thornton
SNIDER, Peter	1792	White
SNIDER, Peter	1794	Thornton
SNIDER, Peter	1795	Thornton
SNIDER, Peter (Over age)	1791	White
SNITIER, Peter	1798	Biddle
SNODGRASS, William	1821	Jones
Solomon	1806	Payn
Solomon (man of colour)	1821	Hale
SOLOMON, Burs	1805	Jas Parker
SOLT, John	1816	Harrison
SOLTS, Andrew	1821	Hampton
SOLTS, Daniel	1821	Hampton
SOLTS, John	1811	McCray
SOUT, John	1812	Crawford [2]
SOUT, Moses	1812	Crawford [2]
SOUTHERLAND, Isaac	1798	Duncan
SPACIER, Jacob	1817	Riley
SPALDING, John	1818	Harris
SPAN, Henrey	1808	Gwin
SPEAKER, Benjamin	1815	Haire
SPEAKER, Benjamin	1816	Hair
SPEAKER, Benjamin	1817	Haire
SPEARS, Leven	1814	McCray
SPECK, Julias	1818	Harris
SPERENKEL, Peter	1812	McCray
SPIRGEN, William	1819	Grisham
SPIVEY, Zadock	1805	Parker
SPIVEY, Zadock	1807	Parker
SPIVEY, Zadock	1808	Parker
SPIVY, Jacob	1811	
SPORE, Henry	1812	Waddill
SPOUR, Henry	1811	Green
SPOUR, Jacob	1811	Green
SPOUR, Jacob	1815	Waddell
SPRING, Nicholas	1795	Calvert
SPRING, Nicholas	1797	Calvert
SPRING, Nicholus	1799	Robertson
SPRING, Nicklas	1794	Scot
SPRING, Nicolas	1798	Roberson
SPRINGS, Nicholis	1793	Brown
SPRINKLE, Peter	1812	McCray
SPROUSE, Jacob	1816	Waddell
SPROUSE, Jessee	1799	Duncan
SPURGEN, William	1811	Britten
SPURGEN, William	1813	Copas
SPURGEN, William	1815	Copas
SPURGENT, William	1805	Doak
SPURGEON, William	1814	Copes
SPURGEON, William	1816	Copas
SPURGEON, William	1817	Grisham
SPURGEON, William	1821	Hale
SPURGIN, William	1806	Doke
SPURGIN, William	1812	Britton
SPURGIN, William	1818	Grisham
SQIBB, John	1797	Hannah
SQIBB, John	1798	Hannah
SQUIB, Caleb	1808	Guin
SQUIB, Caleb	1814	McLin
SQUIB, Caleb	1818	Hunt
SQUIB, Calip	1806	Guin
SQUIB, John	1806	Guin
SQUIB, John	1808	Guin
SQUIB, John	1814	McLin
SQUIB, John	1818	Hunt
SQUIBB, Cabel	1807	Givins
SQUIBB, Caleb	1812	McLin
SQUIBB, Caleb	1816	Hunt
SQUIBB, Caleb	1819	Hunt
SQUIBB, Calip	1809	Gwin
SQUIBB, Calip	1811	Davis
SQUIBB, Cobb	1815	McLin
SQUIBB, Cobb	1821	Hunt
SQUIBB, George	1819	Hunt
SQUIBB, George	1821	Hunt
SQUIBB, John	1796	Millikin
SQUIBB, John	1799	Hannah
SQUIBB, John	1801	Squibb
SQUIBB, John	1807	Givins
SQUIBB, John	1809	Gwin
SQUIBB, John	1811	Davis
SQUIBB, John	1812	McLin
SQUIBB, John	1815	McLin
SQUIBB, John	1816	Hunt
SQUIBB, John	1819	Hunt

Surname, Given names	Year	Comp./Dist.
SQUIBB, John	1821	Hunt
SQUIL, Caleb	1817	Hunt
SQUIL, John	1817	Hunt
STAFFORD, Benjamin	1819	Brown
STAIMER, George	1815	Fines
STAINEL, Wm	1795	Ford
STAN, Mychal	1811	Barron
STANBACK, Michael	1793	Murray
STANBERRY, Ezecal	1812	Crawford [2]
STANBERRY, Samuel	1821	McClure
STANDBACK, Michael	1790	Shipley
STANDBACK, Michel	1791	Shipley
STANDSBERRY, James	1812	Ellis
STANFIELD, Samuel	1799	Duncan
STANFIELD, Samuel	1814	McLin
STANSBERRY, Samuel	1819	McClure
STANSBERY, Elijah	1819	Hair
STANSBERY, Elijah	1821	Louis
STANSBURY, Elijah	1817	Haire
STANSBURY, Elijah	1818	Hair
STANSBURY, Enid	1815	Crookshanks
STANSBURY, Samuel	1815	Crookshanks
STANSBURY, Samuel	1816	Crookshanks
STANSBURY, Samuel	1817	McClure
STANSBURY, Samuel	1818	McClure
STANSBURY, William	1815	Haire
STANSBURY, William	1816	Hair
STANSBURY, William	1817	McClure
STANSBURY, William	1818	McClure
STANTON, John	1814	Brown
STAR, Michael	1807	Britton
STAR, Michel	1806	Doke
STAR, Michel	1809	Cade
STARKES, Joshua	1797	Shipley
STARMAN, George	1806	Parker
STARMEN, George	1796	Young
STARMEN, George	1810	Hartzel
STARMEN, George	1812	Hartsell
STARMER, George	1797	Young
STARMER, George	1814	Hartsell
STARMER, Gorge	1805	Parker
STARMER, Gorge Jr.	1807	Parker
STARMER, John	1797	Calvert
STARMER, John	1799	Stuart
STARMER, John	1801	Calvert
STARMER, John	1805	Jas Parker
STARMER, John	1808	Parker
STARMER, John	1811	McCray
STARMER, John	1812	McCray
STARMER, John	1812	McCray
STARMER, John	1815	Harris
STARN, Christian	1819	Jones
STARNER, George	1809	Par
STARNER, Jno	1809	Parker
STARNES, Christin	1813	Hoss
STARNES, David	1819	Jones
STARNES, Federick	1808	Parker
STARNES, Frederick	1815	Hartsell
STARNES, Frederick	1816	Brown
STARNES, Frederick	1818	Brown [2]
STARNES, Frederock	1816	Hampton
STARNES, George	1817	Fine
STARNES, George	1819	Howard
STARNES, Henry	1819	Jones
STARNES, Jacob	1801	Calvert
STARNES, Jacob	1818	Smith
STARNES, Jacob	1819	Smith
STARNES, James	1819	Smith
STARNES, Jesse	1816	Harrison
STARNES, Jesse	1817	Harris
STARNES, Jesse	1818	Harris
STARNES, Jesse	1819	Harris
STARNES, Jessie	1815	Harris
STARNES, John	1797	Calvert
STARNES, John	1814	McCray
STARNES, John	1816	Harrison
STARNES, John	1817	Harris
STARNES, John	1818	Harris
STARNES, John	1819	Harris
STARNES, Margaret	1819	Jones
STARNES, Meical	1810	Barron
STARNES, Peter	1790	Stone
STARNES, Peter	1791	Stone
STARNES, Peter	1793	Melvan
STARNES, Peter	1798	Crouch
STARNES, Peter	1806	Brown
STARNES, Thomas	1819	Jones
STARNS, Adam	1781	
STARNS, Adam	1780-1781 (Undated)	
STARNS, Fed	1809	Parker
STARNS, Fedick	1821	Brown
STARNS, Frederick	1817	Hampton
STARNS, Frederick	1819	Brown
STARNS, Fredrick	1814	McCray
STARNS, Jacob	1805	Jas Parker
STARNS, Jacob	1808	McAllister
STARNS, Jacob	1809	Bayles
STARNS, Jacob	1809	Parker
STARNS, Jacob	1811	McCray
STARNS, Jacob	1812	Crawford
STARNS, Jacob	1812	Crawford [2]
STARNS, Jacob	1812	McCray

Surname, Given names	Year	Comp./Dist.
STARNS, Jacob	1812	McCray
STARNS, Jacob	1814	McCray
STARNS, Jacob	1819	Smith
STARNS, Jacob	1820	Smith
STARNS, Jacob	1821	Smith
STARNS, Jesse	1805	Jas Parker
STARNS, Jesse	1808	Parker
STARNS, Jesse	1809	Parker
STARNS, Jesse	1811	McCray
STARNS, Jesse	1812	McCray
STARNS, Jesse	1814	McCray
STARNS, Jesse	1821	Hampton
STARNS, Jessee	1812	McCray
STARNS, Miceal	1814	Barns
STARNS, Peter	1794	Melvan
STARNS, Peter	1795	Melvan
STARNS, Peter	1796	Melvin
STARNS, Peter	1799	Morrison
STARNS, Peter	1801	Morrison
STARNS, Peter	1808	Bayles
STARNS, Peter	1809	Bayles
STARNS, Peter	1812	Crawford [2]
STARNS, William	1801	Norwood
STARNS, William	1806	Brown
STARR, Michael	1812	Barnes
STARR, Michael	1815	Grimsley
STARR, Michael	1816	Grimsley
STARR, Michael	1817	Grimsley
STARR, Richard	1818	Grimsley
STATE, Donnal	1795	Thornton
STATLOCK, Zachariah	1806	Crouch
STEALE, Andrew	1801	Taylor
STEEL, Andrew	1806	Guin
STEEL, Andrew	1807	Givins
STEEL, Andrew	1811	Davis
STEEL, Robert	1781	
STEEL, Robert	1780-1781 (undated)	
STEEL, William	1780-1781 (undated)	
STEELE, Andrew	1812	McLin
STEFASEN, Margaret	1808	Carr
STELEL, Will	1801	Biddle
STEPENSON, William	1795	Milliken
STEPESON, Margaret	1801	Morrison
STEPHANSON, Mathew	1798	Hannah
Stephen (man of colour)	1821	Hale
STEPHEN, Alice	1797	Hannah
STEPHEN, Margaret	1807	Carr
STEPHENS, Felex	1808	McAllister
STEPHENS, Henrey	1791	Tullis
STEPHENS, John	1815	Hoss
STEPHENS, Margaret	1815	Hoss
STEPHENS, William	1821	Martin
STEPHENSON, Alice	1799	Hannah
STEPHENSON, Ellis	1801	Squibb
STEPHENSON, James	1778	
STEPHENSON, John	1805	Carson
STEPHENSON, John	1806	Carson
STEPHENSON, John	1808	Guin
STEPHENSON, John	1809	Patterson
STEPHENSON, John	1810	Dimmons
STEPHENSON, John	1811	Davis
STEPHENSON, John	1812	McLin
STEPHENSON, John	1814	Couthers
STEPHENSON, John	1815	Carcathers
STEPHENSON, John	1816	Crookshanks
STEPHENSON, John	1818	McClure
STEPHENSON, John	1819	McClure
STEPHENSON, John V.	1817	McClure
STEPHENSON, M & I	1821	Hunt
STEPHENSON, Mathew	1811	McAlister
STEPHENSON, Mathew	1815	Crookshanks
STEPHENSON, Mathew	1816	Crookshanks
STEPHENSON, Mathew	1818	McClure
STEPHENSON, Mathew	1819	McClure
STEPHENSON, Matthew	1807	Payne
STEPHENSON, Robert	1780-1781 (Undated)	
STEPHENSON, William	1793	Milliken
STEPHENSON, William	1796	Millikin
STEPHENSON, William	1805	Rector
STEPHENSON, William	1808	Cade
STEPHENSON, William	1812	Barnes
STEPHENSON, William	1815	Grimsley
STEPHENSON, William	1816	Grimsley
STEPHENSON, William	1817	Grimsley
STEPHENSON, William	1818	Grimsley
STEPHENSON, William	1819	Grimsley
STEPHENSON, Wm	1790	Milleken
STEPHENSON, Wm	1791	Milliken
STEPHENSON, Wm	1794	Milliken
STEPHESON, Mathew	1808	McAllister
STEPHESON, Mathew	1812	Crawford
STEPHESON, Mathew	1812	Crawford [2]
STEPHESON, William	1814	Barns
STEPHINS, Henry	1793	Morrison
STEPHINS, Henry	1794	Morrison
STEPHONSON, Mathew	1814	Crookshanks
STEPHSENSON, Elece	1812	Crawford [2]
STEPHSON, Wm	1792	Milliken
STERENS, Margart	1813	Hoss
STETSON, William	1818	Grisham
STEVENS, David	1817	Little

Surname, Given names	Year	Comp./Dist.
STEVENS, Henry	1792	Tulley
STEVENS, Henry	1798	Morrison
STEVENS, Henry	1798	Morrison
STEVENS, Henry	1798	Morrison
STEVENS, Henry	1799	Morrison
STEVENS, Henry	[1796] 1797	Morris
STEVENS, John	1814	Hoss
STEVENS, John	1817	Little
STEVENS, Margarate	1806	Carr
STEVENS, Margaret	1814	Hoss
STEVENS, Margaret	1817	Little
STEVENS, Margaret	1821	Jones
STEVENS, Marget	1809	Carr
STEVENS, Thomas	1816	Hoss
STEVENS, Thomas	1817	Little
STEVENS, William	1813	Hoss
STEVENS, William	1817	Little
STEVENS, Wm	1814	Hoss
STEVENSON, Mathew	1809	McAlister
STEVENSON, Mathew	1809	McAlister
STEVENSON, Robert	1781	
STEVENSON, William	1805	Carson
STEVENSON, William	1807	Cade
STEVENSON, William	1809	Cade
STEVENSON, William	1810	Barron
STEVENSON, William	1811	Barron
STEVESON, Henry	1795	Morrison
STEVESON, Wm	1801	Glasscock
STEVINS, David	1818	Jones
STEVINS, Henry	1818	Jones
STEVINS, Henry	1821	Jones
STEVINS, Margaret	1818	Jones
STEVINS, Thomas	1818	Jones
STEWARD, Alexander	1811	Davis
STEWARD, Charles	1790	Biddle
STEWARD, Charles	1791	Biddle
STEWARD, Charles	1792	Biddle
STEWARD, David	1811	Davis
STEWARD, John Sr.	1811	Davis
STEWART,	1812	McLin
STEWART, Alaxander	1798	Duncan
STEWART, Alex	1821	Hunt
STEWART, Alexander	1794	Depew
STEWART, Alexander	1797	Duncan
STEWART, Alexander	1798	Duncan
STEWART, Alexander	1808	Guin
STEWART, Alexander	1809	Gwin
STEWART, Alexander	1812	McLin
STEWART, Alexander	1814	McLin
STEWART, David	1794	Depew
STEWART, David	1794	Depew

Surname, Given names	Year	Comp./Dist.
STEWART, David	1797	Duncan
STEWART, David	1797	Duncan
STEWART, David	1801	Taylor
STEWART, David	1807	Givins
STEWART, David	1808	Guin
STEWART, David	1809	Gwin
STEWART, David	1814	McLin
STEWART, David Jr.	1792	Depew
STEWART, David Jr.	1793	Depew
STEWART, David Jr.	1798	Duncan
STEWART, David Jr.	1821	Hunt
STEWART, David Sr.	1792	Depew
STEWART, David Sr.	1793	Depew
STEWART, David Sr.	1798	Duncan
STEWART, James	1801	Taylor
STEWART, James	1809	Roadmas
STEWART, John	1794	Depew
STEWART, John	1814	McLin
STEWART, John	1821	Hunt
STEWART, John Jr.	1809	Gwin
STEWART, John Jr.	1812	McLin
STEWART, John Jr.	1814	McLin
STEWART, John Sr.	1808	Guin
STEWART, John Sr.	1809	Gwin
STEWART, John Sr.	1812	McLin
STEWART, Montgomery	1811	Rodman
STEWART, Robert	1798	Duncan
STEWART, Robert	1821	Hunt
STEWART, Thomas	1809	Roadmas
STEWART, Thos	1797	Calvert
STEWERT, Alexander	1806	Guin
STEWERT, David	1806	Guin
STIGAR, Adam	1815	Harris
STIGAR, Gasper	1799	Stuart
STIGER, Adam	1815	Harris
STIGER, Henry	1798	Roberson
STILL, Jesse	1817	Brown
STILL, Jesse	1818	Harris
STOCKLEY, Jehu	1798	Morrison
STOCTON, Wm	1780-1781 (Undated)	
STOFER, Christopher	1808	Carr
STOKELY, Jehue	1798	Morrison
STON, Jacob	1814	Waddell
STONE, George	1796	Longmire
STONE, George	1799	Stuart
STONE, George	1801	Aiken
STONE, Robart	1794	Melvan
STONE, Robart	1796	Melvin
STONE, Robert	1790	Stone
STONE, Robert	1791	Stone
STONE, Robert	1793	Melvan

Surname, Given names	Year	Comp./Dist.
STONE, Robert	1795	Melvan
STONE, William	1790	Stone
STONE, William	1791	Stone
STONE, William	1793	Melvan
STONE, William	1794	Melvan
STONE, William	1795	Melvan
STONE, William (Capt.)	1791	
STONE, Wm	1796	Melvin
STOREY, William	1778	
STORM, Coonrod	1795	Ford
STORM, John	1795	Ford
STORM, Peter	1794	Thornton
STORM, Peter	1795	Thornton
STORMER, George	1801	Taylor
STORMER, John	1798	Calvert
STORMER, John	1821	Hampton
STOUER, Christian	1795	Carriger
STOUGHT, Daniel	1793	Thornton
STOUT, Daniel	1794	Thornton
STOUT, Daniel	1819	Findley
STOUT, Daniel	1821	McGee
STOUT, Hosea	1778	
STOUT, John	1806	Parker
STOUT, John	1807	Parker
STOUT, John	1809	McAlister
STOUT, John	1811	McAlister
STOUT, John	1812	Crawford
STOUT, John	1814	Crookshanks
STOUT, John	1815	Crookshanks
STOUT, John	1819	Findley
STOUT, John	1821	McGee
STOUT, Joseph	1801	Taylor
STOUT, Joseph	1807	Parker
STOUT, Peter	1798	Roberson
STOUT, Peter	1801	Taylor
STOVER, Christian	1792	Carriger
STOVER, Christian	1792	Greer
STOVER, Christian	1794	Carriger
STOVER, Christian	1801	Morrison
STOVER, Christian	1809	Carr
STOVER, Christian	1814	Hoss
STOVER, Christian	1816	Hoss
STOVER, Christian	1817	Little
STOVER, Christian	1818	Jones
STOVER, Christian	1821	Jones
STOVER, Christopher	1791	Willey
STOVER, Cristian	1811	Mitchell
STOVER, Daniel	1809	Carr
STOVER, Jacob	1816	Brown
STOVER, Jacob	1817	Brown
STOVER, John	[1796] 1797	Morris

Surname, Given names	Year	Comp./Dist.
STRAIN, John	1781	
STRAIN, John	1797	Duncan
STRAIN, John	1798	Duncan
STRAIN, John	1798	Duncan
STRAIN, John	1799	Duncan
STRAIN, John	1801	Taylor
STRAIN, John	1806	Guin
STRAIN, John	1807	Givins
STRAIN, John	1808	Guin
STRAIN, John	1809	Gwin
STRAIN, John	1811	Davis
STRAIN, John	1812	McLin
STRAIN, John	1814	McLin
STRAIN, John	1815	McLin
STRAIN, John	1816	Hunt
STRAIN, John	1817	Hunt
STRAIN, John	1818	Hunt
STRAIN, John (Esqr.)	1821	Hunt
STRAIN, John Esquire	1819	Hunt
STRAIN, John Jr.	1819	Hunt
STRAIN, Robert	1812	McLin
STRAIN, Robert	1815	McLin
STRAIN, Robert	1816	Hunt
STRAIN, Robert	1817	Hunt
STRAIN, Robert	1819	Hunt
STRAIN, Robert W.	1814	McLin
STRAIN, William	1821	Hunt
STRANGE, Obadiah	1807	
STRANGE, Obadiah	1809	Carr
STRANGE, Obediah	1811	Britten
STRINGER, William	1778	
STRONG, Obadiah (Reverent)	1806	Crouch
STUARCE, David	1815	McLin
STUARCE, Robert	1815	McLin
STUARD, Alexander	1815	McLin
STUARD, David	1781	
STUARD, John	1815	McLin
STUART, Alex	1799	Duncan
STUART, Alexander	1807	Givins
STUART, Alexander	1816	Hunt
STUART, Alexander	1817	Hunt
STUART, Alexander	1818	Hunt
STUART, Alexander	1819	Hunt
STUART, Benjamin	1781	
STUART, Charles	1797	Biddle
STUART, Charles	1783 [after]	Depew
STUART, David	1798	Duncan
STUART, David	1799	Duncan
STUART, David	1816	Hunt
STUART, David	1817	Hunt
STUART, David	1818	Hunt

Surname, Given names	Year	Comp./Dist.
STUART, David	1819	Hunt
STUART, David	1780-1781 (undated)	
STUART, David	1780-1781 (Undated)	
STUART, James	1778	
STUART, James	1779	
STUART, James	1795	Calvert
STUART, James	1797	Calvert
STUART, James	1798	Calvert
STUART, James	1801	Aiken
STUART, James	1801	
STUART, James	1805	Aikin
STUART, James	1805	Guir
STUART, James	1806	Anderson
STUART, James	1806	Grur
STUART, James	1809	
STUART, James	1817	Smith
STUART, James	1818	Smith
STUART, James	1819	Smith
STUART, James	1820	Smith
STUART, James	1821	Smith
STUART, James	1780-1781 (Undated)	
STUART, James (Esq.)	1790	Williams
STUART, James (Esq.)	1791	Williams
STUART, James (heirs of)	1817	Smith
STUART, James (heirs of)	1818	Smith
STUART, James (heirs of)	1821	Smith
STUART, James (heirs)	1819	Smith
STUART, James (heirs)	1820	Smith
STUART, John	1778	
STUART, John	1797	Biddle
STUART, John	1801	Biddle
STUART, John	1816	Hunt
STUART, John	1818	Hunt
STUART, John	1819	Hunt
STUART, John (Buffilaw)	1779	
STUART, Joseph	1781	
STUART, Joseph	1780-1781 (Undated)	
STUART, Mongomary	1807	Anderson
STUART, Montgomery	1805	Aikin
STUART, Montgomery	1806	Anderson
STUART, Montgomery	1814	McCracken
STUART, Montgomery	1815	Garner
STUART, Montgomery	1816	Smith
STUART, Montgomery	1817	Riley
STUART, Montgomery	1818	Riley
STUART, Montgomery	1819	Findley
STUART, Montgr	1820	Smith
STUART, Montgr	1821	Smith
STUART, Robert	1779	
STUART, Robert	1814	McCracken
STUART, Robert	1815	Garner
STUART, Robert	1816	Hunt
STUART, Robert	1819	Hunt
STUART, Thomas	1799	Stuart
STUART, Thomas	1801	Gann
STUART, Thomas	1805	Aikin
STUART, Thomas	1806	Anderson
STUART, Thomas	1807	Anderson
STUART, Thomas	1816	Smith
STUART, Thomas	1817	Smith
STUART, Thomas	1818	Smith
STUART, Thomas	1819	Smith
STUART, Thomas	1820	Smith
STUART, Thos	1801	Aiken
STUART, Thos	1821	Smith
STUDARD, David	1780-1781 (Undated)	
STUEART, James (Esq.)	1793	Handley
STURGEN, Simpson	1798	Hannah
STURGEON, Robt	1801	Squibb
STURGEON, Simpson	1801	Squibb
STURGEON, Sympson	1797	Hannah
STURGEON, Sympson	1799	Hannah
STURM, Coonrad	1794	Ford
STURM, John	1794	Ford
STYGER, John	1817	Hunt
SUCKERS, George	1812	McCray
SUE-, William	1808	Guin
SUELE, Abraham	1795	Thornton
SUELE, Dosson	1795	Thornton
SUELE, Joseph	1795	Thornton
SUEMAN, Jacob	1808	Guin
SUIT, Thomas	1795	Ford
SULLAVAN, Saml	1780-1781 (Undated)	
SULLEN, Willm	1797	Calvert
SULLENS, Richard	1812	Ellis
SULLINGS, William	1805	Aikin
SULLINGS, William	1807	Anderson
SULLINGS, Wm	1799	Stuart
SUMAN, Jacob	1799	Duncan
SUMAN, Jacob	1809	Gwin
SUMMERS, Isaac	1814	Bean
SUMMERS, Isaac	1815	Hartsell
SUMMERS, Isaac	1816	Hampton
SUMMERS, Isaac	1817	Brown
SUMMERS, Isaac	1819	Brown
SUMMERS, Isaac	1821	Haines
SUMMERS, Jonson	1814	Bean
SUMMERS, William	1815	Haire
SUMMERS, William	1816	Hair

Surname, Given names	Year	Comp./Dist.
SUMMERS, William	1817	Haire
SUMMERS, William	1819	Hair
SUMMERS, William	1821	Louis
SUMMERS, Wm	1814	Bean
SUMMONS, Micjah	1816	Hampton
SUNDERLAND, Isaac	1791	Milliken
SURNEY, William	1790	White
SUTHERLAIN, Isaac	1793	Depew
SUTHERLAIN, Thomas	1801	Taylor
SUTHERLAND, Isaac	1792	Milliken
SUTTON, Armstrong	1818	Brown
SUTTON, Buck	1806	Grur
SUTTON, Buck	1810	Green
SUTTON, Buck	1811	Green
SWANEGER, John	1801	Taylor
SWANER, John	1801	Morrison
SWANER, John	1809	Carr
SWANER, John	1810	Hartzel
SWANGER, John	1797	Young
SWANGER, John	1798	Young
SWANGER, John	1807	Parker
SWANGER, John	1808	Carr
SWANGER, John	1813	Hoss
SWATZELL, Henry	1812	Waddill
SWEENEY, Hiram	1821	Smith
SWEENEY, Wm	1821	Smith
SWEET, John	1797	Biddle
SWERINS, John	1781	
SWINEY, William	1791	White
SWINEY, William	1793	Thornton
SWINGEL, George	1808	Odell
SWINGLE, George	1806	Odel
SWINGLE, George	1807	Odell
SWINGLE, George	1809	Viney
SWINGLE, George	1810	Cove
SWINGLE, George	1811	Brown
SWINGLE, George	1812	Brown
SWINGLE, George	1814	Brown
SWINGLE, George	1815	Hartsell
SWINGLE, George	1816	Brown
SWINGLE, George	1817	Brown
SWINGLE, George	1818	Brown
SWINGLE, George	1819	Brown
SWINGLE, George	1821	Haines
SWINGLE, John	1801	Longmire
SWONGER, John	1814	Hoss
SYKE, John	1780-1781 (Undated)	
SYMPSON, James	1798	Hannah
TADLOCK, John	1780-1781 (undated)	
TADLOCK, Joshuah	1780-1781 (undated)	

Surname, Given names	Year	Comp./Dist.
TADLOCK, Lewis	1794	Blair
TADLOCK, Lewis	1783 [after]	Depew
TADLOCK, Thos	1781	
TAIN, Reuben	1797	Gann
TALBERT, Hail	1778	
TALBERT, Matthew	1778	
TALBERT, Matthew Jr.	1778	
TALBOT, Mathew	1795	Taylor
TALBOT, Matthew	1779	
TALBOT, Matthew Jr.	1779	
TALBOT, Matthew Sr.	1779	
TALLEY, John	1811	Barron
TALLEY, John	1815	Grimsley
TALLEY, John	1816	Grimsley
TALLO, John	1807	Cade
TALLY, Henry	1821	Martin
TALLY, John	1808	Cade
TALLY, John	1810	Barron
TALLY, John	1812	Barnes
TALOR, Critofor	1794	Scot
TANER, Masey	1814	Hartsell
TANNER, Mosy	1815	McLin
TANNOR, Massey	1810	Hartzel
TAPLY, Wm	1796	Longmire
TAPP, Isaac	1780-1781	District 7
TAPP, John	1780-1781	District 7
TAPPAN, James	1798	Roberson
TARBOT, James	1781	
TARFOR, Matthew	1794	Taylor
TATE, John	1790	White
TATE, John	1791	White
TATE, John	1793	Campbell
TATE, John	1794	Ford
TATE, John	1795	Ford
TATE, Saml	1790	Greer
TATE, Samuel	1778	
TATE, Samuel	1791	
TATE, Samuel	1792	
TATE, Samuel	1794	Ford
TATE, Samuel	1795	Ford
TAYLER, Micajah	1812	McCray
TAYLOR, Abraham	1797	Calvert
TAYLOR, Andrew	1779	
TAYLOR, Andrew	1779	
TAYLOR, Andrew	1790	Williams
TAYLOR, Andrew	1791	Williams
TAYLOR, Andrew	1792	Maxwell
TAYLOR, Andrew	1793	Maxwell
TAYLOR, Andrew	1794	Taylor
TAYLOR, Andrew	1795	Taylor
TAYLOR, Chris	1781	

Surname, Given names	Year	Comp./Dist.
TAYLOR, Chris	1795	Calvert
TAYLOR, Chris	1809	Parker
TAYLOR, Christepher	1780-1781 (Undated)	
TAYLOR, Christipher	1796	Calvert
TAYLOR, Christopher	1778	
TAYLOR, Christopher	1792	Scott
TAYLOR, Christopher	1793	Scott
TAYLOR, Christopher	1797	Calvert
TAYLOR, Christopher	1799	Stuart
TAYLOR, Christopher	1801	Calvert
TAYLOR, Christopher	1805	Jas Parker
TAYLOR, Christopher	1808	Parker
TAYLOR, Christopher	1811	McCray
TAYLOR, Christopher	1812	McCray
TAYLOR, Christopher	1812	McCray
TAYLOR, Christopher	1814	McCray
TAYLOR, Christopher	1816	Harrison
TAYLOR, Christopher	1817	Harris
TAYLOR, Christopher	1818	Harris
TAYLOR, Christopher	1819	Harris
TAYLOR, Christopher	1821	Hampton
TAYLOR, David	1790	Milleken
TAYLOR, David	1791	Milliken
TAYLOR, David	1792	Milliken
TAYLOR, David	1793	Milliken
TAYLOR, David	1794	Milliken
TAYLOR, George (Single)	1779	
TAYLOR, Henery	1797	Young
TAYLOR, Henery	1798	Young
TAYLOR, Henry	1795	Calvert
TAYLOR, Henry	1796	Calvert
TAYLOR, Henry	1801	Taylor
TAYLOR, Henry	1805	Parker
TAYLOR, Henry	1808	Parker
TAYLOR, Henry	1809	Par
TAYLOR, Henry	1810	Hartzel
TAYLOR, Henry	1812	Hartsell
TAYLOR, Henry	1814	Hartsell
TAYLOR, Henry	1815	Fines
TAYLOR, Henry	1816	Fine
TAYLOR, Henry	1817	Fine
TAYLOR, Henry	1818	Fine
TAYLOR, Henry	1819	Harris
TAYLOR, Henry	1821	Hampton
TAYLOR, Isaac	1778	
TAYLOR, Isaac	1790	Williams
TAYLOR, Isaac	1791	Williams
TAYLOR, Isaac	1794	Taylor
TAYLOR, Isaac (Single)	1779	
TAYLOR, Isaac Sr.	1779	
TAYLOR, James	1813	Hoss

Surname, Given names	Year	Comp./Dist.
TAYLOR, John	1801	Taylor
TAYLOR, John	1807	Anderson
TAYLOR, John Fearguson	1808	Guin
TAYLOR, John Furguson	1814	McLin
TAYLOR, John H.	1819	Harris
TAYLOR, Joseph	1821	Hunt
TAYLOR, Lacy	1817	Hunt
TAYLOR, Leeroy	1792	Depew
TAYLOR, Leeroy	1793	Depew
TAYLOR, Leeroy	1794	Depew
TAYLOR, Leeroy	1797	Duncan
TAYLOR, Leeroy	1798	Duncan
TAYLOR, Leeroy	1801	Taylor
TAYLOR, Leeroy	1808	Guin
TAYLOR, Leeroy	1811	Davis
TAYLOR, Leeroy	1812	McLin
TAYLOR, Leeroy	1814	McLin
TAYLOR, Leeroy	1818	Hunt
TAYLOR, Leeroy	1780-1781 (Undated)	
TAYLOR, Leeroy	1783 [after]	Depew
TAYLOR, Leroy	1781	
TAYLOR, Leroy	1798	Duncan
TAYLOR, Leroy	1799	Duncan
TAYLOR, Leroy	1806	Guin
TAYLOR, Leroy	1812	McLin
TAYLOR, Leroy	1815	McLin
TAYLOR, Leroy	1816	Hunt
TAYLOR, Leroy	1819	Hunt
TAYLOR, Levi	1807	Givins
TAYLOR, Levi	1809	Gwin
TAYLOR, Levi	1811	Davis
TAYLOR, Levi	1815	McLin
TAYLOR, Levi	1816	Hunt
TAYLOR, Levi	1817	Hunt
TAYLOR, Levy	1808	Guin
TAYLOR, Levy	1814	McLin
TAYLOR, Matthew	1790	Williams
TAYLOR, Matthew	1791	Williams
TAYLOR, Matthew	1792	Maxwell
TAYLOR, Matthew	1793	Maxwell
TAYLOR, Nathanial	1801	Longmire
TAYLOR, Nathaniel	1790	Williams
TAYLOR, Nathaniel	1791	Williams
TAYLOR, Nathaniel	1792	Maxwell
TAYLOR, Nathaniel	1799	Stuart
TAYLOR, Nathaniel (Capt.)	1793	Maxwell
TAYLOR, Nathl	1794	Taylor
TAYLOR, Robert	1814	Couthers
TAYLOR, Robert	1815	Carcathers
TAYLOR, Robert	1816	Giles
TAYLOR, Robert	1817	Gillises

Surname, Given names	Year	Comp./Dist.
TAYLOR, William	1798	Duncan
TAYLOR, William	1798	Duncan
TAYLOR, William	1806	Guin
TAYLOR, William	1809	Gwin
TAYLOR, Wm	1799	Duncan
TAYLOR, Wm (Capt.)	1801	Taylor
TAYLOR, Wm (estate of)	1816	Harrison
TEADLOCK, Sam	1817	Gillises
TEADLOCK, Tom	1818	Land
TEDDLOCK, John	1780-1781 (Undated)	
TEDLOCK, James	1818	Grimsley
TEDLOCK, James	1819	Grimsley
TEDLOCK, Jane	1816	Giles
TEDLOCK, Jean	1821	Sands
TEDLOCK, John	1779	Wilson
TEDLOCK, John	1791	North
TEDLOCK, John	1792	Brown
TEDLOCK, Lewes	1805	Carson
TEDLOCK, Lewis	1797	Biddle
TEDLOCK, Lewis	1801	Biddle
TEDLOCK, Lewis	1807	Shields
TEDLOCK, Lewis	1809	Patterson
TEDLOCK, Lewis	1810	Dimmons
TEDLOCK, Lewis	1811	
TEDLOCK, Lewis	1814	Couthers
TEDLOCK, Lewis	1815	Carcathers
TEDLOCK, Lomas	1798	Biddle
TEDLOCK, Luis	1798	Biddle
TEDLOCK, Thom	1819	Sands
TEDLOCKE, John	1793	Brown
TEENSOON, Mose	1780-1781	District 7
TELFORD, John	1816	Crookshanks
TELFORD, Marvin	1817	McClure
TELFORD, Miriam	1816	Crookshanks
TELFORD, Mirow	1818	McClure
TELFORD, Mirriam	1819	McClure
TELFORD, Thomas	1795	Milliken
TELFORD, Thomas	1807	Payne
TELFORD, Thomas	1811	McAlister
TELFORD, Thomas	1812	Waddill
TELFORD, Thomas	1814	Waddell
TELFORD, Thomas	1815	Crookshanks
TELFOUR, Thomas	1801	Squibb
TELOR, Hnenry	1794	Scot
TEMPEL, James	1797	Duncan
TEMPLE, James	1798	Duncan
TEMPLE, James	1799	Stuart
TEMPLE, Mayer	1781	
TEMPLE, Mayor	1780-1781 (Undated)	
TEMPLE, William	1816	Hampton
TEMPLEN, Leml (estate of)	1808	Parker
TEMPLIN, Jacob	1807	Anderson
TEMPLIN, Jacob	1809	Roadmas
TEMPLIN, Jacob	1821	Brown
TEMPLIN, Lemuel	1807	Anderson
TEMPLIN, Saml	1801	Aiken
TEMPLIN, Samuel	1805	Aikin
TEMPLIN, Samuel	1806	Anderson
TEMPLIN, Samuel	1817	Hampton
TEMPLIN, Samuel	1818	Brown [2]
TEMPLIN, Samuel	1819	Brown
TEMPLIN, Samuel	1821	Brown
TEMPLIN, William	1796	Brown
TEMPLIN, William	1798	Roberson
TEMPLIN, William	1801	Roberson
TEMPLIN, William	1806	Brown
TEMPLIN, William	1807	Bayles
TEMPLIN, William	1808	Bayles
TEMPLIN, William	1817	Hampton
TEMPLIN, William	1818	Brown [2]
TEMPLIN, William	1819	Brown
TEMPLIN, William	1821	Brown
TEMPLIN, Willim	1797	Robertson
TEMPLIN, Wm	1799	Robertson
TEMPLIN, Wm	1809	Bayles
TEMPLIN, Wm	1814	Hampton
TERRY, Fanncy	1795	Taylor
TERRY, John	1793	Brown
TERRY, William	1795	Taylor
TERRY, William	1819	Hunt
TETZ, Adam	1809	Green
TETZ, Adam	1810	Green
THACKER, Isaac	1817	Hunt
THACKER, Thomas	1815	McLin
THACKER, Thomas	1818	Land
THACKER, Thomas	1819	Sands
THACKER, Thomas	1821	Hampton
THACKER, William	1819	Harris
THARP, James	1816	Hoss
THARP, James	1817	Haire
THIRSET, Joel	1796	Young
THISEL, Philip	1817	Riley
THISTLE, Philip	1818	Riley
Thomas (man of colour)	1821	Hale
THOMAS, Isaac	1778	
THOMAS, Isaac Sr.	1791	Chisom
THOMAS, Isaac Sr.	1792	Chisolm
THOMAS, John	1787	Fains
THOMAS, John	1795	Morrison
THOMAS, Weslam	1795	Calvert
THOMPKINS, Joseph	1795	Thornton

Surname, Given names	Year	Comp./Dist.
THOMPON, David	1794	Depew
THOMPSON, Absolom	1778	
THOMPSON, Adam	1806	Carson
THOMPSON, Adam	1811	
THOMPSON, Adam	1814	Couthers
THOMPSON, Adam	1815	Carcathers
THOMPSON, Adam	1816	Giles
THOMPSON, Adam	1817	Gillises
THOMPSON, Adam	1818	Land
THOMPSON, Andes	1814	Couthers
THOMPSON, Andrew	1778	
THOMPSON, Andrew	1778	
THOMPSON, Andrew	1790	Milleken
THOMPSON, Andrew	1794	Depew
THOMPSON, Andrew	1797	Biddle
THOMPSON, Andrew	1798	Hannah
THOMPSON, Andrew	1799	Hannah
THOMPSON, Andrew	1801	Biddle
THOMPSON, Andrew	1809	Patterson
THOMPSON, Andrew	1811	
THOMPSON, Andrew	1815	Carcathers
THOMPSON, Andrew	1816	Giles
THOMPSON, Andrew	1817	Gillises
THOMPSON, Andrew	1818	Land
THOMPSON, Andw	1806	Carson
THOMPSON, Andw	1807	Shields
THOMPSON, Ann	1821	Hunt
THOMPSON, Charles	1778	
THOMPSON, David	1799	Duncan
THOMPSON, David	1816	Smith
THOMPSON, David	1817	Smith
THOMPSON, David	1818	Smith
THOMPSON, David	1819	Smith
THOMPSON, David	1821	Smith
THOMPSON, Jesse	1817	Smith
THOMPSON, Jesse	1818	Smith
THOMPSON, Jesse	1819	Smith
THOMPSON, Jesse	1820	Smith
THOMPSON, Jesse	1821	Smith
THOMPSON, John	1805	Rector
THOMPSON, John	1806	Carson
THOMPSON, John	1817	Harris
THOMPSON, Joseph	1819	Harris
THOMPSON, Seth	1815	Hoss
THOMPSON, Seth	1816	Hoss
THOMPSON, Seth	1817	Little
THOMPSON, Seth	1818	Jones
THOMPSON, Seth	1819	Jones
THOMPSON, Seth	1821	Jones
THOMPSON, William	1811	McCray
THOMPSON, William	1816	Harrison
THOMPSON, William	1817	Brown
THOMPSON, William	1817	Harris
THOMPSON, William	1818	Harris
THOMPSON, William	1819	Harris
THOMPSON, William	1819	Smith
THOMPSON, William	1820	Smith
THOMPSON, William	1821	Smith
THOMSON, Adam	1805	Carson
THOMSON, Andrew	1779	Wilson
THOMSON, Andrew	1781	
THOMSON, Andrew	1790	Biddle
THOMSON, Andrew	1791	Biddle
THOMSON, Andrew	1792	Biddle
THOMSON, Andrew	1798	Biddle
THOMSON, Andrew	1805	Carson
THOMSON, Andrew	1783 [after]	Blair
THOMSON, David	1792	Depew
THOMSON, David	1793	Depew
THOMSON, David	1797	Duncan
THOMSON, David	1798	Duncan
THOMSON, David	1798	Duncan
THOMSON, Mark	1808	Odell
THOMSON, Richard	1793	Melvan
THOMSON, Richard	1795	Melvan
THOMSON, William	1805	Jas Parker
THOMSON, William	1812	McCray
THOMSON, William	1814	McCray
THOMSON, William	1821	Hampton
THOMSON, Wm	1808	Parker
THOMSON, Wm	1809	Parker
THORNBERG, John	1818	Harris
THORNBERRY, Thomas	1799	Hannah
THORNBUGE, John	1812	McCray
THORNBURG, John	1819	Hunt
THORNBURGH, John	1812	McCray
THORNBURGH, John	1816	Harrison
THORNBURGH, John	1821	Hampton
THORNBURY, John	1811	McCray
THORNTON, R.N.	1794	Thornton
THORNTON, Reubin	1793	Campbell
THORNTON, Wm	1778	
THORP, James	1813	Hoss
THRASH, Isaac	1808	Cade
THRASHER, Isaac	1809	Cade
THRASHER, Isaac	1815	McLin
THRASHER, William	1809	Patterson
THREATHER, Isack	1805	Carson
THRESHER, Isaac	1807	Cade
THRESHER, Isaac	1812	McLin
THRESHER, Isaac	1814	McLin
THRESHER, Isaac	1816	Hunt

Surname, Given names	Year	Comp./Dist.
THRESHER, Isaac	1818	Hunt
THRESHER, Isaac	1819	Hunt
THRESHER, Thomas	1816	Hunt
THURMOND, John (Single)	1779	
TIDWELL, George	1778	
TIDWELL, John	1778	
TIFFEN, Henery	1801	Glasscock
TIFFEN, Henry	1808	Cade
TIFFIN, Henry	1793	Biddle
TIFFIN, Henry	1794	Blair
TIFFIN, Henry	1797	Biddle
TIFFIN, Henry	1798	Shipley
TIFFIN, Henry	1805	Rector
TIFFIN, Henry	1807	Cade
TILER, Adam	1791	Willey
TILFORD, Maria	1821	McClure
TILFORD, Thomas	1796	Millikin
TILFORD, Thomas	1797	Hannah
TILFORD, Thomas	1798	Hannah
TILFORD, Thomas	1809	McAlister
TILFORD, Thos	1799	Hannah
TILSON, john	1816	Brown
TILSON, John	1810	Cove
TILSON, John	1811	Brown
TILSON, John	1812	Brown
TILSON, John	1814	Brown
TILSON, John	1815	Hartsell
TILSON, John	1817	Brown
TILSON, John	1818	Brown
TILSON, John	1819	Brown
TILSON, John	1821	Haines
TILSON, Joseph	1816	Brown
TILSON, Joseph	1817	Brown
TILSON, Joseph	1819	Brown
TILSON, Joseph	1821	Haines
TILSON, Peleg	1806	Odel
TILSON, Peleg	1807	Odell
TILSON, Peleg	1808	Odell
TILSON, Peleg	1809	Viney
TILSON, Peleg	1810	Cove
TILSON, Peleg	1811	Brown
TILSON, Peleg	1814	Brown
TILSON, Peleg	1815	Hartsell
TILSON, Peleg	1816	Brown
TILSON, Peleg	1819	Brown
TILSON, Peleg	1821	Haines
TILSON, Peleg Jr.	1817	Brown
TILSON, Peleg Jr.	1819	Brown
TILSON, Peleg Jr.	1821	Haines
TILSON, Peleg Sr.	1817	Brown
TILSON, Peleg Sr.	1818	Brown
TILSON, Polig	1812	Brown
TILSON, Stephen	1812	Brown
TILSON, Stephen	1815	Hartsell
TILSON, Stephen	1816	Brown
TILSON, Stephen (constable)	1814	Brown
TILSON, Thomas	1815	Hartsell
TILSON, Thomas	1816	Brown
TILSON, Thomas	1817	Brown
TILSON, Thomas	1818	Brown
TILSON, Thomas	1819	Brown
TILSON, Thomas	1821	Haines
TILSON, Thommas	1814	Brown
TILSON, William	1806	Odel
TILSON, William	1807	Odell
TILSON, William	1808	Odell
TILSON, William	1809	Viney
TILSON, William	1810	Cove
TILSON, William	1811	Brown
TILSON, William	1812	Brown
TILSON, William	1814	Brown
TILSON, William	1815	Hartsell
TILSON, William	1816	Brown
TILSON, William	1817	Brown
TILSON, William	1818	Brown
TILSON, William	1819	Brown
TILSON, William	1821	Haines
TILSON, William Jr.	1819	Brown
TILSON, William Jr.	1821	Haines
TINKER, Abraham	1806	Odel
TINKER, Abraham	1807	Odell
TINKER, Abraham	1810	Cove
TINKER, Abraham	1811	Brown
TINKER, Abraham	1812	Brown
TINKER, Abraham	1814	Brown
TINKER, Abraham	1815	Hartsell
TINKER, Abraham	1817	Brown
TINKER, Abraham	1819	Brown
TINKER, Abraham	1821	Haines
TINKER, John	1806	Odel
TINKER, John	1807	Odell
TINKER, John	1816	Brown
TINKER, John	1817	Brown
TINKER, Joseph	1808	Guin
TINKER, Moses	1806	Odel
TINKER, Moses	1809	Viney
TINKER, Moses	1810	Cove
TINKER, William	1796	Longmire
TINKER, William	1806	Odel
TINKER, William	1807	Odell
TINKER, William	1808	Odell
TINKER, William	1810	Cove

Surname, Given names	Year	Comp./Dist.
TINKER, Wm	1801	Longmire
TINSON, Joseph	1778	
TINTER, Andrew	1809	Green
TIPTON, Abraham	1806	Parker
TIPTON, Abraham	1814	Hoss
TIPTON, Abraham	1815	Hoss
TIPTON, Abraham	1816	Hoss
TIPTON, Abraham	1817	Little
TIPTON, Abraham	1818	Jones
TIPTON, Abraham	1819	Jones
TIPTON, Abraham (heirs)	1821	Jones
TIPTON, Abriham	1813	Hoss
TIPTON, Brient	1806	Carr
TIPTON, Isaac	1790	Greer
TIPTON, Isaac	1792	Carriger
TIPTON, Isaac	1792	Greer
TIPTON, John	1795	Taylor
TIPTON, John	1801	Taylor
TIPTON, John	1805	Aikin
TIPTON, John (Col.)	1790	Williams
TIPTON, John (Col.)	1791	Williams
TIPTON, John (Col.)	1792	Maxwell
TIPTON, John (Col.)	1793	Maxwell
TIPTON, John (Col.)	1794	Taylor
TIPTON, John (Col.)	1796	Young
TIPTON, John (Col.)	1797	Young
TIPTON, John Jr.	1792	Maxwell
TIPTON, John Sr.	1801	Aiken
TIPTON, Jonathan	1778	
TIPTON, Jonathan	1778	
TIPTON, Jonathan	1791	North
TIPTON, Jonathan	1792	Maxwell
TIPTON, Jonathan	1792	North
TIPTON, Jonathan	1793	Maxwell
TIPTON, Jonathan	1794	North
TIPTON, Jonathan	1795	Taylor
TIPTON, Jonathan	1795	Young
TIPTON, Jonathan	1798	Morrison
TIPTON, Jonathon	1793	North
TIPTON, Jonethan	1794	Taylor
TIPTON, Joseph	1778	
TIPTON, Joseph	1779	
TIPTON, Joseph	1792	Maxwell
TIPTON, Joseph	1794	Taylor
TIPTON, Joseph	1795	Taylor
TIPTON, Joshua	1798	Morrison
TIPTON, Joshua	1798	Morrison
TIPTON, Joshua	1801	Morrison
TIPTON, Joshua	1801	Taylor
TIPTON, Mary	1801	Taylor
TIPTON, Mary	1806	Parker
TIPTON, Mary	1807	Parker
TIPTON, Mary	1808	Parker
TIPTON, Mary	1809	Hartzell
TIPTON, Polly	1821	Howard
TIPTON, Recae Boring	1799	Morrison
TIPTON, Rece B.	1806	Carr
TIPTON, Reece	1801	Morrison
TIPTON, Rees	1798	Morrison
TIPTON, Rees	1798	Morrison
TIPTON, Samuel	1790	Greer
TIPTON, Samuel	1792	Carriger
TIPTON, Samuel	1792	Greer
TIPTON, Samuel	1794	Carriger
TIPTON, Samuel	1795	Carriger
TIPTON, Thomas	1792	Greer
TIPTON, Thomas	1794	Carriger
TIPTON, Thomas	1795	Carriger
TIPTON, Thos	1792	Carriger
TIPTONS, John	1794	Taylor
TIPTONS, Joseph	1779	
TITLE, John	1797	Longmire
TITSWORTH, Isaac	1778	
TITSWORTH, Thomas	1778	
TITTEL, John	1808	Odell
TITTLE, Allen	1780-1781	District 7
TITTLE, John	1796	Longmire
TITTLE, John	1798	Longmire
TITTLE, John	1801	Longmire
TITTLE, John	1806	Odel
TITTLE, John	1807	Odell
TITTLE, John	1809	Viney
TITTLE, John	1810	Cove
TITTLE, John	1816	Brown
TITTLE, John	1817	Brown
TITTLE, John	1819	Brown
TITTLE, John	1821	Haines
TITTLE, John	1780-1781	District 7
TITTLE, John Jr.	1815	Hartsell
TOLAND, Jacob	1801	Taylor
TOLAND, Jacob	1805	Parker
TOLBET, James	1780-1781 (Undated)	
TOLER, Joshua	1807	Cade
TOLEY, Jonathan	1791	Tullis
TOLLEY, Dudley	1801	Glasscock
TOLLEY, Dudley Jr.	1801	Glasscock
TOLLEY, Henery	1801	Glasscock
TOLLEY, John	1805	Rector
TOLLY, Dudly	1812	Barnes
TOLLY, Henry	1812	Barnes
TOLLY, John	1801	Glasscock
TOLLY, John	1809	Cade

Surname, Given names	Year	Comp./Dist.
TOMPKINS, James	1821	Haines
TOMPSON, Andrew	1780-1781 (Undated)	
TOMPSON, Richart	1794	Melvan
TOMPSON, W. Gorge	1821	Sands
TOMPSON, Wm	1796	Melvin
TOMSON, John	1805	Carson
TOMSON, John	1807	Cade
TOMSON, John	1808	Cade
TOMSON, William	1812	McCray
TOOLEY, John	1781	
TOP, Roger (Virga)	1778	
TOPP, Roger	1779	
TOPPIN, James	1799	Robertson
TOUL, John	1818	Riley
TOW, John	1817	Riley
TRATER, James	1798	Biddle
TREADWAY, John	1814	Brown
TREADWAY, John	1815	Hartsell
TREADWAY, John	1816	Brown
TREADWAY, John	1818	Brown
TREADWAY, John	1819	Brown
TREADWAY, John	1821	Haines
TREMBLE, John	1780-1781 (undated)	
TRENT, William	1815	Waddell
TRENT, William	1816	Fine
TRENT, William	1816	Waddell
TRENT, Wm	1814	Waddell
TREVORY, John	1817	Brown
TREWLLIAM, Richd	1778	
TRICKER, Elisabeth	1795	Calvert
TRIMBLE, John	1778	
TRIMBLE, John	1779	Wilson
TRIMBLE, John	1780-1781 (Undated)	
TRIMBLE, Walter	1781	
TRIMBLE, Walter	1812	Waddill
TRIMBLE, Walter	1780-1781 (Undated)	
TRIMBLE, William	1778	
TRIMBLE, William	1780-1781 (Undated)	
TRIMBLE, Wm	1790	Milleken
TRIMLEY, Daniel	1810	Green
TRIPPLE, Jacob	1810	Dimmons
TROTHAROW, Allen	1797	Gann
TROTTEN, Alexander	1780-1781 (Undated)	
TROTTER, Alexander	1793	Depew
TROTTER, Alexander	1794	Depew
TROTTER, James	1797	Biddle
TROTTER, Jeremiah	1814	Waddell
TROTTER, John	1790	Biddle

Surname, Given names	Year	Comp./Dist.
TROTTER, John	1791	Biddle
TROTTER, John	1792	Biddle
TROTTER, Joseph	1816	Smith
TROTTES, John	1780-1781 (Undated)	
TRUEMAN, Shadrach	1812	McLin
TRUIT, William	1815	Fines
TRUIT, William	1817	Smith
TUCKER, Abraham	1795	Calvert
TUCKER, Abraham	1797	Robertson
TUCKER, Abraham	1799	Robertson
TUCKER, Abraham	1801	Roberson
TUCKER, Abraham	1806	Brown
TUCKER, Abraham	1807	Bayles
TUCKER, Abraham	1816	Brown
TUCKER, Abraham	1818	Brown
TUCKER, Abram	1821	Hunt
TUCKER, Agnes	1817	Hunt
TUCKER, George	1780-1781	District 7
TUCKER, John	1818	Hunt
TUCKER, John	1819	Hunt
TUCKER, John	1821	Hunt
TUCKER, Jonathan	1810	Cove
TUCKER, Jonathan	1812	Brown
TUCKER, Jonathan	1814	Brown
TUCKER, Jonathan	1815	Hartsell
TUCKER, Jonathan	1816	Brown
TUCKER, Jonathan	1817	Brown
TUCKER, Jonathan	1818	Brown
TUCKER, Jonathan	1819	Brown
TUCKER, Jonathan	1821	Haines
TUCKER, Joseph	1792	Depew
TUCKER, Joseph	1793	Depew
TUCKER, Joseph	1794	Depew
TUCKER, Joseph	1795	Calvert
TUCKER, Joseph	1797	Duncan
TUCKER, Joseph	1798	Duncan
TUCKER, Joseph	1798	Duncan
TUCKER, Joseph	1799	Duncan
TUCKER, Joseph	1806	Guin
TUCKER, Joseph	1807	Givins
TUCKER, Joseph	1809	Gwin
TUCKER, Joseph	1811	Davis
TUCKER, Joseph	1812	McLin
TUCKER, Joseph	1814	McLin
TUCKER, Joseph	1815	McLin
TUCKER, Joseph	1816	Hunt
TUCKER, Joseph	1817	Hunt
TUCKER, Joseph	1818	Hunt
TUCKER, Joseph	1819	Hunt
TUCKER, Joseph	1821	Hunt
TUCKER, Joseph	1783 [after]	Depew

Surname, Given names	Year	Comp./Dist.
TUCKER, Josiah	1801	Taylor
TUCKER, Nich	1809	Parker
TUCKER, Nicholas	1792	Depew
TUCKER, Nicholas	1794	Depew
TUCKER, Nicholas	1796	Millikin
TUCKER, Nicholas	1798	Duncan
TUCKER, Nicholas	1799	Duncan
TUCKER, Nicholas	1801	Taylor
TUCKER, Nicholas	1808	Parker
TUCKER, Nicholas	1811	McCray
TUCKER, Nicholas	1812	McCray
TUCKER, Nicholas	1812	McCray
TUCKER, Nicholas	1814	McCray
TUCKER, Nicholas	1818	Harris
TUCKER, Nicholas	1819	Harris
TUCKER, Nicholas	1821	Hampton
TUCKER, Nicholis	1797	Duncan
TUCKER, Nicholis	1816	Harrison
TUCKER, Nicholis	1817	Harris
TUCKER, Nicolas	1793	Depew
TUCKER, Reece	1816	Harrison
TUCKER, Reece	1816	Hunt
TUCKER, Rees	1811	Davis
TUCKER, Rees	1815	McLin
TUCKER, Rees	1821	Hampton
TUCKER, Reese	1812	McLin
TUCKER, Riis	1817	Harris
TUCKER, Rus	1818	Harris
TUCKER, Thomas	1817	Hunt
TUCKER, William	1821	Hampton
TUCKHOR, Abraham	1798	Roberson
TULLES, Jonathan	1787	Fains
TULLES, Jonthen	1798	Morrison
TULLEY, Samel	1795	Thornton
TULLIS, Jonathan	1793	Morrison
TULLIS, Jonathan	1794	Morrison
TULLIS, Jonathan	1795	Morrison
TULLIS, Jonathan	1798	Morrison
TULLIS, Jonathan	1798	Morrison
TULLIS, Jonathan	1799	Morrison
TULLIS, Jonathan (Capt.)	1791	
TULLY, Jonathan (Capt.)	1792	Tulley
TUMON, Jacob	1806	Guin
TURBUT, John	1779	
TURBUT, Samuel (Single)	1779	
TURDEN, John	1812	Crawford
TURDEN, Lewis	1806	Payn
TURNER, William	1798	Shipley
TURNER, William	1807	Cade
TURNER, William	1808	Cade
TURNER, William	1809	Cade
TURNER, Wm	1801	Glasscock
TUSSAN, William	1799	Morrison
TWEEDY, James	1797	Biddle
TWEEDY, James	1798	Biddle
TWEEDY, James	1798	Biddle
TWEEDY, James	1801	Biddle
TWEEDY, James	1805	Carson
TWEEDY, James	1806	Carson
TWEEDY, James	1807	Shields
TYE, John	1781	
TYLER, William	1806	Brown
TYLER, William	1807	Bayles
TYLER, William	1808	Bayles
TYLER, William	1809	Bayles
TYLER, William	1816	Hampton
TYLER, William	1817	Hampton
TYLER, William	1818	Brown [2]
TYLER, William	1819	Brown
TYLER, William (Deceased)	1821	Brown
TYLER, Wm	1814	Hampton
ULUT, Samuel	1780-1781 (Undated)	
UMPHERY, Richard	1780-1781 (Undated)	
UMPHREYS, Robert	1780-1781 (undated)	
UNDERWOOD, George	1778	
UNDERWOOD, Saml	1787	Fains
UNDERWOOD, Samuel	1778	
URWIN, Elec	1808	Cade
URWIN, Gorge	1808	Cade
VA--AL, Jacob	1779	Wilson
VAICH, Jeremiah	1778	
VAN VACTOR, Benjaman	1796	Shipley
VAN VACTOR, Benjamin	1795	Murray
VAN VACTOR, Benjamin	1812	Britton
VAN VACTOR, Benjamon	1797	Shipley
VAN VICTOR, Benjaman	1814	Copes
VAN, Resevred	1807	Cade
VANCE, D Q	1807	Anderson
VANCE, D.G.	1820	Smith
VANCE, D.G.	1821	Smith
VANCE, David	1799	Stuart
VANCE, David	1801	Aiken
VANCE, David G.	1806	Anderson
VANCE, David G.	1809	Roadmas
VANCE, David G.	1811	Rodman
VANCE, David G.	1814	McCracken
VANCE, David G.	1815	Garner
VANCE, David G.	1816	Smith
VANCE, David G.	1817	Smith
VANCE, David G.	1818	Smith
VANCE, David G.	1819	Smith

Surname, Given names	Year	Comp./Dist.
VANCE, Handale	1797	Biddle
VANCE, Handil	1805	Carson
VANCE, Hugh	1819	Harris
VANCE, Jacob	1821	Brown
VANCE, John	1778	
VANCE, John	1778	
VANCE, Soloman	1821	Sands
VANCE, U. L.	1807	Anderson
VANCE, William H.	1811	Rodman
VANCE, William H.	1814	McCracken
VANCE, William K.	1815	Garner
VANCE, William K.	1816	Smith
VANCE, William K.	1817	Smith
VANCE, William K.	1819	Brown
VANCE, William K.	1821	Brown
VANCE, William R.	1809	Roadmas
VANDEGRIF, Lanerd	1799	Gann
VANDERGRIFF, Leonard	1795	Ford
VANDERGRIFT, Leonard	1797	Gann
VANDERPOLE, Abraham (Deceased)	1779	
VANDER-RIFF, Jacob	1790	White
VANHOUSER, John	1781	
VANHOUSER, John	1780-1781 (Undated)	
VANN, David G.	1805	Aikin
VANN, John	1797	Calvert
VANN, Sherewood	1797	Calvert
VANSEKEL, Vardenan	1809	Cade
VANSICKLE, Vadd	1808	Cade
VANSICKLE, Vardenan	1805	Rector
VANTREES, John	1790	White
VANTRICE, John	1794	Ford
VANTRUCE, John	1791	White
VANVACTER, Benja	1813	Copas
VANVACTER, Benjamin	1811	Britten
VANVACTOR, Benjamin	1815	Copas
VANVARTER, Benjamin	1816	Copas
VANWIKLE, Vardanan	1801	Glasscock
VARNED, Jacob	1818	Brown [2]
VARNER, Jacob	1812	Crawford [2]
VARNER, Jacob	1816	Hampton
VARNER, Jacob	1819	Brown
VASICKLE, Vardeman	1798	Shipley
VA--TER, Jesse (In Virga.)	1778	
VAUGHAN, Sheredan	1812	Barnes
VAUGHN, Jno	1798	Calvert
VAUGHN, John	1799	Stuart
VAUGHN, John	1801	Calvert
VAUGHN, Sharid	1805	Aikin
VAUGHN, Sharrad	1799	Stuart
VAUGHN, Sherred	1811	Barron
VAUGHN, Sherred	1815	Grimsley
VAUGHN, Sherrod	1816	Grimsley
VAUGHT, John	1794	Thornton
VAUGHT, John	1795	Thornton
VAUGHT, William	1816	Crookshanks
VAUGHT, William	1817	McClure
VAUGHT, William	1818	McClure
VAUGHT, William	1819	McClure
VAUGHT, William	1821	McClure
VAUN, Richard	1818	Smith
VERMILLION, Jessie	1781	
VICKERY, Francis	1790	Milleken
VINAGAR, David	1821	Hampton
VINECENT, Lewell	1821	Smith
VINEGAR, David	1819	Harris
VINEY, Andrew	1811	Brown
VINEY, Andrien	1809	Viney
VINEY, Andrien	1810	Cove
VINEY, Jesse	1808	Odell
VINEY, Jesse	1809	Viney
VINEY, William	1817	Brown
VINKREY, Francis	1790	Biddle
VINKREY, Francis	1791	Biddle
VINKREY, Francis	1792	Biddle
VINTREES, John	1795	Ford
VON, Shered	1814	Barns
VOST, Gerge	1795	Thornton
W., Jessy	1793	Brown
WADAL, John	1780-1781 (Undated)	
WADDEL, Charles	1821	Jones
WADDEL, John	1778	
WADDEL, John	1779	Wilson
WADDELL, Charles	1816	Hoss
WADDELL, Charles	1817	Little
WADDELL, James	1805	Guir
WADDELL, Jno	1798	Calvert
WADDELL, John	1793	Scott
WADDELL, John	1795	Calvert
WADDELL, John	1796	Calvert
WADDELL, John	1815	Waddell
WADDELL, John	1816	Waddell
WADDELL, John	1817	Riley
WADDELL, John	1818	Riley
WADDELL, John Sr.	1794	Handly
WADDELL, John Sr.	1795	Handly
WADDELL, Jonathan	1810	Green
WADDELL, Jonathan	1815	Waddell
WADDELL, Jonathan	1816	Waddell
WADDELL, Jonathan	1817	Riley
WADDELL, Jonathan	1818	Riley
WADDILE, James	1812	Waddill

Surname, Given names	Year	Comp./Dist.
WADDILE, John	1814	Waddell
WADDILE, Jonathan	1809	Green
WADDILE, Jonathan	1814	Waddell
WADDILL, Charles	1799	Moore
WADDILL, Charles	1805	Guir
WADDILL, Charles	1813	Hoss
WADDILL, Charles	1814	Hoss
WADDILL, Charles	1815	Hoss
WADDILL, James	1801	Gann
WADDILL, James	1808	Gwin
WADDILL, James	1810	Green
WADDILL, James	1811	Green
WADDILL, John	1793	Handley
WADDILL, John	1799	Moore
WADDILL, John	1805	Guir
WADDILL, John	1808	Gwin
WADDILL, John	1809	Green
WADDILL, John	1810	Green
WADDILL, John	1812	Waddill
WADDILL, John	1821	McGee
WADDILL, John Sr.	1796	Handly
WADDILL, John Sr.	1801	Gann
WADDILL, John Sr.	1811	Green
WADDILL, Jonathan	1808	Gwin
WADDILL, Jonathan	1811	Green
WADDILL, Jonathan	1812	Waddill
WADDILL, Jonathan	1821	McGee
WADDILL, Jonithan	1805	Guir
WADDILL, Joseth	1799	Moore
WADDILL, Loame	1821	McGee
WADDILL, Saml	1799	Moore
WADDILL, Seth	1795	Handly
WADDILL, Seth	1821	McGee
WADDILL, Sethque	1794	Handly
WADDILL, Sethque	1796	Handly
WADDILLE, Charles	1797	Gann
WADDILLE, John	1797	Gann
WADDLE, Charles	1806	Grur
WADDLE, Charles	1808	Carr
WADDLE, Charles	1809	Carr
WADDLE, Charles	1811	Mitchell
WADDLE, Charles	1818	Jones
WADDLE, Charles	1819	Jones
WADDLE, Charls	1798	Gann
WADDLE, Charls	1799	Gann
WADDLE, Charls	1801	Gann
WADDLE, James	1806	Grur
WADDLE, John	1790	Hanley
WADDLE, John	1791	Hanley
WADDLE, John	1797	Calvert
WADDLE, John	1798	Gann
WADDLE, John	1799	Gann
WADDLE, John	1806	Grur
WADDLE, John	1819	Findley
WADDLE, John	1821	McGee
WADDLE, John Jr.	1819	Findley
WADDLE, Johnathan	1806	Grur
WADDLE, Jonathan	1819	Findley
WADDLE, Samuel	1798	Gann
WADDLE, Samuel	1801	Gann
WADDLE, Seth	1799	Gann
WADDLE, Seth	1801	Gann
WADDLE, Sethq	1798	Gann
WADEL, John	1790	Hanley
WADEL, John	1791	Hanley
WADKINS, Thos G.	1814	Hampton
WADLE, John	1799	Gann
WADLEE, Samuel	1799	Gann
WADREN, John	1816	Hair
WAGGONER, David	1790	White
WAGGONER, David	1791	White
WAGGONER, David	1792	White
WAGGONER, David	1793	Campbell
WAGGONER, David	1794	Thornton
WAGGONER, Mathew	1792	White
WAGGONER, Mathias	1793	Campbell
WAGGONER, Matthew	1794	Thornton
WAGGONER, Philip	1805	Guir
WAGGONER, Phillip	1792	Scott
WAGGONER, Phillip	1801	Gann
WAGMAN, David	1795	Thornton
WAGMAN, Mathias	1795	Thornton
WAGMON, Mathias	1795	Thornton
WAGONER, Phillip	1795	Calvert
WAGONER, Phillip	1806	Grur
WAHLIS, George	1807	Shields
WAID, David	1814	McCracken
WAIR, John	1796	Longmire
WAIRE, Nancy	1817	McClure
WAKER, John	1808	Parker
WAKER, John	1810	Hartzel
WAKES, John	1812	Hartsell
WALASE, George	1806	Carson
WALDDEN, John	1809	Right
WALDDEN, John	1812	Ellis
WALDEN, John	1814	Bean
WALDREN, John	1817	Haire
WALDREN, John	1819	Hair
WALDREN, John	1821	Louis
WALDRIN, John	1815	Haire
WALDRIP, James	1798	Gann
WALDRIP, James	1799	Gann

Surname, Given names	Year	Comp./Dist.
WALDRIP, James	1799	Moore
WALDRIP, James	1801	Roberson
WALDRON, John	1818	Hair
WALDRUP, James	1797	Gann
WALINGLUR, Adam Jr.	1812	Crawford
WALKER, Alec	1818	Fine
WALKER, Barbary	1797	Young
WALKER, Barbary	1801	Taylor
WALKER, Barbary (Widow)	1796	Young
WALKER, Barbra	1794	North
WALKER, Barbrah (Widow)	1792	North
WALKER, Danial	1780-1781 (Undated)	
WALKER, Danl	1778	
WALKER, Elias	1819	Howard
WALKER, Ellis	1815	Fines
WALKER, Ellis	1816	Fine
WALKER, Ellis	1817	Fine
WALKER, Ellis	1821	Howard
WALKER, Gabrell	1792	North
WALKER, Jessy	1809	Gwin
WALKER, Jno	1809	Par
WALKER, John	1814	Hartsell
WALKER, John	1815	Fines
WALKER, John	1816	Fine
WALKER, John	1817	Fine
WALKER, John	1818	Fine
WALKER, John	1819	Howard
WALKER, John	1821	Brown
WALKER, John	1821	Howard
WALKER, Richard	1778	
WALKER, Richard	1780-1781 (Undated)	
WALKER, Thomas	1819	Smith
WALKER, William	1793	Depew
WALKER, William	1794	Depew
WALKER, William	1797	Duncan
WALKER, William	1798	Duncan
WALKER, William	1798	Duncan
WALKER, William	1801	Taylor
WALKER, William	1806	Guin
WALKER, William	1807	Givins
WALKER, William	1808	Guin
WALKER, William	1809	Gwin
WALKER, William	1811	Davis
WALKER, William	1812	McLin
WALKER, William	1814	McLin
WALKER, William	1815	McLin
WALKER, William	1816	Hunt
WALKER, William	1817	Hunt
WALKER, William	1818	Hunt
WALKER, William	1819	Hunt
WALKER, William	1821	Hunt
WALKER, William	1783 [after]	Depew
WALKER, Wm	1799	Duncan
WALKERS, James	1778	
WALLA, Aaron	1792	White
WALLACE, Aaron	1790	White
WALLACE, Aaron	1791	White
WALLACE, Aaron	1793	Campbell
WALLACE, Davis	1815	Crookshanks
WALLACE, Davis	1816	Crookshanks
WALLACE, Davis	1819	McClure
WALLACE, George	1805	Carson
WALLACE, George	1810	Dimmons
WALLACE, James	1798	Hannah
WALLACE, James Jr.	1796	Millikin
WALLACE, James Sr.	1796	Millikin
WALLACE, James Sr.	1797	Hannah
WALLACE, Pleasant	1816	Crookshanks
WALLACE, Thomas	1796	Millikin
WALLACE, Thomas	1798	Hannah
WALLAN, Pleasant	1815	Waddell
WALLAS, James	1792	Milliken
WALLAS, James	1794	Milliken
WALLAS, James	1795	Milliken
WALLAS, John	1794	Milliken
WALLER, Peter	1798	Calvert
WALLES, David	1812	Crawford [2]
WALLES, David	1814	Crookshanks
WALLES, Dever	1812	Crawford
WALLES, James	1812	Crawford [2]
WALLES, Plesent	1808	McAllister
WALLIS, David	1818	McClure
WALLIS, Davis	1817	McClure
WALLIS, George	1809	Patterson
WALLIS, Pleasent	1814	Crookshanks
WALLIS, Thomas	1805	Aikin
WALLS, Adam	1815	Waddell
WALLS, Plesent	1812	Crawford
WALLS, Plesent	1812	Crawford [2]
WALLTERS, Robart	1795	Thornton
WALSEY, Mathew	1818	Grimsley
WALSON, Jonathan	1792	North
WALSY, Israel	1818	Grimsley
WALTER, George	1791	White
WALTER, Peter	1793	Scott
WALTER, Peter	1795	Calvert
WALTER, Peter	1797	Calvert
WALTER, Peter	1797	Calvert
WALTER, Peter	1801	Calvert
WALTER, Peter	1805	Jas Parker
WALTER, Peter	1808	Parker

Surname, Given names	Year	Comp./Dist.
WALTER, Peter	1809	Parker
WALTER, Petter	1796	Calvert
WALTER, Putter	1794	Scot
WALTERS, Claricy	1816	Harrison
WALTERS, Clary	1815	Harris
WALTERS, Clary	1817	Harris
WALTERS, Clay	1819	Harris
WALTERS, Cleary	1818	Harris
WALTERS, Cleary	1821	Hampton
WALTERS, George	1815	Harris
WALTERS, George	1817	Harris
WALTERS, George	1818	Harris
WALTERS, George	1819	Harris
WALTERS, George	1821	Hampton
WALTERS, John	1795	Thornton
WALTERS, Peter	1799	Stuart
WALTERS, Peter (estate of)	1811	McCray
WALTERS, Peter (estate)	1812	McCray
WALTERS, Peter (estate)	1814	McCray
WALTHERS, John	1794	Thornton
WALTON, Jesse (Esq.)	1778	
WALTON, Peter	1791	Willey
WANNER, Jacob	1817	Hampton
WARD, Benjamin	1778	
WARD, Demsey	1778	
WARD, William	1778	
WARD, William	1779	
WARD, William	1790	Stone
WARD, William	1791	Stone
WARD, William	1792	Tulley
WARD, William	1793	Maxwell
WARD, William	1794	Taylor
WARD, William	1795	Morrison
WARD, William	1798	Morrison
WARD, William	1806	Carr
WARD, William	1808	Carr
WARD, William (Doctor)	1793	Morrison
WARD, William (Doctor)	1794	Morrison
WARDRISS, James	1796	Handly
WARE, John (Esq.)	1793	Handley
WARE, Nancy	1816	Crookshanks
WARNER, Jacob	1812	Crawford
WARREN, Edmond	1816	Giles
WARREN, Edmond	1817	Gillises
WARREN, Edmond	1818	Land
WATENBARGER, Adam	1814	Crookshanks
WATENBARGER, Jacob	1819	Hunt
WATENBERGER, Adam	1807	Payne
WATENBERGER, Adam	1819	McClure
WATENBERGER, Adam Jr.	1819	McClure
WATENBERGER, Peter	1819	McClure
WATERS, George	1792	White
WATINBURGHES, William	1812	Crawford [2]
WATINBURGTER, Adam	1812	Crawford [2]
WATINGBRIGHER, Aarn Jr.	1812	Crawford [2]
WATINGBURGE, Adam	1808	McAllister
WATKEN, Barbara	1791	North
WATKINS, Jesse	1809	Right
WATSON, Abagel	1809	Par
WATSON, Agnes	1807	Parker
WATSON, John	1781	
WATSON, John	1796	Young
WATSON, John	1797	Young
WATSON, John	1801	Norwood
WATSON, John	1821	Haines
WATSON, Johnathan	1781	
WATSON, Jonathan	1791	North
WATSON, Jonathan	1794	North
WATSON, Jonathan	1796	Young
WATSON, Jonathan	1797	Young
WATSON, Jonathan	1807	Parker
WATSON, Martha	1801	Taylor
WATSON, Martha	1805	Parker
WATSON, Martha	1807	Parker
WATSON, Mary	1801	Taylor
WATSON, Mathew	1809	Hartzell
WATSON, Nancy	1801	Taylor
WATSON, Nancy	1805	Parker
WATSON, Nancy	1806	Parker
WATSON, Nancy	1809	Par
WATSON, Saml (Revd.)	1821	Jones
WATSON, Samual	1805	Parker
WATSON, Samuel	1781	
WATSON, Samuel	1816	Hoss
WATSON, Samuel	1821	Haines
WATSON, Samuel (Rev.)	1817	Little
WATSON, Samuel (Rev.)	1818	Jones
WATSON, Samuel (Rev.)	1819	Jones
WATSON, Stephen	1795	Ford
WATSON, Susannah	1801	Taylor
WATSON, William	1779	
WATSON, William	1790	Williams
WATSON, William	1791	Williams
WATSON, William	1795	Young
WATSON, William	1796	Young
WATSON, William	1797	Young
WATSON, William	1806	Parker
WATSON, Wm	1793	North
WATSON, Wm	1794	North
WATSON, Wm	1801	Taylor
WATTENBARGER, Adam	1809	McAlister
WATTENBARGER, Adam	1809	McAlister

Surname, Given names	Year	Comp./Dist.
WATTENBARGER, Adam	1809	McAlister
WATTENBARGER, Adam	1811	McAlister
WATTENBARGER, Adam	1814	Crookshanks
WATTENBARGER, Adam Jr.	1811	McAlister
WATTENBARGER, Willm	1811	McAlister
WATTENBARGER, Willm	1814	Crookshanks
WATTENBERG, Adam	1817	McClure
WATTENBERGER, Adair	1818	McClure
WATTENBERGER, Adam	1815	Crookshanks
WATTENBERGER, Adam	1816	Crookshanks
WATTENBERGER, Adam Jr.	1818	McClure
WATTENBERGER, Adams	1821	McClure
WATTENBERGER, Alexander Jr.	1815	Crookshanks
WATTENBERGER, William	1816	Crookshanks
WATTENBERGER, William	1818	McClure
WATTENBERGER, William	1821	McClure
WATTENBORGER, Jacob	1821	Hunt
WATTENBURG, William	1817	McClure
WATTERS, George	1814	McCray
WATTINGBURGHER, Adam	1812	Crawford
WATTON, Martha	1810	Hartzel
WAUREN, Jacob	1780-1781 (Undated)	
WEAER, Hugh	1811	Green
WEAR, Agnes	1805	Aikin
WEAR, Agness	1806	Grur
WEAR, Agnis	1801	Gann
WEAR, Benjamin	1801	Gann
WEAR, Benjamin	1805	Guir
WEAR, Benjamin	1806	Grur
WEAR, George	1801	Gann
WEAR, Hugh	1812	Waddill
WEAR, Hugh	1815	McLin
WEAR, Hugh	1819	Sands
WEAR, Hugh	1821	Sands
WEAR, John	1797	Robertson
WEAR, John	1799	Robertson
WEAR, John	1801	Roberson
WEAR, Lewis	1806	Anderson
WEAR, Robert	1781	
WEAR, Robert	1781	
WEAR, Waddon	1808	Gwin
WEAR, Widdow	1805	Guir
WEAR, Widdow	1810	Green
WEAR, Widdow	1812	Waddill
WEARE, John	1797	Calvert
WEATHER, Zebulon	1780-1781 (undated)	
WEATHERFORD, Daniel	1821	Brown
WEATHERS, John	1798	Crouch
WEATHERS, John	1799	Duncan
WEATHERS, William	1795	Melvan
WEATHERS, Wm	1796	Melvin
WEATHERSPOON, James	1797	Calvert
WEAVER, Christian	1778	
WEAVER, Christian	1779	
WEAVER, Michael	1779	
WEAVER, Samuel	1778	
WEAVR, Nancy	1811	Green
WEBB, Benjamin	1779	
WEBB, Farrist	1779	
WEBB, Henry	1818	Brown
WEBB, James	1818	Grimsley
WEBB, John	1778	
WEBB, John	1792	Coye
WEBB, John	1799	Duncan
WEBB, John	1801	Taylor
WEBB, John	1806	Carson
WEBB, John	1807	Shields
WEBB, John (In trust for William Young)	1792	Coye
WEBB, Jonathan	1778	
WEBB, Jonathan	1779	
WEBB, Martin	1778	
WEBB, Mary	1810	Cove
WEBB, Mary	1817	Brown
WEBB, Mercy	1808	Odell
WEBB, Merry	1806	Odel
WEBB, Merry	1807	Odell
WEBB, Merry	1811	Brown
WEBB, Merry	1812	Brown
WEBB, Merry	1815	Hartsell
WEBB, Merry	1816	Brown
WEBB, Merry	1821	Haines
WEBB, Mery	1814	Brown
WEEN, Peter	1818	Smith
WEER, John	1781	
WEER, John	1790	Hanley
WEER, John	1780-1781 (Undated)	
WEER, Saml	1781	
WEIR, Benjemin	1798	Gann
WEIR, Benjemin	1799	Gann
WEIR, George	1798	Gann
WEIR, Gorge	1799	Gann
WEIR, John	1791	Chisom
WEIR, John	1792	Chisolm
WEIR, John	1796	Handly
WEIR, John	1798	Gann
WEIR, John	1799	Gann
WEIRED, Lews	1807	Anderson
WELCH, John	1805	Carson
WELEY, James (Capt.)	1791	Willey
WELISH, John	1821	Martin

Surname, Given names	Year	Comp./Dist.
WELL, Jesse	1811	Barron
WELLET, Zodoc	1798	Hannah
WELLS, Adam	1814	Waddell
WELLS, James	1798	Hannah
WELLS, Merry	1819	Brown
WELLS, William	1779	
WENKLE, Henry	1805	Guir
WENLES, James	1798	Biddle
WENNSY, James	1806	Grur
WERE, Benja	1799	Moore
WERE, Benje	1797	Gann
WERE, George	1797	Gann
WERE, George	1799	Moore
WERE, John	1791	Hanley
WERE, John	1799	Moore
WERIN, Edmond	1809	Patterson
WERIN, Edmond	1814	Couthers
WERRIN, Edward	1815	Carcathers
WESSON, Edward	1819	Sands
WEST, Edward	1814	Hampton
WEST, Edward	1816	Hampton
WEST, Edward	1819	Brown
WEST, Edward	1821	Brown
WEST, Edward Jr.	1821	Brown
WEST, Samuel	1819	Brown
WEST, Thomas	1781	
WESTAIN, Joseph	1819	Sands
WESTEN, Fulgham	1798	Shipley
WESTER, Fulgim	1797	Duncan
WESTER, Fulgim	1799	Duncan
WESTERN, Joseph	1795	Carriger
WESTERN, William	1795	Carriger
WHALEN, Steph	1795	Thornton
WHALEY, William	1790	Stone
WHALEY, William	1791	Stone
WHEALLER, William Jr.	1813	Hoss
WHEALLER, William Sr.	1813	Hoss
WHEELER, Isaac	1801	Glasscock
WHEELER, John	1778	
WHEELER, Stephen	1794	Thornton
WHEELER, William	1805	Jas Parker
WHEELER, William	1816	Hoss
WHEELER, William	1817	Little
WHEELER, William	1818	Jones
WHEELER, William	1819	Jones
WHEELER, William	1821	Jones
WHEELER, Wm	1801	Taylor
WHEELOCK, Alexander	1816	Grimsley
WHEELOCK, Alexander	1817	Grimsley
WHEELOCK, Enoch	1817	Grimsley
WHEELOCK, James	1807	
WHEELOCK, James	1812	Barnes
WHEELOCK, James	1815	Grimsley
WHEELOCK, James	1816	Grimsley
WHEELOCK, James	1817	Grimsley
WHEELOCK, John	1793	Murray
WHEELOCK, John	1795	Murray
WHEELOCK, John	1801	Glasscock
WHEELOCK, John	1812	Barnes
WHEELOCK, John	1815	Grimsley
WHEELOCK, John	1816	Grimsley
WHEELOCK, John	1816	Grimsley
WHEELOCK, John	1817	Grimsley
WHEELOCK, John Jr.	1815	Grimsley
WHEELOCK, John Jr.	1816	Grimsley
WHEELOCK, John Jr.	1817	Grimsley
WHEELOCK, John Sr.	1812	Barnes
WHELEHITE, Reubin	1805	Parker
WHELEHITE, Reubin	1807	Parker
WHELLOCK, John	1807	Cade
WHELOCK, Enock	1821	Martin
WHELOCK, John	1794	Murray
WHELOCK, John	1797	Shipley
WHELOCK, John	1821	Martin
WHELOCK, John Sr.	1798	Shipley
WHETHERE, William	1790	Stone
WHETHERE, William	1791	Stone
WHETHERS, William	1794	Melvan
WHETSON, Thomas	1816	Smith
WHEYLEY, Thomas	1797	Shipley
WHIGHT, Rheubin	1810	Dimmons
WHILLOCK, James	1807	Cade
WHILLOCK, James	1810	Barron
WHILLOCK, John	1807	Cade
WHILLOCK, John	1808	Cade
WHILLOCK, John	1808	Cade
WHILLOCK, John Jr.	1810	Barron
WHILLOCKS, John	1810	Barron
WHILLOT, Zedock	1807	Payne
WHILOCK, Charles	1809	Cade
WHILOCK, James	1809	Cade
WHILOCK, James	1821	Martin
WHILOCK, John	1821	Martin
WHILOCK, John Jr.	1809	Cade
WHILOCK, John Sr.	1809	Cade
WHISLER, Jacob	1821	McClure
WHISTER, Jacob	1819	McClure
WHIT, Alexander	1807	Cade
WHITAKER, Thomas	1817	Grimsley
WHITAKR, Mark	1798	Crouch
WHITANBARGER, Joseph	1780-1781 (Undated)	
WHITE, Adam	1813	Hoss

Surname, Given names	Year	Comp./Dist.
WHITE, Adam	1814	Hoss
WHITE, Adam	1815	Hoss
WHITE, Adam	1816	Hoss
WHITE, Adam	1817	Little
WHITE, Adam	1818	Jones
WHITE, Ann	1799	Morrison
WHITE, Ann	1801	Morrison
WHITE, Ann	1806	Carr
WHITE, Ann	1807	Carr
WHITE, Ann	1809	Carr
WHITE, Ann	1811	Mitchell
WHITE, Ann	1813	Hoss
WHITE, Ann (widow)	1814	Hoss
WHITE, Archable	1790	Shipley
WHITE, Archable	1791	Shipley
WHITE, Archable	1793	Murray
WHITE, Archable	1795	Murray
WHITE, Archebel	1794	Murray
WHITE, Archeble	1796	Shipley
WHITE, David	1801	Glasscock
WHITE, David	1805	Rector
WHITE, David	1807	Cade
WHITE, David	1808	Cade
WHITE, David	1809	Cade
WHITE, David	1810	Barron
WHITE, David	1811	Barron
WHITE, David	1812	Barnes
WHITE, David	1814	Barns
WHITE, David	1815	Grimsley
WHITE, David	1816	Grimsley
WHITE, David	1817	Grimsley
WHITE, David	1818	Grimsley
WHITE, David	1819	Grimsley
WHITE, David	1821	Martin
WHITE, David	1780-1781	District 7
WHITE, Ezekiel	1819	Grisham
WHITE, George	1815	McLin
WHITE, George	1816	Brown
WHITE, George	1816	Hunt
WHITE, George	1817	Brown
WHITE, George	1818	Brown
WHITE, Henry	1818	Grimsley
WHITE, Isaac	1781	
WHITE, Isaac	1795	Murray
WHITE, Isaac	1797	Duncan
WHITE, Isaac	1798	Shipley
WHITE, Isaac	1801	Glasscock
WHITE, Isaac	1805	Rector
WHITE, Isaac	1807	Cade
WHITE, Isaac	1808	Cade
WHITE, Isaac	1809	Cade
WHITE, Isaac	1810	Barron
WHITE, Isaac	1811	Barron
WHITE, Isaac	1812	Barnes
WHITE, Isaac	1814	Barns
WHITE, Isaac	1815	Grimsley
WHITE, Isaac	1816	Grimsley
WHITE, Isaac	1817	Grimsley
WHITE, Isaac	1818	Grimsley
WHITE, Isaac	1819	Grimsley
WHITE, James	1781	
WHITE, James	1795	Morrison
WHITE, James	1795	Thornton
WHITE, James	1806	Carr
WHITE, James	1807	Carr
WHITE, James	1808	Carr
WHITE, James	1809	Carr
WHITE, James	1811	Mitchell
WHITE, James	1813	Hoss
WHITE, James	1814	Hoss
WHITE, James	1816	Hoss
WHITE, James	1817	Little
WHITE, James	1818	Jones
WHITE, James	1819	Jones
WHITE, James	1821	Jones
WHITE, Jeremiah	1819	Grimsley
WHITE, Jerrey	1821	Martin
WHITE, Jesse	1814	McCracken
WHITE, Jesse	1817	Hunt
WHITE, Jesse	1818	Hunt
WHITE, Jesse	1819	Smith
WHITE, Jesse	1821	Smith
WHITE, Job	1817	Hunt
WHITE, John	1778	
WHITE, John	1781	
WHITE, John	1787	Fains
WHITE, John	1791	Tullis
WHITE, John	1792	Tulley
WHITE, John	1793	Morrison
WHITE, John	1794	Morrison
WHITE, John	1795	Morrison
WHITE, John	1808	Odell
WHITE, John	1809	Viney
WHITE, John	1810	Cove
WHITE, John	1811	Brown
WHITE, John	1812	Brown
WHITE, John	1814	Barns
WHITE, John	1814	Brown
WHITE, John	1815	Grimsley
WHITE, John	1815	Hartsell
WHITE, John	1816	Brown
WHITE, John	1816	Grimsley

Surname, Given names	Year	Comp./Dist.
WHITE, John	1817	Brown
WHITE, John	1818	Brown
WHITE, John	1818	Smith
WHITE, John	1819	Brown
WHITE, John	1819	Grimsley
WHITE, John	1821	Haines
WHITE, John	1821	Martin
WHITE, John	[1796] 1797	Morris
WHITE, Joseph	1808	McAllister
WHITE, Joseph	1811	McAlister
WHITE, Lewis	1801	Taylor
WHITE, Lois	1798	Duncan
WHITE, Richard	1778	
WHITE, Richard	1793	Thornton
WHITE, Richard	1794	Ford
WHITE, Richard	1808	Cade
WHITE, Richard	1809	Cade
WHITE, Richard	1810	Barron
WHITE, Richard	1811	Barron
WHITE, Richard	1812	Barnes
WHITE, Richard	1814	Barns
WHITE, Richard	1815	Grimsley
WHITE, Richard	1816	Grimsley
WHITE, Ruth	1808	Guin
WHITE, Ruth	1809	Gwin
WHITE, Ruth	1811	Davis
WHITE, Ruth	1812	McLin
WHITE, Stephen	1805	Rector
WHITE, Stephen	1808	Cade
WHITE, Stephen	1810	Barron
WHITE, Stephen	1811	Barron
WHITE, Stephen	1812	Barnes
WHITE, Sterling	1821	Smith
WHITE, Steven	1809	Cade
WHITE, Terance	1812	Barnes
WHITE, Terry	1815	Grimsley
WHITE, Terry	1816	Grimsley
WHITE, Terry	1817	Grimsley
WHITE, Thomas	1811	Barron
WHITE, Thomas	1812	Barnes
WHITE, Thomas	1814	Barns
WHITE, Thomas	1815	Grimsley
WHITE, Thomas	1816	Grimsley
WHITE, Thomas	1817	Grimsley
WHITE, Thomas	1818	Grimsley
WHITE, Thomas	1819	Grimsley
WHITE, Thos	1821	Martin
WHITE, Tony	1814	Barns
WHITE, William	1805	Rector
WHITE, William	1812	McCray
WHITE, William	1812	McCray
WHITE, William	1814	McCray
WHITE, William	1815	Harris
WHITE, William	1815	Hoss
WHITE, William	1816	Harrison
WHITE, William	1816	Hoss
WHITE, William	1817	Harris
WHITE, William	1817	Little
WHITE, William	1818	Harris
WHITE, William	1818	Jones
WHITE, William	1819	Harris
WHITE, William	1819	Jones
WHITE, William	1821	Hampton
WHITE, William	1821	Jones
WHITE, William Jr.	1811	McCray
WHITE, Wm	1809	Parker
WHITEAKER, Thomas	1812	Barnes
WHITENBERGER, Joseph	1781	
WHITERIAR, Isaac	1811	Rodman
WHITICAR, Mark	1793	Morrison
WHITICAR, Mark	1794	Morrison
WHITLOCK, Alaxandrew	1821	Martin
WHITLOCK, Alex	1801	Glasscock
WHITLOCK, Alexander	1805	Rector
WHITLOCK, Alexander	1808	Cade
WHITLOCK, Alexander	1809	Cade
WHITLOCK, Alexander	1810	Barron
WHITLOCK, Alexander	1811	Barron
WHITLOCK, Alexander	1812	Barnes
WHITLOCK, Alexander	1814	Barns
WHITLOCK, Alexander	1815	Grimsley
WHITLOCK, Alexander	1818	Grimsley
WHITLOCK, Alexander	1819	Grimsley
WHITLOCK, Charles	1807	Cade
WHITLOCK, Charles	1811	Barron
WHITLOCK, Enoch	1818	Grimsley
WHITLOCK, Enoch	1819	Grimsley
WHITLOCK, James	1808	Cade
WHITLOCK, James	1811	Barron
WHITLOCK, James	1814	Barns
WHITLOCK, James	1819	Grimsley
WHITLOCK, John	1801	Aiken
WHITLOCK, John	1811	Barron
WHITLOCK, John	1811	Barron
WHITLOCK, John	1814	Barns
WHITLOCK, John	1814	Barns
WHITLOCK, John	1818	Grimsley
WHITLOCK, John	1818	Grimsley
WHITLOCK, John	1818	Grimsley
WHITLOCK, John	1819	Grimsley
WHITLOCK, John	1819	Grimsley
WHITLOCK, John	1821	Martin

Surname, Given names	Year	Comp./Dist.
WHITLOCK, John Jr.	1818	Grimsley
WHITLOCK, John Sr.	1819	Grimsley
WHITLOCK, Thomas	1818	Grimsley
WHITMON, James	1814	Brown
WHITSON, Abraham	1794	Taylor
WHITSON, Abraham	1795	Taylor
WHITSON, Charles	1795	Carriger
WHITSON, Charles	1806	Odel
WHITSON, Charles	1807	Odell
WHITSON, Charles	1808	Odell
WHITSON, Isaac	1808	Odell
WHITSON, Isaac	1809	Viney
WHITSON, James	1806	Odel
WHITSON, James	1808	Odell
WHITSON, James	1809	Viney
WHITSON, James	1810	Cove
WHITSON, James	1811	Brown
WHITSON, James	1812	Brown
WHITSON, James	1815	Hartsell
WHITSON, James	1816	Brown
WHITSON, James	1817	Brown
WHITSON, James	1818	Brown
WHITSON, James	1819	Brown
WHITSON, James	1821	Haines
WHITSON, James	1780-1781	District 7
WHITSON, Jarimah	1794	Taylor
WHITSON, Jeremiah	1795	Taylor
WHITSON, Jerremiah	1793	Maxwell
WHITSON, Jese	1794	Taylor
WHITSON, Jesse	1790	Williams
WHITSON, Jesse	1791	Williams
WHITSON, Jesse	1792	Maxwell
WHITSON, Jessie	1793	Maxwell
WHITSON, John	1792	Maxwell
WHITSON, John	1793	Maxwell
WHITSON, John	1793	Thornton
WHITSON, John	1794	Taylor
WHITSON, John	1795	Ford
WHITSON, John	1795	Taylor
WHITSON, John	1810	Cove
WHITSON, John (Son of Tho Whitson)	1795	Taylor
WHITSON, Tho	1795	Taylor
WHITSON, Tho	1795	Taylor
WHITSON, Thomas	1793	Thornton
WHITSON, Thomas	1794	Thornton
WHITSON, Thomas	1814	McCracken
WHITSON, Thomas	1815	Garner
WHITSON, Thomas	1817	Smith
WHITSON, Thomas	1818	Smith
WHITSON, Thomas	1819	Jones
WHITSON, Thomas	1821	Jones

Surname, Given names	Year	Comp./Dist.
WHITSON, Thomas (Over age)	1790	White
WHITSON, William	1779	
WHITSON, William	1806	Odel
WHITSON, William	1807	Odell
WHITSON, William	1808	Odell
WHITSON, William	1809	Viney
WHITSON, William	1810	Cove
WHITSON, William	1811	Brown
WHITSON, William	1812	Brown
WHITSON, William	1814	Brown
WHITSON, William	1815	Hartsell
WHITSON, William	1816	Brown
WHITSON, William	1817	Brown
WHITSON, William	1817	Riley
WHITSON, William	1818	Brown
WHITSON, William	1819	Brown
WHITSON, William	1821	Haines
WHITTE, Richard	1795	Ford
WHITTECAR, Mark	1795	Morrison
WHITTECKER, Thomas	1811	Barron
WHITTER, James	1778	
WHITTIKER, Mark	[1796] 1797	Morris
WHOLEWHITE, Rubin	1808	Parker
WHOOD, William	1778	
WHORTER, James W.	1807	Shields
WIDBY, William Jr.	1794	Thornton
WIDLES, James	1798	Biddle
WIER, John	1792	Brown
WIETT, Ares	1798	Young
WIETT, James	1798	Young
WIETT, Jesse	1819	Howard
WILBORN, John	1798	Crouch
WILBY, Abell	1816	Giles
WILCOTT, Francis	1818	Jones
WILCOX, Thomas	1816	Smith
WILDER, Jacob	1793	Campbell
WILDER, Joab (Over age)	1790	White
WILDER, Joab (Over age)	1791	White
WILDER, Joab Sr.; (Over age)	1792	White
WILDER, Joal	1795	Ford
WILES, John	1795	Taylor
WILESON, Isaac	1799	Moore
WILEY, Abel	1817	Gillises
WILEY, Able	1815	Harris
WILEY, James (Capt.)	1791	
WILEY, Thomas	1795	Melvan
WILEY, Thomas	1796	Brown
WILEY, Thomas	1798	Shipley
WILHITE, Reeves	1818	Fine
WILHITE, Reuben	1815	Fines
WILHITE, Reuben	1816	Fine

Surname, Given names	Year	Comp./Dist.
WILLIAMS, Isaac	1821	Brown
WILLIAMS, James	1812	Hartsell
WILLIAMS, Jarrett	1778	
WILLIAMS, Joel	1821	Brown
WILLIAMS, John	1779	Wilson
WILLIAMS, John	1790	Biddle
WILLIAMS, John	1791	Biddle
WILLIAMS, John	1792	Biddle
WILLIAMS, John	1793	Biddle
WILLIAMS, John	1794	Blair
WILLIAMS, John	1796	Handly
WILLIAMS, John	1797	Biddle
WILLIAMS, John	1798	Biddle
WILLIAMS, John	1798	Biddle
WILLIAMS, John	1806	Carson
WILLIAMS, John	1807	Shields
WILLIAMS, John	1808	
WILLIAMS, John	1810	Dimmons
WILLIAMS, John	1811	
WILLIAMS, John	1814	Couthers
WILLIAMS, John	1815	Carcathers
WILLIAMS, John	1816	Giles
WILLIAMS, John	1817	Gillises
WILLIAMS, John	1818	Land
WILLIAMS, John	1819	Sands
WILLIAMS, John	1821	Brown
WILLIAMS, John	1821	Sands
WILLIAMS, John	1780-1781 (Undated)	
WILLIAMS, Jonathan	1817	Hampton
WILLIAMS, Joshua	1778	
WILLIAMS, Samuel	1778	
WILLIAMS, Samuel	1793	Maxwell
WILLIAMS, Tho	1778	
WILLIAMS, Thomas	1795	Carriger
WILLIAMS, Thomas	1816	Giles
WILLIAMS, Thomas	1817	Gillises
WILLIAMS, Thomas	1818	Land
WILLIAMS, Tom	1819	Brown
WILLIAMS, Umphrey	1810	Hartzel
WILLIAMS, Umphrey	1814	Hampton
WILLIAMS, William	1779	
WILLIAMS, Wm	1821	McGee
WILLIT, Fedock	1806	Payn
WILLIT, Franses	1813	Hoss
WILLIT, James	1807	Payne
WILLIT, James	1809	McAlister
WILLIT, James	1811	McAlister
WILLIT, Teddock	1814	Crookshanks
WILLOCK, Charles	1805	Rector
WILLOCK, Charles	1808	Cade
WILLOCK, James	1805	Rector
WILLOCK, John Jr.	1805	Rector
WILLOCK, John Sr.	1805	Rector
WILLOT, Hannah	1807	Payne
WILLOT, Zadock	1818	McClure
WILLOT, Zadock	1821	McClure
WILLOT, Zeddock	1809	McAlister
WILLOT, Zeddock	1811	McAlister
WILLOUGHBY, Matthew	1779	
WILLS, Mvr	1801	Biddle
WILLSON,	1778	
WILLSON, Adam	1778	
WILLSON, Benjamin	1778	
WILLSON, Isaac	1778	
WILLSON, Isaac	1791	Milliken
WILLSON, Isaac	1797	Hannah
WILLSON, Isack	1809	McAlister
WILLSON, James	1780-1781 (Undated)	
WILLSON, John	1795	Thornton
WILLSON, John	1795	Thornton
WILLSON, Joseph	1778	
WILLSON, Joseph	1795	Thornton
WILLSON, Richd	1778	
WILLSON, Robert	1778	
WILLSON, Samuel	1794	Thornton
WILLSON, William	1815	Waddell
WILLSON, William	1780-1781 (Undated)	
WILLY, Thomas	1793	Melvan
WILMBLES, James	1798	Longmire
WILSON, Alexander	1821	Smith
WILSON, Amos	1813	Copas
WILSON, Amos	1815	Copas
WILSON, Amos	1816	Copas
WILSON, Anos	1814	Copes
WILSON, Benja	1813	Copas
WILSON, Benjaman	1814	Copes
WILSON, Benjamin	1815	Copas
WILSON, Benjamin	1816	Copas
WILSON, C. Robert	1821	Sands
WILSON, Charles	1819	McClure
WILSON, Charles	1821	McClure
WILSON, David	1801	Biddle
WILSON, David	1805	Carson
WILSON, David	1806	Carson
WILSON, David	1807	Shields
WILSON, David	1810	Dimmons
WILSON, David	1811	
WILSON, David	1814	Couthers
WILSON, David	1815	Carcathers
WILSON, David	1816	Giles
WILSON, David	1818	Land

Surname, Given names	Year	Comp./Dist.
WILSON, David	1819	Sands
WILSON, David	1821	Sands
WILSON, Garland	1794	Thornton
WILSON, Henry	1806	Anderson
WILSON, Isaac	1792	Milliken
WILSON, Isaac	1793	Milliken
WILSON, Isaac	1799	Hannah
WILSON, Isaac	1801	Gann
WILSON, Isaac	1801	Squibb
WILSON, Isaac	1808	Gwin
WILSON, Isaac	1811	Green
WILSON, Isaac	1812	Crawford [2]
WILSON, Isaac	1814	Waddell
WILSON, Isaac	1815	Crookshanks
WILSON, Isaac	1816	Crookshanks
WILSON, Isaac	1817	McClure
WILSON, Isaac	1818	McClure
WILSON, Isaac	1819	McClure
WILSON, Isaac	1821	McClure
WILSON, Isaack	1796	Millikin
WILSON, Isaack	1812	Waddill
WILSON, Isac	1806	Payn
WILSON, Isack	1798	Gann
WILSON, Isack	1807	Payne
WILSON, James	1779	Wilson
WILSON, Jas (Capt.)	1781	
WILSON, Jassoe	1799	Gann
WILSON, John	1781	
WILSON, John	1781	
WILSON, John	1792	White
WILSON, John	1792	White
WILSON, John	1793	Thornton
WILSON, John	1821	McClure
WILSON, John Jr.	1791	White
WILSON, John Jr.	1794	Thornton
WILSON, John Sr.	1793	Thornton
WILSON, John Sr.	1794	Thornton
WILSON, John Sr.; (Over age)	1790	White
WILSON, John Sr.; (Over age)	1791	White
WILSON, Joseph	1779	Wilson
WILSON, Joseph	1781	
WILSON, Joseph	1781	
WILSON, Joseph	1781	
WILSON, Joseph	1793	Thornton
WILSON, Joseph	1794	Thornton
WILSON, Joseph	1821	Louis
WILSON, Joseph	1780-1781 (Undated)	
WILSON, Robert	1779	Wilson
WILSON, Robert	1781	
WILSON, Samuel	1790	White
WILSON, Samuel	1791	White
WILSON, Samuel	1792	White
WILSON, Samuel	1795	Ford
WILSON, William	1781	
WILSON, William	1790	White
WILSON, William	1791	White
WILSON, William	1792	White
WILSON, William	1793	Thornton
WILSON, William	1794	Thornton
WILSON, William	1809	Green
WILSON, William	1811	Green
WILSON, William	1812	Waddill
WILSON, William	1816	Waddell
WILSON, William	1818	Riley
WILSON, William	1819	Findley
WILSON, William	1780-1781 (Undated)	
WILSON, Wm	1806	Grur
WILSON, Wm	1808	Gwin
WILSON, Wm	1810	Green
WILSON, Wm	1814	Waddell
WILSON, Wm	1821	McGee
WILSONS, Adam	1781	
WILTON, Abraham	1794	Carriger
WIMON, Hannery	1795	Thornton
WINCLE, Peter	1808	Gwin
WINKEL, Christopher	1811	Green
WINKEL, John	1811	Green
WINKLE, Abraham	1819	Findley
WINKLE, Abraham	1821	McGee
WINKLE, Christefor	1806	Grur
WINKLE, Christopher	1809	Green
WINKLE, Christopher	1810	Green
WINKLE, Christopher	1812	Waddill
WINKLE, Henry	1808	Gwin
WINKLE, Henry	1809	Green
WINKLE, Hinry	1806	Grur
WINKLE, John	1805	Guir
WINKLE, John	1806	Grur
WINKLE, John	1808	Gwin
WINKLE, John	1809	Green
WINKLE, John	1812	Waddill
WINKLE, John	1814	Waddell
WINKLE, John	1815	Waddell
WINKLE, John	1816	Waddell
WINKLE, John	1817	Riley
WINKLE, John	1819	Findley
WINKLE, John	1821	McGee
WINKLE, Peter	1809	Green
WINKLE, Peter	1810	Green
WINKLE, William John	1818	Riley
WINKLES, James	1801	Roberson
WISHER, John	1798	Duncan

Surname, Given names	Year	Comp./Dist.
WISHER, John	1798	Duncan
WISSOM, Frances	1798	Morrison
WITHERSPOON, James	1798	Calvert
WITT, Airs	1796	Longmire
WITT, Barges	1796	Calvert
WITT, Birges	1807	Parker
WITT, Birges	1808	Parker
WITT, Bugis	1797	Calvert
WITT, Burgers	1817	Brown
WITT, Burges	1801	Taylor
WITT, Burges	1814	Brown
WITT, Burges	1816	Brown
WITT, Burgess	1795	Young
WITT, Burgess	1798	Calvert
WITT, Burgess	1806	Parker
WITT, Burgess	1809	Parker
WITT, Burgess	1812	Brown
WITT, Burgin	1801	
WITT, Burgis	1818	Brown
WITT, Burgiss	1799	Stuart
WITT, Burjis	1797	Calvert
WITT, Burpp	1815	Hartsell
WITT, Edward	1817	Hampton
WITT, Hevis	1797	Young
WITT, James	1797	Young
WITT, Jess	1796	Calvert
WITT, Jess	1801	Longmire
WITT, Jesse	1798	Roberson
WITT, Jesse	1807	Parker
WITT, Jesse	1817	Fine
WITT, Jesse	1818	Fine
WITT, Jessey	1821	Howard
WITT, Rutheford	1797	Calvert
WITT, Rutherford	1798	Roberson
WITT, Solomon	1801	Taylor
WITT, Stephan	1807	Cade
WOLF, Andrew	1814	Hoss
WOLF, Henry	1816	Harrison
WOLF, Henry	1819	Hunt
WOLF, Lewis	1817	Harris
WOLLAS, Pleasant	1811	McAlister
WOMACK, Jacob	1778	
WOOD, Abraham (executor)	1801	Calvert
WOOD, Absolom	1780-1781 (Undated)	
WOOD, Agnes	1815	Waddell
WOOD, Bartholomew	1781	
WOOD, Barthow Jr.	1781	
WOOD, Batholomew	1779	Wilson
WOOD, Betholeny	1780-1781 (Undated)	
WOOD, Charles	1797	Calvert
WOOD, Daniel	1816	Fine
WOOD, Daniel	1821	Brown
WOOD, Daniel Jr.	1819	Brown
WOOD, James	1796	Longmire
WOOD, James	1797	Calvert
WOOD, James	1798	Calvert
WOOD, Jno	1780-1781 (Undated)	
WOOD, John	1778	
WOOD, John	1780-1781 (undated)	
WOOD, Michal	1797	Gann
WOOD, Milon	1819	McClure
WOOD, Ritchard	1781	
WOOD, Saml Jr.	1797	Calvert
WOOD, Saml Sr.	1797	Calvert
WOOD, Samuel	1791	Willey
WOOD, Samuel	1793	Scott
WOOD, Samuel	1799	Stuart
WOOD, Samuel (Agent for Wm Wood)	1798	Calvert
WOOD, Samuel Jr.	1797	Calvert
WOOD, Samuel Jr.	1798	Calvert
WOOD, Samuel Sr.	1798	Calvert
WOOD, Thomas	1801	Calvert
WOOD, Thomas	1808	Parker
WOOD, William	1790	Williams
WOOD, William	1791	Williams
WOOD, William	1792	Tulley
WOOD, William	1793	Morrison
WOOD, William	1794	Morrison
WOOD, William	1795	Morrison
WOOD, William	1796	Calvert
WOOD, William	1796	Morrison
WOOD, William	1797	Calvert
WOOD, William	1798	Morrison
WOOD, William	1798	Morrison
WOOD, William	1799	Morrison
WOOD, William	1801	Morrison
WOOD, William	1815	Waddell
WOOD, William	1818	Riley
WOOD, William	[1796] 1797	Morris
WOOD, Wm	1798	Calvert
WOODARD, Thomas	1781	
WOODARD, Thomas	1780-1781 (Undated)	
WOODBY, William	1795	Thornton
WOODS, Abraham	1810	Barron
WOODS, Abraham	1811	Barron
WOODS, Abraham	1812	Barnes
WOODS, Agnes	1811	Green
WOODS, Agness	1814	Waddell
WOODS, Arch	1793	Milliken

Surname, Given names	Year	Comp./Dist.
WOODS, Archable	1796	Millikin
WOODS, Bartholomew	1778	
WOODS, Daniel	1817	Fine
WOODS, Gwen	1814	Waddell
WOODS, Isaac	1806	Guin
WOODS, Michael	1794	Handly
WOODS, Michael	1801	Gann
WOODS, Michael	1806	Grur
WOODS, Michael (Decd.)	1810	
WOODS, Michal	1799	Gann
WOODS, Micheal	1805	Guir
WOODS, Michial	1795	Handly
WOODS, Michial	1796	Handly
WOODS, Michl	1778	
WOODS, Michl	1790	Hanley
WOODS, Michl	1791	Hanley
WOODS, Michl	1793	Handley
WOODS, Michl	1798	Gann
WOODS, Michl	1799	Moore
WOODS, Samuel	1792	Scott
WOODS, Samuel	1794	Scot
WOODS, Samuel	1795	Calvert
WOODS, Samuel	1796	Calvert
WOODS, Whiley	1795	Murray
WOODS, Widdow	1810	Green
WOODS, William	1781	
WOODS, William	1792	Depew
WOODS, William	1793	Depew
WOODS, William	1794	Depew
WOODS, William	1798	Duncan
WOODS, William	1801	Morrison
WOODS, William	1801	Taylor
WOODS, William	1806	Guin
WOODS, William (estate of)	1808	Carr
WOODS, Wm	1795	Calvert
WOODS, Wm	1799	Duncan
WOODS, Wm	1801	Gann
WOODWARD, Thomas (Single)	1779	Wilson
WOOLDRIDGE, Richard	1778	
WOOLF, Andrew	1815	Hoss
WOOLF, Andrew	1816	Hoss
WOOLF, Andrew	1817	Little
WOOLF, Andrew	1818	Jones
WOOLF, Andrew	1819	Jones
WOOLF, Andrew	1821	Jones
WOOLF, John	1819	Jones
WOOLF, Joseph	1819	Jones
WOOLSEY, Essau	1819	Grimsley
WOOLSEY, Faltnas	1819	Grimsley
WOOLSEY, Isaac	1815	Grimsley
WOOLSEY, Israel	1816	Grimsley
WOOLSEY, Israel	1817	Grimsley
WORKMAN, Benjamin	1811	Ellis
WORKMAN, John	1809	Patterson
WORLEY, John	1792	Greer
WORLEY, John	1793	Maxwell
WORLEY, John	1794	Carriger
WORLEY, John	1795	Carriger
WORTMAN, John	1807	Givins
WRAIG, James	1778	
WRAY, Joseph	1778	
WRIGHT, Ezekial	1811	Britten
WRIGHT, Ezekiel	1813	Copas
WRIGHT, Ezekiel	1814	Copes
WRIGHT, Ezekiel	1815	Copas
WRIGHT, Ezekiel	1816	Copas
WRIGHT, Ezekiel	1817	Grisham
WRIGHT, Ezekiel	1818	Grisham
WRIGHT, Ezekiel	1821	Hale
WRIGHT, Isaac	1798	Crouch
WRIGHT, James	1792	Greer
WRIGHT, James	1780-1781 (undated)	
WRIGHT, James	1780-1781 (Undated)	
WRIGHT, Jas	1792	Carriger
WRIGHT, Samuel	1821	Howard
WRIGHT, Thomas	1792	Tulley
WRIGHT, Thomas	1794	Melvan
WRIGHT, Thomas	1795	Morrison
WRIGHTE, Thomas	1793	Melvan
WRIT, Thomas	1794	Taylor
WRIT, William	1794	Taylor
WYATT, Thomas	1792	Maxwell
WYATT, Thos	1793	Maxwell
WYATT, William	1780-1781 (undated)	
WYATT, Wm	1792	Tulley
WYATT, Wm	1793	Maxwell
WYDOM, Frances	1799	Morrison
WYET, Wm	1780-1781 (Undated)	
WYLES, Abel	1818	Land
WYLEY, Abel	1814	McCray
WYLY, Searah	1821	Sands
YAGER, Daniel	1817	McClure
YAGER, Daniel	1821	McClure
YAGER, Sold	1794	Milliken
YATES, Benjamin	1809	Viney
YATES, Samuel	1792	White
YATES, Samuel	1793	Thornton
YATES, Samuel	1794	Ford
YEAGER, Danel	1806	Payn
YEAGER, Daniel	1815	Crookshanks

Surname, Given names	Year	Comp./Dist.
YEAGER, Daniel	1816	Crookshanks
YEAGER, Daniel	1818	McClure
YEAGER, Daniel	1819	McClure
YEAGER, Soloman	1790	Milleken
YEAGER, Soloman	1797	Hannah
YEAGER, Soloman (For Wm Breeding)	1797	Hannah
YEAGER, Solomon	1791	Milliken
YEAGER, Solomon	1795	Milliken
YEAGER, Solomon	1801	Squibb
YEARLY, Benjamen	1807	Parker
YEARLY, Benjamin	1806	Parker
YEARLY, Benjamin	1810	Hartzel
YEARLY, Benjamin	1812	Hartsell
YEARLY, Fichen	1812	Hartsell
YEARLY, Samuel	1810	Hartzel
YEARLY, Samuel	1812	Hartsell
YEARLY, Samuel	1814	Hartsell
YEARLY, Samuel	1815	Fines
YEARLY, Thomas	1814	Hartsell
YEARLY, Thomas	1815	Fines
YEATES, Samuel	1795	Ford
YEGAR, Daniel	1807	Payne
YEGAR, Daniel	1811	McAlister
YEGAR, Joel	1811	McAlister
YEGAR, Solloman	1807	Payne
YEGAR, Solloman	1809	McAlister
YEGAR, Solomon	1796	Millikin
YEGAR, Solomon	1811	McAlister
YEGER, Daniel	1808	McAllister
YEGER, Daniel	1809	McAlister
YEGER, Daniel	1812	Crawford [2]
YEGER, Joel	1809	McAlister
YEGER, Joel	1812	Crawford [2]
YEGER, Joll	1812	Crawford
YEGER, Samel	1812	Crawford
YEGER, Soloman	1798	Hannah
YEGER, Solomon	1792	Milliken
YEGER, Solomon	1808	McAllister
YEGER, Solomon	1812	Crawford
YEGER, Solomon	1812	Crawford [2]
YERBY, Ham	1780-1781 (undated)	
YESAN, Daniel	1814	Crookshanks
YESAN, Solomon	1814	Crookshanks
YICKERY, Fancie	1795	Milliken
YORK, Henry	1812	Waddill
YORK, Henry	1814	Waddell
YORK, William	1795	Melvan
YORK, William	1798	Crouch
YORK, Wm	1801	Norwood
YORK, Wy	1796	Melvin

Surname, Given names	Year	Comp./Dist.
YOUNG, Catherine	1816	Fine
YOUNG, Catherine	1817	Fine
YOUNG, Catherine	1819	Howard
YOUNG, Caty	1821	Howard
YOUNG, Charles	1779	
YOUNG, Charles	1791	North
YOUNG, Charles	1792	North
YOUNG, Charles	1793	North
YOUNG, Charles	1794	North
YOUNG, Coty	1812	Hartsell
YOUNG, Coty	1814	Hartsell
YOUNG, Coty	1815	Fines
YOUNG, Hugh	1821	Jones
YOUNG, Isabel	1807	Carr
YOUNG, Isabel (widow)	1814	Hoss
YOUNG, Isabella	1813	Hoss
YOUNG, Isalelt	1818	Jones
YOUNG, Isbell	1815	Hoss
YOUNG, Isbell	1816	Hoss
YOUNG, Isbell	1817	Little
YOUNG, Isebil	1808	Carr
YOUNG, Izable	1806	Carr
YOUNG, James	1798	Morrison
YOUNG, James	1805	Parker
YOUNG, James	1806	Parker
YOUNG, James	1807	Carr
YOUNG, James	1807	Parker
YOUNG, James	1808	Carr
YOUNG, James	1809	Par
YOUNG, James	1810	Hartzel
YOUNG, James	1811	Mitchell
YOUNG, James	1811	Mitchell
YOUNG, James	1812	Hartsell
YOUNG, James	1813	Hoss
YOUNG, James	1814	Hartsell
YOUNG, James	1814	Hoss
YOUNG, James	1815	Fines
YOUNG, James	1815	Hoss
YOUNG, James	1816	Fine
YOUNG, James	1817	Fine
YOUNG, James	1817	Little
YOUNG, James	1818	Fine
YOUNG, James	1818	Jones
YOUNG, James	1819	Howard
YOUNG, James	1819	Jones
YOUNG, James	1821	Jones
YOUNG, James W.	1821	Howard
YOUNG, Jasn	1793	North
YOUNG, John	1779	
YOUNG, John	1791	Tullis
YOUNG, John	1792	Coye

Surname, Given names	Year	Comp./Dist.
YOUNG, Thomas	1819	Jones
YOUNG, Thos	1793	North
YOUNG, Wilbur	1816	Fine
YOUNG, Wilkens	1821	Howard
YOUNG, Wilkes	1815	Fines
YOUNG, Wilkins	1817	Fine
YOUNG, Wilks	1814	Hartsell
YOUNG, Wilks	1818	Fine
YOUNG, Wilks	1819	Howard
YOUNG, William	1792	Coye
YOUNG, William	1798	Morrison
YOUNG, William	1798	Morrison
YOUNG, William	1812	Hartsell
YOUNG, William	1814	Hartsell
YOUNG, William	1815	Fines
YOUNG, William	1816	Fine
YOUNG, William	1817	Fine
YOUNG, William	1818	Fine
YOUNG, William	1819	Howard
YOUNG, William	1821	Howard
YOUNGE, Isabella	1809	Carr
YOUNGE, Isabella	1811	Mitchell
YOUNGE, James	1809	Carr
YOUNGE, Jonathan	1809	Carr
YOUNGE, Jonathan	1811	Mitchell
YOUNGE, Pheba	1809	Carr
YOUNGE, Thomas	1809	Carr
YOUNGS, Robert	1806	Carr
YUTS, Adam	1811	Green
ZEALAR, Robert	1821	Sands
ZEMERMAN, Daniel	1811	Ellis
ZETTY, Christen	1811	Davis
ZETTY, Christeon	1809	Gwin
ZETTY, Christian	1812	McLin
ZETTY, Christian	1814	McLin
ZETTY, Christian	1815	McLin
ZETTY, Christian	1816	Hunt
ZETTY, Christian	1816	Hunt
ZETTY, Christian	1817	Hunt
ZETTY, Christian	1818	Hunt
ZETTY, Christian	1819	Hunt
ZETTY, Christian Jr.	1821	Hunt
ZETTY, Christian Sr.	1821	Hunt
ZETTY, Christopher	1806	Guin
ZETTY, Samuel (Rev.)	1819	Hunt
ZIMMERMAN, Daniel	1807	Britton
ZIMMERMAN, Daniel	1809	Right
ZORING, Wm	1778	
ZORK, William	1790	Stone
ZORK, William	1791	Stone

www.ingramcontent.com/pod-product-compliance
Lightning Source LLC
LaVergne TN
LVHW061241100826
845148LV00008B/1001

* 9 7 8 0 7 8 8 4 3 8 0 7 3 *